There's a
& that stra

Children's Writers'

A CIP catalogue record for this book is available
from the British Library.

ISBN 10 0-7136-7711-2
ISBN 13 978-0-7136-7711-9

Typeset by QPM from David Lewis XML
Associates Ltd

Printed in Great Britain by
William Clowes Ltd, Beccles, Suffolk

Children's Writers' & Artists'
YEARBOOK
2007

Third Edition

A directory for children's writers and artists containing children's media contacts and practical advice and information

A & C Black · London

Contents

Foreword

Meg Cabot is the author of over 40 books for adult and young adult readers, including *The Princess Diaries*, the *Mediator* and the *1-800-Where-R-You?* series, *All American Girl*, *Ready or Not*, *Avalon High*, and *Size 12 Is Not Fat*. She divides her time between New York City and Key West with her husband and their one-eyed cat, Henrietta. Visit Meg's websites at www.megcabot.com and www.megcabotbookclub.com

The only redeeming quality of the small Midwestern town I grew up in was that it was home to a large state university. My father taught at that university, and so did the fathers – and many of the mothers – of all my friends and classmates. Every single one of those parents, including my own, was published. It seemed to me, growing up, that getting published was something you did as a matter of course – like learning to drive, or voting.

It wasn't until I became a teenager and was old enough to babysit that I realised that getting published wasn't easy. Often, I would be asked by young couples who were new to the university and not yet tenured to look after their children while they shut themselves away in an upstairs study to write a book that, if published, would help them secure a permanent place at the university.

I spent most of my Saturday afternoons and every summer vacation, from the ages of 13 to 18, keeping small children from 'bothering' Mommy or Daddy … 'They're WRITING. A BOOK. Come on, let's play Barbies.'

After the book was completed, there was the tense wait … would a publisher accept it? I saw firsthand the joyous celebrations, but also tears and crushing, bitter disappointment. ('Mommy's going to have an aspirin and a nap. Let's go play Barbies now.')

It was only when it was time for me to publish my own book (because growing up in a town like that, how could I not at least *try?*) that I realised I had absolutely no clue how my father and his peers had gone about actually getting their books to a publisher.

That's why a book like the *Children's Writers' & Artists' Yearbook* is so crucial to the novice writer. How else can we learn the complicated ins and outs of the publishing process … a process that even a girl who'd grown up in a town of published authors couldn't understand?

I don't know how I stumbled across my first guide to getting published, but I do remember thinking it was worth every cent I paid for it. I sent query letters to every single agent listed in the guide.

And every single one of them sent back a rejection … except one, who replied that she liked my work and would represent me. Several years – and many rejected manuscripts later – she managed to sell a book I had written at my day job (*The Princess Diaries*) not just to a publisher but to a major motion picture studio as well.

Suddenly, I was not only a published author, but also an author who was in a financial position to be able to quit the day job and write full time. I was like my father and his peers … but without the pesky teaching part. It was a dream come true for me – but a dream that wouldn't have happened if it hadn't been for a book like the *Children's Writers' & Artists' Yearbook*.

On the road to becoming a published author, every writer has to take a first step. Make the *Children's Writers' & Artists' Yearbook* yours. I'm glad I made it mine.

Meg Cabot

Books

Getting started

You just have! By buying or borrowing the *Children's Writers' & Artists' Yearbook* you have taken the first step towards a potential new career in the field of children's publishing. Alison Stanley gives the benefit of her experience for success in this expanding market.

Whether you want to write for magazines, television, write or illustrate books, adapt for radio, get published in the UK or overseas, find an agent, illustrate greetings' cards, attend a festival, course or conference, or surf the children's literature websites, you will find the information on how to do it in this *Yearbook*.

But to help you on your way, here are 10 top tips:

1. Read, read, read

● Read as many children's books as you can – picture books, young fiction, novels, teen reads, non-fiction, the classics, the prize-winners – and find out just what is being published... and what children like to read.

● Look at children's magazines and newspaper supplements as they will give you ideas about current trends.

● Read reviews in national newspapers, read children's literary magazines such as *Books for Keeps* and *Carousel* (see *Magazines about children's literature and education* on page 278).

2. Get out and about

● Visit your local bookshop and browse in the children's section.

● Go to your library and talk to the children's librarian. Children's books are read by children but usually bought by adults – so find out what parents, teachers, librarians and other professionals are recommending for young people.

● Visit Seven Stories, the Centre for Children's Books (see page 337).

● If you have children, don't just go by what they are reading, ask their friends too – children have wide reading tastes, just like adults. Ask permission to sit in on their school 'storytime' (or a literacy hour or a guided reading session if educational publishing is what you are interested in).

● Go to a festival! There are many literature festivals held throughout the year and most have children's literary events (see page 375). All children's literature festivals will have a sprinkling of new and well-known authors and illustrators in attendance, and most authors and illustrators will be accompanied by a representative from their publishing company. So you can see and hear the author/illustrator and even do a bit of networking with the publisher! You will also be guaranteed some fun. Festivals are also a useful way of seeing children's reactions to their favourite authors and books in an informal situation.

3. Watch... and listen

● Familiarise yourself with the children's media: watch children's television and listen to children's radio programmes (see the *Television, film and radio* section beginning on page 283), and check out the websites listed throughout the *Yearbook*. Look at children's character merchandising and greetings cards.

4. Network
● Being an author or illustrator can be a lonely business – don't work in a vacuum. Talk to others of your discipline at festivals, conferences and book groups. Join the Federation of Children's Book Groups (see page 350) where you can network to your heart's content. Find out if there are any writer/illustrator groups in your area. If you are already published, join the Scattered Authors Society (see page 357).

5. Never underestimate the job in hand
● Writing and illustrating for children is not an easy option. Many people think they can dash off a children's story and a few sketchy illustrations and that they will be good enough to publish. But if you have researched the marketplace you will realise that it is a hugely competitive area and you have to be talented, have something original to say, have an unique style… and know how to persevere in order to get your work published and out to a wider audience.

6. Use your experiences
● Having your own children, or working in a child-related profession is helpful but shouldn't be relied on to bring you a new career as a children's writer or illustrator. (Never use this line when submitting a manuscript: 'I wrote this story for my children and they enjoyed it so please will you publish it?' Any story you write for your own children, grand-children, nieces, nephews, etc is likely to be enjoyed by them because children love atten-tion.) Publishers will only want to take on something that has appeal for a wide range of children – both nationally and internationally – never forget that publishing is a business. However, do use your experiences in terms of ideas, especially the more unusual ones, like seeing your first alien fall from the sky!

7. Research catalogues and websites
● Look at publishers' catalogues and websites, not just to find out what they are publishing, but because many of them give guidance for new writers and illustrators. When submitting a manuscript or portfolio to a publisher, it is a good idea to let them know that you know (and admire!) what they already publish. You can then make your case about where your submission will fit in their list. Let them know that you mean business and have researched the marketplace.

8. Submit your material with care
● First decide whether to approach an agent or to go it alone and submit your material direct to a publisher (see *How to get an agent* on page 165, *Do you have to have an agent to succeed?* on page 169 and *Publishing agreements* on page 219 for the pros and cons of each approach.) Check that the agent or publisher you are thinking of approaching accepts (a) unsolicited material, and (b) is interested in the type of work you are doing. For example, don't send your potential prize-winning novel to an educational publisher, and don't send your ideas for a Guided Reading Series at Key Stage 1 to a 'trade' publisher without an

educational list. And don't send your illustrations for a children's picture book to an agent who only deals with teenage fiction – there will be zero interest from them and you will be very disappointed.

● Submit your work to the right publisher/agent and the right person within the company. Ring first to find out who the best person for your work might be, whether it be in a publishing company, an agency, a television production company or a children's magazine. Also ask whether they want a synopsis and sample chapters or the complete manuscript or, for artwork, a selection of illustrations or your whole portfolio.

● Presentation is important. For example, no editor will read a handwritten manuscript. It should be typed/word processed, using double spacing with each page clearly numbered. (Should an editor be interested in your work, it will be photocopied for all involved in the acquisition process to read. Photocopiers have a habit of chewing up pages and there's nothing worse than pages being missing at a crucial part of a novel.) If your manuscript is accepted for publication, the editor will want the text electronically.

● For illustrations, select work on a paper that can be easily photocopied – a white/cream background with no unusual textures for your first pitch (such as sandpaper or glass – yes it really has happened!) And remember, publishers' photocopiers are notoriously bad at reproducing colour accurately, so if you are relying on the vibrancy of your colour to wow an art director, bear in mind that by the time they have been photocopied a few times for interested parties to see, the colours will not be the same. If your artwork is computer generated, send hard copies with your disk – it saves time when being shown around.

9. Identify your USP

● Ask yourself what the unique selling point (USP) of the material you are submitting for publication is. You may have an original authorial 'voice', you may have a particularly innovative illustration style or technique, or you may have come up with an amazingly brilliant idea for a series. If, after checking out the marketplace, you think you have something truly original to offer, then believe in yourself and be convincing when you offer it for publication.

10. Don't give up!

● Editors receive hundreds of manuscripts, and art directors receive hundreds of illustration samples every day. For a publisher, there are many factors that have to be taken into consideration when evaluating these submissions, the most important of which is 'Can we publish it successfully?' – i.e. 'Will it sell?' Publishing is a big business and it is ever more competitive. Even after an editor or art director has seen and liked your work, there are many other people involved before something is acquired for publication: the marketing manager, the publicist, the rights director, the book club manager, the sales director and, of course, the financial director. You will find this mantra repeated again and again in many of the articles in this book: *Have patience, keep at it*. If you believe in your 'product' eventually someone else will too. And meanwhile, keep perfecting your craft. After all, you are doing it because you enjoy it, aren't you?

Alison Stanley has been a senior commissioning editor of children's fiction at Puffin Books and at HarperCollins Children's Books. She is now selling her USP as a freelance.

See also...

Children's book publishers UK and Ireland

*Member of the Publishers Association or Scottish Publishers Association
†Member of the Irish Book Publishers' Association

Abbey Home Media
435–7 Edgware Road, London W2 1TH
tel 020-7563 3910 *fax* 020-7563 3911
email info@abbeyhomemedia.com
Managing Director James Harding

Activity books, board books, novelty books, picture books, non-fiction, reference books, audiotapes and CDs. Advocates learning through interactive play. Age groups: preschool, 5–10.

Academy of Light Ltd
Unit 1c, Delta Centre, Mount Pleasant, Wembley, Middlesex HA0 1UX
tel 020-8795 2695 *fax* 020-8903 3748
email yubraj@academyoflight.co.uk
website www.academyoflight.co.uk
Managing Director & Chief Editor Dr Yubraj Sharma, *Marketing & Financial Director* Mrs Mita Shah

Spirituality and alternative medicine; children's. Founded 2000.

Allegra Publishing Ltd
15 Quayside Lodge, William Morris Way, London SW6 2UZ
tel 020-7384 3303 *fax* 020-7384 3327
email info@allegrapublishing.com
website www.allegrapublishing.com
Publisher Felicia Law

Specialises in creating bright and innovative, frequently character-led, children's learning projects which often contain extended add-ons, such as audios, DVDs, toys and learning tools and games. Novelty books, picture books, reference series, ELT, science. Age groups: preschool, 5–14. Founded 2002.

Alligator Books Ltd
Gadd House, Arcadia Avenue, London N3 2JU
tel 020-8371 6622 *fax* 020-8371 6633
website www.alligatorbooks.co.uk
Joint Managing Directors Neil Rodol and Andrew Rabin

Children's fiction, including classics, and non-fiction, including film tie-ins and characters from animated TV shows, and reference, activity and learning books. Founded 1999.

Andersen Press Ltd
20 Vauxhall Bridge Road, London SW1V 2SA
tel 020-7840 8703 (editorial) *fax* 020-7233 6263

email andersenpress@randomhouse.co.uk
website www.andersenpress.co.uk
Managing Director/Publisher Klaus Flugge, *Directors* Philip Durrance, Joëlle Flugge (company secretary), Rona Selby (editorial)

Picture books, and junior and teenage fiction. Recent successes include the *Elmer* series by David McKee and *Doing it* by Melvin Burgess. Other authors include Anne Fine, Michael Foreman, Tony Ross and Jeanne Willis. Illustrators include Ralph Steadman and Max Velthuijs, winner of the the 2004 Hans Christian Andersen Award for Illustration for his *Frog* series.

Submission details For novels, send 3 sample chapters, a synopsis and return postage. Juvenile fiction should be 3000–5000 words long, and older fiction about 15,000–30,000 words. The text for picture books should be under 1000 words long. No poetry or short stories. Do not send MSS via email.

Andromeda Children's Books – see Pinwheel Ltd

Anglia Young Books – see Mill Publishing

Anness Publishing
88–89 Blackfriars Road, London SE1 8HA
tel 020-7401 2077 *fax* 020-7633 9499
email info@anness.com
website www.annesspublishing.com
Managing Director Paul Anness, *Publisher* Joanna Lorenz

Practical illustrated books on lifestyle, cookery, crafts, gardening, Mind, Body & Spirit, health and children's non-fiction. Founded 1989.

Lorenz Books (hardback imprint)
website www.lorenzbooks.com
Lifestyle, cookery, crafts, gardening, Mind, Body & Spirit, health and children's non-fiction.

Southwater (paperback imprint)
website www.southwaterbooks.com
Lifestyle, cookery, crafts, gardening, Mind, Body & Spirit, health and children's non-fiction.

Practical Pictures (image licensing)
Lifestyle, cookery, crafts, gardening, Mind, Body & Spirit, health and children's non-fiction.

Anova Children's Books
151 Freston Road, London W10 6TH
tel 020-7314 1400 *fax* 020-7314 1594

website www.chrysalisbooks.co.uk
Publisher Ben Cameron, Associate Publisher,
Education Joyce Bentley, Associate Publisher, Fiction &
Preschool Hannah Wilson

Children's books: from baby and picture books to
illustrated classics and educational books.
    Education: non-fiction in all curriculum areas.
Recent successful titles include *Speaking and
Listening, Start Writing, A First Look at Art, World
Issues, Start Science, Start Poetry, Shaping Britain* and
Our Lives, Our World.
    Trade: picture books, novelty and gift books for
ages 0–10. Also publishes innovative and interactive
children's books. Recent successes include *The Shory
of the Little Mole, War Boy, If Elephants Wore
Trousers, The Lady Who Lived in a Car* and *Adrenalin!*
series. Part of the Anova Books Group.
    Submission details Will not consider unsolicited
MSS; submit via an agent. Founded 2003 as Chrysalis
Children's Books.

Anvil Books/The Children's Press†
45 Palmerston Road, Dublin 6, Republic of Ireland
tel (01) 4973628
Directors Rena Dardis (managing), Margaret Dardis
(editorial)

Children's Press: adventure fiction, ages 9–14. Anvil:
Irish history and biography. Only considers MSS by
Irish-based authors and of Irish interest. Send
synopsis with IRCs (no UK stamps); unsolicited MSS
not returned. Founded 1964.

Arcturus Publishing Ltd
26–27 Bickels Yard, 151–3 Bermondsey Street,
London SE1 3HA
tel 020-7407 9400 fax 020-7407 9444
email roberta.bailey@arcturuspublishing.com
Managing Director, Arcturus Children's Publishing
Roberta Bailey

Children's fiction, non-fiction and school library
books, including activity books, reference, education,
geography, history and science.

Atlantic Europe Publishing Co. Ltd
Greys Court Farm, Greys Court, Henley-on-Thames,
Oxon RG9 4PG
tel (01491) 628188 fax (01491) 628189
email enquiries@atlanticeurope.com
Director Dr B.J. Knapp

Educational: children's colour illustrated information
books, co-editions and primary school class books
covering science, geography, technology,
mathematics, history, religious education. Recent
successes include the *Curriculum Visions* series and
Science at School series. Founded 1990.
    Submission details Submit via email to
contactus@atlanticeurope.com with no attachments.
No MSS accepted by post. Established teacher
authors only.

Autumn Publishing
Appledram Barns, Birdham Road, Chichester, West
Sussex PO20 7EQ
tel (01243) 531660 fax (01243) 774433
email autumn@autumpublishing.co.uk
website www.autumpublishing.co.uk

Autumn Publishing's philosophy is that children
should enjoy learning with its books. Byeway Books is
the imprint for all titles. Founded 1976.

Byeway Books (imprint)
Activity books, novelty books and picture books to
enable children to learn whilst they play. Also lift-the-
flap board books, sticker books, wall charts, colouring
books and colourful flash cards designed to help
young children have fun while learning the alphabet
and counting. Publishes approx. 200 titles each year
and has 600 in print. Recent successes include *Help
with Homework* range, wall chart range and *Practice
Makes Perfect* range.
    Submission details No responsibility is accepted for
the return of unsolicited MSS.

Award Publications Ltd
The Old Riding School, The Welbeck Estate,
Worksop, Notts. S80 3LR
tel (01909) 478170 fax (01909) 484632
email info@awardpublications.co.uk

Children's books: full colour picture story books;
early learning, information and activity books. No
unsolicited material. Founded 1954.

b small publishing
The Book Shed, 36 Leyborne Park, Kew, Richmond,
Surrey TW9 3HA
tel 020-8948 2884 fax 020-8948 6458
email info@bsmall.co.uk
website www.bsmall.co.uk
Publisher Catherine Bruzzone

Activity books and foreign language learning books
for 2–12 year-olds. No unsolicited MSS. Founded
1990.

Barefoot Books Ltd ✓
124 Walcot Street, Bath BA1 5BG
tel (01225) 322400 fax (01225) 322499
email info@barefootbooks.co.uk
website www.barefootbooks.co.uk
Editor-in-Chief Tessa Strickland, Group Project
Manager Jo Collins

Children's picture books and audiobooks: myth,
legend, fairytale, cross-cultural stories. Picture book
MSS only with return p&p. Founded 1993.

Barn Owl Books
157 Fortis Green Road, London N10 3LX
email ann@barnowlbooks.com
website barnowlbooks.com, www.franceslincoln.co.uk
Contact Ann Jungman

Specialises in publishing out-of-print children's books from the recent past by authors such as Jacqueline Wilson, Michael Rosen, Joan Aiken, Margaret Mahy, Jeremy Strong, Ann Jungman and illustrator Quentin Blake. Reprints only: no new submissions.

Barrington Stoke*
18 Walker Street, Edinburgh EH3 7LP
tel 0131-225 4113 *fax* 0131-225 4140
email anna.gibbons@barringtonstoke.co.uk
website www.barringtonstoke.co.uk
Managing Director Sonia Raphael, *Editorial Manager* Katie Paice

Fiction for reluctant, dyslexic or under-confident readers: fiction for 8–12 year-olds with a reading age of 8+, fiction for teenagers with a reading age of 8+, fiction for 8–12 year-olds with a reading age of below 8, fiction for teenagers with a reading age of below 8. Resources for readers and their teachers. Publishes approx. 50 titles a year and has over 200 books in print. Founded 1998.
Submission details No unsolicited MSS. All work is commissioned from well-known authors and adapted for reluctant readers.

BBC Active*
80 Strand, London WC2R 0RL
tel 020-7010 2701 *fax* 020-7010 6965
website www.bbcactive.com,
www.bbcschoolshop.com
Director of BBC Active Susan Ross

Educational and textbooks, resources for teachers; electronic, audio and video, CD-Roms and DVDs, activity books, and interactive whiteboard resources. Publishes for preschool–15+.

BBC Audiobooks Ltd*
St James House, The Square, Lower Bristol Road, Bath BA2 3BH
tel (01225) 878000 *fax* (01225) 310771
website www.bbcaudiobooks.com
Directors Paul Dempsey (managing), Jan Paterson (publishing)

Large print books and complete and unabridged audiobooks. Does not publish original books. Children's imprint: Galaxy Children's Large Print. Recent successes include *Midnight* by Jacqueline Wilson, *Artemis Fowl: The Eternity Code* by Eoin Colfer and *Shadowmancer* by G.P. Taylor – all published in audio and large print. Formed in 2002 from the amalgamation of Chivers Press, Cover To Cover and BBC Radio Collection.

BBC Children's Books – see Penguin Group (UK)

Beautiful Books
117 Sugden Road, London SW11 5ED
020-7738 2428 020-7223 4841

email office@beautiful-books.co.uk,
submissions@beautiful-books.co.uk
website www.beautiful-books.co.uk
Managing Director Simon Petherick

Children's and adult fiction and non-fiction. Picture books include *Young Travellers Club* series, European travel guides for children.
Submission details Send a 2-page synopsis, the first 10 pages of text, plus a short biography about yourself with sae for return of material. Alternatively submit by email. Founded 2004.

Belair – see Folens Publishers

Bite – see Hodder Headline Ltd

A & C Black Publishers Ltd*
38 Soho Square, London W1D 3HB
tel 020-7758 0200 *fax* 020-7758 0222
email enquiries@acblack.com
website www.acblack.com
Chairman Nigel Newton, *Managing Director* Jill Coleman, *Deputy Managing Director* Jonathan Glasspool, *Directors* Colin Adams, Oscar Heini (production), Janet Murphy (Adlard Coles Nautical), Kathy Rooney, David Wightman (sales)

Children's and educational books (including music); ceramics, art and craft, drama, ornithology, reference (*Who's Who*, *Whitaker's Almanack*), sport, theatre, books for writers. Subsidiary of Bloomsbury Publishing plc. Founded 1807.

A & C Black/Andrew Brodie Publications (imprints)
Commissioning Editors Susila Bayhars (fiction), David Norris (educational resources), Helen Diamond (home learning)

Fiction for 5–8 and 9–12 year-olds, series non-fiction, reference, plays, poetry. A & C Black publishes approx. 65 titles each year. Andrew Brodie Publications are a range of educational books for primary and secondary schools and about 20 titles are published each year.
Recent fiction successes include, for 5–8 year-olds: *Brick-a-Brek* by Julia Donaldson in the *Chameleons* series; fiction for 7–9 year-olds: *Live the Dream!* by Jenny Oldfield in the *White Wolves* series; fiction for 8–11 year-olds: *Bryony Bell Tops the Bill* by Frankeska G. Ewart in the *Black Cat* series. Recent non-fiction successes include *Science Works* by Jacqui Bailey and Matthew Lilly, *Real Lives* by Sallie Purkis and *Going Up* by Jen Alexander. Recent education successes include *Developing Science* by Christine Moorcroft, *Best Handwriting* by Andrew Brodie and *Foundations Activity Packs*.
Submission details For fiction please enquire about current guidelines before submitting work as the content of each seasonal list varies. Allow 6–8 weeks for a response. No submissions by email. Look at recently published titles and in catalogues to gauge a feel of current publishing interests. Much of the

fiction list has been commissioned to appeal to the educational market and to be part of large series, but increasingly fiction books are being presented to appeal to the trade as standalone titles. For education books the focus is on materials related to the National Curriculum.

Blackwater Press – see Folens Publishers

Bloomsbury Publishing Plc*

36 Soho Square, London W1D 3QY
tel 020-7494 2111 fax 020-7434 0151
website www.bloomsbury.com
Chairman & Chief Executive Nigel Newton, Directors Liz Calder (publishing), Alexandra Pringle (publishing), Michael Fishwick (publishing), Kathleen Farrar (international), Karen Rinaldi (Bloomsbury USA), David Ward (sales), Minna Fry (marketing), Katie Bond (publicity), Ruth Logan (rights), Penny Edwards (production), Arzu Tahsin (paperbacks), Sarah Odedina (children's), Colin Adams (finance), Will Webb (design), Jill Coleman (A & C Black), Kathy Rooney (Berlin Verlag), Elisabeth Ruge (Berlin Verlag), Stephanie Duncan (Dot.com), Charles Black (non-executive), Paul Scherer (non-executive), Mike Mayer (non-executive), Jeremy Wilson (non-executive), Company Secretary Richard Cordeschi

Fiction, biography, illustrated, travel, children's, trade paperbacks and mass market paperbacks. Founded 1986.

Bloomsbury Children's Books (imprint)

website www.bloomsbury.com/childrens
Chairman & Chief Executive Nigel Newton, Publishing Director Sarah Odedina, Deputy Editorial Director Emma Matthewson, Commissioning Editors Ele Fountain, Smriti Prasadam, Design Director Val Brathwaite, Production Manager Helena Coryndon, Publicity Managers Lucy Holden, Ian Lamb, Rights Director Ruth Logan, Children's Key Accounts Manager Rosamund de la Hey, Sales Director David Ward, Marketing Managers Colette Whitehouse, Joanne Owen, Finance Director Colin Adams
Baby books, picture books, fiction for children of all ages. Publishes approx. 100 titles a year and has over 500 books in print. Recent publications include the Harry Potter series, Whispering to Witches by Anna Dale and Marvin Wanted More by Joseph Theobalds (picture book). Company founded 1986; children's list launched 1994.

Submission details Send a synopsis of the book together with 3 chapters. No unsolicited MSS.

Bookmart Ltd

Blaby Road, Wigston, Leicester LE18 4SE
tel 0116-275 9060 fax 0116-275 9090
email books@bookmart.co.uk
website www.bookmart.co.uk
Publishing Director Linda Williams

Colour illustrated titles: children's fiction and non-fiction, poetry, novelty books, pop-up books, activity books. Age groups: preschool, 5–10, 10–15.

Boxer Books Ltd

107 Charterhouse Street, London EC1M 6PT
tel 020-7490 9614
email pa@boxerbooks.com
website www.boxerbooks.com

Innovative books for babies and toddlers: board books, novelty books, picture books. Age groups: 0–6.

Brilliant Publications*

1 Church View, Sparrow Hall Farm, Edlesborough, Dunstable LU6 2ES
tel (01525) 229720 fax (01525) 229725
email editorial@brilliantpublications.co.uk
website www.brilliantpublications.co.uk
Managing Director Priscilla Hannaford

Resource books for teachers and others concerned with the education of 0–13 year-olds. All areas of the curriculum published. Series for reluctant readers, aimed at 7–11 year-olds. Does not publish children's picture books. Study catalogue or visit website before sending proposal. Founded 1993.

Brimax – see Autumn Publishing

British Museum Company Ltd*

38 Russell Square, London WC1B 3QQ
tel 020-7323 1234 fax 020-7436 7315
website www.britishmuseum.co.uk
Director of Publishing Rosemary Bradley, Senior Commissioning Editor Carolyn Jones

The world's leading museum publisher, with a growing children's list encompassing authoritative illustrated reference and information titles as well as a range of activity and colouring books. Founded 1973.

Buster Books

9 Lion Yard, Tremadoc Road, London SW4 7NQ
tel 020-7720 8643 fax 020-7627 8953
email busterbooks@michaelomarabooks.com
website www.mombooks.com/busterbooks
Managing Director Lesley O'Mara, Publishing Director Philippa Wingate, Managing Editor David Sinden

Novelty books, board books, non-fiction and gift books for young children. Publishes approx. 40 titles a year. Recent successes include Kids' Sudoku, boxes of books and children's miscellanies.

Submission details Submit novelty and non-fiction (no fiction) with sae. Allow 1–2 months for response.

Cambridge University Press*

The Edinburgh Building, Shaftesbury Road, Cambridge CB2 2RU
tel (01223) 325892 fax (01223) 325891
email information@cambridge.org
website www.cambridge.org

Chief Executive of the Press Stephen R.R. Bourne, *Managing Director, Europe, Middle East & Africa* Michael Holdsworth, *Managing Director, Academic Publishing* Andrew Brown, *Publishing Director, Humanities & Social Sciences* Richard Fisher, *Publishing Director, Science, Technology & Medicine* Richard Barling, *Managing Director, Cambridge Learning*, Andrew Gilfillan, *Chief Executive, Cambridge-Hitachi*, John Tuttle, *Editorial Director, Journals* Geoffrey Nuttall

For children: curriculum-based education books and software for schools and colleges (primary, secondary and international). Part of the National Grid for Learning. English language teaching for adult and younger learners.

For adults: anthropology and archaeology,astronomy, biological sciences, classical studies, computer science, dictionaries, earth sciences, economics, e-learning products, engineering, English language teaching, history, language and literature, law, mathematics, medical sciences, music, philosophy, physical sciences, politics, psychology, reference, technology, social sciences, theology, religion. Journals (humanities, social sciences, STM). The Bible and Prayer Book. Founded 1534.

Campbell Books – see Macmillan Publishers Ltd

Caterpillar Books – see Magi Publications

Catnip Publishing Ltd

Islington Business Centre, 3–5 Islington High Street, London N1 9LQ
tel 020-7745 2370 *fax* 020-7745 2372
website www.catnippublishing.co.uk
Directors Robert Snuggs (managing), Andrea Reece (publishing), Martin West (editorial)

Children's books. New and previously published titles for children up to the age of 11, with the emphasis on 5–7 year-olds, from foreign publishers or UK houses that have let them go out of print. New titles include *The Riddle of the Poisoned Monk* by Sarah Matthias; republished titles include *Granny Was a Buffer Girl* by Berlie Doherty (twice winner of the Carnegie Prize) and the *Fairy Charm* series by Emily Rodda. Publishes 40 books a year. Created from the merger of Happy Cat Books and Southwood Books. Founded 2005.

CGP

Coordination Group Publications, Kirkby-in-Furness, Cumbria LA17 7WZ
tel (0870) 750 1282 *fax* (0870) 750 1292
email info@cgpbooks.co.uk
website cgpbooks.co.uk

Educational books centred around the National Curriculum, including revision guides and study books for GCSE, KS3, KS2, KS1 and A level. Subjects include maths, English, science, history, geography, ICT, psychology, business studies, religious studies, child development, design and techology, PE, music, French, German, Spanish, sociology.

Submission details On the lookout for top teachers at all levels, in all subjects. Potential authors and proofreaders should send an email to carolinehornby@cgpbooks.co.uk with their name, subject area, level and experience, plus contact address, ready for when a project comes up in their subject area.

Paul Chapman Publishing – see SAGE Publications Ltd

The Chicken House

2 Palmer Street, Frome, Somerset BA11 1DS
tel (01373) 454488 *fax* (01373) 454499
email chickenhouse@doublecluck.com
website www.doublecluck.com
Managing Director & Publisher Barry Cunningham, *Deputy Managing Director* Rachel Hickman

Novelty books, picture books, fiction for ages 5–8 and 9–11 and teenage fiction. Publishes approx. 25 titles a year. Recent successes include *Candy* by Kevin Brooks, *Dragon Rider* by Cornelia Funke and *The Cry of the Icemark* by Stuart Hill. Acquired by Scholastic Inc.

Submission details Will consider unsolicited MSS. Send synopsis and 2–3 sample chapters. Allow 12 weeks for response.

Child's Play (International) Ltd

Ashworth Road, Bridgemead, Swindon, Wilts. SN5 7YD
tel (01793) 616286 *fax* (01793) 512795
email allday@childs-play.com
website www.childs-play.com
Chairman Adriana Twinn, *Publisher* Neil Burden

Children's educational books: board, picture, activity and play books; fiction and non-fiction. Founded 1972.

Chivers Press

St James House, The Square, Windsor Bridge Road, Bath BA2 3AX
tel (01225) 335336 *fax* (01225) 310771
email christine@chivers.co.uk
website www.chivers.co.uk
Publishing Director Jan Paterson, *Contact* Christine Graham

One of the most prolific publishers of large print books and unabridged audiobooks in the world. Has over 3000 titles, encompassing a wide range of best-selling authors and catering for all tastes, including children's titles (*Galaxy Large Print* series). Imprint of **BBC Audiobooks Ltd**. Founded 1979.

Christian Education*

(incorporating RE Today Services and International Bible Reading Association)
1020 Bristol Road, Selly Oak, Birmingham B29 6LB
tel 0121-472 4242 *fax* 0121-472 7575
email enquiries@christianeducation.org.uk
website www.christianeducation.org.uk

Publications and services for teachers of RE including *RE today* magazine, curriculum booklets, training material for children and youth workers in the Church. Worship resources for use in primary schools. Christian drama and musicals, Activity Club material and Bible reading resources.

Chrysalis Children's Books – see Anova Children's Books

Claire Publications

Unit 8, Tey Brook Craft Centre, Great Tey, Colchester, Essex CO6 1JE
tel (01206) 211020 *fax* (01206) 212755
email mail@clairepublications.com
website www.clairepublications.com

Educational publisher of mathematics materials for primary and secondary schools. Also literacy and language materials, including games, puzzles and photocopiable teachers' resources. Supplies training workshops.

Colourpoint Books

Colourpoint House, Jubilee Business Park, 21 Jubilee Road, Newtownards, Co. Down, Northern Ireland BT23 4YH
tel (028) 9182 0505 *fax* (028) 9182 1900
email info@colourpoint.co.uk
website www.colourpoint.co.uk
Commissioning Editor Sheila Johnston

Educational textbooks for KS3 (11–14 year-olds), KS3 Special Needs (10–14 year-olds), GCSE (14–16 year-olds) and A-Level/undergraduates (age 17+). Subjects include English, geography, history and politics, home economics, ICT, maths and religious education. Founded 1993.

Submission details Because Northern Ireland is a small market, Colourpoint concentrates on pupil books which are bought in class set quantities. Potential authors should send some sample pages of their material to show that they can connect with their target age group and not write above or below the ability range, say how long they have been successfully teaching a particular subject and whether they have been involved in writing before. Include return postage.

The Continuum International Publishing Group Ltd

The Tower Building, 11 York Road, London SE1 7NX
tel 020-7922 0880 *fax* 020-7922 0881
email info@continuumbooks.com
website www.continuumbooks.com
Chairman & Ceo Philip Sturrock, *Directors* Robin Baird-Smith (general trade and Continuum religion: publishes under Continuum, Burns & Oates, Morehouse), Anthony Haynes (academic humanities: publishes education, social sciences, literature, film and music, philosophy (including Thoemmes imprint), linguistics, biblical studies and theology printed under T&T Clark), Frank Roney (finance), Ed Suthon (sales & marketing), Benn Linfield (publishing services)

Serious non-fiction, academic and professional, including scholarly monographs and educational texts and reference works in history, politics and social thought; literature, criticism, performing arts; religion and spirituality; education, psychology, women's studies, business. Imprints: Burns & Oates, Continuum, Hambledon, Morehouse, T&T Clark International, Thoemmes Press.

Education books include *Getting the Buggers to Write* and *Getting the Buggers to be Creative* by Sue Cowley.

cp publishing

The Children's Project Ltd, PO Box 2, Richmond, Surrey TW10 7FL
tel 020-8546 8750 *fax* 020-8974 5849
email info@childrensproject.co.uk
website www.childrensproject.co.uk
Directors/Co-founders Helen Dorman, Clive Dorman

High-quality visual books that help parents and carers better understand and communicate with their children from birth. The Children's Project is dedicated exclusively to supporting the family and improved outcomes for children. It draws upon the experience and expertise of parents, health professionals and academics to provide up-to-date information in a form that is easily accessible to everyone – parents, carers and practitioners. Founded in 1995; first books published 2000.

Crown House Publishing Ltd

Crown Buildings, Bancyfelin, Carmarthen SA33 5ND
tel (01267) 211345 *fax* (01267) 211882
email books@crownhouse.co.uk
website www.crownhouse.co.uk
Chairman Martin Roberts, *Directors* David Bowman (managing director), Glenys Roberts, David Bowman, Karen Bowman, Caroline Lenton

Publishes a range of teacher resources detailing the latest and best techniques for enhancing learning and teaching ability. List includes accelerated learning, thinking skills, multiple intelligence, emotional intelligence, mindmapping and music. Also publishes titles in the areas of psychotherapy, business training and development, Mind, Body & Spirit. Founded 1998.

Crowswing Books

PO Box 301, King's Lynn, Norfolk PE33 0XW
tel (01553) 840694

email submissions@crowswingbooks.co.uk
website www.crowswingbooks.co.uk
Contact Patricia Cole

Limited edition science fiction, fantasy and horror fiction for children and adults. Founded 2003.
Submission details Writers and illustrators should always enquire first with a brief one-page synopsis of the work they have to offer. Writers should submit no more than the first 2 sample chapters. Illustrators should submit a small portfolio of work, 6 pieces max. Include a publication history to date (if any) and a brief biographical paragraph about yourself. A personal response to your work cannot be guaranteed beyond acknowledgement. Include sae or IRC for return of material.

Dean – see Egmont Books

Dorling Kindersley – see Penguin Group (UK)

Dref Wen

28 Church Road, Whitchurch, Cardiff CF14 2EA
tel 029-2061 7860 fax 029-2061 0507
Directors Roger Boore, Anne Boore, Gwilym Boore, Alun Boore, Editor Catrin Hughes

Welsh language publisher. Original, adaptations and translations of foreign and English language full-colour picture story books for children. Also activity books, novelty books, Welsh language fiction for 7–14 year-olds, teenage fiction, reference, religion, audiobooks and poetry. Educational material for primary and secondary schoolchildren in Wales and England, including dictionaries, revision guides and Welsh as a Second Language. Publishes approx. 50 titles a year and has 450 in print. Founded 1970.
Submission details No unsolicited MSS. Phone first.

Dublar Scripts

204 Mercer Way, Romsey, Hants SO51 7QJ
tel (01794) 501377 fax (01794) 502538
email scripts@dublar.freeserve.co.uk
website www.dublar.co.uk
Managing Director Robert Heather

Pantomimes. Imprint: Sleepy Hollow Pantomimes. Founded 1994.

The Educational Company of Ireland[†]

Ballymount Road, Walkinstown, Dublin 12, Republic of Ireland
tel (01) 4500611 fax (01) 4500993
email info@edco.ie
website www.edco.ie
Executive Directors Frank Maguire (chief executive), R. McLoughlin, Financial Controller A. Harrold, Sales & Marketing Manager M. Harford-Hughes, Publisher Frank Fahy

Educational (primary and post-primary) books in the Irish language. Publishes approx. 60–70 titles each year and has 600–700 in print. Ancillary materials

include CD-Roms, CDs and audiotapes. Recent successes include Sunny Street/Streets Ahead Primary English Langue Programme, Fonn 1, 2, 3 (Irish language publications for post-primary) and Geo (geography publication for post-primary). Trading unit of Smurfit Kappa Group – Ireland. Founded 1910.
Submission details Send an A4 page outlining the selling points and proposal, a draft table of contents and a sample chapter. Allow 3 months for response.

Educational Explorers (Publishers)

Unit 5, Feidr Castell Business Park, Fishguard SA65 9BB
tel/fax (08456) 123912
email explorers@cuisenaire.co.uk
website www.cuisenaire.co.uk
Directors M.J. Hollyfield, D.M. Gattegno

Educational. Mathematics: Numbers in colour with Cuisenaire Rods; languages: The Silent Way; literacy, reading: Words in Colour; educational films. No unsolicited material. Founded 1962.

Egmont Books*

239 Kensington High Street, London W8 6SA
tel 020-7761 3500 fax 020-7761 3510
email firstname.surname@ecb.egmont.com
website www.egmont.co.uk
Managing Director Robert McMenemy, Publishing Director David Riley, Senior Publishers Susan Reuben (licensing), Cally Poplak (fiction & picture books), Sue Parish (annuals, Dean & stationery)

Annuals, activity books, novelty books, picture books, fiction for 5–8 and 9–12 year-olds, teenage fiction, series fiction, film/TV tie-ins, home learning, stationery and gift books. Characters include Thomas the Tank Engine, Barbie, Mr Men, Miffy, Postman Pat and Action Man. Recent successes include A Series of Unfortunate Events by Lemony Snicket, The Barbie Annual 2004 and Thomas the Tank Engine Story Library. Imprints: Egmont, Dean. Founded 1878.
Submission details Will consider unsolicited MSS. For picture books send some sample pages. For longer fiction send the first 3 chapters and a synopsis. Include an sae. No submissions by email. Allow 3–6 months for response.

Evans Brothers Ltd*

2A Portman Mansions, Chiltern Street, London W1U 6NR
tel 020-7487 0920 fax 020-7487 0921
email sales@evansbooks.co.uk
website www.evansbooks.co.uk
Directors Stephen Pawley (managing), Brian D. Jones (international publishing), A.O. Ojora (Nigeria), UK Publisher Su Swallow

Educational books, particularly preschool, school library and teachers' books for the UK, primary and secondary for Africa, the Caribbean. Part of the Evans Publishing Group. Founded 1908.

Faber and Faber Ltd*

3 Queen Square, London WC1N 3AU
tel 020-7465 0045 fax 020-7465 0034
website www.faber.co.uk
Chief Executive Stephen Page, Publicity Director
Rachel Alexander, Marketing Director Noel Murphy,
Production Director Nigel Marsh, Rights Director
Camilla Smallwood, Children's Director Suzy Jenvey,
Senior Commissioning Editor Julia Wells

High-quality general fiction and non-fiction, drama,
film, music, poetry. For children: fiction for 5–8 and
9–12 year-olds, teenage fiction, poetry and some non-
fiction. Authors include Paul McCartney, Ricky
Gervais, G.P. Taylor, Ted Hughes, Philip Ardagh,
Margaret Mahy, Pauline Fisk, Steve Voake, Harry
Hill, Graham Joyce.
    Submission details Only accepts submissions
through an agent; no unsolicited MSS.

CJ Fallon

Ground Floor, Block B, Liffey Valley Office Campus,
Dublin 22, Republic of Ireland
tel (01) 6166400 fax (01) 6166499
email editorial@cjfallon.ie
website www.cjfallon.ie
Executive Directors H.J. McNicholas (managing),
P. Tolan (financial), N. White (editorial)

Educational textbooks. Founded 1927.

David Fickling Books – see Random House Group Ltd

First and Best in Education Ltd

Earlstrees Court, Earlstrees Road, Corby, Northants.
NN17 4HH
tel (01536) 399004 fax (01536) 399012
email info@firstandbest.co.uk
website www.firstandbest.co.uk
Contact Anne Cockburn (editor)

Education-related books (no fiction). Currently
actively recruiting new writers for schools; ideas
welcome. Sae must accompany submissions.
Founded 1992.

Flame Tree Publishing

Crabtree Hall, Crabtree Lane, London SW6 6TY
tel 020-7386 4700 fax 020-7386 4701
email info@flametreepublishing.com
website www.flametreepublishing.com
Managing Director Frances Bodiam, Publisher/
Creative Director Nick Wells

Education (preschool and Key Stages 1 and 2). Also
for adults: music, reference, art, cookery. Part of The
Foundry Creative Media Company Ltd. Founded
1992.

Floris Books*

15 Harrison Gardens, Edinburgh EH11 1SH
tel 0131-337 2372 fax 0131-347 9919
email floris@florisbooks.co.uk
website www.florisbooks.co.uk
Editors Christopher Moore, Gale Winskill, Children's
Editor Gale Winskill

Children's activity books, picture books, fiction for
5–8 and 9–12 year-olds. Publishes approx. 20 titles
each year and has 120 in print. Recent successes
include West: The Christmas Owls. Also for adults:
religion, science, Celtic studies and craft books.
Founded 1978.
    Submission details No unsolicited picture books.

Kelpies (imprint)

Contemporary Scottish children's fiction for 9–12
year-olds. Recent successes include Arbuthnott: The
Chaos Clock.
    Submission details Will consider unsolicited MSS.
Send synopsis and sample chapter. Must be Scottish
in theme.

Folens Publishers*

Apex Business Centre, Boscombe Road, Dunstable
LU5 4RL
tel (0870) 609 1237 fax (0870) 609 1236
email folens@folens.com
website www.folens.com
Managing Director Malcolm Watson, Director of
Publishing Peter Burton, Primary Publisher Zoe
Nichols

Educational (primary, secondary and tertiary) books
and learn-at-home books for QCA Schemes of Work,
numeracy/literacy frameworks, special needs and
exam board-specific publishing. Publishes atlases,
dictionaries and revision guides. Subject areas include
history, geography, science, maths, French, PSHE,
citizenship, English, RE, PE and ICT. Recent
successes include GCSE RE, Citizenship and PE, plus
11–13 History, Citizenship and English. Imprints:
Folens, Belair. Founded 1987.
    Submission details Will consider unsolicited MSS.
Send synopsis, rationale and sample section by post
or email. Material will be acknowledged on receipt;
reply with decision to publish within 1–3 months.

Folens Publishers

Hibernian Industrial Estate, Greenhills Road,
Tallaght, Dublin 24, Republic of Ireland
tel (01) 4137200 fax (01) 4137282
website www.folens.ie
Chairman Dirk Folens, Managing Director John
O'Connor, Primary Managing & Commissioning
Editor Deirdre Whelan, Secondary Managing Editor
Margaret Burns

Educational (primary, secondary, comprehensive,
technical, in English and Irish). Founded 1956.

Blackwater Press (imprint)

Fiction for 9–12 year-olds, teenage fiction, picture
books and Brainstorm series of activity books. Recent
successes include Irish Lengend series, Reaching the

Heights by Peter Gunning (novel for 8–12 year-olds) and *Izzy and the Skunk* by Marie-Louise Fitzpatrick (picture book). Also general/adult non-fiction and Irish interest. Founded 1993.

Submission details Will consider unsolicited MSS. Send synopsis and first chapter. Allow 6 weeks for response.

David Fulton Publishers Ltd*

Chiswick Centre, 414 Chiswick High Road, London W4 5TF
tel 020-8996 3610 *fax* 020-8996 3622
email mail@fultonpublishers.co.uk
website www.fultonpublishers.co.uk
Publishing Director Tracey Alcock

Books for trainee and working teachers at all levels of the curriculum (foundation stage to post compulsory), with particular emphasis on special educational needs (SEN) and inclusion. SEN books also published in collaboration with the National Association for Special Educational Needs (NASEN); some overlap into other areas of health and social care, therapy, educational psychology, and speech and language therapy. A growing list of books for preschool and nursery staff. About 100 titles per year. No unsolicited MSS; synopses and ideas for books welcome. Founded 1987.

Galaxy Large Print – see Chivers Press

Galore Park Publishing Ltd*

19–21 Sayers Lane, Tenterden, Kent TN30 6BW
tel (0870) 234 2304
website www.galorepark.co.uk

So You Really Want To Learn range of textbooks for children aged 8+. Courses include Latin, French, English, Spanish, maths and science. Founded 1999.

Gardner Education Ltd

168ᴇ High Street, Egham, Surrey TW20 9HP
tel (0845) 230 0775 *fax* (0845) 230 0899
email education@gardnereducation.com
website www.gardnereducation.com

Specialists in literacy books and resources.

Geddes & Grosset*

David Dale House, New Lanark ML11 9DJ
tel (01555) 665000 *fax* (01555) 665694
email info@gandg.sol.co.uk
Publishers Ron Grosset, Mike Miller

Popular reference, children's non-fiction and activity books. Founded 1988.

Ginn & Co. – see Harcourt Education Ltd

Glowworm Books Ltd

Broxburn EH52 5LH
tel (01506) 857570 *fax* (01506) 858100
website www.glowwormbooks.co.uk

The company was formed by the amalgamation of Glowworm Books and The Amaising Publishing House (established in 1988 with the publication of the first 4 titles in its *Maisie* series, written by Aileen Paterson). Recent successes include further books in the *Maisie* series and *The History of Scotland for Children* by Judy Paterson. It has 42 titles in print written by 10 authors. Founded 1999.

Submission details MSS are not accepted without prior arrangement.

Golden Books for Young Readers – see Random House Inc.

Gomer Press

Llandysul, Ceredigion SA44 4JL
tel (01559) 363090 *fax* (01559) 363758
email gwasg@gomer.co.uk
website www.gomer.co.uk
Managing Director Jonathan Lewis, *Publishing Director* Mairwen Prys Jones, *Editors* Bethan Mair, Bryan James (Adult, Welsh), Ceri Wyn Jones (Adult, English), Sioned Lleinau, Helen Evans, Rhiannon Davies (Children's, Welsh), Viv Sayer (Children's, English)

Picture books, novels, stories, poetry and teaching resources all relevant to Welsh culture. No unsolicited MSS; preliminary enquiry essential. English books for children are printed under the imprint Pont Books. Founded 1892.

W.F. Graham

2 Pondwood Close, Moulton Park, Northampton NN3 6RT
tel (01604) 645537 *fax* (01604) 648414
email books@wfgraham.co.uk
website www.wfgraham.co.uk

Activity books including colouring, dot-to-dot, magic painting, puzzle, word search and sticker books. Also picture books and story books.

Granada Learning*

The Chiswick Centre, 414 Chiswick High Road, London W4 5TF
tel 020-8996-3333 *fax* 020-8742-8390
website www.granada-learning.com

Educational multimedia company publishing innovative, curriculum-based resources for the UK and abroad. It has a catalogue of over 800 software and hardware products for preschool children, primary and secondary, through to A level and adult education. Products are developed by teachers and educationalsts. The Granada Learning Group includes ASE, BlackCat (educational software for primary schools), David Fulton Publishers (see separate entry), Granada Learning Software, Granada Learning Professional Development, LearnWise (e-learning products), Leckie & Leckie (see separate entry), Letts Educational (see separate entry), nferNelson (see separate entry), SEMERC (see separate entry) and The Skills Factory.

Alison Green Books – see Scholastic Ltd

Gullane Children's Books – see Pinwheel Ltd

Hachette Children's Books*
338 Euston Road, London NW1 3BH
tel 020-7873 6000 *fax* 020-7873 6024
Managing Director Marlene Johnson

Hodder Children's Books (imprint)
Publishing Director Anne McNeil
Fiction, picture books, novelty, general non-fiction and audiobooks.

Orchard Books (imprint)
Publishing Director Ann-Janine Murtagh
Fiction, picture and novelty books.

Franklin Watts (imprint)
Publishing Director Rachel Cooke
Non-fiction and information books.

Wayland (imprint)
Publishing Director Joyce Bentley
Non-fiction and information books.

Haldane Mason Ltd
PO Box 34196, London NW10 3YB
tel 020-8459 2131 *fax* 020-8728 1216
email info@haldanemason.com
Directors Sydney Francis, Ron Samuel

Illustrated non-fiction books and box sets, mainly for children. Imprint: Red Kite Books (children's). Founded 1995.
   Submission details Will consider unsolicited MSS. Phone or email first to check interest.

Harcourt Education Ltd*
Halley Court, Jordan Hill, Oxford OX2 8EJ
tel (01865) 310533 *fax* (01865) 314641
email uk.schools@harcourteducation.co.uk
website www.harcourteducation.co.uk
Chief Executive Chris Jones

Division of Reed Elsevier (UK) Ltd.

Ginn & Co. (imprint)
fax (01865) 314189
Textbook/other educational resources for primary schools.

Heinemann Educational (imprint)
website www.heinemann.co.uk
Textbooks, literature and other educational resources for all levels.

Rigby Heinemann (imprint)
fax (01865) 314189
website www.myprimary.co.u

Textbook/other educational resources for primary schools.

Patrick Hardy Books – see James Clarke & Co. Ltd

HarperCollins Publishers*
77–85 Fulham Palace Road, London W6 8JB
tel 020-8741 7070 *fax* 020-8307 4440
also at Westerhill Road, Bishopbriggs, Glasgow G64 2QT
tel 0141-772 3200 *fax* 0141-306 3119
website www.harpercollins.co.uk
Ceo/Publisher Victoria Barnsley

For adults: fiction (commercial and literary) and non-fiction. Subjects include history, celebrity memoirs, biographies, popular science, Mind, Body & Spirit, dictionaries, maps and reference. Imprints include Collins Crime, Collins Dictionaries/COBUILD, Collins/Times Maps and Atlases, Collins Willow, Estates, Fourth Estate, HarperCollins, HarperCollins Entertainment, Thorsons/Element. All fiction and trade non-fiction must be submitted through an agent. Owned by News Corporation. Founded 1819.

HarperCollins Audio (imprint)
*Publishing Director*tba
See under *Audio publishers*.

HarperCollins Children's Books
website www.harpercollinschildrensbooks.co.uk
Managing Director Sally Gritten, *Publishing Directors* Gillie Russell (fiction), Sue Buswell (picture books)
Annuals, activity books, novelty books, picture books, painting and colouring books, pop-up books and book and tape sets. Fiction for 5–8 and 9–12 year-olds, teenage fiction and series fiction; poetry; film/TV tie-ins. Publishes approx. 265 titles each year. Recent successes include *Private Peaceful* by Michael Morpurgo, *Goodbye Mog* by Judith Kerr and *Noddy*. Properties include *Paddington, Narnia, Little Grey Rabbit, Brambly Hedge, Percy the Parkeeper, Animal Stories*. Imprints: HarperCollins Children's Books.
   Submission details No unsolicited MSS: only accepts submissions via agents.

Collins Education (division)
Managing Director Jim Green, *Publishing Director* Paul Cherry
Books, CD-Roms and online material for UK primary and secondary schools and colleges.

Collins Maps and Road Atlases (division and imprint)
Maps, atlases, street plans and leisure guides.

Heinemann Educational – see Harcourt Education Ltd

Hippo Books – see Scholastic Ltd

Hodder Children's Books – see Hachette Children's Books

Hodder Gibson*

2A Christie Street, Paisley PA1 1NB
tel 0141-848 1609 *fax* 0141-889 6315
email hoddergibson@hodder.co.uk
website www.hoddergibson.co.uk,
www.hoddereducation.co.uk,
www.madaboutbooks.com
Managing Director John Mitchell

Educational books specifically for Scotland. No
unsolicited MSS. Formed by an amalgamation of
Robert Gibson & Sons (Glasgow) and the Scottish
branch of Hodder & Stoughton Educational. Part of
the Hodder Headline Group.

Hodder Headline Ltd*

338 Euston Road, London NW1 3BH
tel 020-7873 6000 *fax* 020-7873 6024
website www.hodderheadline.co.uk
Group Chief Executive Tim Hely Hutchinson,
Directors Martin Neild (managing, Hodder
Headline), Jamie Hodder-Williams (managing,
Hodder & Stoughton General), Malcolm Edwards
(managing, Australia & New Zealand), Philip Walters
(managing, Hodder Education), Pierre de Cacqueray
(finance), Graham Money (managing, Bookpoint),
Mary Tapissier (group personnel/training/admin)

For adults: fiction (commercial and literary) and
non-fiction. Subjects include autobiography,
biography, food and wine, gardening, history,
humour, Mind, Body & Spirit, popular science,
religion, self-help, sport, travel and TV tie-ins.
Imprints include Headline, Help Yourself, Hodder &
Stoughton, Hodder Christian Books, Lir, Mobius,
New English Library, Review and Sceptre. Owned by
Hachette Livre. Founded 1986.

Hodder Education (division)

Directors Philip Walters (managing), Elisabeth Tribe
(schools publishing), Katie Roden (consumer
education), Joanna Koster (health sciences), Peter
McKay (journals & reference books), Alyssum Ross
(production & design), Catherine Newman (sales &
marketing)

Textbooks for the primary, secondary, tertiary and
further education sectors and for self-improvement.
Academic and professional books and journals.
Publishes under Hodder & Stoughton Educational,
Teach Yourself, Headway.

Hopscotch Educational Publishing Ltd

Unit 2, 56 Pickwick Road, Corsham, Wilts. SN13 9BX
tel (01249) 701701 *fax* (01249) 701987
email sales@hopscotchbooks.com
website www.hopscotchbooks.com
Editorial Director Margot O'Keeffe, *Creative Director*
Frances Mackay

National Curriculum teaching resources for primary
schools. Founded 1997.

John Hunt Publishing Ltd

(incorporating O-Books)
The Bothy, Deershot Lodge, Park Lane, Ropley,
Hants SO24 0BE
email john.hunt@o-books.net
Director John Hunt

Children's and adult religious full-colour books for
the international market. MSS welcome; send sae.
Founded 1989.

The Islamic Foundation*

Markfield Conference Centre, Ratby Lane, Markfield,
Leics. LE67 9SY
tel (01530) 244944 *fax* (01530) 244946
email publications@islamic-foundation.org.uk
website www.islamic-foundation.org.uk
Director General Dr Manazir Ahsan, *Executive
Director* Irshad Baqui

Books on Islam for adults and children. Founded
1973.

Jolly Learning Ltd

Tailours House, High Road, Chigwell, Essex IG7 6DL
tel 020-8501 0405 *fax* 020-8500 1696
email info@jollylearning.co.uk
website www.jollylearning.co.uk
Director Christopher Jolly

Educational: primary and English as a Foreign
Lanuage. The company is committed to enabling
high standards in the teaching of reading and writing.
Jolly Phonics provides a foundation for reading and
writing. Publishes approx. 25 titles each year and has
200 in print. Recent successes include *Jolly Dictionary*,
Jolly Readers and *Jolly Phonics Starter Kit*. Imprint:
Jolly Phonics. Founded 1987.

Submission details Unsolicited MSS are only
considered for add-ons to existing products.

Miles Kelly Publishing

The Bradfield Centre, Great Bardfield, Essex
CM7 4SL
tel (01371) 811309 *fax* (01371) 811393
email info@mileskelly.net
website www.mileskelly.net
Directors Kelly Gerard, Jim Miles, Kate Miles

High-quality illustrated non-fiction titles for children
and family: activity books, board books, story books,
poetry, reference, posters and wallcharts. Age groups:
preschool, 5–10, 10–15, 15+. See also entry in *Book
packagers*. Founded 1996.

Kelpies – see Floris Books

Kingfisher Publications plc

(formerly Larousse plc)
New Penderel House, 283–288 High Holborn,
London WC1V 7HZ
tel 020-7903 9999 *fax* 020-7242 4979
email sales@kingfisherpub.co.uk
website www.kingfisherpub.com

Kingfisher (imprint)

Non-fiction Publishing Director Melissa Fairley, *Fiction
Publishing Director* Anne Marie Ryan

Novelty books, picture books, fiction for 5–8 and 9–12 year-olds, series fiction, reference and poetry. Publishes approx. 50 new non-fiction titles and 25 new fiction titles each year and has about 500 in print. Recent successes include *Kingfisher Young Knowledge* (science for age 5+) and *Kingfisher Knowledge* (general knowledge for age 8+), *The Kingfisher Book of Nursery Tales* by Vivian French and *Small Bad Wolf* by Sean Taylor (from the *I am Reading* series. Imprint of Houghton Mifflin Company in Boston, US.

Submission details Will not consider unsolicited MSS.

The King's England Press

Cambertown House, Commercial Road, Goldthorpe, Rotherham, South Yorkshire S63 9BL
tel/fax (01484) 663790
email sales@kingsengland.com
website www.kingsengland.com, www.pottypoets.com

Poetry collections for both adults and children. Successes include *The Spot on My Bum: Horrible Poems for Horrible Children* by Gez Walsh, *Always Eat Your Bogies and Other Rotten Rhymes* by Andrew Collett, *Wang Foo the Kung Fu Shrew and Other Freaky Poems Too* by Chris White and *Vikings Don't Wear Pants* by Roger Stevens and Celia Warren.

Also publishes reprints of Arthur Mee's *King's England* series of 1930s guidebooks and books on folklore, and local and ecclesiastical history.

Submission details Writers should read the contributors' guidelines on the website before submitting material. Founded 1989.

Kingscourt/McGraw-Hill*

McGraw-Hill House, Shoppenhangers Road, Maidenhead, Berks. SL6 2QL
tel (01628) 502500 *fax* (01628) 635895
email enquiries@kingscourt.co.uk
website www.kingscourt.co.uk
Editorial/New Product Barbara Davison

Educational publisher of resources for KS1–3, including *Big Books for Shared Reading, Guided Reading, Story Chest, Literacy Links Plus* and *Maths Links Plus*. Resources support National Literacy and Numeracy Strategies, the Scottish Guidelines 5–14, Northern Ireland curriculum and Curriculum 2000 in Wales. Part of the McGraw-Hill Companies. Founded in 1988.

Jessica Kingsley Publishers*

116 Pentonville Road, London N1 9JB
tel 020-7833 2307 *fax* 020-7837 2917
email post@jkp.com
website www.jkp.com
Managing Director Jessica Kingsley

Psychology, psychiatry, arts therapies, social work, special needs (especially autism and Asperger Syndrome), education, law, practical theology and a small children's list focusing on books for children with special needs. Founded 1987.

Klutz – see Scholastic Ltd

Ladybird – see Penguin Group (UK)

Leckie & Leckie*

3rd Floor, 4 Queen Street, Edinburgh EH2 1JF
tel (0131) 220 6831 *fax* (0131) 225 9987
email enquiries@leckieandleckie.co.uk
website www.leckieandleckie.co.uk

Educational resources. Dedicated to the ongoing development of materials specifically for education in Scotland, from Standard Grade, Foundation to Higher Level. Over 50 titles are currently available in Leckie & Leckie's study guide range. Part of Granada Learning.

Letts Educational*

Chiswick Centre, 414 Chiswick High Road, London W4 5TF
tel 020-8996 3333 *fax* 020-8742 8390
email mail@lettsed.co.uk
website www.lettsed.co.uk
Directors Nigel Ward (managing), Andrew Thraves (publishing, education group), Helen Jacobs (publishing), Lee Warren (finance)

Children's activity books, home study publications for 0–18 year-olds and homework and revision books. Also for adults: accountancy and taxation; computer science; economics; industry, business and management; mathematics and statistics; vocational training and careers. Associate and subsidiary companies: Granada Learning, nferNelson, Black Cat, Granada Media, SEMERC. Founded 1979.

Frances Lincoln Ltd

4 Torriano Mews, Torriano Avenue, London NW5 2RZ
tel 020-7284 4009 *fax* 020-7485 0490
email reception@frances-lincoln.com
website www.frances-lincoln.com
Directors John Nicoll (managing), Anne Fraser (editorial, adult books), Janetta Otter-Barry (editorial, children's books), Jon Rippon (finance), Martin Oestreicher (sales), Andrew Dunn (rights), Tim Rix, David Kewley, Sarah Roberts (non-executive)

Illustrated, international co-editions: gardening, architecture, environment, interiors, art, walking and climbing, gift, children's books. Founded 1977.

Frances Lincoln Children's Books (imprint)

Novelty books, picture books, fiction for 5–12 year-olds, religion, poetry.

Submission details Submit material either through an agent or direct to Antonia Parkin.

Lion Hudson plc*

Mayfield House, 256 Banbury Road, Oxford OX2 7DH

tel (01865) 302750 *fax* (01865) 302757
email enquiries@lionhudson.com
website www.lionhudson.com
Managing Director Paul Clifford

Books for children and adults. Children's books include fiction, picture stories, illustrated non-fiction and information books on the Christian faith. Also specialises in children's Bibles and prayer collections. Founded 1971 as Angus Hudson; merged with Lion Publishing in 2004.

Little, Brown Book Group*

Brettenham House, Lancaster Place, London
WC2E 7EN
tel 020-7911 8000 *fax* 020-7911 8100
email uk@littlebrown.co.uk
website www.littlebrown.co.uk
Ceo & Publisher Ursula Mackenzie, *Coo* Nigel Batt, *Directors* Richard Beswick (editorial), Antonia Hodgson (editorial), Peter Cotton (design), David Kent (group sales), Melanee Winder (export sales), Robert Manser (deputy group sales), Roger Cazalet (marketing), Karen Blewett (commercial), Rosalie MacFarlane (publicity), Diane Spivey (rights)

Hardback and paperback fiction and general non-fiction. No unsolicited MSS. Acquired by Hachette Livre Group of Companies in 2006. Founded 1988.

Atom (division)

website www.atombooks.co.uk
Editorial Director Tim Holman, *Senior Editor* Darren Nash

Teen fiction with a fantastical edge.

Little Hippo – see Scholastic Ltd

Little Tiger Press – see Magi Publications

Livewire – see The Women's Press

Marion Lloyd Books – see Scholastic Ltd

Longman – see Pearson Education

Lutterworth Press – see James Clarke & Co. Ltd

Macmillan Education Ltd – see Macmillan Publishers Ltd

Macmillan Publishers Ltd*

The Macmillan Building, 4 Crinan Street, London
N1 9XW
tel 020-7833 4000 *fax* 020-7843 4640
website www.macmillan.com
Chief Executive Richard Charkin, *Chief Operating Officer* Julian Drinkall, *Directors* G.R.U. Todd, M. Barnard, C.J. Paterson, D.J.G. Knight, D. North, Dr A. Thomas, D. Macmillan, N. Byam Shaw, G. Elliot, J. Gutbrod (Germany), S. von Holtzbrinck (Germany), R. Gibb (Australia)

Pan Macmillan (division)

20 New Wharf Road, London N1 9RR
tel 020-7014 6000 *fax* 020-7014 6001
website www.panmacmillan.com
Managing Director David North, *Publishers* Andrew Kidd (Macmillan fiction & Picador), Richard Milner (Macmillan non-fiction, Sidgwick & Jackson, Boxtree), *Publishing Manager* Alison Muirden (Macmillan Audio)

Novels, literary, crime, thrillers, romance, science fiction, fantasy and horror. Autobiography, biography, business, gift books, health and beauty, history, humour, natural history, travel, philosophy, politics, world affairs, theatre, film, gardening, cookery, popular reference. Publishes under Macmillan, Tor, Pan, Picador, Sidgwick & Jackson, Boxtree, Macmillan Audio, Macmillan New Writing. No unsolicited MSS except through Macmillan New Writing. Founded 1843.

For adults: novels, literary, crime, thrillers, romance, science fiction, fantasy and horror. Autobiography, biography, business, gift books, health and beauty, history, humour, travel, philosophy, politics, world affairs, theatre, film, gardening, cookery, popular reference. Publishes under Macmillan, Tor, Pan, Picador, Sidgwick & Jackson, Boxtree, Macmillan Audio, Macmillan New Writing. No unsolicited MSS except through Macmillan New Writing. Founded 1843.

Boxtree (imprint)

Publisher Richard Milner

Brand and media tie-in titles, including TV, film, music and internet, plus entertainment licences, pop culture, humour in hardback and paperback.

Macmillan Children's Books (division)

20 New Wharf Road, London N1 9RR
tel 020-7014 6000 *fax* 020-7014 6001
website www.panmacmillan.com
Managing Director & Publisher Emma Hopkin, *Publishing Director* Sarah Davies, *Editorial Directors* Sarah Dudman (fiction), Gaby Morgan (non-fiction & poetry), Suzanne Carnell (picture books)

Fiction, non-fiction, poetry, picture books, early learning, pop-up, novelty, board books for 0–16 year-olds. Publishes approx. 200 titles each year and has 1750 in print. Recent successes include *The Gruffalo's Child* by Julia Donaldson and Axel Scheffler, *The Princess Diaries: Sixsational* by Meg Cabot, and *Millions* by Frank Cottrell Boyce. Publishes under Macmillan Children's Books, Campbell Books, Young Picador.

Submission details Will not consider unsolicited MSS.

Campbell Books (imprint)

Editorial Director Sarah Fabiny

Early learning, pop-up, novelty, board books for the preschool market.

Young Picador (imprint)

Editorial Director Sarah Dudman

Literary fiction in paperback and hardback for the young adult market.

Macmillan Education Ltd (division)

Macmillan Oxford, 4 Between Towns Road, Oxford OX4 3PP
tel (01865) 405700 *fax* (01865) 405701
email info@macmillan.com
website www.macmillaneducation.com
Executive Chairman Christopher Paterson, *Managing Director* Christopher Harrison, *Publishing Directors* Alison Hubert (Africa, Central & Eastern Europe, Middle East), Ian Johnstone (internet), *Publishers* David Riley (ELT), Gwyneth Fox (dictionaries), David Williamson (Asia), Kate Melliss (Iberia), Susan Jones (Latin America), Fiona McKenzie (internet)

ELT titles and school and college textbooks and materials in all subjects for the international education market in both book and electronic formats.

Magi Publications

1 The Coda Centre, 189 Munster Road, London SW6 6AW
tel 020-7385 6333 *fax* 020-7385 7333
website www.littletigerpress.com
Publisher Monty Bhatia, *Editors* Jude Evans, Ellena Mann

Caterpillar Books (imprint)

email jasher@caterpillarbooks.com
Publisher Jamie Asher

Books for preschool children, including pop-ups, board books, cloth books and activity books.

Little Tiger Press (imprint)

email info@littletiger.co.uk

Children's picture books, novelty books, board books, pop-up books and activity books for preschool age to 10 year-olds. Will consider new material from authors and illustrators; see website for guidelines. Founded 1987.

Mantra Lingua

Global House, 303 Ballards Lane, London N12 8NP
tel 020-8445 5123 *fax* 020-8446 7745
email sales@mantralingua.com
website www.mantralingua.com
Managing Director M. Chatterji

Children's multicultural picture books; multilingual friezes/posters; dual language books/cassettes; South Asian literature/teenage fiction; CD-Roms and videos. Founded 1984.

Marshall Cavendish Partworks Ltd*

119 Wardour Street, London W1F 0UW
tel 020-7565 6000 *fax* 020-7734 6221
email editorial@marshallcavendish.co.uk
website www.marshallcavendish.co.uk
Managing Editor Clive Gregory

Cookery, crafts, gardening, do-it-yourself, history, children's fiction and children's interests, football and sport, general illustrated non-fiction, English language teaching. Founded 1969.

Kevin Mayhew Ltd

Buxhall, Stowmarket, Suffolk IP14 3BW
tel (01449) 737978 *fax* (01449) 737834
email info@kevinmayhew.com
website www.kevinmayhew.com
Directors Kevin Mayhew (chairman), Kevin Whomes (production)

Christianity: prayer and spirituality, pastoral care, preaching, liturgy worship, children's, youth work, drama, instant art. Music: hymns, organ and choral, contemporary worship, piano and instrumental. Contact Manuscript Submissions Dept before sending MSS/synopses. Founded 1976.

Meadowside Children's Books

185 Fleet Street, London EC4A 2HS
tel 020-7400 1061 *fax* 020-7400 1037
email info@meadowsidebooks.com
website www.meadowsidebooks.com
Publisher Simon Rosenheim

Picture books and children's fiction. Founded 2003.

Mentor Books†

43 Furze Road, Sandyford Industrial Estate, Dublin 18, Republic of Ireland
tel (353) 1 295 2112 *fax* (353) 1 295 2114
email all@mentorbooks.ie
website www.mentorbooks.ie
Managing Director Daniel McCarthy, *Managing Editor* Claire Haugh

Fiction for 5–8 and 9–12 year-olds, teenage fiction, series fiction, film/TV tie-ins. Educational (primary and secondary): languages, history, geography, business, maths, science. Also, for adults: fiction, non-fiction, guidebooks, biographies and history. Publishes approx. 60 titles each year and has 300 in print. Founded 1980.

Submission details Will not consider unsolicited MSS or even letters from prospective authors.

The Mercier Press†

Douglas Village, Cork, Republic of Ireland
tel (021) 4899858 *fax* (021) 4899887
email pr@mercierpress.ie
website www.mercierpress.ie
Directors J.F. Spillane (chairman), C. Feehan (managing), M.P. Feehan

Books for adults and children. Subjects include Irish literature, folklore, history, politics, humour, current affairs, health, mind and spirit and general non-fiction. Imprint: Marino Books. Founded 1944.

Mill Publishing

PO Box 120, 4, Balloo Avenue, County Down BT19 7BX
tel (0800) 731 2837
email info@millpublishing.co.uk
website www.millpublishing.co.uk

Produces material to meet the needs of the National Curriculum. The Skillbuilder system, in its separate

Literacy and Numeracy versions, provides schools with a means of achieving the objectives required by the National Literacy Strategy and National Numeracy Strategy. The *Write into History* series develops key writing skills using the approach set out in *Grammar for Writing*. The *Crosslinks* series covers reading, writing and thinking across the curriculum.

Anglia Young Books (imprint)
website www.angliayoungbooks.co.uk
Educational publisher. Historical fiction for use in the KS2 classroom. Also publishes cross-curricular material; the *Write into History* series delivers grammar in the context of historical stories and *Crosslinks* focuses on reading, writing and thinking across the curriculum.Welcomes suggestions from teachers for new resources. Authors and illustrators should send a brief synopsis of their intended title or portfolio.

National Association for the Teaching of English (NATE)
50 Broadfield Road, Sheffield S8 0XJ
tel 0114-255 5419 *fax* 0114-255 5296
email natehq@btconnect.com
website www.nate.org.uk
Chair Simon Wrigley, *Vice-chair* Craig Morrison, *Company Secretary* Lyn Fairfax, *Development & Communications Officer* Ian McNeilly, *Publications Manager* Anne Fairhall, *Publications Coordinator* Julie Selwood

Educational (primary, secondary and tertiary): teaching English, drama and media. Publishes approx. 4 titles each year and has 70 in print. Recent publications include *Guided Reading* packs (KS3 focus), *Cracking Good Picture Books* (KS1 focus) and *Drama Packs* (KS3/4 focus). Imprint: NATE. Founded 1963.
Submission details Submissions should be made via a 'Publication Proposal' form for consideration by the Publications Manager and 3 members of the Editorial Board. Allow 3–6 weeks for response. Will consider unsolicited MSS.

Neate Publishing
33 Downside Road, Winchester SO22 5LT
tel (01962) 841479 *fax* (01962) 841743
email sales@neatepublishing.co.uk
website www.neatepublishing.co.uk
Directors Bobbie Neate (managing), Ann Langran, Maggie Threadingham

Non-fiction books, educational packs, CDs and posters for primary schoolchildren. Founded 1999.

Thomas Nelson Ltd – see Nelson Thornes Ltd

Nelson Thornes Ltd*
Delta Place, 27 Bath Road, Cheltenham, Glos.
GL53 7TH
tel (01242) 267100 *fax* (01242) 221914

email name@nelsonthornes.com
website www.nelsonthornes.com
Managing Director Mary O'Connor

Print and electronic publishers for the educational market: primary, secondary, further education, professional. Part of the Wolters Kluwer Group of Companies.

nferNelson Publishing Co. Ltd*
The Chiswick Centre, 414 Chiswick High Road, London W4 5TF
tel (0845) 602 1937 *fax* 020-8996 3660
email information@nfer-nelson.co.uk
website www.nfer-nelson.co.uk
Managing Director Nigel Ward

Independent provider of tests, assessments and assessment services for education. Its aim is to help educational professionals to understand and maximise the potential of their pupils and students. Publishes assessments for the 0–19 age group, though the majority of its assessments are aimed at 5–14 year-olds. Testing and assessment services include literacy, numeracy, thinking skills, ability, learning support and online testing. Founded 1981.

Jane Nissen Books
Swan House, Chiswick Mall, London W4 2PS
tel 020-8994 8203 *fax* 020-8742 8198
email jane@nissen.demon.co.uk

Reprinted fiction for 5–8 and 9–12 year-olds, teenage fiction and poetry. Publishes approx. 4 titles each year and has 25 in print. Recent successes include *My Friend Mr Leakey* by J.B.S. Haldane, *Kings and Queens* by Eleanor and Herbert Farjeon and *Tennis Shoes* by Noel Streatfeild. Seeking to publish more children's 'forgotten' classics. Founded 2000.
Submission details Personal recommendations welcome.

The O'Brien Press Ltd†
20 Victoria Road, Rathgar, Dublin 6, Republic of Ireland
tel (01) 492 3333 *fax* (01) 492 2777
email books@obrien.ie
website www.obrien.ie
Directors Michael O'Brien, Ide ní Laoghaire, Ivan O'Brien

For children: fiction for all ages; illustrated fiction series – *Solos* (age 3+), *Pandas* (age 5+), *Flyers* (age 6+) and *Red Flag* (8+); substantial novels (10+) – contemporary, historical, fantasy; also non-fiction. Also for adults: biography, politics, local history, true crime, sport, humour, reference. No adult fiction, poetry or academic. Founded 1974.
Submission details Unsolicited MSS (sample chapters only), synopses and ideas for books welcome – submissions will not be returned.

Orchard Books – see Hachette Children's Books

The Orion Publishing Group Ltd*

Orion House, 5 Upper St Martin's Lane, London WC2H 9EA
tel 020-7240 3444 *fax* 020-7240 4822
website www.orionbooks.co.uk
Directors Arnaud Nourry (chairman), Peter Roche (chief executive), Malcolm Edwards (deputy chief executive)

For adults: fiction and non-fiction and audio. Imprints include Everyman, Gollancz, Orion, Phoenix and Weidenfeld & Nicolson. Founded 1992.

Orion Children's Books (division)

Publisher Fiona Kennedy, *Editorial Manager* Jane Hughes

Picture books, fiction for 5–8 and 9–12 year-olds, teenage fiction, series fiction and audio. Publishes approx. 50 titles each year and has about 350 in print. Recent successes include books by Francesca Simon, Michelle Paver and Sally Gardner. Imprints: Orion Children's Books.
Submission details Will consider unsolicited MSS. Allow 2 months for response. Submissions via agents take priority.

Oxford University Press*

Great Clarendon Street, Oxford OX2 6DP
tel (01865) 556767 *fax* (01865) 556646
email enquiry@oup.com
website www.oup.com
Ceo Henry Reece, *Group Finance Director* Roger Boning, *Academic Division Managing Director* Tim Barton, *UK Children's & Educational Division Managing Director* Kate Harris, *ELT Division Managing Director* Peter Marshall, *Publishing Director Journals* Martin Richardson, *UK Human Resources Director* John Williams, *Sales Directors* Phil Garratt, Alastair Lewis

Anthropology, archaeology, architecture, art, belles-lettres, bibles, bibliography, children's books (fiction, non-fiction, picture), commerce, current affairs, dictionaries, drama, economics, educational (infants, primary, secondary, technical, university), encyclopedias, English language teaching, electronic publishing, essays, foreign language learning, general history, hymn and service books, journals, law, maps and atlases, medical, music, oriental, philosophy, political economy, prayer books, reference, science, sociology, theology and religion; educational software; *Grove Dictionaries of Music & Art*. Trade paperbacks published under the imprint of Oxford Paperbacks. Founded 1478.

Children's and Educational Division

Managing Director, Children's & Education Kate Harris, *Children's Publisher, Fiction & Picture Books* Liz Cross, *Head of Dictionaries & Reference* Vineeta Gupta; *Schoolbooks: Publishing Director* Denise Cripps, *Publisher, English & Geography* Rachel Houghton, *Publisher, Modern Foreign Languages &*

Classics Dick Capel-Davies, *Publisher, Science, Maths & Technology* Elspeth Boardley, *Primary Publisher* Jane Harley, *Publisher, Primary Literacy* Fiona Undrill
Picture books, fiction, poetry and dictionaries. Authors include Tim Bowler, Gillian Cross, Julie Hearne and Geraldine McCaughrean.

Pan – see Macmillan Publishers Ltd

Parragon

4 Queen Street, Bath BA1 1HE
tel (01225) 478888 *fax* (01225) 478897
email info@parragon.com
Directors Trevor McCurdie, Guy Parr, Catherine Hardy (publishing), *Commissioning Editors* Jane Walker, Catherine Jones

Activity books, novelty books, picture books, fiction for 5–8 year-olds, poetry, reference, religion and audio. Publishes approx. 400 titles each year and has about 4500 in print. Imprints: Parragon, Bright Sparks. Founded 1988.
Submission details Any material submitted cannot be returned. Telephone calls cannot be accepted.

PCET Publishing

27 Kirchen Road, London W13 0UD
tel 020-8567 9206 *fax* 020-8566 5120
email info@pcet.co.uk
website www.pcet.co.uk

Pictorial Charts Educational Trust (PCET) publishes visual resources for primary and secondary education: wallcharts, photopacks, activity books and other classroom accessories to support the National Curriculum. Also has a charitable arm which provides funding and teaching resources for the developing world.

Pearson Education*

Edinburgh Gate, Harlow, Essex CM20 2JE
tel (01279) 623623 *fax* (01279) 414130
email firstname.lastname@pearsoned-ema.com
website www.pearsoned.co.uk
President, Pearson Education Ltd Rod Bristow

Materials for school pupils, students and practitioners globally.

Longman (imprint)

Edinburgh Gate, Harlow, Essex CM20 2JE
tel (0800) 579579 *fax* (01279) 414130
email schools.enq@pearsoned-ema.com
website www.longman.co.uk
Educational: primary and secondary. Primary: literacy and numeracy. Secondary: English, maths, science, history, geography, modern languages, design and technology, business and economics, psychology and sociology.

Penguin Longman (imprint)

English language teaching.

York Notes (imprint)

Literature guides for students.

Penguin Group (UK)*

80 Strand, London WC2R 0RL
tel 020-7010 3000 *fax* 020-7010 6060
website www.penguin.co.uk
Ceo John Makinson, *Managing Directors* Helen Fraser
(Penguin), Gary June (Dorling Kindersley)

Books for adults and children (see below and BBC
Children's Books). Adult subjects include biography,
fiction, current affairs, fiction, general leisure, health,
history, humour, literature, politics, spirituality and
relationships, sports, travel and TV/film tie-ins. Adult
imprints include Allen Lane, Dorling Kindersley,
Hamish Hamilton, Hugo's Language Books, Michael
Joseph, Penguin, Penguin Press, Rough Guides,
Viking. Owned by Pearson plc.

Puffin (division)

Managing Director Francesca Dow, *Publishing
Directors* Rebecca McNally (fiction), Mandy Suhr
(picture books)

Children's paperback and hardback books: picture
books, board books, novelty books, fiction, poetry,
non-fiction, popular culture; and audio. Recent
successes include *The English Roses* by Madonna,
Eoin Colfer's *Artemis Fowl* series and Jeremy Strong's
humorous titles for younger readers. Backlist titles by
authors such as Roald Dahl, Gene Kemp, Jill Paton
Walsh, Leon Garfield, Mildred D. Taylor, as well as
the *Puffin Classics* and *Puffin Modern Classics*.
Operates the Puffin Book Club (see page 74).
Submission details No unsolicited MSS or synopses.

Warne (division)

website www.funwithspot.com,
www.flowerfairies.com, www.peterrabbit.com
Managing Director Sally Floyer, *Publishing Director*
Stephanie Barton

Specialises in preschool illustrated developmental
books for 0–6, non-fiction 0–8; licensed brands;
children's classic publishing and merchandising
properties. No unsolicited MSS.

Ladybird (division)

website www.ladybird.co.uk
Managing Director Sally Floyer

Dorling Kindersley (division)

Managing Director Gary Dune, *Publisher* Christopher
Davis, *Adult Publisher* John Roberts, *Children's
Publisher* Miriam Farbey

Illustrated non-fiction for adults and children:
gardening, medical, travel, food and drink, Mind,
Body & Spirit, history, reference, pregnancy and
childcare, antiques. Age groups: preschool, 5–8, 8+.

BBC Children's Books (division)

Managing Director Sally Floyer, *Editorial Director*
Catherine Johnson

Piccadilly Press

5 Castle Road, London NW1 8PR
tel 020-7267 4492 *fax* 020-7267 4493
email books@piccadillypress.co.uk
website www.piccadillypress.co.uk
Managing Director & Publisher Brenda Gardner,
Senior Editor Yasemin Uçar, *Commissioning Editors*
Ruth Williams, Anne Clark, *Assistant Editor* Melissa
Patey

Picture books, humorous tween/teenage fiction, series
fiction, parental advice trade paperbacks. Publishes
approx. 25–30 titles each year and has 200 in print.
Recent successes include *Mates Dates* series by Cathy
Hopkins and *Butterfly Fairy* by Fran Evans. Founded
1983.
Submission details Will consider unsolicited MSS.
Send synopsis and 3 sample chapters. Allow 6 weeks
for response. Looking to publish humorous teenage
books which deal with contemporary issues.

Picthall & Gunzi Ltd

21A Widmore Road, Bromley, Kent BR1 1RW
tel 020-8460 4032 *fax* 020-8460 4021
email chez@picthallandgunzi.demon.co.uk,
chris@picthallandgunzi.demon.co.uk
website www.picthallandgunzi.co.uk
Director Chez Picthall (managing director), *Publisher
& Editorial Director* Christiane Gunzi

High-quality, photographically illustrated non-fiction
for children: activity books, board books, novelty
books, early learning. Age groups: preschool and Key
Stage 1. See also page 71.

Pinwheel Ltd

Winchester House, 259–269 Old Marylebone Road,
London NW1 5XJ
tel 020-7616 7200 *fax* 020-7616 7201
email sales@pinwheel.co.uk
website www.pinwheel.co.uk
Managing Director Andrew Flatt

Children's non-fiction, picture books and novelty
titles. Unsolicited MSS will not be returned.

Andromeda Children's Books (imprint)

Publishing/Creative Director Linda Cole
Illustrated non-fiction for children aged 3–12 years.

Gullane Children's Books (imprint)

Creative Director Paula Burgess
Picture books for children aged 0–8 years.

Pinwheel Children's Books (imprint)

Publishing/Creative Director Linda Cole
Cloth and novelty books for children aged 0–5 years.

The Playwrights Publishing Company

70 Nottingham Road, Burton Joyce, Notts.
NG14 5AL
tel 0115-931 3356
email playwrightspublishingco@yahoo.com
website www.geocities.com/playwrightspublishingco
Proprietor Liz Breeze, *Consultant* Tony Breeze

One-act and full-length drama published first on the
internet and if popular, later in hard copy: serious

work and comedies, for mixed cast, all women or schools. Reading fee unless professionally produced; sae required. Founded 1990.

Point – see Scholastic Ltd

Poolbeg Press Ltd
123 Grange Hill, Baldoyle, Dublin 13, Republic of Ireland
tel (01) 8321477 *fax* (01) 8321430
email poolbeg@poolbeg.com
website www.poolbeg.com
Directors Kieran Devlin (managing), Paula Campbell (publisher)

Children's and teenage fiction. Also adult popular fiction, non-fiction, current affairs. Imprint: Poolbeg. Founded 1976.

Portland Press Ltd
3rd Floor, Eagle House, 16 Procter Street, London WC1V 6NX
tel 020-7280 4100 *fax* 020-7280 4170
email editorial@portlandpress.com
website www.portlandpress.com
Directors Rhonda C. Oliver (managing), Chris J. Finch (finance), John Day (IT), Adam Marshall (marketing)

Biochemistry and molecular life science books for graduate, postgraduate and research students. Illustrated science books for children: *Making Sense of Science* series. Founded 1990.

Mathew Price Ltd
The Old Glove Factory, Bristol Road, Sherborne, Dorset DT9 4HP
tel (01935) 816010 *fax* (01935) 816310
email mathewp@mathewprice.com
Chairman Mathew Price

Illustrated fiction and non-fiction children's books for all ages for the UK and international market. Specialist in flap, pop-up, paper-engineered titles as well as conventional books. Founded 1983.

Priddy Books
4 Crinan Street, London N1 9XW
020-7418 5515 *fax* 020-7418 85507
email claire.cartwright@priddybooks.com
website www.priddybooks.com
Publisher Roger Priddy, *Editorial Director* Jo Douglass, *Art Director* Robert Tainsh, *International Sales Director* Sally Poulson

Specialises in photographic baby/toddler and preschool books: activity books, board books, novelty books, picture books.

Prim-Ed Publishing
PO Box 2840, Coventry CV6 5ZY
tel (0870) 876 0151 *fax* (0870) 876 0152
website www.prim-ed.com

Contact Seamus McGuinness

Educational publisher specialising in copymasters (photocopiable teaching resources) for primary school and special needs lower secondary pupils. Books written by practising classroom teachers.

QED Publishing
226 City Road, London EC1V 2TT
tel 020-7812 8600 *fax* 020-7253 4370
email qedpublishing@quarto.com
website www.qed-publishing.co.uk
Publisher Steve Evans, *Editorial Director* Jean Coppendale

Education. High-quality curriculum-based books designed to stimulate early learning in the classroom, as well as in the home. Series include *QED Start Talking, QED Start Reading, QED Start Writing*. QED is from the Latin *quod erat demonstrandum* (that which was to be demonstrated). Imprint of the Quarto Group. Founded 2003.

Ragged Bears Publishing Ltd
Unit 14A, Bennett's Field Trading Estate, Southgate Road, Wincanton, Somerset BA9 9DT
tel (01963) 824184 *fax* (01963) 31147
email info@raggedbears.co.uk
website www.raggedbears.co.uk
Managing Director Henrietta Stickland, *Submissions Editor* Barbara Lamb

Activity books, picture books, novelty books and fiction for 5–8 year-olds. Publishes 5–10 titles each year and has 150 in print. Recent successes include *Big Dig* by Paul Stickland, *Lovely Ruby & The Mermaid* by Nancy Trott and *We're Going on an Aeroplane* by Steve Augarde. *Dinosaur Roar!* has sold over 10 million copies since its publication almost 10 years ago. *Little Robots* by Mike Brownlow is now an animated TV series on Cbeebies. Founded 1994.

Submission details Will consider unsolicited MSS. Allow 3–4 months for response. Takes very few unsolicited ideas as the list is small. Include sae for return of MSS; do not send original artwork.

Random House Group Ltd*
20 Vauxhall Bridge Road, London SW1V 2SA
tel 020-7840 8400 *fax* 020-7233 8791
website www.randomhouse.co.uk
Chairman/Ceo Gail Rebuck, *Deputy Ceo* Ian Hudson, *Directors* Larry Finlay (managing, Transworld), Mark Gardiner (finance), Brian Davies (managing director, overseas operations), Peter Bowron (group managing), Clare Harington (group communications), Philippa Dickinson (managing, children's), Richard Cable (managing, Random House Division), Mark Booth (publishing), Dan Franklin (publisher, CCV)

For adults: fiction (commercial and literary) and non-fiction. Subjects include art, autobiography, belles-lettres, biography, business, cookery, current affairs, diet and fitness, drama, essays, film and TV tie-ins, health and beauty, history, humour, lifestyle, music, parenting, personal development, poetry, politics, philosophy, reference, science, spirituality, sport, translations and travel. Imprints include Arrow Books, Jonathan Cape, Century, Chatto & Windus, Ebury Press, Fodor Guides, Harvill Secker, William Heinemann, Hutchinson, Pimlico, Rider, Time Out, Vermilion, Vintage, Yellow Jersey Press. Subsidiary of Bertelsmann AG.

Random House Audio Books
tel 020-7840 8419 *fax* 020-7233 6127
Editor Zoe Howes

Random House Children's Books (division)
61–63 Uxbridge Road, London W5 5SA
tel 020-8579 2652 *fax* 020-8579 5479
Managing Director Philippa Dickinson, *Publishing Director – Fiction* Annie Eaton, *Publisher – Doubleday Picture Books* Penny Walker, *Senior Commissioning Editor – Fiction* Alex Antscherl, *Senior Commissioning Editor* Natascha Biebow, *Senior Commissioning Editor – Jonathan Cape Picture Books* Helen Mackenzie-Smith, *Editorial Director (Fiction)* Charlie Sheppard, *Publishing Director (Custom Publishing)* Fiona Macmillan, *Publicity Director* Clare Hall-Craggs

Picture books, fiction, poetry, non-fiction and audio cassettes. Authors include Jacqueline Wilson, Anne Fine, Michael Morpurgo, Philip Pullman and Roald Dahl, and illustrators include Quentin Blake, Helen Cooper, Shirley Hughes, John Burningham and Babette Cole. Publishes approx. 240 titles each year.

Imprints: Bodley Head Children's Books, Corgi Children's Books, Doubleday Children's Books, Hutchinson Children's Books, Jonathan Cape Children's Books, Red Fox Children's Books, David Fickling Books. Merged with Transworld Children's books in November 2001; now ranks amongst the top 5 children's publishers in the UK.

David Fickling Books (imprint)
31 Beaumont Street, Oxford OX1 2NP
tel (01865) 339000 *fax* (01865) 339009
email dfickling@randomhouse.co.uk
website davidficklingbooks.co.uk
Publisher David Fickling, *Editor* Bella Pearson
Picture books, fiction for 5–8 and 9–12 year-olds, teenage fiction and poetry. Publishes approx. 12 titles each year. Recent successes include: *The Curious Incident of the Dog in the Night-Time* by Mark Haddon, *Pants* by Giles Andreae and Nick Sharratt and *The Various* by Steve Augarde. Publishes books simultaneously with Random House Inc. Founded 2000.
Submission details Will consider unsolicited MSS; allow 3 months for response and include a covering letter and sae. If possible find an agent first.

Ransom Publishing Ltd
Rose Cottage, Howe Hill, Watlington, Oxon
OX49 5HB

tel (01491) 613711 *fax* (01491) 613733
email ransom@ransom.co.uk
website www.ransom.co.uk
Directors Jenny Ertle (managing), Steve Rickard (creative)

Books for preschool to teens, including fiction, non-fiction and special needs (high interest age, low reading age). Range of digital content from preschool to secondary for literacy, numeracy, science and goegraphy. Publishes approx. 50 titles each year and has about 100 in print. Recent successes include *Rainbow Readers, Living Phonics, Trailblazers* and *Dark Man*. Looking to publish books for older children struggling to learn to read, i.e. Key Stages 2 and 3. Founded 1995.
Submission details Will consider unsolicited MSS but prefers a preliminary email. Selects very little as material needs to correspond to Ransom key publishing areas.

Reader's Digest Children's Publishing Ltd
The Ice House, 124–126 Walcot Street, Bath
BA1 5BG
tel (01225) 473200 *fax* (01225) 460942
email jo_o'hagan@readersdigest.co.uk
Publisher Rosanne McManus, *Contact* Jo O'Hagan
Innovative, high-quality books designed to encourage children to use their creativity and imagination. Board, novelty, cinema and TV tie-ins. Licensed characters and brands. Also a wide range of children's religious titles. Fully owned subsidiary of Reader's Digest Association Inc. Founded 1981.

Red Bird Publishing
Kiln Farm, East End Green, Brightlingsea, Colchester, Essex CO7 0SX
tel (01206) 303525 *fax* (01206) 304545
email info@red-bird.co.uk
website www.red-bird.co.uk
Publisher Marin Rhodes-Schofield

Innovative children's activity packs and books produced with a mix of techniques and materials such as Glow in the Dark, Mirrors, Stereoscopic 3D, Moiré and other optical illusions. Authors are specialists in their fields. Activity books, novelty books, picture books, painting and colouring books, teaching books, posters: hobbies, nature and the environment, science. Age groups: preschool, 5–10, 10–15.

Red Kite Books – see Haldane Mason Ltd

Religious and Moral Education Press (RMEP)*
St Mary's Works, St Mary's Plain, Norwich NR3 3BH
tel (01603) 612914 *fax* (01603) 624483
email admin@scm-canterburypress.co.uk
website www.rmep.co.uk

Chief Executive Andrew Moore, *Editorial Director* Mary Mears

Educational books and teachers' resources (primary and secondary): religious education, citizenship, PSHE, assembly resources (collective worship). Publishes approx. 10–20 titles each year and has about 150 in print. Recent successes include *Speaking for Ourselves* (developing oral and literacy skills in religious education), the *Superstars* series, *Faith in Action* and *Round the Year* (99 stories for the primary school assembly). Division of SCM-Canterbury Press Ltd. Founded 1980.

Submission details Will consider unsolicited MSS. Send an outline or synopsis to the Editorial Director, indicating how the proposed publication would meet school curriculum requirements. Allow 4–6 weeks for a response. Most RMEP authors are, or have been, school teachers or college lecturers – mostly specialists in religious education.

Rigby Heinemann – see Harcourt Education Ltd

RoutledgeFalmer – see Taylor and Francis Books Ltd

SAGE Publications Ltd*
1 Oliver's Yard, 55 City Road, London EC1Y 1SP
tel 020-7324 8500 *fax* 020-7324 8600
email info@sagepub.co.uk
website www.sagepub.co.uk
Directors Stephen Barr (managing), Katharine Jackson, Ziyad Marar, Richard Fidczuk, Phil Denvir, Clive Parry, Jane Quick, Blaise Simqu (USA), Sara Miller McCune (USA), Paul R. Chapman

Primary/elementary education, children's development. Social sciences, behavioural sciences, humanities, STM. Founded 1971.

Paul Chapman Publishing (imprint)
website www.paulchapmanpublishing.co.uk
Publisher Marianne Lagrange

Education: academic and professional books for students, practitioners and school leaders.

St Pauls
St Pauls Publishing, 187 Battersea Bridge Road, London SW11 3AS
tel 020-7978 4300 *fax* 020-7978 4370
email editions@stpauls.org.uk
website www.stpauls.ie

Theology, ethics, spirituality, biography, education, general books of Roman Catholic and Christian interest. Founded 1948.

Salariya Book Company Ltd
Book House, 25 Marlborough Place, Brighton BN1 1UB
tel (01273) 603306 *fax* (01273) 693857
email salariya@salariya.com
website www.salariya.com
Director David Salariya

Children's non-fiction. Imprint: Book House. Founded 1989.

Schofield & Sims Ltd
Dogley Mill, Fenay Bridge, Huddersfield HD8 0NQ
tel (01484) 607080 *fax* (01484) 606815
email sales@schofieldandsims.co.uk
website www.schofieldandsims.co.uk
Chairman C.N. Platts

Educational: nursery, infants, primary; posters. Founded 1901.

Scholastic Ltd*
Villiers House, Clarendon Avenue, Leamington Spa CV32 5PR
tel (01926) 887799 *fax* (01926) 883881
website www.scholastic.co.uk
Chairman M.R. Robinson, *Group Managing Director* Kate Wilson

Children's fiction and non-fiction and education for primary schools. Owned by Scholastic Inc. Founded 1964.

Scholastic Children's Books (division)
Euston House, 24 Eversholt Street, London NW1 1DB
tel 020-7756 7756 *fax* 020-7756 7795
email publicity@scholastic.co.uk
Managing Director Elaine McQuaide, *Editorial Director, Non-fiction* Lisa Edwards, *Editorial Director, Fiction* Kristen Skidmore, *Senior Commissioning Editor, Preschool* Paulina Malinen, *International Trade Director* Gavin Lang, *Rights Director* Antonia Pelari, *Sales & Marketing Director* Hilary Murray Hill

Activity books, novelty books, picture books, fiction for 5–12 year-olds, teenage fiction, series fiction and film/TV tie-ins. Recent successes include *Horrible Histories* by Terry Deary and Martin Brown, *His Dark Materials Trilogy* by Philip Pullman and *Mortal Engines* by Philip Reeve. Imprints include Young Hippo, Scholastic Press, Alison Green Books, Marion Lloyd Books, Klutz, Hippo Books, Little Hippo, Point.

Submission details Will consider unsolicited submissions: send synopsis and sample chapter only.

The Chicken House
See page 9.

Scholastic Educational Publishing (division)
Villiers House, Clarendon Avenue, Leamington Spa CV32 5PR
tel (01926) 887799 *fax* (01926) 883881
Managing Director Denise Cripps

Professional books and classroom materials for primary teachers and magazines (*Child Education, Junior Education, Junior Focus, Child Education Topics, Nursery Education, Litreracy Time*).

Scholastic Book Clubs (division)
See page 75.

Scholastic Book Fairs (division)
See page 75.

SCP Childrens Ltd
(trading as Scottish Children's Press)
Unit 6, Newbattle Abbey Business Park, Newbattle
Road, Dalkeith EH22 3LJ
tel 0131-660 4757 *fax* 0131-660 4666
email info@scottishbooks.com
website www.scottishbooks.com
Directors Brian Pugh, Avril Gray
'Scottish books for children.' Picture books, fiction
for 5–8 and 9–12 year-olds, reference, poetry and
cookery. Publishes approx. 3 titles each year and has
32 in print. Recent successes include *Wee Willie
Winkie* (nursery rhymes and songs), *Teach the Bairns
to Cook/Bake* and *Danger by Gaslight* (fiction for age
8+). Also, for adults: Scottish fiction, Scottish non-
fiction and Scots language. Founded 1992.
Submission details Will not accept unsolicited MSS.
See website or send for submission guidelines.

Scripture Union
207–209 Queensway, Bletchley, Milton Keynes,
Bucks. MK2 2EB
tel (01908) 856000 *fax* (01908) 856111
email postmaster@scriptureunion.org.uk
website www.scriptureunion.org.uk
Head of Resource Development Terry Clutterham

Christian books and Bible reading materials for
people of all ages; educational and worship resources
for churches; adult fiction and non-fiction; children's
fiction and non-fiction (age groups: under 6, 6–7,
8–10 and youth). Publishes approx. 30 titles each year
for children/young people and has 200–250 in print.
Recent successes include *Fabulous Phoebe* by Kathy
Lee, *Friends First* by Claire Pedrick and Andy Morgan
and *An Alien at Christmas* by Brian Ogden. Scripture
Union works as a charity in over 120 countries and
publishes in approx. 20. Founded 1867.
Submission details Will consider unsolicited MSS.
Send sample and outline to Christina Simms in
Publishing Dept. Authors should note that Scripture
Union is a ministry as well as a publishing house. All
books have an overt Christian or Biblical content.

SEMERC
The Chiswick Centre, 414 Chiswick High Road,
London W4 5TF
tel 020-8996 3333 *fax* 020-8742 8390
website www.semerc.com
'Solutions for inclusion.' Publisher of ICT resources
for learners of all ages with special educational needs.
Part of Granada Learning.

Short Books Ltd
3ᴀ Exmouth House, Pine Street, London EC1R 0JH
tel 020-7833 9429 *fax* 020-7833 9500

email emily@shortbooks.biz
website www.shortbooks.co.uk
Editorial Directors Rebecca Nicolson, Aurea
Carpenter
Children's books: biographies of famous people from
the past. Also non-fiction for adults, mainly
biography and journalism. No unsolicited MSS.
Founded 2000.

Simon & Schuster UK Ltd*
Africa House, 64–78 Kingsway, London WC2B 6AH
tel 020-7316 1900 *fax* 020-7316 0331/2
website www.simonsays.co.uk
Directors Ian Chapman (managing), Suzanne
Baboneau (publishing), Charlotte Robertson (sales),
Alex Maramenides (children's rights), Ingrid Selberg
(children's publishing)

For adults: fiction (commercial and literary) and
serious non-fiction. Subjects include biography,
current affairs, history and science. Imprints include
Free Press, Pocket Books, Scribner and Simon &
Schuster Audio. No unsolicited MSS. Founded 1986.

Simon & Schuster Children's Publishing
Children's Publishing Director Ingrid Selberg,
Children's Rights Director Alex Maramenides, *Fiction
Editorial Director* Venetia Gosling, *Senior
Commissioning Editor, Picture Books* Katherine
Halligan, *Art Director* Margaret Hope
Activity books, novelty books, picture books, fiction
for 5–8 and 9–12 year-olds, teenage fiction, series
fiction, film/TV tie-ins. Publishes approx. 180–200
titles each year. Recent successes include *The
Spiderwick Chronicles* by Holly Black and Tony
Diterlizzi, *Alice's Adventures in Wonderland* (Robert
Sabuda, pop-up book) and *Wendy* by Karen Wallace.
Submission details No unsolicited MSS. Will only
consider MSS via agents.

Smart Learning
PO Box 321, Cambridge CB1 2XU
tel (01223) 477550 *fax* (01223) 477551
email admin@smart-learning.co.uk
website www.smart-learning.co.uk
High-quality teaching and learning resources for both
teachers and children – from the Foundation stage
through to Year 6. Publishes teacher's books, pupil
activity books, photocopiable resource sheets, poster
packs to support and enhance the teaching and
learning of ICT, PSHE and Citizenship throughout
the primary years.

Stacey International
128 Kensington Church Street, London W8 4BH
tel 020-7221 7166 *fax* 020-7792 9288
email enquiries@stacey-international.co.uk
website www.stacey-international.co.uk
Chairman Tom Stacey, *Managing Director* Max Scott,
Commissioning Editor Caroline Singer
Illustrated non-fiction, encyclopedic books on
regions and countries, Islamic and Arab subjects,

world affairs, art, travel, belles-lettres, children's books (picture books, fiction for 5–8 and 9–12 year-olds and reference). Publishers of the *Musgrove* series.

Storysack Ltd

Resource House, Kay Street, Bury BL9 6BU
tel 0161-763 6232 *fax* 0161-763 5366
email hello@resourcehouse.co.uk
website www.storysack.com

Storysacks for children aged 3+. Storysacks are cloth bags of resources to encourage children and parents to enjoy reading together. Each sack is based around a picture story book with a supporting fact book on a similar theme, a parent guide, characters and a game. Founded 1999.

Tamarind Ltd

PO Box 52, Northwood, Middlesex HA6 1UN
tel 020-8866 8808 *fax* 020-8866 5627
email info@tamarindbooks.co.uk
website www.tamarindbooks.co.uk
Managing Director Verna Wilkins

Multicultural children's books. Fiction: picture books (ages 4–8), board books for babies (ages 0–3), board books for toddlers (ages 2–5). Non-fiction: biography (ages 8–12). Books feature on National Curriculum. Founded 1987.

Submission details Will consider unsolicited MSS with sae. Allow one month for response. Looking for books which give black children a high positive profile.

Tango Books

PO Box 32595, London W4 5YD
tel 020-8996 9970 *fax* 020-8996 9977
email sales@tangobooks.co.uk
website www.tangobooks.co.uk
Directors Sheri Safran, David Fielder

Children's novelty books, including pop-up, touch-and-feel and cloth books.

Tarquin Publications

99 Hatfield Road, St Albans AL1 4ET
tel (0870) 1432568 *fax* (0845) 4566385
email editorial@tarquinbooks.com
website www.tarquinbooks.com
Director Andrew Griffin

Mathematical models and paper engineering books for intelligent children. Publishes 7–8 titles each year and has 103 in print. Recent successes include *Mathematical Merry-go-round, A Handbook of Paper Automata Mechanisms* and *Paper Gliders*. Founded 1970.

Submission details Do not send unsolicited MSS. Send a one-page proposal of idea.

Taylor and Francis Books Ltd*

4 Park Road, Milton Park, Abingdon, Oxon OX14 4RN

tel (01235) 828600 *fax* (01235) 828000
email info@tandf.co.uk
website www.tandf.co.uk, www.tfinforma.com
Managing Director, Taylor & Francis Books Ltd Roger Horton

Academic and reference books. Imprints include BIOS Scientific Publishers, CRC Press, Dunitz, Europa Publications, Fitzroy-Dearborn, Garland Science, Institute of Physics, Parthenon Press, Pschology Press, Routledge, RoutledgeCurzon, RoutledgeFalmer, Spon Press and Taylor & Francis.

RoutledgeFalmer (imprint)

website www.routledgefalmer.com
Education books for teachers.

The Templar Company plc

Pippbrook Mill, London Road, Dorking, Surrey RH4 1JE
tel (01306) 876361 *fax* (01306) 889097
email info@templar.co.uk
website www.templarco.co.uk
Managing Director Amanda Wood, *Publishing Manager* Rebecca Elliott, *Sales & Marketing Director* Ruth Huddleston

High-quality illustrated children's books, including novelty books, picture books, pop-up books, board books, non-fiction and gift titles. See also page 72.

D.C. Thomson & Co. Ltd – Publications

2 Albert Square, Dundee DD1 9QJ
London office 185 Fleet Street, London EC4A 2HS

Publishers of newspapers and periodicals. Children's books (annuals), based on weekly magazine characters; fiction. For fiction guidelines, send a large sae to Central Fiction Dept.

Ticktock Media

2 Orchard Business Centre, North Farm Road, Tunbridge Wells, Kent TN2 3XF
tel (01892) 509400 *fax* (01892) 509401
website www.ticktock.co.uk

Children's non-fiction; specialises in the schools market.

Titan Books

144 Southwark Street, London SE1 0UP
tel 020-7620 0200 *fax* 020-7620 0032
email editorial@titanemail.com
website www.titanbooks.com
Publisher & Managing Director Nick Landau, *Editorial Director* Katy Wild

Graphic novels, including *Simpsons* and *Batman*, featuring comic strip material; film and TV tie-ins and cinema reference books. No fiction or children's proposals, no email submissions and no unsolicited material without preliminary letter; email or send large sae for current author guidelines. Division of Titan Publishing Group Ltd. Founded 1981.

Top That! Publishing plc
Marine House, Tide Mill Way, Woodbridge, Suffolk IP12 1AP
tel (01394) 386651 fax (01394) 386011
email info@topthatpublishing.com
website www.topthatpublishing.com
Directors Barrie Henderson (managing), Simon Couchman (creative), Dave Greggor (sales)

Top That! Kids (imprint)
Activity books, novelty books, reference books and CD-Roms. Publishes 150 titles each year and has 300 titles in print. Recent successes include *Mini Maestro* activity series and *Early Days* series (preschool). Founded 1998.
Submission details Phone the Editorial Dept before sending MS to ascertain interest.

Treehouse Children's Books
2nd Floor Offices, Old Brewhouse, Lower Charlton Trading Estate, Shepton Mallet, Somerset BA4 5QE
tel (01749) 330529 fax (01749) 330544
email treehouse-books@btconnect.com
Editorial Director Richard Powell

Preschool children's books and novelty books. Imprint of Emma Treehouse Ltd (see page 72). Founded 1989.

Trentham Books Ltd
Westview House, 734 London Road, Oakhill, Stoke-on-Trent, Staffs. ST4 5NP
tel (01782) 745567 fax (01782) 745553
email tb@trentham.books.co.uk
Editorial office 28 Hillside Gardens, London N6 5ST
tel 020-8348 2174
website www.trentham-books.co.uk
Directors Dr Gillian Klein (editorial), Barbara Wiggins (executive)

Education (including specialist fields – multi-ethnic issues, equal opportunities, bullying, design and technology, early years), social policy, sociology of education, European education, women's studies. Does not publish books for use by parents or children, or fiction, biography, reminiscences and poetry. Founded 1978.

Trotman & Company Ltd
2 The Green, Richmond, Surrey TW9 1PL
tel 020-8486 1150 fax 020-8486 1161
website www.trotman.co.uk
Publishing Director Mina Patria, *Commissioning Editor* Rachel Lockhart

Independent advice and guidance on careers and higher education. Founded 1970.

Usborne Publishing Ltd
Usborne House, 83–85 Saffron Hill, London EC1N 8RT
tel 020-7430 2800 fax 020-8636 3758
email mail@usborne.co.uk
website www.usborne.com
Publishing Director Jenny Tyler, *Editorial Director, Fiction* Megan Larkin, *General Manager* Robert Jones

Activity books, novelty books, picture books, fiction for 5–8 and 9–12 year-olds, series fiction, reference, poetry and audio. Reference subjects include practical, craft, natural history, science, languages, history, art, activities, geography. Publishes 120 titles each year and has about 1000 in print. Recent successes include *That's Not My Dolly* (touchy-feely board book) and *Fairy Things to Make and Do* (activity book). Imprint: Usborne. Founded 1973.
Submission details Looking for high-quality imaginative children's fiction. Send non-fiction correspondence to Jenny Tyler and fiction correspondence to Megan Larkin.

Walker Books Ltd
87 Vauxhall Walk, London SE11 5HJ
tel 020-7793 0909 fax 020-7587 1123
website www.walkerbooks.co.uk
Directors David Lloyd (chairman), David Heatherwick (managing), Mark Briars (finance), Michel Blake (production), Jane Winterbotham (publishing), Henryk Wesolowski (sales & marketing), *Publishers* Deirdre McDermott, Caroline Royds, Lorraine Taylor, Denise Johnstone-Burt, Gill Evans

Activity books, novelty books, picture books, fiction for 5–8 and 9–12 year-olds, teenage fiction, series fiction, film/TV tie-ins, plays, poetry and audio. Publishes approx. 300 titles each year and has 2300 in print. Recent successes include the *Alex Rider* series by Anthony Horowitz, *Dear Tooth Fairy* by Alan Durant and Vanessa Cabban and *Maisy's Rainbow Dream* by Lucy Cousins. Imprint: Walker Books. Founded 1980.
Submission details Write to the Editor. Allow 3 months for response.

Ward Lock Educational Co. Ltd
BIC Ling Kee House, 1 Christopher Road, East Grinstead, West Sussex RH19 3BT
tel (01342) 318980 fax (01342) 410980
email wle@lingkee.com
website www.wardlockeducational.com
Directors Au Bak Ling (chairman, Hong Kong), Au King Kwok (Hong Kong), Au Wai Kwok (Hong Kong), Albert Kw Au (Hong Kong), *Company Secretary* Eileen Parsons

Primary and secondary pupil materials, Kent Mathematics Project: *KMP BASIC* and *KMP Main* series covering Reception to GCSE, *Reading Workshops*, *Take Part* series and *Take Part* starters, teachers' books, music books, *Target* series for the National Curriculum: *Target Science* and *Target Geography*, religious education. Founded 1952.

Warne – see Penguin Group (UK)

Franklin Watts – see Hachette Children's Books

The Watts Publishing Group Ltd – see Hachette Children's Books

Wayland – see Hachette Children's Books

Wizard Books Ltd

The Old Dairy, Brook Road, Thriplow, Cambridge SG8 7RG
tel (01763) 208008 *fax* (01763) 208080
email wizard@iconbooks.co.uk
website www.iconbooks.co.uk/wizard
Directors Peter Pugh (managing), Simon Flynn (publishing)

Gamebooks for 5–8 and 9–12 year-olds, reference and narrative non-fiction. Publishes approx. 15 titles each year. Recent successes include *Fighting Fantasy Gamebooks* by Steve Jackson and Ian Livingstone, *Big Numbers* by Mary and John Gribbin and *Darkness Visible: Inside the World of Philip Pullman* by Nicholas Tucker. Imprint of Icon Books Ltd.
Submission details Will consider unsolicited MSS.

The Women's Press

Top Floor, 27 Goodge Street, London W1P 2LD
tel 020-7580 7806 *fax* 020-7637 1866
website www.the-womens-press.com
Acting Managing Director Stella Kane

Books by women in the areas of literary and crime fiction, biography and autobiography, health, culture, politics, handbooks, literary criticism, psychology and self-help, the arts. Founded 1978.

Livewire (imprint)

Books for teenagers and young women.

Wordsworth Editions Ltd

8B East Street, Ware, Herts. SG12 9HJ
tel (01920) 465167 *fax* (01920) 462267
email enquiries@wordsworth-editions.com
website www.wordsworth.editions.com
Directors Helen Trayler (managing), Dennis Hart (sales)

Reprints of classic books: literary, children's; poetry; reference; Special Editions; mystery and supernatural. Founded 1987.

Y Lolfa Cyf.

Talybont, Ceredigion SY24 5AP
tel (01970) 832304 *fax* (01970) 832782
email ylolfa@ylolfa.com
website www.ylolfa.com
Director Garmon Gruffudd, *Editor* Lefi Gruffudd

Welsh-language popular fiction and non-fiction, music, children's books (recent successes include *Iawn Boi!* by Caryl Lewis and *Stori Dafydd ap Gwilym* by Gwyn Thomas and Margaret Jones); Welsh-language tutors; Welsh politics in English and a range of Welsh-interest books for the tourist market. Founded 1967.

York Notes – see Pearson Education

Young Hippo – see Scholastic Ltd

Young Picador – see Macmillan Publishers Ltd

Zero to Ten Ltd*

2A Portman Mansions, Chiltern Street, London W1U 6NR
tel 020-7487 0920 *fax* 020-7487 0921
email sales@evansbrothers.co.uk
Publishing Director Su Swallow

Non-fiction for children aged 0–10: board books, toddler books, first story books, etc. Part of the Evans Publishing Group. Founded 1997.

Cherrytree Books (imprint)

UK Publisher Su Swallow

Children's non-fiction illustrated books mainly for schools and libraries.

Zoë Books

15 Worthy Lane, Winchester, Hants SO23 7AB
tel (01962) 851318
email enquiries@zoebooks.co.uk
website www.zoebooks.co.uk
Managing/Publishing Director Imogen Dawson

Children's information books for schools (primary and secondary) libraries. Has over 100 titles in print. Recent successes include *Postcards From* series, *Clothes and Crafts* series and *World Habitats* series. Founded 1990.
Submission details Will not consider unsolicited MSS. No opportunities for freelances. Not looking for new writers.

ZooBooKoo International Ltd

4 Gurdon Road, Grundisburgh, Woodbridge, Suffolk IP13 6XA
tel (01473) 735346 *fax* (01473) 735346
email karen@zoobookoo.com
website www.zoobookoo.com
Sales Director Karen Wattleworth

Designer/manufacturer of ZooBooKoo Original Cube Books, multi-level educational folding cube books. Recent successes include *World Football, Human Body, Magic Maze, Add and Subtract, Planets, Natural Europe* and *Dolphins & Whales.*

Children's book publishers overseas

Listings are given for children's book publishers in Australia (below), Canada (page 31), France (page 35), Germany (page 35), Italy (page 36), the Netherlands (page 36), New Zealand (page 36), South Africa (page 38), Spain (page 39) and the USA (page 40).

AUSTRALIA

*Member of the Australian Publishers Association

Allen & Unwin Pty Ltd*
83 Alexander Street, Crows Nest, NSW 2065
postal address PO Box 8500, St Leonards, NSW 1590
tel (02) 8425 0100 *fax* (02) 9906 2218
email info@allenandunwin.com
website www.allenandunwin.com
Directors Patrick Gallagher (publishing), Paul Donovan (managing), Peter Eichhorn (finance), *Publishers, Children & Teenagers* Rosalind Price, Erica Wagner

Picture books, fiction for 5–8 and 9–12 year-olds, teenage fiction, series fiction, narrative non-fiction and poetry. Also adult/general trade books, including fiction, academic, especially social science and history. Publishes approx. 40 titles each year and has about 310 in print. Recent successes include *Horrible Harriet* by Leigh Hobbs (picture book), *Think Smart, Hazel Green* by Odo Hirsch (junior fiction) and *How to Make a Bird* by Martine Murray. Imprint: Allen & Unwin. Founded 1990.
Submission details Will consider unsolicited MSS (but not picture book texts). Prefers to receive full MSS by post, with a brief synopsis and biography. Allow 3 months for response. Seeking junior fiction, quirkey non-fiction by wise, funny, inventive authors with a dinstinctive voice.

Michelle Anderson Publishing Pty Ltd*
PO Box 6032, Chapel Street North, South Yarra 3141
tel (03) 9826 9028 *fax* (03) 9826 8552
email mapubl@bigpond.net.au
website www.michelleandersonpublishing.com
Director Michelle Anderson

Picture books for children aged 3–8. Also for adults: general health and mind/body, babies and motherhood. Publishes 2 children's titles each year and has 6 in print. Recent successes include *Broken Beaks* (explaining homelessness to children), *What About Me?* (story for siblings of sick children) and *Who Am I?* (yoga for children). Imprint: Michelle Anderson Publishing. Founded 1965.
Submission details Will consider unsolicited synopses but not MSS. Allow 3 weeks for response.

The Australian Council *for* Educational Research
19 Prospect Hill Road, Private Bag 55, Camberwell, Victoria 3124
tel (03) 9277 5555 *fax* (03) 9277 5500
email info@acer.edu.au
website www.acer.edu.au
Ceo Prof. Geoff Masters

Range of books and kits: for teachers, trainee teachers, parents, psychologists, counsellors, students of education, researchers.

Cygnet – see University of Western Australia Press

Hachette Livre Australia Pty Ltd*
Level 17, 207 Kent Street, Sydney, NSW 2000
tel (02) 8248 0800 *fax* (02) 2848 0810
email auspub@hachette.com.au
website www.hachette.com.au
Directors Malcolm Edwards (managing), Mary Drum, Chris Raine, David Cocking, Louise Sherwin-Stark, Matt Richell, Sandy Weir, Fiona Hazard

General, children's. No unsolicited MSS.

HarperCollins Publishers (Australia) Pty Ltd Group*
postal address PO Box 321, 25 Ryde Road, Pymble, NSW 2073
tel (02) 9952 5000 *fax* (02) 9952 5555
Managing Director Robert Gorman, *Publishing Director* Shona Martyn, *Publishers* Linda Funnell (fiction), Amruta Slee (non-fiction), Alison Urquhart (non-fiction), Lisa Berryman (children's)

Literary fiction and non-fiction, popular fiction, children's, reference, biography, autobiography, current affairs, sport, lifestyle, health/self-help, humour, true crime, travel, Australiana, history, business, gift, religion.

Lothian Books*
132 Albert Road, South Melbourne, Victoria 3205
tel 613-9694-4900 *fax* 613-9645-0705
email books@lothian.com.au
website www.lothian.com.au
Ceo Peter Lothian, *Sales & Marketing Manager* Bruce Hilliard, *Children's Publisher* Helen Chamberlin, *Children's Book Publicist* Georgina Way

Picture books, fiction for 5–8 and 9–12 year-olds, teenage fiction and series fiction. Publishes approx. 65 titles each year and has 750 in print. Recent successes include *The Quentaris Chronicles and Woolly Jumpers* by Nette Hilton (junior fiction) and *Jacko Moran and Robert Moran* by Ken Catran (young adult). Imprints: Start-Ups, Junior Fiction, Lothian Young Adult Fiction, The Quentaris Chronicles. Also for adults: health, gardening, reference, Australian history, business, sport, biography, New Age, humour, Buddhism. Imprint of Time Warner Book Group.

Submission details Will not accept unsolicited MSS. Submit MSS via an agent. List is full until 2008.

McGraw-Hill Education*

Level 2, The Everglade Building, 82 Waterloo Road, North Ryde NSW 2113
Private Bag 2233, Business Centre, North Ryde, NSW 1670
tel (02) 9900 1905, 9900 1800
email eiko_bron@mcgraw-hill.com
website www.macgraw-hill.com.au
Publishing Manager Michael Tully, *Schools Acquisitions Editor* Eiko Bron

Educational publisher: higher education, primary and secondary education (grades K–12) and professional (including medical, general and reference). Division of the McGraw-Hill Companies. Founded 1964.

Submission details Always looking for new potential authors. Has a rapidly expanding publishing programme. See website for author's guide.

Macmillan Education Australia Pty Ltd*

Melbourne office Level 4, 627 Chapel Street, South Yarra, Victoria 3141
tel (03) 9825 1025 *fax* (03) 9825 1010
email mea@macmillan.com.au
Sydney office Level 2, St Martin's Tower, 31 Market Street, Sydney, NSW 2000
tel (02) 9285 9200 *fax* (02) 9285 9290
Directors Shane Armstrong (managing), Peter Huntley (sales), Sandra Iversen (primary publishing), Rex Parry (secondary publishing), George Smith (production), *Company Secretary/Financial Controller* Terry White, *Children's Publisher* Sandra Iverson

Educational books.

New Frontier Publishing*

Forest Central Building 7, 4–49 Frenchs Forest Road, Frenchs Forest, NSW 2086
tel (02) 9453 1525 *fax* (02) 9975 2531
Director Peter Whitfield

Aims to uplift, educate and inspire through its range of children's books. Activity books, picture books, fiction, dictionaries, textbooks. Caters for 5–10 year-olds.

Pan Macmillan Australia Pty Ltd*

Level 25, 1 Market Street, Sydney, NSW 2000
tel (02) 9285 9100 *fax* (02) 9285 9190
email pansyd@macmillan.com.au
website www.macmillan.com.au
Directors Ross Gibb (chairman), James Fraser (publishing), Roxarne Burns (publishing), Siv Toigo

(finance), Peter Phillips (sales), Jeannine Fowler (publicity & marketing)

Commercial and literary fiction; children's fiction, non-fiction and character products; non-fiction; sport.

Pearson Education Australia*

Level 9, 5 Queens Road, Melbourne 3004
tel (3) 9811 2878 *fax* (3) 9811 2999
email rosaleen.stewart@pearsoned.com.au
website www.pearsoned.com.au/schools
Primary Publisher Rosaleen Stewart

Early fiction, non-fiction, geography, history, mathematics, textbooks, CD-Roms, interactive websites.

Penguin Group (Australia)*

250 Camberwell Road, Camberwell, Victoria 3124
tel (03) 9811 2400 *fax* (03) 9811 2620
postal address PO Box 701, Hawthorn, Victoria 3122
website www.penguin.com.au
Managing Director Gabrielle Coyne, *Publishing Director* Robert Sessions, *Executive Publisher – Books for Children & Young Adults* Julie Watts, *Publisher – Books for Children & Young Adults* Laura Harris, *Commissioning Editor* Lisa Riley

Picture books, fiction for 5–8 and 9–12 year-olds, teenage fiction, series fiction and film/TV tie-ins. Also for adults: fiction and general non-fiction. Publishes approx. 85 titles each year and has about 500 in print. Recent successes include *Cuthbert's Babies* by Pamela Allen (picture book), *Rascal* books by Paul Jennings (younger readers) and *Saving Francesca* by Melina Marchetta (young adult). Children's imprints: Puffin (paperback). A Pearson company. Founded 1935.

Submission details Will consider unsolicited MSS but submit only one MS at a time. Send proposals to The Editor, Books for Children and Young Adults at the postal address (above). Enclose an sae for the return of material. Does not accept proposals by email or fax.

Prim-Ed Publishing Pty Ltd

4 Bendsten Place, Balcatta, WA 6021
tel 618-9240-9888 *fax* 618-9240-1513
website www.prim-ed.com

Educational publisher specialising in blackline master or copymasters and student workbooks for schools and homeschoolers.

Puffin – see Penguin Group (Australia)

University of Queensland Press*

PO Box 6042, St Lucia, Queensland 4067
tel (07) 3365 2127 *fax* (07) 3365 7579
email uqp@uqp.uq.edu.au
website www.uqp.uq.edu.au
General Manager Greg Bain

Scholarly works, tertiary texts, indigenous Australian writing, Australian fiction, young adult fiction, poetry, history, general interest. Founded 1948.

Random House Australia Pty Ltd*

20 Alfred Street, Milsons Point, NSW 2061
tel (02) 9954 9966 *fax* (02) 9954 4562
email random@randomhouse.com.au
website www.randomhouse.com.au
Managing Director Margaret Seale, *Head of Publishing, Random House* Jane Palfreyman, *Head of Publishing, Bantam Doubleday* Fiona Henderson, *Children's Publisher* Lindsay Knight, *Illustrated Publisher* Jude McGee, *Sales & Marketing Director* Carol Davidson, *Publicity Director* Karen Reid

General fiction and non-fiction; children's, illustrated. Imprints: Arrow, Avon, Ballantine, Bantam, Black Swan, Broadway, Century, Chatto & Windus, Corgi, Crown, Dell, Doubleday, Ebury, Fodor, Heinemann, Hutchinson, Jonathan Cape, Knopf, Mammoth UK, Minerva, Pantheon, Pavilion, Pimlico, Random House, Red Fox, Rider, Vermilion, Vintage, Virgin.Subsidiary of Bertelsmann AG.

Submission details For Random House and Transworld Publishing, unsolicited non-fiction accepted, unbound in hard copy addressed to Submissions Editor. Fiction submissions are only accepted from previously published authors, or authors represented by an agent or accompanied by a report from an accredited assessment service.

Scholastic Australia Pty Ltd*

PO Box 579, Gosford, NSW 2250
tel (02) 4328 3555 *fax* (02) 4323 3827
website www.scholastic.com.au
Managing Director Ken Jolly, *Publisher* Andrew Berkhut

Children's fiction and non-fiction. Founded 1968.

Start-Ups – see Lothian Books

Takeaways – see Lothian Books

The Quentaris Chronicles – see Lothian Books

Thomson Learning Australia*

Level 7, 80 Dorcas Street, South Melbourne, Victoria 3205
tel (03) 9685 4111 *fax* (03) 9685 4199
email customerservice@thomsonlearning.com.au
website www.thomsonlearning.com.au

Educational books.

University of Western Australia Press*

UWA, 35 Stirling Hwy, Crawley 6009, Western Australia
tel (618) 6488 3670 *fax* (618) 6488 1027
email admin@uwapress.uwa.edu.au
website www.uwapress.uwa.edu.au
Acting Director Terri-Ann White

Fiction for 5–8 and 9–12 year-olds and teenage fiction. Also for adults: natural history, history,

maritime history, critical studies, women's studies, general non-fiction, contemporary issues. Publishes approx. 6 children's titles each year. Recent successes include *Eyes in the Night* by Jan Ramage, *Corroboree* by Angus Wallam and Suzanne Kelly, and *Saving Tippy* by Jenny Shepherd. Children's imprints: Cygnet, Cygnet Young Fiction. Founded 1954.

Submission details Will consider unsolicited MSS. Contact UWAP for guidelines. Seeking to publish books with Australian themes, an environmental message and historical topics.

CANADA

*Member of the Canadian Publishers' Council
†Member of the Association of Canadian Publishers

Annick Press Ltd†

15 Patricia Avenue, Toronto, Ontario M2M 1H9
tel 416-221-4802 *fax* 416-221-8400
email annickpress@annickpress.com
website www.annickpress.com
Co-editors Rick Wilks, Colleen MacMillan, *Creative Director* Sheryl Shapiro

Preschool to young adult fiction and non-fiction. Publishes 8 picture books, 3 young readers, 3 middle readers and 8 young adult titles each year. Recent successes include *The Research Virtuoso: Brilliant Methods for Normal Brains, My Kind of Sad: What it's Like to be Young and Depressed, Torrie and the Firebird* and *Into the World of the Dead: Astonishing Adventures in the Underworld.* Founded 1975.

Submission details Approx. 25% of books are by first-time authors. No unsolicited MSS. For illustrations, query with samples and sase to Creative Director. Responds in 6 months.

Boardwalk Books – see Dundurn Press

Doubleday Canada

1 Toronto Street, Suite 300, Toronto, Ontario M5C 2V6
tel 416-364-4449 *fax* 416-957-1587
website www.randomhouse.ca
Chairman John Neale, *Publisher* Maya Mavjee

General trade non-fiction; fiction; young adults. Division of **Random House of Canada Ltd**. Founded 1942.

Dundurn Press†

3 Church Street, Suite 500, Toronto, Ontario M5E 1MZ
tel 416-214-5544 *fax* 416-214-5556
email info@dundurn.com
website www.dundurn.com
Directors J. Kirk Howard (President), Beth Bruder (Vic-President, sales & marketing), Tony Hawke (editorial)

Popular non-fiction, fiction, scholarship, history, biography, young adult, art. Part of the Dundurn Group. Founded 1973.

Boardwalk Books (imprint); Sandcastle Books (imprint)
Young adult fiction.

Fitzhenry & Whiteside Ltd†
195 Allstate Parkway, Markham, Ontario L3R 4T8
tel 800-387-9776 *fax* 800-260-9777
email godwit@fitzhenry.ca
website www.fitzhenry.ca
Director Sharon Fitzhenry, *Children's Publisher* Gail Winskill

Fiction and non-fiction (social studies, visual arts, biography, environment). Publishes 10 picture books, 5 early readers/chapter books, 6 middle novels and 7 young adult books each year. Founded 1966.
   Submission details Approx. 10% of books are by first-time authors. Emphasis is on Canadian authors and illustrators, subject or perspective. Will review MS/illustration packages from artists. Submit outline and copy of sample illustration. For illustrations only, send samples and promotional scheet. Responds in 3 months. Samples returned with sase.

Harcourt Canada Ltd
55 Horner Avenue, Toronto, Ontario M8Z 4X6
tel 800-268-2222 *fax* 800-430-4445
website www.nelson.com

Educational materials from K–Grade 12, testing and assessment. Imprints: Harcourt Religion (formerly Brown-ROA), Harcourt Brace & Company, Holt, Rinehart and Winston, MeadowBrook Press, The Psychological Corporation, Therapy Skill Builders/ Communications Skill Builders. Distributed by Thomson Nelson. Founded 1922.

HarperCollins Publishers Ltd*
2 Bloor Street East, 20th Floor, Toronto, Ontario M4W 1A8
tel 416-975-9334 *fax* 416-975-9884
website www.harpercollins.ca
President David Kent

Publishers of literary fiction and non-fiction, history, politics, biography, spiritual and children's books. Founded 1989.

Key Porter Books Ltd†
6 Adelaide Street East, 10th Floor, Toronto, Ontario M5C 1H6
tel 416-862-7777 *fax* 416-862-2304
email info@keyporter.com
website www.keyporter.com
Publisher Jordan Fenn

Fiction and non-fiction for all ages. Recent successes include *Rose in New York: Gotcha!* by Carol Matas (fiction, young adult), *The Dinosaur Atlas* by Don Lessem (non-fiction, ages 8–10) and *Rude Ramsey and The Roaming Radishes* by Margaret Atwood (non-fiction, ages 4–7). For adults: fiction and non-fiction (nature, history, Canadian politics, conservation, humour, biography, autobiography, health). Founded 1981.

Submission details Approx. 30% of books are by first-time authors. No unsolicited MSS: only interested in submissions via literary agents. Responds to queries/proposals in 6 months. Length: picture books – 1500 words; young readers, fiction – 5000 words; middle readers, non-fiction – 15,000 words.

Kids Can Press Ltd†
29 Birch Avenue, Toronto, Ontario M4V 1E2
tel 416-925-5437 *fax* 416-960-5437
email info@kidscan.com
website www.kidscanpress.com
Publisher Valerie Hussey, Karen Boersma

Juvenile/young adult fiction and non-fiction. Publishes 6–10 pciture books, 10–15 young readers, 20–30 middle readers and 2–3 young adult titles each year. Recent successes include *Suki's Kimono* by Chieri Ugaki, illustrated by Stephane Jorlisch (picture book), *The Secret of Sagawa Lake* by Mary Labatt (early novel), *The Kids' Winter Handbook* by Jane Drake and Ann Love, illustrated by Heather Collings (informational activity) and *Animals at Work* by Etta Kaner, illustrated by Pat Stephens. Publishers of *Franklin the Turtle* and *Elliot Moose* characters. Founded 1973.
   Submission details Approx. 10–15% of books are by first-time authors. Submit outline/synopsis and 2–3 sample chapters. For picture books, submit complete MS. Responds in 6 months. Only accepts MSS from Canadian authors. Fiction length: picture books – 1000–2000 words; young readers – 750–1500 words; middle readers – 10,000–15,000 words; young adult – over 15,000 words. Non-fiction length: picture books – 500–1250 words; young readers – 750–2000 words; middle readers – 5000–15,000 words.

McGraw-Hill Ryerson Ltd*
300 Water Street, Whitby, Ontario L1N 9B6
tel 905-430-5000 *fax* 905-430-5020
website www.mcgrawhill.ca
Executive Vice-President Robert Bahash

Educational and trade books.

Madison Press Books
1000 Yonge Street, Suite 200, Toronto, Ontario M4W 2K2
tel 416-923-5027 *fax* 416-923-9708
website www.madisonpressbooks.com
Editorial Director Wanda Nowakowska

Illustrated non-fiction for 8–12 year-olds.

Napoleon Publishing/Rendez Vous Press†
178 Willowdale Avenue, Suite 201, Toronto, Ontario M2N 4Y8
tel 416-730-9052 *fax* 416-730-8096
email napoleon.publishing@transmedia95.com
website www.napoleonpublishing.com

Publisher Sylvia McConnell, *Editor* Allister Thompson
Children's books and adult fiction. Founded 1990.

Orca Book Publishers

Box 5626, Station B, Victoria, BC, V8R 6S4
tel 800-210-5277 *fax* 877-408-1551
email orca@orcabook.com
website www.orcabook.com

Books for children and young adults. No poetry. *Orca Echoes* (7–8 year-olds), *Young Readers* (8–11 year-olds), juvenile novels (9–13 year-olds), *Orca Currents* (intermediate novels aimed at reluctant readers with simple language and short, high-interest chapters), young adult fiction, *Orca Soundings* (high-interest teen novels aimed at reluctant readers). Recent successes include *Hero an Orca Young Reader* by Martha Attema and *The Puppet Wrangler* by Vicki Grant.

Submission details Currently seeking MS of picture books. Length: up to 1500 words. Submit complete MS FAO Maggie deVries, Children's Book Editor. No queries.

Orca Echoes, Orca Young Readers (also called chapter books) and juvenile fiction: Contemporary stories or fantasy with a universal theme, a compelling, unified plot and a strong, sympathetic child protagonist who grows through the course of the story and solves the central problem him/herself. Well-researched stories dealing with, or taking their inspiration from, historical subjects, but not thinly disguised history lessons. Length: Orca Echoes 5500–6000 words; Young Readers 14,000–18,000 words; juvenile fiction 25,000–35,000 words. *Orca Echoes, Young Reader* and juvenile novel queries should be sent with sample chapters FAO Maggie deVries, Children's Book Editor.

Stories for *Orca Currents* should have appropriate story lines for middle school (family issues, humour, sports, adventure, mystery/suspense, fantasy, etc) with strong plots, credible characters/situations. Awkward moralising should be avoided. Protagonists are between 12–14 years old and should be appealing and believable. Length: 14,000–16,000 words; 12–16 short chapters. Send a chapter-by-chapter outline and one sample chapter FAO Melanie Jeffs, Editor.

Teen or young adult fiction: Issue-oriented contemporary stories exploring a universal theme, with a compelling, unified plot and strong, sympathetic protagonist(s). Well-researched stories dealing with, or taking their inspiration from, historical subjects, but not thinly disguised history lessons. Length: up to 50,000 words. Send queries to Teen Fiction Editor.

Orca Soundings: These stories should reflect the universal struggles that young people face. They need not be limited to 'gritty' urban tales but can include adventures, mystery/suspense, fantasy, etc. Interested in humorous stories that will appeal to teens of both sexes. 'Disease-of-the-week' potboilers or awkward moralising should be avoided. Protagonists are

between 14–17 years old and should be appealing and believable. Length: 14,000–16,000 words, 12–16 short chapters. Send a chapter-by-chapter outline and one sample chapter FAO Andrew Wooldridge, Editor.

Will consider MMS from Canadian writers only. No submissions by fax or email. Inappropriate queries and submissions that arrive without a sase will be fed to the shredder. Founded 1984.

Pearson Education Canada*

(formerly Prentice Hall Canada and Addison-Wesley Canada)
26 Prince Andrew Place, Toronto, Ontario M3C 2T8
tel 416-447-5101 *fax* 416-443-0948
website www.pearsoned.ca
President Allan Reynolds

Academic, technical, educational, children's and adult, trade.

Penguin Group (Canada)*

90 Eglinton Avenue East, Suite 700, Toronto, Ontario M4P 2Y3
tel 416-925-2249 *fax* 416-925-0068
email info@penguin.ca
website www.penguin.ca

Literary fiction, memoir, non-fiction (history, business, current events). No unsolicited MSS; submissions via an agent only. Imprints: Penguin Canada, Viking Canada, Puffin Canada. Founded 1974.

Pippin Publishing Corporation

PO Box 242, Don Mills, Ontario M3C 2S2
tel 416-510-2918 *fax* 416-510-3359
email cynthia@pippinpub.com
website www.pippinpub.com
President/Editorial Director Jonathan Lovat Dickson

ESL/EFL, teacher reference, adult basic education, school texts (all subjects), general trade (non-fiction).

Raincoast Books[†]

9050 Shaughnessy Street, Vancouver, BC V6P 6E5
tel 604-323-7100 *fax* 604-323-2600
email publishing@raincoast.com
website www.raincoast.com

Fiction and non-fiction for adults and children. Recent successes include *The Song Within my Heart* by David Bouchard, paintings by Allen Sapp (picture book), *Tess* by Jocelyn Reekie (juvenile fiction), *Albertosaurus Death of a Predator* by Monique Keiran (non-fiction) and *A Young Dancer's Apprenticeship* by Olympia Dowd (non-fiction). Imprints: Polestar, Press Gang.

Submission details Will not accept unsolicited MSS. Send a query letter via regular mail for the attention of the Editorial Department. For young adult fiction, submit query letter with a list of publication credits plus one-page outline of the plot. No queries via email. Allow 8–16 weeks for reply. Only accepts material from Canadian residents.

Red Deer Press

MacKimmie Library Tower, Room 813, 2500
University Drive NW, Calgary, AB T2N 1N4
tel (403) 220-4334
email rdp@ucalgary.ca
website www.reddeerpress.com
Managing Editor Dennis Johnson, *Children's Editor*
Peter Carver

Literary fiction, non-fiction, drama, poetry, children's
illustrated books, young adult fiction, teen fiction.
Publishes books that are written or illustrated by
Canadians and that are about or of interest to
Canadians. Imprints: Discovery Books, Prairie
Garden Books, History Along the Highway Books,
Roundup Books, Writing West, Northern Lights
Books for Children (illustrated books), Northern
Lights Young Novels (juvenile and young adult
fiction), Sirrocco Books (teen fiction for 14–20 year-
olds). Also series in Canadian drama, adult fiction,
and children's first chapter books. Publishes 18–20
new books per year.
    Submission details The publishing program is full
for 2005–6 and for the next 3 years in the children's
picture book, juvenile and teen fiction categories. For
children's picture books MSS from established
authors with a demonstrable record of publishing
success are preferred. Founded 1975.

Sandcastle Books – see Dundurn Press

Scholastic Canada Ltd*

Scholastic Canada Ltd, 604 King Street West,
Toronto, Ontario M5V 1E1
website www.scholastic.ca
Art Director Ms Yüksel Hassan

Serves children, parents and teachers through a
variety of businesses including Scholastic Book Clubs
and Book Fairs, Scholastic Education, Classroom
Magazines, Trade, and Les éditions Scholastic.
Publishes recreational reading for children and young
people from kindergarten to Grade 8 and educational
materials in both official languages. Its publishing
focus is on books by Canadians. Scholastic Canada
Ltd is a wholly owned subsidiary of Scholastic Inc.
    Submission details No unsolicited MSS. Fiction –
length: picture books (4–8 years) under 1000 words;
first chapter books (7–9 years) 7000–10,000 words;
junior novels 9–14 years 25,000–40,000 words. Non-
fiction subjects: up to 4 years – animals, school,
seasons, etc; 5–6 years – biography, Canadiana,
history, etc; 7–10 years – adventure, animals, sports,
etc; 11–14 years – crafts, friendship, technology, etc.
    Artists may submit several photocopied samples of
their work and a brief résumé to the art director.
Never send originals or anything that cannot be
replaced.

Thomson Nelson*

1120 Birchmount Road, Scarborough, Ontario
M1K 5G4

tel 416-752-9100 *fax* 416-752-9646
email inquire@nelson.com
website www.nelson.com
President George W. Bergquist, *Vice President, Market
Development* Chris Besse, *Senior Vice President, School*
Greg Pilon, *Senior Vice President, Media Services*
Susan Cline, *Senior Vice President, Higher Education*
Lesley Gouldie

Educational publishing: school (K–12), college and
university, career education, measurement and
guidance, professional and reference, ESL titles.
Division of Thomson Canada Ltd. Founded 1914.

Total Publishing

7 Bates Road, Outermont, Quebec H2V 4V7
tel 514-270-6860 *fax* 514-276-2533
website www.total-publishing.com
Contact Stephanie Labbe

Activity books, novelty books, picture books,
biography, fairy tales, history. Age groups: preschool,
5–10, 10–15.

Tundra Books Inc.[†]

75 Sherbourne Street, 5th Floor, Toronto, Ontario
M5A 2P9
tel 416-598-4786 *fax* 416-598-0247
website www.tundrabooks.com
Children's Publisher Kathy Lowinger

High-quality children's picture books.

Whitecap Books Ltd[†] ✓

351 Lynn Avenue, North Vancouver, BC V7J 2C4
website www.whitecap.ca
President Michael E. Burch, *Vice-President* Nicholas
S.M. Rundall, *Publisher* Robert McCullough

General: children's, cooking, gardening, crafts and
home, health and well-being, history, biography,
nature and the environment, travel, wine and spirit.
Juvenile fiction, young adult fiction, non-fiction,
picture books for young children (nature, wildlife
and animals), *Young Nature* series. Recent successes
include *Saddle Island* series No 1: *Gallop to the Sea* by
Sharon Siamon, *Take it to the Extreme* No 6: *Vertical
Limits* by Pam Withers, *Jane Ray's Wildlife Rescue*
series No 1: *Flight or Fight* by Diane Haynes, *Digging
Canadian History* by Rebecca Grambo, and *Eleven
Lazy Llamas* written and illustrated by Dianna
Bonder.
    Submission details For children's illustrated fiction,
send complete MS. For all other submissions, send a
synopsis, a table of contents listing the chapters or
stories and their length, information about proposed
illustrations or photographs (number planned, b&w
or colour), 1–3 sample chapters and information
about the author, including educational and
professional background and previous publishing
credits. Include a sase with sufficient return postage,
and if submitting from outside of Canada, include an
international postal voucher.

Women's Press[†]

180 Bloor Street West, Suite 801, Toronto, Ontario
M5S 2V6
tel 416-929-2774 *fax* 416-929-1926
email info@cspi.org
website www.womenspress.ca
President & Publisher Dr Jack Wayne, *General
Manager* C. Dick Yu, *Editorial Director* Megan
Mueller

The ideas and experiences of women: fiction, creative
non-fiction, children's books, plays, biography,
autobiography, memoirs, poetry. Owned by
Canadian Scholars' Press. Founded 1987.

FRANCE

Flammarion

4 Rue Casimir Delavigne, 75006 Paris
tel (1) 40 51 31 60 *fax* (1) 46 33 59 45
email jho@flammarion.fr
website www.flammarion.fr

Leading French publisher. Children's imprints
include: Albums du Père Castor, Castor Poche,
Tribal, Etonnants Classiques, GF – Flammarion.
Founded 1875.

Père Castor (imprint)
Children's Publisher Hélène Wadowski
Children's picture books, junior fiction, activity
books, board books, how-to books, comics, gift
books, fairy tales, dictionaries and records and tapes.
Covers preschool, 5–10, 10–15 age groups.

Gallimard Jeunesse

5 rue Sebastien Bottin, 75007 Paris
tel (1) 49 54 42 00 *fax* (1) 45 44 94 03
email enquiries@gallimard-jeunesse.fr
website www.gallimard-jeunesse.fr
Children's Publisher Christine Baker, *Editor, Young
Children's Books* Anne de Bouchony

Publisher of high-quality children's fiction and non-
fiction including board books, novelty books, picture
books, pop-up books. Founded 1911.

Hachette Livre/Gautier-Languereau

43 quai de Grenelle, 75905 Paris Cedex 15
tel (43) 92 33 34 *fax* (43) 92 33 38
Director Frederique de Buron, *Editorial Director*
Emmanuelle Massonaud, *Publisher* Emmanuelle
Henry, *Artistic Manager* Maryvonne Denizet

Novelty books, picture books and poetry. Publishes
approx. 55 titles each year. Recent successes include
Bayayaga by Tai-Marc Le Thanh and Rébecca
Dautremer and *Cache-Lune* by Eric Puybaret.
Founded 1992.
    Submission details Will consider unsolicited MSS.
Allow 2 months for response.

Kaléidoscope

Kaléidoscope, 11 Rue de Sèvres, F–75006 Paris
tel (1) 45 44 07 07 *fax* (1) 45 44 53 71

email infos@editions-kaleidoscope.com
website www.editions-kaleidoscope.com
Children's Publisher Isabel Finkenstaedt

Specialises in up-market picture books for 0–6 year-
olds. Founded 1988.

Universpoche-Pocket Jeunesse

12 avenue d'Italie, 75013 Paris
tel (10) 44 16 07 96 *fax* (01) 44 16 05 20
email cecile.burgard@universpoche.com
website www.pocketjeunesse.fr
Publishing Director Jean-Claude Dubost, *Literary
Director* Natacha Derevitsky

Fiction for 5–8 and 9–12 year-olds, teenage fiction,
series, fiction and film/TV tie-ins. Publishes approx.
150–160 titles each year.
    Submission details Will consider unsolicited MSS.
Allow one month for response.

GERMANY

Carl Hanser Verlag

Vilshofener Strasse 10, 81679 München
tel (89-99) 830191 *fax* (89-99) 830461
email info@hanser.de
website www.hanser.de
Children's Publisher Friedbert Stohner

High-quality hardcover books for all ages from
preschool to young adults. Board books, picture
books, cinema and TV tie-ins, fiction and non-
fiction. Age groups: 5–10, 10–15, 15+. Founded 1928.

Carlsen Verlag

Kinderbuchlektorat, Völckersstrasse 14–20, D22765
Hamburg
tel (40) 398040 *fax* (40) 39804390
email info@carlsen.de
website www.carlsen.de
Children's Publisher Klaus Humann

Children's picture books, board books and novelty
books. Illustrated fiction and non-fiction. Teenage
fiction and non-fiction. Publishes both German and
international authors. Publisher of the *Harry Potter*
series. Age groups: preschool, 5–10, 10–15, 15+.
Founded 1953.
    Submission details Unsolicited MSS welcome but
must include an sae for its return. Do not follow up
by phone or post. For illustrations, submit no more
than 3 colour photocopies and unlimited b&w copies.

Deutscher Taschenbuch Verlag (DTV)

Friedrichstrasse 1/A, D–80801 München
tel (89) 381 67281 *fax* (89) 381 67482
website www.dtvjunior.de
Children's Publishing Director Anne Schieckel

Fiction and non-fiction for children and teenagers.
Authors include Astrid Lindgren, Uwe Timm and
Joan Aiken. Founded 1971.

Ravensburger Buchverlage

Robert-Bosch-Straße 1, 88214 Ravensburg
tel (49) 751860 *fax* (49) 751 861289
email buchverlag@ravensburger.de
website www.ravensburger.de/buchverlag
Managing Directors Renate Herre, Johannes
Hauenstein, *Commissioning Editors* Caroline Jacobi,
Ulrike Metzger, Sandra Schwarz, Sabine Zürn

Activity books, novelty books, picture books, fiction
for 5–8 and 9–12 year-olds, teenage fiction, series
fiction and educational games and puzzles. Publishes
approx. 450 titles each year and has 1500 in print.
Founded 1883.

Submission details Will consider unsolicited MSS
for fiction only. Allow 2 months for response.

ITALY

Edizioni El/Einaudi Ragazzi/Emme Edizioni

Via J. Ressel 5, 34018 San Dorligo della Valle TS
tel (040) 3880311 *fax* (040) 3880330
email edizionel@edizioniel.it
website www.edizionel.com
Children's Publisher Orietta Fatucci

Activity books, board books, picture books, pop-up
books, non-fiction, novels, poetry, fairy tales, fiction.
Age groups: preschool, 5–10, 10–15, 15+. Publishes
over 270 new titles per year.

Fabbri Editori

R.C.S. Libri S.pA, Via Mecenate 91, 20138 Milano
tel (02) 50951 *fax* (02) 50952387
website www.rcslibri.it/fabbri

Children's fiction, especially fantasy: Clive Barker,
Michael Chabon, Paolini's *Eragon*, Aidan Chambers.
Children's picture books: *The Flower Fairies, The
Ologies, Spot, Winx Club.*

Arnoldo Mondadori Editore S.p.A (Mondadori)

Via Arnoldo Mondadori, 15–37131, Verona
tel (045) 934111 *fax* (045) 934566
website www.mondadori.it
Children's Publisher Margherita Forstan, Fiammette
Giorgi

Activity books, board books, novelty books, picture
books, painting and colouring books, pop-up books,
how-to books, hobbies, leisure, pets, sport, comics,
poetry, fairy tales, education, fiction and non-fiction.
Age groups: preschool, 5–10, 10–15, 15+. Founded
1907.

Adriano Salani Editore S.P.A.

Via Gherardini 10, 20145 Milano
tel (02) 34597624 *fax* (02) 34597206
email info@salani.it

website www.salani.it
Publisher Grazia Maria Mazzitelli

Picture books, how-to books, comics, gift books,
fiction, novels, poetry, fairy tales. Age groups:
preschool, 5–10, 10–15, 15.

THE NETHERLANDS

De Fontein

Prinses Marielaan, 8-3740, AA Baarn
tel (35) 5422141 *fax* (35) 5423855
Children's Publisher Joriz VoLeur

Encyclopedias, non-fiction, fiction, poetry.

Sjaloom & Wildeboer, Uitgevers

PO Box 1895, NL–1000BW, Amsterdam
tel (20) 6206263 *fax* (20) 4288540
email post@sjaloom.nl
website www.sjaloon.nl
Children's Publisher Willem Wildeboer

Board books, novelty books, picture books, pop-up
books, non-fiction, fiction for ages preschool, 5–10
and 10–15.

Submission details Welcomes new submissions (no
disks) and illustrations. Include sae for return of
material.

Uitgeverij Hillen bv

W.G. Plein 512, NL–1054, Amsterdam
tel (20) 6124088 *fax* (20) 4120481
website www.hillenboeken.nl
Publishers Jacqueline Wilson, Clara Hillen

Prize-winning children's books for ages 6 months to
10+ years. New submissions welcome with sae for
return. No disks. Founded 2000.

Zirkoon Uitgevers bv

PO Box 598608, 1040 LC, Amsterdam
tel (20) 6233426 *fax* (20) 6234031
website www.zircoon.nl
Children's Publisher Iris Zuydewijn van de Roy

High-quality picture books, activity books, board
books, novelty books, pop-up books, poetry, fiction
and some non-fiction.

NEW ZEALAND

*Member of the New Zealand Book Publishers'
Association*

David Bateman Ltd*

30 Tarndale Grove, Albany, Auckland
tel (09) 415-7664 *fax* (09) 415-8892
email bateman@bateman.co.nz
postal address PO Box 100242, North Shore Mail
Centre, Auckland 1330

website www.bateman.co.nz
Chairman/Publisher David L. Bateman, *Directors* Janet Bateman, Paul Bateman (joint managing), Paul Parkinson (joint managing)

Natural history, gardening, encyclopedias, sport, art, cookery, historical, juvenile, travel, motoring, maritime history, business, art, lifestyle. Founded 1979.

Blue Balloon – see Scholastic New Zealand Ltd

Dunmore Press Ltd*
PO Box 2580, Wellington
tel (04) 472-2705 *fax* (04) 471-0604
email books@dunmore.co.nz
website www.dunmore.co.nz
Directors Murray Gatenby, Sharmian Firth

Education, history, sociology, business studies, general non-fiction. Founded 1970.

HarperCollins Publishers (New Zealand) Ltd*
PO Box 1, Auckland
tel (09) 443-9400 *fax* (09) 443-9403
Postal address PO Box 1, Auckland
website www.harpercollins.co.nz
Managing Director Tony Fisk, *Commissioning Editor* Lorain Day

General literature, non-fiction, reference, children's.

McGraw-Hill Book Company New Zealand Ltd*
56–60 Cawley Street, Level 8, Ellerslie, Auckland
Private Bag 11904, Ellerslie, Auckland 1005
tel (09) 526 6200 *fax* (09) 526 6216
website www.mcgrawhill.com.au

Educational publisher: higher education, primary and secondary education (grades K–12) and professional (including medical, general and reference). Division of the McGraw-Hill Companies. Founded 1974.
Submission details Always looking for new potential authors. Has a rapidly expanding publishing programme. See website for author's guide.

Mallinson Rendel Publishers Ltd*
Level 5, 15 Courtenay Place, PO Box 9409, Wellington
tel (04) 802-5012 *fax* (04) 802-5013
email publisher@mallinsonrendel.co.nz
Publisher & Managing Director Ann Mallinson, *Editor* Carol Dee

Picture books, fiction for 5–8 and 9–12 year-olds and teenage fiction. Publishes approx. 7 titles each year and has over 100 in print. Recent successes include *The Other Ark* by Lynley Dodd, *Right Where It Hurts* by David Hill and *The Real Thing* by Brian Falkner. Imprint: Mallinson Rendel. Founded 1980.
Submission details Will accept unsolicited MSS but is only interested in submissions from New Zealand authors.

MM House Publishing
752 Gladstone Road, Gisborne 3815, PO Box 539
tel (06) 8687769 *fax* (06) 8687767
email john@millymolly.com
website www.millymolly.com
Managing Director John Pittar

Picture books, gift books, fiction, education, interactive CD-Roms for preschool children and 4–8 year-olds. Promotes acceptance of diversity and sound values worldwide.

Nelson Price Milburn Ltd
1 Te Puni Street, Petone
tel (04) 568-7179 *fax* (04) 568-2115
email jacqui.rivera@thomson.com
postal address PO Box 38–945, Wellington Mail Centre, Wellington

Children's fiction, primary school texts, especially school readers and maths, secondary educational.

New Zealand Council for Educational Research
Box 3237, Education House, 178–182 Willis Street, Wellington 1
tel (04) 384-7939 *fax* (04) 384-7933
email info@nzcer.org.nz
website www.nzcer.org.nz
Director Robyn Baker, *Publisher* Bev Webber

Education, including educational policy and institutions, early childhood education, educational achievement tests, Maori education, curriculum and assessment, etc. Founded 1934.

Pearson Education New Zealand Ltd*
Private Bag 102908, North Shore Mail Centre, Glenfield, Auckland 10
tel (09) 414-9980 *fax* (09) 414-9981
email firstname.lastname@pearsoned.co.nz
Managing Director Rosemary Stagg

New Zealand educational books.

Penguin Books NZ Ltd
Corner Rosedale & Airborne Roads, Albany, Private Bag 102902, NSMC, Auckland
tel (09) 415 4700 *fax* (09) 415 4701
website www.penguin.co.nz
Managing Director Tony Harkins, *Publishing Director* Geoff Walker

Adult and children's fiction and non-fiction. Imprints: Penguin, Viking, Puffin Books. Founded 1973.

Reed Publishing (New Zealand) Ltd*
(incorporating Reed Books and Heinemann Education)
39 Rawene Road, PO Box 34901, Birkenhead, Auckland 10
tel (09) 441 2960 *fax* (09) 480-4999

Chairman Chris Jones, *Managing Director* David O'Brien, *Publishing Manager* Peter Dowling

NZ specialist and general titles, primary and secondary textbooks, children's titles.

RSVP Publishing Company*
PO Box 47166, Ponsonby, Auckland
tel (09) 372-3480 *fax* (09) 372 8480
email rsvppub@iconz.co.nz
website www.rsvp-publishing.co.nz
Managing Director/Publisher Stephen Picard

Fiction, metaphysical, children's. Founded 1990.

Scholastic New Zealand Ltd*
21 Lady Ruby Drive, East Tamaki, Auckland
tel (09) 274-8112 *fax* (09) 274-8114
email publishing@scholastic.co.nz
postal address Private Bag 94407, Greenmount, Auckland
website www.scholastic.co.nz
Manager Neil Welham, *Publishing Manager* Christine Dale, *Senior Editor* Penny Scown

Picture books, fiction for 5–8 and 9–12 year-olds, teenage fiction and series fiction. Publishes approx. 50 titles each year and has over 200 in print. Imprints: Scholastic NZ, Blue Balloon. Founded 1962.

Submission details Will consider unsolicited MSS from New Zealand citizens or residents only. Include an sae for its return. For picture books send copies of illustrations (though not essential), *not* original artwork.

Shortland Publications*
PO Box 11–904, Auckland 5
tel (09) 687-0128 *fax* (09) 6203-0143
website www.mcgraw-hill.com.au
Managing Director Avelyn Davidson

International primary reading market: potential authors should familiarise themselves with Shortland products. Looking for fresh ideas. *Cocky Circle* series 24pp read-to books for 2–6 year-olds. Acquired by McGraw-Hill Australia & New Zealand. Founded 1984.

Submission details Currently seeking submissions for emergent/early and fluency reading material (8–24pp): stories need to be simple and to feature supports for the child learning to read, e.g. repetition of vocabulary and sentence structure. Also short fiction (ages 9–12): MSS up to 1500 words long. Stories must lend themselves to a different illustration on each page. Fantasy and humour are always good sellers. All submissions should cater for an international market; include sae.

Weldon Owen Education
Level 1, 39 Market Place, Auckland 1015
tel (09) 358-0190 *fax* (09) 358-0793
website www.weldonowen.com

Supplementary educational titles for school systems internationally. Produces literacy-teaching programmes for kindergarten through to Grade 6. Also resources for home-schooling. Series include *Wings* (8–10 year-olds), *Infoquest* and *Explorers* for 8–12 year-olds. Founded 2001.

SOUTH AFRICA

*Member of the Publishers' Association of South Africa

Cambridge University Press*
(African Branch)
Lower Ground Floor, Nautica Building, The Water Club, Beach Road, Granger Bay, Cape Town 8005
tel (021) 412-7800 *fax* (021) 419-0594
email capetown@cambridge.org
website www.cambridge.org
Director Hanri Pieterse

African Branch of CUP, responsible for sub-Saharan Africa and English-speaking Caribbean. Publishes distance learning materials and textbooks for various African countries, as well as primary reading materials in 28 local African languages.

Chart Studio Publishing (Pty) Ltd
Portion 58 Kromdraai, Krugersdorp, Johannesburg 1740
tel (11) 9570151 *fax* (11) 9570313
email chartstudio@chartstudio.com
website www.chartstudio.com

Educational, fun-to-learn products including posters, flip-charts, fun-time fold-out books, flash cards, wooden puzzles, board books. Age groups: preschool, 5–10, 10–15, 15+.

Clever Books Pty Ltd*
PO Box 13816, Hatfield, Pretoria 0028
tel (012) 342-3263 *fax* (012) 430-2376
email cillierss@cleverbooks.co.za
Managing Director Steven Cilliers

Educational titles for the RSA market. Founded 1981.

Human & Rousseau
PO Box 5050, Cape Town 8000
tel (021) 406 3033 *fax* (021) 406 3812
email humanhk@humanrousseau.com
website www.nb.co.za

General Afrikaans and English titles. Quality Afrikaans literature, popular literature, general children's and youth literature, cookery, self-help. Founded 1959.

Best Books (imprint)
Education.

Jacklin Enterprises (Pty) Ltd
PO Box 521, Parklands 2121
tel (011) 265-4200 *fax* (011) 314-2984

email mjacklin@jacklin.co.za
Managing Director M.A.C. Jacklin

Children's fiction and non-fiction; Afrikaans large print books. Subjects include aviation, natural history, romance, general science, technology and transportation. Imprints: Mike Jacklin, Kennis Onbeperk, Daan Retief.

Juta & Company Ltd*

PO Box 14373, Landsdown 7779, Cape Town
tel (021) 797-5101 *fax* (021) 797-5569
email books@juta.co.za
website www.juta.co.za
Ceo Rory Wilson

School, academic, professional, law and electronic. Founded 1853.

Maskew Miller Longman (Pty) Ltd*

PO Box 396, Howard Drive, Pinelands 7405, Cape Town 8000
tel (021) 531-7750 *fax* (021) 531-4877
email firstname@mml.co.za
website www.mml.co.za
Publishing Director Japie Pienaar

Educational and general publishers.

NB Publishers (Pty) Ltd*

PO Box 879, Cape Town 8000
tel (021) 406-3033 *fax* (021) 406-3812
email nb@nb.co.za
website www.nb.co.za
Managing Director Eloise Wessels

General: Afrikaans fiction, politics, children's and youth literature in all the country's languages, non-fiction. Imprints include Tafelberg, Human & Rousseau, Pharos and Kwela. Founded 1950.

New Africa Books (Pty) Ltd

99 Garfield Road, Claremont, Cape Town 7700
tel (21) 674-4136 *fax* (21) 674-3358
website www.newafricabooks.co.za
Managing Director Brian Wafawarowa

General books, textbooks, literary works, contemporary issues, children and young adult. Formed as a result of the merger of David Philip Publishers (founded 1971), Spearhead Press (founded 2000) and New Africa Educational Publishing.

Oxford University Press Southern Africa*

Vasco Boulevard, N1 City, Goodwood, Cape Town 7460
tel (021) 596-2300 *fax* (021) 596-1234
email oxford.za@oup.com.za
postal address PO Box 12119, N1 City, Cape Town 7463
website www.oup.com.za
Managing Director E. Kotze, *Publishing Director* M.R. Griffin

Reference books for children and school books: Preschool and Foundation Phase, Intermediate Phase, Senior Phase, dictionaries, thesauruses, atlases and teaching English as a main and as a second language.

Shuter and Shooter Publishers (Pty) Ltd*

21c Cascades Crescent, Cascades, Pietermaritzburg 3201, KwaZulu-Natal
tel (033) 347-6130 *fax* (033) 347-6100
email dryder@shuter.co.za
postal address PO Box 13016, Cascades 3202, KwaZulu-Natal
website www.shuters.com
Publishing Director D.F. Ryder

Core curriculum-based textbooks for use at foundation, intermediate, senior and further education phases. Supplementary readers in various languages; dictionaries; reading development kits, charts. Literature titles in English, isiXhosa, Sesotho, Sepedi, Setswana, Tshivenda, Xitsonga, Ndebele and Siswati. Founded 1925.

SPAIN

Destino Infantil & Juvenil

Edificio Planeta, Diagonal 662–664, 08034 Barcelona
tel (93) 496 7001 *fax* (93) 496 7041
email destinojoven@edestino.es
website www.edestino.es
Children's Publisher Patrizia Campana, *Children's Editor* Marta Vilagut

Fiction for ages 6–16 years old. Picture books, pop-up books, fiction and some unusual illustrated books. Age groups: preschool, 5–10, 10–15, 15+.

Editorial Cruilla

Balmes 245, 4t, 08006 Barcelona
tel (93) 292 21 72 *fax* (93) 238 01 16
email editorial@cruilla.com
website www.cruilla.com
Publishing Director Josep Herrero, *Literary Director* Montse Ingla

Activity books, novelty books, fiction for 5–8 and 9–12 year-olds, teenage fiction and poetry. Publishes approx. 120–130 titles each year. Recent successes include *El Vaixell de Vapor* (series), *Vull Llegir!* and *Molly Moon Stops the World/Molly Moon's Incredible Book of Hypnotism.* Founded 1984.

Random House Mondadori

Travessera de Gracia 47–49, 08021 Barcelona, Spain
tel (34) 93 3660300 *fax* (34) 93 2414823
website www.randomhousemondadori.es

Preschool activity, novelty and picture books through to young adult fiction. Also a packager and printer.

Beasco (division)

Character publishing, including Disney and Fisher-Price.

Lumen (division)
Classics and illustrated books.

Montena (division)
Contemporary literary fiction including fantasy.

Fundación Santa Maria/Ediciones SM
C/Impresores, 15, Urb. Prado des Espino, 28660
Boadilla, Madrid
tel (91) 422 88 00 fax (91) 422 61 16
email communicacion@grupo-sm.com
website www.grupo-sm.com
Publishing Director José Luis Cortes Salinas

Activity books, novelty books, picture books, fiction
for 5–8 and 9–12 year-olds, teenage fiction, series
fiction, reference and religion. Publishes approx. 220
titles each year and has about 100 in print. Recent
successes include El Sindrome de Mozart by Gonzalo
Moure and Cuentos Para Sentir by Begoña Ibarrola.

Submission details Will consider unsolicited MSS
by post or by email. Include sae for return of MS.
Allow 5 months for response. Looking for good
quality literature for children and young readers.

Vicens Vives SA
Avenida Sarriá 130–132, 08017 Barcelona
tel (93) 252 3700 fax (93) 252 3711
website www.vicensvives.es
Managing Director Roser Espona de Rahola

Activity and novelty books, fiction, art, encyclopedias,
dictionaries, education, geography, history, music,
science, textbooks, posters. Age groups: preschool,
5–10, 10–15, 15+.

USA

*Member of the Association of American Publishers Inc.

Abingdon Press
201 Eighth Avenue, PO Box 801, Nashville,
TN 37202–0801
tel 615-749-6290 fax 615-749-6372
website www.abingdonpress.com
President Neil Alexander, Senior Vice President,
Publishing Harriett Jane Olson

General interest, professional, academic and reference
– primarily directed to the religious market;
children's non-fiction.

Harry N. Abrams Books for Young Readers
115 West 18th Street, New York, NY 10011
tel 212-519-1200
Director, Children's Books Howard W. Reeves

Fiction and non-fiction: picture books, young
readers, middle readers, young adult.

Submission details For picture books submit
covering letter and complete MS, for longer works

and non-fiction send query and sample chapter
with sase.

Harry N. Abrams Inc.
115 West 18th Street, New York, NY 10011
tel 212-206-7715 fax 212-519-1210
website www.hnabooks.com
Ceo/President Michael Jacobs

Art and architecture, photography, natural sciences,
performing arts, children's books. No fiction.
Founded 1949.

Absey and Co. Inc.*
23011 Northcrest Drive, Spring, TX 77389
tel 888-412-2739 fax 281-251-4676
website www.absey.com
Publisher Edward Wilson

Mainstream fiction and non-fiction, poetry,
educational books, especially those dealing in
language arts. Recent successes for young adult
readers include Where I'm From by George Ella Lyon,
Poetry After Lunch by Joyce Armstrong Carroll and
Edward E. Wilson and Just People and Paper, Pen,
Poem by Kathi Appelt.

Submission details For fiction query with sase. For
non-fiction query with outline and 1–2 sample
chapters.

Action Publishing, LLC
PO Box 391, Glendale, CA 91209
tel 800-644-2665 fax 323-478-1767
website www.actionpublishing.com

Picture books and fiction for young, middle and
young adult readers.

Submission details See website for submission
guidelines. Founded 1996.

Aladdin Paperbacks – see Simon & Schuster Children's Publishing Division

All About Kids Publising
9333 Benbow Drive, Gilroy, CA 95020
tel 408-846-1833 fax 408-846-1835
website www.aakp.com
Publisher Mike G. Guevara, Editor Linda L. Guevara

Fiction and non-fiction picture books and chapter
books. Recent successes include A, My Name is
Andrew by Mary McManus-Burke (picture book) and
The Titanic Game by Mike Warner (chapter book).
Founded 1999.

Submission details See website.

Alyson Publications, Inc.
PO Box 4371, Los Angeles, CA 90078
tel 323-860-6065 fax 323-467-0152

Picture books and young adult titles that deal with
gay or lesbian issues. Recent successes include
Daddy's Wedding by Michael Willhoite.

Submission details Picture books are only
considered if text and illustrations are submitted

together. For young adult books submit synopsis and sample chapters with sase. Send sase for submission guidelines.

American Girl Publications
8400 Fairway Place, Middleton, WI 53562
website www.americangirl.com

Age-appropriate books and playthings to 'foster girls' individuality, intellectual curiosity and imagination'.

American Girl Library® (imprint)
Advice and activity books for 8–12 year-old girls. Also Hopscotch Hill School™, a line of integrated early reader books.
Submission details Publishes material to encourage girls' dreams and to reinforce their self-confidence and curiosity as they prepare to navigate adolescence in the years ahead. Invites proposals for well-focused concepts for activity books, craft books, or advice books. Also non-fiction specifically targeted to girls – if the approach would appeal to boys as well as to girls, submission is not appropriate. Proposals should include a detailed description of the concept, sample chapters or spreads, and lists or samples of previous publications, plus sase. Complete MSS are also acceptable. Founded 1985.

Atheneum Books for Young Readers – see Simon & Schuster Children's Publishing Division

A/V Concepts Corp.
30 Montauk Blvd, Oakdale, NY 11769
tel 631-567-7227 *fax* 631-567-8745
email info@edcompublishing.com
Editorial Director Laura Solimene

Educational books and multimedia: classic literature, maths, science, language, arts, self esteem.

Avisson Press, Inc.
3007 Taliaferro Road, Greensboro, NC 27408
tel 336-288-6989 *fax* 336-288-6989
Publisher Martin Hester

Biography for young adults. Recent successes include *Freedom's Martyr: The Story of Jose Rizal, National Hero of the Philippines* by Suzanne Middendorf Arruda.
Submission details Submit synopsis and 2 sample chapters. Founded 1995.

Bantam Books for Young Readers – see Random House Inc.

Barefoot Books ✓
2067 Massachusetts Avenue, Cambridge, MA 02140
tel 617-576-0660 *fax* 617-576-0049
website www.barefootbooks.com

Barefoot Books 'celebrates art and story with books that open the hearts and minds of children from all

walks of life'. Recent successes include *The Boy Who Grew Flowers* by Jen Wojtowicz, illustrated by Steve Adams (age 4–9, picture book).
Submission details Length: 500–1000 words (picture books), 2000–3000 young readers.Inspiration for books is taken from different cultures and the focus is on themes that encourage 'independence of spirit, enthusiasm for learning, and sharing of the world's diversity'. Founded 1993 in UK; 1998 in USA.

Barron's Educational Series Inc.
250 Wireless Boulevard, Hauppage, NY 11788
800-645-3476*fax* 631-434-3723
email waynebarr@barronseduc.com
website www.barronseduc.com
Chairman/Ceo Manuel H. Barron, *President/Publisher* Ellen Sibley

Series books for children aged 7–11, 12–16. Publishes 20 picture books, 20 young reader titles, 20 middle reader titles and 10 young adult titles each year. Recent successes include *Everyday Witch* by Sandra Forrester and *Word Wizardry* by Margaret and William Kenda. Also for adults: cookbooks, Mind, Body & Spirit, crafts, business, pets, gardening, family and health, art. Founded 1941.
Submission details Approx. 25% of books are by first-time authors. For fiction, query by email. For non-fiction, submit outline/synopsis and sample chapters with sase for response. Responds to queries in 2 months; MSS in 4 months. Send to Wayne R. Barr, Acquisitions Manager
Reviews MS/illustration packages from artists: send query letter with 3 chapters of MS with one piece of final art, remainder roughs. For illustrations only send tearsheets or slides plus résumé. Responds in 2 months. Send to Bill Kuchler, Art Director.

Behop Books
95 Madison Avenue, New York, NY 10016
tel 212-779-4400 *fax* 212-683-1894
email general@bebopbooks.com
website www.bebopbooks.com
Editor-in-Chief Louise May

Fiction and non-fiction with multicultural content. Imprint of Lee & Low Books, Inc.
Submission details Child-centered stories that support literacy learning and provide multicultural content for beginning readers. See website. Founded 2000.

Bick Publishing House
307 Neck Road, Madison, CT 06443
tel 203-245-0073 *fax* 203-245-5990
email bickpubhse@aol.com
website www.bickpubhouse.com

Adults: health and recovery, living with disabilities, wildlife rehabilitation. Non-fiction for young adults: philosophy, psychology, self help, social issues, science. Recent successes include *What Are You Doing with Your Life? Books on Living for Teenagers* by J. Krishnamurti; *The Teen Brain Book: Who and What Are You?* and *Talk: Teen Art of Communication* by Dale Carlson. Founded 1993.

Bloomsbury USA

Suite 315, 175 Fifth Avenue, New York, NY 10010
tel 212-674-5151 *fax* 212-982-2837
email bloomsbury.kids@bloomsburyusa.com
Associate Publisher, Children's Books Victoria Wells Arms, *Director of Sales & Marketing (Children's)* Diana Blough, *Executive Editor* Melanie Cecka

Literary fiction, general non-fiction and children's. Branch of **Bloomsbury UK**. Founded 1998.

Bloomsbury Children's (USA)

Novelty books, picture books, fiction for 5–8 and 9–12 year-olds, teenage fiction, series fiction and poetry. Publishes 40 titles each year and has 80 in print. Recent successes include *Pirates!* by Celia Rees, *Bill in a China Shop* by Katie McAllaster Weaver and Tim Raglin and *The Alphabet Room* by Sara Pinto. Founded 2002.
  Submission details Approx. 25% of books are by first-time authors. Will consider unsolicited MSS with sase. Allow 6 months for response. Will review MS/illustration packages from artists; send query letter or submit MS with dummy.

Blue Sky Press – see Scholastic Inc.

Boyds Mills Press

815 Church Street, Honesdale, PA 18431
tel 570-253-1164 *fax* 570-253-0179
email contact@boydsmillspress.com
website www.boydsmillspress.com
President Clay Winters, *Publisher* Kent L. Brown Jr, *Associate Publisher* Stephen Roxburgh, *Editorial Director* Larry Rosler, *Art Director* Tim Gillner

Activity books, picture books, fiction, non-fiction, and poetry for ages 18 and under. Recent successes include *My Red Balloon* by Eve Bunting, *A Splendid Friend, Indeed* by Suzanne Bloom, and *Cat Poems* by Dave Crawley. Publishes approx. 70 titles each year. Founded 1991.
  Submission details Will consider both unsolicited MSS and queries; send to Jeanna DeLuca, Manuscript Coordinator. Looking for middle-grade fiction with fresh ideas and subject matter, and young adult novels of real literary merit. Non-fiction should be fun and entertaining as well as informative, and non-fiction MSS should be accompanied by a detailed bibliography. Interested in imaginative picture books and welcomes submissions from both writers and illustrators. Submit samples as b&w and/or colour copies or transparencies; submissions will not be returned. Include sase with all submissions. Send art samples to Tim Gillner, Art Director.

Calkins Creek Books (imprint)

Editor Carolyn P. Yoder
History.

Front Street (imprint)

See page 46.

Wordsong (imprint)

Editor Stephen Roxburgh
Poetry.

Calkins Creek Books – see Boyds Mills Press

Candlewick Press

2067 Massachusetts Avenue, Cambridge, MA 02140
tel 617-661-3330 *fax* 617-661-0565
email bigbear@candlewick.com
website www.candlewick.com
President/Publisher Karen Lotz, *Editorial Director/Associate Publisher* Liz Bicknell, *Executive Editor* Mary Lee Donovan, *Editor-at-Large, Non-fiction Picture Books* Joan Powers

Books for 6 months–18 year-olds: board books, picture books, novels, non-fiction, novelty books. Publishes 160 picture books, 15 middle readers and 15 young adult titles each year. Recent successes include *The Earth, My Butt, and Other Big Round Things* by Carolyn Mackler (young adult fiction), *The Tales of Despereaux* by Kate DiCamillo (middle-grade fiction) and *Surprising Sharks* by Nicola Davies, illustrated by James Croft (non-fiction picture book). Subsidiary of **Walker Books Ltd**, UK.
  Submission details Approx. 5% of books are by first-time authors. Submit MSS via a literary agent. For illustrations, send résumé and portfolio for the attention of Anne Moore. Responds in 6 weeks. Samples returned with sase. Founded 1991.

Carolrhoda Books – see Lerner Publishing Group

Cartwheel Books – see Scholastic Inc.

Charlesbridge Publishing

(Trade Division)
85 Main Street, Watertown, MA 02472
tel 617-926-0329 *fax* 617-926-5720
email tradeeditorial@charlesbridge.com
website www.charlesbridge.com
President & Publisher Brent Farmer, *Vice President & Associate Publisher* Mary Ann Sabia

Board books, novelty books, fiction and non-fiction picture books and transitional books for preschool–12 year-olds. Lively, plot-driven story books plus nursery rhymes, fairy tales and humorous stories for the very young. Non-fiction list specialises in nature, concept and multicultural books. Publishes 60% non-fiction, 40% fiction picture books and transitional books. Recent successes include *Ace Lacewing: Bug Detective* by David Biedrzycki and *Jingle Bells* by Iza Trapani (fiction), and *Amelia to Zora: Twenty-six Women Who Changed the World* by Cynthia Chin-Lee, and *Yum! Yuck!* by Linda Sue Park (non-ficton). Founded 1980.

Submission details Send full MSS with sase; no queries. Responds to MSS in 3 months. Length: 1000–10,000 words. For illustrations, send query with samples, tearsheets and résumé.

Chicago Review Press

814 Franklin Street, Chicago, IL 60610
tel 312-337-0747 *fax* 312-337-5110
email frontdesk@chicagoreviewpress.com
website www.chicagoreviewpress.com
Associate Publisher Cynthia Sherry

General publisher. Non-fiction activity books for children. Recent successes include *Exploring the Solar System: A History with 22 Activities* by Mary Kay Carson.
Submission details Interested in hands-on educational books. See website for submission guidelines. Founded 1973.

Children's Press – see Scholastic Education

Chronicle Books

85 Second Street, 6th Floor, San Francisco, CA 94105
tel 415-537-4200 *fax* 415-537-4460
email frontdesk@chroniclebooks.com
website www.chroniclebooks.com,
www.chroniclekids.com
Chairman & Ceo Nion McEvoy, *President & Publisher* Jay Schaefer, *Associate Publishers* Debra Lande, Victoria Rock, Alan Rapp

Traditional and innovative children's books. Looking for projects that have a unique bent – in subject matter, writing style or illustrative technique – that will add a distinctive flair. Interested in fiction and non-fiction for children of all ages as well as board books, decks, activity kits, and other unusual or 'novelty' formats. Publishes 60–100 books each year. Recent successes include *Just a Minute* (picture book) and *The Man Who Went to the Far Side of the Moon* (non-fiction chapter book). Also for adults: cooking, how-to books, nature, art, biographies, fiction, gift. Founded 1967.
Submission details For picture books submit MS. For older readers, submit outline/synopsis and 3 sample chapters. Projects will not be returned without a sase. Responds to queries in one month; to MSS in 3–5 months.

Clarion Books – see Houghton Mifflin Company

Clear Light Books

823 Don Diego, Santa Fe, NM 87505
tel 505-989-9590 *fax* 505-989-9519
website www.clearlightbooks.com
Publisher Harmon Houghton

For adults: art and photography, cookbooks, ecology/environment, health, gift books, history, Native America, Tibet, Western Americana. Non-fiction for children and young adults: multicultural, American Indian, Hispanic.
Submission details Looking for authentic American Indian art and folklore. Send complete MS with sase.

Continental Press Educational Publishers

520 East Bainbridge Street, Elizabethtown, PA 17022
tel 800-233-0759 *fax* 888-834-1303

K–12 educational materials and professional resources for educators. Subjects include reading, language skills, maths, social studies, science, state testing, teacher resources, Spanish materials. Founded 1937.

Seedlings Publications

Books to support pre-K–2 readers, and parent and volunteer training materials. Founded 1991.

The Continuum International Publishing Group Inc.

80 Maiden Lane, Suite 704, New York, NY 10038
tel 212-953-5858 *fax* 212-953-5944
email info@continuum-books.com
website www.continuum-books.com
Chairman/Publisher Philip Sturrock

General non-fiction, education, literature, psychology, politics, sociology, history, literary criticism, religious studies. Founded 1999.

Copper Beach – see Millbrook Press

Cricket Books

Carus Publishing Company, Cricket Magazine Group, PO Box 300, Peru, IL 61354
email mmiklavcic@caruspub.com,
cricketbooks@caruspub.com
website www.cricketbooks.net

Picture books, chapter books, poetry, non-fiction and novels for children and young adults. Recent successes include *Breakout* by Paul Fleischman and *Robert and the Weird & Wacky Facts* by Barbara Sterling, illustrated by Paul Brewer. Also publishes *Cricket*, the award-winning magazine of outstanding stories and art for 9–14 year-olds (see page 267), and other magazines for young readers. Founded 1999. Division of Carus Publishing.
Submission details Primarily interested in chapter books, middle-grade fiction, and young adult novels, as well as exceptional non-fiction for all ages, but will also consider picture books. Send MSS to Submissions Editor, Cricket Books, Carus Publishing Company, 332 South Michigan Avenue, Suite 1100, Chicago, IL 60604, USA. For illustrations, send samples and tearsheets to Ron McCutchan, 315 Fifth Street, Peru, IL 61354, USA. Samples returned with sase.

Marcato Books (imprint)

Exceptional non-fiction and innovative fiction for young readers of all ages, especially teenagers.

Crown Books for Young Readers – see Random House Inc.

Darby Creek Publishing
7858 Industrial Parkway, Plain City, OH 43064
tel 614-873-7955 fax 614-873-7135
email info@darbycreekpublishing.com
website www.darbycreekpublishing.com

Fiction and non-fiction for children and young adults. Recent successes include *Albino Animals* by Kelly Milner Halls (age 10+).

Submission details Interested in non-fiction works for ages 8–14 with themes that relate to sports, science, history or biography, and fiction from early chapter books through to young adult. For short projects submit entire MS. For longer works submit 2–3 sample chapters with a synopsis and brief chapter summary outline. Also include a CV and sase.

Interested in seeing illustration samples of all styles, in both colour and b&w. Do not send originals. Send to Submissions Editor. Founded 2002.

Dawn Publications
12402 Bitney Springs Road, Nevada City, CA 95959
website www.dawnpub.com
Editor & Co-Publisher Glenn Hovemann, *Art Director & Co-Publisher* Muffy Weaver

Picture books and biographies 'to assist parents and educators to open the minds and hearts of children to the transforming influence of Nature'. Recent successes include *Near One Cattail: Turtles, Logs and Leaping Frogs* by Anthony D. Fredericks (picture book).

Submission details See website.

DC Comics
1700 Broadway, New York, NY 10019
tel 212-636-5400 fax 212-636-5975
website www.dccomics.com

Activity books, board books, novelty books, picture books, painting and colouring books, pop-up books, fiction, fairy tales, art, hobbies, how-to books, leisure, entertainment, film/TV tie-ins, calendars, comics, gift books, periodicals, picture cards, posters, CD-Roms, CD-I, internet for preschool age to 15+.

DC Comics has published and licensed comic books for over 60 years in all genres for all ages, including super heroes, fantasy, horror, mystery and high-quality graphic stories for mature readers. Imprints: WildStorm, Vertigo. A Warner Bros. Company.

Dial Books for Young Readers – see Penguin Putnam Books for Young Readers

Discovery Enterprises Ltd
31 Laurelwood Drive, Carlisle, MA 01741
tel 978-287-5401 fax 978-287-5402
website www.ushistorydocs.com

The history of the USA presented through the study of primary source documents. Recent successes include *Get a Clue!* (grades 2–8) and *Adventures in History* series (grades 4–8). Other series include *Perspectives on History* (grades 5–12+) and *Researching American History* (8–15 year-olds and ESL students). Also historical fiction for younger readers. Acquired by History Compass LLC in 2005; founded 1990.

Dog-Eared Publications
PO Box 620863, Middletown, WI 53562–0863
tel/fax 608-831-1410
email field@dog-eared.com
website www.dog-eared.com

Children's nature books.
Submission details No unsolicited MSS.

Dominie Press Inc.
1949 Kellogg Avenue, Carlsbad, CA 92008
tel 760-431-8000 fax 760-431-8777
website www.dominie.com

Educational children's publisher dedicated to providing the finest learning materials to children of ages 3–16. Subjects include nature and environment, biographies, science, fiction, fairy tales and teaching. High-quality photographic books on animals, insects, amphibians, marine and ocean life, habitats, etc. Part of the Pearson Learning Group.

Doubleday Books for Young Readers – see Random House Inc.

Dover Publications Inc.
31 East 2nd Street, Mineola, NY 11501
tel 516-294-7000 fax 516-742-5049
website www.doverpublications.com
President, Dover Publications Paul Negri, *Editor-in-Chief* Mary Carolyn Waldrep

Activity books, novelty books, picture books, fiction for 5–8 and 9–12 year-olds, teenage fiction, series fiction, reference, plays, religion, poetry, audio and CD-Roms. Also adult non-fiction. Publishes approx. 150 children's titles and has over 2500 in print. Recent successes include *Easy Noah's Ark Sticker Picture, How to Draw a Funny Monster* and *Pretty Ballerina Sticker Paper Doll*. Founded 1941.

Submission details Will consider unsolicited MSS but write for guidelines.

Dragon Books – see Pacific View Press

Dutton Children's Books – see Penguin Putnam Books for Young Readers

EDCON Publishing Group
30 Montauk Boulevard, Oakdale, NY 11769–1399
tel 631-567-7227 fax 631-567-8745
email info@edconpublishing.com

website www.edconpublishing.com

Supplemental instructional materials for use by education professionals to improve reading and maths skills. Includes early reading, Classics series, Easy Shakespeare, fiction and non-fiction, reading diagnosis and vocabulary books. Recent successes include adaptations of *A Midsummer Night's Dream* and *The Merchant of Venice*. Founded 1970.

Edupress

W5527 State Road 106, PO Box 800, Fort Atkinson, WI 53538–0800
tel 800-835-7978 *fax* 800-558-9332
email edupress@highsmith.com
website www.edupressinc.com

Educational materials. Founded 1979.

Eerdmans Publishing Company

255 Jefferson Avenue SE, Grand Rapids, MI 49503
tel 616-459-4591 *fax* 616-459-6540
website www.eerdmans.com
President William B. Eerdmans

Independent publisher of a wide range of religious books, from academic works in theology, biblical studies, religious history, and reference to popular titles in spirituality, social and cultural criticism and literature. Founded 1911.

Eerdmans Books for Young Readers (imprint)

website www.eerdmans.com/youngreaders
Acquisitions Editor Judy Zylstra, *Art Director* Gayle Brown

Picture books, biographies, middle reader and young adult fiction and non-ficiton. Publishes 12–18 books a year. Seeks MSS that are honest, wise and hopeful but also publishes stories that delight with their storyline, characters or good humour. Stories that celebrate diversity, stories of historical significance, and stories that relate to current issues are of special interest.
Submission details Only considers exclusive submissions; include sase for reply. Send to Judy Zylstra; responds in 3 months. For illustrations, send photocopies or printed media and include a list of books you have illustrated. Send to Gayle Brown. Samples returned with sase.

Encyclopaedia Britannica Inc.

310 South Michigan Avenue, Chicago, Illinois 60604
fax 312-294-2108
email international@eb.com
website www.britannica.com

Encyclopedias, reference books, almanacs, videos and CD-Roms for adults and children aged 5–15+.

Enslow Publishers, Inc.

Box 398, 40 Industrial Road, Berkeley Heights, NJ 07922–0398
tel 908-771-9400 *fax* 908-771-0925

email customerservice@enslow.com
website www.enslow.com
President Mark Enslow, *Vice President/Publisher* Brian Enslow

Non-fiction library books for children and young adults. Founded 1976.

Evan-Moor Educational Publishers

18 Lower Ragsdale Drive, Monterey, CA 93940
tel 831 649 5901 *fax* 831 649 6256
email editorial@evan-moor.com
website www.evan-moor.com
President William Evans, *Senior Editor* Marilyn Evans, *Art Director* Cheryl Pucket

Educational materials for parents and teachers of children (ages 3–12): activity books, textbooks, how-to books, CD-Roms. Subjects include maths, geography, history, science, reading, writing, social studies, art and craft. Publishes approx. 50 titles each year and has over 450 in print. Recent successes include *Daily Paragraph Editing* (5-book series, grades 2–5) and *Nonfiction Reading Practice* (6-book series, grades 1–6). Founded 1979.
Submission details Less than 10% of books are by first-time authors. Query or submit outline, table of contents and sample pages. Responds to queries in 2 months; MSS in 4 months. See website for submission guidelines. For illustrations, send résumé, samples and tearsheets to the Art Director. Primarily uses b&w material.

Facts On File

132 West 31st Street, New York, NY 10001
tel 212-967-8800 *fax* 212-967-9196
website www.factsonfile.com
Editorial Director Laurie Likoff

Print and electronic products for schools and libraries. 'Committed to publishing timely, comprehensive, and curriculum-driven references'. Subjects include history, science, literature, multicultural studies.

Faith Kidz

4050 Lee Vance View, Colorado Springs, CO 80918
tel 719-536-0100 *fax* 719-536-3243
website www.cookministries.com

Preschool–elementary books with Christian values in English and Spanish. Imprint of Cook Communications Ministries.

Farrar, Straus and Giroux, Inc.

19 Union Square West, New York, NY 10003
tel 212-741-6900 *fax* 212-633-9385
website www.fsgbooks.com, www.fsgkidsbooks.com
President/Publisher Jonathan Galassi

General publishers: literary fiction, non-fiction, poetry, children's. Founded 1946.

Farrar, Straus and Giroux Books for Young Readers

Editorial Director Margaret Ferguson, *Publisher*,
Frances Foster Books Frances Foster, *Publisher*,

Melanie Kroupa Books Melanie Kroupa, *Executive Editors* Wesley Adams, Beverly Reingold, *Editors* Robert Mayes, Janine O-Malley, *Art Director* Robbin Gourley

Books for toddlers through to young adults: picture books, fiction for 5–8 and 9–12 year-olds, teenage fiction and poetry (occasionally). Publishes 80 hardcover originals plus 20 paperback reprints each year and has approx. 500 titles in print. Recent successes include *The Tree of Life* by Peter Sís, *The Canning Season* by Polly Horvath and *Buddha Boy* by Kathe Koja. Imprints: Frances Foster Books, Melanie Kroupa Books, Sunburst (paperback).

Submission details Approx. 5% of books are by first-time authors. Send query letter first but will consider unsolicited MSS. Include a covering letter containing any pertinent information about yourself, your writing, your MSS, etc and a sase for return of MSS. Address submissions to Children's Editorial Department. Allow 3 months for response. Looking to publish books of high literary merit. For illustrations, send only 2–3 samples; do *not* send original artwork.

Flux – see Llewellyn Worldwide

Walter Foster Publishing Inc.
23062 La Cadena Drive, Laguna Hills, Irvine, CA 92653
tel 949-380-7510 *fax* 949-380-7575
website www.walterfoster.com
Chief Executive Ross Sarracino

'Fostering creativity for more than 80 years.'
Instructional art books for children and adults. Also art and activity kits for children.

Free Spirit Publishing
217 Fifth Avenue North, Suite 200, Minneapolis, MN 55401
tel 612 338 2068 *fax* 612 337 5050
email help4kids@freespirit.com
website www.freespirit.com
President Judy Galbraith

Award-winning publisher of non-fiction materials for children and teens, parents, educators, and counsellors. Specialises in SELF-HELP FOR KIDS® and SELF-HELP FOR TEENS® materials which empower young people and promote positive self-esteem through improved social and learning skills. Topics include self-esteem and self-awareness, stress management, school success, creativity, friends and family, peacemaking, social action, and special needs (i.e. gifted and talented, children with learning differences). Publishes approx. 18–22 new products each year, adding to a backlist of over 100 books, audio tapes, and posters. Free Spirit authors are expert educators and mental health professionals who have been honoured nationally for their contributions on behalf of children. Founded 1983.

Front Street
862 Haywood Road, Asheville, NC 28806
tel 828-236-5940 *fax* 828-236-5935

email contactus@frontstreetbooks.com
website www.frontstreetbooks.com
Director of Institutional Marketing & Subsidiary Rights Nancy Hogan, *Associate Publisher, Boyds Mills Press Inc.* Stephen Roxburgh, *Art Director* Helen Robinson, *Editor* Joy Neaves

Books for children and young adults: picture books, fiction (5–8, 9–12, teenage), non-fiction, poetry, anthologies. Publishes 10–15 books each year. Recent successes include *Heck Superhero* by Martine Leavitt, *Honeysuckle House* by Andrea Cheng and *The Big House* by Carolyn Coman. Imprints: Front Street, Front Street/Lemniscaat. Imprint of Boyds Mills Press Inc. Founded 1994.

Submission details For fiction, submit 2–3 sample chapters and a plot summary. For picture books, do not send MSS but send a query letter describing your project as fully as possible. For poetry, send up to 25 poems that are representative of your work. For non-fiction send a detailed proposal and sample chapter. Include sase. Allow 3–4 months for response.

Fulcrum Resources
Fulcrum Publishing, 16100 Table Mountain Parkway, Suite 300, Golden, CO 80403
tel 303-277-1623 *fax* 303-279-7111
website www.fulcrum-books.com

Books and support materials for teachers, librarians, parents and elementary through middle school children in the subjects of science and nature, literature and storytelling, history, multicultural studies, and Native American and Hispanic cultures. Imprint of Fulcrum Publishing.

Laura Geringer Books – see HarperCollins Publishers

Graphia – see Houghton Mifflin Company

Greenhaven Press – see Thomson Gale

Greenwillow Books – see HarperCollins Publishers

Grolier – see Scholastic Inc.

Grosset & Dunlap – see Penguin Putnam Books for Young Readers

Gryphon House, Inc.
PO Box 207, Beltsville, MD 20704
tel 301-595-9500 *fax* 301-595-0051
website www.gryphonhouse.com
Editor-in-Chief Kathy Charner

Early childhood (age 0–8) books for teachers and parents.

Submission details 'We look for books that are developmentally appropriate for the intended age group, are well researched and based on current trends in the field, and include creative, participatory learning experiences with a common conceptual theme to tie them together.' Send query and/or a proposal.

Hachai Publishing

762 Park Place, Brooklyn, NY 11216
tel 718-633-0100 *fax* 718-633-0103
website www.hachai.com

Jewish books for children aged 0–8+.
Submission details Welcomes unsolicited MSS. Specialises in books for 2–4 year-olds and 3–6 year-olds. Looking for stories that convey the traditional Jewish experience in modern times or long ago, traditional Jewish observance, and positive character traits.

Handprint Books

413 Sixth Avenue, Brooklyn, New York 11215
tel 718-768-3696 *fax* 718-369-0844
email submissions@handprintbooks.com
website www.handprintbooks.com
Publisher Christopher Franceschelli

A range of children's books: picture and story books through to young adult fiction. Imprints: Handprint Books, Ragged Bears, Blue Apple.
Submission details Welcomes submissions of MSS of quality for works ranging from board books to young adult novels. For novels, first query interest on the subject and submit a 7500-word max. sample. Accepts MSS on an e-submission basis only, sent as attachments in a word processing format readily readable on a PC. Artwork should be sent as jpg files and total size should not exceed 200K and website addresses containing artists' illustrations may be submitted. Submission of the following is discouraged: series fiction, licensed character (or characters whose primary avatar is meant to be as licenses), 'I-Can-Read'- type books, titles intended primarily for mass merchandise outlets.

Harcourt School Publishers*

6277 Sea Harbor Drive, Orlando, FL 32887
tel 407-345-2000
website www.harcourtschool.com

Textbooks and related instructional materials for school and home use by students (grades PreK-6): reading, language arts, ESL, maths, science, social studies, art, health, professional development. Division of Harcourt Inc. Founded 1919.

Harcourt Trade Publishers*

525 B Street, Suite 1900, San Diego, CA 92101
tel 619-231-6616 *fax* 619-699-6320
website www.harcourt.com
President/Publisher, Adult Books Dan Farley, *Vice President/Publisher, Children's Books* Louise Pelan

Fiction and non-fiction (history, biography, etc) for readers of all ages. Imprints: Harcourt (hardcover books), Harvest Books (paperbacks), Harcourt Children's Books. Division of Harcourt Inc.

Harcourt Children's Books

Editorial Director, Harcourt Children's Books Allyn Johnston

Quality picture books, contemporary and historical fiction for teen readers, board and novelty books, gift items, and non-fiction for children of all ages. Also reading and teacher guides for teachers of children aged 8–14+. The original publisher of such classics as *The Little Prince, Mary Poppins, The Borrowers, Half Magic, Ginger Pye,* and *The Moffats.* Recent successes include *Where Did That Baby Come From?* by Debi Gliori and *Juliet Dove, Queen of Love* by Bruce Coville (fiction, age 8–12). Imprints: Gulliver Books, Silver Whistle, Red Wagon Books, Harcourt Young Classics, Green Light Readers, Voyager Books/Libros Viajeros, Harcourt Paperbacks, Odyssey Classics, Magic Carpet Books.
Submission details Does not accept unsolicited query letters or emails, MSS and illustrations. Only accepts material via literary agents.

HarperCollins Publishers*

10 East 53rd Street, New York, NY 10022
tel 212-207-7000 *fax* 212-207-7145
HarperCollins SanFrancisco 1160 Battery Street, San Francisco, CA 94111
tel 415-477-4400 *fax* 415-477-4444
website www.harpercollins.com
President/Ceo Jane Friedman

Adult fiction (commercial and literary) and non-fiction. Subjects include biography, business, cookbooks, educational, history, juvenile, poetry, religious, science, technical and travel. Imprints include Access, Amistad, Avon, Cliff Street Books, Ecco, Eos, Fourth Estate, HarperAudio, HarperBusiness, HarperCollins, HarperEntertainment, HarperResource, HarperSanFrancisco, HarperTorch, Large Print Editions, William Morrow, William Morrow Cookbooks, Perennial, PerfectBound (e-books), Quill, Rayo and ReganBooks. No unsolicited material; all submissions must come through a literary agent. Founded 1817.

HarperCollins Children's Books Group

1350 6th Avenue, New York, NY 10019
tel 212-261-6500
website www.harperchildrens.com
President/Publisher Susan Katz

Imprints: Avon, Joanna Cotler Books, Laura Geringer Books, Greenwillow Books, HarperCollins Children's Books, HarperFestival, HarperTempest, HarperTrophy.

Laura Geringer Books (imprint)

1350 6th Avenue, New York, NY 10019
Publisher Laura Geringer

Fiction. Publishes 6 picture books, 2 young readers, 4 middle readers and one young adult title each year.

Recent successes include *If You Take a Mouse to School* by Laura Numeroff, illustrated by Felicia Band (ages 3–7) and *The Dulcimer Boy* by Tor Seidler, illustrated by Brian Selznick (ages 8+).

Submission details Approx. 15% of books are by first-time authors. Only interested in submissions via a literary agent. Length: picture books – 500 words; young readers – 1000 words; middle readers – 25,000 words; young adult – 40,000 words. For illustrations, send query with colour photocopies to Laura Geringer. Samples returned with sase.

Greenwillow Books (imprint)
1350 6th Avenue, New York, NY 10019
tel 212-261-6500
Vice-President & Publisher Virginia Duncan,
Art Director Paul Zakris

Publishes 40 picture books, 5 middle readers and 5 young adult books each year. Recent successes indlue *Olive's Ocean* by Kevin Henkes.

Submission details No unsolicited MSS or queries. Unsolicited mail will not be opened or returned. Call 212-261-6627 for update on submissions. For illustrations, art samples (postcards only) should be sent in duplicate to Paul Zakris and Virginia Duncan.

HarperCollins Children's Books (imprint)
1350 Avenues of the Americas, New York, NY 10019
tel 212-261-6588 *fax* 212-261-6603
website www.harperchildrens.com
President/Publisher Susan Katz, *Editorial Director* Alix Reid, *Art Director* Stephanie Berth-Horvath

Activity books, board books, novelty books, picture books, pop-up books, nature, environment, non-fiction, calendars, gift books, audio tapes, fiction, poetry, fairy tales for ages 5–15. Imprints: HarperCollins Hardcover, HarperTrophy Paperbacks, HarperFestival, HarperChildren's Audio.

Submission details No unsolicited MSS or queries; such submissions will not be reviewed or returned. All submissions must be via a literary agent. For illustrations, send samples with sase to the Art Director.

Health Press NA Inc.
PO Box 37470, Albuquerque, NM 87176
tel 505-888-1394
email goodbooks@healthpress.com
website www.healthpress.com

Books for children and adults on a wide variety of medical conditions to meet the need for easy access to responsible, accurate patient education materials.

Submission details Not currently accepting new MSS submissions.

Holiday House
425 Madison Avenue, New York, NY 10017
tel 212-421-6134
website www.holidayhouse.com
Vice-President/Editor-in-Chief Regina Griffin

General. Publishes 35 picture books, 3 young reader, 15 middle reader and 8 young adult titles each year. Recent successes include *My Family Plays Music*, illustrated by Elbrite Brown.

Submission details Approx. 20% of books are by first-time authors. Send query letter with sase before submitting MSS. Responds in 3 months. Will review MS/illustration packages from artists: send MS with dummy and colour photocopies.

Henry Holt and Company LLC*
175 Fifth Avenue, New York, NY 10010
tel 646-307-5095 *fax* 646-307-5285
website www.henryholt.com
President/Publisher John Sterling

Books for young readers. Publishes 20–40 picture books, 4–6 chapter books, 10–15 middle-grade titles and 8–10 young adult titles each year. Recent successes include *The Way a Door Closes* by Hope Anita Smith. For adults: history, biography, nature, science, self-help, novels, mysteries, computer books. Founded 1866.

Submission details Approx. 15% of books are by first-time authors. For fiction and non-fiction, submit complete MS with sase to Laura Godwin, Editor-in-Chief/Associate Publisher of Books for Young Readers. Responds in 4 months. Will not consider simultaneous or multiple submissions. For illustrations, send tearsheets and/or slides to Patrick Collins, Creative Director. Responds in one month.

Houghton Mifflin Company*
222 Berkeley Street, Boston, MA 02116
tel 617-351-5000
website www.houghtonmifflinbooks.com

Fiction and non-fiction – cookbooks, history, political science, biography, nature (Peterson Guides), and gardening guides; reference, both adult and juvenile. No unsolicited MSS. Imprints: Mariner (original and reprint paperbacks); Houghton Mifflin Children's Books; American Heritage® Dictionaries. Founded 1832.

Houghton Mifflin Children's Books (imprint)
222 Berkeley Street, Boston, MA 02116-3764
tel 617-351-5000 *fax* 617-351-1111
email childrens_books@hmco.com
website www.houghtonmifflinbooks.com
Editorial Associate Hannah Rodgers, *Managing Editor* Jenny Lattanzio, *Creative Director* Sheila Smallwood

Fiction and non-fiction for all ages. Recent successes include *What Do You Do With a Tail Like This?* written and illustrated by Steve Jenkins and Robin Page and *On Sand Island* by Jacqueline Briggs Martin, illustrated by David A. Johnson (picture books). Imprints include Clarion Books, Graphia and Walter Lorraine.

Submission details For fiction, submit complete MS. For non-fiction, submit outline/synopsis and sample chapters. Responds within 4 months only if interested. For illustrations, query with samples (colour photocopies and tearsheets). Responds in 4 months. Samples returned with sase.

Clarion Books (imprint)
215 Park Avenue South, New York, NY 10003
tel 212-420-5800 *fax* 212-420-5850
website www.houghtonmifflinbooks.com/trade
Vice-President & Associate Publisher, Clarion Books Dinah Stevenson,
Director, Children's Rights Rebecca Mancini, *Editor* Jennifer Green, *Art Director* Joann Hill
Board books, picture books, biographies, non-fiction, fiction, poetry and fairy tales for ages 5–15. Recent successes include *An American Plague: The True and Terrifying Story of the Yellow Fever Epidemic of 1793* by Jim Murphy. Founded 1965.
Submission details For fiction and picture books, send complete MSS. For non-fiction, send query with up to 3 sample chapters. Include sase.

Graphia (imprint)
222 Berkeley Street, Boston, MA 02116-3764
tel 617-351-5000 *fax* 617-351-1111
website www.graphiabooks.com
Manuscript Acquisitions Eden Edwards
Fiction and non-fiction for young adults, including poetry and graphic novels. Recent successes include *Zazoo* by Richard Mosher, *I Can't Tell You* by Hillary Frank and *48 Shades of Brown* by Nick Earls.

Kingfisher (imprint)
215 Park Avenue South, New York, NY 10003
tel 212-420-5800 *fax* 212-420-5899
website www.houghtonmifflinbooks.com/kingfisher
Contact Phil Gray
Non-fiction, illustrated reference, fiction. Recent successes include *Kingfisher Knowledge* (grades 4–8) and *Kingfisher Young Knowledge* (K–3) series and *Mythology of the World* by Neil Philip.
Submission details No unsolicited MSS. All submissions must by via a literary agent.

Hunter House Publishers
PO Box 2914, Alameda, CA 94501–0914
tel 510-865-5282 *fax* 510-865-4295
email acquisitions@hunterhouse.com
website www.hunterhouse.com

Non-fiction books on physical, mental, and emotional health, including sexuality and relationships for adults and teens and life skills and trauma recovery workbooks for young people. Recent successes include *Helping Teens Stop Violence*, *No More Hurt* and *Someone I Love Died* in the *Growth and Recovery Workbook* series. Founded 1978.

Hyperion*
77 West 66 Street, New York, NY 10023–6298
tel 212-456-0100 *fax* 212-456-0157
website www.hyperionbooks.com

President Robert Miller, *Vice-President/Publisher* Ellen Archer, *Vice-President/Publisher (Hyperion Books for Children)* Lisa Holton

Hyperion Books for Children
114 Fifth Avenue, New York, NY 10010–5690
tel 212-633-4400
website www.hyperionbooksforchildren.com
Board and novelty books, picture books, young readers, middle grade, young adult, non-fiction (all subjects at all levels). Recent successes include *Don't Let the Pigeon Drive the Bus*, written and ilustrated by Mo Willems, *Dumpy The Dump Truck* series by Julie Andrews Edwards and Emma Walton Hamilton (ages 3–7) and *Artemis Fowl* by Eoin Colfer (young adult novel, *New York Times* bestseller).
Submission details Approx. 10% of books are by first-time authors. Only interested in submissions via literary agents. For illustrations, send résumé, business card, promotional literature or tearsheets to be kept on file to Anne Diebel, Art Director.

Ideals Publications LLC
535 Metroplex Drive, Suite 250, Nashville, TN 37211
website www.idealsbooks.com
Picture books and board books for young children. Imprints: Ideals Children's Books, Candy Cane Press, Williamson Books. A Guideposts company.
Submission details Send sase for submission guidelines.

Illumination Arts Publishing
PO Box 1865, Bellevue, WA 98009
tel 925-644-7185
website www.illumin.com
Editorial Director Ruth Thompson
Picture books. 'Books to inspire the mind, touch the heart and uplift the spirit.'
Submission details Length: 300–1500 words. Founded 1987.

Impact Publishers Inc.*
PO Box 6016, Atascadero, CA 93423–6016
tel 805-466-5917
email editor@impactpublishers.com
website www.impactpublishers.com
Psychology and self-improvement books and audio tapes for adults, children, families, organisations, and communities. Recent successes include *The Divorce Helpbook for Kids* by Cynthia MacGregor and *Teen Esteem: A Self-Direction Manual for Young Adults* by Pat Palmer and Melissa Alberti Froehner. Founded 1970.
Submission details Only publishes books which serve human development. Written by highly respected psychologists and other human service professionals. See website for guidelines.

Incentive Publications Inc.
2400 Crestmoor Road, Suite 211, Nashville, TN 37215

tel 800-421-2830
website www.incentivepublications.com
President Imogene Forte, *Editor* Patience Camplair

Supplemental resources for K–8 educators and students. Founded 1969.

Submission details Send a letter of introduction, table of contents, a sample chapter, and sase for return of.

Innovative Kids

18 Ann Street, Norwalk, CT 06854
tel 203-838-6400 *fax* 203-855-5582

Non-fiction picture books and activity books with educational content. Recent successes include *Math Gear* series and *Now I'm Reading Teacher's Activity Packs*. Founded 1999.

Just Us Books, Inc.

356 Glenwood Avenue East Orange, NJ 07017
tel 973-672-7701
email justusbooks@mindspring.com
website www.justusbooks.com

'Publishers of Black interest books for young people,' including preschool materials, picture books, biographies, chapter books, young adult fiction. Focuses on Black history, Black culture and Black experiences.

Submission details Currently accepting queries for young adult titles only, targeted to 13–16 year-old readers. Work should contain realistic, contemporary characters, compelling plot lines that introduce conflict and resolution, and cultural authenticity. Send a query letter, 1–2 page synopsis, a brief author bio that includes any previously published work, plus a sase. Founded 1988.

Kaeden Books

PO Box 16190, Rocky River, OH 44116
tel 440-617-1400 *fax* 440-617-1403
website www.kaeden.com

Educational publisher specialising in early literacy books and beginning chapter books.

Submission details Seeking beginning chapter books and unique non-fiction MSS (25–2000 words). Vocabularly and sentence structure must be appropriate for young readers. No sentence fragments. See website for complete guidelines.

Accepts samples of all styles of illustration but is primarily looking for samples that match the often humorous style appropriate for juvenile literature. Send samples, no larger than 8.5 x 11ins to keep on file. Founded 1986.

Kar-Ben Publishing – see Lerner Publishing Group

KidHave Press – see Thomson Gale

Kids Story Book LLC

5135 Avenida Encinas, Suite B, Carlsbad, CA 92008
tel 800-849-9960
email info@kidsstorybook.com
website http://kidsstorybook.com

Kids Story Book is a personalised, interactive, animated, audio CD story book that automatically reads the story, written for 3–7 year-olds.

Kingfisher – see Houghton Mifflin Company

Klutz – see Scholastic Inc.

Wendy Lamb – see Random House Inc.

Lee & Low Books

95 Madison Avenue, Suite 606, New York, NY 10016
tel 212-779-4400 *fax* 212-683-1894
email general@leeandlow.com
website www.leeandlow.com
Editor-in-Chief Louise May

Children's book publisher specialising multicultural literature that is relevant to young readers. The company's goal is 'to meet the need for stories that children of colour can identify with and that all children can enjoy and which promote a greater understanding of one another'.

Focuses on fiction and non-fiction for children aged 5–12 which feature children/people of colour. Of special interest are realistic fiction, historical fiction, and non-fiction with a distinct voice or unique approach. Does not consider folktales or animal stories.

Submission details MSS should be no longer 1500 words for fiction and 3000 words for non-fiction. Send MSS with a covering letter that includes a brief biography of the author, including publishing history, and stating if the MS is a simultaneous or an exclusive submission. Include sase, or for international submissions send an international money order to pay for return postage. No submissions via email. Makes a special effort to work with artists of colour. Founded 1991.

Lerner Publishing Group

241 First Avenue North, Minneapolis,
MN 55401–1607
tel 612-332-3344 *fax* 612-332-7615
email info@lernerbooks.com
website www.lernerbooks.com
Publisher Adam Lerner, *Non-fiction Submisions Editor* Jennifer Zimian, *Fiction Submisions Editor* Zelda Wagner

Independent publisher of high-quality children's books for K–12 schools and libraries: picture books, fiction for 5–8 and 9–12 year-olds, teenage fiction, series fiction and non-fiction. Subjects include biography, social studies, science, sports and curriculum. Publishes approx. 200 titles each year and has about 1500 in print. Imprints: Lerner Publications, Carolrhoda Books, First Avenue Editions, Kar-Ben Publishing, LernerSports and LernerClassroom. Founded 1959.

Submission details Only accepts submissions during November; submissions received in any other month will be returned to the sender unopened. A sase, addressed to either Ms Zimian or Ms Wagner is required; allow 8 months for a response. No telephone calls. For guidelines, address to 'Guideline request' and send a business-sized sase. *For illustrations* Accepts unsolicited artists' samples at all times of the year. Submit slides, jpg or pdf files on disk, colour photocopies or tearsheets; do not send original artwork. Include a résumé detailing previous work. Address to the Art Director.

Carolrhoda Books (imprint)
website www.carolrhodabooks.com
Picture books aimed at 5–8 year-olds; longer fiction for age 7+, including chapter books and middle-grade and young adult novels; biographies. Interested in unique, honest stories that stay away from moralising and religious themes; also science fiction/fantasy for young readers. Popular characters include Little Wolf and Harriet. Authors and illustrators include Nancy Carlson and Jan Wahl. Recent successes include *Almost to Freedom* by Vaunda Micheaux Nelson, illustrated by Colin Bootman. Founded 1969.
Submission details All submissions must have a sufficiently posted sase otherwise there will be no response and MSS will not be returned. For non-fiction, send the complete MS with a one-page outline/synopsis and a résumé to Ms Zimian. For picture book submissions send the whole MS to Ms Wagner; dummy books are not necessary. For longer fiction send a brief outline/synopsis and a few sample chapters not exceeding 50pp, to Ms Wagner.

Kar-Ben Publishing (imprint)
6800 Tildenwood Lane, Rockville, MD 20852-4371
tel 301-984-8733 *fax* 301-881-9195
website www.karben.com
Contact Judye Groner, Madeline Wikler
Books on Jewish themes for children and families. Subjects include the High Holidays, Passover, Sukkot and Simchat Torah, Hanukkah, Purim, Selichot, Tu B'Shevat, crafts, cooking, folk tales, and contemporary stories, Jewish calendars, music, and activity books. Founded 1974.
Submission details Welcomes unsolicited MSS and artists' samples at all times of the year. Include a sase for a response and allow 3–5 weeks for a reply. Will consider fiction and non-fiction for preschool through to high school age, including holiday books, life-cycle stories, Bible tales, folk tales, board books and activity books. Illustrators should send colour photocopies or tearsheets, not original artwork.

LernerClassroom (imprint)
website www.lernerclassroom.com
Non-fiction books and teaching guides for grades K-8 in social studies, science, reading/literacy and mathematics. Books are paired with teaching guides that are correlated to national and state standards.

Millbrook Press (imprint)
Maths, science, American history, social studies and biography for a younger age bracket.
Submission details See above.

Twenty-First Century Books (imprint)
Maths, science, American history, social studies and biography for Secondary school age bracket.
Submission details See above.

LernerClassroom – see Lerner Publishing Group

Little, Brown & Company
1271 Avenue of the Americas, New York, NY 10020
tel 212-522-8700 *fax* 212-522-7997
website www.hachettebookgroupusa.com
Publisher Megan Tingley

General literature, fiction, non-fiction, biography, history, trade paperbacks, children's.

Little, Brown Books for Young Readers
website www.lb-kids.com, www.lb-teens.com
Publisher Megan Tingley, *Creative Director* Alyssa Morris
Fiction and non-fiction for all ages including young adult. Subjects include art, biographies, fairy tales, film/TV tie-ins, entertainment, how-to books, pets, sport. Also activity books, board books, novelty books, picture books, pop-up books, poetry, calendars and gift books. Recent successes include *I Know an Old Lady Who Swallowed a Fly* by Mary Ann Hoberman and Nadine Bernard Westcott (ages 0–3), *You Read to Me, I'll Read to You: Very Short Fairy Tales to Read Together* by Mary Ann Hoberman and Michael Emberley (ages 4–8) and *How to Train Your Dragon* by Cressida Cowell ages 8–12.
Submission details Only interested in submissions via literary agents. For illustrations, query Art Director with b&w and colour samples; provide résumé, promotional sheet or tearsheets to be kept on file.

Llewellyn Worldwide
2143 Wooddale Drive, Woodbury, MN 55125
tel 800-843-666
email info@llewellyn.com
website www.llewellyn.com
President & Publisher Carl L. Weschcke

New Age: alternative health and healing, astrology, earth-based religions, shamanism, Gnostic Christianity and Kabbalah; mystery novels. Founded 1901.

Flux (imprint)
email submissions@fluxnow.com
website www.fluxnow.com
Young adult: fiction for ages 12+ in all genres. Seeks to publish authors who see young adult as a point of view rather than a reading level. Looks for edgy,

challenging books that try to capture a slice of teenage experience. Particularly interested in books that tell the stories of young adults in unexpected or surprising situations around the globe. Recent successes include *Blue is for Nightmares* and sequels by Laurie Faria Stolarz and *How It's Done* by Christine Kole MacLean.

Submission details Seeking high-quality novels of all genres for ages 12+. No middle-grade or picture books. See website for submission guidlines.

Lucent Books – see Thomson Gale

Margaret K. McElderry Books – see Simon & Schuster Children's Publishing Division

McGraw-Hill*

2 Penn Plaza, New York, NY 10121
tel 212-512-2000
website www.books.mcgraw-hill.com
Group Vice-President Theodore Nardin

Professional and reference: engineering, scientific, business, architecture, encyclopedias; college textbooks; high school and vocational textbooks: business, secretarial, career; trade books; training materials for industry. Division of The McGraw-Hill Companies.

Marcato Books – see Cricket Books

Marshall Cavendish Benchmark

Marshall Cavendish Corporation, 99 White Plains Road, PO Box 2001, Tarrytown, NY 10591
tel 914-332-8888 *fax* 914-332-1082
email customerservice@marshallcavendish.us
website www.marshallcavendish.com

Information books for young, middle and young adult readers. Subjects include activities, American studies, the arts, biographies, health, human behaviour, mathematics, science, social studies, world cultures. Imprint of Marshall Cavendish Corporation.

Submission details Non-fiction subjects should be curriculum related and are published in series form. Length: 4000–20,000 words. Either send complete MS or synopsis with one or more sample chapters.

Marshall Cavendish Children's Books

Marshall Cavendish Corporation, 99 White Plains Road, PO Box 2001, Tarrytown, NY 10591
tel 914-332-8888 *fax* 914-332-1082
email customerservice@marshallcavendish.com
website www.marshallcavendish.us

Picture books, non-fiction and fiction for young readers. Imprint of Marshall Cavendish Corporation.

Milet Publishing Ltd

333 North Michigan Avenue, Suite 530, Chicago, IL 60601
email info@milet.com

website www.milet.com

Picture books in English; bilingual picture books; adventurous and international young fiction.

Submission details Will consider unsolicited submissions by post only. No email submissions. See website for guidelines and profile of list.

Milkweed Editions

1011 Washington Avenue South, Suite 300, Minneapolis, MN 55415
tel 612-332-3192 *fax* 612-215-2550
email editor@milkweed.org
website www.milkweed.org
Editor Daniel Slager

Children's novels (ages 8–14). Recent successes include *Perfect* (contemporary) and *Trudy* (contemporary). For adults: fiction, poetry, essays, the natural world. Founded 1979.

Submission details For fiction, submit complete MS. Responds in 6 months. Will consider simultaneous submissions. For illustrations, query with samples: provide résumé, promotional sheet, slides, tearsheets and client list. Samples files or returned with sase.

Millbrook Press – see Lerner Publishing Group

Mitchell Lane Publishers, Inc.

PO Box 196, Hockessin, DE 19707
tel 302-234-9426
email customerservice@mitchelllane.com
website www.mitchelllane.com
President Barbara Mitchell

Non-fiction for young readers, middle readers and young adults. Recent successes include *Uncharted, Unexplored and Unexplained* series (middle-grade readers) and *Clay Aiken: From Second Place to the Top of the Charts* by Kathleen Tracy (12+).

Mondo Publishing

980 Avenue of the Americas, New York, NY 10018
tel 212-268-3560 *fax* 212-268-3561
email info@mondopub.com
website www.mondopub.com

Classroom materials and professional development for K–5 educators.

Morehouse Publishing Co.

PO Box 1321, Harrisburg, PA 17105
tel 717-541-8130 *fax* 717-541-8136
email morehouse@morehousegroup.com
website www.morehousepublishing.org
Vice President & Publisher Ken Arnold

Religious books, spirituality, children's.

Morgan Reynolds Publishing

620 South Elm Street, Suite 223, Greensboro, NC 27406
tel 800-535-1504 *fax* 800-535-5725

website www.morganreynolds.com

Non-fiction for young adults. Recent successes include *Elizabeth I of England in the European Queens* series and *Ulysses S. Grant: Defender of the Union in the Civil War Generals* series. Founded 1993.

Thomas Nelson Publisher

501 Nelson Place, Nashville, TN 37214–1000
tel 800-251-4000 *fax* 615-391-5225
email publicity@thomasnelson.com
website www.thomasnelson.com
Executive Vice President, Thomas Nelson Publishing Group Lee Gessner

Bibles, religious, non-fiction and fiction general trade books for adults and children. Founded 1798.

NorthWord Books for Young Readers

T & N Children's Publishing, 11571 K–Tel Drive, Minnetonka, MN 55343
tel 952-933-7537 *fax* 952-933-3630
website www.tnkidsbooks.com

Picture books and non-fiction nature and wildlife books in interactive and fun-to-read formats. Imrprint of T & N Children's Publishing. Founded 1989.

The Oliver Press, Inc.

Charlotte Square, 5707 West 36th Street, Minneapolis, MN 55416–2510
tel 952-926-8981 *fax* 952-926-8965
website www.oliverpress.com

Non-fiction for young adults: history, biography, science.

Submission details Interested in receiving proposals that fit into an established series. Submit proposal, a resume of previously published works and any applicable education or experience together with a writing sample similar to the reading level, style and subject to the book that is being proposed. No unsolicited MSS.

Orchard Books – see Scholastic Inc.

The Overlook Press*

141 Wooster Street, New York, New York 10012
tel 212-673-2210 *fax* 212-673-2296
website www.overlookpress.com
President & Publisher Peter Mayer

Non-fiction, fiction, children's books (*Freddy the Pig* series). Founded 1971.

Richard C. Owen Publishers, Inc.

PO Box 585, Katonah, NY 10536
tel 800-262-0787 *fax* 914-232-3977
Children's Books Editor Janice Boland

Classroom materials for grades K–8 and professional books for teachers and administrators.

Submission details Books for Young Learners: Seeks high-interest stories with charm and appeal that 5–7

year-olds can read by themselves. Interested in original, realistic, contemporary stories, as well as folktales, legends, and myths of all cultures. Non-fiction topics should be presented in language accessible to 5–7 year-olds; no dry encyclopedia-type pieces. Content must be supported with details and accurate facts. Length: 45–1000 words. Publishes a variety of genres, styles and subjects that support the curriculum including science, technology, history and geography.

Books for Older Learners: Seeks short, high-interest, easy-reading MSS that
will appeal to and inform 8–10 year-olds.
Submissions should have the economy of words, vitality, focus, impact, and energy of a magazine or newspaper article but written for 8–10 year-olds. Children should be able to read the piece in
one sitting with understanding and enthusiasm.
Topics and genres include: adventure, action, mysteries, magic, humour, science, science fiction, simple scientific observations, journals, diaries, photo essays, current trends, sports, music, how-to, letters, nature and the environment, careers, technology, geography, architecture, travel, interviews, plays, and the retelling of myths and legends.

Do not submit queries, MS summaries, resumes, chapter books or lengthy MSS.

Oxford University Press Inc.*

198 Madison Avenue, New York, NY 10016
tel 212-726-6000 *fax* 212-726-6455
website www.oup.com/us
President Laura Brown

Children's fiction and non-fiction. Subjects include art, history, literature, music, myths and fairy tales, poetry, reference, science. Also scholarly, professional, reference, bibles, college textbooks, religion, medical, music.

Pacific View Press

PO Box 2657, Berkeley, CA 94702
tel 415-285-8538 *fax* 415-285-2620
email pvp2@mindspring.com
website www.pacificviewpress.com

Multicultural children's books, acupuncture and Traditional Chinese Medicine, Asia and Asian–American affairs.

Dragon Books (imprint)

Multicultural non-fiction and literature for children. Focuses on the culture and history of China, Japan, the Philippines, Mexico, and other countries on the Pacific Rim. Books are intended to encourage pride in and respect for the shared history that makes a people unique, as well as an awareness of universal human experiences. Recent successes include *Cloud Weavers: Ancient Chinese Legends* by Rena Krasno and Yeng-Fong Chiang and *Exploring Chinatown: A Children's Guide to Chinese Culture* by Carol Stepanchuk, illustrated by Leland Wong. Founded 1992.

Parenting Press, Inc.

PO Box 75267, Seattle, WA 98175–0267
tel 206-364-2900 fax 206-364-0702
Acquisitions Carolyn Threadgill

How-to information for child guidance, problem solving, emotional competence, and children's personal safety issues. Recent successful picture books include The Way I Feel by Janan Cain (ages 18 months–8), When You're Mad and You Know It in the Feelings for Little Children series by Elizabeth Crary and Shari Steelsmith, illustrated by Mits Katayama (ages 1–3) and What About Me?: 12 Ways to Get Your Parents' Attention Without Hitting Your Sister by Eileen Kennedy-Moore, illustrated by Mits Katayama (ages 4–8).

Parragon Publishing

440 Park Avenue South, 13th Floor, New York, NY 10006
tel 212-629-9773
email usinfo@parragon.com
website www.parragon.com

The world's largest 'value-orientated' publisher of children's titles.

Paula Wiseman – see Simon & Schuster Children's Publishing Division

Peachtree Publishers

1700 Chattahoochee Avenue, Atlanta, GA 30318–2112
tel 404-876-8761 fax 404-875-2578
email hello@peachtree-online.com
website www.peachtree-online.com
President & Publisher Margaret Quinlin, Editorial Director Kathy Landwehr, Art Director Loraine Joyner

Children's picture books, novels and non-fiction. Adult non-fiction subjects include self-help, parenting, education, health, regional guides. No adult fiction.

Children's picture books, novels and non-fiction. Publishes 30–35 titles each year. Recent successes include Dad, Jackie and Me by Myron Uhlberg and Colin Bootman. Adult non-fiction subjects include self-help, parenting, education, health, regional guides. No adult fiction. Founded 1977.

Submission details For children's books, send complete MSS; for all others, send query letter with 3 sample chapters and table of contents to Helen Harriss with sase for response and/or return of material. For illustrations, query with samples, résumé, slides, colour photocopies to keep on file. Samples returned with sase.

Pearson Prentice Hall*

One Lake Street, Upper Saddle River, NJ 07458
tel 201-236-7000
email communications@pearsoned.com
website www.phschool.com

Educational secondary publisher of scientifically researched and standards-based instruction materials for today's Grade 6–12 classrooms with a mission is to create exceptional educational tools that ensure student and teacher success in language arts, mathematics, modern and classical languages, science, social studies, career and technology, and advanced placement, electives, and honors. Division of Pearson Education.

Pelican Publishing Company*

1000 Burmaster Street, Gretna, LA 70053
tel 504-368-1175 fax 504-368-1195
email editorial@pelicanpub.com
website www.pelicanpub.com, www.epelican.com
Publisher/President Milburn Calhoun

Children's books. Also travel guides, art and architecture books, Christmas stories, local and international cookbooks, motivational and inspirational works, social commentary, history, fiction.

Submission details Send a query letter and sase. No queries or submissions by email. No unsolicited MSS. Most young children's books are 32 illustrated pages when published; their MSS cover about 7pp when typed continuously. Proposed books for middle readers (ages 8+) should be at least 150pp. Brief books for readers under 9 may be submitted in their entirety. Founded 1926.

Penguin Putnam Books for Young Readers*

345 Hudson Street, New York, NY 10014
tel 212-366-2000 fax 212-366-2666
email online@penguinputnam.com
website www.penguinputnam.com
President & Publisher Douglas Whiteman

Children's picture books, board and novelty books, young adult novels, mass merchandise products. Imprints: Dial Books for Young Readers, Dutton Children's Books, Dutton Interactive, Phyllis Fogelman Books, Grosset & Dunlap, PaperStar, Philomel, Planet Dexter, Platt & Munk, Playskool, Price Stern Sloan, PSS, Puffin Books, G.P. Putnam's Sons, Viking Children's Books, Frederick Warne. Division of Penguin Putnam Inc. Founded 1997.

Dial Books for Young Readers (imprint)

fax 212-414-3394
President/Publisher Nancy Paulsen, Editorial Director Laura Hornik, Vice President/Publisher, Phyllis Fogelman Books Phyllis Fogelman, Acquisitions Editor Nancy Mercado, Senior Editor Cecile Goyette, Art Director Lily Malcom

Children's fiction and non-fiction, picture books, board books, interactive books, novels. Publishes 35 picture books, 3 young reader titles, 6 middle reader titles and 9 young adult titles each year. Recent successes include A Year Down Yonder by Richard Peck (fiction, age 10+), The Sea Chest by Toni

Buzzeo, illustrated by Mary Grand (fiction picture book, all ages), *A Strong Right Arm* by Michelle Y. Green (non-fiction, age 10+) and *Dirt on Their Skirts* by Doreen Rappaport and Lyndall Callan (non-fiction picture book, ages 4–8).

Submission details For picture books, send MSS. For longer works, query with no more than 10pp of MSS. Responds in 4 months. Send sase. No email queries. For illustrations, send samples with sase to Design Dept.

Dutton Children's Books (imprint)
tel 212-366 2792 *fax* 212-243-6002
President/Publisher Stephanie Lurie, *Editorial Director, Dutton Children's Trade* Donna Brooks, *Art Director* Sara Reynolds

Picture books, young adult novels, non-fiction photographic books. Publishes 50% fiction, mostly young adult and middle-grade. Recent successes include *Leonard: Beautiful Dreamer* by Robert Byrd (non-fiction), *The Boy Who Spoke Dog* by Clay Morgan (middle-grade fiction), *Skippyjon Jones* by Judy Schachner (picture book) and *PREP* by Jake Coburn (young adult fiction). Founded 1852.

Submission details Approx. 10% of books are by first-time authors. No unsolicited MSS. Send query letter only; responds in 3 months. Send to Lucia Mondfried (easy-to-read, middle-grade fiction), Meredith Mundy Wasinger (middle-grade fiction, picture books), Michele Coppola (picture books, middle-gradde fiction, upper young adult fiction), Julie Strauss-Gabel (picture books, middle-grade fiction, young adult). For illustrations, query with samples. Samples returned with sase.

Grosset & Dunlap (imprint)
President/Publisher, Grosset & Dunlap Debra Dorfman

Children's picture books, activity books, fiction and non-fiction. Publishes 175 books each year. Recent successes include *Zenda* (series) and *Strawberry Shortcake* (license). Imprints: Grosset & Dunlap, Platt & Munk, Somerville House USA, Planet Dexter. Founded 1898.

Submission details Only interested in material via literary agent.

Philomel Books (imprint)
Fiction and non-fiction for all ages. Publishes 18 picture books, 2 middle-grade books, 2 young readers and 4 young adult books each year. Founded 1980.

Submission details Approx. 5% of books are by first-time authors. No unsolicited MSS. Fiction length: picture books – 1000 words; young readers – 1500 words; middle readers – 14,000 words; young adult – 20,000 words. Non-fiction length: picture books – 2000 words; young readers – 3000 words; middle readers – 10,000 words. For illustrations, query with samples: send résumé and tearsheets. Responds in one month. Samples returned with sase.

Price Stern Sloan (imprint)
President/Publisher Debra Dorfman

Children's novelty/lift-flap books, activity books, picture books, middle-grade fiction, middle-grade

and young adult non-fiction, graphic readers, books plus. Recent successes include *Inside the Little Old Woman's Shoe* by Chuck Reasoner, *Fear Factor Mad Libs* and *Elf*. Imprints: Crazy Games, Doodle Art, Planet Dexter, Serendipity, Troubador Press, Wee Sing. Founded 1963.

Submission details Send query; responds in 3 weeks.

Puffin Books (imprint)
President & Publisher Tracy Tang, *Executive Editor* Kristin Gilson, *Senior Editor* Sharyn November

Picture books, fiction for 5–8 and 9–12 year-olds, teenage fiction, series fiction and film/TV tie-ins. Publishes approx. 225–275 titles each year. Recent successes include *Rules of the Road* by Joan Bauer, *A Long Way from Chicago* by Richard Peck and *26 Fairmount Avenue* by Tomie dePaola. Founded 1941.

Submission details Approx. 1% of books are by first-time authors. Will consider unsolicited MSS for novels only. Send with sase to Submissions Editor. Seeking to publish mysteries.

G.P. Putnam's Sons (imprint)
tel 212-414-3610
President/Publisher Nancy Paulsen, *Executive Editor* Kathy Dawson, *Art Director* Cecilia Yung

Children's hardcover and paperback books. Recent successes include *Fat Kid Rules the World* by K.L. Going (ages 12+), *Locomotion* by Jacqueline Woodson and *Atlantic* by G. Brian Karas (ages 4–8, non-fiction). Founded 1838.

Submission details For fiction, query with outline/synopsis and 1–3 sample chapters. Fiction length: picture books – 200–1000 words; middle readers – 10,000–30,000 words; young adult – 40,000–50,000 words. For non-fiction, query with outline/synopsis, 1–2 sample chapters and table of contents. Non-fiction length: picture books – 200–1500 words. Responds to queries in 3 weeks and to MS in 2 months. Write for illustrator guidelines.

Viking Children's Books (imprint)
tel 212-414-3600
President Regina Hayes

Fiction, non-fiction and picture books for preschool–young adult. Publishes 70 books each year. Recent successes include *Strange Mr Satie* by M.T. Anderson (ages 5–8, picture book), *Restless* by Richard Wallace (ages 12) fiction, and *Open Your Eyes: Extraordinary Experiences in Far Away Places* (ages 12+, non-fiction). Founded 1925.

Submission details Approx. 25% of books are by first-time authors; receives 7500 queries a year. No unsolicited MSS. Responds to artists' queries/submissions only if interested. Samples returned with sase.

Frederick Warne (imprint)
Original publisher of Beatrix Potter's *Tales of Peter Rabbit*. Founded 1865.

Penguin Putnam Inc.*

(formerly Penguin USA and Putnam Berkley)
375 Hudson Street, New York, NY10014
tel 212-366-2000 *fax* 212-366-2666
email online@penguinputnam.com
website www.penguinputnam.com
President, The Penguin Group David Wan, *Chairman*
John McKinson, *Ceo* David Shanks

Consumer books in both hardcover and paperback
for adults and children; also maps, calendars, audio
books and mass merchandise products. Children's
imprints: Dial Books for Young Readers, Dutton
Children's Books, Grosset & Dunlap, PaperStar,
Philomel Books, Planet Dexter, Price Stern Sloan
Inc., Puffin, G.P. Putnam's Sons, Viking Children's
Books, Wee Sing, Frederick Warne.

Adult imprints: Ace, Ace/Putnam, Allen Lane The
Penguin Press, Avery, Berkley Books, BlueHen,
Boulevard, DAW, Dutton, Grosset/Putnam, HP
Books, Jove, Mentor, Meridian, Onyx, Penguin,
Penguin Classics, Penguin Compass, Perigee, Plume,
Prime Crime, Price Stern Sloan Inc., Putnam, G.P.
Putnam's Sons, Riverhead Books, Roc, Signet, Signet
Classics, Jeremy P. Tarcher, Topaz, Viking, Viking
Compass, Viking Studio, Marian Wood Books.
Divisions: Berkley Publishing Group, Dutton, Plume,
NAL, Penguin Putnam Books for Young Readers (see
separate entry), The Putnam Publishing Group,
Viking Penguin.

Penguin Putnam Books for Young Readers
345 Hudson Street, New York, NY 10014
tel 212-366-2000 *fax* 212-366-2666
email online@penguinputnam.com
website www.penguinputnam.com
President & Publisher Douglas Whiteman
Children's picture books, board and novelty books,
young adult novels, mass merchandise products.
Imprints: Dial Books for Young Readers, Dutton
Children's Books, Dutton Interactive, Phyllis
Fogelman Books, Grosset & Dunlap, PaperStar,
Philomel, Planet Dexter, Platt & Munk, Playskool,
Price Stern Sloan, PSS, Puffin Books, G.P. Putnam's
Sons, Viking Children's Books, Frederick Warne.
Division of **Penguin Putnam Inc.** Founded 1997.

Dial Books for Young Readers (imprint)
fax 212-414-3394
President/Publisher Nancy Paulsen, *Editorial Director*
Laura Hornik, *Vice President/Publisher, Phyllis
Fogelman Books* Phyllis Fogelman, *Acquisitions Editor*
Nancy Mercado, *Senior Editor* Cecile Goyette, *Art
Director* Lily Malcom
Children's fiction and non-fiction, picture books,
board books, interactive books, novels. Publishes 35
picture books, 3 young reader titles, 6 middle reader
titles and 9 young adult titles each year. Recent
successes include *A Year Down Yonder* by Richard
Peck (fiction, age 10+), *The Sea Chest* by Toni
Buzzeo, illustrated by Mary Grand (fiction picture

book, all ages), *A Strong Right Arm* by Michelle Y.
Green (non-fiction, age 10+) and *Dirt on Their Skirts*
by Doreen Rappaport and Lyndall Callan (non-
fiction picture book, ages 4–8).
Submission details For picture books, send MSS.
For longer works, query with no more than 10pp of
MSS. Responds in 4 months. Send sase. No email
queries. For illustrations, send samples with sase to
Design Dept.

Dutton Children's Books (imprint)
tel 212-366 2792 *fax* 212-243-6002
President/Publisher Stephanie Lurie, *Editorial Director,
Dutton Children's Trade* Donna Brooks, *Art Director*
Sara Reynolds
Picture books, young adult novels, non-fiction
photographic books. Publishes 50% fiction, mostly
young adult and middle-grade. Recent successes
include *Leonard: Beautiful Dreamer* by Robert Byrd
(non-fiction), *The Boy Who Spoke Dog* by Clay
Morgan (middle-grade fiction), *Skippyjon Jones* by
Judy Schachner (picture book) and *PREP* by Jake
Coburn (young adult fiction). Founded 1852.
Submission details Approx. 10% of books are by
first-time authors. No unsolicited MSS. Send query
letter only; responds in 3 months. Send to Lucia
Mondfried (easy-to-read, middle-grade fiction),
Meredith Mundy Wasinger (middle-grade fiction,
picture books), Michele Coppola (picture books,
middle-gradde fiction, upper young adult fiction),
Julie Strauss-Gabel (picture books, middle-grade
fiction, young adult). For illustrations, query with
samples. Samples returned with sase.

Grosset & Dunlap (imprint)
President/Publisher, Grosset & Dunlap Debra
Dorfman
Children's picture books, activity books, fiction and
non-fiction. Publishes 175 books each year. Recent
successes include *Zenda* (series) and *Strawberry
Shortcake* (license). Imprints: Grosset & Dunlap, Platt
& Munk, Somerville House USA, Planet Dexter.
Founded 1898.
Submission details Only interested in material via
literary agent.

Philomel Books (imprint)
Fiction and non-fiction for all ages. Publishes 18
picture books, 2 middle-grade books, 2 young readers
and 4 young adult books each year. Founded 1980.
Submission details Approx. 5% of books are by
first-time authors. No unsolicited MSS. Fiction
length: picture books – 1000 words; young readers –
1500 words; middle readers – 14,000 words; young
adult – 20,000 words. Non-fiction length: picture
books – 2000 words; young readers – 3000 words;
middle readers – 10,000 words. For illustrations,
query with samples: send résumé and tearsheets.
Responds in one month. Samples returned with sase.

Price Stern Sloan (imprint)
President/Publisher Debra Dorfman
Children's novelty/lift-flap books, activity books,
picture books, middle-grade fiction, middle-grade

and young adult non-fiction, graphic readers, books plus. Recent successes include *Inside the Little Old Woman's Shoe* by Chuck Reasoner, *Fear Factor Mad Libs* and *Elf*. Imprints: Crazy Games, Doodle Art, Planet Dexter, Serendipity, Troubador Press, Wee Sing. Founded 1963.

Submission details Send query; responds in 3 weeks.

Puffin Books (imprint)

President & Publisher Tracy Tang, *Executive Editor* Kristin Gilson, *Senior Editor* Sharyn November

Picture books, fiction for 5–8 and 9–12 year-olds, teenage fiction, series fiction and film/TV tie-ins. Publishes approx. 225–275 titles each year. Recent successes include *Rules of the Road* by Joan Bauer, *A Long Way from Chicago* by Richard Peck and *26 Fairmount Avenue* by Tomie dePaola. Founded 1941.

Submission details Approx. 1% of books are by first-time authors. Will consider unsolicited MSS for novels only. Send with sase to Submissions Editor. Seeking to publish mysteries.

G.P. Putnam's Sons (imprint)

tel 212-414-3610

President/Publisher Nancy Paulsen, *Executive Editor* Kathy Dawson, *Art Director* Cecilia Yung

Children's hardcover and paperback books. Recent successes include *Fat Kid Rules the World* by K.L. Going (ages 12+), *Locomotion* by Jacqueline Woodson and *Atlantic* by G. Brian Karas (ages 4–8, non-fiction). Founded 1838.

Submission details For fiction, query with outline/synopsis and 1–3 sample chapters. Fiction length: picture books – 200–1000 words; middle readers – 10,000–30,000 words; young adult – 40,000–50,000 words. For non-fiction, query with outline/synopsis, 1–2 sample chapters and table of contents. Non-fiction length: picture books – 200–1500 words. Responds to queries in 3 weeks and to MS in 2 months. Write for illustrator guidelines.

Viking Children's Books (imprint)

tel 212-414-3600

President Regina Hayes

Fiction, non-fiction and picture books for preschool–young adult. Publishes 70 books each year. Recent successes include *Strange Mr Satie* by M.T. Anderson (ages 5–8, picture book), *Restless* by Richard Wallace (ages 12) fiction, and *Open Your Eyes: Extraordinary Experiences in Far Away Places* (ages 12+, non-fiction). Founded 1925.

Submission details Approx. 25% of books are by first-time authors; receives 7500 queries a year. No unsolicited MSS. Responds to artists' queries/submissions only if interested. Samples returned with sase.

Frederick Warne (imprint)

Original publisher of Beatrix Potter's *Tales of Peter Rabbit*. Founded 1865.

Philomel Books – see Penguin Putnam Inc.

Phoenix Learning Resources

2349 Chaffee Drive, Saint Louis, MO 63146
tel 314-569-0211 *fax* 314-569-2834
website www.phoenixlearninggroup.com
Vice President, Phoenix Learning Resources John Rothermich

Remedial reading, language arts, arithmetic. Division of The Phoenix Learning Group, Inc.

Price Stern Sloan – see Penguin Putnam Books for Young Readers

Puffin Books – see Penguin Putnam Books for Young Readers

Simon Pulse Paperback Books – see Simon & Schuster Children's Publishing Division

G.P. Putnam's Sons – see Penguin Putnam Books for Young Readers

G.P. Putnam's Sons (children's) – see Penguin Putnam Books for Young Readers

Random House Inc.*

1745 Broadway, 10th Floor, New York, NY 10019
tel 212-782-9000 *fax* 212-302-7985
website www.randomhouse.com
Chairman/Ceo Peter Olson, *President/Coo* Erik Engstrom

Adult general fiction and non-fiction and audio publishing. Imprints include Fodors Travel Publications, Living Language, The Modern Library, Princeton Review, Random House Adult Trade Books, Random House Large Print Publishing, Random House Puzzles and Games, Random House Reference, Random House Value Publishing (Children's Classics, Crescent Books, Derrydale, Gramercy Books, Testament Books, Wings Books) and Villard Books. Subsidiary of Bertelsmann AG.

Knopf Publishing Group (division)

Chairman Sonny Mehta, *Vice-President & Senior Editor* Judith Jones

Literature, fiction, poetry, cooking, biography, history, nature, travel. Imprints: Alfred A. Knopf, Anchor Books, Everyman's Library (including *Pocket Poets* and *Children's Classics* series), Pantheon Books, Schocken Books, Vintage.

Random House Children's Media Group (division)

President & Publisher Craig W. Virden

Children's imprints: Bantam Books for Young Readers, Crown Books for Young Readers, Delacorte Press Books for Young Readers, Disney Books for Young Readers, Doubleday Books for Young Readers, Dragonfly Books, David Fickling Books, Golden Books for Young Readers, Alfred A. Knopf Books for

Young Readers, Wendy Lamb Books, Laurel-Leaf Books, Lucas Books, Random House Books for Young Readers, Yearling Books.

Bantam Books for Young Readers (imprint)
website www.randomhouse.com/kids
Submission details Not seeking new MSS at the moment.

Crown Books for Young Readers (imprint)
website www.randomhouse.com/kids
Juvenile fiction and non-fiction for ages 0–18.
Submission details Send query letter with sase to Acquisitions Editor. For illustrations, send samples to Isabel Warren-Lynch, *Executive Director, Art & Design.* Responds only if interested. Samples returned with sase.

Delacorte Press Books for Young Readers (imprint)
website www.randomhouse.com/kids
Submission details Approx. 90% of books are published via literary agents. Unsolicited MSS are only accepted as submissions to either the Delacorte Dell Yearling Contest for a Mid-Grade Novel or the Delacorte Press Contest for a First Young Adult Novel. See website for details. For illustrations, send samples to Isabel Warren-Lynch, *Executive Director, Art & Design.* Responds only if interested. Samples returned with sase.

Doubleday Books for Young Readers (imprint)
website www.randomhouse.com/kids
Submission details Approx. 90% of books are published via literary agents. Unsolicited MSS are only accepted as submissions to either the Delacorte Dell Yearling Contest for a Mid-Grade Novel or the Delacorte Press Contest for a First Young Adult Novel. See website for details. For illustrations, send samples to Isabel Warren-Lynch, *Executive Director, Art & Design.* Responds only if interested. Samples returned with sase.

Golden Books for Young Readers (imprint)
website www.goldenbooks.com
Ceo Peter Olsen, *Editorial Directors* Courtney Silk (colour & activity), Chris Angelilli (storybooks), Denise Shealy (novelty), *Executive Art Director* Tracey Tyler
Children's books, educational workbooks and products, electronic books and software, children's videos.
Submission details Approx. 2% of books are by first-time authors. No unsolicited MSS: reserves the right to not return unsolicited material. All acquisitions are made via literary agents.

Alfred A. Knopf Books for Young Readers (imprint)
website www.randomhouse.com/kids
Juvenile fiction and non-fiction for ages 0–18. Recent successes include *Milkweed* by Jerry Spinelli.
Submission details Send query letter with sase to Acquisitions Editor. For illustrations, send samples to

Isabel Warren-Lynch, *Executive Director, Art & Design.* Responds only if interested. Samples returned with sase.

Wendy Lamb (imprint)
website www.randomhouse.com/kids
Trade books, fiction, multicultural material. Publishes 12 middle readers and young adult books each year. Recent successes include *Island Boy* by Graham Salisbury, *Brian's Hunt* by Gary Paulsen and *Dust* by Arthur Slade.
Submission details Approx. 15% of books are by first-time authors. Receives 300–400 submissions a year. Send query letter with sase and no more than 5pp (picture books) or 10pp (novels) to Wendy Lamb. Will review MS/illustrations packages from artists: query with sase for reply.

Random House Books for Young Readers (imprint)
website www.goldenbooks.com
Ceo Peter Olsen, *Editorial Directors* Courtney Silk (colour & activity), Chris Angelilli (storybooks), Denise Shealy (novelty), *Executive Art Director* Tracey Tyler, *Associate Publisher/Art Director* Cathy Goldsmith
Books, educational workbooks and products, and electronic books and software for ages 6 months–12 years.
Submission details Approx. 2% of books are by first-time authors. No unsolicited MSS: reserves the right to not return unsolicited material. All acquisitions are made via literary agents.

Random House/Golden Books for Young Readers Group*
1745 Broadway, New York, NY 10019
tel 212-782-9000
website www.goldenbooks.com
Ceo Peter Olsen, *Editorial Directors* Courtney Silk (colour & activity), Chris Angelilli (storybooks), Denise Shealy (novelty), *Executive Art Director* Tracey Tyler
Children's books, educational workbooks and products, electronic books and software, children's videos.

Rising Moon – Luna Rising
PO Box 1389, Flagstaff, AZ 86002–1389
tel 928-774-5251 *fax* 928-774-0592
website www.risingmoonbooks.com
Illustrated, entertaining, and thought-provoking picture books for children, including Spanish–English bilingual titles.
Submission details Seeking fresh picture book MSS about contemporary everyday life of children: edgy, innovative, spirited (e.g. *Do Princesses Wear Hiking Boots?* and *It's a Bad Day*). Also seeking exceptional Latino-themed picture books about multicultural living, contemporary issues, Latino role models (e.g. *My Name is Celia* and *Lupe Vargas and Her Super*

Best Friend). Additionally seeking picture books that relate to western and southwestern USA, original stories with a Southwest flavour, fractured fairytales (e.g. *The Treasure of Ghostwood Gully* and *The Three Little Javelinas*). Founded 1997.

Roaring Brook Press

175 Fifth Avenue, New York, NY 10010
tel 203-740-2220 *fax* 203-740-2526
website www.holtzbrincks.com
Publisher Simon Broughton, *Publishers* Neil Porter, Deborah Brodie, Lauren Wohl

Picture books, fiction (including graphic novels) and non-fiction for young readers, from toddler to teen. Publishes about 40 titles a year. Recent successes include *My Friend Rabbit* by Eric Rohmann (Caldecott Medal winner, 2003), and *The Man Who Walked Between the Towers* by Mordicai Gerstein (Caldecott Medal winner, 2004). Division of Holtzbrink Publishers.
  Submission details Does not accept unsolicited MSS or submissions.

Running Press Book Publishers

125 South 22 Street, Philadelphia, PA 19103–4399
tel 215-567-5080 *fax* 215-568 2919
website www.runningpress.com
Publisher Jon Anderson, *Directors* Bill Jones (design), Greg Jones (editorial), Joanne Cassetti (production), Craig Herman (marketing)

Art, craft/how-to, general non-fiction, children's books. Imprints: Courage Books, Running Press Miniature Editions, Running Press Kids. Founded 1972.

Running Press Kids (imprint)

Picture books, activity books for young/middle readers. Publishes 10 picture books each year. Recent successes include *Halloween Night* by Charles Gigna (picture book, poetry), *The Three Funny Friends* by Charlotte Zolotow and *The Thread of Life*, illustrated by Mary Grand Pre (picture book).
  Submission details Approx. 20% of submissions are by first-time authors. For fiction, send complete MSS. Length: 500 words. For non-fiction, query. Responds to queries in one month and MSS in 2 months. Will review MS/illustration packages from artists: send MS with dummy. For illustrations only, send postcard sample. Responds only if interested.

Scholastic Education*

557 Broadway, New York, NY 10012
tel 212-343-6100
website www.scholastic.com

Educational publisher of research-based core and supplementary instructional materials. A leading provider in reading improvement and professional development products, as well as learning services that address the needs of the developing reader – from grades pre-K to high school.

Publishes 34 curriculum-based classroom magazines used by teachers in grades pre-K–12 as supplementary educational materials to raise awareness about current events in an age-appropriate manner and to help children develop reading skills. Magazines include *Scholastic News®*, *Junior Scholastic®*, *The New York Times Upfront®*, *Science World®*, *Scope®* and others, covering subjects such as English, maths, science, social studies, current events, and foreign languages. The magazine's online companion, *Scholastic News Online* is the leading news source for students and teachers on the internet.

Scholastic Education has also developed technology-based reading assessment and management products to help administrators and educators quickly and accurately assess student reading levels, match students to the appropriate books, predict how well they will do on district and state standardised tests, and inform instruction to improve reading skills.

Its wholly owned operations in Australia, Canada, New Zealand, and the UK have original trade and educational publishing programmes.

Scholastic Library Publishing (division)

90 Sherman Turnpike, Danbury, CT 06816
tel 203-797-3500
website www.scholastic.com

Online and print publisher of reference products. Major reference sets include *Encyclopedia Americana®*, *The New Book of Knowledge®*, *Nueva Enciclopedia Cumbre®*, *Lands and Peoples* and *The New Book of Popular Science*.

Children's Press and Franklin Watts (imprints)

Children's fiction and non-fiction: all subjects and all grades. Has over 2400 titles in print.

Grolier (imprint)

website www.publishing.grolier.com
Children's non-fiction and reference materials in print and online.

Scholastic Inc.*

557 Broadway, New York, NY 10012
tel 212-343-6100 *fax* 212-343-6930
website www.scholastic.com
Chairman/President/Ceo Richard Robinson, *Editorial Director* Elizabeth Szabla

Innovative textbooks, magazines, technology and teacher materials for use in both school and the home. Scholastic is a global children's publishing and media company with a corporate mission to instill the love of reading and learning for lifelong pleasure in all children. Founded 1920.

Scholastic Trade Press

557 Broadway, New York, NY 10012
tel 212 343 6100
website www.scholastic.com
Award-winning publisher of original children's books. Publishes over 750 different titles per year

including the branding publishing properties *Harry Potter®* and *Captain Underpants®*, the series *Clifford The Big Red Dog®*, *I Spy*™, and Scholastic's *The Magic School Bus®*, as well as licensed properties such as *Barney®*, *Star Wars®* and *Scooby Doo*™. Imprints: Blue Sky Press®, Cartwheel Books®, The Chicken House™, Arthur A. Levine Books, Orchard Books®, Scholastic Paperbacks, Scholastic Press and Scholastic Reference™.

Blue Sky Press (imprint)
Acquisitions Bonnie Verburg
Hardcover fiction and non-fiction, including novels and picture books. Publishes 15–20 titles a year. Recent successes include *To Every Thing There is a Season* illustrated by Leo and Diane Dillon (all ages, picture book) and *How Do Dinosaurs Say Good Night?* by Jane Yolen, illustrated by Mark Teague.
  Submission details Approx. 1% of which are by first-time authors. Not currently accepting unsolicited submissions due to a large backlog of books. For illustrations, query with samples or tearsheets. Responds only if interested; samples only returned with sase.

Cartwheel Books (imprint)
Vice-President/Editorial Director Ken Geist
Fiction and non-fiction for very young readers. Non-fiction is mostly written on assignment or is within a series. Publishes 25–30 picture books, 30–35 easy readers and 15–20 novelty books each year.
  Submission details Submissions via literary agents only: send complete MSS. Will respond in 6 months. All unsolicited material will be returned unread. Length: 100–3000 words (picture books, easy readers). For illustrations, send samples and tearsheets to the Art Director with sase.

Klutz
How-to books packaged with the tools of their trade (from juggling cubes to face paints to yo-yos). Includes an educational product line for pre K–Grade 4 children in maths, reading and general knowledge. Products are designed for doing, not just reading: 'We think people learn best through their hands, nose, feet, mouth and ears. Then their eyes. So we design multi-sensory books'.

Orchard Books (imprint)
555 Broadway, New York, NY 10012
tel 212-343-6782 *fax* 212-343-4890
website www.scholastic.com
Editorial Director Ken Geist, *Art Director* David Saylor
Picture books, fiction and poetry for children and fiction for young adults. Publishes approx. 55 books each year. Recent successes include *Stuart's Cape* by Sara Pennypacker, illustrated by Martin Matje and *Where Are You Going? To See My Friend!* by Eric Carle and Kazuo Iwamura (picture book). Founded 1987.
  Submission details Approx. 10% of books are by first-time authors. Send query letter only (responds

in 3 months): no unsolicited MSS. For illustrations, send tearsheets or photocopies (not disks or slides). Responds in one month. Samples returned with sase.

Scholastic Press (imprint)
Editorial Director Elizabeth Stabla, *Executive Editors* Tracy Mach, Dianne Hess, *Senior Editor* Lauren Thompson, *Associate Editors* Jennifer Ress, Leslie Budrich
Picture books, fiction for 5–8 and 9–12 year-olds, teenage fiction, poetry, religion and non-fiction for 3 year-olds–teenage. Publishes approx. 35–50 titles each year. Recent successes include *A Corner of the Universe* by Ann M. Martin, *Gregor the Overlander* by Suzanne Collins and *Old Turtle and the Broken Truth* by Douglas Wood and Jon J. Muth.
  Submission details Will not consider unsolicited MSS. Send query letter or submit via an agent. Currently considering picture books, non-fiction and fresh, literary middle grade and young adult fiction. Also especially interested in subtly handled treatments of the key relationships in children's lives: unusual approaches to commonly dry subjects, such as biography, history, maths, science, etc. Not interested in board books, flap books or other novelty formats; books intended mainly as resources for teachers and librarians; genre or series fiction such as mystery, fantasy, historical (fiction should stand out first as excellent literature).

Scott Foresman
One Lake Street, Upper Saddle River, NJ 07458
tel 201-236-7000
email communications@pearsoned.com
Elementary educational publisher. Publishes high-quality teacher and student materials in all school disciplines: reading, science, mathematics, language arts, social studies, music, technology, and religion. Imprints include: Scott Foresman, Silver Burdett Ginn.
  Generations of children learned to read with the company's highly successful *Dick and Jane* series. The company's continued commitment to reading education is best exemplified with the *Scott Foresman Reading* and *Lectura Scott Foresman* programmes, available for K–Grade 6 students. Part of Pearson Education. Founded 1896.

Silver Moon Press
160 Fifth Avenue, New York, New York 10010
tel 800-874-3320 *fax* 212-242-6799
email customerservice@silvermoonpress.com
website www.silvermoonpress.com
Children's book publisher: test preparation, science, multiculture, biographies, historical fiction. Recent series successes include *Stories of the States*, *Mysteries in Time* and *Adventures in America* series.

Simon & Schuster Children's Publishing Division*
1230 Avenue of the Americas, New York, NY 10020
tel 212-698-7200 *fax* 212-698-2793

website www.simonsayskids.com
President Rick Richter

Preschool to young adult, fiction and non-fiction, trade, library and mass market. Imprints: Aladdin Paperbacks, Atheneum Books for Young Readers, Libros para niños, Little Simon, Little Simon Inspirations, Margaret K. McElderry Books, Simon & Schuster Books for Young Readers, Simon Scribbles, Simon Pulse, Simon Spotlight. Division of Simon & Schuster, Inc. Founded 1924.

Aladdin Paperbacks (imprint)
Vice-President & Associate Publisher Ellen Krieger, *Executive Editor* Jen Klonsky, *Editorial Director* Julia Richardson

Reprints successful hardcovers from other Simon & Schuster imprints (primarily). Recent successes include the *Pendragon* series and *Edgar & Ellen* series.

Submission details Accepts query letters with proposals for middle-grade series and single-title fiction, beginning readers, middle-grade and commercial non-fiction. Send MSS for the attention of the Submissions Editor. Send artwork submissions to Debra Sfetsios.

Atheneum Books for Young Readers (imprint)
Vice-President & Editorial Director Emma Dryden, *Editorial Director* Ginnee Seo, *Executive Editors* Justin Chanda, Caitlyn Dlouhy

Picture books, chapter books, mysteries, biography, science fiction, fantasy, graphic novels, middle-grade and young adult fiction and non-fiction. Covers preschool–young adult. Publishes 20–30 picture books, 4–5 young readers, 20–25 middle readers and 10–15 young adult books each year. Successes include *Inexcusable* by Chris Lynch, *Once Upon a Time, the End (Asleep in 60 Seconds)* by Geoffrey Kloske and Barry Blittt, *Click Clack Quackity-Quack* by Doreen Cronin and Betsy Lewin, and *Kira-Kira* by Cynthia Kadohata. Includes Ginnee Seo Books and Richard Jackson Books.

Submission details Approx. 10% of books are by first-time authors. No unsolicited MSS. Send query letter only. Responds in one month. For illustrations, send résumé, samples and tearsheets to Ann Bobco, Design Dept.

Margaret K. McElderry Books (imprint)
Vice-President & Associate Publisher Emma Dryden, *Executive Editor* Karen Wojtyla

Picture books, easy-to-read books, fiction (8–12 year-olds, young adult), poetry, fantasy. Covers preschool–young adult. Publishes 10–12 pciture books, 2–4 young reader titles, 8–10 middle reader titles, 5–7 young adult books each year. Recent successes include *Bear Stays Up for Christmas* by Karma Wilson and Jane Chapman, *The Water Mirror* by Kai Meyer, *Freaks* by Annette Curtis Klause, and *Where Did They Hide My Presents: Silly Dilly Christmas Songs* by Alan Katz and David Catrow.

Submission details Approx. 10% of books are by first-time authors. No unsolicited MSS. Fiction

length: picture books – 500 words; young readers – 2000; middle readers – 10,000–20,000; young adult – 45,000–50,000. Non-fiction length: picture books – 500–1000 words; young readers – 1500–3000 words; middle readers – 10,000–20,000 words; young adult – 30,000–45,000 words. For illustrations, query with samples to Ann Bobco, Executive Art Director. Responds in 3 months. Samples returned with sase.

Simon Pulse Paperback Books (imprint)
Associate Publisher Bethany Buck, *Senior Editor* Michelle Nagler

Young adult series and fiction (primarily) and some reprints of successful hardcovers from other Simon & Schuster imprints. Recent successes include the *Uglies* trilogy by Scott Westerfield and the *Au Pair* books by Melissa de la Cruz.

Submission details Accepts query letters. Send MSS for the attention of the Submission Editor. Send artwork submissions to Russel Gordon.

Simon & Schuster Books for Young Readers (imprint)
Vice-President & Associate Publisher Elizabeth Law, *Editorial Director* David Gale, *Executive Editor* Kevin Lewis

Fiction and non-fiction, all ages. Recent successes include the *Pendragon* series including *The Rivers of Zadaa* by D.J. MacHale, *Arthur Spiderwick's Field Guide to the Fantastical World Around You* by Tony DiTerlizzi and Holly Black, and *And Tango Makes Three* by Pete Parnell, Justin Richardson and Henry Cole.

Submission details No unsolicited MSS. Send query letter only. Responds to queries in 2 months. Seeking young adult novels that are challenging and psychologically complex; also imaginative and humorous middle-grade fiction.

Paula Wiseman (imprint)
email paulawiseman@simonandschuster.com
Vice-President & Editorial Director Paula Wiseman

Picture books, fiction and non-fiction. Publishes 10 picture books, 2 middle readers and 2 young adult titles each year. Recent successes include *Double Pink* by Kate Feiffer and the *Amelia Notebook* series by Marissa Moss.

Submission details Approx. 10% of books are by first-time authors. Submit complete MSS. Length: picture books – 500 words; others standard length. Considers all categories of fiction. Will review MS/illustration packages from artists. Send MS with dummy.

Sterling Publishing Co., Inc.
387 Park Avenue South, New York, NY 10016
tel 212-532-7160
website www.sterlingpublishing.com
President/Ceo Charles G. Nurnberg

Adult non-fiction and children's board books, picture books, juvenile fiction and non-fiction. Juvenile non-fiction includes: crafts, hobbies, games, activities, origami, optical illusions, mazes, dot-to-dots, science experiments, puzzles (maths/word/picture/logic), chess, card games and tricks, sports, magic. Fiction in the following categories only: riddles and jokes, ghost stories, mystery and detective short stories. Recent successes include *Sometimes I Like to Curl Up in a Ball* by by Vicki Churchill and Charles Fuge and *I Know a Rhino* by Charles Fuge.

Submission details Accepts children's fiction only in those categories listed above. For non-fiction write explaining the idea and enclose an outline and a sample chapter of the proposed book. Include information a bio with regard to the subject area and your publishing history, and a sase if you wish your material to be returned. No email submissions. Submissions should be sent FAO Children's Book Editor. Founded in 1949.

Gareth Stevens Publishing

330 West Olive Street, Suite 100, Milwaukee, WI 53212
tel 414-332-3520 *fax* 414-332-3567
email info@gspub.com
website www.garethstevens.com
Publisher Robert Famighetti, *Art Director* Tammy Guenewald, *Production Director* Jessica Morris, *Creative Director* Mark Sachner

Educational books and high-quality fiction for 4–16 year-olds. Subjects include atlases and reference, arts and crafts, emergent readers, nature, science, social studies, history and Spanish/bilingual. Publishes approx. 300 new titles each year and has over 100 in print. Part of WRC Media Inc. Founded 1983.

Ten Speed Press

PO Box 7123, Berkeley, CA 94707
tel 510-559-1600 *fax* 510-524-1052
email order@tenspeed.com
website www.tenspeed.com
President Philip Wood, *Publisher* Lorena Jones

Career/business, cooking, practical non-fiction, health, women's interest, self-help, children's. Founded 1971.

Tricycle Press (division)
Publisher Nicole Geiger

Children's picture books, activity books, fiction and non-fiction. Subjects include arts and crafts, folktales and multicultural, history, language arts, cooking, life lessons and social skills, maths, science, nature. Recent successes include *Pretend Soup* by Mollie Katzen, *Don't Laugh at Me* by Steve Seskin and illustrated by Glin Dibley, *G is for Googol* by David M. Schwartz and illustrated by Marissa Moss and *Hey, Little Ant* by Phillip and Hannah Hoose and illustrated by Debbie Tilley. Founded 1993.

Thomson Gale*

15822 Bernardo Center Drive, Suite C, San Diego, CA 92127

tel 858-485-7474 *fax* 858-485-9542
website www.gale.com
Executive Vice President Dedria Bryfonski

Serves information and education needs through its vast content pools, which are used by students and consumers in their libraries, schools and on the internet. Listed below are its children's imprints serving the 4–12 market. Part of The Thomson Corporation.

Greenhaven Press (imprint)
website www.thomson.com/greenhaven
Senior Acquisitions Editor Chandra Howard

High-quality non-fiction resources for the education community. Publishes 300 young adult academic reference titles each year. Recent successes include the *Opposing Viewpoints* series. Founded 1970.

Submission details Approx. 35% of books are by first-time authors. No unsolicited MSS. All writing is done on a work-to-hire basis. Send query, résumé and list of published works.

KidHave Press (imprint)
website wwwl.gale.com/kidhaven

Non-fiction references for younger researchers.

Lucent Books (imprint)
email chandra.howard@thomson.com
website www.gale.com/lucent
Senior Acquisitions Editor Chandra Howard

Non-fiction resources for upper-elementary to high school students. Recent successes include *Women in the American Revolution* and *Civil Liberties and the War on Terrorism*.

Submission details No unsolicited MSS. Query with résumé.

Tor Books

175 Fifth Avenue, 14th Floor, New York, NY 10010
tel 212-388-0100 *fax* 212-388-0191
website www.tor.com

Fiction and non-fiction for middle readers and young adults. Publishes 5–10 middle readers and 5–10 young adult books each year. Recent successes include *Hidden Talents, Flip* by David Lubar (fantasy, ages 10+), *Briar Rose* by Jane Yolen (fiction, age 12+), *Strange Unsolved Mysteries* by Phyllis Rabin Amert (non-fiction). For adults: fiction – general, historical, western, suspense, mystery, horror, science fiction, fantasy, humour, juvenile, classics (English language); non-fiction. Affiliate of Holtzbrinck Publishers. Founded 1980.

Submission details For both fiction and non-fiction, submit outline/synopsis and complete MS. Responds to queries in one month; MSS in 6 months for unsolicited work. Fiction length: middle readers – 30,000 words; young adult – 60,000–100,000 words. Non-fiction length: middle readers – 25,000–35,000 words; young adult – 70,000 words. For illustrations, query with samples to Irene Gallo, Art Director. Responds only if interested.

Tricycle Press – see Ten Speed Press

Twenty-first Century Books – see
Millbrook Press

Two-Can Publishing
T & N Children's Publishing, 11571 K-Tel Drive,
Minnetonka, MN 55343
tel 952-933-7537 *fax* 952-933-3630
website www.two-canpublishing.com

Non-fiction books and multimedia products to
entertain and educate 2–12 year-olds. Imprint of
T & N Children's Publishing.

Viking Children's Books – see Penguin
Putnam Books for Young Readers

VSP Books
PO Box 17011, Alexandria, VA 22302
tel 703-684-8142 *fax* 703-684-7955
email mail@vspbooks.com
website www.vspbooks.com

Educational books for children about special and
historic places. Recent successes inlcude the *Mice
Way to Learn* series and *Heartsongs* (poetry).
Founded 1992.

Walker & Co.
104 Fifth Avenue, New York, NY 10011
tel 212-727-8300 *fax* 212-727-0984
website www.walkerbooks.com,
www.walkeryoungreaders.com
Publisher Emily Easton

Picture books, non-fiction and fiction (middle grade
and young adult). Publishes 20 picture books, 2–4
middle readers and 2–4 young adult books each year.
Recent successes include *Testing Miss Malarkey* by
Judy Finchler and Kevin O'Malley and *Stella the Star*
by Mark Shulman and Vincent Nguyen. General
publishers for adults: biography, popular science,
health, business, mystery, history. Founded 1960;
acquired by Bloomsbury USA 2004.
   Submission details Approx. 5% of books are by
first-time authors. Approx. 65% of books are
acquired via literary agents. Particularly interested in
picture books, illustrated non-fiction, middle grade
and young adult fiction. No series ideas. Send
50–75pp and synopsis for longer works; send the
entire MSS for picture books. Include sase for return
of material.

Frederick Warne – see Penguin Putnam Books
for Young Readers

Franklin Watts – see Scholastic Education

Weigl Publishers Inc.
350 5th Avenue, Suite 3304, New York,
NY 10118–0069

tel 866-649-3445 *fax* 866-449-3445
email info@weigl.com
website www.weigl.com

Educational publisher: non-fiction titles only. Recent
successes include *My Favorite Writer* series and
Natural Wonders series.

Albert Whitman & Company
6340 Oakton Street, Morton Grove,
Illinois 60053–2723
tel 847-581-0033 *fax* 847-581-0039
email mail@awhitmanco.com
website www.albertwhitman.com

Children's books.
   Submission details Interested in reviewing the
following: picture book MSS for ages 2–8; novels and
chapter books for ages 8–12. Currently not seeking
MS for the *Boxcar Children® Mysteries* series. For
picture books send complete MS; for longer works
send a query letter with 3 sample chapters. Also
interested in art samples showing pictures of
children. Founded 1919.

John Wiley & Sons Inc.*
111 River Street, Hoboken, NJ 07030
tel 201-748-6000 *fax* 201-748-6088
email info@wiley.com
website www.wiley.com
President/Ceo William J. Pesce

Specialises in scientific and technical books and
journals, textbooks and educational materials for
colleges and universities, as well as professional and
consumer books and subscription services. Subjects
include business, computer science, electronics,
engineering, environmental studies, reference books,
science, social sciences, multimedia, and trade
paperbacks. Founded 1807.

Wiley Children's Division
General K–12, K–12 teaching and learning, history,
cooking, parenting. Recent successes include *Secrets of
Ancient Cultures: The Inca: Activities and Crafts from a
Mysterious Land* by Arlette N. Braman, *The Complete
Handbook of Science Fair Projects* by Julianne Blair
Bochinski and *The United States Cookbook: Fabulous
Foods and Fascinating Facts From All 50 States* by Joan
D'Amico and Karen Eich Drummond.

Wordsong – see Boyds Mills Press

Workman Publishing Company
708 Broadway, New York, NY 10003–9555
tel 212-254-5900 *fax* 212-254-8098
email info@workman.com
website www.workman.com

Adult and juvenile books: art and architecture,
biography and memoirs, BRAIN QUEST®, business,
children's, cooking, food and wine, crafts, fiction,
gardening, gift books, health, history, home

reference/how-to, humour, film and TV, music, parenting and families, pets and animals, poetry, science, sport, travel. Founded 1968.

World Book, Inc.

233 North Michigan Avenue, Suite 2000, Chicago, Illinois 60601

tel 312-729-5800 *fax* 312-729-5600

Encyclopedias, reference sources, and multimedia products for the home and schools, including *World Book*. Recent publications include *World Book Student Discovery Encyclopedia*, a new *Childcraft – The How and Why Library* and *Animals of the World*. Founded 1917.

Children's audio publishers

Many of the audio publishers listed below are also publishers of books.

Abbey Home Entertainment plc
435–437 Edgware Road, London W2 1TH
tel 020-7563 3910 *fax* 020-7563 3911
Contact Anne Miles

Specialises in the acquisition, production and distribution of quality audio/visual entertainment for children. Bestselling children's spoken word and music titles are available on CD and cassette in the Tempo range including *Postman Pat*, *Watership Down*, *Michael Rosen*, *Baby Bright*, *Wide Eye*, *SuperTed* and *Golden Nursery Rhymes*.

Barefoot Books Ltd
124 Walcot Street, Bath BA1 5BG
tel (01225) 322400 *fax* (01225) 322499
email info@barefootbooks.co.uk
website www.barefootbooks.co.uk
Publisher Tessa Stickland, *Group Project Manager* Emma Parkin

Narrative unabridged audiobooks, spoken and sung. Established 1993.

Barrington Stoke
18 Walker Street, Edinburgh EH3 7LP
tel 0131-225 4113 *fax* 0131-225 4140
email info@barringtonstoke.co.uk
website www.barringtonstoke.co.uk
Chairman David Croom, *Managing Director* Sonia Raphael, *Editorial Manager* Kate Paice

Cassette tapes accompanied by 2 books: *Virtual Friends* and *Virtual Friends Again* by Mary Hoffman, *Problems with a Python* and *Living with Vampires* by Jeremy Strong, *Tod in Biker City* and *Bicycle Blues* by Anthony Masters, *Hat Trick* and *Ghost for Sale* by Terry Deary. Limited output. Founded 1998.

BBC Audio – Children's
St James House, The Square, Lower Bristol Road, Bath BA2 3BH
tel (01225) 335336 *fax* (01225) 310771
email bbcaudiobooks@bbc.co.uk
website www.bbcshopcom
Managing Director Paul Dempsey, *Publishing Director* Jan Paterson, *Children's Commissioning Editor* Kate Walsh

Spoken word entertainment for parents and children, from preschool nursery rhymes to modern classics such as *The Chronicles of Narnia* and *His Dark Materials* trilogy by Philip Pullman. Imprint of BBC Audiobooks Ltd. Other children's imprints include: Chivers Children's Audiobooks. Formed in 2003 from the amalgamation of Chivers Press, Cover To Cover and BBC Radio Collection.

BBC Cover to Cover
St James House, The Square, Lower Bristol Road, Bath BA2 3BH
tel (01225) 878000 *fax* (01225) 310771
website www.bbcaudiobooks.com

Unabridged children's bestselling titles. List includes readings of stories by today's major children's authors, such as Philip Pullman, Eoin Colfer and Jacqueline Wilson. Imprint of BBC Audiobooks Ltd.

Bloomsbury Publishing Plc
36 Soho Square, London W1D 3QY
tel 020-7494 2111 *fax* 020-7734 8656
website www.bloomsbury.com
Contact Sarah Odedina

A broad selection of fiction and non-fiction. Baby books, picture books and fiction for children of all ages.

Bolinda Publishing Ltd
2 Ivanhoe Road, London SE5 8DH
tel 020-7733 1088
email marisa@bolinda.com
website www.bolinda.com
UK Publisher Marisa McGreevy

CDs and cassettes of children's, teenage and adult fiction titles. Based in Melbourne, Australia; established in the UK in 2003.

Chivers Children's Audiobooks
St James House, The Square, Lower Bristol Road, Bath BA2 3BH
tel (01225) 878000 *fax* (01225) 310771
website www.bbcaudiobooks.com

Both the adult and children's lists feature current bestselling fiction and popular classics by some of Britain and the USA's best authors, read by some of the world's most celebrated actors. In addition, there is an extensive monthly programme of titles available on CD. Chivers Press pioneered the recording of complete and unabridged books with the first titles being published in 1980 and it now has a backlist in excess of 3000 titles ranged from 2-cassette to 16-cassette formats. Imprint of BBC Audiobooks Ltd.

Cló Iar-Chonnachta Teo.
Indreabhán, Conamara, Co. Galway, Republic of Ireland
tel (091) 593307 *fax* (091) 593362
email cic@iol.ie
website www.cic.ie
Ceo Micheál Ó Conghaile, *General Manager* Deirdre O'Toole

Predominantly Irish-language children's books with accompanying CD/cassette of stories/folklore/poetry. Established 1985.

CSA Word

6A Archway Mews, London SW15 2PE
tel 020-8871 0220 *fax* 020-8877 0712
email info@csaword.co.uk
website www.csaword.co.uk
Managing Director Clive Stanhope, *Audio Director* Victoria Williams

CDs and cassettes of classic children's literature such as *Just William*, *Billy Bunter* and *Black Beauty*; also adult, classic and current literary authors. Founded 1991.

Dref Wen

28 Church Road, Whitchurch, Cardiff CF14 2EA
tel 029-2061 7860 *fax* 029-2061 0507
Directors Roger Boore, Anne Boore, Gwilym Boore, Alun Boore

Welsh language audiobooks. Founded 1970.

The Educational Company of Ireland

Ballymount Road, Walkinstown, Dublin 12, Republic of Ireland
tel (01) 4500611 *fax* (01) 4500993
email info@edco.ie
website www.edco.ie
Executive Directors Frank Maguire (chief executive), R. McLoughlin, *Financial Controller* A. Harrold, *Sales & Marketing Manager* M. Harford-Hughes, *Publisher* Frank Fahy

Irish language CDs and audiotapes. Trading unit of Smurfit Ireland Ltd. Founded 1910.

HarperCollins Audio

77–85 Fulham Palace Road, London W6 8JB
tel 020-8741 7070 *fax* 020-8307 4517
website www.harpercollins.co.uk
Editorial Nicola Townsend

Publishers of a wide range of genres including fiction, non-fiction, poetry, Classics, Shakespeare, comedy, personal development and children's. All works are read by famous actors. Established 1990.

Hodder Headline Audiobooks

338 Euston Road, London NW1 3BH
tel 020-7873 6000 *fax* 020-7873 6024

Publishes outstanding authors from within the Hodder Headline group and from elsewhere. The list is made up of quality non-fiction; fiction, from John le Carré to Louis de Bernieres to Ardal O'Hanlon; WHSmith's Classic Collection; self-help titles from authors such as Susan Jeffers and Richard Carlson; religious titles; children's (i.e. the highly acclaimed dramatised *Winnie the Pooh*); sporting autobiographies including Alex Ferguson, Brian Moore and Dickie Bird; comedy titles such as *Wallace*

& Gromit and the *Magic Roundabout Adventures*, bestselling collaborations with Classic FM; Derek Jacobi's acclaimed readings of the *Brother Cadfael* mysteries, and C.S. Forester's *Hornblower* novels read by Ioan Gruffudd. Founded 1994.

Ladybird Books

80 Strand, London WC2R 0RL
tel 020-7010 3000 *fax* 020-7010 6707
Marketing Director Rachel Partridge

Ladybird Books in book-and-CD format for children aged 0–8 years, including nursery rhymes, fairytales and classic stories as well as licensed character publishing.

Macmillan Audio Books

20 New Wharf Road, London N1 9RR
tel 020-7014 6040 *fax* 020-7014 6023
email a.muirden@macmillan.co.uk
website www.panmacmillan.com
Audio Publisher Alison Muirden

Children's book and tape packs include *The Gruffalo*, *Room on the Broom* and *The Smartest Giant in Town* by Julia Donaldson and Axel Scheffler. Also adult fiction, non-fiction and autobiography. Publishes approx. 20 titles each year and has 80+ available. Established 1995.

Naxos AudioBooks

18 High Street, Welwyn, Herts. AL6 9EQ
tel (01438) 717808 *fax* (01438) 717809
email naxos_audiobooks@compuserve.com
website www.naxosaudiobooks.com
Managing Director Nicolas Soames

Classic literature, modern fiction, non-fiction, drama and poetry on CD. Also junior classics and classical music. Founded 1994.

The Orion Publishing Group Ltd

5 Upper St Martin's Lane, London WC2H 9EA
tel 020-7520 4425 *fax* 020-7379 6158
email pandora.white@orionbooks.co.uk
Audio Manager Pandora White

Adult and children's fiction and non-fiction. Established 1998.

Penguin Audiobooks

Penguin Books Ltd, 80 Strand, London WC2R 0RL
tel 020-7010 3000
email audio@penguin.co.uk
website www.penguin.co.uk/audio
Audio Publisher Jeremy Ettinghausen

The audiobooks list reflects the diversity of the Penguin book range, including classic and contemporary fiction and non-fiction, autobiography, poetry, drama and, in Puffin Audiobooks, the best of contemporary and classic literature for younger listeners. Authors include Nick Hornby, Sue Townsend, Seamus Heaney, Roald Dahl and Eoin Colfer. Readings are by talented and recognisable actors. Over 500 titles are now available. Founded 1993.

Puffin Audiobooks – see Penguin Audiobooks

SmartPass Ltd
15 Park Road, Rottingdean, Brighton BN2 7HL
tel (01273) 300742
email info@smartpass.co.uk
website www.smartpass.co.uk,
www.spaudiobooks.com
Managing Director Phil Viner, *Creative Director* Jools Viner

SmartPass audio guides present English literature texts for Key Stage 3, SATS and GCSE as full-cast dramas with an educational twist. The *PassMaster* comments, explains and explores the novel, play or poetry, as well as its background in history and in society. Includes dramatised debate and discussion to tease out information about themes, the author's biography and study strategies. Publishes approx. 3 titles each year and has 13 available.

SPAudiobooks: the first full-cast unabridged drama has been released, read by the author with fully dramatised dialogue. Established 1999.

Usborne Publishing Ltd
Usborne House, 83–85 Saffron Hill, London EC1N 8RT
tel 020-7430 2800 *fax* 020-7430 1562
email mail@usborne.co.uk

website www.usborne.com
Publishing Director Jenny Tyler, *General Manager* Robert Jones

First Book of the Piano with CD for 5–7 year-olds.
Founded 1973.

Walker Books Ltd
87 Vauxhall Walk, London SE11 5HJ
tel 020-7793 0909 *fax* 020-7587 1123
Publisher Lorraine Taylor

Audiobooks include bestselling fiction titles such as the *Alex Rider* series, *Judy Moody* and *Confessions of a Teenage Drama Queen*. For younger children, the *Listen and Join In* audio range comprises entertaining story-based activities based on favourite picture books, including *We're Going on a Bear Hunt*, *Guess How Much I Love You* and *Can't You Sleep Little Bear?*

Walking Oliver
The Manning Partnership Ltd, 6 The Old Dairy, Melcombe Road, Bath BA2 3LR
tel (01225) 478444 *fax* (01225) 478440
email sales@manning-partnership.co.uk
website www.manning-partnership.co.uk

Managing Director Garry Manning, *Sales Director* Rober Hibbert

Committed to producing traditional yet innovative music for children that is fun, enriching and of the highest quality. Features world-renowned tenor Paul Austin Kelly. Established 2003.

Children's book packagers

Many modern illustrated books are created by book packagers, whose special skills are in the areas of book design and graphic content. In-house editors match up the expertise of specialist writers, artists and photographers who usually work on a freelance basis.

Aladdin Books Ltd
2–3 Fitzroy Mews, London W1T 6DF
tel 020-7383 2084 fax 020-7388 6391
email firstname.surname@aladdinbooks.co.uk
website www.aladdinbooks.co.uk
Directors Charles Nicholas, Bibby Whittaker

Full design and book packaging facility specialising in children's non-fiction and reference. Founded 1980.

The Albion Press Ltd
Spring Hill, Idbury, Oxon OX7 6RU
tel (01993) 831094 fax (01993) 831982
Directors Emma Bradford (managing), Neil Philip (editorial)

Produces quality integrated illustrated titles from the initial idea to the printed copy. Specialises in children's books: poetry, fairy tales, myths, Native Americans. Produces 4 titles each year. Founded 1984.
Submission details Will not consider unsolicited MSS. Interested in seeing fine samples of illustrations but no cartoons or technical drawings. Include an sae.

Amber Books Ltd
Bradley's Close, 74–77 White Lion Street, London N1 9PF
tel 020-7520 7600 fax 020-7520 7606/7607
email enquiries@amberbooks.co.uk
website www.amberbooks.co.uk
Managing Director Stasz Gnych, Deputy Managing Director Sara Ballard, Publishing Manager Charles Catton, Head of Production Peter Thompson, Design Manager Mark Batley, Picture Manager Terry Forshaw

Illustrated non-fiction. Subject areas include history, military technology, aviation, transport, sport, crime, music, natural history, encyclopedias and children's books. Opportunities for freelances. Imprints: Brown Books Ltd. Founded 1989.

Nicola Baxter
PO Box 215, Framingham Earl, Yelverton, Norwich NR14 7UR
tel (01508) 491111
email nb@nicolabaxter.co.uk
website www.nicolabaxter.co.uk
Proprietor, Commissioning Editor & Author Nicola Baxter, Design Manager Amy Barton, Submissions Sally Delaney

Full packaging service for children's books, from concept to film or any part of the process in between.

Produces both fiction and non-fiction titles in a wide range of formats, from board books to encyclopedias. Experienced in novelty books and licensed publishing. Opportunities for freelances. Founded 1990.

Bender Richardson White
PO Box 266, Uxbridge, Middlesex UB9 5NX
tel (01895) 832444 fax (01895) 835213
email brw@brw.co.uk
website www.brw.co.uk
Directors Lionel Bender (editorial), Kim Richardson (sales & production), Ben White (design)

Design, editorial and production of activity books, non-fiction and reference books. Specialises in non-fiction: natural history, science, history and educational. Packages approx. 60–70 titles each year. Founded 1990.
Submission details Writers should send a letter and synopsis of their proposal. Opportunities for freelances.

The Book Guild Ltd
Temple House, 25 High Street, Lewes, East Sussex BN7 2LU
tel (01273) 472534 fax (01273) 476472
email info@bookguild.co.uk
website www.bookguild.co.uk
Directors G.M. Nissen CBE (chairman), Carol Biss (managing), Anthony Nissen, Paul White (financial), Janet Wrench (production)

Fiction for 5–8 and 9–12 year-olds. Produces approx. 10 children's titles each year. Offers a range of publishing options: a comprehensive package for authors incorporating editorial, design, production, marketing, publicity and distribution; editorial and production only for authors requiring private editions; or a complete service for companies and organisations requiring books for internal or promotional purposes – from brief to finished book. Founded 1982.
Submission details Write for submission information.

Book Street Ltd
Foresters Hall, 25–27 Westow Street, London SE19 3RY
tel 020-8771 5115 fax 020-8771 9994
email graham@bwj-ltd.com

Designers and packagers of large format children's books for the international market.

Bookwork Ltd

Unit 17, Piccadilly Mill, Lower Street, Stroud, Glos.
GL5 2HT
tel (01453) 752521 *fax* (01453) 751544
email bookwork@compuserve.com
Directors Louise Pritchard (editorial), Alan Plank
(production), Jill Plank (design), *Editor* Annabel
Blackledge, *Art Editor* Kate Mullins

Creates innovative books for children of all ages:
activity books, board books, picture books, how-to
books, reference books. Also supplies a full editorial
and design service to other publishers. Imprint:
Pangolin.

Brainwaves Ltd

31 Chart Lane, Reigate, Surrey RH2 7DY
tel (01737) 224444 *fax* (01737) 225777
Editorial Director Keith Faulkner

Packager of activity books, board books, novelty
books, picture books, pop-up books and gift books.

Breslich & Foss Ltd

2ᴀ Union Court, 20–22 Union Road, London
SW4 6JP
tel 020-7819 3990 *fax* 020-7819 3998
Directors Paula G. Breslich, K.B. Dunning

Books produced from MS to bound copy stage from
in-house ideas. Specialising in crafts, interiors, health
and beauty, children's non-fiction. Founded 1978.

John Brown Junior

The New Boathouse, 136–142 Bramley Road, London
W10 6SR
tel 020-7565 3000 *fax* 020-7565 3060
email info@jbjunior.com
website www.jbjunior.com
Directors Andrew Jarvis (operations), Sara Lynn
(creative)

Creative development and packaging of children's
products including books, magazines, partworks, CD-
Roms and websites.

The Brown Reference Group Plc

8 Chapel Place, Rivington Street, London EC2A 3DQ
tel 020-7920 7500 *fax* 020-7920 7501
email info@brownreference.com
website www.brownreference.com
Managing Director Sharon Hutton, *Children's
Publisher* Anne O'Daly

Specialises in high-quality illustrated reference books
and multi-volume sets for trade and educational
markets. Opportunities for freelances. Founded 1989.

Brown Wells & Jacobs Ltd

Foresters Hall, 25–27 Westow Street, London
SE19 3RY
tel 020-8771 5115 *fax* 020-8771 9994
email graham@bwj-ltd.com

website www.bwj.org
Director Graham Brown

Design, editorial, illustration and production of high-
quality non-fiction illustrated children's books.
Specialities include pop-up and novelty books.
Packages approx. 30–40 titles each year. Founded
1979.
Submission details Opportunities for freelances.

Cambridge Publishing Management Ltd

Unit 2, Burr Elm Court, Main Street, Caldecote,
Cambs. CB3 7NU
tel (01954) 214000 *fax* (01954) 214001
email initial.surname@cambridgepm.co.uk
website www.cambridgepm.co.uk
Managing Director Jackie Dobbyne, *Managing Editor*
Karen Beaulah

Creative and highly skilled editorial and book
production company specialising in complete project
management of business, education, ELT, travel and
illustrated non-fiction titles, from MS to delivery of
final files on disk. Opportunities for freelances; send
CV to Managing Editor. Founded 1999.

Cowley Robinson Publishing Ltd

(incorporating David Hawcock Books)
8 Belmont, Bath BA1 5DZ
tel (01225) 339999 *fax* (01225) 339995
website www.cowleyrobinson.com
Directors Stewart Cowley (publishing), Rob Kendrew
(production), David Hawcock

Specialises in children's novelty and paper-engineered
formats for international co-editions. Licence and
character publishing developments. Information and
early learning. Imprint: Whizz Kids. Founded 1998.

Creations for Children International

Steenweg op Deinze 150, 9810 Nazareth, Belgium
tel (9) 2446090 *fax* (9) 2446099
email info@c4ci.com, jan.meeuws@c4ci.com,
marc.jomgbloet@inkypress.com
website www.c4ci.com, www.inkypress.com
Directors Marc Barbier (business & sales), Marc
Jambloet (book publishing & sales), *Production
Manager* Joost Demuynck, *Chief Editor* Mr Jan
Meeuws

Packagers of high-quality mass market children's
illustrated books, including fairy tale and classic
adventure story books. Activity books, board books,
colouring books, pop-up books, novelty books,
picture books and non-fiction books. Acquired Inky
Press in 2005.

Design Eye Ltd

226 City Road, London EC1V 2TT
tel 020-7700 9000 *fax* 020-7812 8601
email sueg@quarto.com, geoffs@quarto.com
Publisher Sue Grabham, *Art Director* Geoff Sida

Co-edition publisher of innovative Books-Plus for
children and adults. Children's: highly illustrated

paper-engineered, novelty and component-based titles for all ages, but primarily children's preschool (3+), 5–8 and 8+ years. Mainly non-fiction, early concepts and curriculum-based topics for the trade in all international markets. Adults: highly illustrated component-based kits and books for arts, crafts, lifestyle and hobbies. Opportunities for freelance paper engineers, artists, authors, editors and designers. Founded 1988.

Elm Grove Books Ltd

Elm Grove, Henstridge, Somerset BA8 0TQ
tel (01963) 362498
email hugh@elmgrovebooks.com,
susie@elmgrovebooks.com
Directors Hugh Elwes, Susie Elwes

Packager of children's books. Opportunities for freelances. Founded 1993.

Graham-Cameron Publishing & Illustration

The Studio, 23 Holt Road, Sheringham, Norfolk NR26 8NB
tel (01263) 821333 *fax* (01263) 821334
email enquiry@graham-cameron-illustration.com
and Duncan Graham-Cameron, 59 Redvers Road, Brighton BN2 4BF
tel (01273) 385890
website www.graham-cameron-illustration.com
Partners Mike Graham-Cameron, Helen Graham-Cameron, Duncan Graham-Cameron

Offers illustration and editorial services for picture books and educational materials. Handles activity books, picture books, fiction for 5–8 and 9–12 year-olds, non-fiction, reference and poetry. Illustration agency with 37 artists. No unsolicited MSS. Founded 1985.

Gusto

PO Box 4, 1393 Vollen, Norway
tel (47) 22 43 4005 *fax* (47) 85 03 4316
email accounts@gusto.tv
website www.gusto.tv
Art Director Jan Chr. Danielsen

Packager of gift books, children's books, cookbooks and handbooks. Children's books include *Jeff the Chef*, *Funnymals* and *Men at Work*. Board books, novelty books, picture books and how-to books. Based in Norway. Established in 2000 as SmallWorld Publishing; renamed Gusto in 2004.

Hart McLeod Ltd

14 Greenside, Waterbeach, Cambridge CB5 9HP
tel (01223) 861495 *fax* (01223) 862902
email inhouse@hartmcleod.co.uk
website www.hartmcleod.co.uk
Directors Graham Hart, Chris McLeod, Joanne Barker

Primarily educational and general non-fiction with particular expertise in revision books, school texts,

ELT and electronic content. Opportunities for freelances and work experience. Founded 1985.

Hawcock Books

Grafton House, High Street, Norton St Philip, Nr Bath BA2 7LG
tel (01373) 834055 *fax* (01373) 834622
email popupbooks@aol.com Hawcock
website http://hawcockbooks.co.uk

Company devoted to the design and production of highly creative and original pop-up art and 3D paper-engineered concepts. Most of its experience is in developing, providing editorial for, printing and manufacturing pop-up books and novelty items for the publishing industry. Also undertakes demanding commissions from the advertising world for model-making, point-of-sale and all printed 3D aspects of major campaigns.

HL Studios Ltd

17 Fenlock Court, Blenheim Office Park, Long Hanborough, Oxford OX29 8LN
tel (01993) 881010 *fax* (01993) 882713
email info@hlstudios.eu.com
website www.hlstudios.eu.com
Managing Director Robin Hickey

Primary, secondary academic education (geography, science, modern languages) and co-editions (travel guides, gardening, cookery). Multimedia (CD-Rom programming and animations). Opportunities for freelances. Founded 1985.

Inky Press – see Creations for Children International

Miles Kelly Packaging

The Bradfield Centre, Great Bardfield, Essex CM7 4SL
tel (01371) 811309 *fax* (01371) 811393
email info@mileskelly.net
website www.mileskelly.net
Directors Kelly Gerard, Jim Miles, Kate Miles

Offers a complete packaging service from conception through to finished copies of high-quality illustrated non-fiction titles for children and family. See also page 15. Founded 1996.

Little People Books

The Home of BookBod, Knighton, Radnorshire LD7 1UP
tel (01547) 520925
email littlepeoplebooks@thehobb.tv
website www.thehobb.tv/postings/000182.php
Directors Grant Jessé (production & managing), Helen Wallis (rights & finance)

Packager of audio, children's educational and textbooks, digital publications. Parent company: Grant Jessé UK.

Marshall Editions Ltd

The Old Brewery, 6 Blundell Street, London N7 9BH
tel 020-7700 6764 *fax* 020-7700 4191

email info@marshalleditions.com
Publisher Richard Green

Highly illustrated non-fiction for adults and children, including history, health, gardening, home design, pets, natural history, popular science.

Monkey Puzzle Media Ltd
Gissing's Farm, Fressingfield, Eye, Suffolk IP21 5SH
tel (01379) 588044 *fax* (01379) 588055
email info@monkeypuzzlemedia.com
Director Roger Goddard-Coote

Offers a full packaging service from concept or commission through to delivery of repro-ready disks or film. Specialises in children's non-fiction and reference. Produces approx. 60 titles each year. Founded 1998.

Submission details Will consider unsolicited MSS and copies of illustrations with an sae.

Orpheus Books Ltd
6 Church Green, Witney, Oxon OX28 4AW
tel (01993) 774949 *fax* (01993) 700330
email info@orpheusbooks.com
website www.orpheusbooks.com
Executive Director Nicholas Harris (editorial, design & marketing)

Produces children's non-fiction books for the international co-editions market: activity books, novelty books, non-fiction and reference. Produces approx. 8–20 titles each year. Founded 1993.

Submission details Welcomes samples from illustrators and CVs from writers.

Picthall & Gunzi Ltd
21A Widmore Road, Bromley BR1 1RW
tel 020-8460 4032 *fax* 020-8460 4021
email chez@picthallandgunzi.demon.co.uk, chris@picthallandgunzi.demon.co.uk
website www.picthallandgunzi.co.uk
Managing Director Chez Picthall, *Editorial Director & Publisher* Christiane Gunzi

Offers a complete package, from initial concept to publication, producing high-quality, illustrated non-fiction for children: early learning, novelty, activity, board books, non-fiction.

Pinwheel Ltd
Winchester House, 259–269 Old Marylebone Road, London NW1 5XJ
tel 020-7616 7200 *fax* 020-7616 7201
website www.pinwheel.co.uk
Directors Andrew Flatt (managing), Linda Cole (publishing), Paula Burgess (creative)

Packages unique and innovative children's books for the international market, across 3 imprints (see page 21).

Playne Books Ltd
Park Court Barn, Trefin, Haverfordwest, Pembrokeshire SA62 5AU

tel (01348) 837073 *fax* (01348) 837063
email playne.books@virgin.net
Design & Production Director David Playne, *Editor* Gill Davies

Specialises in highly illustrated adult non-fiction and books for very young children. All stages of production undertaken from initial concept (editorial, design and manufacture) to delivery of completed books. Include sae for return of work. Founded 1987.

Tony Potter Publishing Ltd
1 Stairbridge Court, Bolney Grange Business Park, Stairbridge Lane, Bolney, West Sussex RH17 5PA
tel (01444) 232889 *fax* (01444) 232142
email sheilamortimer@zoo.co.uk
website www.tonypotter.com
Directors Tony Potter (managing), Christine Potter, Sheila Mortimer

Creates custom children's book and own brand innovative paper-based products for children and adults. Also creates high-quality children's titles as a packager and occasionally publishes under its own imprint: Over the Moon. Opportunities for freelance designers and illustrators. Founded 1997.

The Puzzle House
Ivy Cottage, Battlesea Green, Stradbroke, Suffolk IP21 5NE
tel (01379) 384656 *fax* (01379) 384656
email puzzlehouse@btinternet.com
Partners Roy Preston and Sue Preston

Editorial service creating crossword, quiz, puzzle and activity material for all ages. Founded 1988.

Quarto Children's Books Ltd
226 City Road, London EC1V 2TT
tel 020-7700 9000 *fax* 020-7812 8601
email sueg@quarto.com, jonathang@quarto.com
Publisher Sue Grabham, *Art Director* Jonathan Gilbert

Co-edition publisher of innovative Books-Plus for children. Highly illustrated paper-engineered, novelty and component-based titles for all ages, but primarily preschool (3+), 5–8 and 8+ years. Mainly non-fiction, early concepts and curriculum-based topics for the trade in all international markets. Opportunities for freelance paper engineers, artists, authors, editors and designers.

Small World Design
72A Pope Lane, Penwortham, Preston, Lancs. PR1 9DA
tel (01772) 750885 *fax* (01772) 750885
email sue.chadwick@smallworlddesign.co.uk
website www.smallworlddesign.co.uk
Partners Sue Chadwick, David Peet

Offers a writing, illustration, design and packaging service for preschool material, books, novelty books, games, jigsaw puzzles, activity packs, licensed products, creative and educational products. Founded 1995.

Tangerine Designs Ltd

2 High Street, Freshford, Bath BA2 7WE
tel/fax (01225) 720001
email tangerinedesigns@btinternet.com
Managing Director Christine Swift

Packagers and co-edition publishers of children's books including novelty books and licensed titles. Submissions only accepted if sae is enclosed. Founded 2000.

Tango Books

PO Box 32595, London W4 5YD
tel 020-8996 9970 *fax* 020-8996 9977
email sheri@tangobooks.co.uk,
edith@tangobooks.co.uk
website www.tangobooks.co.uk
Directors Sheri Safran, David Fielder, *Submissions* Edith Fricker (*tel* 020-8996 9973)

Creates and produces international co-productions of children's novelty books only (touch-and-feel, flaps, pop-ups, foils, etc). No flat picture books. Produces mainly for the 0–6 age group but some for up to age 12. Books are highly visual with lots of illustrations and minimal text, except for non-fiction where there is scope for longer texts. Publishes in the UK under Tango. Founded 1983.

Submission details The max. word count for ages 0–6 is 750 words. Text should be for novelty format (repetition works well). No particularly British themes or characters. No poetry. Artwork: modern style, fresh and fun. Likes collage, bright and bold styles, pen and ink coloured in. Less keen on watercolour unless very special. Send submissions with sae for their return. Allow one month for reply.

The Templar Company plc

Pippbrook Mill, London Road, Dorking, Surrey RH4 1JE
tel (01306) 876361 *fax* (01306) 889097
email info@templarco.co.uk
website www.templarco.co.uk
Directors Amanda Wood, Ruth Huddleston, Elaine Hunt

High-quality children's gift, novelty, picture and illustrated information books; most titles aimed at international co-edition market. Established links with major co-publishers in USA, Australia and throughout Europe. Imprints: Templar Publishing, Amazing Baby.

TKC Design

105 Sladedale Road, London SE18 1PX
tel/fax 020-8855 7602
mobile (07973) 828923
email TracyCarrington@tkcdesign@aol.com
Contact Tracy Carrington

Packager for the international children's market in the 0–11 age group (fiction and non-fiction). Also promotional and marketing design for print. Offers a complete service from origination to print-ready disks. Also offers the creation of branding styles and design for new and existing licensed characters; concept development; project management including scheduling, budgeting and setting up teams for large-scale, multi-component projects; creative original and innovative design. Has a bank of experienced freelancers/consultants (authors, illustrators, designers and editorial services). Founded 2004.

Toucan Books Ltd

3rd Floor, 89 Charterhouse Street, London EC1M 6HR
tel 020-7250 3388 *fax* 020-7250 3123
website www.toucanbooks.co.uk
Directors Robert Sackville West, Ellen Dupont

International co-editions; editorial, design and production services. Founded 1985.

Emma Treehouse Ltd

Little Orchard House, Mill Lane, Beckington, Somerset BA11 6SN
tel (01373) 831215 *fax* (01373) 831216
email sales@emmatreehouse.com
website www.emmatreehouse.com
Directors David Bailey, Richard Powell (creative & editorial)

Specialist creator of novelty books for children aged 0–7: bath books, books with a sound concept, cloth books, novelty books, flap books, touch-and-feel books. Packager and co-edition publisher with international recognition for its innovative and often unique concepts. The company has produced over 30 million books, translated into 33 different languages. Opportunities for freelance artists. Founded 1992

Tucker Slingsby Ltd

5th Floor, Regal House, 70 London Road, Twickenham TW1 3QS
tel 020-8744 1007 *fax* 020-8744 0041
email firstname@tuckerslingsby.co.uk
Directors Janet Slingsby, Del Tucker

Highly illustrated adult and children's books and magazines from concept to delivery of film, disk or finished copies. Produces for preschool to teenage: annuals, activity books, novelty books, picture books, film/TV tie-ins, non-fiction, religion and reference. Produces approx. 100 titles each year. Founded 1992.

Submission details Opportunities for freelances and picture book artists. Submit by post.

David West Children's Books

7 Princeton Court, 55 Felsham Road, London SW15 1AZ
tel 020-8780 3836 *fax* 020-8780 9313
email dww@btinternet.com

website www.davidwestchildrensbooks.com
Proprietor David West, *Partner* Lynn Lockett

Packagers of children's illustrated reference books. Specialises in science, art, geography, history, sport and flight. Produces 40 titles each year. Opportunities for freelances. Founded 1986.

Working Partners Ltd

1 Albion Place, London W6 0QT
tel 020-8748 7477 *fax* 020-8748 7450
email enquiries@workingpartnersltd.co.uk
website www.workingpartnersltd.co.uk

Chairman Ben Baglio, *Managing Director* Chris Snowdon, *Creative Director* Rod Ritchie

Children's and young adult fiction series. Genres include: animal fiction, fantasy, horror, historical fiction, detective, magical, adventure. Recent successes include *Animal Ark*, *Rainbow Magic* and *My Secret Unicorn*.

Submission details Unable to accept any MS or illustration submissions. Pays advance and royalty; retains copyright on all work created. Selects writers from unpaid writing samples based on specific brief provided. Always looking to add writers to database: contact writers@workingpartnersltd.co.uk to register details. Founded 1995.

Children's book clubs

Not all the companies listed here are 'clubs' in the true sense: some are mail order operations and others sell their books via book fairs.

Baker Books
Manfield Park, Cranleigh, Surrey GU6 8NU
tel (01483) 267888 *fax* (01483) 267409
email bakerbooks@dial.pipex.com
website www.bakerbooks.co.uk

School book club for children aged 3–13. Operates in the UK and reaches English medium schools overseas.

BFC Books for Children
Greater London House, Hampstead Road, London NW1 7TZ
tel (0870) 165 0292 (customer services)
fax (0870) 165 0222
website www.booksforchildren.co.uk

Offers a wide range of books, tapes, toys and CD-Roms for babies through to teenagers. Books include fiction, non-fiction and national curriculum-related material. Membership gives access to Books for Children website, and 4-weekly colour magazines offering books for sale. Conditions of membership: 6 books in first year must be ordered through the website or magazine. Part of the BCA Group.

Bibliophile
5 Thomas Road, London E14 7BN
tel 020-7515 9222 *fax* 020-7538 4115
email orders@bibliophilebooks.com
website www.bibliophilebooks.com
Secretary Annie Quigley

To promote value-for-money reading. Upmarket literature and classical music on CD available from mail order catalogue (10 p.a.). Over 3000 titles covering art and fiction to travel, history and children's books. Founded 1978.

The Book People Ltd
Catteshall Manor, Catteshall Lane, Godalming, Surrey GU7 1UU
tel (01483) 861144 *fax* (01483) 861256
website www.thebookpeople.co.uk

Popular general fiction and non-fiction, including children's and travel. Monthly.

Children's Poetry Bookshelf
website www.childrenspoetrybookshelf.co.uk

Newly relaunched, this poetry book club offers poetry for 7–11-year-olds and its membership schemes are for parents and grandparents (with a gift membership), teachers and libraries. Its open access website has a lively and child-friendly area. See also the Poetry Book Society on page 159.

Disney Book Club
Customer services Grolier Ltd, PO Box 49, Norwich NR5 9PP
tel (0870) 240 4385
email customerservice@grolier.co.uk
website www.disneybookclub.co.uk

Offers books based on Disney characters, Disney storybooks, year books, calendars and supplements. Six free books on joining. New books sent every 4 weeks. Membership may be cancelled after acceptance of 3 shipments.

Letterbox Library
71–73 Allen Road, London N16 8RY
tel 020-7503 4801 *fax* 020-7503 4800
email info@letterboxlibrary.com
website www.letterboxlibrary.com

Specialises in children's books that celebrate equality and diversity. Also provides pre-selected packs for Sure Starts and nurseries. Quarterly annotated catalogues. Operates as a non-profit-driven workers' co-operative. Orders taken online, by fax or by post.

The Poetry Book Society
4th Floor, 2 Tavistock Place, London WC1H 9RA
tel 020-8870 8403 *fax* 020-8870 0865
email info@poetrybooks.co.uk
website www.poetrybooks.co.uk,
www.poetrybookshoponline.com,
www.childrenspoetrybookshelf.co.uk

Runs the Children's Poetry Bookshelf, a 3 times yearly book club offering children's poetry to teachers, parents and grandparents. See also page 159.

Puffin Book Club
Penguin Books, 80 The Strand, London WC2R 0RL
Freephone tel (0500) 454 444 (UK), (1) 800 340 131 (ROI) *fax* 020-7010 6667, (01279) 621 102
email pbccustomerservice@penguin.co.uk
Customer services Edinburgh Gate, Harlow, Essex CM20 2JE
website www.puffinbookclub.co.uk

A schools-based club from Puffin Books giving access to a range of discounted books for 5 age ranges: Junior for 0–5, Xtra for 5–7, Zone for 7–9, Word for 9–11, Max for 11+. The club offers selections from Puffin, Penguin, Dorling Kindersley and Ladybird as well as bestsellers from other publishers. The *Puffin Book Club* magazine features books on offer as well as editorial features, activities and competitions.

Red House
PO Box 142, Bangor LL57 4ZP
email arrabella.hall@redhouse.co.uk

website www.redhouse.co.uk

Helps parents to select the right books for their children at affordable prices. A free monthly magazine features the best of the latest titles on offer, young reader reviews and fascinating insight into the minds of popular children's writers. Sponsors the Red House Children's Book Award (page 369). Founded 1979.

Red House International Schools Book Club (ISBC)

Scholastic Ltd, Windrush Park, Witney, Oxon OX29 0YD
tel (01993) 893474 *fax* (01993) 708159
email intschool@scholastic.co.uk

International book club service for schools worldwide.

Scholastic Book Clubs

Windrush Park, Range Road, Witney, Oxon OX29 0YZ
tel (01993) 893456 *fax* (01993) 776813
website www.scholastic.co.uk
Managing Director Miles Stevens-Hoare

Leading schools book club. Offers 5 age-specific clubs.

Scholastic Book Fairs

Dolomite Avenue, Coventry Business Park, Coventry CV5 6UE
tel 0800 212281 (freephone)
website www.scholastic.co.uk/bookfairs
Managing Director Miles Stevens-Hoare

Sells directly to children, parents and teachers in schools through 25,000 week-long events held in schools throughout the UK.

Travelling Book Company

(also known as Troubadour)
Express House, Crow Arch Lane, Ringwood, Hants BH24 1PD
tel (0800) 7315758
email customer.services@travellingbooks.co.uk
website www.travellingbooks.co.uk

Book fair operation selling books to children in schools in the UK (Celtic Travelling Book Company in Ireland) through easy-to-manage, well-stocked bookcases containing a wide range of books for all age groups. An editorial team works closely with teachers and parents to ensure a balanced collection and is headed up by Fiona Waters, the well-known writer, reviewer, publisher and bookseller.

Children's bookshops

The bookshops in the first part of this list specialise in selling new children's books and are good places for writers and illustrators to check out the marketplace. Most of them are members of the Booksellers Association and are well known to publishers. A list of secondhand and antiquarian children's bookshops follows.

Askews
218–222 North Road, Preston, Lancs. PRI 1SV
tel (01772) 254860 fax (01772) 254860
website www.askews.co.uk

Libraries and schools supplier with particular emphasis on children's books. Sponsors of the Askews Torchlight Award.

Bags of Books
1 South Street, Lewes, East Sussex BN7 2BT
tel (01273) 479320 fax (01273) 478404
website www.bags-of-books.co.uk

Specialist children's bookshop including a mail-order service for audio tapes. Also distributes big books and some hard-to-get US children's books.

Balloons Children's Boookshop
41a Killigrew Street, Falmouth, Cornwall TR11 3PW
tel/fax (01326) 211505

School bookshop and book fair service. Also accommodates class visits and caters for special needs. Stocks dual language and storytapes.

BfS (Books for Students)
22–28 George Street, Hull HU1 3AP
tel (01482) 384660 fax (01482) 384677
email schools@bfs.co.uk
website www.bfsnavigator.net

Supplies children's books and any book in print to schools, colleges and international schools. Full school servicing of books on request.

Blast-Off Books
103 High Street, Linlithgow, Scotland EH49 7EQ
tel (01506) 844645 fax (01506) 844346
email info@blastoffbooks.co.uk
website www.blastoffbooks.co.uk

A dedicated children's bookshop for babies through to young adults, also stocking support materials for the Standard Grades and Highers. An important aspect of the shop is the range of materials for parents of, and teachers working with, children with specific learning needs such as dyslexia, autism, ADHD and Down's Syndrome.

The Book House
93 High Street, Thame, Oxon OX9 3HJ
tel (01844) 213032 fax (01844) 213311

Bookspread Ltd
311 Upper Elmers End Road, Beckingham BR3 3QP
tel (0845) 200 4954 fax (0845) 200 4964

website www.bookspread.co.uk

A bookshop run by ex-teachers who offer advice and consultation as well as a mobile book service for schools. Also organises workshops and author visits to schools. Works in conjunction with the educational charity, the Children's Discovery Centre.

Bookworm
1177 Finchley Road, London NW11 0AA
tel 020-8201 9811 fax 020-8201 9311
website www.thebookworm.uk.com

Brook Green Bookshop
72 Blythe Road, Brook Green, London W14 0HB
tel 020-7603 5999
email brookgreenbooks@btconnect.com

Children's bookshop started by former Macmillan sales director Michael Halden and his wife Loma Slater in spring 2003, situated in West London.

Charlotte's Web
59 Newton Road, Mumbles, Swansea SA3 4BL
tel (01792) 366654

Childrens@Blackwells
Blackwells Bookshop, 48–51 Broad Street, Oxford OX1 3BQ
tel (01865) 333694

Children's Book Centre
237 Kensington High Street, London W8 6SA
tel 020-7937 7497 fax 020-7938 4968
website www.childrensbookcentre.co.uk

Children's books, videos, tapes, audiobooks, toys and multimedia products.

The Children's Bookshop
1 Red Lion Parade, Bridge Street, Pinner, Middlesex HA5 3JD
tel 020-8866 9116 fax 020-8866 9116

Children's Bookshop (Huddersfield)
37–39 Lidget Street, Lindley, Huddersfield, West Yorkshire HD3 3JF
tel (01484) 658013 fax (01484) 460020

Children's Bookshop (Muswell Hill)
29 Fortis Green Road, London N10 3HP
tel 020-8444 5500 fax 020-8883 8632

Daisy & Tom Ltd
181 Kings Road, London SW3 5EB
tel 020-7349 5814 fax 020-7349 5818
website www.daisyandtom.com

Daisy & Tom Ltd
118 Deansgate, Manchester M3 2QR
tel 0161-835 5000 *fax* 0161-834 6608

Enchanted Wood
3–5 Kings Road, Shalford, Guildford, Surrey
GU4 8JU
tel (01483) 570088 *fax* (0870) 7052342
email sales@enchanted-wood.co.uk
website www.enchanted-wood.co.uk

Golden Treasury (Southfields)
29 Replingham Road, London SW18 5LT
tel 020-8333 0167

Jubilee Books
Eltham Green School Complex, Middle Park Avenue,
London SE9 5EQ
tel 020-8850 7676 *fax* 020-8294 0345
email enquiries@jubileebooks.co.uk
website www.jubileebooks.co.uk

Offers a wide range of books and resources to
schools. Organises book-related events including
visits by the bookbus, author/illustrator sessions and
creative workshops for schools, LEAs and other
education organisations. Established 1996.

Kendrake Children's Bookshop
St Nicholas Centre, 16 St Nicholas Way, Sutton,
Surrey SM1 1AX
tel 020-8255 7744 *fax* 020-8255 7744
website www.kendrakebooks.co.uk

Independent children's bookshop selling books for all
ages, including wide range of preschool books and
teachers' resources. Allows customers access to search
their database for titles.

The Lion and Unicorn Bookshop
19 King Street, Richmond, Surrey TW9 1ND
tel 020-8940 0483 *fax* 020-8332 6133
email services@lionunicornbooks.co.uk
website www.lionunicornbooks.co.uk

A specialist independent children's bookshop. Holds
regular author/illustrator events, Saturday storytelling
and publishes the *Roar*, a termly newsletter archived
on the website. Offers services to schools. Winner of
Independent Bookseller of the Year Award, the
British Book Awards 2000. Founded 1977.

Madeleine Lindley Ltd
Broadgate, Broadway Business Park, Chadderton,
Oldham OL9 9XA
tel 0161-683 4400 *fax* 0161-682 6801
website www.madeleinelindley.com

Supplies children's books to schools, provides
information services and runs open days for teachers.
Hosts author/publisher events for teachers and
children.

Norfolk Children's Book Centre
Alby, Norwich NR11 7HB
tel (01263) 761402 *fax* (01263) 768167
email marilyn@ncbc.co.uk
website www.ncbc.co.uk

Specialist children's bookshop for readers of all ages.
Offers services to schools in East Anglia including
storytelling, talks to children and parents, approval
services and INSET for teachers.

Oundle School Bookshop
13 Market Place, Oundle, Peterborough PE8 4BA
tel (01832) 273523 *fax* (01832) 274611
email bookshop@oundle.co.uk

Peters Bookselling Services
120 Bromsgrove Street, Birmingham B5 6RJ
tel 0121-666 6646 *fax* 0121-666 7033
website www.peters-books.co.uk

Libraries and schools supplier which provides book-
related promotional material for schools such as
posters, information booklets and magazines,
including *Author Zone* and *tBkmag*.

Rhyme & Reason
681 Ecclesall Road, Sheffield S11 8TG
tel 0114-266 1950
email richard@rhyme-reason.co.uk
website www.rhyme-reason.co.uk

New books for children of all ages.

Roving Books Ltd (The Roving Bookshop)
Administration 3 Kirkby Road, Desford, Leicester
LE9 9GL
tel (01455) 822192 *fax* (07005) 982306
email mail@rovingbooks.com
Showroom inside the Leicester Wholefood Co-op,
Unit 3, Freehold Street, Leicester LE1 9LX
tel 0116-2519151
website www.rovingbooks.com, www.xybacard.com

Children's specialist bookseller, taking a
comprehensive children's bookshop into schools for
purchases by children, parents, teachers and schools.
Promoting reading with the Jolly Roger Book Club
and Xybacard. Specialist advice and supply of
children's books for individuals and institutions.

Willesden Bookshop
Willesden Green Library Centre, 95 High Road,
London NW10 4QU
tel 020-8451 7000 *fax* 020-8830 1233
email books@willesdenbookshop.co.uk
website www.willesdenbookshop.co.uk

Specialist supplier of multicultural children's books
(including many unusual and imported titles) to
schools, nurseries, libraries and professional
development agencies.

Young Browsers Bookshop
33 The Thoroughfare, Woodbridge, Suffolk
IP12 1AH
tel (01394) 382832

CHILDREN'S BOOKSELLERS FOR COLLECTORS

Ampersand Books
Ludford Mill, Ludlow, Shrops. SY8 1PP
tel (01584) 877813 *fax* (01584) 877519
email popups@ampersandbooks.co.uk
website www.ampersandbooks.co.uk
Contact Michael Dawson

The only dealer in Britain specialising exclusively in three-dimensional and interactive books, with a permanent stock of about 1000 pop-ups, movables, panoramas, carousels, peepshows, split-page and flick books – in fact, all types of paper-engineering, whether antiquarian, secondhand, remaindered or new. Ampersand Books also repair, research and write about books of this sort. Private premises: open at any time but strictly by prior appointment. Established 1982.

Blackwell's Rare Books
48–51 Broad Street, Oxford OX1 3BQ
tel (01865) 333555 *fax* (01865) 794143
email rarebooks@blackwell.co.uk
website www.rarebooks.blackwell.co.uk

The Rare Books Department within Blackwell's deals in early and modern first editions of children's books, among other subjects. Catalogues are issued periodically, which include modern and antiquarian children's books.

Bookmark Children's Books
Fortnight, Broad Hinton, Swindon, Wilts. SN4 9NR
tel (01793) 731693 *fax* (01793) 731782
email leonora-excell@btconnect.com
Contact Anne Excell, Leonora Excell

A mail-order bookseller, specialising in books for collectors, ranging from antiquarian to modern. A wide range of first editions, novelty and picture books, chap-books, ABCs, annuals, etc. Also a selection of vintage toys, games, dolls and nursery china. Catalogues of children's books and related juvenilia issued. Book search service available within this specialist area. Member of PBFA, exhibiting at PBFA book fairs in London, Oxford and Bath. Established 1973.

Mary Butts Books
219 Church Road, Earley, Reading, Berks. RG6 1HW
tel 0118-926 1793
email mary.butts@tiscali.co.uk

Secondhand bookseller specialising in 19th- and 20th-century children's books for readers and students rather than collectors. Mainly postal business, but bookroom available on request. Free book search.

Paul Embleton
12 Greenfields, Stansted, Essex CM24 8AH
tel (01279) 812627
email paulembleton@btconnect.com

Sells by post via the internet (some stock is on ABE) and sends subject lists to regular customers. Receives visitors by appointment. Specialises in books and ephemera for the picture postcard collector and maintains a good stock of children's books and ephemera, mostly Victorian and Edwardian chromolithographic by such publishers as Nister and Raphael Tuck, and items of any age by collectable illustrators.

Ian Hodgkins & Co Ltd
Upper Vatch Mill, The Vatch, Slad, Stroud, Glos. GL6 7JY
tel (01453) 764270 *fax* (01453) 755233
email i.hodgkins@dial.pipex.com
Contact Simon Weager

Dealer in rare and out-of-print books and related material. Specialist in Beatrix Potter and fairy tales and 19th-century British art and literature. Free catalogues in all specialist areas published regularly.

Robert J. Kirkpatrick
6 Osterley Park View Road, London W7 2HH
(private premises)
tel 020-8567 4521

Secondhand bookseller specialising in stories about boys' schools from 1800 to the present day. Also public school studies, histories, etc.

Marchpane Children's Books
16 Cecil Court, Charing Cross Road, London WC2N 4HE
tel 020-7836 8661 *fax* 020-7497 0567

Specialises in illustrated children's books. Open Mon–Sat 11am–6.30pm.

Plurabelle Books
The Grey Barn (Building 3), Michael Young Centre, Purbeck Road, Cambridge CB2 2HN
tel (01223) 415671 *fax* (01223) 413241
email books@plurabelle.co.uk
website www.plurabelle.co.uk
Contact Michael Cahn

Secondhand bookseller specialising in academic books on literature, reading, history of education and children's literature. Free book search for out-of-print books. Catalogue published 3 times a year. Visitors welcome by appointment.

Ripping Yarns Bookshop
355 Archway Road, London N6 4EJ
tel 020-8341 6111 *fax* 020-7482 5056

email yarns@rippingyarns.co.uk
website www.rippingyarns.co.uk

Bookshop specialising in children's books – particularly in 19th and 20th century children's fiction – annuals, Puffins and picture books.

Rose's Books

14 Broad Street, Hay-on-Wye, Herefordshire HR3 5DB
tel (01497) 820013 *fax* (01497) 820031
email enquiry@rosesbooks.com
website www.rosesbooks.com
Contact Maria Goddard

Bookshop specialising solely in rare out-of-print children's books and located in the international book town of Hay-on-Wye. Stock available via website. Catalogues and specialist lists issued on a regular basis. Open daily 9.30am–5.00pm. Free want match service. Children's books purchased – single items or collections. Established 1986.

Henry Sotheran Ltd

2–5 Sackville Street, Piccadilly, London W1X 2DP
tel 020-7439 6151 *fax* 020-7434 2019
Contact Rosie Hodge

A large showroom with hundreds of important children's books spanning two centuries, specialising in first editions and attractive illustrated works by pivotal artists. Issues two specialist children's book catalogues free, on request.

Talatin Books

21 Parkstone Avenue, Emerson Park, Hornchurch, Essex RM11 3LX
tel (01708) 447561 *fax* (01708) 442238
email talatin-books@talk21.com
Contact Maggie Stevenson

Dealer in antiquarian and modern children's books. A wide range available, including reference books. Visitors are welcome by appointment (private premises, parking at door). Catalogues sent worldwide. Exhibits at the occasional book fair.

A word from J.K. Rowling

J.K. Rowling shares her first experience of becoming a writing success.

I can remember writing *Harry Potter and the Philosopher's Stone* in a café in Oporto. I was employed as a teacher at the language institute three doors along the road at the time, and this café was a kind of unofficial staffroom. My friend and colleague joined me at my table. When I realised I was no longer alone I hastily shuffled worksheets over my notebook, but not before Paul had seen exactly what I was doing. 'Writing a novel, eh?' he asked wearily, as though he had seen this sort of behaviour in foolish young teachers only too often before. '*Writers' & Artists' Yearbook*, that's what you need,' he said. 'Lists all the publishers and… stuff' he advised before ordering a lager and starting to talk about the previous night's episode of *The Simpsons*.

I had almost no knowledge of the practical aspects of getting published; I knew nobody in the publishing world, I didn't even know anybody who knew anybody. It had never occurred to me that assistance might be available in book form.

Nearly three years later and a long way from Oporto, I had almost finished *Harry Potter and the Philosopher's Stone*. I felt oddly as though I was setting out on a blind date as I took a copy of the *Writers' & Artists' Yearbook* from the shelf in Edinburgh's Central Library. Paul had been right and the *Yearbook* answered my every question, and after I had read and re-read the invaluable advice on preparing a manuscript, and noted the time-lapse between sending said manuscript and trying to get information back from the publisher, I made two lists: one of publishers, the other of agents.

The first agent on my list sent my sample three chapters and synopsis back by return of post. The first two publishers took slightly longer to return them, but the 'no' was just as firm. Oddly, these rejections didn't upset me much. I was braced to be turned down by the entire list, and in any case, these were real rejection letters – even real writers had got them. And then the second agent, who was high on the list purely because I like his name, wrote back with the most magical words I have ever read: 'We would be pleased to read the balance of your manuscript on an exclusive basis…'

J.K. Rowling is the best-selling author of the *Harry Potter* series (Bloomsbury). The first in the series, *Harry Potter and the Philosopher's Stone*, was the winner of the 1997 Nestlé Smarties Gold Prize and *Harry Potter and the Goblet of Fire* (2000) broke all records for the number of books sold on the first day of publication. The sixth book in the series, *Harry Potter and the Half-Blood Prince*, was published in 2005. All four of the published *Harry Potter* novels were voted into the BBC Big Read's top 100 in April 2003.

See also...
- *Spotting talent*, page 83
- *How it all began*, page 81
- *The amazing picture book story*, page 197
- *Fiction for 6–9 year-olds*, page 103
- *Teenage fiction*, page 119
- *Getting started*, page 1

How it all began

Eoin Colfer shares his first experience of becoming a writing success.

I have in my time purchased several copies of the *Writers' & Artists' Yearbook*, yet there is only one copy on my bookshelf. This, I suspect, is a condition common to most authors. When other writers visit my bat-cave – sorry, office – they don't bother asking for a signed first edition of my book, instead they make off with my *Yearbook* secreted up their jumpers. This inevitably happens shortly after I have completed the laborious task of attaching colour-coded paperclips to pages of interest. I know what you're thinking. Colour-coded paperclips. That explains a lot.

My obsession with the *Yearbook* began in the dark era of glitter eye shadow and ozone-puncturing hairdos known as the Eighties. I had recently finished college, and like all males in their twenties, knew all there was to know about the world. The population in general, I decided with humble altruism, deserved the benefit of my wisdom. And the best way to reach my prospective public was through literature.

So I wrote a book. Not content with that, I designed the cover. Multi-tasking even before the phrase was coined. This book qualified as a book because it had many words and quite a few pages. Secure in my sublime self delusion, I got hold of an industrial stapler, bound the whole lot together and crammed a copy into the nearest postbox. One copy would be sufficient, to the country's foremost publishers. I settled back on the family chaise longue and waited for the publisher's helicopter to land in the garden.

Seasons passed and the helicopter never materialised. Not so much as a postcard from the honoured house. Sighing mightily I widened my net, sending copies of my book to several other publishers. I got some replies this time. Would that I had not. Most were civil enough. We regret to inform you, etc … the opening phrase that haunts every writer's dreams. Still, at least they were polite. But a few less generic replies dropped onto my doormat. There was one note in which the handwriting deteriorated in spots, as the editor suffered from sporadic fits of laughter. A pattern was beginning to emerge. Could it be possible that my manuscript was flawed? Was there a chance that my presentation was not all that it could be? Did genius have to be packaged?

Help arrived in the form of an editor's response. 'We regret to inform you …' it began. Nothing new there. I was becoming inured. But there was an addendum pencilled below the type. Get the *Writers' & Artists' Yearbook*. It's worth the investment.

Reluctant as any Irish man in his twenties is to take advice from anyone besides his mother, I decided to act on this particular recommendation. The *Yearbook* paid for itself almost immediately. The mere act of purchasing the fat volume made me feel like a legitimate writer. I left the shop, making certain that my grip did not obscure the book title.

At home, I was amazed to discover that the *Yearbook* was not just a list of publishers. Every possible scrap of information needed by the upcoming or established writer was included (for more details buy the book. And if there are paperclips on this book, it is mine: please return it!) but what I needed to know was detailed under the heading 'Submitting material'. Next time, I vowed. Next time.

Next time turned out to be nearly a decade later. My self esteem had recovered sufficiently to brave the sae trail once more. So I wrote an introductory letter and an interesting summary of the book, and included the first 50 pages – double-spaced.

It worked. Two weeks later I had a publisher. Now I can't put the entire thing down to the *Yearbook*, but it certainly played its part. In public of course, I take all the credit myself. I am a writer after all. But packaging and presentation in my opinion made the difference between desktop and trash, to use a computer analogy.

A few years later my brothers advised me that I needed an agent, as they were running short on beer money. Once again the *Yearbook* was consulted. Not only were the agents listed but they were categorised. These *Yearbook* people were cut from the same cloth as myself. I could almost imagine their desks stacked with coloured paperclips.

My research paid off, and within weeks I was sitting in a top-class hotel treating my new agent to a flute of champagne. Although she insists it was a glass of Guinness in a Dublin pub and she paid.

Since then, I haven't looked back. Things are going well enough for me to be invited to write this Foreword. If you are published and reading this book, hide it away and beware those with baggy jumpers. If you are as yet unpublished, then keep the faith and make sure that all around you can see the title.

Eoin Colfer has written several bestselling children's novels, including the *Artemis Fowl* series. The books have been translated into 43 languages and have won awards including British Children's Book of the Year, WHSmith Children's Book of the Year, Bisto Merit Awards and the South African Book Club Book of the Year. The first *Artemis Fowl* film is currently in production.

See also...

- *Spotting talent*, page 83
- *The amazing picture book story*, page 197
- *Fiction for 6–9 year-olds*, page 103
- *Teenage fiction*, page 119
- *A word from J.K. Rowling*, page 80
- *Getting started*, page 1

Spotting talent

Publishers and literary agents are not looking for what *they* like but for what children will like. Barry Cunningham famously accepted the manuscript of the first Harry Potter book which – as everyone knows – turned out to be the first of an international bestselling series. He explains here what he is looking for when he reads a new manuscript.

I'm a fan: I love reading and I love great stories. My background is in sales and marketing, and for many years I travelled with Penguin the length and breadth of the country – on tours with authors like Roald Dahl, to schools with the Puffin Book Club or to lonely writers' festivals.

It was during that time that I learnt the most important part of my trade – how children react to the books they love, the authors that they adore, and how they put up with the material that they are coerced into reading. Reluctant readers indeed!

So what I'm looking for is what *they* want, not what I like or what you think is good. More of this later.

First steps

All publishers get streams of brown envelopes – especially, like divorces, after Christmas or the summer holidays – when writers finally feel something must be done with that story they've been working on.

We read some part of everything we get. But, be warned, not every publisher does. So, ring up and find out what the publisher wants: sample, complete manuscript, or perhaps they won't accept it at all!

For most editors, first on the reading list are the submissions from agents, manuscripts recommended by other authors or by someone whose judgement they trust. So, if you know someone who knows someone – use the contact.

Next, know a little about the list you are submitting to: look at their catalogue or read some of their books. Let publishers know how much you like their publications (we all like those sorts of comments!) and how you think your novel might sit with the rest of their titles.

Then, write a short snappy synopsis – a page will do (I've had some that are as long as half the novel itself!). It should tell the publisher what the book is about, its characters and why they should read it.

Also include a little bit about you, the author. Don't forget that. It can be almost as important as anything else in these days of marketing and personality promotion (no, you don't *have* to be a vicar or an ex-glamour model, but it does give an impetus to read on…).

I worked with a very famous editor in my first job who was talking one day about her regular advice to first-time writers. Her advice began with a simple question – 'Have you thought of starting at Chapter 2?'

Strangely, I find myself repeating this regularly. Often I find the first chapter is tortured and difficult, before the writer relaxes into the flow of the story in Chapter 2. And often things improve if we start straight into the action, and come back and explain later. But more importantly, first novels often fail because the editor doesn't get past a poor opening section. Beginnings are crucial, because I know children won't persevere if the story has a poor start, either.

So what am I looking for?

Back to the heart of things...

There are writers who know a lot about children – they might be teachers or parents – so does this mean they can write more relevantly for young people? There are authors who know nothing about modern children, don't even really like children – does this mean they will never understand what a child wants? There are 'crossover' books that don't appear to be for real children at all. There are books with children in them that aren't children's books. Confused?

To me it's simple. Books that really work for children are written from a child's perspective through an age-appropriate memory of how the author felt and dreamed and wondered. The best children's writers carry that childhood wonder, its worry and concern, or even its fear and disappointment, around with them. They have kept the child within alive – so writing is not a professional task of storytelling for tiny tots but a simple glorious act of recreating the excitement of childhood.

That's part one of what you need. Part two, in my view, is a concentration on your audience. I've worked with adult writers too and there is a difference here. Children's authors are creating for a distinctly different readership – they need to think in a more *humble* way than if their work was for their contemporaries. What I mean is that they have to be mindful of how their work will impact on children. Characters must have convincing voices, descriptions must be good enough for children to visualise, and authors must be aware of things like children's attention span when it comes to detailed explanations.

But perhaps even more important is an awareness of the emotional effect of a story on a child. We must always remember their hunger for hope and a bright tomorrow, the closeness and importance of relationships – how easily a world can be upset by parents, or loss of an animal or a friend – and the way in which action really does speak to children, for fantasy and adventure is part of the process of literally growing an imagination.

(If all this means nothing to you, and writing for children is just another category, then I don't think you should bother. That's not to say all this should operate consciously in the mind of the new writer – but that's what a publisher seeks, and that's what I'm looking for.)

Categories and concepts

Everyone has read about the older children's market, and its lucrative crossover into the kind of children's book that adults buy for themselves. I think this will continue to be a growing phenomenon – but the best books in the field will still be clear in their intent: not looking 'over their shoulder' at adults, but true to themselves and their subjects.

I'm sure fantasy will continue to hold a firm following – but with the best books based around character and not simply wild lands and strange people. And historical fiction is poised for a come back for older children – showing the rich material and heritage we have in our shared everyday culture, as well as the 'big battles' of yore!

At last all kinds of young adult fiction has found a firm market and any number of clear voices: hard edged, romantic, comic, or a wild mixture of all three! Both here and in the United States the 13–17 age group has really started buying for themselves, and this is sure to demand more than just conventional 'problem issues' fare.

But my favourite category is the most neglected – real stories and novels for the 7–9 year-olds. This really was once the classic area of children's books, with the biggest names and the greatest longevity of appeal. Sadly, it has become the haunt of derivative series and boring chapter books. I predict a considerable revival, and it will be a great area for new talent.

Picture books seem to have had a much quieter time lately and are, perhaps, awaiting a revival with some newer attitudes. The success of cartoon novels and graphic story treatments for older readers must also hint at a new market here.

Language and setting

It's often said that, like exams, children's books are getting easier, that the language is getting 'younger' while the plots are getting more sophisticated. I don't think this is true. Certainly, for all markets, dialogue is more important than ever – and less time is taken in description.

Children are used to characters who say what they mean, and whose motivations and subtleties emerge in speech. But largely I think this makes for more interpretation and imagination. Descriptions now concentrate on setting and atmosphere, rather than telling us authoritatively what the hero or heroine feels. All to the good in my view, and something new writers for children should absorb.

Also welcome in contemporary children's books is the freeing up of the adult! These characters are no longer confined to small walk-on parts and 'parental' or 'villainous' roles. Nowadays, adults in children's novels are as well drawn as the children, sometimes as touchingly vulnerable people themselves. But as in life, the most potent and frightening image in any children's book remains the bad or exploitative parent.

International scope

Children's literature is truly one of our most glorious 'hidden exports'. British writers continue to be very successful around the world, particularly in the USA and Europe. It is worth remembering this – while setting is not so important as inspiration, obviously UK-centred plots, regional dialogue and purely domestic issues, if not absolutely necessary, are best avoided. But there is no need either – like a creaky old British film – to introduce 'an American boy' or mid-Atlantic slang to your work to appeal to another audience. This seldom works and is often excruciating!

The marketplace

The market still remains delightfully unpredictable. It is hopeless to look at last year's trends and try to speculate. The sound and timelessly good advice is to find your own voice and, above all, to write from the heart. If you can touch what moved you as a child or still moves the child within you, then there's your 'market appeal'. Whether it's aboard the frigate of your imagination or in the quieter, but equally dangerous seas of the lonely soul, skill and inspiration will win you your readership.

Oh, and finally, don't give up. As I once said to a certain young woman about a boy called Harry...

Barry Cunningham was the editor who originally signed J.K. Rowling to Bloomsbury Children's Books. He now runs his own company, The Chicken House, specialising in introducing new children's writers to the UK and USA. Notable recent successes include Cornelia Funke and Kevin Brooks.

See also...
• *A word from J.K. Rowling,* page 80

Writing and the children's book market

Around 10,000 new children's titles are published in the UK every year. Chris Kloet suggests how a potential author can best ensure that their work is published.

The profile of children's books has never been higher, yet it can be difficult for the first-time writer to get published. It is a diverse, overcrowded market, with many thousands of titles currently in print, available both in the UK and from elsewhere via the internet. Children's publishers tend to fill their lists with commissioned books by writers they publish regularly, so they may have little space for the untried writer, even though they seek exceptional new talent. This is a selective, highly competitive, market-led business. Since every new book is expected to meet its projected sales target, your writing must demonstrate solid sales potential, as well as strength and originality, if it is to stand a chance of being published.

Is your work right for today's market? Literary tastes and fashions change. Publishers cater to children whose reading is now almost certainly different from that of your own childhood. In the present electronic media-driven age, few want cosy tales about fairies and bunnies, jolly talking cars or magic teapots. Nor anything remotely imitative. Editors choose *original*, lively material – something witty, innovative and pacey. They look for polished writing with a fresh, contemporary voice that speaks directly and engages today's critical, media-savvy young readers, who are often easily bored.

Develop a sense of the market so that you can judge the potential for your work. Read widely and critically across the children's book spectrum for an overview, especially noting recent titles. Talk to children's librarians, who are expert in current tastes, and visit children's bookshops and dedicated children's books websites, such as Achuka. As you read, pay attention to the different categories, series, genres and publishers' imprints. This will help you to pinpoint likely publishers. Before submitting your typescript, ensure that your targeted publisher currently publishes in your particular form or genre. Request catalogues from their marketing department; check out their website. Consult the publisher's entry under *Children's book publishers UK and Ireland* (see page 5). Many publishing houses now stipulate 'No unsolicited MSS or synopses'. Don't spend your time and postage sending work to them; choose instead a publisher who accepts unsolicited work.

You might consider approaching a literary agent who knows market trends, publishers' lists and the faces behind them. Most editors regard agents as filters and may prefer submissions from them, knowing that a preliminary critical eye has been cast over them.

Picture books

Books for babies and toddlers are often board books and novelties. Unless you are also a professional illustrator (see *Illustrating for children's books*, page 201) they present few opportunities for a writer. Picture books are aimed at children aged between two and five or six, and are usually 32 pages long, giving 12–14 double-page spreads, and illustrated in colour.

Although a story written for this format should be simple, it must be structured, with a compelling beginning, middle and end. The theme should interest and be appropriate for the age and experience of its audience. As the text is likely to be reread, it should possess a satisfying rhythm (but beware of rhymes). Ideally, it should be fewer than 1000 words (and could be much shorter), must offer scope for illustration and, finally, it needs strong international appeal. Reproducing full-colour artwork is costly and the originating publisher must be confident of achieving co-productions with publishers overseas, to keep unit costs down. It has to be said: it is a tough field.

Submit a picture book text typed either on single-sided A4 sheets, showing page breaks, or as a series of numbered pages, each with its own text. Do not go into details about illustrations, but simply note anything that is not obvious from the text that needs to be included in the pictures.

Younger fiction

This area of publishing may present opportunities for the new writer. It covers stories written for the post-picture book stage, when children are reading their first whole novels. Texts vary in length and complexity, depending on the age and fluency of the reader, but tend to be between 1000 and 6000 words long.

Some publishers continue to bring out titles under the umbrella of various series, each targeted at a particular level of reading experience and competency, although these are now often replaced by individual author series. Categories are: beginning or first readers, developing or newly confident, confident, and fluent readers. Note that these are not the same as reading schemes published for the schools market and do not require such a restricted vocabulary. Stories for the bottom end of the age range are usually short, straight-through narratives illustrated throughout in colour, whereas those for older children are broken down into chapters and may be illustrated in black and white. The table on page 88 lists publishers' requirements for some currently published series. Check that your material is correct in terms of length and interest level when approaching a publisher with a submission for a series.

General fiction

Many novels for children aged 9–12+ are published, not in series, but as 'standalone' titles, each judged on its own merits. The scope for different types of stories is wide – adventure stories, fantasies, historical novels (increasingly popular), science fiction, ghost and horror stories, humour, and stories of everyday life. Generally, their length is 20,000– 40,000 words. This is a rough guide and is by no means fixed. For example, J.K. Rowling's recent *Harry Potter* novels weigh in at between 600–750+ closely printed pages, and publishers now seem more willing to publish longer texts, particularly fantasies, although the market is presently overloaded with hefty trilogies.

Perhaps more than in other areas of juvenile fiction, the individual editor's tastes will play a significant part in the publishing decision, i.e they want authors' work which *they* like. They, and their sales and marketing departments, also need to feel confident of a new writer's ability to go on to write further books for their lists – nobody is keen to invest in an author who is just a one-book wonder.

When submitting your work it is probably best to send the entire typescript. Although some people advise sending in a synopsis with the first three chapters, a prospective publisher will need to see whether you can sustain a reader's interest to the end of the book.

Publisher	Series name	Length	Age group	Comments
Andersen Press	Tiger Cubs	1000–3000 words; 64 pages	5–8	B&w illustrations throughout
	Tigers	3000–5000 words; 64 pages	6–9	B&w illustrations throughout
A & C Black	Chameleons	1200 words; 48 pages	5–7	Colour illustrations throughout
	Black Cats	9000–14,000 words; 80–128 pages	7–10	B&w illustrations throughout
	Flashbacks	12,000–14,000 words; 96 pages	8+	Historical fiction
Egmont Books	Green Bananas	500 words; 48 pages	4+	Colour illustrations
	Blue Bananas	1000 words; 48 pages	5+	Colour illustrations
	Red Bananas	2000 words; 48 pages	6+	Colour illustrations
Franklin Watts	Tadpoles	70 words; 24 pages	4–6	Colour illustrations throughout
	Leapfrog	180 words; 32 pages	4–6	Colour illustrations throughout
	Hopscotch	350–400 words; 32 pages	5–7	Colour illustrations throughout
Hodder Children's Books	Bite	35,000+ words	12+	Contemporary fiction
Kingfisher	I Am Reading	1200 words; 48 pages	5–7	Colour illustrations throughout
Orchard Books	Crunchies	1000–1500 words	5–7	B&w line illustrations
	Colour Crunchies	1000–1500 words	5–7	Colour illustrations
	Super Crunchies	5000 words	7–9	B&w line illustrations
	Red Apples	20,000–25,000 words	9–12	
	Black Apples	30,000–40,000 words	12+	
Penguin Group	Colour Young Puffin	2500 words; 64 pages	5–7	Colour illustrations
Walker Books	Walker Stories	1800 words; 64 pages	5+	B&w illustrations throughout
	Racing Reads	8000 words; 80–96 pages	7–9	B&w illustrations throughout

Teenage fiction

Some of the published output for teenaged readers is published in series but increasingly, publishers are targeting this area of the market with edgy, hard-hitting novels about contemporary teenagers, which they publish as standalone titles. There is also a current vogue for 'young adult' novels that have a crossover appeal to an adult readership. Indeed, recent award-winning titles such as Philip Pullman's *His Dark Materials* sequence and Mark Haddon's *The Curious Incident of the Dog at Night-time* and J.K. Rowling's *Harry Potter* books, have all been published in both juvenile and adult editions.

Non-fiction

The last few years have seen fundamental and striking changes in the type of information books published for the young. Hitherto the province, by and large, of specialist publishers catering for the educational market, the field has now broadened to encompass an astonishing range of presentations and formats which are attractive to the young reader. Increasingly, children who use the internet to furnish their information needs are wooed into learning about many topics via entertaining and accessible paperback series such as the *Horrible Histories* published by Scholastic, and similar series from other publishers. In writing for this market, it goes without saying that you must research your subject thoroughly and be able to put it across clearly, with an engaging style. Familiarise yourself with the relevant parts of the National Curriculum. Check out the various series and ask the publishers for any guidelines. You will be well advised to check that there is a market for your book before you actually write it, as researching a subject can be both time consuming and costly. Submit a proposal to your targeted publisher, outlining the subject matter and the level of treatment, and your ideas about the audience for your book.

Chris Kloet worked as Children's Publisher at Victor Gollancz Ltd, and is now Editor-at-Large at Walker Books. She has written and reviewed children's books and has lectured widely on the subject.

See also...
● *A word from J.K. Rowling,* page 80

Books for babies

Books for babies can be wonderfully enjoyable for both infant and reader, and can give the child a head start in learning to learn. Wendy Cooling looks at what makes a successful book for a baby.

Over the last few years reading has become big news with the phenomenal success of the *Harry Potter* series, *His Dark Materials, Lord of the Rings* and such memorable events as the National Year of Reading, World Book Day and the Big Read. Children's books are now being read by adults and people outside the book business have stopped asking in sympathetic voices: 'Do you ever do anything with adult books?'. Within this context the baby book market has been an area of real growth.

For babies

Publishers are not the kinds of people who miss opportunities and they have responded with great creativity to this growing market. For five years the Sainsbury's Baby Book Award (now the Booktrust Early Years Awards; see page 365) has celebrated the rich achievements of this publishing and looked at what it is that makes a good book for a baby. The first winner was Helen Oxenbury's *Tickle, Tickle* (Walker Books); it has been hugely successful and demonstrates many of the ingredients that add up to a really good book for a baby. The text is a joy to read aloud – very necessary as anyone with children will know that favourite books must be read again, and again, and again. Children don't understand all the words but they respond to the sound of the voice of someone who loves them and to the sound of the words. 'Splish, splash' and 'Tickle, tickle' resonate in the head because they sound good, they're great words to say and help the very youngest children to develop an ear for language that will later take them into reading. The invitation to adult and child to join in with the 'Tickle, tickle' is a winner too as the shared reading experience is always better if there's an element of fun and interaction. The illustrations are a delight as babies rule in this book; they fill every page as they squelch in the mud, splash in the bath and take readers through the pages to bedtime. Helen Oxenbury draws wonderful babies, both black and white, yet children just starting to talk will point to every one of them saying, 'Me, me, me, me.' So this is a book, a tough board book, for a baby to listen to, look at, play with and enjoy in the first two years of life. And, for those parents who worry excessively about learning, children who've enjoyed this book will find that they understand such things as alliteration and onomatopoeia when they come to them at school!

Even before *Tickle, Tickle* babies needed books made from cloth, books for the bath and books with no words at all. Helen Oxenbury's wordless books, first published in 1981, are still the best as her pictures are perfectly observed yet deceivingly simple. *Dressing* (Walker Books) is a good example as it really encourages the adult to talk as each page reveals a clear picture of a toddler progressing with the very complicated business of getting dressed. Many others have tried the wordless book but to do it well is no easy task. My favourite bath book is a small duck-shaped book *My First Duck* (published long ago by Blackie and now sadly out of print). It fits into a baby's hand and feels squidgy and wonderful when wet; it's a great first book as it tells a simple story in clear words and pictures. With a book like this babies learn to love books before they have any real idea about what books and stories – and ducks – are. They just know that the experience is fun and the voice of mum or dad is lovely and they want more of it!

Cloth books too are quite a creative challenge. A good one is *Farm* (Baby Campbell), a stuffed cloth book that crackles and crinkles as it's touched and uses black and white alongside just a little red – colours good for the very young child to pick out.

For innovation it's hard to beat another Baby Book Award winner, *Baby Faces* (Baby Campbell). This is a small board book with round pages joined by a string on which there is also a rattle. You can't move this book, or even turn a page without it making a noise – great, for shared reading with tiny children is often not quiet time! The title of this book describes it accurately as each round page reveals a baby's face and a minimal text as babies say 'hello', demonstrate moods and say 'goodbye'. This time the illustrations are black and white photographs, by Sandra Lousada, and they really do appeal to babies. The publisher has put lots of thought into this, picked up on the research that tells us that babies can focus on black and white long before they can pick out colours, and produced a superb first book for any baby. Baby Campbell also gave us another winning innovation – the buggy buddies – a series of tiny board books that can be attached to a buggy, cot or high chair and so always be accessible to the baby. These books look good and are very close to being toys but with them babies and toddlers learn how books work, learn to turn the pages and to look at the pictures even when no one has time to read to them.

Nursery rhymes

Nursery rhymes, traditional songs and action rhymes are great for all preschool children but there are never enough good, small collections for the very young. Some rhymes are quite violent but many are ideal to start with – hopefully they remind adults of the rhymes they listened to when they were young, because of course talking and singing to children is just as good as reading to them. Too often, nursery rhyme books are packed so full of words and pictures that they're too much for the early years, although children will of course love all the detail on the page as they get older. *Head, Shoulders, Knees and Toes*, illustrated by Annie Kubler (Child's Play), another prize-winner, is a good example for the youngest of children. It is quite a large board book and Annie Kubler's babies fill every page as they touch their head, shoulders, and laugh and giggle as they do it! This is a book that absolutely demands participation and is totally focused on the baby and on fun!

For a more sophisticated edition of a well-known rhyme there's *Twinkle, Twinkle!* (Templar). 'Twinkle, twinkle little star' is told on uncluttered backgrounds with star-shaped cut-outs that are perfect for little fingers to feel and explore. This is a tough and stylish board book that invites talk about shapes as it introduces a traditional poem – it's part of the excellent amazing baby series.

For a big nursery rhyme book it's hard to beat Sam Childs' *The Rainbow Book of Nursery Rhymes* (Hutchinson), for its generous page design, clear and warm pictures and wide range of rhymes – this is a book to last, a book for the bookshelf so it can be dipped into again and again well up to starting school. There is, however, no doubt that babies under one year old prefer the small book that they can hold themselves and keep in the toy box.

For toddlers

As babies grow into toddlers and develop better coordination there's nothing they like more than the lift-the-flap book – unless it's the touch-and-feel book! A newish one for really young children is Debi Gliori's *Where, oh where, is Baby Bear?* (Orchard Books), offering a good introduction to her positive dad character, Mr Bear. Mr Bear is searching for Baby Bear and there's a flap to be lifted on every page until Baby Bear is discovered on the last page – and in the most obvious place. This is great for under one year-olds, with its delicious pictures and good rhyming text that children will try and gurgle along with before they start to talk. There are several bigger board books featuring Mr Bear for babies to move on to.

It's probably not necessary to mention two long-time winning lift-the-flap titles but I must. Eric Hill's *Where's Spot?* (Puffin) shows exactly what it takes to make a lasting baby book and so does *Dear Zoo* by Rod Campbell (Macmillan and Puffin) These books are worth examining by all would-be authors and illustrators of books for babies. What is it that makes children want to look and listen again and again once they know exactly where Spot is, and what will make the perfect pet?

Young children love to find characters they can read more and more about. As well as Spot and Mr Bear, current stars are Lucy Cousins' Maisy (Walker), Mick Inkpen's Kipper (Hodder), David McKee's Elmer (Andersen) and Tony Ross' Little Princess (Andersen). These characters all appear in board books as well as picture books and will still be enjoyed as children start school. *Weather*, a Little Princess board book, is one of the most delightful non-fiction books ever produced for babies; children who know her will happily learn with her many of the important things of life. All the characters mentioned are drawn with charm and love; all are very original and have the capacity to become friends. Many characters lack these qualities and never get beyond the third book. An interesting new one to look out for is Ted Dewan's *Bing*, a slightly anarchic character with great appeal to one and two year-olds – watch out for him!

What makes a classic picture book?

Babies who experience these exciting early books – and there are many more I could have mentioned – will soon be taking off into wonderful classic picture books such as *Each Peach Pear Plum* by Janet and Allan Ahlberg, *Where the Wild Things Are* by Maurice Sendak, *We're Going on a Bear Hunt* by Michael Rosen and Helen Oxenbury, and Eric Carle's *The Very Hungry Caterpillar*. If you're contemplating a career as an author and/orillustrator of picture books, look at these and at other great picture books carefully for there's a lot to learn – not least that every single word counts in a book for the very young.

What doesn't make a good picture book? The perfect picture book that has been reduced to board book format (why do publishers do it?) simply doesn't work – picture books are more sophisticated than that. Texts that lack rhythm and so really can't be read aloud should not be used. Crowded pages packed with the sort of detail that will intrigue a six year-old are obviously inappropriate for babies. Illustration that lacks quality and offers no interest to the child – and certainly none to the adult – should be abandoned.

So what *does* make a good picture book? Let's have great language packed with fine-sounding words that children will enjoy listening to. Let's have rhythm and rhyme that makes the reader want to turn the page and look/read on. Let's remember that the books are for the babies – it helps if adults enjoy them too but the baby must be at the heart of it. Let's value books for babies and celebrate them – they take children into a love of books and the start of a life as readers, and what could be more important? The right books can be nothing but good for babies, parents, carers, authors, illustrators and publishers – they make commercial and social sense.

About Bookstart

We've always known that an enormous amount of learning takes place in the preschool years and that reading books to babies can do nothing but good. Yet it took the Bookstart research to really prove to us all that sharing books with children from a very early age can give them a positive advantage when they start school and can change family attitudes to books and book-buying. Bookstart was piloted by Booktrust in Birmingham in 1992 and aimed simply to give books to families when they attended the 7–9 month health check at their Health Centre, and to invite them to join the local public library.

Professor Barrie Wade and Doctor Maggie Moore of Birmingham University evaluated the project and continue to follow the progress of the first babies involved with Bookstart. When they started school this group of children were way ahead of the control group in all literacy-based tests and, rather unexpectedly, in all the numeracy tests. The children who had been read to at home were really ready for school and were able to start with confidence. They knew about stories, about rhyme and rhythm, and about shapes and numbers and most importantly, they knew that books could give great pleasure and that sharing could be fun – their learning from this early book experience was accidental, but very important learning.

Bookstart became established and grew into a nationwide project as the Government was extending nursery education and starting the Surestart scheme – a brilliant initiative working with disadvantaged families. Not all those Bookstart parents have enrolled their babies at the library but many more than ever before have, and many are buying books whether it be in bookshops, by mail order or at car boot sales, which has to be good for books and for babies.

Wendy Cooling is a highly respected children's book consultant and reviewer. She taught English in Inner London comprehensives for many years before becoming head of the Children's Book Foundation (now Booktrust) where she initiated the Bookstart project. She is a regular guest on book-related radio and television programmes, and is the compiler of several children's fiction and poetry anthologies.

Writing for boys

Everyone knows that boys and girls develop differently, and their reading preferences are similarly as diverse. Russell Ash writes about non-fiction and explains what boys like to read.

Reluctant readers?

When my annual *The Top 10 of Everything* (Hamlyn) was chosen by the American Library Association (ALA) as a 'Book for Reluctant Young Adult Readers', I felt slightly miffed. Then I realised it was something of an accolade: getting someone who didn't generally read books to read one is something of an achievement.

As well as my book, the ALA's recent non-fiction picks for reluctant readers have included subjects of which the following is a random selection: basketball, film plots, biographies of rap and pop stars, manga comics, natural disasters, *Star Wars*, vampires, tattoos, young people's rights, superheroes, robots, James Bond, the artist M.C. Escher, phobias, skeletons, the *Titanic* and racing cars.

Note the common thread? Predominantly, though not exclusively, these represent 'boys' interests'. And since American culture is closer to our own than many would like to think, the interests of British boys would not diverge much. Nor are the reluctant readers' subjects likely to be that different from those of the enthusiastic readers: the latter just read more and their tastes may be somewhat broader.

Although my books are not deliberately targeted at boys (nor even only at children), they constitute the majority of readers because they fulfil several criteria of 'things boys like', including lists, amazing facts, records and trivia. As both a male author of non-fiction books and the father of two teenaged boys, I have a sense of what we/they appreciate – though I stress at the outset that these views are my own and are inevitably generalisations: there are plenty of 'boy' subjects that girls like too, and *vice versa*. Also, many comments that relate to books are also relevant to magazine articles.

A century of non-fiction for boys

It is almost the centenary of the publication of one of the bestselling non-fiction boys' books of all time, Robert Baden Powell's *Scouting for Boys* (1908). It was written at a time when, firstly, its mildly double-entendre title was not even considered, and, secondly, there was a very clear distinction between boys' and girls' interests, and hence their books.

In my own pre-computer youth, 'boys' fiction was often set in public schools or featured militaristic heroes such as Biggles, pirates and cowboys, while boys' non-fiction similarly reflected the actual or imagined interests of boys – transport, warfare, science, exploration and endeavour and so on. Boys' pursuits were firmly acknowledged as totally different from those of their female peers: we shot airguns, built things guided by books with titles like *Hundreds of Things a Boy Can Make* or played with Meccano. Girls probably had other obsessions – dolls? ponies? ballet? – we never discovered, since we were too busy devoting incalculable boy-hours to constructing unfeasibly huge gantry cranes.

Ward Lock's endless series of Wonder Books often included '...for Girls and Boys' in their titles, but their subjects (*Railways, Aircraft* – even the *Wonder Book of Wonders*) belied the claim. By 1960, over five million copies of them had been sold. Yet despite such numbers, juvenile non-fiction remained the poor relative of 'proper' books – novels. A US survey of books that had sold more than a million copies up to 1975 could muster only a handful of children's non-fiction bestsellers, including an atlas, a dictionary, a cookbook and, perhaps surprisingly, a sex manual for teenagers published in 1950 – although all of them had, astonishingly, outsold *Mary Poppins* and *Winnie-the-Pooh*.

From the 1970s onwards, in both juvenile fiction and non-fiction, various initiatives were launched to overcome gender stereotyping, but it really didn't work, and since the 1990s, the focus in schools at least has shifted from this issue to the problem of underachieving boys, which is today a worldwide phenomenon, irrespective of national variations in school systems.

Popular non-fiction themes for boys

Adventure – thrilling true-life stories of exploration and survival against the odds

Biographies – the lives of heroes and individuals whose achievements boys respect

Cars, trucks, and big machines

Computer games-based books

Crime and criminals – general villainy (pirates and other free spirits are as popular in books as on the screen) and the work of the police and detectives

Fact books – generally, and especially books of lists and statistics, are perennially popular; from such almost exclusively male activities as memorising cricket scores to train-spotting, boys in particular have long been fascinated by numbers and rankings, so information books like *Guinness World Records*, my own books and those that compare and contrast things are of special appeal, while such books have the advantage of selling into the 'crossover market' (children and adults), some even attracting a good proportion of girl readers. *Blue Peter* offers an annual award for the 'Best Book with Facts' – the 2005 winner was *Explorers Wanted! At the North Pole* by Simon Chapman (Egmont Books)

Fitness – despite alarmist press reports about levels of childhood obesity, many boys are concerned with achieving the levels of fitness required to compete in their favourite sports

History – provided it is presented in an amusing and entertaining style, popular history is an exceptionally strong genre, with Ancient Egypt, Rome, the Middle Ages and World War II among the most notable periods. Almost deserving of a case study of its own, Public Lending Right data indicate that history titles are the most-borrowed children's non-fiction in public libraries, but this should be qualified by noting that at the last count Terry Deary's *Horrible Histories* titles (*The Terrible Tudors, et al*) occupied 14 of the top 20 places! He describes his enormously popular style as, 'Look, kids, I am not an expert – but you'll never guess what I discovered about these people!' – a far cry from the 'I'm the expert, so listen to me...' approach of more traditional school history textbooks. Deary has his imitators, but he would be a hard act for any would-be writer to follow unless they come up with an approach as refreshingly original as the one he has created

Hobbies – as with their choice of magazines and comics, at age 11–16 some 34% of boys compared with 15.38% of girls choose books because they relate to their hobby

Humour – boys respond well to humour and (especially sick) joke books

Magic tricks – a long-standing and ever-popular genre among boys

Military – warfare, derring-do, chivalry, weapons, the work of the SAS, and so on

Music – especially guitars, bands and music technology for the iPod generation

Mysteries – from unsolved crime to the occult fringe (aliens, ghosts, the Bermuda Triangle, etc)

Nature – boys are notably fond of killer creatures, sharks, dinosaurs and creepy-crawlies

Science – including inventions, technology, how things work technically and computers; the Aventis Prize for Science Books has a junior award – the 2005 winner was *What Makes Me, Me?* by Robert Winston (Dorling Kindersley) (see page 364)

Sport – football and 'cool' sports such as basketball, extreme sports (surfing, skateboarding, mountain biking, etc) and martial arts have a captive boy audience: a study showed that 46.55% of boys aged 11–16 like to read about sport, compared with only 6.15% of girls!

It's different for boys

A survey of reading habits generally by the National Literacy Trust showed that among children in early years education, one girl in five said she would rather read than watch television or use computers, but less than one boy in 10 expressed this preference. Some 63% of boys and 82% of girls liked reading at home, but the boys' stronger preference for non-fiction revealed itself. When provided with a list of genres from which to select, 28% of boys chose non-fiction as one of their top three genres, but only 13% of girls did so.

Children's non-fiction author John Malam put it succinctly: 'Non-fiction is definitely a "boy thing" more than a "girl thing". In the past I've been commissioned to write specifically for boys on subjects that should appeal to them (cars, planes, trucks, football, etc). In some cases the books were high-low readers, targeted at boys with high ages but low reading abilities, where the choice of pictures seems to be as critical as the choice of facts (pictures being the hook to lure them in to reading captions, then the main text).'

Research by the Exeter Extending Literacy Project (EXEL) showed that boys were more likely than girls to be reading non-fiction books (a ratio of 56.6% boys to 43.3% girls), but the gender difference was far greater among those choosing information books as their favourite category (61.9% to 38.0%).

All the evidence shows that girls develop differently from boys. In her *Differently Literate: Boys, Girls and the Schooling of Literacy* (RoutledgeFalmer 1997), Elaine Millard explains: 'The largest contrast is between boys' interest in action and adventure, and girls' preference for emotion and relationships.' Girls' reading skills are often superior to those of boys, they enjoy reading fiction more, socialise and discuss their feelings about the books more readily, whereas boys want to interact with the world and expend their surplus energy through sport and other activities. They are much less inclined to 'curl up with a book' – but they can surprise: one of my sons didn't read a book for months, then suddenly became absorbed in a 500-page account of the Siege of Stalingrad.

Boys, in the words of non-fiction author Anna Claybourne, '...don't like to be fobbed off, they want the real thing... boys at schools I visit are the ones who say (for example, of a picture in a book), "Is that a *real* operation, is that a *real live* person cut open... cool". Boys don't just like non-fiction, they like genuine reality and of course that's where things like oversensitive US restrictions can be really depressing – when I'm told not to show an arrow sticking through a soldier's neck, or elephant seals tearing each other apart, or photos of shark-inflicted wounds, for fear of being frightening or distressing, I always think "boring for the boys"! I know some girls (and probably some boys) may find such pictures distressing, but I also think that's often a cultural affectation, whereby girls demonstrate their femininity by reacting with stage horror to things like that, when in fact they are interested too – so I think it's important to keep these things in non-fiction books.'

This concern for 'reality' extends into other attributes that are typically male and are often considered in non-fiction. As exemplified by 'gross-out' films and television shows, boys like yuckiness – a well-known series of books often featured a minuscule person sitting on a toilet, posing a *Where's Wally?*-type challenge to its (mainly male) readers. Such elements may actually be a plus or a minus: with children, the ultimate reader is often not the purchaser, since books are bought by parents and other relatives or by teachers and librarians who may find offensive the very thing boys consider 'cool'.

Boys love the 'wow!' factor – the discovery of some remarkable fact they can quote as a sort of one-upmanship. The quoting of such facts and statistics, telling jokes, reciting comic catch-phrases and exchanging stickers for sticker books reinforces the bonds among many boys: it is a shared activity that forms part of their social development, with non-fiction books a source and component of the whole equation.

Facts about non-fiction

Illustrated non-fiction has a see-at-a-glance advantage over fiction in that the child can tell instantly whether this is a book that appeals, whereas they might get pages into a novel before they find they don't like it. A clear subject focus also has an obvious advantage – if a boy is interested in trucks, he will respond well to a book that is targeted at this specific interest (and being aware of his enthusiasm will make it easier to buy a book for him).

Non-fiction has the advantage that it can be read non-lineally – readers can dip in and select what they read in portions to suit their reading ability. While fiction may be read aloud to younger children, many are left to their own devices with an integrated text and picture information book – although the opportunities for questions and discussion about the content are actually often greater with non-fiction subjects. We should emphasise to children of both sexes that non-fiction is an important means of obtaining information, that the internet is not the only source, and that looking up and checking facts in books are skills worth acquiring.

A third of boys in the UK say they never read for enjoyment. When they do read they tend to go for magazines and comics rather than books. However, neither should be discounted as 'unsuitable' since they may be the stepping stones to books. We must also face up to the fact that not all children are going to become avid readers: all we can do is provide the tools and encourage them. Some parents, teachers and librarians still retain the prejudice that non-fiction books are not 'proper' books, and it remains true that many lists of recommended books are restricted to fiction. The force-feeding of fiction to the exclusion of non-fiction may hamper the progress of the reluctant reader: fiction reading and comprehension skills highlight gender differences and revealing boys' relatively poor skills in this area may embarrass them and cut them off still further.

Certain other prejudices and often unwitting censorship also persist: librarians often refuse to stock books about wars and weaponry (just as many parents discourage their children from playing with toy guns, whereupon the child fashions one out of Lego). And – though, again, this is a generalisation – many publishers' commissioning editors are women to whom 'boys' interests' are to some extent unknown territory.

The publisher's perspective

In the UK some 10,000 new children's books are published every year, while 48.8 million books in total worth £243.7 million were sold in 2005. The statistics do not separate children's fiction and non-fiction as precisely as adults', but Public Lending Right figures suggest a ratio of almost four fiction borrowings to every one non-fiction. A visual check in the average children's bookshop indicates that the space devoted to non-fiction is smaller than that for fiction, but whatever the figures, children's non-fiction – with boys as its principal consumers – is big business.

As the publishers' listings in this *Yearbook* show (see page 5), most companies produce non-fiction for children. Whether they exert positive discrimination and commission writers with boys specifically in mind is less apparent. However, while publishers rarely indicate that a book is aimed squarely at boys, its presentation and content are often clearly designed with boys as the perceived principal readers. (There are, of course, certain differences between books created for schools, where teachers use them as both literacy and learning tools, and trade books where the emphasis is more on impulse purchase.)

In an ideal world, publishers would like to sell their fiction and non-fiction to both sexes, but as with books for adults, if the reality is that girls gravitate to fiction and boys to non-fiction, whether tacitly or avowedly, they target each group separately in terms both of topic and presentation (the latter is graphically shown by such signs as the sea of pink on the girls' shelves and the graffiti-style lettering on the boys' books).

The illustrative content and style of illustration in non-fiction is paramount – boys respond well to a magazine-style presentation: captioned pictures and short entries can overcome the often short concentration spans of boys (frankly, we literate adults have to grin and bear this – there is no way the average boy is going to read swathes of narrative text). The high illustrative content of boys' non-fiction is also a response to the psychological facts of the case: because they are better at it than girls, boys prefer to decode meaning from visual symbols rather than words, this advantage often compensating for or masking their inferior reading skills.

Perhaps unfortunately for the novice author, in terms of commissioning (and unlike fiction where publishers tend to wait for books to come along from existing authors, agents, and – vary rarely – from unpublished authors) with non-fiction they customarily identify the gaps in the market themselves, create the ideas and seek an (often well-established) author. Much less commonly a publisher responds positively to an approach from a writer with a convincing idea – unless it is overwhelmingly original and obviously commercial.

Writing for boys

Do you feel competent to write about the themes listed in the box on page 95, or allied areas? If so, consider whether – although you may be a specialist, perhaps with a teaching background – you are able to convey information entertainingly to boys. Even if you do not possess specialist skills, research ability counts for a lot: many non-fiction titles can be written by non-specialists provided they undertake their research conscientiously.

Can you accommodate girl readers without alienating the boys? Anna Claybourne again: 'As for traditionally "girly" stuff, I think boys can cope with it in a book on a general topic – for example, I won't eschew mentioning painting your nails in a book on the human body, a fashion picture when dealing with silk moths, or romantic love in a biography, where it adds interest. Firstly, boys can identify this as "for the girls" and choose to perceive it from the outside; secondly, as with the reverse situation, boys will sneer at things like this to assert masculinity, but they may well strike a chord with them internally. So the more inclusion of both "girl" and "boy" things in a non-fiction book the better; the more variety and extremes the better; the more restriction and uniformity and dumbing-down, the worse.'

With the filtering out of content from many National Curriculum subjects, creating entertaining and informative non-fiction books for boys could be your opportunity to give them the facts they crave. It is not an overcrowded market and the rewards from a successful book or series, where books can stay in print and sell steadily for many years, can be considerable. Good luck!

Russell Ash is is the author of *The Top 10 of Everything* (Hamlyn, annual, 1989–) and *Whitaker's World of Facts* (A & C Black 2006), as well as over 100 other non-fiction titles for boys (and girls, and adults). For further information see www.russellash.com, www.top10ofeverything.com, www.whitakersworld.com, www.whitakersworld.co.uk

Writing for girls

Louise Rennison shares her thoughts about writing books for girls.

It still amuses me *a lot* when so called grown-ups have to read the titles of my books out loud. At one of my book launches, a middle-aged respectable-looking bloke in a suit was forced to say: 'And we are really looking forward to seeing *It's OK I'm Wearing Really BIG Knickers* at the top of the bestselling list'. Tee hee hee. I had to be practically carried to the loos because I was laughing so much when the same bloke announced the publication of my new book *Knocked Out By My Nunga-Nungas*. And this you see, in a nutshell, is the secret of my geniosity. I don't have to unleash my teenager within when I write Georgia's diaries because it is already unleashed and wandering around like a fool. (As I write this I am wearing my fluffy mules and a tiara, just in case I suddenly get asked to a party.) It is very restful being yourself(ish).

One of my first readings was in a bookshop in Brighton. It was a mixed adult and teenage audience and as usual I did *ad hoc* rambling. I told the audience that everything in the books was based on real life – my life – and that I had written *Angus, Thongs and Full Frontal Snogging* really quickly and used real people's names. I said I meant to change them before the book was published but forgot.

For instance, my loony school caretaker was nicknamed 'Elvis' because he once came to a school dance and did some exhibition twisting on stage until his back went and he had to be taken to casualty. Well, in the book he is called 'Elvis Attwood'. And guess what his name was in real life? Yes, Mr Attwood. Now you get the picture. Ditto 'Nauseating P. Green' and 'Wet Lindsay'.

Anyway, I was telling the audience that all the characters were real and the family in the book was my family in real life and so on and a woman said 'Well, how does your family feel about having all of their secrets revealed?' My mum was in the audience and I replied 'I don't know. Mum, how do you feel about having all of your secrets revealed?' Mum was slightly flustered by this because she wanted to be proud but also wanted to keep her distance, so she said 'Well, on the whole I think this is a very good book but of course the bits about me are grossly exaggerated.'

Another member of the audience said 'So did you really go to a fancy dress party dressed as a stuffed olive?' And, sadly, I had to admit it was true. I made the 'olive' bit out of green crepe paper and chicken wire to make the round shape. Then I dyed my face, neck and head red for a pimento effect. It was quite funny at the time – well, it was when I was still in my room. The difficulty came when I tried to get out of my room. I had to go down the stairs sideways and I couldn't get in dad's Volvo. He told me I'd have to walk but offered to drive really slowly alongside me. I announced I would walk there by myself in that case and he got all dadish and said 'I don't want you wandering around the streets at night by yourself.' And I replied 'What would I be doing wandering the streets at night dressed as a stuffed olive? Gate crashing cocktail parties?'

But he didn't get it. Anyway, when I did get to the party (walking with dad driving his Volvo alongside me at five miles an hour) I had a horrible time. Initially, everyone laughed but later ignored me. I did have a dance by myself, but things kept crashing to the floor around me. In the end, the host asked me to sit down. I tried – but failed. Still, I did find out that I am not on my own *vis à vis* childishosity. At the end of the reading, a woman confided in me that she'd gone to a fancy dress party as a fried egg! We both shared a chuckle and I said 'Blimey what were we like?'And she replied 'No Louise, you don't understand, this was last week!'

What was I rambling on about? Oh yes – writing for girls. It's a hoot and I thoroughly recommend it. All you do is think about jokes, boys, snogging and lipstick. Perfect. I wish I had a useful tale to tell about how to write for girls, but the fact is that everything I have done has been sort of accidental. I wasn't intending to write books. In fact, years ago, I used to perform my own show entitled 'Stevie Wonder felt my face'. (He did actually feel my face... hang on a minute... 'Stevie Wonder' was also based on my real life. I am sensing a theme here...) Anyway, I was at the Edinburgh Festival doing my show and my first instinct was to reply 'Oooh no, I don't want to be stuck in a room writing by myself'.

I did eventually write my first book in 1999. I was a columnist on the London *Evening Standard* and I wrote a piece about having to have my shoes surgically removed. (Once again based on a real incident. I had forced my big fat feet into tiny strappy stilettoes out of sheer vanity, and then I fell out with my boyfriend and clip clopped off home in a high dudgeon (I lived on the other side of London). When I eventually got home, in the early hours, I fell asleep on the sofa fully clothed and still wearing my shoes. I woke up in the morning to find my feet had swollen up and my shoes were cutting into my feet. The shoes were embedded in my feet. I had shoefeet. My friends carried me to Charing Cross Hospital casualty to have them cut off.

The day after publication, Brenda Gardener from Piccadilly Press phoned me up and asked me to write a teenage girls diary and I asked why me? She said 'Because I have never read anything so childish and self obsessed as your article and I think you could do a really good job.' And the rest is historosity. But not very good advice for getting a book deal!

When I attempted to write the book, quite a few people pointed out that I am in fact not a teenager and haven't been one for quite some time. A very long time. A very very long time. Their advice was that I go and talk to some teenagers. I tried this straight away because I assumed it was possible to talk to teenagers – but it isn't – it is a hopeless task. You can't get any sense out of them at all and very often they do that helpless laughing thing. They know they should just stop it because if they don't someone will kill them, but they still can't stop. Anyway, I did attempt to speak to them for 'research' purposes. I asked one group of girls if they still did snogging. And they looked at me as if I had fallen out of someone's nose. They said 'SNOGGING? You say snogging. Snogging? How sad is that?' Then when I asked another group of girls, they looked at me in the same way and said 'Yeah, we say snogging, what else would you say you sad person?'

So, on the whole I more or less ignore what 'the youth' say. When I do readings and signings I am very often asked which are my favourite teenage books. My answer is – none. I don't read teenage books because I am not a teenager. In truth, I really am very ignorant about the whole 'teen' thing and that's how I want to stay. I deliberately don't read anyone else's books. I just plug into what I remember about my own teen times.

I recall parts of my teens very vividly. When I was 15 my family emigrated from Leeds to Whakatane, New Zealand. I'm sure I remember things around that time because of the high drama of what I went through. But I think that if I hadn't had any major drama to star in I would have made some up for myself. After all, every teenager is the star of their own melodrama. *Everything* matters and can potentially ruin your life – the way your fringe lies, a spot under your skin (*aka* a lurker) and I won't even go into the nose slimming measures.

Having an excellent memory definitely helps and I do credit myself with a head made for trivia. Did you know that your memory is like a muscle? The more I go back in time to remember, for example, my teenage friend's and my scoring system for snogging (graded one to 10 – number five being a three-minute kiss with no breaks) the more I remember.

Of course, it helps if you are still on speaking terms with other people who were there at the same time. I am still in touch with my 'Ace Gang' from school and they can sometimes fill in the gaps in my memory. For instance, I was talking to my friend Rosie about one of our school teachers, Herr Kamyer. He had the double comedy value of being the only male teacher in an all-girls school and being German. I recalled a physics experiment he did using billiard balls on a tea towel to explain how molecules vibrate. At the time, I found this very funny and I put my hand up and said 'Herr Kamyer, what part does the tea towel play in the molecular structure?' And Herr Kamyer made his fateful mistake and replied 'Ach no, I merely use the tea towel to keep my balls still.' It was absolute pandemonium. I could not stop laughing even as I was taken to see the headmistress. Anyway, while Rosie and I were talking about this incident, she remembered something else about Herr Kamyer that I had completely forgotten. She recalled when he had taken our class by train to the Lake District. The train had slam doors on each side of the carriage and when the train pulled into the station Herr Kamyer leapt up said 'Ach here ve are' and stepped out of the door on the wrong side of the train and disappeared onto the track. Oh – happy days.

Writing for teenage girls is somehow timeless. The rites of passage that my mates and I went through in the Sixties are not so very different – emotionally – from girls now. Fashions have changed and the bands have different names but girls still strop around worrying about boys liking them and ignoring their long-suffering dads. Somewhere, even as I write this, a girl will be thinking 'For the teenage vampire party I could make one big eyebrow out of theatrical fur. That will be vair vair funny.'

Louise Rennison is the author of six books for teenage girls. Her most recent book is *Startled By His Furry Shorts* in the *Confessions of Georgia Nicolson* series (2006).

Fiction for 6–9 year-olds

Alison Stanley is an experienced commissioning editor of young fiction. She gives here what she regards as essential components of a good fiction book for younger readers.

When teaching six year-olds in the mid-1970s, 'reading' was something that involved a queue of children at my desk, waiting to be heard struggling through their less than stimulating reading-scheme books. There had to be a better way of developing reading skills, especially as the delight of sharing real books with the children during 'storytime' at the end of the day, was such a marked contrast. I had no idea in those days about the business of publishing, and I certainly never imagined that many years later I would be commissioning books for that very same age group to read and enjoy. But without that classroom experience, I doubt that I would have begun to appreciate the needs of the young beginner reader. Nor would I have experienced that magical moment when a child just breaks through the reading skills barrier and begins to read unaided for the very first time. The anticipation in excitedly turning over the page to find out what happens next; the thrill of a guessed word being right; and the beginning of reading for pleasure are all magical moments to witness.

Books for younger readers

Here are some of my favourite books for younger readers that have stood the test of time. Read them and you'll know what I mean!

Happy Families series by Janet and Allan Ahlberg (Puffin)

Horrid Henry by Francesca Simon (Orion)

The Littlest Dragon by Margaret Ryan (Collins)

Mr Majeika by Humphrey Carpenter (Puffin)

The Worst Witch by Jill Murphy (Puffin)

Spider McDrew by Alan Durant (Collins)

The Black Queen by Michael Morpurgo (Random House)

Morris the Mouse Hunter by Vivian French (Collins)

Clarice Bean by Lauren Child (Orchard Books)

Lizzie Zipmouth by Jacqueline Wilson (Random House)

There's a Viking in My Bed by Jeremy Strong (Puffin)

Beginner readers

What makes a good book for children just beginning to read on their own – one that will stimulate and motivate them, and let them know that reading is an enjoyable and rewarding activity?

Firstly and simply – beginner readers need good stories. Strong plots that are easy to follow, so that when faced with an unrecognisable word, the child can predict what is going to happen and be able to have a go at reading that 'difficult' word. Lively and appealing characters are essential too, especially if featured in more than one book.

Beginner readers like stories that reflect their experiences of the world but also ones that will stretch their imaginations. Stories with a fantasy element rooted in the real world where something ordinary becomes extraordinary in a familiar world, are always popular. The language of the stories should be rhythmic with plenty of repetition and alliteration. Sentences need to be short enough so they don't get split by a page turn, but long enough so that the story doesn't read in a stilted fashion.

Books for beginner readers require a generous typeface and good clear layout with plenty of illustrations giving clues to the text. This will help make the transition from shared picture books to reading alone a smooth one.

Last, but definitely not least, there is one vital thing to remember when writing stories for the beginner reader… beginner readers read *slowly*. Wacky, fast-paced humour within the text does not work when read word for word, very slowly. Humour in the text needs to be obvious, relate to the child's world and work when read at a snail's pace (see *Writing humour for young children* on page 105 for inspirational advice on writing funny fiction).

Top 10 questions

To summarise, the 10 questions I ask when assessing manuscripts for younger readers are:

Plot
- Is it a good story?
- Will it make sense when read slowly?
- Will it keep the reader wanting to turn over the pages?
- Is the story strong enough to stand up to the competition?

Setting
- Is the story set in a world that children will be familiar with?
- Are there events in the story that children will relate to?

Characters
- Are the characters appealing and original?
- Are the characters rounded enough for the beginner reader to want further books about them?

Language
- Is the vocabulary suitable for the young beginner reader?
- Is there plenty of repetition, alliteration and rhythmic writing?

I would also want to know about the author. I'd want to know if the manuscript was written by a published author, and if so, do his or her books sell? (Never forget that publishing is a commercial venture!) If it is a new author, I'd like to know if he or she is seen to be a major new talent who will progress to write further books.

The editorial process can help with many of these points, but the originality and uniqueness of a story belong to the author. Because there are so many books written for this age group, it takes a special author to create something new and appealing, something that will stand the test of time.

Confident readers

Once children become fluent readers, there's usually no stopping them in their quest to read more, and soon move on to longer novels. It's at this stage that they are exploring the different genres – humour, horror, adventure, or themes such as school stories, animal stories and football stories, amongst others. They're also finding out which authors they like to read and will be actively seeking out new books by that author. Confident readers come in all shapes, sizes, ages and with different backgrounds and personalities and it is essential that this is reflected in a broad range of reading matter.

Alison Stanley was a commissioning editor at Puffin Books and at HarperCollins Children's Books, where she was responsible for developing the younger end of the fiction list.

See also...
- *Writing humour for young children*, page 105
- *Getting started*, page 1

Writing humour for young children

Like most adults, children love humour. But in both cases the joke will fall flat unless it is aimed at the right audience. Jeremy Strong has 10 rules for writing humour for young children.

The snappy bit: some simple rules

1. Never allow your bum to become gratuitous.
2. Write wrong.
3. Self mutilation is highly recommended.
4. Words are essential.
5. Pulchritude? No way.
6. Inside every 20-plus there's an eight year-old trying to get out.
7. You calling me a wozzer? Mankynora!
8. Just who do you think you're talking to?
9. Surprise!
10. Ha! I laugh at death.

The expansive bit. We begin at the beginning, with **Rule Nine. Surprise!** Ha ha! That's pretty much self explanatory.

Rule Six: Inside every 20-plus there's an eight year-old trying to get out.

Years ago, when I first began writing for children, I was often asked (by adults) why it was that the stories I wrote seemed to appeal to children. You have to imagine an adult asking this question, in a tone of voice that mixes one part admiration to 10 parts complete bewilderment. I used to answer, fairly truthfully, that only my exterior had aged along with my chronological age, and that I was still aged about eight inside. The adult would usually laugh and would go away as bewildered as they were before they'd asked the question. The point here is, I think, that it isn't possible to really understand except from a child's viewpoint. If you have forgotten what it was like to be a child then you're unlikely to understand.

Rule One: Never allow your bum to become gratuitous.

To make matters worse, adults often think the things that make children laugh are puerile. To some extent this is true and it is easy to make a child laugh by playing 'lowest common denominator' jokes – jokes that refer to farts, snot, bums, knickers, etc. But whilst employing these guaranteed tickle-sticks it is easy to forget that children also like quite sophisticated jokes.

As for the bums and farts, it's okay to pop them in here and there but, for the sake of at least some self respect, keep them to a minimum. Never let your bum be gratuitous.

Rule Four: Words are essential.

Children love word play, and they love 'knowing' jokes – for example, jokes that are aware of how bad they are, or referential jokes that make use of things familiar to them, the things that mark out their lives, such as school, parents, family.

Then there is the matter of what children can read and understand. Obviously, this is going to vary not only with age but with ability. Anyone who has taught junior age children knows that there are children of six who can read like 11 year-olds, and *vice versa*, with all shades in between and quite frequently further beyond. Nevertheless, as a writer, you need to aim towards the centre. In this article I am going to concentrate on 6–11 year-olds because those are the ages I taught for 17 years.

Let's look at language. Things need to be fairly simple. Shorter, rather than longer sentences work best. But like all rules this one can be deliberately misused. For example, at some appropriate point in a story you might wish to hurl yourself into some ever-increasing sentence that just seems to plunge on and on at a relentless pace and with reckless abandon like a runaway car because that happens to be one of the best ways your writing can capture the manic activity that is going on in your story at that particular point. Maybe it is a description of a runaway car. You get the point. Children respond to this positively because, anchored as it is in a normally short and simple style of writing, the over-long sentence becomes not only a writing device, but also a source of humour.

Rule 10: Ha! I laugh at death.

As with comedy for other age groups, nothing is held sacred. You will, however, have to obey the obvious rules that generally apply to writing for children, and also steer clear of the PC police. You can be smutty, but not dirty. You can be unkind to animals, but they mustn't be in a circus, unless you're a signed up freedom fighter for 'Say no! to performing dumb creatures'.

You can laugh about death. (It's an emotional release. Honest.) You can even have stereotypes and clichés – but in this instance don't expect to get published.

Rule Two: Write wrong.

Children love to recognise things that are wrong, and this is where word play often has great effect. Characters that get their words or spellings wrong are a good source of humour, not only because it is funny in its own right, but because children love the empowerment of recognising what's wrong. (You will, incidentally, lose brownie points for using words like 'empowerment'.)

Rule Seven: You calling me a wozzer? Mankynora!

Invented words can also be a terrific source of enjoyment for both writer and reader, especially when they are used as expletives – sort of coded (and therefore safe) swear words. Mankynora! Wozzer yourself! Let's also take a look at sophistication. You have to ask yourself, am I writing a joke for an adult or a child? I know for a fact that I am guilty of putting jokes for adults in some stories – jokes I know only an adult will understand. (Or sometimes a joke that a child will get on one level, but where the adult will see a second 'hidden' joke or implication.) The reason I do this is because (a) I can't resist the temptation if it's a good one, (b) I like to remember that many of my books are read to children by adults, and so I am putting in something to make it more enjoyable for them, and (c) I don't do it often and I make sure that the vast majority of the humour is firmly in the child's grasp.

Rule Five: Pulchritude? No way.

Whilst on the subject of sophistication it is worth thinking about the words you use. With each word you need to ask yourself: can a child of 'x' years read and understand this word? Apply a bit of common sense. There are some words a child might not understand but it might be worthwhile introducing it to them, allowing the context to help reveal its meaning.

The word sophistication itself is a reasonable example. Many junior children would not understand it but, although it's long, it's not too difficult to work out what it says and you could argue that it's a good word for a child to know. On the other hand, the word 'pulchritudinous' is not only very hard for a child to work out but it is extremely unlikely you would need to use such a word when writing for junior children and if you do then you seriously need to reconsider what you are doing.

Rule Three: Self mutilation is highly recommended.

You have to be rigorously self disciplined about this. No matter how good a joke is you have to cut it out if it's not actually funny to your audience. The humour also needs to arrive and leave quickly. Anything that takes pages to set up is not worth it and the longer it takes the more likely it is that your writing will become increasingly false and unnatural as you struggle with all the scaffolding you require to hold up the joke.

Rule Eight: Just who do you think you're talking to?

It is a mistake to think that the things adults laugh at in children make good material for children's books. They don't, for the simple reason that it's funny to the adult watching the child, and not the other way round. All of this points to one of the cardinal rules for writing anything: be aware of your audience. Keep that firmly in mind and you can't go far wrong. I was going to finish by writing: May the fart be with you. Then I realised that it would be out of place and one fart too many. See what I mean?

Jeremy Strong's humorous fiction is hugely popular with 8–11 year-olds. His books include *The Karate Princess* titles, and three Viking stories which were made into a popular television series. Jeremy won the Federation of Children's Book Groups Children's Book Award for *The Hundred-Mile-an-Hour Dog*. Recent books include *Let's Do The Pharoah* and *My Brother's Famous Bottom*, all published by Puffin.

See also...

- *Writing comedy for children's television*, page 286
- *Fiction for 6–9 year-olds*, page 103

Writing horror for children

'Nine stories you'll wish you'd never read' it warns on the cover of *Horowitz Horror*. Anthony Horowitz writes about writing horror for children and, aware of children's thirst for blood and intestines, airs the question of just how far an author can go.

As much as it's fun to be asked to write about writing, I hope anyone reading this will take it all with a medium-sized pinch of salt. The only incontrovertible law of writing I ever came upon was set down by my great hero, the American screenwriter William Goldman in *Adventures in the Screen Trade*. NOBODY KNOWS ANYTHING. It deserves the capital letters. If you're setting out to write a horror story for children, what follows may be useful. But your own instincts are probably better. Anyway, here is my experience for what it's worth.

I am currently about halfway through writing a series of supernatural thrillers with the overall title of *The Power of Five*. The hero is a 14-year-old boy called Matt Freeman and in the first book, *Raven's Gate*, he finds himself arrested for attempted murder and sent on a fostering programme which lands him in the middle of a Yorkshire village, inhabited – as it turns out – by a coven of witches. Matt is chased by ferocious devil dogs and by the animated skeletons of dinosaurs. He is sucked into a bog, kidnapped and set up to be sacrificed. Anyone who tries to help him dies horribly. A policeman is killed in a car accident. A farmer is frightened to death. His own parents, of course, died long ago.

The second volume, *Evil Star,* begins with a madwoman immolating herself in a petrol tanker, shortly after murdering her live-in lover. The villain is a South American businessman who has been purposefully mutilated at birth. This time, Matt is beaten up by Peruvian police, robbed, starved, attacked by savage condors and … well, you probably get the idea.

Children love horror. You need look no further than the worldwide success of writers like Darren Shan to see it. Years ago, the *Goosebumps* series had covers that promised far more than the contents ever delivered but for a time they were littered across every school yard and made their author – R.L. Stine – a millionaire. Even the *Harry Potter* films have become progressively darker until the most recent instalment, which had one character cutting off his own hand, the death of a teenager and the truly hideous appearance of 'he who should not be named'.

And yet, the first – indeed the most crucial – question you have to ask yourself is: how far can you go? This is something of which I'm always painfully aware. Go into a classroom and talk to the children and you will discover that far enough is never enough. They want the blood, the intestines, the knife cutting through the flesh … the full monty. The problem, of course, is that if you give it to them you risk alienating the school librarians, bookshop buyers and the parents, and your book may never actually reach its intended audience.

When I visit schools, I always advise children to keep their own writing blood-free. Teachers don't like it, I tell them. I remind them that the scariest moment in any horror film is when the hand reaches for the door handle in the dark. That's when the music jangles and your imagination runs riot. What happens after the door is open is almost incidental. It seems to me that what you imagine will always be scarier than what you see – and this is a rule I apply to my own writing. For my money, the most effective passage in *Raven's Gate* comes when Matt gets lost, cycling through a wood in the dark. Every road brings him back to the same point. Slowly he begins to realise that he is never going to escape. There's no blood. No monsters. But it seems to work.

But at the same time – if you don't actually deliver, you're going to disappoint and so lose your audience. In my view, this is what went wrong with *Goosebumps* and it's the reason why they're no longer so popular. There has to be blood. How much of it and how far you go is up to you. Like I say, there are no rules. Take a look at the opening of Darren Shan's *Lord Loss*. The death of the parents leaves nothing to the imagination but teachers still love him. I don't know how he gets away with it.

Perhaps it's a question of context. A random act of violence or mutilation might seem very horrible in a book by, say, Jacqueline Wilson. But that's because her characters are so real, her world so recognisable. But when you write a horror story, you have a different departure point. Even before your readers buy the book, they know what to expect and they open it in exactly the same way as they might get on a ghost train at a fairground. They expect a certain number of skeletons and monsters and read the book in the knowledge that (a) it's only a ride, and (b) it will eventually deliver them back into the daylight.

The daylight, though, I think is important. I was genuinely shocked by the death of the teenager – Cedric Diggory – in *Harry Potter and the Goblet of Fire*. Not that J.K. Rowling needs to worry about the rules. But I've always thought that although it's reasonable to slap around your heroes, to frighten them and to hurt them, it's somehow irresponsible and wrong to kill them. No children have ever died in any of my books. Actually, none of them have ever felt real pain – again, because of the context. A child being chased by devil dogs through the swamps of Yorkshire may seem to be having a tough time. But that's nothing compared to a child in a London supermarket being slapped and screamed at by his mother. That, to me, is real horror.

Enough of these generalities. If you're thinking of writing something dark and scary for a young audience, here are just a few thoughts that might help.

- **You need an original story.** It may seem obvious but the realm of horror is stuffed with haunted castles, wicked stepmothers, evil magicians and all the rest of it. I know because I've used plenty of them myself. But a strong, simple idea will set you apart from the pack. Look at Justin Somper's success with *Vampirates*, a clever collision of swashbuckling and blood. Or Garth Nix (*Mister Monday*) who time and time again comes up with hugely imaginative universes, completely new ideas.
- **Think about your central characters.** If they're likeable enough and idiosyncratic enough, you can – and will – get away with murder. There are some quite horrible things in Philip Pullman's *Northern Lights* with children kidnapped, stripped of their souls and turned into zombies. But we never doubt that Will and Lyra will win through.
- **Don't lose your sense of humour.** Mixing a few laughs in with the general mayhem doesn't lessen the horror. It helps the reader to deal with it. Paul Jennings, the Australian author, has produced some wonderfully twisted stories that would be far nastier if he didn't write with a smile.
- **Forget that you're writing for children.** This advice may seem incompatible with what I've already written but for me it's always been vital. If you sit at your desk with children in mind, it's all too easy for your work to become patronising and flabby. Of course it's important to consider levels of violence, what sort of language is applicable, how far you

can go – but these should all be at the back of your mind. When I write horror, I try to scare myself. Darkness, solitude, the sense of being lost, the figure glimpsed out of the corner of your eye. I'm pretty sure that what scares children scares adults too. There's no need to cherry-pick, or to filter, the frissons!

• **Think visually.** The awful truth is that children are seeing more and more horror films with a 15 certificate, and they're also playing computer games with an incredible amount of electronic gore. Both films and games have a language which, I think, translates well to books. My generation was literary. Today's generation is visual. That's my theory, anyway, and I hope my audience will 'see' as much as read my work.

My intention has always been to entertain children – by which I mean neither educating them, improving them nor terrorising them. As to the last of these, I only ever got it wrong once. I wrote a short horror story (it's in *Horowitz Horror 2*) where the first letter of each sentence spelled out a message to the reader. That message went something along the lines of: 'As soon as you have read this, I'm coming to your house to kill you.'

About a year later, I received a note from a very angry and distressed mother who told me that she now had a traumatised daughter. My story, she said, was wilfully irresponsible and she suggested that I write a letter to her daughter, apologising.

I totally agreed. The next day I wrote a nice letter to the girl, explaining that I had intended to be mischievous rather than malevolent, that it was only a story, that she shouldn't have taken it so seriously.

Unfortunately, the first letter of every sentence in my letter spelled out: 'I am going to kill you too.'

Anthony Horowitz knew he wanted to be a writer when he was eight years old and was published for the first time when he was 22. He writes for up to 10 hours a day in a studio at the bottom of his garden. He is perhaps best known for his *Alex Rider* novels, the first of which, *Stormbreaker*, was released as a major film in 2006. He has also written extensively for television, creating *Midsomer Murders* and *Foyle's War*. He is currently writing *Nightrise*, the third volume in *The Power of Fi*.

Writing historical novels for children

Michelle Paver shares her thoughts on how to approach writing historical novels for children and the importance of focusing on the story.

Books about how to get published sometimes advise new writers to research the market thoroughly. Read the competition, see what sells – that sort of thing. If that appeals to you, fine. But I've never liked the idea and have never done it. In my view it isn't necessary, or even a good thing. You might just find it confusing and intimidating, and it could put you off what you really want to write.

I think it's better to concentrate on the story *you* want to write. The characters. The premise. The historical setting. You may not even know *why* you want to write it. But you do, and that's the main thing.

The period

Before you make a start, though, it's worth asking yourself why you want to set the story in your chosen historical period. Are you especially attracted to it? Did you day-dream about it as a child (maybe you still do)? Or does it simply have a vague appeal, perhaps based on having seen a few films or read some novels set in that time?

There's no harm in being drawn to a particular period for tenuous reasons. But if that is the case, I'd suggest that you become a little more familiar with it before deciding whether to use that time for your story. You'll need to know your chosen period pretty thoroughly; and if you decide halfway through writing your novel that it isn't quite as fascinating as you'd thought, then the chances are that the reader won't either and your story probably won't work. In short, you must be prepared to live and breathe it for months or even years.

The story is king

This would seem to be the logical point to talk about research, but I'm going to leave that for later because I don't think it's the most important thing. The most important thing is the story. Always. And particularly for children. In general, children don't read a book because it got a great review in *The Times*, or because they want to look impressive reading it on the train. They read it because they want to know what's going to happen next.

That might seem trite, but it's amazing how easy it is to forget, especially when you've done a ton of research on a particular period, and there are so many terrific things about it that you just can't wait to share with everybody else.

So it's worth reminding yourself that the basics of any good story need to be firmly in place: characters about whom you care passionately; a protagonist who wants or needs something desperately; perhaps a powerful villain or opposing force which poses a significant threat. Big emotions: anger, envy, pride, hate, loyalty, love, grief. And just because the book will be read by children, don't shy away from the bad stuff (although obviously, you'll need to handle it responsibly). Death, violence, neglect, loneliness. Children want to know. They're curious about everything.

The beginning

Everyone knows that the first page of a story is critical, but this is especially so for children. In fact, the first paragraph is even more critical. And the first sentence is the most critical of all.

This poses a special challenge if you're writing a historical novel. How do you root the story in the past without getting bogged down in clunky exposition?

There's no magic formula, but the idea of 'show, don't tell' is a good place to start. Perhaps you could begin with a situation that's specifically of that period, like a witch-burning. Or, as part of the story, weave in an object of the period, like a flint knife.

You might be tempted to write a 'prologue', like the ones they used to have at the beginning of old movies ('London, England. The Cavaliers and Roundheads are at War...'). By all means write one of these. I did, for the first draft of *Wolf Brother*. But you may well ditch it before you finish the final draft. You may find that by then it has done its work by helping to anchor you in the period. If you leave it in, it might have a distancing effect, diminishing the immediacy of the story.

Telling the story

What I said about the beginning of the story goes for the rest of it, too. The challenge for the writer of historical novels is to make the reader 'live' the story along with the characters. Somehow you've got to make them see, feel, touch, taste that period – without resorting to wodges of boring description that might slow things down, or overdone 'period' dialogue which is tiring to read and may distance the reader.

Again, there's no formula, but a good guiding principle is to make the essential exposition an integral part of the story. Make this a story that couldn't really have happened at any other time in history – even though the emotions involved are universals with which the reader can readily identify.

If you do this, then it'll become fairly clear what needs to stay in and what should come out. And there will probably be a lot of cutting. Pare down the exposition to what's essential. For instance, you may not need to explain the background to the entire war; just the particular skirmish in which your heroine has been caught up.

And for the essential exposition, it can help to introduce it in a highly charged emotional way: perhaps an argument or a fight. 'Exposition as ammunition' was a favourite motto of the film-maker Ingmar Bergman and it's one that can serve you well. But don't get so hung up on explaining things that you lose sight of the emotional focus of the scene.

The same goes for 'period atmosphere'. I would think long and hard before including anything for this reason alone. Try to make your period details part of the story. Then cut them back, then cut them back some more. What you need is a swift, vivid, unforgettable image with *just* enough detail to bring it alive – but no more.

Research

Which brings me (finally) to research. Some novelists don't do any. If that works for them, that's great. But if you're setting your story in the past, I don't think you can get by without doing at least some. And probably rather a lot. You need to know, intimately, what it was like to live back then. It's the little everyday details which interest readers, particularly children. What did people eat, wear, live in? How did they fight, travel, work, entertain themselves? What did they *think*? How were they similar to us? How were they different? And the more you can actually experience some of this for yourself the better – for example, by location research, trying out the food of the period – because it will give you all sorts of intriguing ideas and insights that you couldn't have got in a library.

Bear in mind, too, that research isn't just a matter of getting the details right. It'll probably spark ideas for the story itself: incidents, twists, particular scenes. These are gold dust. Use them. (Provided, of course, that they work in the context of the story as a whole.)

Perhaps the hardest thing about research is that the vast bulk of what you've lovingly unearthed isn't going to make it into the final draft. Be ruthless about keeping *only* those details that you really need: either to move the story along, or to develop character, or to set the scene. And shun any whiff of teaching; this is a story, not a history lesson.

That means that you'll probably go through a rather painful process of cutting over the course of your first, second, and successive drafts. But don't grieve too deeply for your lost treasures. *You* know all that background, and your in-depth knowledge will give your writing an assurance that it wouldn't otherwise have.

Language and style

This can be especially tricky: a kind of balancing act between keeping the story and the characters accessible, while leaving the language with just enough special vocabulary or dialogue to remind us that we're in another time. All this without distancing us too much, or (just as bad) without obvious anachronisms.

I'm often asked if I write differently when I'm writing for children, as opposed to when I'm writing for adults. The answer is, no, not at all. For me, it's the nature of the story that dictates the language and the style. If you're writing a story set in a middle-class Victorian home, your vocabulary and style will be utterly different from that which you'd use if you were writing about a forest of the Stone Age.

Having said that, if children are going to be among your readers, one important thing to bear in mind is that lengthy flashbacks can weaken the force of a story by reducing its immediacy. Because children read to know what's going to happen next, it helps too, to have unexpected twists, surprises, action, high emotion, flashes of humour, and lots of dialogue, as well as the odd cliff-hanger chapter ending. You've got to give them a reason to turn the page; and to keep turning the pages, all the way to the end.

Who are you writing for?

'What age group are you "aiming" at?' is a frequently asked question. For myself, the answer is: none. Apart from a general idea that I'm not writing a picture book for six-year-olds, I prefer to leave age groups to editors and publishers, and concentrate on the story.

Besides, once you start thinking in terms of 'aiming' a story at a particular group of people, where does it end? For instance, say you're 'aiming' a story at 9–12 year-olds. Well, what kind of 9–12 year-olds? They're not a homogeneous mass. Boys or girls, or both? And what kind? Middle-class or underprivileged? Immigrant or home-grown? Gifted, average, or special needs? If you start thinking like that, you run the risk of killing your story.

The same thing goes for the publisher's Holy Grail of the 'crossover' novel that's read by both adults and children. If you have this at the forefront of your mind when you're writing, it's unlikely that you'll do justice to the story. It may well end up being a mess which *nobody* will want to read.

Although this may sound a bit uncompromising, I have the same view when it comes to trying out your story on your own children – if you have them – or on others. This is risky and I prefer not to do it. (Well, in my case, I couldn't, because I don't have children, and don't know any very well!) In fact, quite a few children's writers don't have children of their own, but what many do have is a strong memory of what it was like to be a child and an ability to write from a child's perspective. That's what you need. Not market research.

Being true to your story, knowing your chosen period inside out but only including the most telling of details... Of course, none of this is going to guarantee success. But with luck, it'll improve your chances on the slush pile. *And* you'll have a lot more fun than if you'd been slavishly studying the market!

Michelle Paver is the author of the *Chronicles of Ancient Darkness* series. The first book in the series, *Wolf Brother*, was published in 2004 and a film of it is to be directed by Ridley Scott for Twentieth Century Fox. The second book is *Spirit Walker* (2005) and the latest in the series is *Soul Eater*, due to be published in September 2006.

Writing for teenagers

Meg Rosoff describes how she came to write *How I Live Now* and offers some suggestions to bear in mind when writing for teenagers.

Despite the optimistic title of this piece, I know hardly anything about writing for teenagers.

Here's a metaphor. Let's say you have sex, get pregnant, and give birth to a baby who grows up to be a successful actor/scientist/politician. Everyone wants to know how you did it. You ponder the question. Was it the organic food? Piano lessons? Good genes? State school? Was it benign neglect? Fish oil? Dumb luck?

It may be possible to post-rationalise success, but it rarely rings true. How did I manage to write a book adolescents like? I read a lot. Procrastinated for years. Had five careers. Am a foreigner. Found a good agent. Was desperate.

The answer is probably all of the above, plus a few hundred things I haven't thought of yet. Writing does come easily to me, which (let's face it) helps a lot. I always *wanted* to be a writer. And much as I hate to give it any credit at all, my disastrous career in advertising turned out to be an excellent apprenticeship. I was also desperate to get out of advertising, which helped in a different way. But I never thought I could write a novel.

For one thing, I was never interested in plot and could never figure out where people got their ideas for stories. I am not the sort of mother with an endless supply of charming bedtime tales. I can't even tell a decent joke.

To make matters worse, I compared myself incessantly to the people I most admired – Jose Saramago, George Eliot, William James, Shirley Hazzard – and knew I'd never be able to write a book *that good*. Which turned out to be true enough, but (in retrospect) blindingly irrelevant.

As for writing for teenagers, I am uniquely ill-equipped by virtue of my advanced age. I'll be 50 next year, which disqualifies me from talking like a teenager or knowing much about how teenagers act or dress or think, except insofar as I observe them walking past my North London home most mornings on the way to school, leaving a trail of incomprehensible slang and McDonald's wrappers behind them. My daughter (aged four when I wrote *How I Live Now*) is now eight, which thankfully hints at, but does not yet provide concrete evidence of, the workings of the teenage mind.

So. The answer doesn't lie in storytelling ability, youth, or confidence. Nor will you find it in my powers of observation (mediocre, at best). I don't have an exceptional ear for dialogue or significant recall for past events. I'm terrible at history and hate research.

However … I have always had a morbid imagination (I can imagine a disaster in the most cheerful of scenarios) and a tendency to think like an adolescent. For me, teenage angst and midlife crisis got all caught up together at about the age of 20, and have been going along hand-in-hand ever since.

And I'm not the only hybrid freak around, the phenomenon of the middle-aged teenager is everywhere. Much of my generation was brought up on the idea that we never had to grow up, that we could wait forever to have children (whom we would raise as friends) that we could marry late or not at all, have powerful, well-paid jobs to which we would wear jeans and T-shirts, give ourselves grown-up toys for Christmas and birthdays (wide screen televisions, iPods, snowboarding kit, lava lamps) and never develop the gravitas our parents seemed to acquire magically and effortlessly at age 20.

When I was 25 (at which age my mother had married, bought a house and was pregnant with her second child) my friends and I were mooching around New York City, living in cockroach-riddled apartments, having affairs with inappropriate men, applying to art school, swapping illegal substances and going to all-night clubs. I married so late, my parents were convinced I was a lesbian. (How old was I? 33.)

My professional life followed a similar path. After seven jobs, three careers and a series of disastrous attempts to conform, I ended up in advertising, home to the hipsters at the end of the universe. Here was immaturity taken to its extreme: departments full of so-called creatives with goatee beards and extreme spectacles who played Xbox all day and called it work. The boys were joined by a tiny minority of females who changed their names from Susan and Mary to Cherokee and Zeus. And everyone pretended day after day that selling stuff nobody wanted was incredibly cool.

I got fired a lot from advertising, which seems fine today but at the time was discouraging. In retrospect, my relationship with advertising reminds me of a bad love affair – the sort that happens repeatedly when you lack the insight to realise that your taste in men (or in my case, careers) stinks. Being stuck in perpetual adolescence is all about lacking insight: lacking perspective, lacking wisdom, lacking everything in fact, except an enthusiasm that transcends failure. After failure. After failure.

As I moved from a 30-something adolescent to a 40-something adolescent, I ran up against the sobering consideration of having children. If your kids have parents who wear jeans, listen to Kings of Leon, and still don't understand the stock market, how are they supposed to act? My daughter started asking how to buy a house and the difference between credit and debit cards when she was six. She advises her father and me on how to dress, what car to drive, how to behave in public. She says she'd like to live in the American suburbs when she grows up, with a huge 4 x 4 and a spray-on tan. All her father and I can do is laugh (through our tears) and hope it passes.

But recently, something strange happened. Around my 40th birthday, I began to notice I wasn't quite so lacking in perspective as before. I began to make certain observations, certain wise observations, like: *Life is short. I hate my job. Perhaps I should write a book.*

In July 2002, I gave myself a deadline: two years.

I took a two-month leave of absence from work, stole a plot from the horse books I loved as a kid and wrote a practice novel. It wasn't the finest work of literature, and I sincerely hope it will never see the light of day, but it worked. It had a story (an old story, but a story) and a bunch of characters. It moved smoothly from A to B, was moderately funny and faintly poignant. It looked like a book, it read like a book, and I thought, it may not be Henry James, but it ain't advertising either.

With that book I found myself an agent, who suggested I write another book (she didn't say, 'a better one' but I read between the lines). And when I asked for advice on how to write a 'proper book' for teenagers, she said 'Write the best book you can write'. If I had to condense this long rambling autobiography-disguised-as-advice into seven words, that would be it. Nothing wiser has come my way since.

Having stuck with me so far, you are no doubt panting for the good old-fashioned, opinionated, bullet-pointed advice on how to write for teenagers that this article promises and I'm more than happy to give it a shot. Remember, however, your grain of salt, and that for each suggestion that follows, I can already think of an exception.

- **There are no rules.** There are books for teenagers with sex and drugs and unhappy endings. There are 100-page books and 700-page books, moral and immoral world-views, books with no children in them, books that tackle the Spanish Inquisition, the holocaust, adultery, suicide, football. If you don't believe me about this lack of rules, take note of how many panel discussions at literary festivals are devoted to the subject 'What Makes a Young Adult Novel?' The reason they continue to ask the question is that nobody knows the answer.
- **Know how to write.** Really, it helps. If your true talent lies in baking bread, open a bakery.
- **If you're not lucky enough to be immature, regress.** Haul yourself back to the days when the world was opaque.
- **On the other hand, be wise.** The more you experience in life, the more wisdom you unconsciously stockpile. The broken relationships, the family rows, the children you raise, the friends you manage to hang on to (or not), the careers you try, the journeys you take – all these things separate you, the writer, from a genuine adolescent. I may not know much, but I do know that having to read a book written by an actual 15 year-old makes my blood run cold.
- **Cut to the chase.** Ten pages of exposition will lose all of your readers. Five pages will lose most of them. Even two paragraphs is dicey. So start fast. The average attention span of a 12 year-old these days is about half as long as whatever you're trying to tell them. (And having judged prizes for teenage books, I can tell you that judges with 50 books to read aren't much better.)
- **Don't try to write cool.** You will almost inevitably fail. Even if you have eight teenagers at home, your writing will somehow manage to expose you as the middle-aged person you are. At which point you will embarrass your friends and family and particularly your teenage children. They will gag and run out of the room and shout that you've ruined their lives, and they will be correct. I've often been asked how I managed to write like a teenager in *How I Live Now*. The answer is, I didn't. I wrote like an old jaded person thinking like a teenager.
- **Get a life.** OK, I'm prejudiced. But it helps to know something about a subject, any subject. And despite failed careers in journalism, PR, politics, publishing and advertising, I managed to pick up a great deal of useful training for writing novels, articles, screenplays, etc on the way.
- **Have a good story.** This is true of writing for anyone. It's amazing how many people forget. And as someone who's good at character but lousy at plot, I feel your pain. Steal a plot, if you have to. After all there are only two: (1) Stranger Comes to Town, and (2) The Journey.
- **Don't look for issues, they will find you.** I challenge anyone to write for teenagers without coming up against at least one of the following subjects: sex, drugs, the meaning of life, family conflict, friendship, the future of the world, self-image, self-loathing, difficult siblings, impossible parents, bullying, depression, overachievement, please someone stop me! *Animal Ark* is a wonderful series of books about fixing hurt animals and that's why five to nine year-olds love it; but there's a reason that adults look back on Vonnegut and Dostoevsky and Kundera novels and say their lives were never quite the same afterwards.
- **Lie about everything except emotions.** England can be at war. Boys can read minds. Pigs can fly. But if you can't remember what it felt like to be depressed/vulnerable/in love, get a job writing *Animal Ark*.

- **Be passionate (see above).** Readers are.
- **Listen to what other people have to say.** OK, OK. So 15 publishers turned down *Harry Potter*. But if 15 people say your story is dull, heavy handed and badly written, it's probably not the next *Harry Potter* in its current form.
- **Don't worry about your connections (or lack thereof).** Ask any agent, editor or bookseller and they'll all tell you the same thing: there is not an overabundance of terrific books around. So if you think you can write something amazing, don't worry about selling it. When you're ready to show it around, someone will sit up and take notice.
- **Write the best book you can write.**

It worked for me, anyway.

Meg Rosoff was born in Boston, USA, and lived in New York City before moving to London in 1989. She was fired from an impressive variety of jobs before writing *How I Live Now*, which won the Guardian Children's Fiction prize in 2004. Her second novel is *Just in Case* and is due to be published in August 2006.

Teenage fiction

Gillie Russell writes about teenage fiction from a publisher's pespective.

People often ask what the difference is between writing for teenagers and writing for adults. For me, the one significant difference is that teenagers come to books without a life experience. They are on the brink of self discovery, never having been plunged into the everyday grind of earning a living. They are open, honest and questioning as an audience and this, I believe, is why so many terrific writers want to write for this age group. Teenagers are challenging to write for and satisfyingly able to digest complex ideas. This often means that there are far too many 'issue'-based books on the market – not that these are badly written, often completely the reverse. But every major book fair will offer teenage books on incest, bullying, sibling rivalry, parental separation and drugs. Of course these kinds of books are important, but teenagers, like adults, need a varied diet. Teenagers like well-crafted stories in many genres – they love humour and history and fantasy, just as much as they like books which reflect their own worlds. They like inspirational and aspirational books where they can identify with the protagonists in a real way.

Getting teenagers to read

To lump teenage readers into one, all-encompassing bracket is not only dangerous but will ultimately reduce the choice of books available to them. We all know that teenagers who read don't necessarily want to continue reading 'children's books', that some seem to move seamlessly on to authors as varied as Agatha Christie and Isobel Allende, Ian Rankin and Margaret Atwood. This is partly because, though there are many wonderful writers for teenagers, no self-respecting young adult wants to venture into the 'children's' section of a bookshop – they would much rather hang out in Body Shop or HMV, or find books in the adult book displays or, sadly, stop reading books, entirely.

To attract teenagers to read at all is difficult; they don't like to feel manipulated, and life in secondary school nowadays makes it difficult to find time to read anything other than the books they are studying, The lead-up to major exams and the required reading tends to dominate their lives. This is why it is so important for children to develop the reading habit and reading stamina earlier in their lives – something which, hopefully, will never leave them, and the desire to lose themselves in a book.

As teenagers move away from the influence of their parents, it is important that, as well as having teachers to motivate and inspire them to read, there are bookshops which do the same. In the USA, for example, there are large areas devoted to 'young adult' books, sections of the bookshops which feel right for them, and are 'cool' places to be. Here in the UK it is sadly not the case. In most of the high street chains the children's areas are dominated by books for the much younger child. Hidden in amongst the books for the 8–12 year-olds there may be a few 'teenage' gems – but few teenagers venture into these areas and discover them. How about bookshops ranging teenage books like CDs, for example – in a rack, facing outwards – and organised by theme, with some short reviews?

Variety is the key

It is true that when we talk about books for teenagers, we tend to think automatically of gritty, contemporary fiction – rather like Melvyn Burgess's *Junk*, for example. But there are lots of books that young people like that are not specially written for teenagers. We need to remember that books for teenagers are any books, any genres, for the 12-plus age group. This band of children – from 12 up to young adult – can have any variety of tastes; they may like historical fiction, such as Celia Rees's *Witch Child*, humour, like Louise Rennison's *Angus, Thongs and Full Frontal Snogging* (to name just one of her deliciously funny and timeless teenage books), Philip Pullman's *His Dark Materials*, and David Almond's *Skellig*. A variety of genres, easy visibility in bookshops, the right covers and 'packaging' – all these things are hugely important to attract teenage readers. They are an intelligent and discerning audience, and when they discover an author they like, extremely loyal. Surely this is reason enough to make retailers think about being more imaginative in attracting teenage buyers?

The 'crossover' book

We talk a great deal these days of the 'crossover' book where an adult market has been identified for a children's book, a phenomenon which started with Harry Potter. Perhaps this is because publishers are desperately trying to attract a bigger section of the market for their authors, to make a double killing with one book. How true this *actually* is, I'm not sure, though occasionally a book which is stunningly original and exceptional, like *The Curious Incident of the Dog in the Night-Time*, can appeal to both markets, and even be successful in two editions. Another example of a 'crossover' book is *Across the Nightingale Floor* by Lian Hearn, which to some may feel more 'adult' than 'child', but which is hugely appealing to teenagers and doesn't feel at all patronisingly like a 'children's' book marketed at teens. How we market, package and position these 'crossover' books, such as Isobel Allende's *City of Beasts*, for example, occupies publishers constantly. Should they do one edition, sold into both adult and children's sections, or should there be two separate editions, one following the other? Or will teenagers who read discover Isobel Allende anyway, and thus make the publishing of a 'children's' edition completely redundant? Publishers certainly don't want to cannibalise their own book sales.

Is reading cool?

What we can say, post Harry Potter, is that reading is still 'cool' – that it is OK to be seen with a book on a bus or train. This can only be a good thing. It can only be fantastically exciting that there are queues outside bookshops for authors like Jacqueline Wilson, Philip Pullman, Darren Shan and, of course, J.K. Rowling.

Where do we go from here?

So where does this leave teenage fiction? How do we enable wonderful writers to reach their target audience? We try to keep publishing the talented authors who are offered to us, people like Mark Haddon who make a difference, who may write about 'issues' but don't set out to do so, but simply set out to write an engaging and compelling book. We keep trying to persuade retailers to recognise the importance of good teenage books – and I sincerely believe this is ultimately empowering, liberating and vital to their adult lives – and we have to be as innovative and imaginative as possible in the ways we think about presenting these books to our readers. Fewer books, better publishing, strong authors writing in different genres – this can be the only way forward. We have to keep on trying to publish the culturally important with the commercially successful in order to be able to produce books for our teenagers. We need to remember that, even in this relatively small area of our market, children need variety, complexity and vitality; they need adventure and fantasy and history and thrillers, humour and grit – everything, of course, that adult readers need, too.

We are privileged in our country to have truly wonderful authors writing for the teenage market – Michael Morpurgo's *Private Peaceful*, for example, which shows how world events impact on ordinary lives; Adele Geras, whose novel *Troy* is better than any history lesson; Peter Dickinson, Anthony Horovitz, Sherry Ashworth, Melvyn Burgess, Kevin Brooks, Nicky Singer… one can go on and on. There is new talent emerging all the time. Children's authors are now dominating the market in a way that was unheard of a few years ago, and this can only be a thrilling time for teenage fiction.

Gillie Russell is Fiction Publishing Director at HarperCollins Children's Books.

See also...
- *Getting started,* page 1
- *A word from J.K. Rowling,* page 80
- *How it all began,* page 81
- *What does an editor do?* page 129

Writing for the school market

Changes made to the National Curriculum provide educational writers with the opportunity to create up-to-date teaching aids. Jim Green outlines the relationship between the writer for schools and the publisher.

Picture the scene: a typical school classroom; a teacher, pupils, desks, chairs, a computer in the corner of the room, the atmosphere noisy and intense. The typical classroom is a boisterous environment with a learning focus. What makes this so clearly a place of learning? The presence of a teacher and pupils of course; but it's their interaction with the vast range of available learning resources that makes this such a special place. It's the textbooks, the revision aids, the educational software, the posters on the walls and the vast array of published materials to be found in every classroom that, when expertly used by teachers and eagerly consumed by pupils, make this a centre for learning. How did all these resources find their way into the classroom? Whose thought, creativity and effort went into their development? And how would someone approach the challenge of creating materials that will one day find their way into this exciting environment?

The short answer to all these questions is that most educational resources are the result of an involved collaboration between a writer and a publishing company. A motivated individual wanted to create new materials and a publishing company saw an opportunity to develop and produce them. Individual schools are free to select their own resources and to use a broad range of materials from a number of sources. However, schools in the state sector are obliged to follow the National Curriculum, and it is the context of a National Curriculum that is most significant in determining the nature of published materials for the educational sector.

The National Curriculum

The National Curriculum is an educational framework that covers the entire Primary and Secondary school age range, establishing specific subject-by-subject requirements, desired learning outcomes and thus a very clear route map through the educational system followed by teachers and learners. Published materials must be compliant with, and supportive of, the requirements of the National Curriculum in order for them to be viable for use in the classroom. The template provided by the National Curriculum can be seen as both a very useful guide to an individual school's resource requirements and, less positively, as a rather constricting straitjacket which allows little individuality either in the preparation of resources or the teaching of course subject matter. My favourite National Curriculum analogy is that it can be likened to a classical symphony or a haiku – both have a clear and somewhat rigid framework within which there is infinite space for the creation of uniquely individual content. Indeed, it is the creation of unique content within the framework of the National Curriculum that is the essential challenge facing all prospective educational writers and publishers.

Whilst teachers might find reassurance in the overall structure offered by the National Curriculum, its ongoing development gives teachers the problem of implementing curriculum changes into their classroom teaching on a regular basis. Many teachers complain that the evolving curriculum creates one of their largest challenges – no sooner have they updated teaching notes, assimilated new learning outcomes and developed their own strategies for teaching the curriculum requirements, than the process begins again. However, it is curriculum change that presents the greatest single opportunity for new writers to create new materials and to get them into use in the classroom. Indeed, it is in helping teachers deliver emerging areas of the curriculum that writers and publishers can be of most value to the teaching community. Curriculum change can generally be anticipated some time in advance of implementation, giving prospective writers time to prepare materials and publishers time to assess both the market and the proposed materials. Focusing time and effort on areas of the curriculum that are changing makes good sense for all interested parties – teachers, writers and publishers.

What do publishers look for when assessing educational materials?

The single, overarching requirement is an understanding of the requirements of teachers and learners, which can also be described as market knowledge. What do schools need? What will help teachers do an even better job of delivering the curriculum? What will enhance the educational experience of pupils? A writer with clear and compelling answers to these questions will be of great interest to publishing companies. Other criteria publishers apply when assessing educational materials include:

- **Writing ability.** Is the material coherent, clear and appropriate for the target age group?
- **Knowledge of subject.** Is the writer an expert in the subject matter?
- Does the writer have **experience teaching the material**?
- Is the writer **a known authority in the field**, whose published work will be recognised as coming from an authoritative source? (For example, materials created by a subject examiner are widely coveted by publishers.)
- **Is the material well organised?** Does it have a logical structure?
- How much thought has the writer given to the **visual presentation of the content**? Are there sample illustrations, diagrams or photographs?
- **Is theoretical content applied in a motivating way?** Are the examples relevant and interesting? Do examples clarify or confuse?
- **Will the end product have an advantage** over the products currently available to schools? Is this clear in the materials?
- **Will the writer be fun to work with?** The best resources grow from a genuine partnership between writer and publisher.
- **Does the material give the motivated learner opportunities to go further and learn more?** This could, for example, take the form of a suggested further reading list, a series of links to relevant websites or optional activities that extend the learners' understanding of subject matter.

What publishers do

Assuming the prospective writer has given thought to the above, that there is a curriculum need for the materials and that a publisher is keen to invest in development and production, what happens next? Or more succinctly, what is it that publishers actually do?! Publishers manage every stage of the development, production and promotion of a project. The publisher role is to shape an original idea into an end product that articulates the original idea, whilst also supporting the curriculum and providing teachers with a resource that enhances the way they teach. The writer generally provides the creative impetus, the hard work of writing core content and, frequently, support to the sales and marketing of the end product. A more detailed list of the activities undertaken by a publisher includes:

- 18–24 months before publication: development of proposal; from an author's original idea the proposal is finalised, a contract agreed and the development timeline created.
- 6–24 months before publication: this phase includes the bulk of the writing and is when the writer's involvement is greatest. The publisher will provide input, feedback and guidance to the writer.
- 12 months before publication: initiation of marketing and promotional activities.
- 6–8 months before publication: coordination of reviews of the first draft of the manuscript. An editor will read the typescript and may also take advice from independent reviewers.
- 6–8 months before publication: copy-editing and preparing the typescript, commissioning of artwork, appointment of a picture researcher and clearance of copyright permission for sourced material.
- 6–8 months before publication: internal design and page layout.
- 6 months before publication: publisher will provide the author with a set of proofs for checking, these will also be sent to a professional proof reader and necessary corrections made to typescript.
- 4 months before publication: printing and binding.
- 2 weeks before publication: warehousing and release to market.

This is an overview of the process of creating educational materials that will hopefully be of use to anyone commissioned to write for the education market. However, we still need to look at the challenge of getting commissioned in the first place. This process will vary by publisher, indeed this process will vary between editors working at the same publishing house. What follows is a list of suggestions that will be of help to writers hoping to be commissioned to write for the school sector.

- **Make personal contact with the relevant editor**. The name of the editor responsible for a specific subject area will be available from the company switchboard. Call the editor to introduce yourself and your proposal prior to sending in sample materials. Materials sent to a generic 'Dear Sir/Madam' are rarely published.
- **When the time comes to send in sample materials, follow the publisher's requirements as closely as possible**. Most publishers will request a written overview of the project plus some comments on the needs of the prospective audience, as well as a draft table of contents and sample chapter. It's important to note that sending in too much material to an editor can be as unhelpful as sending in too little.
- **Ensure the material is 'fit for purpose'**. Does it solve a teaching problem? Does it meet an emerging curriculum requirement? Is it obvious to the reader that the material solves a problem/meets a curriculum requirement?
- **Ensure the end product has an advantage over currently available resources**. The existence of the National Curriculum means that there are ever smaller differences between the competing resources. A new product needs an 'edge', a point of distinction, that makes it more attractive to a teacher than the resource they currently use.

Summary

My intention is to provide helpful information that will assist in overcoming the challenges ahead. Should you feel daunted by any of the above it's important to remember that thousands of new products are published for the school market each year and many thousands of once-aspiring writers are now successfully published authors. The average classroom is packed with resources and this breadth of materials gives a lot of scope for new writers. Remember the classroom from the start of this article? A typical classroom will contain the work of around 100 different writers. Of course there will be long, lonely hours involved in the writing itself but once a publisher has committed to your project you'll be working as part of a team. The joy of making a direct contribution to education will make the effort worthwhile and when things get tough just imagine the excitement and interest created by well-written, well-published and genuinely motivating educational resources.

Jim Green is Managing Director of Collins Education and involved in creating a broad range of educational resources for schools.

It could happen to you

Hundreds of manuscripts are sent to literary agents each week and luck and perseverance both play a part in their fate. Matthew Skelton tells the story of how his book was published.

My story begins with three unlikely words: 'No unsolicited manuscripts.' The stark warning appears next to many of the publishers and agents listed in the *Writers' & Artists' Yearbook* and filled me with trepidation each time I daydreamed my way through the guide as an aspiring author. How was I supposed to interest anyone in my manuscript if I couldn't send even the smallest portion without permission? It seemed impossible.

I was fortunate. One of my friends had completed a creative writing course at a UK institution and provided me with the names of two agents I might like to approach. My manuscript was already longer than the suggested word count for its age group, but I followed the rules in the *Yearbook* as closely as possible: I drafted a short synopsis of the plot and requested permission to submit my manuscript at the earliest convenience. I chose the longer-established agency first – more from a sense of reverence than anything else. (I had studied the rise of literary agents in the 1890s as part of my doctoral dissertation and I'd read some of the founder's letters to famous authors at the turn of the century. It seemed as good a connection as any.)

There was only one thing left to do: wait.

And wait.

No answer came.

I waited for more than four months, but I received no invitation to submit my manuscript. Was my proposal *that* bad? At this point, I was unemployed and living in a borrowed room. My confidence was at an all-time low. I didn't have the nerve to pick up the phone to check that my letter had arrived. I didn't even have a phone.

I took this as a sign. My book wasn't going to be published. I had failed. I hid my manuscript from all but my family and closest friends and tried to find that equally elusive thing: an academic job.

Once again, I was lucky. Another friend read my manuscript and urged me to approach the second agent. The text was far from perfect, she agreed with me, but there was something promising inside it … something just waiting to get out. When I pointed out that this agency was located a few streets away from where we stood, she put her foot down and said, 'If you don't send it, I will.'

And that's what she did. With my permission, of course, she printed the first 40 pages and delivered them, together with a revised copy of my covering letter, to the local agency.

In my case, I was extremely lucky. The first person to look at my manuscript took an instant liking to one of my central characters, Duck – a precocious girl who is unwilling to take off her bright yellow raincoat in case it causes her parents to split up. Within days, I had received a reply: the agency asked to see the rest of the manuscript. The name of the reader didn't match the name of the agent I had approached in my letter, but this didn't matter. I was in with a chance …

Once again, my friend came to my aid. She printed the whole manuscript for me and delivered it in person. This time, the wait was longer.

Something promising

What are agents looking for? As my friend wisely suggested, they're looking for something promising … something just waiting to get out. 'Something promising' can take a variety of forms: a gripping storyline; an intriguing character; a new, unusual, or confident voice; or something else completely... I can't presume to know. I wrote my first novel because my characters' lives depended on it. I wrote it for them – and for myself. I wrote it because I've known since I was a small boy that I wanted to be a writer and I had to keep on trying.

Had I realised, then, the number of manuscripts that are submitted to an agency in any given week I might have lost heart. Fortunately, these manuscripts *do* receive attention. Some are sent to the wrong kind of agent and so determine their own fate; others are so full of mistakes they make the agent's decision quite simple; but the majority come from hopeful, hardworking, aspiring writers – like me – and need some refinement before publishers will consider them seriously.

An agent is not merely an arbiter of good writing or potential marketability; increasingly, an agent is also an author's first editor, an experienced reader who happens to have an abundance of networks and contacts within the publishing industry. Someone, in short, who helps prepare a manuscript for its entrance into the fiercely competitive book world.

The wait

I went through the familiar gamut of emotions while I waited: excitement, incredulity, self-doubt … Four weeks later, I received a short note from the agent herself. Her verdict: we should meet.

The meeting was friendly, but professional. I was able to learn more about the kinds of books she represented (and to hear in advance about one of the following year's publishing sensations) while she asked me about my background and my aspirations as a writer. It was not dissimilar to a job interview, except that this was for a job I really wanted. We talked about the manuscript and she voiced many of my own reservations about the plot. She advised me not to give up my day job (well, in my case, my daily hunt for a day job), but more promisingly she told me to keep in touch.

Sadly, there is no instant metamorphosis from an aspiring author into a soon-to-be-published one. Securing an agent is just the first promising step of a long, often arduous process involving a lot of editing and endless daydreaming, but for me it made all the difference. I was back on my own, living in another borrowed room, revising my manuscript for what felt like the ten-thousandth time. Only I now had a renewed sense of hope and ambition. Even though we hadn't yet signed a contract, I had enticed the interest of a reputable agent and I was beginning to believe in my manuscript as a 'book'.

Three months of revision quickly lapsed into eight but something magical was happening: the plot was undergoing a radical transformation – a whole new dimension to the story was added, an historical element that connected most of the loose strands that had bothered me so much before. Every now and then, I would receive an encouraging, enquiring email from *my* agent (as I liked to think of her) which gave me the confidence to persevere, even when I feared my characters had led me into another dead end. It was the spur I needed: an approving voice telling me I was on the right track. Little did I realise, of course, that she was already 'selling' the book in quarters I could never hope to reach on my own: editorial offices, book fairs, publishing houses – both in the UK and overseas. I still remember the occasion she told me that an editor in New York was keen to see the revised version of the text. I was so surprised I jumped up from my seat at the computer terminal in the local public library (where I'd set up my makeshift office) and walked straight into a wall of books.

Nothing, however, could have prepared me for what happened next – not even my agent's cautious optimism. Just a few weeks after I signed the agency's agreement and she submitted the manuscript to London publishers, I was meeting many of the people mentioned in the *Writers' & Artists' Yearbook* face-to-face, hearing flattering things said about my writing, and receiving offers from various countries for translation rights. I was also learning rapidly about other components of the publishing world: interviews, launch parties, power lunches ... And now I'm being asked to write an article for the *Children's Writers' & Artists' Yearbook* on how it feels to be published. Life is sometimes as strange as fiction.

Thanks to the advice of friends, the timely intervention of my agent (who decided when I should stop revising my manuscript and allow other people to read it) and no end of good luck, my first novel appeared in March 2006. Of course, the really hard work is only now beginning. There are publicity tours, television and radio interviews and school visits to consider ... as well as Book Number Two! Nevertheless, I have achieved what initially felt impossible: I've got my foot in that elusive, allusive door. And that's just the start.

(As for the first agent on my list: I received a response – asking to see the manuscript – less than two weeks after I met my current agent. My letter had been buried in a pile of manuscripts. Of course, I wouldn't change a thing. My story had its own very happy ending.)

Matthew Skelton's first novel *Endymion Spring* is published by Puffin (2006) and the film rights have been purchased by Warner Bros.

What does an editor do?

Yvonne Hooker describes the varied and exciting aspects to an editor's job.

What does an editor do? Good question. Answers have ranged from reading all day to drawing the illustrations. However, baldly put, an editor's job is to acquire new titles and to oversee a book's progress from acquisition to publication, bringing the book in on time and on budget. Where the book goes, the editor follows – from finance and contracts, through design and production, to sales and publicity – making sure that their book, their baby, is getting the best possible treatment and the maximum attention. An editor is the book's champion throughout its life.

Acquiring

The demise of the publisher's slush pile in recent years means that most new books now come via agents. No editor wants to miss out on seeing the latest find from an agent. It's always possible that she will turn down a manuscript that will later become a runaway bestseller – publishing remains a gambling business – but the worst scenario of all is just not to have been offered the book in the first place. So, it is absolutely vital for the editor to be on close terms with all the relevant agents. She must make sure that the agent knows her tastes and is generally confident of her editorial skills and judgements, so that when a real plum of a book arrives, the agent will immediately think, 'Ah, x is just the editor for this,' and send it off.

No one can be an editor and not thrill to the sight of a new manuscript, so finding something you want to publish is a pulse-racing moment. What the editor has to do immediately is to get everyone else's pulse racing as well. She has to start the internal buzz. No book is going to succeed unless all the publishing departments are firmly behind it and it is the editor's job to get the enthusiasm going by talking the book up to key figures, and by presenting the book at the publisher's acquisitions meetings.

The editor will probably have to prepare some kind of financial spreadsheet showing that the book can be expected to make a profit. Figures are needed from sales, marketing, rights and so on and, in order to get the best possible forecasts, the editor has to convince all these other departments that here is a terrific new book which is an absolute must for the list.

In the meantime, the editor will have rung the agent to express her enthusiasm. Usually agents will say whether they are sending books to other publishers as well, but it's always prudent to check and to find out if interest has been expressed from any other quarter. If it has, and an auction situation is developing, then the editor has to make sure that everyone is aware of this, and that the offer is going to be ready on time. In these circumstances, the editor may prepare a particular pitch for the book: a presentation which will convince the author that this is the true home for the book with people who really understand it.

Although many other departments will be involved in the mechanics of the offer, it is the editor who will present it to the agent and who will negotiate all the terms of advance, royalties and rights. It would be rare for an offer for a book by a new author to be accepted as it stands. A certain amount of haggling will be expected and this is one instance where a cool head will serve an editor rather better than unbridled enthusiasm.

Sometimes, before the deal is concluded, the agent will want to have a beauty parade and take the author round to meet competing publishers. This is the editor's chance to woo the author face-to-face and, very often, though not always, the choice of editor will be the deciding factor. The author should be well aware that this is the person with whom he or she will be working most closely and that this will be a vital and all-important relationship. It is, of course, a professional one, and it is perfectly possible for author and editor to work together harmoniously even if they would never choose each other's company outside of publishing, but it does help to have a sense of rapport. No one else has as much contact with the author, and no one else fights as fiercely for the author's voice to be heard. Once the book is hers, the editor will be the author's champion. But she also has to remember that the book is required to make money for the publisher as well as the author.

Editing

The first stage the manuscript of the book goes through is editing: the process to arrive at a final text which is agreed upon by both the editor and the author. This is, rightly, a stage largely hidden from the rest of the world though, for both author and editor, it is the most rewarding part of the whole process. The editor is the first professional reader of the manuscript and her aim is to make the book the best it can possibly be. She will read it with a fine critical eye, checking for problems and seeing what can be done to put them right. These can range from the simple glitch (a week that lasts 10 days or a dog that changes breed in the course of the story), to the emotional core (does a relationship have enough depth, would this character actually do or say this, is the emotional focus clear enough?) and the overall narrative structure (is the beginning punchy enough, does it take too long to get going, does it feel rushed at the end?).

This is the stage which cements the relationship between editor and author. It is a curiously intimate process, relying as it does on a basis of trust and a sharing of the creative process. There has to be absolute trust between author and editor. The author has to feel that he or she can rely upon the editor's critical skill and judgement; the editor has to feel that the author will receive editorial suggestions with serenity. It is taken for granted that editors will not make changes for the sake of it. Nor will they try to rewrite the book as they would have written it. It is, and will remain, the author's book. The whole process should be one of discussion and cooperation, with author and editor working together to make the book the very best it can be.

Every author has a different way of working with his or her editor. Some like to submit a finished manuscript, while others like to send in first ideas and chapters for editorial input as they go along. Any way the author wants to play it is fine with the editor. Sometimes, even the most experienced authors get stuck for some reason – finding the right voice, for instance – and it helps to meet with and talk to the editor. This is a vital and important part of the editorial role as writing is an incredibly lonely occupation and to be able to talk problems through with an interested and experienced reader can be a lifeline. The author–editor relationship can develop to the point where the editor will be one of the first people to be told about quite personal things – impending marriages and babies – and her advice can be sought about things which have nothing to do with work: the best way to cook roast potatoes, for instance (this has actually happened!). Editorial trust can extend beyond the book!

Copy-editing and proofing

When a final manuscript has been agreed between the author and editor, the text is ready to be copy-edited. Not many editors do this themselves nowadays, though most will have copy-editorial experience. This is not just because they do not have the time but it's good to have a fresh eye on the manuscript at this stage. The copy-editor marks up the manuscript for the typesetter, checks the grammar and spelling and acts as a safety net for any glitches which may have slipped through. Any word changes are checked with the author and, in any case, most authors are given the opportunity of seeing the copy-edited manuscript. This is the last opportunity to get everything right before the manuscript is typeset (and changes start costing money) so it is vitally important that everyone should be happy with it at this stage.

The copy-edited manuscript will then go off to be typeset. The editor, with the designer or text designer, will have chosen an appropriate text setting and any flourishes to chapter heads. If the book is to be illustrated, the editor will have marked appropriate places in the text for the illustrations. Both editor and author will be involved in choosing an illustrator, but this aspect is the responsibility of the design department.

When the proofs arrive from the typesetter a set will be sent to the author and another set will be proofread by a professional proofreader. The editor will see the proofs but will very rarely proofread the text, though every editor has the skill. This is a last opportunity for another fresh eye on the text to check for any errors.

While all this is going on, the editor will be busy with other aspects of the book. Having a final manuscript or bound proofs, if there are any, is an opportunity to remind everyone how good the book is, making sure it's not forgotten as other, newer titles are coming through. The editor may send the book out to well-known people in the hope of getting a useful quote for publicity purposes.

The cover

Getting the right cover for a book is of paramount importance. Although this is the design department's province, the editor has a vital role to play. She will need to discuss the book with the designer, and with the sales and marketing teams. Together they will decide on the approach to take, though the choice of artist will generally be in the hands of the designer. The editor may also have to write the cover copy if the publishing house does not have a separate blurb-writing department.

Because getting the right cover is so important, other departments such as sales and marketing will be involved and will have to approve. Of course, publishers want authors to be happy with the covers but authors very rarely have final approval of covers; it is generally accepted that this is an area where the publisher's judgement is final. It is the editor's job to send roughs and visuals of the cover to the author and, in rare cases of disagreement, to persuade them that the cover is absolutely the right one, or to suggest acceptable compromises.

Proof covers have to be ready at least six months before publication to allow for sell-in time. If that date slips, then the publication date has to move, so getting the cover through on time is a major editorial preoccupation.

Publication

Once the cover is done and the final text is going through, the editor's major work on the book is done. But she must keep it in the forefront of everyone's minds and keep the internal buzz growing. She will present the book at internal launch meetings and possibly also at sales conferences and presentations of lead and highlight titles. She will also be liaising with publicity and marketing on their plans to launch the book and will make sure that the author knows the publisher's publicity contact.

About a month before publication, early finished copies of the book will arrive on the editor's desk, hopefully looking wonderful. The editor will check through to make sure that everything is all right, and send an early copy to the author.

All the editor has to do then is to send the author a card on publication day, raise a glass at the launch party if there is one, read the reviews circulated by the publicity department, and make sure that the book is entered for every relevant prize going.

An editor has to have sound judgement, a fine critical eye and enormous funds of patience and sensitivity. It also helps to be a fast reader! Above all, she must be a consummate juggler, handling books at all their different stages – yet be able to drop everything in a crisis to concentrate on the one thing that matters: getting an author's book absolutely right, the book that he or she always hoped it would be.

Yvonne Hooker is Senior Editor at Puffin Books.

See also...
- *Getting started*, page 1
- *A word from J.K. Rowling*, page 80
- *How it all began*, page 81
- *Marketing, publicising and selling children's books*, page 133

Marketing, publicising and selling children's books

The way in which books for children are marketed and publicised is different to the way the adult market is targeted. Rosamund de la Hey identifies the target audience for children's books and explains the various ways in which publishers can reach that audience.

What is marketing?

Marketing can be seen as an umbrella term that includes all the work a publisher does to promote or sell a book. Many people are not clear about the difference between marketing and publicity. Traditionally, marketing is categorised as anything paid for (posters, advertising, catalogues, etc) and publicity (such as review coverage and radio interviews) is free. There is a useful saying that every book must be sold three times – by the editor to the rest of the company, by the sales/marketing/publicity departments to the bookseller, and by the bookseller to the consumer.

How can authors help?

There are many ways authors can help to market their books from the start. Most publishers will send out an author questionnaire soon after acquiring the book. This will generally ask for information ranging from the name of his or her local bookshop, to background details which may offer a marketing or publicity hook. It can help to think of a biography as a series of tabloid headlines – for instance, a children's novelist whose previous career was that of a fighter pilot would be very interesting to teenage magazine editors with a young male readership. On the other hand, if there are areas an author would rather the press did not know about, he or she should tell the publicist, as otherwise innocent, but upsetting, mistakes may happen. Sometimes a mock interview with the publisher's publicist may help the author.

If a book covers a specialist area or issue – for example, Benjamin Zephaniah's *Face* deals with severe facial scarring – it's likely that the author will be able to give the publisher information about relevant organisations which would be interested in hearing about the book, and whose members may indeed buy it.

Events can form a crucial part of promoting a children's book. However, it's worth remembering that not all authors are comfortable in front of a room full of six year-olds.

Marketing children's books

One of the differences between marketing children's books and marketing adults' books is the timescale. Adult book launches are all tied round a very specific window of publication, whereas a children's publication, even if there is a splashy launch, tends to work more like a slow-burn candle.

Children's advertising is also dictated by both the target market – children and their parents – and by more limited budgets. While adult campaigns can assume that adults read a newspaper, take public transport and go shopping, children's sphere of influence tends to be more limited – school, the local sports centre, the library, the internet or television. Publishers must also decide whether they are targeting the child or the parent in advertising.

Publicity

In publicity terms, children's review space is more limited than for adult books, so the coverage happens when the space allows. Additionally, many of the important reviews for children's books happen in specialist magazines such as *Books for Keeps* and *Carousel* which are published only bimonthly or quarterly.

Libraries

Libraries often receive the books some time after publication as each book needs to be adapted for library use. In school libraries, budgets can also be very tight so it may be months or years after publication that a school can afford to stock new titles.

Events

Unlike adult authors who will normally only do a book tour around publication, many children's authors and illustrators spend a great deal of their time doing events and workshops in schools and bookshops, and at the numerous literary festivals around the country throughout the year (see *Children's literature festivals and trade fairs* on page 375). For those who do get involved, the word-of-mouth benefits are well worth the effort. One of the best examples of this is Jacqueline Wilson, who was visiting schools up to three times a week long before her books became bestsellers. She still visits schools regularly year round, as well as touring bookshops and festivals with her new publications.

Direct marketing to schools

The children's market lends itself to direct marketing more than many other areas of trade publishing. This is largely because there is a captive market sitting in school for much of the year. However, marketing directly to schools does have its drawbacks. Teachers are very busy people who have to wade through enough paperwork without being sent endless publishers' catalogues. So, it is important for publishers to be clear and realistic about why they are sending material to schools. A children's educational publisher which also publishes a trade fiction list, may be more likely to be picked up by the Head of English because he or she is expecting to order course books from that catalogue.

Mailing a full trade publisher catalogue to every primary school headteacher in the country is also a very expensive exercise, for potentially little return. Some publishers do have a schools sales force who sell their list directly into schools; others use freelance reps to sell a limited selection from their list into schools. The appropriateness of either of these approaches will depend entirely on the type of list a publisher has.

World Book Day, however, provides many trade publishers with a positive platform to market to schools. For the past few years, a schools' pack has been sent out giving information to teachers and their pupils about World Book Day. Publishers that support World Book Day have the opportunity to insert marketing material (flyers, posters, etc) into the schools pack and know that the investment is more likely to pay dividends because it's more targeted.

Advertising in schools

Media agencies now sell poster sites within schools themselves. Books are arguably the perfect 'product' to advertise in this way – the teachers are keen to encourage reading and hopefully the advertisement will spark the interest of the children. This is an example of where jacketdesign is crucial. If the jacket is not sufficiently strong, it's unlikely to make an eye-catching design that will stand up to the advertising-savvy children.

This type of advertising is not cheap and so is likely to be used rarely and be carefully timed. *Holes* by Louis Sachar, although winner of the prestigious Newbury Medal in the USA, was unknown in the UK until 1999. Bloomsbury marketed the hardback with a successful publicity-led campaign and when the paperback was published nine months later it targeted schools and ran a poster campaign within secondary schools. It is always hard to gauge the exact response to advertising of this type without commissioning expensive research (which is often more expensive than the original advertising costs). However, *Holes* has now sold half a million copies, helped in no small way by being extensively read for course work in schools.

Playground marketing

The phrase 'playground marketing' was widely used after the publication of *Harry Potter and the Philosopher's Stone* in 1997 and partly as a result of the book winning theGold Smarties Book Prize that year. It is very hard to pin down exactly how playground marketing works except to say that it is a combination of many factors: school events, word of mouth, in-school advertising and the prizes network all play their part. The latter is especially important when the children themselves are involved in selecting the winner of a book prize. This now happens for many prizes, from the big national ones such as the Nestle Children's Book Prize and the Children's Book Award, to strongly championed local prizes such as the Angus Book Award (see *Children's book and illustration prizes and awards* on page 363).

Playground marketing only works in tandem with mainstream publicity and child-focused campaigns. For example, when *Harry Potter and the Prisoner of Azkaban* was released in 1999, it was timed for 3.45pm, just after school finished for the day. This caused massive publicity as children streamed out of school and into bookshop queues to buy the book, giving the television cameras a visual hook.

Internet marketing

Many children's publishers are putting more emphasis on internet marketing. The reasons for this are fairly straightforward. In general, children are far more internet-aware than their parents, and tend to spend a lot more time on their computers than reading a book.

Most publishers have their own website and it's worth having a look at some examples to get an idea about what's out there. Some lead titles will be marketed on a specially created independent site as a key part of the overall marketing plan. For example, fantasy fiction often inspires addictive online games and quizzes, such as www.faeriewars.co.uk and www.artemisfowl.co.uk. However, these are expensive to set up and a great deal can be done to promote a book on the existing publisher website. Many publishers also use their sites to run readers' clubs and offer information to teachers.

Design

One of the key marketing tools for any book is the jacket image. If the book is fantastic but has a dull, or inappropriate jacket, not only will the bookseller be unwilling to stock it, but the reader will not be attracted to it, nor understand what kind of a reading experience it's 'selling'.

A good example of where a jacket can help to raise an already successful writer to the next level, is *Witch Child* by Celia Rees. Staring out of the jacket is the beautiful face of a young girl who commands the passer-by's attention with her piercing stare. The book jacket was cited by many booksellers as one of the key reasons why customers picked it up and it was subsequently shortlisted for the British Book Awards in their Book Cover image of the year.

Book jacket design is not only important in bookshops, it is also crucial in advertising. This is true for all advertising from standing out in a small trade advert in *The Bookseller* or *The School Librarian*, to staring down from the side of a London bus.

Trade sales and marketing

Sales and marketing have become more and more closely allied since the demise of the Net Book Agreement (NBA). This was abolished in 1995 and has meant the inexorable rise of the big discount as a way for booksellers to market to the consumer. The knock-on effect of this in the high street has been for publishers to compete with one another for their books to claim valued places in bookshop promotions, be they '3 for 2' offers or '£2 off' schemes. Although these do almost always generate higher sales for a title, they come at a price, and more and more publishers' marketing budgets are being devoted to funding bookshops to run these promotions.

As a result, the trend is for big books to get bigger and small titles to get lost and often disappear without trace. This in turn is polarising publishers' lists and making it a much harder business to break into.

Non-traditional book markets

Another knock-on effect of the NBA's demise is the rise of the supermarket as bookseller. Big supermarket chains such as Asda, Tesco and Sainsbury's are getting more and more involved in selling books, and it is now almost impossible to get onto the general bestseller lists without a supermarket presence for your title. They usually stock a very narrow range of titles but some, such as Asda, will occasionally try less well-known authors who publishers are pushing strongly. Bearing in mind that the likes of Tesco have in the region of 800 stores, this can transform the sales of a title on the basis of one retailer.

Book clubs/direct marketing sales

Book clubs have always marketed themselves using price and heavy advertising in the national press. Usually they offer deals whereby if you join you get several books very cheaply and you are then tied into a minimum level of book buying through the club for a specific period. Direct marketing companies such as The Book People have been incredibly successful in selling to customers in their workplace and through catalogues.

In the children's world, book clubs are especially important as there are more clubs devoted to children and their parents than there are for adults (see *Children's book clubs* on page 74). The children's market also has schools as a captive audience. Several clubs, including Scholastic and Troubadour, are set up to run 'book fairs' in schools in tandem with their mail order operations. They offer a hand-picked selection of what the club deems to be the most commercial and appropriate selection of titles. It is therefore crucial that any children's publisher has a very strong relationship with the clubs. They may stock a more narrow range than the high street, but they order in bulk and in many cases that one order can radically improve the viability of a book's print run.

The changing face of the children's marketplace

The past five or six years has seen a huge change in attitudes to children's publishing. One of the effects of this has been to generate far more high-profile – and expensive – marketing campaigns to launch new writers such as Eoin Colfer and Lemony Snicket. In the past, these authors might have expected a publicity campaign and perhaps a poster for book-shops and libraries. However, for a small number of lead titles, now you will see major 'outdoor' advertising and read about them as front page news. Children's books are now winning the big prizes and taking up the kind of column inches that used to be reserved for the Salman Rushdies of this world.

However, this can distort the market and it should be emphasised that, generally speaking, children's books attract smaller marketing budgets than adults' books. This is down to simple economics: in general, children's books cost less than their adult equivalent. On the positive side, all this publicity has meant that the public awareness of good children's writing has been massively raised by the success of authors such as Rowling, Pullman and Wilson.

The 'crossover' book

The rise of the children's book prompted adults to find out what all the fuss is about and as a result the 'crossover' book was born. When Bloomsbury first published the Harry Potter books for the adult market with a specially designed discreet black and white jacket in 1998, it was for several reasons. Firstly, anecdotal evidence suggested that adults were reading the books already but that some felt embarrassed to be seen in public with a children's book. Secondly, even when *Harry Potter and the Chamber of Secrets* reached number one in the overall bestseller charts, booksellers refused to stock the books at the front of store. And finally, as a marketing concept, for fun, to see if it worked.

The results speak for themselves with the advent of adult editions of the Philip Pullman trilogy *His Dark Materials*, *Holes* by Louis Sachar and *Face* by Benjamin Zephaniah, the 'crossover' book has become a recognised marketing strategy that works when used for the right book.

This theory has been taken a step further by the simultaneous publication of Mark Haddon's *The Curious Incident of the Dog in the Night-Time* in 2003 when Jonathan Cape and David Fickling Books brought out editions for both markets. This has proved a huge critical and commercial success.

Champion the book

One thing that will never change in marketing children's books is the very first sale that is made – by the editor to the publishing company. He or she must be able to inspire people to read and love the book they champion. In children's books, as with adult books, a very great deal comes down to the individual championing of one book above all others. This passion can make all the difference in marketing and selling, and it costs nothing.

Rosamund de la Hey was formerly Children's Marketing Director of Bloomsbury Publishing plc and has been responsible for marketing J.K. Rowling's *Harry Potter* books, as well as other notable successes such as *Holes* by Louis Sachar and *Witch Child* by Celia Rees. She now manages the children's trade sales at Bloomsbury.

See also...

- *Getting started*, page 1
- *What does an editor do?* page 129
- *Children's books and the US market*, page 144
- *Magazines about children's literature and education*, page 278

Notes from a successful self-publisher

G.P. Taylor shares his experiences of writing and self-publishing success.

Lying in bed and hearing that horrendous thud on the doormat is the unpublished author's worst nightmare. It is the thud of a returned manuscript – the tell-tale sound of rejection. Nevertheless, you get out of bed and grimly hold on to *faux* hope that this time the letter will read differently and that you've been accepted and will be published. But no, nothing is further from the truth. Instead, you're faced with a note, hastily typed by a spotty faced 16 year-old who says she enjoyed your manuscript but it doesn't 'fit in' with the list and the niche in the market for romantic-fantasy-gothic literature isn't as big as it once was.

The trouble is, there are just too many people writing these days. Since a certain young lady put pen to paper, fiction (especially children's fiction) has become a *perceived* means of gathering fame and fortune. Even the prestigious Faber and Faber have now closed its doors to the unsolicited manuscript. So why bother? Only a few titles get produced each year from new authors but I don't feel all is lost. The writer has now, thanks to the advent of the internet and email, a publishing house at their fingertips.

Once self-publishing was known as the 'vanity press' – for those failed authors who didn't feel their pride would allow them to die without first seeing a book in print. For a monumental fee, you would receive five copies of your book along with the promise that your book would appear in their magazine for the entire world to see and that copies would be sent to reviewers so that they could herald your arrival to a greater world. Sadly, editors and reviewers knew the names of all the vanity press imprints and, once spotted, would be heaped at the back of the office and sent to the local charity shop once a year.

It was when I found out this information that I decided to avoid the usual route to publication and go it *alone*. In a nutshell, Mount Publishing Ltd was born – established via Companies House and a credit card. I became the director, editor and tea boy of the newest and most prestigious name in publishing! However, I knew nothing and it showed. A PDF what? Typeset? Margins? All these were very new concepts, but thankfully there is help out there.

The first problem I faced was the printing. Very quickly I realised that the prices varied immensely. One company wanted to charge me £6 per paperback, which would have meant pricing my book at £12 – who would buy it at that price? This is the area where you have to be very careful. If you are self-publishing you have to keep the costs of your book down and there are many hidden overheads to look out for (don't forget postage!).

So, once again, reach out for help that's available. My blessing came in the shape of Mr David Sowter, who I found courtesy of the Society of Authors. David was the UK rep for W.S. Bookwell of Finland and quickly became the fount of all knowledge and good advice at the end of a phone. He knew what I wanted and where I should go, and was a guiding hand through the difficulties of file preparation and submission.

Within two weeks of sending off the manuscript to the printer I was greeted with 2000 copies of my first book *Shadowmancer*. They filled my house – they were under the bed, in the toilet, I couldn't even enter my small office. All these books with nowhere to go. Now I faced my biggest problem so far: how to sell them.

Thankfully for us self-publishers, there is a ready supply of independent bookshops all too willing to help the new author on a 'sale or return' basis. The Whitby Bookshop quickly set me off on the right foot. A book signing and press call were all arranged for a rainy October morning, and as my wife tramped through the wet streets with a pram full of books, she turned to me and said 'I bet J.K. Rowling didn't have to do this'. Too true – but the excitement and hope I was feeling at this point more than made up for it.

Very quickly I came across another hurdle – the national bookshop chains (known to self-publishers as the Mafia). No one would deal with me, no one would talk to me. 'Graham who?' Was all they asked. 'Self-publisher? No thank you.' The kindly manager of my local Waterstone's suggested I contact a book distributor but when I did they turned me down flat. I then went to Bertram Books, another wholesaler which supplies Waterstone's, and thankfully they opted to give me a chance. Bingo! I was now selling my book to the shops.

Luck was well and truly on my side. Somewhere around this time, the story of *Shadowmancer* was spreading by word of mouth. From nowhere, people from all over the country were ringing my home wanting copies of the book. I couldn't believe it! Suddenly, hundreds of people wanted to read *Shadowmancer* and my house started to empty of books. I knew I was doing well when copies were selling on Ebay for large sums of money – I was outbidding J.K. Rowling!

Within a matter of weeks of the start of my self-publishing venture, I was signed to Faber and Faber. It was good timing because everyday was a constant stream of wrapping and posting books, an operation so large that my local Post Office could no longer accommodate me and I was forced to find alternative arrangements. Self-publishing is definitely not for the faint hearted!

From then on, the path to notoriety has been a fast one. *Shadowmancer* spent many weeks at the number one spot on the bestseller lists in both the USA and UK. The film rights were quickly bought by Universal Pictures and a multi-book deal was in the bag. I had sold out and gone the way of the establishment!

Would I recommend others to self-publish? Definitely. In fact, I receive several emails a day asking me what to do and how to do it. Ultimately, my advice is simple – research the area and check prices, get quotes and be as wary as a fox. Be prepared for disappointment as self-publishing is certainly not a get-rich-quick scheme. It cost me all I had in time, money and resources – and more! Finally, it is always best to set up a limited company just in case all goes wrong, oh and *never* remortgage your house – sell your vintage motorbike instead.

G.P. Taylor self-published his debut novel *Shadowmancer* in 2002. He was soon signed to Faber and Faber and G.P. Putnam & Son in the USA. The book became an international bestseller, translated into 42 languages. His subsequent book *Wormwood* has also been an international bestseller and both books are to be turned into film and video games. Until recently, he was an Anglican Vicar, but now writes full-time and guests on television and radio programmes.

Notes from a self-starter self-publisher

Despite having proof that children liked what he had written, John Howard's novel was repeatedly rejected by literary agents (as was his bogus submission). Undeterred, he self-published his book and drew upon his creative resources to gain national and international recognition.

When I dispatched three chapters of my children's novel *The Key to Chintak* to literary agents in late 2003, along with appreciative letters and emails from children who'd read and commented on it for me, I had very high hopes.

The children's reaction to my book had been very enthusiastic, and to me that was the acid test. I thought literary agents would take a similar view.

Then, after the usual long wait for a response, something amazing happened. Every single agent I'd contacted rejected it.

But had any of these agents, I wondered, actually read a word of what I'd sent them?

It was at this point that a new washing machine arrived in the house. Determined to test my theory that many unsolicited manuscripts to agents and publishers never even warrant a second glance, I took the washing machine user guide and scanned it into my computer. Once I'd removed the pictures and tidied the text into chapters, *The Tin Drum* was ready.

As the first chapter was entitled 'Jumbo Drum', and the first words extolled the virtues of said drum, it was fairly obvious what I was up to.

The first line actually read: 'LG's jumbo drum can wash about 40% more load than conventional washing machines.' Another chapter began: 'If the washing machine is turned off by a power failure, it will restart automatically from the position it stopped at, adjusting accordingly.'

Yet of the three agents I sent this bogus manuscript to, two replied with the same standard rejection letter as before, saying they had read and enjoyed my submission but 'it wasn't for them'.

It is hard to describe the feeling of continually being rejected in this way, although I'm sure many aspiring authors all around the UK would know exactly what I'm talking about.

On a scale of one to 100 in bloody-mindedness, though, I rank at about a 99 – give or take one. No way was I going to lay down so easily this time. Besides, writing was now my chosen profession and our family savings were starting to dwindle. There's nothing quite like a few brown envelopes on the doormat to snap you out of a bout of self-pity. No, I was going to make it, *and* the publishing industry would regret not being along for the ride. Time, I decided, to self-publish.

Writing the right book

Around 12 months earlier, I had decided the time was right to ditch my IT career and finally have a go at full-time writing. It's something I've always wanted to do, even though I'm dyslexic and because of that, actually failed my English 'O' level at school. So my plan was not necessarily a wise one, particularly from a financial point of view. But money wasn't the main motivation. If it was, I would have stuck with IT. But my wife and I had built up a healthy savings fund, and she fully supported my decision. For my part, I simply wanted to earn a fair living doing something that I loved – creating something new for children to explore and enjoy.

The basic plot of *The Key to Chintak* had been swirling around in my head for quite a while, and once I started writing my story – about a 12-year-old girl who can read the pages of a blank book no one else can see – it all came together fairly quickly. My idea was to write a story for children aged 10 and over that mixed fact and fiction, and where the central character was a young girl, because in my view there aren't enough strong young heroines in modern children's literature.

Once it was written, I then took the radical decision to actually ask children if they liked it before, and after, submitting it to any literary agents. This was because in 1997, I'd had an earlier stab at writing, producing a few chapters of a novel about the life and adventures of a young James Bond. I had no experience of writing a book but my head has always been overflowing with ideas. Though immersed in full-time work at that time, I managed to snatch the odd hour here and there to pen my planned masterpiece. Alas, the many publishing agents I contacted did not agree with my future career plans. After months of waiting, all returned my work with a dismissive, pre-printed reply – 'Thanks but no thanks', basically.

To find out why, I phoned one up, only to be told that James Bond was 'old hat'. If I believed *that* was what children wanted to read, then I should stick to my day job. So I did.

Roll forward to 2004 to find that young James Bond clone Alex Rider, the teenage spy created by author Anthony Horowitz, is an international multi-million bestseller. And since then, Master Bond himself has topped the charts in the book *Silverfin*, by Charlie Higson.

So, when it came to getting *The Key to Chintak* published, I reasoned that if the agents didn't appear to know what children wanted – based on my unfortunate experience with Master Bond – and the agents in turn didn't think *I* knew, then maybe I should ask children themselves?

As I understand it, most children's books fail to turn a profit. Surely this has got to be, I thought, because most are written by adults, reviewed by adult agents, passed to adult publishers, and circulated by adult buyers?

So, for my own little market testing exercise, I had 50 copies of *The Key to Chintak* printed, and after visiting two local schools near my home in East Sussex to distribute the copies and then talking directly to the children who'd read it, I came away certain I was onto a winner. They all absolutely loved the book. Hence my decision to go it alone once I'd been knocked back by the agents.

On the self-publishing road

Self-publishing is, however, a minefield. To start with, a good cover and good editor – and both are essential – will set you back over £1000. But that's just one part of the jigsaw. If you want to succeed as a self-published author, you also need an iron will, outstanding marketing and presentation skills, and a good website. Most importantly, you must be able to deal with anyone or anything that blocks your way. And a lot will block your way.

From the off, I decided I wanted to sell a large number of books – at the time I thought around 1000 should be enough – to convince a publisher to take me on without an agent.

To do this, I needed exposure and to get into the bookshops, fairly obviously. But don't think for a minute that as soon as you print your work, people will be queuing up to buy it. Once you have exhausted family and friends, who else knows your book exists?

So I decided the best way to drum up sales was to continue touring schools around Sussex. To convince headteachers to take a chance on an unknown like me, I offered my services free – and soon built up a long list of schools willing to have me in. Visiting both primary and secondary schools, I'd talk for an hour or so to an interested and enthusiastic young audience about my struggle to get published, then read from the book and act out a scene or two.

I then used these visits, and the enthusiastic response I met with, to blag some local press coverage, and then used the local press to blag some local radio airtime. Oh, yes, I should mention, you need to be able to blag a lot. Yet initially, all of this effort did not sell me many books in the shops. Instead it filled up my email inbox with people telling me they couldn't get *The Key To Chintak* anywhere.

I'd signed up with a very helpful print-on-demand specialist, and through this company, managed to get my book listed at a distributor. But this system let me down, and cost me sales.

As I discovered, the current system for supply of books is cumbersome and flawed when it comes to print-on-demand for a mass market title. The theory is fantastic but the reality is not. The theory goes like this: somehow convince people to go into a shop and ask for my book. Being print-on-demand it will not be on the shelf, but once ordered it will be printed overnight and shipped to the store the next day. Fantastic.

It turned out, though, that when people were going into bookshops and asking for *The Key to Chintak*, they were often told it was out of print. I remedied this by convincing the wholesaler to actually stock pre-printed copies of the book, and once this happened, sales started to move. So a golden rule for all aspiring self-publishers is to never let your stock drop to zero at the wholesaler otherwise you will lose sales.

Because a lot of people were requesting *The Key to Chintak,* some local stores then decided to stock it on their shelves. My delight at this was short-lived when I discovered that one shop, which had sold some 200 copies of my book, was not scanning it at the till but manually keying the price in. This makes a lot of difference, because if your books are not scanned, they will not register on Nielsen BookScan (which records all book sales nationwide). If your sales do not register with them, then it is very hard to prove that you've had any in the first place. And no sales equals no credibility: I know this because I had a huge row with Nielsen about it. Apart from the bookshop scanning problem, I had also sold some 2500 books direct to schools. Nielsen would not accept these sales either. Only by hooking up with a local bookshop that supplies schools did I overcome this problem but it took months to remedy and lots of pushing.

Gaining national recognition

By February 2006, I had visited 40 more schools around Sussex, and spoken to loads of local booksellers, journalists and television people. I had also received around a thousand glowing emails from readers through the book's website (www.zamorian.com). Sales were going well. There was one remaining problem: outside of Sussex, nobody knew me. I needed national exposure. Specifically I needed to convince a major book retailer to stock *The Key to Chintak* nationwide, expand my school tour to coincide with this, and a new cover.

Up until then, everything I earned went back into the deep hole in the ground that is self-publishing. Visiting schools free and printing bookmarks and posters takes its toll on the bank balance. With no marketing budget to speak of, I believed a fancy cover would help persuade people who knew nothing about me to pick up my book and give it a chance – providing I could get into the shops nationally, of course.

I sent a cold-call email to Scott Pack, the head buyer at Waterstones, who, according to at least one newspaper has a fearsome reputation. My email was written with a lot of tongue and a lot of cheek. I didn't have Scott's email address, as nobody at Waterstones would give it to me, so I guessed a few and one got through.

Scott replied straight away, saying that if the book was any good, Waterstones would stock it. After reading it, he ordered 3000 copies in March, and included it in the stores' 'three books for the price of two' promotion. Oh, how lovely it was to see that order! Airport branches of WHSmith have also now followed suit, as have the Sussex schools library service. *The Key to Chintak* is now outselling a lot of mainstream-published books in the same Waterstones' promotion as mine. As for school visits to coincide with this, I am currently in the middle of a nationwide tour that will take in 30 schools scattered far and wide around the country.

Not all of my promotional approaches have worked but both Terry Wogan and Chris Evans were kind enough to spare me some time when, after standing in the rain for two hours, I pounced on them as they left the BBC Radio 2 studios. And *Shadowmancer* author G.P. Taylor has kindly provided a foreword for the second edition.

Now, I have several US film studios and one UK media company showing a keen interest in acquiring the film rights to *The Key to Chintak* and its sequels. I also have numerous international publishers looking at making offers for the foreign publishing rights. If they fall into place, I may just stay self-published in the UK.

After three years of trying, blagging, ducking, diving, rejection, rejection, rejection, and a lot of hard work, it is very tempting to say: 'Told you so' to the odd agent or publisher. But the truth is that I've still got a long way to go. I'll get there, though.

Mind you, I'll get there a lot quicker if everyone reading this article buys my book.

John Howard is author of *The Key to Chintak: The Zamorian Chronicles* and is available from all good bookshops. His website is www.zamorian.com

Children's books and the US market

Richard Scrivener outlines the possibilities for breaking into the US children's book market.

As L.P. Hartley once said of the past, America is a foreign country, they do things differently there. It is the biggest territory in the world for books, with immense opportunities, but with just as many pitfalls. Of course, the Brits have those US senators to thank, who some 200 years ago decided to make English the national language of their young nation. This does give British writers an edge over their Italian and French counterparts, although the competition for places is intense. So this article will briefly consider and note the general state of the US market, and then offer some general thoughts on what awaits a British writer who finds themselves about to be published in the United States of America.

Getting through the door

It's an old joke: the British and the Americans find their respective sandwiches very amusing. We think theirs are ridiculously big, they think ours are ridiculously small. The good news for authors is the 'big sandwich culture' has an enormous sales potential. The even better news is that, unlike their rock and pop counterparts, British authors have a brilliant track record in doing very well 'over there'. From A.A. Milne to J.K. Rowling, from Beatrix Potter to Philip Pullman, time and again the US market has shown itself more than receptive to the stories written on these wet islands. The knack is how to get in through the door.

I wouldn't recommend that a writer research the American market, then write a novel with that specifically in mind. One would most likely end up with a series of novels featuring a Christian wizard who loved *Star Trek* and looked after horses. No. As a writer, you simply have to write what you think is right. Practicalities say that you should begin with a UK publisher and editor in mind. However, you may choose to avoid subjects that might alienate the American market, though it's probably true to say the same issues apply in the UK.

The US market

Here are some basic facts and figures. (With apologies if this is a little like an economics lesson.) The US market is six times bigger than the UK's. The US publish just about the same number of titles as in the UK – somewhere a little north of 110,000, of which around a quarter are children's books in various formats. The independent bookshop is still viable in the US, and that's despite the massive growth of online sales via Amazon and the growing importance of retail chains such as Barnes and Noble and Borders. The library and institutional market whilst having suffered severe funding issues of late, still plays a stronger role in US publishing than its much ravaged British counterpart. The area of the greatest volume at retail, the mass market, is dominated by a couple of key players, with Walmart by far the largest company. The Asda-owning supermarket behemoth has a turnover larger than most countries. When it takes a book it will sell in great quantities.

Immediately one can see parallels with the UK, yet there is one noticeable difference and it's a crucial one for authors. In the delightful vicious pond that is the UK publishing market, publishers and retailers agree different discounts depending on the size of the account. In the US you can't do that. It's basically the same discount if you're Mr Barnes

Books of Biloxi or if you're Mr Barnes and Noble, though of course there are various legitimate ways around this. Nonetheless it sets the tone for the business.

As in the UK, the US is dominated by the big 'conglomerate' publishers: Random House, Penguin, HarperCollins and Scholastic. They all carry large lists, publishing sometimes as many as 800 books a year. Hardback publication is still the much preferred initial route for most novels and picture books with a paperback following sometime later. Review coverage in the US for children's books is noticeably better than in the UK. *Publishers Weekly* (the US equivalent of *The Bookseller*; see *Magazines about children's literature and education* on page 278) always carries a children's section and features many thoughtful – and detailed – reviews. It would certainly be worth getting hold of a few copies of this excellent magazine to get a sense of the US market.

Alongside the usual names are other publishers which are less well known in the UK, but highly respected in the US: Harcourt Brace, Farrar Straus-Giroux, Houghton Mifflin and Little, Brown. Some of these publishers have affiliates in the UK, others are part of major media companies. They have considerable clout in the marketplace and can certainly make things happen. For example: Farrar Strauss-Giroux is the US publisher of Louis Sachar's *Holes* and sold it to Bloomsbury in the UK which then published it to great acclaim. And then there was the film…

There are also a host of small hardback houses, independent general publishers who have children's lists, as well as mass market publishers who service the supermarkets. There is plethora of choice, each company with its own dynamic and ethos.

So how do I make it over there?

The principal question of interest to any author is how do I get published in the US? As Bill Clinton used to say: that depends. If your book has been sold in the UK and the publisher has world rights and if that publisher has a US affiliate then most likely the affiliate will be the first port of call. This has the advantage of them knowing who to send it to and the fact that it's being published in the UK by the sister company will help. There should be a financial benefit to the author too – in that the royalty is paid 'straight through'. From a marketing perspective it could also mean that the publisher feels a global ownership of the author, and that would certainly help justify the necessary marketing investment.

But publishing isn't always that simple. The US affiliate may not like your book but this needn't be an issue *per se*. Nor indeed should it be a problem if the UK publisher doesn't have a US office because a good rights department will look to sell the title elsewhere. The cost of doing this for the publisher and the author is reflected in the cut of the deal retained by publisher.

If you have an agent, he or she may suggest selling US rights separately, in which case your manuscript or book will be submitted direct to US publishers. If you're really lucky, the agent may even be able to conduct an auction, but you have to be confident the book concerned will generate sufficient interest. There's nothing more embarrassing than a one-publisher auction.

In the case of picture books – there is no question of the publisher *not* getting world rights. Co-editions will need to be set up, so as broad a territory as possible is required to offset the high origination costs of publishing in full colour.

Changes, changes

Once your book has been sold, be prepared for further editorial comments! American editors nearly always make changes to the text to Americanise it. For example, rubbish becomes garbage, nappy becomes diaper and sausage becomes hot dog. And it's not un-usual for a US editor to give more line by line comments and even request a different ending. Take these in your stride, sometimes it will help sell the book. On other occasions you may think it's a bridge too far. You'll have to take each battle as it comes.

Covers, too, require a sharp intake of breath. Invariably the US cover will be different. For reasons no one can understand, British and American cover sensibilities vary consid-erably. It's best really to let them get on with it. You have to trust that the publisher will know what sells in Des Moines. It may not look pretty to you, but if it sells, does it matter?

As in the UK, marketing is a critical factor in determining a book's success. Dumpbins, publicity, review coverage all add to the mix. The key thing is to have an editor who's supportive and a publishing organisation which supports the editor. The best marketing plans in the world can fall flat, whilst the unexpected bestseller can come from nowhere.

Being published in the US means you'll get US fanmail! And, unless you happen to live there, you won't have that 'I'll just the check the stock in my local bookshop' opportunity, that is unless you have American friends prepared to do it for you. (Though if you ring your US publisher to tell them about this, expect the same frosty response as you'd get from your UK publisher.)

Schools

Another point of difference with the US is the schools market. School book clubs and book fairs are enormously important sales channels in the US. A typical order quantity would be 75,000 units. Through club mailings and touring fairs, the principal player in this market is Scholastic, reaching virtually every American child at some stage or other. These titles are often discounted and acquired under licence from US publishers who grant schools rights. Royalties are generated via the net receipts from the sale of those rights and the ongoing sale of the book. And of course there is a promotional benefit in having your book displayed in schools.

How did they do it?

It all sounds very exciting doesn't it? So how do I get invited to the party? Luck as much as anything plays an important part. Certainly you can't sit down and think I'm going to write a children's bestseller. Did J.K. Rowling ever think: 'I bet kids in Montana are going to love a story about an orphan trainee wizard attending a summer public school?' Who would have thought that Philip Pullman's version of *Paradise Lost* in which religion is castigated and God dies, would have been so popular in a country with such a wide Bible Belt?

So write what you want to write. Certainly it might be an idea to have more than one book in mind. America is after all the ultimate consumer country, if they like one, they'll want another – quickly. Though not what it once was, series publishing is still popular in the US. *Goosebumps* holds the record for the largest number of books sold, at its peak subscribing over a million copies on publication. Lemony Snicket is currently king of this castle, but there's always something else around the corner. And most likely a popular series will be made into a television show or even film – and then there's merchandising. But that's a whole other story.

Genres

As anywhere in the publishing world, genres come and go out of fashion. Fiction has been a hot category for some time now, with a particular emphasis on fantasy. It may well be this bubble will burst as publishers' lists fill with titles featuring weird creatures in various forms. Picture books have had a tough few years, but that said there are writers and artists who continue to sell very well in the US. Again it will depend on the strength of the book – it will have to be outstanding. Probably the most difficult area is publishing for the 5–8 year-olds. These books tend to feature school scenarios or make assumptions about reading levels. It is very difficult to sell these books in the US, so I wouldn't have high hopes if that's your milieu. That's not saying, like a local wine, that there's anything wrong with it – it just doesn't travel long distances.

Teenage books have actually found a much greater audience in recent years. That's as much a British thing as an American factor. Though I personally would avoid writing what I call 'My Dad killed my Step Mum' fiction, there are plenty of American writers doing that. Non-fiction certainly can travel extremely well – although for some reason, humorous non-fiction is less successful.

In short, there are many reasons to be interested in the American market. And the obvious point is the sales potential. Imagine if all of Europe spoke English – okay they do, but at least no American cities have been trashed by English football fans. The infrastructure of US publishing is immensely impressive, it's full of talented and dedicated people who, like their British counterparts, love books. Find a home. Find an editor. Find a publisher. If you get all three in the US, you'd be lucky, you may earn a few pennies. But whatever, if you're successful you'll have the satisfaction of knowing you're better than Oasis and Robbie Williams. *You* made it in America.

Richard Scrivener is an entertainment and publishing consultant.

Categorising children's books

When you walk into any high street bookstore the range of children's books can seem overwhelming. Once you look beyond the promotions and offers on the centre tables, however, the selections and layout start to make sense. Caroline Horn explains.

Retailers generally organise their children's book displays according to age ranges, making it easier for buyers to go straight to the section they want, be it baby board books or teen fiction. This approach also reflects how publishers 'segment' their lists.

Categorising children's books according to age groups is helpful as these categories generally reflect children's interests and reading abilities at key stages in their development. A book's format and subject matter, the presence of illustrations and the size of text and pagination, signal the intended age of its reader. So, for example, toddlers and preschool titles comprise short, illustrated picture books while young fiction books are mainly black and white text with short chapters, large text and some illustrations.

Large publishing houses will tend to cover the whole gamut of age ranges for children, from naught to young adult. They want their titles to win the loyalty of new parents from day one and to keep that loyalty all the way through to that child's teen years. Smaller, specialist publishers will often focus their lists on specific areas of children's publishing that reflect their in-house skills. Piccadilly Press, for example, is strong in teen fiction while Templar Publishing has developed a strong range of baby books.

Broadly speaking, children's books fit one of the following age groups: baby books (one to two years), picture books (two to five years), beginner readers (five to seven years), young fiction (six to eight years) and core fiction (8–12 years).

Teen titles and 'crossover books' (those that appeal to children or teenagers, as well as to adults) are in the top age range, i.e. 12 years plus. Non-fiction is also categorised according to age range and, often, National Curriculum subject areas.

There are, though, always exceptions and children's varied abilities and interests will mean that young readers will often cross these age bands. This is why publishers are not more specific about a book's intended audience. Indeed, including a recommended age on the cover (as manufacturers do, for example, on toys) is a contentious issue and one that publishers actively avoid because of the wide variation in children's abilities. A nine year-old boy with reading difficulties could, for example, find himself reading a title that is recommended for a child aged six years, and there's nothing more guaranteed to put off a child from picking up another book – ever! New lists have been developed by publishers like A & C Black (*White Wolves* series) and Barrington Stoke to fill the gap for titles that can be enjoyed by older readers who are still struggling to read fluently, and reluctant readers.

In other cases, where perhaps an eight year-old child has the reading ability of an 11 or 12 year-old, that child would probably struggle with the subject matter intended for older readers.

Age ranging

Being more specific about a book's intended audience can also restrict the book's potential market since the same book can appeal to many different age groups. Teenagers, for example, are among the fans of Anthony Horowitz's *Alex Rider* books (Walker Books) although the identified age range for the titles is the 'core fiction' market of 9–11 years. Among younger children, a picture book can be as appealing to a three year-old who enjoys being read to, as a five or six year-old child who can read the book themselves. Sophisticated picture books by authors such as Lauren Child and Clarissa Cowell are highly rated among children aged up to six or seven years (as well as many grown-up readers).

While there are very good reasons for not giving specific age recommendations on book covers, this does not help parents and other book buyers who are struggling to find the right title for children. Research by Book Marketing Ltd ('Expanding the Market') indicates a high level of confusion by consumers when buying books for children and publishers remain heavily reliant on booksellers' ability to recommend the best book for individual children. This is why age ranging on displays and shelving in bookshops remains so essential.

Age ranging is the broadest tool publishers can use in categorising their lists but they will also build their lists' depth and range according to a variety of other factors, particularly genres that are popular such as fantasy, historical fiction, horror, thrillers, etc. Publishers will frequently revisit their lists to check where their 'gaps' are and how well each area is doing at any particular time. They pay special attention to how well their list serves the core market of 8–12 year-old readers.

Recent developments in fiction

In recent years, the British and American markets for children's fiction, particularly fantasy, have flourished thanks to authors such as J.K. Rowling (*Harry Potter*) and Philip Pullman (*His Dark Materials*) and the appetite among young readers for more 'big' fiction books seems insatiable. This has helped drive up author advances to unprecedented heights in the children's market, with the popularity of strong fantasy titles both here and in the US continuing to hold. This was not always the case. One of the reasons why *Harry Potter* was originally turned down was its length – publishers were wary of any books that were more than 40,000 words long, believing that children would not pick up hefty or challenging reads. Children's fantasy was also distinctly out of fashion, both among UK booksellers and foreign publishers, whereas today publishers are keen to find imaginative and challenging reads for children.

The market for 'crossover' fiction is another recent development – it was hard to envisage any demand by adults for children's books prior to *His Dark Materials* trilogy and *Harry Potter*. Today, though, publishers will look closely at a title's potential for crossover appeal. After all, selling to adults as well as to children instantly doubles a book's market. David Fickling Books and Random House exploited this by creating separate covers, for children and for adults, for *The Curious Incident of the Dog in the Night-time* by Mark Haddon – the text was identical for both versions. Although very few novels can do so successfully, titles like Jonathan Stroud's *Bartimaeus Trilogy* (Random House Children's Books) and Jennifer Donnelly's *A Gathering Light* (Bloomsbury) can appeal to both adults and children or teen readers, and publishers are keen to find more books like these.

A more recent development in how books are categorised is by author 'brand'. Authors such as Jacqueline Wilson, Michael Morpurgo, Dick King-Smith and Eoin Colfer are all regarded as brands in their own right and, although these authors write for many different age ranges, their titles will often be displayed together on an author's 'shelf' in bookshops. Waterstone's, for example, has introduced new display cases in its children's sections to do just that, highlighting bestselling authors' work in individual sections. These key author 'brands' have a guaranteed – and large – audience. Jacqueline Wilson, who has sold more than 20 million copies across her titles, will regularly outsell adult bestseller titles with sales of her children's titles averaging about 50,000 copies a month. Readers are also loyal to series and Lemony Snicket's *A Series of Unfortunate Events* (Egmont) as well as Darren Shan's *The Saga of Darren Shan* series (one million UK sales) have shown how successful these can be.

At the younger end of the market, sales of the *Horrid Henry* series by Francesca Simon (Orion) have encouraged publishers to develop more mass market series such as those based on the Felicity Wishes character (Hodder Children's Books) and *Rainbow Fairies* (Orchard Books), as well as Random House Children's Books new *Astrosaurs* series. Mass market series like these help to get children aged six to eight years into the reading habit because they can recognise the books they have enjoyed and go back for more. Since young fiction books also tend to be relatively thin, a set of five or six books will help them to stand out on booksellers' shelves. More 'literary' series have also been developed for younger readers, with the production quality of the *Judy Moody* titles by Megan McDonald (Walker Books) and *The Spiderwick Chronicles* by Tony DiTerlizzi and Holly Black (Simon & Schuster) ensuring that they stand out from the crowd.

The next 'big thing'

But publishers know that they would be unwise to focus exclusively on areas that are ahead in today's climate – children's books is a cyclical business and what works today could be out of favour a few months down the line. Dorling Kindersley's approach to production was key to driving non-fiction sales in the Eighties while *Guess How Much I Love You* by Sam McBratney and illustrated by Anita Jeram (Walker Books) achieved a similar status for the picture book in the Nineties. In today's climate, however, non-fiction and picture books are struggling but it will only take a new taste, design or development to turn that around. People could easily be saying the same thing about fantasy fiction just a few years from now.

Publishers will regularly revisit and reshape their lists as a result of market changes like these. Walker Books, a notable picture book publisher, has in recent years strengthened its fiction list with lead authors including Anthony Horowitz and Kate DiCamillo, while Bloomsbury, which has traditionally focused on fiction, is now strengthening its picture book list. Traditional non-fiction publishers Kingfisher and Usborne have both recently moved into the fiction market, reflecting the greater focus on fiction.

Demographics are also responsible for changing tastes and shifting emphasis in publishers' lists. The number of children aged under 12 years is falling while the teen market is growing and this accounts for the increasing interest in young adult and crossover books. The demographic picture is similar in the US, a key market for British publishers, so interest in teen fiction is likely to be maintained for some time. Teenage titles are, themselves, also categorised according to genres such as 'issue' books, crime, thrillers, etc. What is proving most successful among teen readers today, largely thanks to Louise Rennison's *Angus* series (Piccadilly Press, HarperCollins) and Meg Cabot's *Princess Diaries* (Macmillan Children's Books) are contemporary, humorous and very commercial books for teenage girls.

It goes without saying that writers need to know what areas a publisher specialises in before approaching them with manuscripts. A brilliant teenage title is likely to be rejected if the publisher's list does not include teenage books. Still worse, an inexperienced publisher could take on a teen novel but let it fall into oblivion by failing to market it to the correct audience.

That said, it is hard to second-guess what type of book publishers are looking for at any one time. A picture book publisher may still turn down a title, no matter how much they like it, if they have over-commissioned in that area or it is too similar to a title they are already publishing. Equally, even though booksellers' shelves are groaning under the weight of fantasy titles, a book that stands out from the crowd will always find a home – publishers are continuously hunting for talented 'new voices'. In fact, 'debut author' has almost become a category in its own right as publishers strive to get unknown but promising authors into retail outlets.

It is also worth remembering that across the board, large publishing houses are reducing their children's output and that their lists are more structured and more focused than ever before. If a company has filled the gap for a dragon fantasy for a 10 year-old reader, then they won't be looking for any more. Another publisher, however, might be looking for exactly that.

Caroline Horn is children's books editor at *The Bookseller* and director of children's books website Reading Zone (www.readingzone.com).

Poetry

Riding on the poetry roundabout

Poet and anthologist John Foster writes about the difficulties involved in getting children's poetry published and offers some practical advice.

Today's children's poetry roundabout started spinning in the 1960s, when it was given a push-start by Spike Milligan, gathered momentum in the 1970s and 1980s with helping hands from the likes of Roger McGough, Allan Ahlberg and Michael Rosen, and has been gathering speed ever since. You would think, therefore, that it might be easier for a new-comer to break in and to get their poems published these days than it was when I started anthologising and writing poetry some 25 years ago. Yet, in spite of the upsurge in children's poetry publishing in recent decades, for the aspiring children's poet it can seem as hard as ever to get your poems published.

One reason, of course, is that there are now many more people specialising in writing children's poetry than there used to be and the competition is more fierce. Another is that there's an increasing number of established children's poets and that those people inevitably stand much more chance of getting a collection of their poems into print than someone who is unknown.

That said, anthologists like myself are always on the lookout for new voices, and if a good poem is submitted for an anthology, it doesn't matter who has written it – it will go in. When you're starting out, you have far more chance of getting one or two of your poems into some of the anthologies that are published annually than you have of getting a complete collection of your poems published. So if you are keen to find a ride on the poetry roundabout, it is better to discover what anthologies are in the pipeline and what specific poems are required than to try to place a single author collection. I had been anthologising and contributing poems to other anthologies for over 10 years before my first book of original poems, *Four O'Clock Friday*, was accepted. And there are some very good children's poets – Julie Holder and John Kitching, for example – who have contributed to anthologies for many years, yet have never had collections of their own published.

Ask a publisher why there are many more anthologies than single poet collections and they will give you a simple answer: anthologies sell more copies. It is much easier to sell an anthology of school poems, such as 'Why do we have to go to school today?' than it is to sell 'The Very Best of A.N.Other Children's Poet'.

Get inspired by children

If you are undaunted by what I have said so far and still determined that you are going to write children's poetry and get it published, what tips can I offer?

Starting with the most obvious, get to know children's language. If you are writing poems about children's experiences from a child's point of view you must get the language right. It is, perhaps, not surprising that many of the most successful children's poets are from a teaching background – for example, Tony Mitton, Wes Magee, Judith Nicholls, Paul Cookson and Brian Moses. Teachers not only know what children's interests are, but they also know how children think and how they express themselves. So steep yourself in children's language, not just the language of your children or the children of friends, but of children from all sorts of backgrounds and cultures.

Try to arrange to visit schools in different areas. But always go through the correct channels with a letter to the literacy coordinator, copied to the head teacher, explaining the reasons you would like to visit. Schools these days are, quite rightly, very security-conscious. Visiting schools will give you the opportunity not only to talk with children, but to try out your poems too. There's nothing like a deafening wall of silence greeting that punchline you thought they would find so amusing to let you know that, in fact, the poem doesn't work!

Schools are also a good source of ideas. Many a poem comes from a child's tale or a teacher's comment. In one school I met a teacher called Mr Little, who was six foot six inches tall. He told me a story about a girl who had asked him: Were you big when you were little? This led to my poem 'Size-Wise' (below).

> Our teacher Mr Little's really tall.
> He's twice the size of our helper Mrs Small.
> 'Were you big when you were little?'
> Sandra asked him.
> 'I was Little when I was little,
> but I've always been big!'
> he said with a grin.
> 'Have you always been small?'
> Sandra asked Mrs Small.
> 'No,' said Mrs Small.
> 'I was Short before I got married,
> then I became Small.
> But,' she added, 'I've always been little.'
> 'That's the long and the short of it,'
> said Mr Little.
> 'I've always been big and Little,
> but she used to be little and Short,
> and now she's little and Small.'

Visiting schools is worthwhile, too, because you can bring yourself up to date with how poetry is being used in the classroom. The National Literacy Strategy requires that children be introduced in the primary years to a wide range of poetic forms. There is an educational as well as a trade market for children's poems and it is worth knowing what the educational publishers might be looking out for.

Anthologies

Successful children's poets will tell you that many of their poems have been triggered by an anthologist's request for a poem on a particular theme. What then is the secret of getting a poem into an anthology?

It may seem to be stating the obvious but the first thing to do is to read the submissions letter closely. My filing cabinets are full of poems that have been given only a cursory glance, because it has become apparent from the first line that they are neither relevant to the theme of the anthology in question nor appropriate for the age group at which the anthology is aimed.

Having read the letter, one's first impulse is to consider whether any of the poems you have already written are suitable. There may well be one or two, particularly among those that are already published, but simply trawling through your file of unpublished poems to see if some of them can be made to fit in with the anthologist's demands is less likely to be successful than actually writing something new.

The key very often is to come up with something slightly different. Let's say you have been asked to contribute to a book of poems about pirates. You probably stand more chance of getting your poem selected if you write a poem about pirates who have become film stars, specialising in gangster parts, than if you write a poem about traditional pirates burying their treasure or making a captive walk the plank. Similarly, if you are writing about dragons, you are more likely to succeed in placing a poem about young dragons having a flying lesson (as I have done myself), or about a young dragon doing his party trick of lighting the candles on his birthday cake (as Ian McMillan has done) than a poem about a dragon fighting a knight. The wackier and more bizarre your idea is, the more chance you will have of your poem being chosen.

Another way of making your poem stand out from the crowd is to write it in a more unusual form. For example, instead of writing your poem about St George and the dragon in couplets, you could write it in the form of an encyclopedia entry, as a series of extracts from St George's diary or even as a text message. The more contemporary the form, the more likely it is to appeal, both to the anthologist and the reader.

Getting the idea is, of course, the hardest part. If you are stuck for a humorous idea, one way of trying to find one is to look in a book of jokes. I was racking my brains to come up with a new poem for a book of magic poems, when I came across this joke: Why are the ghosts of magicians no good at conjuring? Because you can see right through their tricks! This led to:

The ghost of the magician said:
'I'm really in a fix.
The trouble is the audience
Sees right through all my tricks!'

A word of caution: whereas it can pay to be risqué, both in terms of getting your poem selected and entertaining your readers, don't be rude just for the sake of it and, especially, don't be crude. Besides, you could easily get yourself labelled! During a performance in Glasgow, I included one or two poems which made references to 'bottoms' and 'knickers', getting the usual delighted response from the audience. However, I was taken aback when I asked them to suggest why the publishers won't allow me to illustrate my poetry books. Instead of giving me the expected – and correct – answer that my drawings are no good, the first boy I asked said: 'Because your poems are dirty!'

Before sending off your poems, make sure your name and contact details are given clearly beneath every poem. It is usually better, too, to put each poem on a separate page. Check with the anthologist before you submit your poems by email. Many anthologists prefer to receive hard copies, since they assemble the anthology by hand, rather than on the computer, and it saves them the chore of having to print out the poems themselves.

Also, don't send too many poems. As a rule of thumb it's usually best to send about five, and not more than 10. Of course, you will include what you think is your best and most suitable poem. But don't be surprised if it's not chosen and another one is. I'm constantly being asked why that happens. Usually it's because someone else has written a poem that's similar in content or form to your best one and it would not be appropriate to include two such similar poems. Whereas, with regard to your other poem, it either looks at the topic from a different angle or fills a gap that needs to be filled.

You won't make a fortune from getting your poem into an anthology, but once it is in print there's also the chance that it will be picked up and used by another anthologist. So my advice is: be prepared to accept any minor changes that the editor proposes, even if you prefer your original version of the poem. My own experience is that nine times out of 10 any changes that have been suggested to my poems have actually improved them. One established poet actually calls me 'the poetry surgeon' because on several occasions I have suggested cutting whole verses from some of his poems. Professional that he is, he has agreed to accept the cuts, even if privately he knows, and I know, that he does not totally agree with them. And, of course, he has pocketed the fee!

Finally, the big question: how do you get yourself onto the anthologists' mailing lists? A simple request to have your name added won't necessarily do the trick. The anthologist needs to know that it is worth taking the time to send you a letter. So it's worth sending a sample of your poems (about five is enough) with a covering letter. But don't expect to be flooded with requests. There are only a limited number of anthologies published annually. However, if the anthologist thinks your poems have potential, your name will be added to the list – the first step towards getting a ride on the children's poetry roundabout.

John Foster's latest collection of his own poems, *Our Teacher's Gone Bananas*, is published by Oxford University Press. 'Size-Wise' is from *Making Waves* (Oxford University Press) ©John Foster; 'The Ghost of the Magician' ©John Foster.

An interview with my shadow

Brian Patten talks about writing poetry.

Who are you?
I'm your shadow.

What's that you're eating?
It's the shadow of an apple.

Surely shadows can't detach themselves from walls and eat shadow-apples?
They can if they are writers' and poets' shadows.

Why do you write for children as well as for adults?
I don't know, it just happened that way. But I really do believe that writing for one is no easier than writing for the other. If somebody tries to write for adults and finds they aren't any good at it, then they will very likely be even worse at writing for children.

Can you really appreciate poetry at seven or even 11 years old?
Of course you can! Adults have no monopoly on feelings. I suspect that many adults never feel as intensely about things as they did when they were younger.

What are the best kinds of things to write about?
You can write about anything you want. Sometimes the weirder the better. At 10 you will probably write very different poems than when you're 14 and when you are 40 you'll write different poems again.

How about telling stories through poems?
Very short stories, yes. But not long stories. For long stories children prefer prose, and quite rightly I think. Part of poetry is to do with condensing, not expanding. It is different if you are writing a series of poems about the same character or about a particular situation or unusual creatures, or seeing certain themes from different angles. Then snapshots can build up into a story. But there have been very few successful long story-poems written for children.

I thought poets were supposed to be daydreamers. Some people think poetry is a bit soft.
Modern poetry for children is usually anarchic – anything but soft. Having said this, there is an awful lot of bad so-called 'children's poetry' about. Almost as much as bad 'adult poetry'.

How so?
Well, there is more rhyme and word play in contemporary children's poetry than in contemporary adult poetry. People can make things rhyme, but they either don't or can't work on the scansion, and then the whole metrical structure falls apart. No matter how good an idea, it is the execution of the work that brings it to life.

Did you intend that last sentence to be ironic?
Yes. And it is true. Would-be writers forget it at their peril! Children won't be fobbed off with lazy work.

Why did you begin writing poetry? Did anyone teach you?

No, one day I just started writing things down. You see, as a child I lived in this tiny house with three adults. They were all unhappy people. My mother was young and couldn't afford a place of her own, so we lived with my grandmother. My grandmother wore callipers and she dragged herself round the house by her hands. I remember thinking they were like talons.

What has this got to do with poetry and beginning to write it?

Everybody in that little house was miserable and they didn't talk to each other, and although they knew they were miserable and why they were miserable, they couldn't explain why.

You mean they could not express themselves?

Yes, and because they could not express themselves they kept everything walled up inside them, where it hurt and festered for want of light.

Were you like this as well?

To begin with. I don't know how it happened, or why, but I realised the only way I could express my feelings was by writing them down. I think that is how I started to become a poet. I began writing down what I felt. So really, I began writing poetry before I even began reading it. I needed to express my feelings and writing poetry was like writing a very intense diary.

Would you say you were a 'real' poet at that age? I mean, when you began writing did you think that you would ever become a professional poet?

No. That happened when I began changing words and moving lines around. When you begin to *make* something out of the words is when the professional element comes into play. A good poem is something that carries your feelings and ideas inside it. People remember a good poem because of the way it is written, just as much as because of what it says.

Would you like a bit of my apple?

I'm not sure. What does a shadow-apple taste like?

Brian Patten was born and bred in Liverpool. He writes poetry for adults and children.

Poetry organisations

Poetry is one of the easiest writing art forms to begin with, though the hardest to excel at or earn any money from. Carl Dhiman, Membership Manager at the Poetry Society, lists below the organisations which can help poets take their poetry further.

WHERE TO GET INVOLVED

Academi

Mount Stuart House, Mount Stuart Square, Cardiff Bay, Cardiff CF10 5FQ
tel 029-204 72266
email post@academi.org
website www.academi.org
Coordinator Peter Finch

The Welsh National Literature Promotion Agency which has a huge resource available for poets and poetry. It organises events and tours, promotes poets and poetry, offers poetry advice, locates poetry publishers, offers financial help to poets and to organisers wishing to book poets, and much more. To take advantage of their services you have to live or be in Wales, which has the largest number of poets per 1000 population anywhere in the Western World.

Brightside

33 Churchill Street, Leicester LE2 1FH
website www.brightside.mcmail.com

Opened in April 1996 as a poetry cabaret event in Leicester, the Brightside is now a performance poetry organisation made up of professional performance poets who have backgrounds in teaching, youth work, theatre, mental health and stand-up comedy.

The British Haiku Society

Lenacre Ford, Woolhope, Hereford HR1 4RF
tel (01432) 860328
email davidawalker@btinternet.com
website www.britishhaikusociety.org
Secretary David Walker

The Society runs the prestigious annual James W. Hackett International Haiku Award, the Nobuyuki Yuasa Annual International Award for Haibun and the bienniel Sasakawa Prize worth £2500 for original contributions in the field of haikai. It is active in promoting the teaching of haiku in schools and colleges, and is able to provide readers, course/workshop leaders and speakers for poetry groups, etc. It has created a haiku teaching/learning kit for schools. Write for membership details. Founded 1990.

Commonword

6 Mount Street, Manchester M2 5NS
tel 0161-832 3777
email cathy@commonword.org.uk
website www.commonword.org.uk
Contact Cathy Bolton

Commonword is a valuable resource for poets and writers in the North West. It provides support, training and publishing opportunities for new writers. It has helped to launch the careers of many of the region's leading poets and strives to seek out new talent in unexpected places.

Creative Arts East

Griffin Court, Market Street, Wymondham, Norfolk NR18 0GU
tel (01603) 774789
email lisa.d'onofrio@cae.norfolk.gov.uk
website www.creativeartseast.co.uk
Coodinator Lisa D'Onofrio

Creative Arts East is a fast-growing arts development agency which provides practical support to the arts community in Norfolk; directly promotes tours, exhibitions, and one-off performances and readings by professional artists and companies; and develops community-based arts projects which address social issues around isolation and disadvantage.

The agency was formally launched in 2002, and was set up to combine the collective expertise and energy of 4 smaller arts organisations: Rural Arts East, Norfolk Arts Marketing, Norfolk Literature Development and Create! Members receive the Norfolk Literature Network newsletter containing information, news, events listings and competitions.

Mini Mushaira

c/o 11 Donnington Road, Sheffield S2 2RF
tel (01743) 245004, 0114-272390
email simon@shrews1.fsnet.co.uk
Coordinators Simon Fletcher, Debjani Chatterjee

Mushaira is the Arabic word for 'a gathering of poets' and the Mini Mushaira writers (Debjani Chatterjee in Sheffield, Simon Fletcher in Shrewsbury, Basir Sultan Kazmi in Manchester and Brian G. D'Arcy in Sheffield) are a group of multicultural poets and storytellers who seek to build cultural 'bridges' through their work with both children and adults. Mini Mushaira have given excellent multilingual poetry performances and run poetry workshops throughout the country. While each is a well-published poet, they also have a Mini Mushaira anthology: *A Little Bridge* published by Pennine Pens.

The Poetry Book Society

4th Floor, 2 Tavistock Place, London WC1H 9RA
tel 020-7833 9247 *fax* 020-7833 5990

email info@poetrybooks.co.uk
website www.poetrybooks.co.uk,
www.poetrybookshoponline.com,
www.childrenspoetrybookshelf.co.uk
Chair Daisy Goodwin, *Director* Chris Holifield

This unique book club for readers of poetry was founded in 1953 by T.S. Eliot, and is funded by the Arts Council England. Every quarter, selectors choose one outstanding publication (the PBS Choice), and recommend 4 other titles, which are sent to members, who are also offered substantial discounts on other poetry books. The Poetry Book Society also administers the T.S. Eliot Prize, produces the quarterly membership magazine, the *Bulletin*, and has an education service providing teaching materials for primary and secondary schools. In addition, the PBS runs the Children's Poetry Bookshelf, offering children's poetry for 7–11 year-olds, with parent, school and library memberships and a new child-friendly website.

The Poetry Business
Byram Arcade, Huddersfield HD1 1ND
email edit@poetrybusiness.co.uk
Contact Peter Sansom

Dedicated to helping writers reach their full potential by running supportive workshops.

The Poetry Can
Unit 11, 20–22 Hepburn Road, Bristol BS2 8UD
tel 0117-943 6976
email colin@poetrycan.demon.co.uk
website www.poetrycan.com
Coordinator Colin Brown

The Poetry Can is one of the few literature organisations in the UK specialising in poetry. It organises events such as the Bristol Poetry Festival; runs a lifelong learning programme; offers information and advice in all aspects of poetry.

Poetry Ireland
120 St Stephen's Green, Dublin 2, Republic of Ireland
tel (01) 478 9974 *fax* (0) 478 0205
email poetry@iol.ie
website www.poetryireland.ie

Poetry Ireland is the national organisation dedicated to developing, supporting and promoting poetry throughout Ireland. It is a resource and information point for any member of the public with an interest in poetry and works towards creating opportunities for poets working or living in Ireland. It is grant-aided by both the Northern and Southern Arts Councils of Ireland and is a resource centre with the Austin Clarke Library of over 10,000 titles. It publishes the quarterly magazine *Poetry Ireland Review* and the bi-monthly newsletter *Poetry Ireland News*. Poetry Ireland organises readings in Dublin and nationally, and runs a Writers-in-Schools Scheme.

Poetry on Loan
Unit 116, The Custard Factory, Gibb Street,
Birmingham B9 4AA
tel 0121-246 2770
email jonathan@bookcommunications.co.uk
Coordinator Jonathan Davidson

Poetry on Loan is a scheme to promote contemporary poetry through libraries in the West Midlands. There are 30 participating libraries and the scheme supports events, displays, stock collections and commissions. It also runs poetry projects for young people.

The Poetry Society
22 Betterton Street, London WC2H 9BX
tel 020-7420 9880 *fax* 020-7240 4818
email info@poetrysociety.org.uk
website www.poetrysociety.org.uk
Membership From £15 p.a.

The Poetry Society was set up to help poetry and poets thrive in Britain and is a registered charity funded by the Arts Council England. The Society offers advice and information to all, with a more comprehensive level of information available to members. Membership is open to anyone interested in poetry and members receive copies of the UK's most prominent poetry magazine, *Poetry Review*, and the Society's newsletter, *Poetry News*, each quarter. The Society's website provides excellent information, news, poetry links and a useful FAQ page, as well as an interactive regional guide to poetry organisations, venues, publishers, magazines and bookshops around the UK through its Poetry Landmarks of Britain section.

The Society also publishes education resources (see later); promotes National Poetry Day; runs Poetry Prescription, a critical appraisal service available to members and non-members (£50 for 100 lines – 20% discount to members); provides an education advisory and training service, school membership, youth membership and a thriving website. A diverse range of events and readings frequently take place at the Poetry Café and the Poetry Studio at the Society's headquarters in London. The Society also programmes events and readings in other regions of the UK.

Competitions run by the Society include the annual National Poetry Competition, which is one of the largest open poetry competitions in the UK with a first prize of £5000, the biannual Corneliu M. Popescu Prize for European Poetry in Translation and the Foyle Young Poets of the Year Award. Founded 1909.

The Seamus Heaney Centre for Poetry
46–48 University Road, Belfast BT7 1NN
tel 028-9097 1070
email shc@qub.ac.uk
website www.qub.ac.uk/heanycentre

The new Seamus Heaney Centre for Poetry (SHC) is designed to celebrate and promote poetry and artistic endeavour by poets from Northern Ireland. The Centre houses an extensive library of contemporary poetry volumes. It hosts regular creative writing workshops, a poetry reading group, and an ongoing series of readings and lectures by visiting poets and critics from all over the world. The SHC is chaired by the eminent poet, Ciaran Carson, and other resident poets include Medbh McGuckian.

Stop All The Clocks

The Marlborough Theatre, Prince's Street, Brighton BN2 1RD
tel (01273) 207562
email simon@stopalltheclocks.co.uk
website www.stopalltheclocks.co.uk
Coordinator Simon Clayton

Stop All The Clocks was formed from an amalgamation of the 3 best poetry promotion stables in Brighton – Don't Feed The Poets, Holy! Holy! Holy! Holy! and Wanderlust Wonderlust. It is by far the most active of Brighton's many poetry organisations and runs year-round genuinely grassroots events and organises the fringe literature festival every May.

Survivors Poetry

Diorama Arts Centre, 34 Osnaburgh Street, London NW1 3ND
tel 020-7916 5317 *fax* 020-7916 0830
email survivor@survivorspoetry.org.uk

Survivors Poetry provides poetry workshops, performances, readings, publishing, networking and training for survivors of mental distress in London and the UK. Survivors Poetry is funded by the Arts Council England and was founded in 1991 by 4 poets who have had first-hand experience of the mental health system. It works in partnership with local and national arts, mental health, community, statutory and disability organisations. Its outreach project has established a network of 30 writers' groups in the UK.

WHERE TO GET INFORMATION

The first place to start is your local library. They usually have information about the local poetry scene. Many libraries are actively involved in promoting poetry as well as having modern poetry available for loan. Local librarians promote writing activities with, for example, projects like Poetry on Loan and Poetry Places information points in West Midlands Libraries.

Arts Council England

website www.artscouncil.org.uk

Arts Council England has 9 regional offices and local literature officers can provide information on local poetry groups, workshops and societies (see page 342). Some give grant aid to local publishers and magazines and help fund festivals, literature projects and readings, and some run critical services.

The Northern Poetry Library

County Library, The Willows, Morpeth, Northumberland NE61 1TA
tel (01670) 534514 (poetry enquiries), (01670) 534524 (poetry dept)
Membership Free to anyone living in the areas of Tyne and Wear, Durham, Northumberland, Cumbria and Cleveland

The Northern Poetry Library has over 14,000 titles and magazines covering poetry published since 1945. For information about epic through to classic poetry, a full text database is available of all poetry from 600–1900. A postal lending service is available to members, who pay for return postage. Founded 1968.

The Poetry Library

Level 5, Royal Festival Hall, London SE1 8XX
tel 020-7921 0943/0664 *fax* 020-7921 0939
email poetrylibrary@rfh.org.uk
website www.poetrylibrary.org.uk
Membership Free with proof of identity and current address

The principal roles of the Poetry Library are to collect and preserve all poetry published in the UK since about 1912 and to act as a public lending library. It also keeps a wide range of international poetry. It has 2 copies of each title available and a collection of about 40,000 titles in English and English translation. The Library also provides an education service (see under 'Help for young poets and teachers', below).

The Library runs an active information service, which includes a unique noticeboard for lost quotations, and tracing authors and publishers from extracts of poems. Current awareness lists are available for magazines, publishers, competitions, bookshops, groups and workshops, evening classes and festivals on receipt of a large sae. The Library also stocks a full range of British poetry magazines as well as a selection from abroad. When visiting the Library, look out for the Voice Box, a performance space for literature; a programme is available from 020-7921 0906. Open 11am–8pm Tuesday to Sunday. Founded in 1953 by the Arts Council.

The Scottish Poetry Library

5 Crichton's Close, Canongate, Edinburgh EH8 8DT
tel 0131-558 2876
email admin@spl.org.uk
website www.spl.org.uk

The Scottish Poetry Library is the place for poetry in Scotland for the regular reader, the serious student or the casual browser. It has a remarkable collection of written works, as well as tapes and videos. The emphasis is on contemporary poetry written in Scotland, in Scots, Gaelic and English, but historic

Scottish poetry – and contemporary works from almost every part of the world – feature too. They also have collections for the visually impaired. All resources, advice and information are readily accessible, free of charge. It holds regular poetry events, details of which are available on the library website. Founded 1984.

ONLINE RESOURCES

You can obtain a wealth of information at the click of a mouse these days. In addition to those listed above, good starting points are:

The Poetry Archive
website www.poetryarchive.org

The Poetry Kit
website www.poetrykit.org

The Poetry Society of America
website www.poetrysociety.org

WHERE TO GET POETRY BOOKS

See the Poetry Book Society, above. The Poetry Library provides a list of bookshops which stock poetry. For second-hand mail order poetry books try:

Baggins Books
19 High Street, Rochester, Kent ME1 1PY
tel (01634) 811651 *fax* (01634) 840591
email godfreygeorge@btconnect.com

Secondhand bookshop with over half a million books in stock.

The Poetry Bookshop
The Ice House, Brook Street, Hay-on-Wye HR3 5BQ
tel (01497) 821812

Peter Riley
27 Sturton Street, Cambridge CB1 2QG
tel (01223) 576422
email priley@dircon.co.uk

WHERE TO CELEBRATE POETRY

Festival information should be available from Arts Council England offices (see page 342). See also *Children's literature festivals and trade fairs* on page 375.

The British Council
Information Officer, Literature Dept, The British Council, 11 Portland Place, London W1N 4EJ
tel 020-7930 8466 *fax* 020-7389 3199
website www.britishcouncil.org/arts/literature

Send a large sae or visit the website for a list of forthcoming festivals.

WHERE TO PERFORM

In London, Express Excess, Short Fuse and Aromapoetry are 3 of the liveliest venues for poetry performances and they regularly feature the best performers. Poetry Unplugged at the Poetry Café is famous for its open mic nights (Tuesdays 7.30pm). Poetry evenings are held all over the UK and those listed below are worth checking out. Others can be found by visiting your local library or your Arts Council office, or by visiting the Landmarks of Britain section of the Poetry Society website (www.poetrysociety.org.uk/landmarks.htm).

Apples and Snakes Performance Poetry
Battersea Arts Centre, Lavender Hill, London SW11
tel 020-7223 2223
website www.applesandsnakes.org

Aromapoetry
Charterhouse Bar, Charterhouse Street, London EC1M 6JH
website www.x-bout.com/aroma

Big Word Performance Poetry
Edinburgh Comedy Room, The Tron Bar, 9 Hunter Square, Royal Mile, Edinburgh EH1 1QW
tel 0131-226 0931
email jemrolls@bigword.fsnet.co.uk
website www.geocities.com/poemsandpints/misc/bigword.htm#ed

Coffee House Poetry
Troubadour Coffee House, 265 Old Brompton Road, London SW5
tel 020-7370 1434

Dead Good Poets Society
96 Bould Street, Liverpool L1 4HY
tel 0151-709 5221
email dgps@blueyonder.co.uk
Contact Cath Nichols

Express Excess
The Enterprise, 2 Haverstock Hill, London NW3
tel 020-7485 2659

Poetry Café
22 Betterton Street, London WC2 9BX
tel 020-7420 9888

Shortfuse
The Camden Head, Camden Walk, Islington, London N1
website www.20six.co.uk/shortfuse

Spiel
20 Coxwell Street, Cirencester, Glos. GL7 2BH
tel (01285) 640470
email spiel@scarum.freeserve.co.uk, spiel@arbury.freeserve.co.uk
website www.author.co.uk/spiel/index.htm

Voice Box
Level 5, Royal Festival Hall, London SE1
tel 020-7960 4242

COMPETITIONS

There are now hundreds of competitions to enter and as the prizes increase, the highest being £5000 (first prize in the National Poetry Competition and the Arvon Foundation International Poetry Competition), so does the prestige associated with winning such competitions.

To decide which competitions are worth entering, make sure you know who the judges are and think twice before paying large sums for an anthology of 'winning' poems which will only be read by entrants wanting to see their own work in print. The Poetry Library publishes a list of competitions each month (available free on receipt of a large sae).

Literary prizes are given annually to published poets and as such are non-competitive. An A–Z guide to literary prizes can be found on the Booktrust website (www.booktrust.org.uk).

WHERE TO WRITE POETRY

The Arvon Foundation
Lumb Bank – The Ted Hughes Arvon Centre, Hebden Bridge, West Yorkshire HX7 6DF
tel (01422) 843714 *fax* (01422) 843714
The Arvon Foundation at Totleigh Barton, Sheepwash, Beaworthy, Devon EX21 5NS
tel (01409) 231338 *fax* (01409) 231144
The Arvon Foundation at Moniack Mhor, Teavarren, Kiltarlity, Beauly, Inverness-shire IV4 7HT
tel (01463) 741675 *fax* (01463) 741733
The Hurst – The John Osborne Arvon Centre, Clunton, Craven Arms, Shrops. SY7 0JA
tel (01588) 640658 *fax* (01588) 640509
email hurst@arvonfoundation.org
website www.arvonfoundation.org

The Arvon Foundation's 4 centres run 5-day residential courses throughout the year to anyone over the age of 16, providing the opportunity to live and work with professional writers. Writing genres explored include poetry, narrative, drama, writing for children, song writing and the performing arts. Bursaries are available to those receiving benefits. Founded in 1968.

The Poetry School
1A Jewel Road, London E17 4QU
tel (0845) 223 5274 *fax* 020-822 30439
email programme@poetryschool.com
website www.poetryschool.com

Using London venues and regional centres in Manchester, York and Exeter, the Poetry School offers a core programme of tuition in reading and writing poetry. It provides a forum to share experience, develop skills and extend appreciation of both traditional and innovative aspects of poetry.

The Poet's House/Teach na hÉigse
Clonbarra, Falcarragh, County Donegal, Republic of Ireland
tel (074) 65470 *fax* (074) 65471
email phouse@iol.ie

The Poet's House runs 3 10-day poetry courses in July and August. An MA degree in creative writing is validated by Lancaster University, and the Irish Language Faculty includes Cathal O'Searcaigh. The poetry faculty comprises 30 writers, including Paul Durcan and John Montagu.

Ty Newydd
Taliesin Trust, Ty Newydd, Llanystumdwy, Criccieth, Gwynedd LL52 0LW
tel (01766) 522811 *fax* (01766) 523095
email post@tynewydd.org
website www.tynewydd.org

Ty Newydd runs week-long writing courses encompassing a wide variety of genres, including poetry, and caters for all levels, from beginners to published poets. All the courses are tutored by published writers. Writing retreats are also available.

GROUPS ON THE INTERNET

It is worth searching for discussion groups and chat rooms on the internet. There are plenty of them; John Kinsella's is highly recommended, which is junk mail-resistant and highly informative:

John Kinsella's
email poetryetc@jiscmail.ac.uk

The Poetry Kit
website www.poetrykit.org/wkshops2.htm

Local groups
Local groups vary enormously so it is worth shopping around to find one that suits your poetry. Up-to-date information can be obtained from Arts Council England regional offices (see page 342).

The Poetry Library publishes a list of groups for the Greater London area which will be sent out on receipt of a large sae.

HELP FOR YOUNG POETS AND TEACHERS

National Association of Writers in Education (NAWE)
PO Box 1, Sheriff Hutton, York YO60 7YU
tel/fax (01653) 618429
email paul@nawe.co.uk

website www.nawe.co.uk

NAWE is a national organisation, which aims to widen the scope of writing in education, and coordinate activities between writers, teachers and funding bodies. It publishes the magazine *Writing in Education* and is author of a writers' database which can identify writers who fit the given criteria (e.g. speaks several languages, works well with special needs, etc) for schools, colleges and the community. Publishes *Reading the Applause: Reflections on Performance Poetry by Various Artists*. Write for membership details.

The Poetry Library

Children's Section, Royal Festival Hall, London SE1 8XX
tel 020-7921 0664
website www.poetrylibrary.org.uk

For young poets, the Poetry Library has about 4000 books incorporating the SIGNAL Collection of Children's Poetry. It also has a multimedia children's section, from which cassettes and videos are available to engage children's interest in poetry.

The Poetry Library has an education service for teachers and writing groups. Its information file covers all aspects of poetry in education. There is a separate collection of books and materials for teachers and poets who work with children in schools, and teachers may join a special membership scheme to borrow books for the classroom.

Poetry Society Education

The Poetry Society, 22 Betterton Street, London WC2H 9BX
tel 020-7420 9894 *fax* 020-7240 4818
email education@poetrysociety.org.uk
website www.poetrysociety.org.uk
Membership £50 secondary schools, £30 primary schools

The Poetry Society has an outstanding reputation for its exciting and innovative education work. For over 30 years it has been introducing poets into classrooms, providing comprehensive teachers' resources and producing colourful, accessible publications for pupils.

Poetry Society Education develops projects and schemes to keep poetry flourishing in schools, libraries and workplaces. Schemes like Poets in Schools, Poet in the City and Poetry Places (a 2-year programme of residencies and placements, funded by the Arts Council's 'Arts for Everyone' lottery budget) have enabled the Poetry Society to give work to hundreds of poets and allowed thousands of children

and adults to experience poetry for themselves. Through projects such as the Respect Slam and The Foyle Young Poets of the Year Award the Poetry Society gives valuable encouragement and exposure to young writers and performers.

Schools membership offers publications, training opportunities for teachers and poets, a free subscription to *Poems on the Underground* and a consultancy service giving advice on working with poets in the classroom. *Poetryclass*, an INSET training project funded by the DfES, employs poets to train teachers at primary and secondary level. Youth membership is available to 11–18 year-olds and provides advice on developing writing skills, access to publication on the Poetry Society website, quarterly issues of *Poetry News*, and poetry books and posters.

Poetry Society publications for schools include *The Poetry Book for Primary Schools* and *Jumpstart – Poetry in the Secondary School*, a young poet's pack and posters for Key Stage 1 to GCSE requirements. Information on resources, membership, the Foyle Young Poets of the Year Award and educational residencies is available from the Education department.

YOUNG POETRY COMPETITIONS

Children's competitions are included in the competition list provided by the Poetry Library (free on receipt of a large sae).

Foyle Young Poets of the Year Award

The Poetry Society, 22 Betterton Street, London WC2H 9BX
tel 020-7420 9894 *fax* 020-7240 4818
email education@poetrysociety.org.uk
website www.poetrysociety.org.uk

Free entry for 11–17 year-olds with unique prizes.

Christopher Tower Poetry Prize

Tower Poetry, Christ Church, Oxford OX1 1DP
tel/fax (01865) 286591
email info@towerpoetry.org.uk
website www.towerpoetry.org.uk/prize/index.html

An annual poetry competition from Christ Church, Oxford, open to 16–18 year-olds in UK schools and colleges. The poems should be no longer than 48 lines, on a different chosen theme each year. Prizes: £1500 (1st), prize £750 (2nd), £500 (3rd). Every winner also receives a prize for their school. Highly commended entries each receive £200.

Literary agents
How to get an agent

Because children's publishing is highly competitive and the market is crowded, in this article Philippa Milnes-Smith explains that finding an agent isn't child's play.

If you are currently just experiencing a vague interest in being a writer or illustrator, stop now. You are unlikely to survive the rigorous commercial assessment to which your work will be subjected. If you are a children's writer or illustrator, do not think that the process of getting published will be any easier than for the adult market. It's just as tough, if not tougher, partly because a lot of writers and would-be writers see writing for children as an easy option. It can't be that difficult to write a kid's book, can it? After all, it is just for kids...

Nowadays, too, there is extra competition in the children's field: the high profile of successes such as J.K. Rowling's *Harry Potter* series and Philip Pullman's *His Dark Materials* have drawn the attention of many professional writers who have previously only written for the adult market and who see it as a new and lucrative area for their talents. So, before embarking on a children's book/script/proposal for an exciting new children's character, remember that it is a highly competitive and crowded market you are entering.

So, what is a literary agent and why would I want one?

You will probably already have noticed that contacts for many publishers are provided in the *Children's Writers' & Artists' Yearbook*. This means that there is nothing to prevent you from pursuing publishers directly yourself. Indeed, if you can answer a confident 'yes' to all the questions below, and have the time and resources to devote to this objective, you probably don't need an agent.

- Do you have a thorough understanding of the publishing market and its dynamics?
- Do you know who are the best publishers for your book and why? Can you evaluate the pros and cons of each?
- Are you financially numerate and confident of being able to negotiate the best commercial deal available in current market conditions?
- Are you confident of being able to understand fully and negotiate a publishing or other media contract?
- Do you enjoy the process of selling yourself and your work?
- Do you want to spend your creative time on these activities?

An agent's job is to deal with all of the above on your behalf. A good agent will do all of these well.

Is that all an agent does?

Agents aren't all the same. Some will provide more editorial and creative support; some will help on longer-term career planning; some will be subject specialists; some will involve themselves more on marketing and promotion. Such extras may well be taken into consideration in the commission rates charged.

If I am writing and/or illustrating for children's books, do I need a specialist children's agent?

Most specialist children's agents would probably say you definitely need a specialist; many general agents will say you don't really need a specialist. In the end you will have to make up your own mind about whether an individual agent is right for your work and right for you as an individual. Knowledge, experience and excellent industry contacts (in the right companies and the right categories) are essential qualities in an agent who is going to represent you. If you are writing younger fiction, an agent whose expertise is in adult books with a few forays into young adult fiction probably won't have a full grasp of its potential. If your project is really something specifically for the schools and educational market it may well require different representation than a project for the consumer market: the audience (children) may be the same but projects for educational publishers tend to have to be tailored to the educational syllabus in a very particular way. You will need an agent who understands this (and there are very few).

If you are only interested in illustrating work by other people rather than developing your own projects and would like to try illustration work across a broad range of genres and formats, you may be best served by an artists' agent rather than a literary agent (see *Illustrators' agents* on page 208).

I am writing a text for an illustrated book – do I need to send illustrations with it for an agent to consider it?

No, not unless you are an accomplished illustrator or intend to do the illustrations yourself. The wrong illustrations will put off an agent as they will a publisher. A good text should be able to speak for itself. And never, in any case, send in original artwork, only send copies.

What if I have a brilliant novelty proposal, like a pop-up book? Do I need to show how it is going to look it its finished state?

If you can do it competently and it helps demonstrate how different and exciting your project is, you can certainly do this. But be prepared for the fact that you may need to make more than one, as the original runs the risk of getting damaged through handling or, when the worst comes to the worst, getting lost.

I have decided I definitely do want an agent. Where do I begin?

When I left publishing and talked generally to the authors and illustrators I knew, a number of them said it was now more difficult to find an agent than a publisher. Why is this? The answer is a commercial one. Running an agency is a costly thing and an agent will only take someone on if they can see how and why they are going to make money for the client and themselves (and, of course, a client who is making no money tends quickly to become an unhappy client). To survive just the basic costs, an agent needs to make commission and if an agent needs to fund sales trips on clients' behalf, often internationally, they need more commission. An agent also knows that if he or she cannot and does not sell a client's work, the relationship isn't going to last long.

So the agent just thinks about money?

Well, some agents may just think about money. And it is certainly what some authors and artists think about a lot. *But* good agents do also care about the quality of work and the clients they take on. They are professional people who commit themselves to doing the best job they can. They also know that good personal relationships count – and that they help everyone enjoy business more. This means that, if and when you get as far as talking to a prospective agent, you should ask yourself the questions: 'Do I have a good rapport with this person? Do I think we will get along? Do I understand and trust what they are saying?' Follow your instinct – more often than not it will be right.

So how do I convince them that I'm worth taking on?

Start with the basics. Make your approach professional. Make sure you only approach an appropriate agent who deals with the category of book you are writing/illustrating. Phone to check to whom you should send your work and whether there are any particular ways your submission should be made (if it's not clear from the listings in this *Yearbook* – see page 173). Only submit neat typed work on single-sided A4 paper. Send a short covering letter with your manuscript explaining what it is, why you wrote it, what the intended audience is and providing any other *relevant* context. Always say if and why you are uniquely placed and qualified to write a particular book. Also, provide a CV (again, neat, typed, relevant). Think of the whole thing in the same way as you would a job application, for which you would expect to prepare thoroughly in advance. You might only get one go at making your big sales pitch to an agent. Don't mess it up by being anything less than thorough.

And if I get to meet them?

Treat it like a job interview (although hopefully it will be more relaxed than this). Be prepared to talk about your work and yourself. An agent knows that a prepossessing personality in an author is a great asset for a publisher in terms of publicity and marketing – they will be looking to see how good your interpersonal skills are. Do also take the chance to find out, if you are discussing children's projects in particular, how and where they submit their clients' work and how well they understand the children's market themselves. Also check that they have good relationships with the sort of publishers/media companies with whom you think your work belongs. Don't be afraid to question them on their credentials and track record. And if you have personal recommendations and referrals from other writers, publishers and other industry contacts, do follow these up. Ask, too, about representation overseas and at the key trade children's book fair(s) such as the one held annually in Bologna. If appropriate, ask about representation in other media. Is this agent going to get their clients' work noticed by the right people in the right places and sold for the best market rates?

Will they expect me to be an expert on children and the children's market?

Not as such, but they might reasonably expect you to have an interest in what children like and enjoy and show an understanding of a child's eye view of the world. Basically, an agent will be looking for a writer/illustrator who is in sympathy with the target audience. It also won't do any harm if you spend time at your local bookshop and/or library and befriend your local librarian or specialist children's bookseller to find out what books and authors are working well and if anyone is doing exactly what you plan to do. It's good, basic market research, as is browsing what else is available through internet retailers. For example, if you are planning a series of picture books about a ballet-dancing mouse you need to be aware that *Angelina Ballerina* is already out there.

And if they turn my work down? Should I ask them to look again? People say you should not accept rejection.

No means no. Don't pester. It won't make an agent change his or her mind. Instead, move on to the next agency who might feel more positive towards your work. The agents who reject you may be wrong. But the loss is theirs.

Even if they turn my work down, isn't it worth asking for help with my creative direction?

No. Agents will often provide editorial advice for clients but won't do so for non-clients. Submissions are usually sorted into two piles of 'yes, worth seeing more' and 'rejections'.

There is not another pile of 'promising writer but requires further tutoring'. To get teaching and advice, creative writing courses (see page 325) and writers' and artists' groups are better options to pursue. It is, however, important to practise and develop your creative skills. You wouldn't expect to be able to play football without working at your ball skills or practise as a lawyer without studying to acquire the relevant knowledge. If you are looking to get your work published, you are going to have to compete with professional writers and artists – and those who have spent years working at their craft.

There are particular considerations that need to be given in the craft of writing children's books. In a picture book, the text needs to work specifically with the illustrations: the fewer words there are, the more they matter. In writing fiction for a young age group, where language and sentence construction have to be simple enough for a seven year-old child, the writer often has to work much harder to generate emotion and excitement and give the story personality. When illustrating children's poetry, the artist has to be able to develop and enhance the meaning of the words to just the right level. Children's books are a demanding business.

Good luck!

Philippa Milnes-Smith is a literary agent and children's specialist at the agency LAW (Lucas Alexander Whitley). She was previously Managing Director of Puffin Books.

See also...
- *Do you have to have an agent to succeed?*, page 169
- *Children's literary agents UK and Ireland*, page 173
- *Children's literary agents overseas*, page 181

Do you *have* to have an agent to succeed?

Bestselling children's author Philip Ardagh has over 60 titles to his credit but chooses not have a literary agent to represent him. In this article he tells us why.

There are a lot of people out there who think that they're children's writers ('I was a child myself once, you know') and who send unsolicited manuscripts directly to publishers in their hundreds – possibly thousands – every year. These manuscripts usually end up on what is called the 'slush pile'. Some publishers won't even read them. Some do but, usually, only after a very long time. Many manuscripts are very badly written or very badly presented. Some are perfectly good but a little too much like something already out there in the bookshops, or they lack that indefinable something that makes them stand out from the crowd. Others are perfectly good but are sent to completely the wrong publisher. The best children's fantasy novel ever isn't going to appeal to a publisher specialising in adult DIY manuals, is it? Getting an agent cuts through this process.

Having an agent

Firstly, if an agent submits a manuscript it's going to be to the publisher they think that it's best suited to, and probably to the most suitable editor within that company – more often than not someone they know or have had dealings with in the past. So your manuscript is being seen by the right people at the right place. It's also neatly bypassed the slush pile. It will actually get read. Hurrah! The agent has acted as a filter. The publisher knows that, if you've been taken on by a reputable agent, your words are probably *worth* reading. You're ahead of the game.

And if a publisher wants to publish your work, an agent knows the ins and outs of advances, royalties, escalators, foreign rights, and a million and one other things that makes the humble writer's head spin. Agents know the 'going rates' and will get you the very best deal they can. And, should there be problems further down the line, your agent can play the bad guy on your behalf – renegotiating contracts and doing the number crunching – whilst you only deal with the nice fluffy creative side with your editor.

That's the theory, of course, and much of it is true. They take their 10%–15% but they're not a charity and, if they're on a percentage of your earnings, it's generally in their interest to make you as much money as possible, isn't it?

The question is: is it possible to be a successful children's author without an agent? Of course it is. Anything's possible. I'm an agentless author and I'm doing okay, but not without help, advice, common sense, good luck and, as time has passed, experience.

So what are the disadvantages of having an agent? If you've got the right agent, the answer is probably very few, if any. Sure, you're not earning the full advance or royalty because you're giving them a percentage but your manuscript may never have become a book (or the advance and royalty may have been much lower) if they didn't represent you in the first place. If you don't have an agent you don't get directly involved in every aspect of negotiation and discussion with your publisher because you've handed that role over. And if you like the on-hands approach (for that read 'are a control freak'), you may miss out on that but, over all, the pros seem to outweigh the cons.

If you're *not* happy with your agent, though, it can be a very different story. You're not your agent's only client and you may feel – rightly or wrongly – that they're not giving you enough attention. Many is the writer and illustrator I know who has said, 'I find more work for myself than my agent does', or who isn't happy with the advance they've received and said, 'I'm not sure why my agent was so keen for me to agree to this deal.' Another familiar lament is, 'She seemed so enthusiastic when I first signed up, but now she's gone really quiet.' Your filter has become a barrier.

There may also be jobs which your agent is reluctant for you to take. In children's non-fiction, many authors are still paid flat fees, and small ones at that. Many agents will tell you not to touch them with a barge pole but – if you are at the beginning of your career – who knows what that little job might lead to? I once wrote the text to a book that owed its subsequent international success not to the beauty of my prose but to the illustrations and brilliant paper engineering. My fee was peanuts and, in immediate financial terms, it made no difference if the book sold three copies or 300,000. But it did my writing career the power of good. My name was associated with a successful title, I got known by various people within that particular publishing house, I went on to write many more books for them *with* royalties, and added to my reputation, generating interest from other publishers.

Going it alone

I enjoy that getting-to-know aspect of developing a relationship with publishers and, when it comes to contracts, I have a very useful not-so-secret secret weapon. I may not have an agent but I can call on the contracts experts at the Society of Authors (see page 333). As a member of the Society, they'll go through a contract line by line for me, free and for nothing, offering comments, suggestions and advice. They also publish excellent easy-to-understand pamphlets on various aspects of publishing. If you're not already a member, rush out and join immediately! If you don't understand something, don't be afraid to ask.

Remember, whatever impression a publisher might give, there is very rarely such thing as a standard contract, written in stone, that can't be altered; sometimes significantly. Be prepared to concede some minor points, maybe, in return for sticking to your guns over a point which may really matter to you. (Different things matter to different writers.)

My big break came by luck, but luck borne out of developing contacts and making real friendships in the course of my agentless foray into the children's publishing world. The bulk of my 60-or-more titles are non-fiction, but the bulk of my income and 95% of my recognition comes from my fiction, but one grew from the other. Because I was involved and enthusiastic, I was invited to promote one of my non-fiction titles at a sales conference. As a result of how I ad libbed at the conference, following a mighty cock-up, I was asked if I wrote fiction. *Awful End* (my first Eddie Dickens book) was pulled out of the drawer and a deal was done. One thing had, indeed, led to another. Eddie's adventures are now in 25 languages and read around the world, picking up a few literary awards along the way. An option for a series of Eddie Dickens films has been signed with Warner Bros.

Your rights

Publishers love to have world rights to your books. Agents love to sell the rights separately. You can see why. An agent will argue that they can get more for you (and therefore more for them) by selling foreign rights separately to foreign publishers – perhaps creating a US auction for your fabulous book, for example – rather than your signing everything over to your UK publisher in one fell swoop. If, however, you sell the world rights to your publisher, and you have a good relationship with them, they're in effect acting as your agent on foreign deals and can still negotiate some excellent ones *in consultation with you*. And, having your world rights, they can share in your international success when it comes, so may be more keen to nurture you (and your money-generating, recognition-building world rights) in the future than, possibly, another writer whom they only publish in the UK.

And remember, an advance is an advance of royalties. If the advance is small and the book is a success, it simply means that the advance is earned out sooner and the cheques start rolling in. My advance for *Awful End* was just a four figure sum, but the money I've earned from additional royalties have been very-nice-thank-you-very-much. And my advance for the latest Eddie Dickens books are significantly larger.

Making the right decision

I know from friends and colleagues that, when you're starting out, you can find it as hard to get an agent as a publisher, which is why some people choose to go straight for the publishing houses. My advice – and this may surprise some of you – is to stick at trying to get an agent. If I was starting out now, I'd do that. Having an agent from the beginning makes sense.

If you're dead against the idea, feeling convinced that you can do a great job (see Philippa Milnes-Smith's check list on page 165) or are exhausted trying, there are a few obvious things you can do. Even now, I sometimes ask myself 'Am I getting the very best deal?' and 'Could an agent do better for me?' Financially, the answers to these are probably 'Maybe not' and 'Yes', but are these the right questions? Surely what I need to ask is: 'Am I happy with this deal?' 'Is it a reasonable sum reflecting what I think I'm worth and showing the commitment and understanding of the publisher?' And the answer to that is, more often than not, 'yes'. And remember, money ain't the be all and end all. A good working relationship with an editor and publisher who understand you, consult with you, nurture you and your writing, promote and market you in a way you're happy with is beyond price!

Approaching a publisher

But let's not get ahead of ourselves. One of the most important, important *important* – it's important, get it? – things you need to be sure of before sending a manuscript to an agent *or* a publisher is that it's ready to be seen. Some unpublished writers are so keen to show their work to others in the hope of getting it published as soon as possible that it's still in a very raw state. They're not doing themselves any favours. In fact, they could be ruining their chances. Sure, there is such a thing as overworking a piece, but you really need to be confident that it's about as good as it's going to get, especially if you're bypassing the agent route and going direct to the publisher. With no agent 'filter', you've got to be sure that you're representing yourself, through your work, in the very best possible light.

Look in bookshops to find out who publishes what. Once you've chosen a publisher, look them up in this *Yearbook*, find out their submissions procedure and ring them up. Ask the receptionist the name of the person you should send your manuscript or sample chapters to. This way you can address and write a letter to a particular person, rather than taking the 'Dear Sir/Madam' approach.

The covering letter you should write to the publisher is almost identical to the one Philippa Milnes-Smith outlines for writing to a prospective agent in her article starting on page 165 except, of course, that you should also include the reason why you think they'd be right people to publish your work.

Finally, do treat the business side of selling yourself as a business. It's not simply that 'the writing's the important bit' and that it'll 'sell itself'. Network, send in invoices on time, get in touch when you say you'll get in touch and be contactable (there's no excuse for dropping off the radar in this age of emails and mobile phones). If you're shy or don't like parties, still go to the ones you're invited to by your publisher. You never know what that chance meeting with that rather scruffy bloke by the chilli dips might lead to. He could end up turning your book into a 24-part television series.

Oh, and one last thing: never admit that, secretly, you enjoy writing so much that you'd happily be published for nothing. Ooops. Me and my big mouth!

Agented or agentless, good luck.

Philip Ardagh has been a full-time writer for over 12 years. His non-fiction includes *The Truth About Christmas*; whilst his novels comprise the very silly *Eddie Dickens* adventures, now in 25 different languages and being developed by Warner Bros. for a proposed series of films. *The Fall of Fergal*, the first of his *Unlikely Exploits*, has been serialised on Radio 4. He collaborated with Sir Paul McCartney and Geoff Dunbar on the children's book *High in the Clouds*.

See also...
- *How to get an agent*, page 165
- *Notes from a successful self-publisher*, page 138
- *Publishing agreements*, page 219
- *The amazing picture book story*, page 197

Children's literary agents UK and Ireland

Cautionary note: The *Children's Writers' & Artists' Yearbook,* along with the Association of Authors Agents and the Society of Authors, takes a dim view of any literary agent who asks potential clients for a fee prior to a manuscript being placed with a publisher. We advise you to treat any such request with caution and to let us know if that agent appears in the listings below. However, agents may charge additional costs later in the process but these should only arise once a book has been accepted by a publisher and the author is earning an income. We urge authors to make the distinction between upfront and additional charges.

*Full member of the Association of Authors' Agents

The Agency (London) Ltd*
24 Pottery Lane, London W11 4LZ
tel 020-7727 1346 *fax* 020-7727 9037
email info@theagency.co.uk
Executives Stephen Durbridge, Leah Schmidt, Julia Kreitman, Bethan Evans, Norman North, Hilary Delamere (children's books), Katie Haines, Ligeia Marsh, Faye Webber, Nick Quinn

Novelty books, picture books, fiction for all ages including teenage fiction and series fiction (home 10%). All adult writers for theatre, film, TV and radio. No unsolicited MSS. No reading fee. Will suggest revision. Works in conjunction with agents in USA and overseas.

Gillon Aitken Associates Ltd*
18–21 Cavaye Place, London SW10 9PT
tel 020-7373 8672 *fax* 020-7373 6002
email reception@gillonaitken.co.uk
website www.gillonaitkenassociates.co.uk
Agent Kate Shaw

Children's fiction (home 10–15%, overseas 20%). Handles fiction for 9–12 year-olds and teenage fiction. Also handles adult fiction and non-fiction; 10% of list is for the children's market. Send preliminary letter with a short synopsis and 3–5 sample chapters with a sae. No reading fee. Will suggest revision. No picture books and no submissions by email.
    Children's authors include Helen Fox, Manjula Padma and Louise Rennison. Founded 1977.

Darley Anderson Literary, TV and Film Agency*
Estelle House, 11 Eustace Road, London SW6 1JB
tel 020-7385 6652 *fax* 020-7386 5571
email enquiries@darleyanderson.com
website www.darleyanderson.com
Contacts Darley Anderson (crime, mystery & thrillers), Lucie Whitehouse (women's & general fiction/foreign rights), Elizabeth Wright (agent), Julia Churchill (children's fiction), Emma White (non-fiction/US, foreign & TV rights), Rosi Bridge (finance), Zoe King, Ella Andrews

Commercial fiction and non-fiction; children's fiction and non-fiction (home 15%, USA/translation 20%, film/TV/radio 20%). No poetry or academic books.
    Send preliminary letter, synopsis and first 3 chapters. Return postage/sae essential for reply. Disk and emailed submissions cannot be considered. Overseas associates: APA Talent & Literary Agency (LA/Hollywood), Cornerstone Literary (LA), Liza Dawson Literary Agency (New York) and 21 leading foreign agents worldwide.

Author Literary Agents
53 Talbot Road, London N6 4QX
tel 020-8341 0442 *mobile* (07767) 022659
email agile@authors.co.uk
Contact John Havergal

Fiction, non-fiction and children's (home 15%, overseas/translations 25%). Send first chapter, scene or section plus a half–one-page outline. Sae essential for reply. No reading fee. Founded 1997.

The Bell Lomax Agency
James House, 1 Babmaes Street, London SW1Y 6HF
tel 020-7930 4447 *fax* 020-7925 0118
email agency@bell-lomax.co.uk
Executives Eddie Bell, Pat Lomax, Paul Moreton, June Bell

Quality fiction and non-fiction, biography, children's, business and sport. No unsolicited MSS without preliminary letter. No scripts. No reading fee. Founded 2000.

Jenny Brown Associates*
33 Argyle Place, Edinburgh EH9 1JT
tel 0131-229 5334
email jenny-brown@blueyonder.co.uk
website www.jennybrownassociates.com

Contact Jenny Brown, Mark Stanton

Literary fiction, crime writing and writing for children; non-fiction: biography, history, sport, music popular culture (home 12.5%, overseas/translation 20%). No poetry, science fiction, fantasy or academic. No reading fee.

Clients include Lin Anderson, Jeff Connor, Mary Contini, Jennie Erdal, Alex Gray, Laura Hird, Laura Marney, Janet Morgan, Tom Pow, Jonathan Rendall, Suhayl Saadi, Paul Torday, Christopher Whyte. Founded 2002.

Felicity Bryan*

2A North Parade, Banbury Road, Oxford OX2 6LX
tel (01865) 513816 fax (01865) 310055
email agency@felicitybryan.com
website www.felicitybryan.com

Fiction for children aged 8–14, and adult fiction and general non-fiction (home 15%, overseas 20%). Translation rights handled by Andrew Nurnberg Associates; works in conjunction with US agents.

Children's authors include Julie Hearn, Liz Kessler, Katherine Langrish, Meg Rosoff, Matthew Skelton, Eleanor Updale, Jeanne Willis.

Celia Catchpole

56 Gilpin Avenue, London SW14 8QY
tel 020-8255 4835
email celiacatchpole@yahoo.co.uk
website www.celiacatchpole.co.uk

Specialises exclusively as agent for children's writers and illustrators (home 10%, overseas 20%). Handles picture books and fiction to age 12. No reading fee. Founded 1996.

Conville & Walsh Ltd*

2 Ganton Street, London W1F 7QL
tel 020-7287 3030 fax 020-7287 4545
email firstname@convilleandwalsh.com
Directors Clare Conville, Patrick Walsh, Peter Tallack

Picture books, fiction for 5–8 and 9–12 year-olds, teenage fiction, series fiction and film/TV tie-ins (home 15%, overseas 20%). Also handles adult literary and commercial fiction and non-fiction. Submit first 3 chapters, cover letter, synopsis and sae. No reading fee.

Children's authors include John Burningham, Kate Cann, Timothy Knapman, P.J. Lynch, Joshua Mowll, Jacqui Murhall, Peadar O'Guilin, Nicky Singer, Steve Voake. Founded 2000.

Curtis Brown Group Ltd*

Haymarket House, 28–29 Haymarket, London SW1Y 4SP
tel 020-7393 4400 fax 020-7393 4401
email cb@curtisbrown.co.uk
website www.curtisbrown.co.uk
Ceo Jonathan Lloyd, Director of Operations Ben Hall,
Directors Jacquie Drewe, Jonny Geller, Nick Marston

Books Jonny Geller (Managing Director, Book Division), Ali Gunn, Camilla Hornby, Jonathan Lloyd, Jonathan Pegg, Vivienne Schuster, Elizabeth Sheinkman, Janice Swanson, Gordon Wise, Foreign Rights (books) Kate Cooper, Carol Jackson, Diana Mackay, Betsy Robbins
Film/TV/Theatre Nick Marston (Managing Director, Media Division), Tally Garner, Ben Hall, Joe Phillips, Sally Whitehill
Actors Grace Clissold, Maxine Hoffman, Sarah MacCormick, Sarah Spear, Kate Staddon, Claire Stannard, Frances Williams
Presenters Jacquie Drewe, Catherine Tapsell Jenkin

Novels, general non-fiction, children's books and associated rights (including multimedia), as well as film, theatre, TV and radio scripts (home 15%, overseas 20%). Send outline for non-fiction and short synopsis for fiction with 2–3 sample chapters and autobiographical note. No reading fee. Return postage essential. No submissions by email. See website for further submission guidelines. Also represents playwrights, film and TV writers and directors, theatre directors and designers, TV and radio presenters and actors. Overseas associates in Australia and the USA. Founded 1914.

Eddison Pearson Ltd

West Hill House, 6 Swains Lane, London N6 6QS
tel 020-7700 7763 fax 020-7700 7866
email info@eddisonpearson.com
Contact Clare Pearson

Children's books, literary fiction and non-fiction, poetry (home 10%, overseas 15–20%). Email enquiries only; email for up-to-date submission guidelines by return. No reading fee. May suggest revision where appropriate.

Authors include Valerie Bloom, Sue Heap, Sally Lloyd-Jones, Robert Muchamore.

Fraser Ross Associates

6 Wellington Place, Edinburgh EH6 7EQ
tel 0131-553 2759, 0131-657 4412
email lindsey.fraser@tiscali.co.uk, kjross@tiscali.co.uk
website www.fraserross.co.uk
Partners Lindsey Fraser, Kathryn Ross

Writing and illustration for children's books, but not exclusively (home 10%). No reading fee. Founded 2002.

Futerman, Rose & Associates*

17 Deanhill Road, London SW14 7DQ
tel 020-8255 7755 fax 020-8286 4860
email guy@futermanrose.co.uk (general enquiries),
betty@futermanrose.co.uk (fiction submissions)
website www.futermanrose.co.uk
Contact Guy Rose

Teen fiction only. Also scripts for film and TV; commercial fiction and non-fiction with film potential, biography, show business (15–20%). No unsolicited MSS, science fiction or fantasy. Send preliminary letter with a brief résumé, detailed synopsis and sae. Overseas associates. Founded 1984.

Annette Green Authors' Agency*

1 East Cliff Road, Tunbridge Wells, Kent TN4 9AD
tel (01892) 514275 fax (01892) 518124
email annettekgreen@aol.com
website www.annettegreenagency.co.uk
Partners Annette Green, David Smith

Full-length MSS (home 15%, overseas 20%). Literary and general fiction and non-fiction, popular culture, history, science, teenage fiction. No dramatic scripts, poetry, science fiction or fantasy. No reading fee. Preliminary letter, synopsis, sample chapter and sae essential.

Children's authors include Julia Bell, Meg Cabot, Mary Hogan. Founded 1998.

Greene & Heaton Ltd*

37 Goldhawk Road, London W12 8QQ
tel 020-8749 0315 fax 020-8749 0318
email info@greeneheaton.co.uk
website www.greeneheaton.co.uk
Contact Linda Davis

Children's fiction and non-fiction (home 15%, overseas 20%). Handles picture books, fiction for 5–8 and 9–12 year-olds, teenage fiction, series fiction, poetry and non-fiction. Also handles adult fiction and non-fiction. Send a covering letter, synopsis and the first 50pp (or less) with an sae and return postage. Email enquiries will be answered but submission attached to emails will not be considered.

Children's authors include Helen Craig, Joshua Doder, Amber Deckers. Founded 1963.

Marianne Gunn O'Connor Literary Agency

Morrison Chambers, Suite 17, 32 Nassau Street, Dublin 2, Republic of Ireland
email mgoclitagency@eircom.net
Contact Marianne Gunn O' Connor

Commercial and literary fiction, non-fiction, biography, children's fiction (UK 15%, overseas 20%, film/TV 20%). Send preliminary letter plus half-page synopsis and first 50pp. Translation rights handled by Vicki Satlow Literary Agency, Milan.

Antony Harwood Ltd

103 Walton Street, Oxford OX2 6EB
tel (01865) 559615 fax (01865) 310660
email mail@antonyharwood.com
website www.antonyharwood.com
Contacts Antony Harwood, James Macdonald Lockhart

General and genre fiction; general non-fiction (home 15%, overseas 20%). Will suggest revision. No reading fee.

Children's authors include Garth Nix. Founded 2000.

A.M. Heath & Co. Ltd*

6 Warwick Court, London WC1R 5DJ
tel 020-7242 2811 fax 020-7242 2711
website www.amheath.com
Contact William Hamilton (managing director), Sara Fisher, Victoria Hobbs, Sarah Molloy

Fiction and non-fiction from age 5 to young adult (home 15%, USA 20%, translation 20%). Handles picture books, fiction for 5–8 and 9–12 year-olds, teenage fiction, series fiction, film/TV tie-ins and non-fiction. Also handles adult literary and commercial fiction and non-fiction; 20% of list is for children's market. Submit synopsis and sample chapters. No reading fee. Will suggest revision. Overseas associates in USA, Europe, South America, Japan and the Far East.

Children's authors include Nicholas Allan, Nick Gifford, Joanna Nadin, Susan Price, Maggie Prince, John Singleton, Rose Wilkins, Leslie Wilson, the Estates of Noel Streatfeild, Helen Cresswell and Joan Aiken. Founded 1919.

David Higham Associates Ltd*

(incorporating Murray Pollinger)
5–8 Lower John Street, Golden Square, London W1F 9HA
tel 020-7434 5900 fax 020-7437 1072
email dha@davidhigham.co.uk
website www.davidhigham.co.uk
Managing Director Anthony Goff, Books Veronique Baxter, Lucy Firth, Anthony Goff, Bruce Hunter, Lizzy Kremer, Caroline Walsh, Foreign Rights Ania Corless, Film/TV/Theatre Gemma Hirst, Nicky Lund, Georgina Ruffhead

Children's fiction, picture books and non-fiction (home 15%, USA/translation 20%, scripts 10%). Handles novelty books, picture books, fiction for 5–8 and 9–12 year-olds, teenage fiction, series fiction, poetry, plays, film/TV tie-ins, non-fiction, audio and CD-Roms. Also handles adult fiction, general non-fiction, plays, film and TV scripts; 35% of list is for the children's market. Submit synopsis and 2–3 sample chapters with a covering letter. For picture books, send complete MS, CV and sae. Address all submissions to Children's Submissions. No reading fee. Represented in all foreign markets.

Also represents 21 illustrators for children's book publishing (home 15%). Submit colour copies of artwork by post or via email. Include samples that show children 'in action' and animals.

Clients (children's market) include Jenny Alexander, Caroline Anstey, Elizabeth Arnold, Antonia Barber, Julie Bertagna, Tim Bowler, Henrietta Branford, Mike Brownlow, Charles Causley, Kathryn Cave, Catherine Charley, Lauren Child, Peter Collington, Trish Cooke, W.J. Corbett, Anne Cottringer, Cressida Cowell, Kady Macdonald Denton, Berlie Doherty, Ruth Dowley, Jonathan Emmett, Jan Fearnley, Anne Fine, Susan Gates,

Jamila Gavin, Hannah Giffard, Julia Golding, Kes Gray, Ann Halam, Carol Hedges, Meredith Hooper, Julia Jarman, Brenda Jobling, Clive King, Bert Kitchen, Rebecca Lisle, Tim Lott, Geraldine McCaughrean, Richard MacSween, Jan Mark, Hazel Marshall, Simon Mason, Gwen Millward, Pratima Mitchell, Tony Mitton, Nicola Moon, Bel Mooney, Michael Morpurgo, Jan Needle, Jenny Nimmo, Martine Oborne, June Oldham, Liz Pichon, Tamora Pierce, Chris Powling, Gwyneth Rees, Adrian Reynolds, Georgie Ripper, Catherine Robinson, Jenny Samuels, Emily Smith, Alexander McCall Smith, Jeremy Strong, Alan Temperley, Frances Thomas, Theresa Tomlinson, Ann Turnbull, Caroline Uff, Martin Waddell, Nick Warburton, Gina Wilson, Jacqueline Wilson and David Wojtowycz. Founded 1935.

Johnson & Alcock Ltd*

Clerkenwell House, 45–47 Clerkenwell Green, London EC1R 0HT
tel 020-7251 0125 *fax* 020-7251 2172
email info@johnsonandalcock.co.uk
Contacts Michael Alcock, Andrew Hewson, Anna Power, Merel Reinink

Full-length MSS (home 15%, US and translation 20%). Literary and commercial fiction, children's fiction; general non-fiction including current affairs, biography and memoirs, history, lifestyle, health and personal development. No poetry, screenplays, science fiction, technical or academic material. No unsolicited MSS; approach by letter in the first instance giving details of writing experience, plus synopsis. For fiction send one-page synopsis and first 3 chapters. Sae essential for response. No reading fee. No email submissions. Founded 1956.

LAW Ltd*

14 Vernon Street, London W14 0RJ
tel 020-7471 7900 *fax* 020-7471 7910
website www.lawagency.co.uk
Contacts Adult: Mark Lucas, Julian Alexander, Araminta Whitley, Alice Saunders, Lucinda Cook, Peta Nightingale, Lizzie Jones; Children's: Philippa Milnes-Smith, Helen Norris

Children's books (home 15%, overseas 20%). Handles novelty books, picture books, fiction for 5–8 and 9–12 year-olds, teenage fiction, series fiction, film/TV tie-ins, poetry, non-fiction, reference and audio. Also handles adult commercial and literary fiction and non-fiction. Send brief covering letter, short synopsis and 2–3 sample chapters. For picture books, send complete text and/or copies of sample artwork. Do *not* send original artwork. Sae essential. No email submissions. Overseas associates worldwide. Founded 1996.

The Christopher Little Literary Agency*

10 Eel Brook Studios, 125 Moore Park Road, London SW6 4PS

tel 020-7736 4455 *fax* 020-7736 4490
email info@christopherlittle.net
website www.christopherlittle.net
Contact Christopher Little

Fiction for 9–12 year-olds and teenage fiction (home 15%, overseas 20%); no illustrated children's or short stories. Also handles adult fiction and non-fiction. Send synopsis and first 3 chapters with an sae. No reading fee.
  Children's authors include J.K. Rowling and Darren Shan. Founded 1979.

London Independent Books

26 Chalcot Crescent, London NW1 8YD
tel 020-7706 0486 *fax* 020-7724 3122
Proprietor Carolyn Whitaker

Specialises in teenage fiction (home 10–15%, overseas 20%). Handles fiction for 9–12 year-olds, teenage fiction and non-fiction. Also handles adult fiction, show business and travel; approx. one-third of list is for the children's market. Submit 2 chapters and a synopsis with return postage. No reading fee. Will suggest revision of promising MSS.
  Authors include Simon Chapman, Joe Delaney, Keith Gray, Elizabeth Kay, Elizabeth Richardson, Chris Wooding. Founded 1971.

Jennifer Luithlen Agency

88 Holmfield Road, Leicester LE2 1SB
tel 0116-273 8863 *fax* 0116-273 5697
Agents Jennifer Luithlen, Penny Luithlen

Not looking for new clients. Children's and adult fiction (home 15%, overseas 20%), performance rights (15%). Founded 1986.

Frances McKay Illustration – see Illustrators' agents

Eunice McMullen Children's Literary Agent Ltd

Low Ibbotsholme Cottage, Off Bridge Lane, Troutbeck Bridge, Windermere, Cumbria LA23 1HU
tel (01539) 448551
email eunicemcmullen@totalise.co.uk
website www.eunicemcmullen.co.uk
Director Eunice McMullen

Specialises exclusively in children's books, especially picture books and older fiction (home 10%, overseas 15%). Handles novelty books, picture books, fiction for all ages including teenage, series fiction and audio. No unsolicited scripts. Telephone enquiries only. No reading fee.
  Authors include Wayne Anderson, Sam Childs, Caroline Jayne Church, Jason Cockcroft, Ross Collins, Charles Fuge, Maggie Kneen, David Melling, Angela McAllister, Angie Sage, Gillian Shields, Susan Winter. Founded 1992.

Andrew Mann Ltd*

(in association with Jane Conway-Gordon)
1 Old Compton Street, London W1D 5JA
tel 020-7734 4751 *fax* 020-7287 9264
email manscript@onetel.com
Contacts Anne Dewe, Tina Betts, Sacha Elliot

Children's fiction and non-fiction (home 15%,
overseas 20%). Handles picture books, fiction for
5–8 and 9–12 year-olds, teenage fiction, series fiction,
film/TV tie-ins and non-fiction. Also handles adult
fiction and scripts for TV, cinema, radio and theatre;
20% of list is for children's market. Submit synopsis
and first 30pp plus a sae. Email synopses submissions
only; no attachments. No reading fee. Will suggest
revision. Founded 1968.

Children's authors include Gina Douthwaite, Joe
Hackett, Judith Heneghan, Shirley Isherwood, Kate
Lennard, Jude Wisdom, Sarah Mussi.

Sarah Manson Literary Agent

6 Totnes Walk, London N2 0AD
tel 020-8442 0396
email info@sarahmanson.com
website www.sarahmanson.com
Proprietor Sarah Manson

Specialises exclusively in fiction for children and
young adults (home 10%, overseas 20%). Send letter,
brief author biography, one-page synopsis, first 3
chapters with sae. See website for full submission
guidelines. Founded 2002.

Marjacq Scripts

34 Devonshire Place, London W1G 6JW
tel 020-7935 9499 *fax* 020-7935 9115
email enquiries@marjacq.com
website www.marjacq.com
Contact Philip Patterson (books), Luke Speed
(film/TV)

All full-length MSS (home 10%, overseas 20%),
including commercial and literary fiction and non-
fiction, crime, thrillers, commercial, women's fiction,
children's, science fiction, history, biography, sport,
travel, health. No poetry. Send first 3 chapters with
synopsis. May suggest revision. Film and TV rights,
screenplays, radio plays, documentaries, screenplays/
radio plays: send full script with 1–2 page short
synopsis/outline. Strong interest in writer/directors:
send show reel with script. Also looking for
documentary concepts and will accept proposals
from writer/directors. Sae essential for return of
submissions.

Miles Stott Literary Agency

East Hook Farm, Lower Quay Road, Hook,
Haverfordwest, Pembrokeshire SA62 4LR
tel/fax (01437) 890570
email miles.stott@virgin.net
Director Nancy Miles

Specialist in children's novelty books, picture books,
fiction for 6–9 and 10–12 year-olds, teenage fiction
and series fiction (from 10% home, 20% overseas).
Send covering letter, brief synopsis and 3 sample
chapters. For picture books send complete text and/
or copies of sample artwork (do not send original
artwork). No reading fee.

Authors include Frances Hardinge, Justin Richards,
Dominic Barker, Ronda Armitage and Sebastien
Braun. Founded 2003.

Maggie Noach Literary Agency*

22 Dorville Crescent, London W6 0HJ
tel 020-8748 2926 *fax* 020-8748 8057
email m-noach@dircon.co.uk

Fiction for 9–12 year-olds and teenage fiction (home
15%, USA 20%). No children's non-fiction or
illustrated books. Also handles adult fiction and non-
fiction; approx. one-third of list is for the children's
market. Send letter plus synopsis and 3 chapters. Will
not accept submissions by email or fax but initial
enquiry may be made by email.

Children's authors include David Almond, Anthony
Horowitz, Graham Marks, Linda Newbery, Katherine
Roberts, Jean Ure. Founded 1982.

PFD (The Peters Fraser & Dunlop Group Ltd)*

Drury House, 34–43 Russell Street, London
WC2B 5HA
tel 020-7344 1000 *fax* 020-7836 9539
website www.pfd.co.uk
Joint Chairmen Maureen Vincent and St John
Donald, *Books* Caroline Dawnay, Michael Sissons, Pat
Kavanagh, Charles Walker, Rosemary Scoular, Robert
Kirby, Simon Trewin, James Gill, Carol Macarthur,
Sophie Laurimore, Anna Webber, *Children's books*
Rosemary Canter, Alison Kain, *Translation rights*
Intercontinental Literary Agency, *PFD New York* Zoë
Pagnamenta, Mark Reiter, *Film/TV/theatre agents*
Natasha Galloway, Anthony Jones, Tim Corrie,
Charles Walker, St John Donald, Rose Cobbe, Jago
Irwin, Hannah Begbie

Represents authors of fiction and non-fiction (home
10%; USA/translation 20%), children's writers,
screenwriters, playwrights, directors, documentary
makers, technicians, presenters and actors
throughout the world. See website for submission
guidelines.

Pollinger Ltd*

(formerly Laurence Pollinger Ltd, successor of Pearn,
Pollinger and Higham)
9 Staple Inn, Holborn, London WC1V 7QH
tel 020-7404 0342 *fax* 020-7242 5737
email info@pollingerltd.com,
permissions@pollingerltd

website www.pollingerltd.com
Managing Director Lesley Pollinger, *Agents* Joanna Devereux, Tim Bates, *Consultants* Leigh Pollinger, Joan Deitch

All types of general trade adult and children's fiction and non-fiction books; intellectual property developments, illustrators/photographers (home 15%, translation 20%). Overseas, media and theatrical associates. No unsolicited material.

Children's clients include Peter Clover, Bridget Crowley, Catherine Fisher, Phillip Gross, Frances Hendry, Catherine Johnson, Kelly McKain, Sue Mongredien. Founded 1935.

Redhammer Management Ltd
186 Bickenhall Mansions, Bickenhall Street, London W1U 6BX
tel 020-7224 1748 *fax* 020-7224 1802
email info@redhammer.info
website www.redhammer.info
Vice President Peter Cox

Specialises in works with international potential (home 17.5%, overseas 20%). Unpublished authors must be professional in their approach and have major international potential, ideally book, film and/ or TV. Submissions must follow the guidelines given on the website. Do not send unsolicited MSS by post. No radio or theatre scripts. No reading fee.

Clients include Martin Bell OBE, Nicholas Booth, Mihir Bose, John Brindley, Brian Clegg, Joe Donnelly, Audrey Eyton, Senator Orrin Hatch, Amanda Lees, Dirk Maggs, David McIntee, Hon. Nicholas Monson, Michelle Paver, Harriet Smart, David Soul, Carolyn Soutar, Carole Stone, Prof. Donald Trelford, Justin Wintle, David Yelland. Founded 1993.

The Lisa Richards Agency
46 Upper Baggot Street, Dublin 4, Republic of Ireland
tel (01) 660 3534 *fax* (01) 660 3545
email faith@lisarichards.ie
website www.lisarichards.ie
Contact Faith O'Grady

Fiction and general non-fiction (home 10%, UK 15%, USA/translation 20%, film/TV 15%). Approach with proposal and sample chapter for non-fiction, and 3–4 sample chapters and synopsis for fiction (sae essential). Translation rights handled by the **Marsh Agency Ltd**. No reading fee.

Authors include June Considine, Judi Curtin, Denise Deegan, Christine Dwyer Hickey, Karen Gillece, Tara Heavey, Paul Howard (Ross O'Carroll-Kelly), Arlene Hunt, Roisin Ingle, Alison Jameson, Declan Lynch, Martin Malone, Roisin Meaney, Jennifer MacCann, Pauline McLynn, Sarah O'Brien (Helena Close and Trisha Rainsford), Hector O'LEochagáin, Damien Owens, Kevin Rafter. Founded 1998.

Rogers, Coleridge & White Ltd*
20 Powis Mews, London W11 1JN
tel 020-7221 3717 *fax* 020-7229 9084
Managing Director Peter Straus, *Directors* Deborah Rogers, Gill Coleridge, Patricia White (USA, children's), David Miller, Laurence Laluyaux, Stephen Edwards, Zoe Waldie

Children's fiction and non-fiction (home 10%, USA 15–20%). Handles novelty books, picture books, fiction for 5–8 and 9–12 year-olds, teenage fiction, series fiction, non-fiction and reference. Also handles adult MSS. No unsolicited MSS. No submissions by fax or email. No reading fee. Will suggest revision.

Children's authors include Mary Hoffman, Valerie Mendes, Karen Wallace. Founded 1967.

Elizabeth Roy Literary Agency
White Cottage, Greatford, Nr Stamford, Lincs. PE9 4PR
tel (01778) 560672 *fax* (01778) 560672

Children's fiction and non-fiction – writers and illustrators (home 15%, overseas 20%). Send preliminary letter, synopsis and sample chapters with names of publishers and agents previously contacted. Return postage essential. No reading fee. Founded 1990.

Uli Rushby-Smith Literary Agency
72 Plimsoll Road, London N4 2EE
tel 020-7354 2718 *fax* 020-7354 2718
Director Uli Rushby-Smith

Fiction and non-fiction, literary and commercial (home 15%, USA/foreign 20%). No poetry, plays or film scripts. Send outline, sample chapters (no disks) and return postage. No reading fee. UK representatives of **Curtis Brown Ltd**, New York (children's books) and Columbia University Press (USA). Founded 1993.

Rosemary Sandberg Ltd
6 Bayley Street, London WC1B 3HE
tel 020-7304 4110 *fax* 020-7304 4109
email rosemary@sandberg.demon.co.uk
Directors Rosemary Sandberg, Ed Victor

Children's writers and illustrators, general fiction and non-fiction. Absolutely no unsolicited MSS: client list is full. Founded 1991.

Caroline Sheldon Literary Agency Ltd*
London office 70–75 Cowcross Street, London EC1M 6EJ
tel 020-7336 6550
Mailing address for MSS Thorley Manor Farm, Thorley, Yarmouth PO41 0SJ
tel (01983) 760205
Contacts Caroline Sheldon, Penny Holroyde

Specialises in full-length children's novels, picture books and authors and artists with a substantial body of work (home 10%, overseas 20%). Handles novelty books, picture books, fiction for 5–8 and 9–12 year-olds, teenage fiction and series fiction. Also handles adult general and women's fiction; 50% of list is for the children's market. Submit first 3 chapters of a novel with a synopsis or photocopies of illustration work. Always enclose with material an intelligent letter of introduction and an sae. No reading fee. Will suggest revision. Founded 1985.

Dorie Simmonds Agency*

67 Upper Berkeley Street, London W1H 7QZ
tel 020-7569 8686 *fax* 020-7569 8696
Contact Dorie Simmonds

Children's fiction (UK/USA 15%; translation 20%). No reading fee but sae required. Send a short synopsis, 2–3 sample chapters and a CV with writing/publishing background.
Clients include award-winning children's authors.

The Standen Literary Agency

20 Twyford Court, Fortis Green, London N10 3ES
tel/fax 020-8444 1641
email info@standenliteraryagency.com
website www.standenliteraryagency.com
Director Yasmin Standen

Children's fiction for all ages and picture books (home 15%, overseas 20%). In particular looking for new writers of fiction for 5–8, 9–12 and teen/young adult age groups. Send first 3 chapters and synopsis (one side of A4) with a covering letter by post only in first instance (no submissions via email) and sae. No reading fee. Also handles literary and commercial fiction for adults. 70% of list is children's writing.
Authors include Zara Kane, Zoe Marriott, Andrew Murray, Jonathan Yeatman-Biggs. Founded 2004.

Abner Stein*

10 Roland Gardens, London SW7 3PH
tel 020-7373 0456 *fax* 020-7370 6316
Contact Caspian Dennis, Arabella Stein

Fiction, general non-fiction and children's (home 10%, overseas 20%). Not taking on any new clients at present.

United Authors Ltd

11–15 Betterton Street, London WC2H 9BP
tel 020-7470 8886 *fax* 020-7470 8887
email editorial@unitedauthors.co.uk

Fiction, non-fiction, children's, biography, travel (home 12%, overseas 20%, film/radio 15%/20%, TV 15%/15%). Will suggest revision.

Ed Victor Ltd*

6 Bayley Street, Bedford Square, London WC1B 3HE
tel 020-7304 4100 *fax* 020-7304 4111
Contact Sophie Hicks

Children's picture books, fiction for 5–8 and 9–12 year-olds, teenage fiction, series fiction, film/TV tie-ins, non-fiction and audio (home 10%, overseas 20%). No short stories or poetry. Also handles adult fiction and non-fiction. No reading fee. No unsolicited MSS. No response to submission by email.
Children's authors include Mary Arrigan, Herbie Brennan, Eoin Colfer, David Lee Stone, Oisín McGann and Kate Thompson. Founded 1976.

Watson, Little Ltd*

Lymehouse Studios, 38 Georgiana Street, London NW1 0EB
tel 020-7486 5935 *fax* 020-7486 6051
email office@watsonlittle.com
Contacts Mandy Little, Sugra Zaman, James Wills

Commercial women's, crime and literary fiction. Non-fiction special interests include history, science, popular psychology, self-help and general leisure books. Also children's fiction and non-fiction (home 15%, USA 20%, translation 20%). No short stories, poetry, TV, play or film scripts. Not interested in purely academic writers. No emails or unsolicited MSS. Informative preliminary letter and synopsis with return postage essential. Film and TV associates: the **Sharland Organisation Ltd** and **MBA Literary Agents Ltd**. Translation rights sold by the **Marsh Agency** in the UK; and Howard Morhaim and Folio Literary Management in the US.
Children's authors include Stephen Biesty, V.M. Jones, Margaret Mahy, Lynne Reid Banks, Stewart Ross.

A.P. Watt Ltd*

20 John Street, London WC1N 2DR
tel 020-7405 6774 *fax* 020-7831 2154 (books), 020-7430 1952 (drama)
email apw@apwatt.co.uk
website www.apwatt.co.uk
Directors Caradoc King, Linda Shaughnessy, Derek Johns, Georgia Garrett, Natasha Fairweather, Sheila Crowley

Adults' and children's full-length MSS; dramatic works for all media (home 15%, USA and foreign 20% including commission to foreign agent). No poetry. No reading fee. Does not accept unsolicited MSS or any other material. In the first instance send a query letter.
Authors include Quentin Blake, Georgia Byng, Zizou Corder, Grace Dent, Helen Dunmore, Sarah Harrison, Dick King-Smith, Philip Pullman, Philip Ridley. Founded 1875.

Eve White

1A High Street, Kintbury, Berks. RG17 9TJ
tel (01488) 657656
email evewhite@btinternet.com
website www.evewhite.co.uk
Contact Eve White

Picture books, fiction for 5–8 and 9–12 year-olds, teenage fiction and film/TV tie-ins (home 15%, overseas 20%). Also handles adult commercial and literary fiction and non-fiction; 50% of list is for the children's market. Send brief synopsis and 2–3 sample chapters and word count with a covering letter, biography and sae. Include email address. No submissions by email. No reading fee. Will suggest revision where appropriate.

Children's clients include Suzanna Corbett, Jimmy Do, Margie Hann-Syme, Abie Longstaff, Peter J. Murray, Gillian Rogerson, Andy Stanton, Emma Tennant. Founded 2003.

Children's literary agents overseas

Before submitting material, writers are advised to send a preliminary letter with an sae or IRC (International Reply Coupon) and to ascertain terms.

AUSTRALIA

Altair-Australia Literary Agency
PO Box 475, Blackwood SA 5051
tel (8) 8278 8995 *fax* (8) 8278 5585
email altair-australia@altair-australia.com
Agent Robert N. Stephenson

Specialises in science fiction and fantasy; also children's literature, mainstream literature, crime and mystery and action/adventure fiction (15%–20%). Non-fiction material may be considered if queried first. Founded 1997.

Submission details Submit the first 3 chapters (up to 15,000 words) and a 2-page synopsis for fiction/novel. Send whole MS plus reference details for non-fiction (do not include original graphics, films or photographs). Allow at least 12 weeks before querying.

Australian Literary Management
2–A Booth Street, Balmain, New South Wales 2041
tel (9) 818 8557 *fax* (9) 818 8569
email alpha@austlit.com
website www.austlit.com

Fiction, non-fiction, fantasy, young readers and cartoons (home 15%). Telephone first, then submit a short synopsis and 2 chapters. No reading fee. Do not email. Does not suggest revision.

Children's authors include Pamela Freeman, Christine Harris, Glyn Parry-Ranulfo, Laurie Stiller. Established 1980.

Bryson Agency Australia Pty Ltd
PO Box 226, Finders Lane PO, Melbourne 8009
tel (613) 9620 9100 *fax* (613) 9621 2788
email agency@bryson.com.au
website www.bryson.com.au
Contact Fran Bryson

Represents writers operating in all media: print, film, TV, radio, the stage and electronic derivatives; specialises in representation of book writers. Query first before sending unsolicited MSS. Not accepting until further notice.

Jenny Darling & Associates
PO Box 413, Toorak, Victoria 3142
tel (03) 9827 3883 *fax* (03) 9827 1270
email jda@jd-associates.com.au
Contact Jenny Darling

Represents only a few children's authors. Open to all genres and ages. For picture books and up to end

primary school, send the complete MS. For young adult, send the first 10pp in the first instance. Submit material by post, including return postage.

Golvan Arts Management
PO Box 766, Kew, Australia 3101
tel (03) 9853 5341 *fax* (03) 9853 8555
website www.golvanarts.com.au
Manager & Director Debbie Golvan, *Director* Colin Golvan

Children's fiction and non-fiction (10%+GST). Handles picture books, fiction for 5–8 and 9–12 year-olds, teenage fiction, series fiction, film/TV tie-ins, non-fiction and plays; educational – primary, secondary and tertiary. Also handles adult fiction and non-fiction, plays, feature film and TV scripts, visual artists and composers; 60% of list is for children's market. Read 'general information' section on website before sending a brief letter. No reading fee. Will suggest revision. Works with Chinese and Korean agents.

Children's authors include Bronwyn Bancroft, Vicki Bennett, Nan Bodsworth, Kim Caraher, Terry Denton, Janine Fraser, Helen Lunn, Gilly McInnes, Paty Marshall-Stace, Sally Morgan, Wendy Orr, Greg Pyers, Alan Sunderland, Mark Svendsen. Founded 1989.

CANADA

Melanie Colbert
17 West Street, Holland Landing, Ontario L9N 1L4
tel 905-853-2435
Contact Melanie Colbert

Children's authors and illustrators. Please send initial query; no unsolicited MSS. Established 1985.

Pamela Paul Agency
12 Westrose Avenue, Toronto, Ontario M8X 2A1
tel 416-410-4395 *fax* 416-410-4949
email agency@interlog.com
Contact Pamela Paul

Children's fiction only. No unsolicited MSS. Established 1989.

Carolyn Swayze Literary Agency Ltd
WRPO Box 39588, White Rock, British Columbia V4B 5L6
tel 604-538-3478
email carolyn@swayzeagency.com
website www.swayzeagency.com

Proprietor Carolyn Swayze

Literary and commercial fiction, some juvenile and teen books. No romance, science fiction, poetry, screenplays, or picture books. Eager to discover lively, thought-provoking narrative non-fiction, especially in the fields of science, history, travel, politics, and memoir. Founded 1994.

Submission details No telephone calls: make contact either by post or send short queries by email, providing a brief résumé which describes who you are. Include publication credits, writing awards, education and experience relevant to your book project. Include a one-page synopsis of the book and – if querying via post – include sase for the return of your materials. Do not include original photographs or artwork. Include sase if acknowledgement of receipt of materials is required. Will not open unsolicited attachments. Allow 6 weeks or longer for a reply.

Transatlantic Literary Agency

72 Glengowan Road, Toronto, Ontario M4N 1G4
tel 416-488-9214 *fax* 416-488-4531
email info@tla1.com
website www.tla1.com
Contact David Bennett, Lynn Bennett

Specialises in children's and young adult books: fiction, non-fiction, illustrated books and picture books. No unsolicited MSS. Founded 1993.

NEW ZEALAND

Glenys Bean Writer's Agent

PO Box 60509, Titirangi, Auckland
tel (09) 812 8486 *fax* (09) 812 8188
email g.bean@clear.net.nz
website www.glenysbean.com
Directors Fay Weldon, Glenys Bean

Adult and children's fiction, educational, non-fiction, film, TV, radio (10–20%). Send preliminary letter, synopsis and sae. No reading fee. Represented by Sanford Greenburger Associates Ltd (USA). Translation/foreign rights: the Marsh Agency Ltd. Founded 1989.

Michael Gifkins & Associates

PO Box 6496, Wellesley Street PO, Auckland 1000
tel (09) 523-5032 *fax* (09) 523-5033
email michael.gifkins@xtra.co.nz
Director Michael Gifkins

Literary and popular fiction, fine arts, children's and young adult fiction, substantial non-fiction (non-academic) co-publications (home 15%, overseas 20%). No reading fee. Will suggest revision. Founded 1985.

Richards Literary Agency

postal address PO Box 31–240, Milford, Auckland 9
tel/fax (09) 410-0209

email rla.richards@clear.net.nz
Partners Ray Richards, Elaine Blake, Judy Bartlam, Frances Plumpton

Children's fiction and non-fiction (home/overseas 15%). Handles picture books, fiction for 5–8 and 9–12 year-olds, teenage fiction, series fiction, film/TV tie-ins, non-fiction and reference; educational (primary). Also handles adult fiction and non-fiction, and film, TV and radio; approx. 50% of list is for the children's market. Concentrates on New Zealand authors. Send book proposal with an outline and biography. No reading fee.

Children's authors include Joy Cowley and Maurice Gee – the agency has approx. 50 on books. Founded 1977.

Total Fiction Services

PO Box 46-031, Park Avenue, Lower Hutt
tel/fax (04) 565 4429
email tfs@elseware.co.nz
website www.elseware.co.nz

General fiction, non-fiction, children's books. No poetry, or individual short stories or articles. Enquiries from New Zealand authors only. Email queries but no attachments. Hard copy preferred. No reading fee. Also offers assessment reports, mentoring and courses.

SOUTH AFRICA

Cherokee Literary Agency

3 Blythwood Road, Rondebosch, Cape 7700, South Africa
tel (021) 671 4508
email dklee@mweb.co.za
Director D.K. Lee

Children's picture books in translation (home 10%). Founded 1988.

USA

*Member of the Association of Authors' Representatives

Adams Literary

295 Greenwich Street, Suite 260, New York, NY 1007
tel 212-786-9140 *fax* 212-786-9170
email info@adamsliterary.com
website www.adamsliterary.com
Agent Tracy Adams

Exclusively children's: from picture books to teenage novels (home 15%, overseas 20%). Strictly no unsolicited submissions. Founded 2004.

Andrea Brown Literary Agency

560 San Antonio Road, Suite 105, Palo Alto, CA 94306
tel 831-422-5925
website www.andreabrownlit.com

President Andrea Brown, *Senior Agent* Laura Rennert, *Associate Agents* Caryn Wiseman, Jennifer Jaeger, Robert Welsh

Exclusively all kinds of children's books. Represents both authors and illustrators.

Submission details For picture books send complete MS (max. 3); for all fiction send short synopsis and first 3 chapters; for non-fiction send proposal and 1–2 sample chapters; for illustrations send 4–5 colour samples (no originals). Include query letter, email and phone number, plus sase for return of material. Founded 1981.

Browne & Miller Literary Associates

(formerly Multimedia Product Development Inc.)
410 South Michigan Avenue, Suite 460, Chicago, IL 60605
tel 312-922-3063 *fax* 312-922-1905
website www.browneandmiller.com
Contact Danielle Egan-Miller

General fiction and non-fiction (home 15%, overseas 20%). Select young adult projects. Works in conjunction with foreign agents. Will suggest revision; no reading fee. Founded 1971.

Maria Carvainis Agency Inc.*

1350 Avenue of the Americas, Suite 2905, New York, NY 10019
tel 212-245-6365 *fax* 212-245-7196
President & Literary Agent Maria Carvainis, *Literary Agent* Donna Bagdasarian

Adult fiction and non-fiction (home 15%, overseas 20%). Fiction: all categories except science fiction and fantasy, especially literary and mainstream; mystery, thrillers and suspense; historical, Regency, young adult. Non-fiction: biography and memoir, health and women's issues, business, finance, psychology, popular science, popular culture. No reading fee. Query first; no unsolicited MSS. No queries by fax or email. Works in conjunction with foreign, TV and movie agents.

The Chudney Agency

750 Kappock Street, Suite 808, Riverdale, NY 10463
tel 917-902-9727 *fax* 718-549-2678
email mail@thechudneyagency.com
website www.thechudneyagency.com
Contact Steven Chudney

Children's books. Focuses particularly on picture books, middle-grade novels and teen fiction. No unsolicited submissions for non-fiction chapter books, middle-grade or teen novels. Not interested in board books or lift-the-flap books; fables, folklore, or traditional fairytales; poetry or 'mood pieces'; stories for 'all ages'; or heavy-handed message-driven stories. Looking for author/illustrators (one individual), who can both write and illustrate picture books. They must really know and understand the prime needs and wants of the child reader.

Submission details Submit full text; include 3–5 art samples (not originals), a brief biography, and a sase for return of material. Founded 2002.

Curtis Brown Ltd*

10 Astor Place, New York, NY 10003
tel 212-473-5400
Branch office 1750 Montgomery Street, San Francisco, CA 94111
tel 415-954 8566
President Peter Ginsberg, *Ceo* Timothy Knowlton, *Contacts* Elizabeth Harding, Ginger Knowlton, Michele Beno

Fiction and non-fiction, juvenile, film and TV rights. No unsolicited MSS; query first with sase. No reading fee; no handling fees.

Dunham Literary, Inc.*

156 Fifth Avenue, Suite 625, New York, NY 10010–7002
website www.dunhamlit.com
Contact Jennie Dunham

Children's books (home 15%, overseas 20%). Handles picture books, fiction for 5–8 and 9–12 year-olds and teenage fiction. Also handles adult literary fiction and non-fiction; 50% of list is for the children's market. Send query letter in first instance by post, not by fax or email. Do not send full MS. No reading fee. Founded 2000.

Dwyer & O'Grady Inc.

PO Box 790, Cedar Key, FL 32625–0790
tel 352-543-9307 *fax* 603-375-5373
website www.dryerogrady.com
Agents Elizabeth O'Grady, Jeff Dwyer

Exclusively children's books (home 15%, overseas 20%). Represents both authors and illustrators. Small agency; not looking for new clients.

Dystel & Goderich Literary Management*

1 Union Square West, New York, NY 10003
tel 212-627-9100 *fax* 212-627-9313
website www.dystel.com
Contact Jane D. Dystel

Children's fiction and non-fiction (home 15%, overseas 19%). Handles picture books, fiction for 5–8 and 9–12 year-olds, teenage fiction, series fiction and non-fiction. Looking for quality young adult fiction. Also handles adult fiction and non-fiction. Send a query letter with a synopsis and up to 50pp of sample MS. No reading fee. Will suggest revision.

Children's authors include Deb Levine, Kelly McWilliams, Soyung Pak, Anne Rockwell, Bernadette Rossetti. Founded 1994.

Educational Design Services LLC

7238 Treviso Lane, Boynton Beach, FL 33437
email linder.eds@juno.com

Contact B. Linder

Specialises in educational texts for K–12 market (home 15%, overseas 25%). No picture books or fiction. Send query with sase, or send outline and one sample chapter by email or with sase for return of material. Founded 1981.

The Ethan Ellenberg Literary Agency
548 Broadway, Suite 5E, New York, NY 10012
tel 212-431-4554 fax 212-941-4652
email agent@ethanellenberg.com
website www.ethanellenberg.com
President & Agent Ethan Ellenberg

Fiction and non-fiction (home 15%, overseas 20%). Commercial fiction: thrillers, mysteries, children's, romance, women's, ethnic, science fiction, fantasy and general fiction; also literary fiction with a strong narrative. Non-fiction: current affairs, health, science, psychology, cookbooks, new age, spirituality, pop-culture, adventure, true crime, biography and memoir. No scholarly works, poetry, short stories or screenplays.

Will accept unsolicited MSS and seriously consider all submissions, including first-time writers. For fiction submit synopsis and first 3 chapters. For non-fiction send a proposal (outline, sample material, author CV, etc). For children's works send complete MS. Illustrators should send a representative selection of colour copies (no orginal artwork). Always include a sase. Founded 1983.

Flannery Literary
1155 South Washing Street, Suite 202, Naperville, IL 60540–3300
tel 630-428-2682 fax 630-428-2683
Contact Jennifer Flannery

Specialises in children's and young adult, juvenile fiction and non-fiction (home 15%, overseas 20%). Send query letter by post in first instance. Founded 1992.

Barry Goldblatt Literary LLC*
320 Seventh Avenue, PMB 266, Brooklyn, New York, NY 11215
tel 718-832-8787 fax 718-832-5558
email bgliterary@earthlink.net
Contact Barry Goldblatt

Specialises in young adult and middle grade fiction, but also handles picture book writers and illustrators. No non-fiction. Has a preference for quirky, offbeat work. Query only.

Ashley Grayson Literary Agency*
1342 18th Street, San Pedro, CA 90732
tel 310-548-4672 fax 310-514-1148
email carolynadg@mac.com
Contact Ashley Grayson, Carolyn Grayson

Commercial fiction and literary fiction for adults and children. Handles foreign rights. No unsolicited MSS.

Submit query letter and first 3 pages of MSS. No calls or queries. No reading fee.
Clients include Bruce Coville, J.B. Cheany, David Lubar, Christopher Pike. Established 1976.

John Hawkins & Associates Inc.*
(formerly Paul R. Reynolds Inc.)
71 West 23rd Street, Suite 1600, New York, NY 10010
tel 212-807-7040 fax 212-807-9555
website www.jhalit.com
President John Hawkins, Vice-President William Reiss, Foreign Rights Moses Cardona, Other Agents Warren Frazier, Anne Hawkins

Fiction, non-fiction, young adult. No reading fee. Founded 1893.

JCA Literary Agency Inc.
174 Sullivan Street, New York, NY 10012
tel 212-807-0888
Contacts Tom Cushman, Melanie Meyers Cushman

Adult fiction, non-fiction and young adult. No unsolicited MSS; query first.

The Kirchoff/Wohlberg Literary Agency
866 United Nation Plaza, New York, New York 10017
tel 212-644-2020 fax 212-223-4387
website www.kirchoffwohlberg.com
Agent Liza Pulitzer-Voges

Children's fiction and non-fiction for all ages from baby to young adult. Represents authors and author/illustrators. Send query letter, outline and sample plus sase.

Barbara S. Kouts, Literary Agent*
PO Box 560, Bellport, NY 11713
tel 631-286-1278 fax 631-286-1538

Fiction and non-fiction, children's (home 15%, overseas 20%). Works with overseas agents. No reading fee. No phone calls. Send query letter first. Founded 1980.

Gina Maccoby Literary Agency
PO Box 60, Chappaqua, NY 10514
tel 914-238-5630
Contact Gina Maccoby

Specialises in children's books: fiction, non-fiction, picture books, MS/illustration packages for middle grade and young adult (home 10%, overseas 20%).
Submission details Send query letter by post in first instance. Founded 1986.

McIntosh & Otis Inc.*
353 Lexington Avenue, New York, NY 10016
tel 212-687-7400 fax 212-687-6894
Head of Children's Dept Edward Necarsulmer IV

Fiction for 5–8 and 9–12 year-olds, teenage fiction, series fiction, poetry and non-fiction for children (home 15%, overseas 20%). Also handles adult fiction and non-fiction. No unsolicited MSS for novels; query first with outline, sample chapters and sase. No submissions by email. No reading fee. Will suggest revision. Founded 1928.

Barbara Markowitz Literary Agency
PO Box 41709, Los Angeles, CA 90041
Agents Barbara Markowitz, Judith Rosenthal

Children's fiction, middle grade, young adult (11–15 year-olds), historical fiction (home 15%, overseas 15%). Seeking contemporary and historical fiction up to 35,000 words for 8–11 and 11–15 year-olds. No fables, fantasy or fairytales; no illustrated books; no sci-fi.

Submission details Send query letter with sase or outline with 3 sample chapters. Send sase for return of material. Founded 1980.

Mews Books
20 Bluewater Hill, Westport, CT 06880
tel 203-227-1836 *fax* 203-227-1144
email mewsbooks@aol.com
Agents Sidney B. Kramer, Fran Pollak

Children's fiction, non-fiction, picture books, middle grade and young adult books (home 15%, overseas 20%). Seeking well-written books with continuity of character and story.

Submission details Send query letter with sase or outline and 2 sample chapters. Send sase for return of material. Founded 1974.

William Morris Agency Inc.*
(incorporating the Writers Shop, formerly Virginia Barber Literary Agency)
1325 Avenue of the Americas, New York, NY 10019
tel 212-586-5100
website www.wma.com
Executive VP Owen Laster, *Senior VPs* Jennifer Rudolph Walsh, Suzanne Gluck, Joni Evans, Mel Berger, Jay Mandel, Tracy Fisher

General fiction and non-fiction (home 15%, overseas 20%, performance rights 15%). Will suggest revision. No reading fee.

Alison Picard, Literary Agent
PO Box 2000, Cotuit, MA 02635
tel 508-477-7192
email ajpicard@aol.com

Adult fiction and non-fiction, children's and young adult (15%). No short stories or poetry. No reading fee. Founded 1985.

Wendy Schmalz Agency
PO Box 831, Hudson, NY 12534
tel 518-672-7697 *fax* 518-672-7662
email wendy@schmalzagency.com
Contact Wendy Schmalz

Children's fiction and non-fiction: middle grade and young adult (home 15%, overseas 20%). Seeking

young adult and middle-grade novels. No picture books, sci-fi or fantasy. Send query letter with sase or by email. Founded 2001.

Susan Schulman Literary & Dramatic Agents Inc.*
454 West 44th Street, New York, NY 10036
tel 212-713-1633 *fax* 212-581-8830
email schulman@aol.com
Branch office 2 Bryan Plaza, Washington Depot, CT 06794
tel 860-868-3700

Agents for negotiation in all markets (with co-agents) of fiction, general non-fiction, children's books, academic and professional works, and associated subsidiary rights including plays and film (home 15%, UK 7.5%, overseas 20%). No reading fee. Return postage required.

Stimola Literary Studio
306 Chase Court, Edgewater, NJ 07020
tel/fax 201-945-9353
email ltrystudio@aol.com
Contact Rosemary B. Stimola

Children's fiction and non-fiction, from preschool to young adult (home 15%, overseas 20%).

Submission details Send query letter with sase, or email (no attachments). Most clients come via referral. Founded 1997.

Ann Tobias, Literary Agent
52 East 84th Street, Apt 4L, New York, NY 10028
Contact Ann Tobias

Exclusively children's fiction and non-fiction: picture books, middle grade, young adult, young readers (home 15%, overseas 20%).

Submission details For picture books send complete MS; for longer works send 30pp and synopsis. Include sase for return of material. No email, fax or phone queries. Founded 1988.

Sc©tt Treimel NY
434 Lafayette Street, New York, NT 10003
tel 212-505-8353 *fax* 212-505-0664
email st.ny@verizon.net
Contact Scott Treimel

Exclusively children's books: middle grade, young adult novels and MS/illustration packages (home 15–20%, overseas 20–25%). Interested in seeing first chapter books, and middle-grade and teenage fiction. No religious books. Send query letter with sase; no fax or email queries. For picture books submit complete MS. Founded 1995.

Writers House LLC*
21 West 26th Street, New York, NY 10010
tel 212-685-2400 *fax* 212-685-1781
website www.writershouse.com
Chairman Albert Zuckerman, *President* Amy Berkower, *Juvenile & Young Adult Agents* Susan Cohen, Rebecca Sherman, Jodi Reamer, Steven Malk

Fiction and non-fiction, including all rights; film and TV rights. No screenplays or software. Send a one-page letter in the first instance, saying what's wonderful about your book, what it is about and why you are the best person to write it. No reading fee. Founded 1974.

Wylie-Merrick Literary Agency*

1138 South Webster Street, Kokomo, IN 46902
tel 765-459-8258

email rbrown@wylie-merrick.com, smartin@wylie-merrick.com
website www.wylie-merrick.com
Partners Robert Brown and Sharene Martin

Adult and juvenile fiction and non-fiction (home 15%, overseas 20%). Interested in romance, sci-fi and fantasy, women's, gay/lesbian, suspense/thrillers. No picture books or graphic novels. Query by email only; no unsolicited MSS. See website for full submission guidelines. Founded 1999.

Illustrating for children
Creating graphic novels
Raymond Briggs has created many graphic novels and here he describes the process.

Book writers have such an easy time of it. They sit down, write their book and when they come to the end they send it off to the publisher. It might be long, it might be short, the publisher doesn't mind.

The writer needs no materials or equipment. He can do it all with a pencil and a Woolworth's pad. Even the typing may be done for him. Unlike the illustrator, he needs no paints, crayons, T-squares, set squares, brushes, dividers, spray cans, handmade paper and mounting boards, light boxes, cutting tables, guillotines, type scales, magnifier lamps, wall-to-wall display boards and masses of space. The writer can scribble it all in bed. (They often do.)

Drawing the book
For the picture book illustrator, when he has finished the writing, that is the easy bit done. His true task then begins.

First he has to design the book. Picture books have to be exactly 32 pages, not 33 or 31. This includes prelims. So the text has to be divided into fewer than 16 spreads. On rare occasions, the publisher may allow 40 pages, or on even rarer occasions 48, though this allowance may contain 'self-ends' which take up eight pages. (This is too technical to explain to book writers.)

Then, the illustrator becomes a typographer. He casts off the MSS, chooses a suitable font, decides on the type size, the measure and the leading, and has it set. Surprisingly, some writers I have met know nothing about typography. Some don't even know the name of the font their own book is set in! Some have never even set foot in a printer's.

If the book is strip cartoon with speech bubbles, the task is even greater as each speech bubble has to be individually designed. The size and shape of it is part of its expressive quality and once the bubble is finalised the illustrator becomes a hand-lettering expert and letters in, possibly many hundreds of words, trying to maintain a consistent style over many days' work. In America strip cartoon work is divided amongst several people: writer, pencilling-in artist, inker-in, and letterer. In England we are made of sterner stuff – 'blood, toil, tears and sweat' and we 'graphic novelists' do it all.

The illustrator then makes a dummy (a blank book) with the correct number of pages and of the exact size. If he is well established and commands respect from the publisher, the publisher may have a dummy made for him – but you need to be at least 60 years old to be granted this privilege. (You might have to show them your Bus Pass.) He then cuts up the type proofs (which used to be called 'galleys') and sticks them onto the dummy, imagining the pictures on the page as he does so. Again, for strip cartoons it is much more complicated – you have to consider not just what text goes on each spread but how many frames the text is to be divided amongst, and what size and shape the frames are to be.

This brings us to the next stage: designing the 'grid', i.e. how many rows of frames per page and the number of frames in each row there are to be. Places where small frames give way to a big picture, either vignetted or bled off, will be determined by the text itself, not only in terms of space but also by the feeling the text is trying to express.

Creating the action

When all this is done, it is time to stop book designing and start making the 'film'. You become the director. Who comes on from the left and who from the right? A slight nuisance is that the character on the left is the one who has to speak first. What are the characters doing and thinking and feeling? We have their words, but is there a subtext? Can this be expressed by body language? Is one of them angrily scrubbing the floor, whilst the other gazes moodily out of the window?

You then become the art director, designing the sets. Where does the scene take place? Indoors or outdoors? In the garden or in the street? What does a 1930s kitchen look like? How big is the room? What is the view from the window?

You also have to be the costume designer and the lighting designer. What would they be wearing at the time? Is it winter or summer? What were overcoats and hats like then? What did they wear on the beach? Should it be daylight or artificial light in this scene? What exactly was the look of gaslight? Does it need a dark ominous light or a happy morning light?

Then as the cameraman you have to decide where to shoot from. Close-up, long shot, or middle distance? Both characters in shot or one off-screen? Perhaps a speech bubble stays in the frame but the speaker is unseen, through a doorway or simply out of shot. Shall it be a high view looking down on the scene or a low angle looking up? It all depends on what the action is trying to convey.

Finally, you have to become the actor and feel yourself inside the character when you're drawing it. This is the essence of good narrative illustration. It is an odd bit of psychology. You have to be mentally in two places at once. One part of you is inside character, feeling what it is like to be huddled and running in the pouring rain, the other part of your brain is detachedly looking at this figure from a certain point of view, taking note of perspective. 'Ah yes, the lower leg will be foreshortened from this angle; we're looking down on the thigh and on the back; we can't see his face as his head is down and his arm is up. Will we see the sole of the shoe that is raised or is it edge on?'

The lucky writer need know nothing about human and animal anatomy, perspective, drawing, line tone or colour. All they have to do is write down some words! It's a doddle.

I wish I could do it.

Raymond Briggs is creator of *The Snowman*, *Fungus the Bogeyman*, *Father Christmas* and many other characters and stories for children, and *When the Wind Blows* for adults. Since leaving art school in 1957 he has been a writer and illustrator, mainly of children's books. He has written plays for the stage and radio and a few 'adult' books. In 2004 he designed the Christmas stamps for the Royal Mail, and was made a Fellow of the Royal Society of Literature, but his proudest achievement is going on the radio programme *Desert Island Discs*, twice. See his fansite (www.toonhound.com/briggs.htm) for further information about him.

Eight great tips to get your picture book published

Tony Ross gives some sound advice for illustrators and writers of children's picture books.

I have always had the uncomfortable feeling that if I can get published, anyone can. A belief that being published is something that only happens to other people, holds some very good writers and illustrators back.

Assuming you have drawings – or a story – to offer, there are several ways to go about it. Probably the best way is to have a publishing house in the family! Failing that, all is not lost.

Work can be sent directly to a publisher's office. Most editors receive a good amount of unsolicited work, so be patient with them for a reply. A stamped addressed envelope for its return is always appreciated, bearing in mind that the majority of work submitted is refused. At the beginning of a career, refusal is quite normal and a great deal about yourself and your talent can be gleaned from this experience. Sometimes, advice gained at this stage can change your future.

Starting on a drawing career is an exciting time and I think it's a good idea to get yourself in perspective. Visit the library and some bookshops to look at all the styles that are around. Get a sense for what's out there: you don't want to regurgitate it, but to get a feel for the parameters. You can learn a lot, maybe more than you learned at art school, from looking at great artists such as Edward Ardizzone, E.H. Shepherd, Maurice Sendak and Chris Van Allsberg.

Great Tip No 1: Use black and white

There is great appeal in working in full colour but it's good to remember black and white. Sometimes a publisher may have a black and white project waiting for an illustrator, while all of the big interest is going into the coloured picture book list. Some of the greatest children's books are illustrated in black and white – A.A. Milne and E.H. Shepherd made one of the greatest partnerships with those tiny black ink drawings contributing so much to a great classic. Not a bad place to start, eh?

Ink drawing is simple, in the hands of a master, but not easy. That unforgiving fluid! Wonder at the uncomplicated, straightforwardness of the Pooh drawings. Consider Toad in *The Wind in the Willows*. When he applied to do the illustrations, Kenneth Graham said to Shepherd: 'I have seen many artists who can draw better than you, but you make the animals live.' Can you learn anything from that? Look at Ardizzone's ability to draw mood. He can show a summer afternoon, or a cold November morning, both using black ink. There is so much to look at, so much to learn from.

Try to include black and white work in your folder. Also include a series of perhaps 30 drawings, such as a fully illustrated story, where you show your ability to be consistent with the characters and the style, without repetition or irrelevance (like the radio programme *Just a Minute*!).

It is a duty of an illustrator to be able to read – that is to try and understand the writer's aims – and to help them rather than to inflict a totally different angle onto the book (think of the Milne and Shepherd partnership). Much of this comes down to being sensitive enough to recognise the tone of the writing, and skilful enough to draw in the same tone. So the importance of really taking an interest in the story cannot be overstressed. In the text, there will be either clues, or blatant instructions to help the drawings gel. Be very aware.

Great Tip No 2: Experiment

I have known illustrators who convinced themselves that they couldn't use black ink. Mostly this was because they were using the wrong ink, the wrong pen, and/or the wrong paper. Types of black ink vary: waterproof behaves differently from water soluble. Fine nibs and broad nibs each give a totally different result, as does an old fountain pen or a sharpened stick. Try 10 different inks, 50 different nibs, odd sticks and all the papers you can find: tracing, layout, calendered, five different cartridges, smooth and rough water-colour, handmade, wrapping paper, anything at all. It's a case of finding the combination that suits your hand and your intention. Your own genius, unrecognised at art school, could surprise you.

Many of the points I've made about black and white work also apply to colour. The marriage of image to text will be in your hands, but it must work.

Great Tip No 3: Choose the right words

I am hesitant to give advice to writers. After all, there are few rules, and the next J.K. Rowling may read this. My own view is really quite simple, and rather obvious. I write mainly for under eight year-olds, so my stories are as short as I can make them. I feel that it is good to have a magnetic first sentence, and an ending that EXPLODES WITH SURPRISE. I think that the ending is the most important part of the story. The bit in the middle should waft the reader along, remembering that the *sound* of words and sentences can be a useful tool.

I like stories to be either funny or scary. *Very* funny, or *very* scary. To be dull is the worst thing in the world! That sounds so obvious, but it gets overlooked. If you are not excited with your work, maybe nobody else will be either.

A picture book has about 23 pages of text (but this can be flexible). I think those pages should have fewer than 2000 words; 1000–1500 is good. One word per page would be great, if the one word was brilliant. As brilliant as the story. Don't be frightened of editing out surplus words. One brilliant one will work better than a dozen mundane ones.

Don't fall into the mindset that writing for children is easy. It has all the disciplines of writing for adults, with the added problem of understanding a child's mind and world. The great writers have a passport to a child's world – think of Roald Dahl. I have seen many brilliant ideas, with less than brilliant pictures, make wonderful books. I have seen a bad idea saved by wonderful illustrations. So, writing style apart, be your own concept's greatest critic. It is quite natural to be protective of your baby, of your story. But try to remember that there are a lot of good editors out there and it will be in your own interest to consider their advice. So don't be a young fogey: be flexible, listen, understand experienced points of view. This can be a good time to change for the better, and to start a relationship with one publishing house that may serve you for a lifetime.

Great Tip No 4: Choose what you draw

Don't plan huge drawing problems into your submitted roughs. They may be accepted, and the editor will expect the final art to be better than the roughs.

I illustrate my own writing. This appeals to me for all sorts of reasons, few of them noble. Firstly, I get all of the available fee or/and royalty. I don't have to let half or more go to a writer. Secondly, if there is something I don't like to draw, I don't write about it! For instance, most of my stories take place in the summer, because I prefer to handle trees with their leaves on.

Illustrations being worked on to be published is not the place to practise your drawing. *Practise, change, experiment* all the time, but not in a publishing project. Your finished illustrations must be as good as you can make them. I know an illustrator who won't draw feet, always hiding the ends of legs in grass, water, behind rocks, etc. This is okay if the text will allow; a well-drawn puddle is better than a badly drawn foot any day. It is better to think around a drawing problem, than just to go along with it.

Great Tip No 5: Experiment with your main character

Before you start, try drawing your main character (the most important visual element of the story) in all sorts of ways. A day spent doing this can be so valuable. Getting the main character right can indicate ways to proceed with the whole book.

Great Tip No 6: Think global

Remember that editors react well to stories with wide appeal, rather than minority groups. Foreign sales are in everyone's interest, so try to allow your work to travel. Rhyme is sometimes difficult to translate, as are unusual plays on words.

Great Tip No 7: Plan the whole book

Do little mock-up books for yourself to plan what text goes on which page. This helps to get the story right throughout the book. A 32-page children's book (the most common extent for a picture book) includes covers, end papers, title and half-title pages. This leaves you 23–25 pages to play with. These little mock-ups are for your own use, not to be presented as roughs, so they can be quite work-a-day.

By working out what text goes on which page you will get some sort of an idea of which illustrations go where. Just as the drawings are creative, so is their use on the page. If you use a full double-page spread, another can be expected on the next page. But imagine the effect if the next page explodes with huge typography, and tiny pictures? I am not suggesting you do this, only reminding you that pages of a book are there to be turned, and the turning can be unpredictable and adventurous. Book design is important, along with everything else.

Great Tip No 8: Persevere

So much to do, so much to remember. The main thing is, every children's illustrator and writer I know who has kept trying has got there in the end and been published. But I've also seen great talents give up far too early. Remember that rejection is normal: it's only someone's point of view. Some great books have had long hunts for a publisher. Be open to change and always bear in mind that editors have the experience that you may lack and an editor's advice is meant to help you, not choke you off. However, not all of their advice may apply in your case, so try to recognise what applies to you. When I worked in advertising, I had an art director who said: 'Half of what I say is rubbish. Trouble is, I don't know which half.'

And a reminder

Don't waste time by sending work to publishers who don't publish material like yours. Libraries and bookshops are worth exploring to familiarise yourself with which publishing houses favour what types of work. Research of this kind is time well spent.

Try to show your work in person so that you get a chance to talk, and learn. Do not, however, just drop in. Make an appointment first and hope that these busy people have some time available.

There are also agents prepared to represent new talent (see *Illustrators' agents* on page 208). Of course, an agent will charge a percentage of work sold, but my dad used to say, 'Seventy-five per cent of something is better than 100% of nothing.'

I am troubled by giving advice. I can't help thinking of the young composer who approached the slightly older Mozart and asked, 'Maestro, how should I compose a concerto?' to which Mozart replied 'You are very young, perhaps you should start with a simple tune'. The young composer frowned, and argued. 'But, Maestro, *you* composed a concerto when you were still a child!' 'Ah yes,' said Mozart, 'but I didn't have to ask how?'

Tony Ross is a renowned illustrator of international repute and the creator of such classics as *The Little Princess* and *I Want My Potty*. His first book was published in 1976 and since then he has illustrated more than 700 books including the *Dr Xargle* series, created with the author Jeanne Willis and the *Horrid Henry* series written by Francesca Simon.

See also...
- *Creating graphic novels,* page 187
- *Writing and illustrating picture books,* page 193
- *The amazing picture book story,* page 197
- *Cartoons and deadlines,* page 259

Writing and illustrating picture books

Debi Gliori tells the story of how she started writing and illustrating children's books.

The prospect of spending your life making children's books has a great deal to recommend it, not least the fact that you will never have to buy those nasty big itchy rolls of rockwool to insulate the walls of your home ever again. Twelve thousand or so volumes will do the job far better. Following the children's books career path will ensure that books will pour into your home, year after year, yours and other people's; foreign editions and large-print versions; pop-ups and boards; collections and anthologies; so many that you might think about studying 'Elementary Bookshelf Building for Beginners and Fumblethumbs' before your piles of books reach to the ceiling. You will also be forced to develop a pronounced and sincerely apologetic grovel each time your postman staggers laden to your door – after all, his sciatica/lower back pain/slipped disc is *entirely your fault*.

Tottering heaps of hardbacks notwithstanding, I can say, with hand-on-heart, that being a children's author and illustrator is the best job in the world. I'm not alone in this opinion. Some years ago, a midwife visited me in the studio I work from in my garden and said, apropos of nothing: 'Eee lass, you've landed with your bum in the butter'.

Unsurprisingly, I looked suitably horrified. (What *was* this, pray? Surely not more indignities to be visited upon my person in the name of childbirth?) Seeing my expression, she hastily explained that what she had *meant* was that I was exceedingly fortunate to be paid to do what I love best. 'Bum in the butter' huh? Takes all sorts. But hey, Gentle Reader, it was not always thus. Back in the mists of that ghastly period of human history known as the Eighties when I set off on this Quest for Publication, I recall that I underwent a long period of major struggle during which many lentils were consumed. This was a lengthy phase which also involved dressing in the morning *in* bed, serious layering of woolly jumpers and, I kid you not, bathrooms so cold that one's toothbrush *froze*.

After graduation from Edinburgh College of Art, I trawled round London publishers with my too-big portfolio and quickly realised that good picture book texts were as rare as talking bears. While illustrators, such as I'd been studying to become, were everywhere in abundance. Encouraging, *not*.

Stubborn is my middle name. That's right, Debi Stubborn Gliori – I know it's weird, but parents... pffff, what can I say? Anyway, stubbornly I decided that there was no way that I was going to take on a badly paid job to 'support' my unpaid non-existent career in children's books. That would be *two* jobs. I mean, get real. Nor did I much fancy the kind of grinding-noble-poverty-consumption-in-a-garret artist's lifestyle afforded by a complete lack of cash. Mercenary little beast that I was, I picked up as many well-paid advertising jobs as possible (illustrating whisky labels and smoked salmon packaging, mainly) and in my spare time, hauled myself off to libraries and bookshops and did my research. Who was publishing what? Why were these books published rather than, say, *mine*? What was fashionable and why? Did retellings work? Were books for babies no-brainers? Trust me, it wasn't all that hard for me to see what was required from a good picture book. I won't insult your intelligence by telling you. You know this stuff. Or if you don't, you'll pick it up quickly.

So, armed with a rough idea of what first publishers, then parents and finally, children might want (the order is, sadly, significant), I holed myself up in a 1.2 square metre cupboard and wrote a book which, joy of joys, was picked off the Walker Books slush pile and published. Read my lips: at that point, I had no 'in' in publishing – no contacts, no money and no influence. I was a single parent living in a freezing cold, damp cottage waaaaay out in the sticks in Scotland. And yet, and yet, and yet, I managed to get my book published. The message here is Take Heart. It *can* be done.

Making a picture book the Gliori way

How I go about starting to make a book from scratch is another matter. All of us approach the process of creating picture books from a multitude of different directions. For what it's worth, here's how I go about it. Although I always start with the text, nine times out of 10 the initial idea for a book arrives in my head as a couple of images that I know I'd love to paint. Unsurprisingly, I never experience a burning desire to make a book that involves cars or horses, mainly because I cannot draw either. On the other hand, I love landscapes. So, for example, there's a scene in one of my early books called *Mr Bear Babysits* in which Mr Bear is walking home by moonlight through trees, and all around him are baby animals, birds and insects being tucked in for the night. Immediately that image sparks off a series of questions. What season would this be set in? Answer – summer, because then I can draw golden moonlit fields and haystacks. What time is it? Probably after midnight. Why is Mr Bear out so late? Maybe he's having a *liaison dangereux* with Mrs Grizzle-Bear... or then again, perhaps not. Let's imagine he's been babysitting for the Grizzle-Bear cubs. How many? Three. Heavens, poor Grizzle-Bears, they must *really* need a night off. What are the cubs like? Rumbustious. Has Mr Bear got kids of his own? Is he going home? Is this the end or is it the beginning? You can see the process, can't you? By trying to supply answers to my own questions, I am effortlessly beginning to build a framework round which I could start to construct a narrative.

I wouldn't like you to think that it's easy though. Frequently, the entire framework begins to assume the tensile properties of overcooked tagliatelle, at which point I will decide that this is an idea that's not ready to be written yet. I have several of these raw and palely loitering things tucked away in various notebooks, and once in a while I'll drag them out into the unforgiving daylight; poke, prod and play with them until they turn to mush at which point, with deep regret, I'll put them back and try a different tack. Sometimes, to my delight, the poking and prodding succeeds and a picture book text emerges, oozing and flubby in parts, but with a decent story at its heart. Over the course of the next month, I'll return to that text and read it out loud until my ears bleed, because reading out loud is the single best way for me to expose flaws, glitches and bumpy bits before I self-edit in what I blithely imagine to be a ruthlessly incisive fashion.

Afterwards, breathless and pink with the unaccustomed exertion, I type it out and email it to my editor. When I was a beginner, I would assemble a thick envelope in which I included the following items for editor-seduction purposes: one lovingly typed covering letter on headed stationery, one double-spaced (with Tippex blobs) manuscript, (both typed and corrected on an ancient manual typewriter bought in a junk shop), a set of thumbnail sketches showing how I anticipated pacing the text and pictures over 32 pages, two hideously expensive colour photocopies of two spreads of artwork and one sae for the return of said hideously expensive samples. And then I would wait... and wait... and wait.

These days, if my editor likes my initial idea, she usually lets me know the same day I emailed it. This has little to do with talent, and everything to do with expediency. These days my editor knows my work and she trusts me. From past experience, she is fairly certain that come hell or high water, or even both, simultaneously, along with some obstetric complications thrown in for good measure, three months after she has read and approved my text, I will deliver detailed black and white pencil roughs showing how I intend each spread to look. For her part, she will comment on the roughs, sending them back to me with a tactful and light powdering of post-it notes. Only *suggestions*, Debi. Put that axe down. Five months afterwards, I will deliver camera-ready artwork and 10 minutes after that, my editor and I will be raising that first of many flutes of champagne to our lips in celebration. What, at 10 o'clock in the morning? Damn straight.

Proofs and publication

Back when I was starting out, nothing much happened after I delivered a book. There was a lull and then the first proofs arrived – a stage I loved, and still love, because suddenly your whole book appears to fall into focus – it looks like a real book at last and it's one of many identical copies, thus saving me from my illustrator's artwork-related paranoia about someone accidentally dropping a slice of raw tomato onto it. Before you dismiss me as neurotic, Gentle Reader, let me say that this tomato-on-watercolour-artwork-falling-incident really happened. He'll never walk again without a limp, though. After the heady rush of seeing my work in proof form, came the not-so heady rush of publication day, which came... and went, unremarked. Sometimes there would be a wee card in the post, signed by everyone who'd had anything to do with the book; sometimes a bunch of flowers would arrive from my publisher, bestowing a kind of temporary London-glamour on my Scottish hovel. Sometimes I'd cook something special for my family, or bake a cake or just sit in my studio and gnaw my fingernails off one by one, wondering just how far we could make 10% of not a lot stretch.

These days, I'm so involved with my next project that I'll have achieved a measure of distance from the book just published; so much so that I have been known to stare at a beautiful bouquet of flowers and wonder if my publisher thinks I've had another baby. Surely not? Maybe I did – perhaps I'd better just go and check the pram, just in case...

The exact timing of Publication Day can become a bit blurred when your book is released early in order to maximise sales at, say, a book festival. Actually, given the levels of author hospitality on offer, *everything* can get a little blurred during book festivals. By the time you get to Publication Day it's quite hard not to feel a little anti-climatic. What happens to your book from now on is, by and large, out of your hands. It's the day that unpublished authors dream of: the day you see *your* book in print. Perhaps I'm just an old cynic, but seeing my book in mint condition in bookshops doesn't press any of my buttons whatsoever. No, what *I* want to see is *my* book being read till it *falls to bits*. I want to see the date-stamp page at the front of a library copy of one of my books full to the brim with the inky evidence of many withdrawals. *That's* the whole point. Being *read* – not being published.

But first you have to get published, and that's why we're here; you reading and me attempting to spout wisdom like an illustrator's version of the Delphic Oracle. Did anyone remember to bring me a goat, by the way? Problem is, I'm not an oracle, and nor am I a teacher. All that I know is based my own experience of the business. Your experience will be significantly different. Without sitting down beside you and looking over your text or your portfolio, the best advice I can give is *keep going*. Be stubborn – if you want to be published, you're going to have to be rhinoceros-like in your determination as well as acquiring a rhino-hide to shrug off those slings and arrows of unkind comment. Follow your own star, even if it's a redundant Russian satellite. Er, learn how to put up bookshelves and develop a series of nifty recipes for lentils. And good luck: like all the best things in life, the process of learning how to make picture books is well worth the effort.

Debi Gliori has written and illustrated many picture books and her best-loved titles include *No Matter What* and the *Mr Bear* series. She is also the author of the *Pure Dead...* series of novels for older children. She lives in Scotland and works from her International Shedquarters at the bottom of her garden.

The amazing picture book story

Oliver Jeffers tells the story of how his first picture book came to be published.

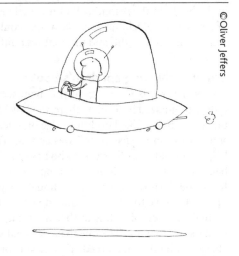

In this, the 21st century, anything is possible. We drive flying cars, live in bubbles, go to the moon for our summer holidays and we can freeze and heat things instantly. People can do whatever they want, and in some cases get paid for it, even writing and illustrating children's books. And in this age of possibility, they can even be picked from the slush pile. That's what happened to me. Although I still believe I'm one of the luckiest people alive, and this article isn't much beyond bragging, hindsight and other people would suggest there is more to it than that. One thing that hasn't changed with all our technological advancements is the fundamental need for children's picture books on a number of levels. From educating enquiring young minds, and entertaining both children and adults alike at bedtime (and not just adults who have children, and not just at bedtime) to pushing the boundaries of style and content within the broader worlds of both art and literature. Children's books are art, and all true artists do what they love first and hope to make a living second. Creating a piece of work to the absolute best of an ability is an artist's priority. Getting paid is a bonus. The same goes for those who create children's books. (I bet if you were to ask someone like Tony Ross, if he wasn't getting paid to make children's books, would he do it anyway and just be poor? He'd probably say 'yes' but also have a second job working at the moon resort.)

Anyway, so back to me bragging about how I'm one of the luckiest people in the world and get to do what I love for a living. Well, sort of living as the money isn't great, and I sell proper paintings as well, and between the two I can pay my mortgage. But I do have a publisher that publishes my books and I'm going to tell you how that happened. The story itself is actually quite business-like and boring so I'll throw in a few creative exaggerations for effect.

The story begins

It all started when I had just defeated the Admiral of the Swiss Navy in a sword fight, and sat at the edge of the pier at the Sydney fish market for a think. I had known all along that I liked to draw pictures and I liked to write, and I had been putting the two together for a while in my paintings. I even bought and collected children's picture books both for my own enjoyment and as research for my paintings. But it wasn't until my good friend Ben suggested I attempt a children's book of my own that I seriously considered it as a direction to take my life. So, as I sat there dangling my legs off the pier, I had my first idea for a children's book, about a boy who tries to catch the reflection of a star in the water, much like the Brer Rabbit story of the *Moon and the Mill Pond*.

After a year out, I carried the idea into my final year studying Visual Communication (specialising in illustration) at the University of Ulster in Belfast in 2000, having to hold down a second job as a racecar driver to pay for my tuition. I developed self-portrait doodles to narrate my thesis that year, which eventually developed into the character used in the book. In the second half of my final year I used my picture book concept as a piece of coursework, deciding to see how far I could take it to a finished product. This involved getting the words right, and the pictures right, and more importantly, the balance between the two right.

Looking, thinking children's books

To get the words right, I read my manuscript to as many six year-olds as I could find (you'd be amazed how many there are: I reckon if they were all to jump at once something big would break, like London Bridge or at least a phone box or two), slowly tweaking the story based on the feedback I was getting. To get the pictures right I used the unending help of my older brother Rory who basically has a lot more sense than I do. And to get the balance right we both looked at hundreds of other picture books to see what everyone else had done. That was when the earthquake happened and Rory had to balance 58 books on his head to save them from falling down a crack to the molten core of the earth.

In the process of getting the balance right, I noticed a few things about how good picture books seem to work. The one that sticks out most is about how they seem to appeal across all ages without being forced. They aren't condescending, but at the same time they aren't inaccessible. There just seems to be a natural universal appeal to both children and adults – and let's face it, they need to appeal to adults, as however well a six year-old is doing, they're unlikely to stick their hand in their pocket and pull out a tenner in a bookshop!

OK, so in the second half of 2001, after I had finished developing my idea and finished my degree, and after the initial euphoria of never having to write another thesis in my life wore off, and during that slightly intimidating, 'I actually have to do something with my life now!' phase, I decided I would get my book published. I looked at what was around

© Oliver Jeffers

in the bookshops and thought that what I had created was as good as, if not better, than anything else that was out there, and confidence and self belief are important tools when you need to be self motivated. My first step was to buy the *Writers' & Artists' Yearbook* (and it's great to see this *Children's Writers' & Artists' Yearbook* out now) and I then began to look at which publisher would be lucky enough to receive my manuscript. Alright, I wasn't that confident, in fact, having worked in Waterstones for a few years and armed with a very minimal knowledge of the publishing world, I knew I was in for a long and trying road of numerous attempts contacting publishers, repeatedly saying 'have you read it yet?'

Apart from using the *Yearbook* to research which publishers I should send my idea to, I also referred to my own collection of children's picture books, the collection that would make any six year-old jealous. I looked to see who had published what, paying particular attention to my favourites, and which publishers popped up more often.

My next step was to figure out what exactly to send them. There are hundreds and thousands of unsolicited ideas that reach publishers every year and my objective was to stand out among those. To be noticed. By asking, I found that what publishers like to see in a proposal for a new book was the manuscript and a few samples of the illustrations to give a broad idea of the feel for the book. I invested a bit of money into producing 100 copies of a small spiral bound 'sample', with the manuscript at the start and 10 full-colour illustrations after, which I put into an envelope with a letter outlining who I was and what I was trying to do, and a self-addressed envelope for them to contact me. I also included a small portfolio (and I mean small, eight prints that were 14cm square each) of other examples of my paintings and illustrations in the hope that if a particular publisher didn't pick up on my book idea, at least I might be able to get a few commissions while I was waiting.

A few phone calls later and I had found out who looked after the children's division in each appropriate publishing house, and addressed my envelope to them. The point being that it would arrive at a real person's desk instead of an anonymous room that was only used for hostage situations or when they ran out of chairs. I spent a while drawing up a big chart showing which publishers I had sent an envelope to, their contact name and number, date last contacted, and room for comments. I sent an envelope to the 10 biggest publishers in the UK, and the 10 biggest in USA, figuring I'd start at the top and work my way down.

© Oliver Jeffers

© Oliver Jeffers

The envelopes were opened

Expecting a healthy dose of being ignored and avoided, you can perhaps imagine my surprise when, the next afternoon, as I was entertaining the Sultan of Brunei and his wonderful wife Delilah, I received a phone call from a publisher in London during the course of which they expressed their desire to publish my book. It had arrived on the desk of a young editorial assistant: she had opened it, liked what she saw, and had immediately decided to do something about it. That offer was followed a week later by one from a US publisher in New York City, where something similar happened. I forgave the US publisher for their delay, as they are geographically further away.

And it was as simple as that. I met with both publishers, and between the three of us we were able to devise a cunning plan that would enable both of them to publish the book.

Told you I was lucky, I may as well have won the lottery. But as someone wiser than me once said, 'It's all about healthy measures of luck and hard work!' or was that 'work and hard luck?' I can't remember, but the point is that I set myself an objective and was quite methodical and logical in my efforts to get there. Like most businesses, I had an idea, I developed it, then invested time, thought, and money in selling it. But if I hadn't already sold it, I'd still be trying to, and I'd still be having the same ideas for my next books, only wearing cheaper shoes, eating Weetabix for dinner, and maybe sending off an application to the moon resort too.

The end. Or rather, the beginning...

Oliver Jeffers' first children's picture book, *How to Catch a Star*, was published in 2004. His second book, *Lost and Found*, was published in 2005 and won the Nestlé Children's Book Prize that year, and both books won the CBI Bisto Merit Award in 2005 and 2006 respectively and are published by HarperCollins.

See also...

Illustrating for children's books

The world of children's publishing is big business. The huge range of books published each year all carry artwork – lots of it. Maggie Mundy offers guidance for people who are at the start of their career in illustrating for children's books.

The portfolio

Your portfolio should reflect the best of you and your work, and should speak for itself. Keep its content simple – if too many styles are included, for instance, your work will not leave a lasting impression.

Include some artwork other than those carried out for college projects, e.g. an illustration from a timeless classic to show your abilities, and something modern which reflects your own taste and the area in which you wish to work.

If your strength is for black and white illustration, include pieces with and without tone and with or without a wash. Some publishers want line and tone and some want only line. As cross hatching and stippling can add a lot of extra time to an illustration deadline, it might be advisable to leave out these samples. If you can, include a selection of humour as it can be used effectively in educational books and elsewhere. It is best not to sign and date your work: some artworks can stand the test of time and still look good after a year or two, but if it looks dated … so is the illustrator!

An A3 portfolio is probably the ideal size. Place your best piece of artwork on the opening page and your next best piece on the last page.

Looking at the market

Start by looking thoroughly at what is being published today for children. Take your studies to branches of big retail chains, some independent bookshops, as well as your local library (a helpful librarian should be able to tell you which are the most borrowed books). Absorb the picture books, explore the novelty books, look at the variety of colour covers, and note the range of black line illustrations inside books for children and teenagers. Make a list of the publishers you think may be able to use your particular style.

By making these investigations you will gain an insight into not only the current trends and styles but also the much favoured, oft-published classic children's literature. Most importantly, it will help you identify your market.

In books for a young age range every picture must tell the story – some books have no text and the illustrations say it all. Artwork should be uncluttered, shapes clear, and colour bright. If this does not appeal to you, go up a year or two and note the extra details that are added to the artwork (which still tells the story). Children now need to see more than just clear shapes: they need extra details added to the scene – e.g. a quirky spider hanging around, or a mouse under the bed.

Children are your most critical audience: never think that you can get away with 'any old thing'. Indeed, at the Bologna Book Fair it is a panel of children which judges what they consider to be the best picture book.

Current trends

Innovative publishers are always on the lookout for something new in illustration styles: something completely different from the tried and tested. More and more they are turning to European and overseas illustrators, often sourced from the Bologna Book Fair exhibitions and illustrators catalogue.

Always strive to improve on your work. Don't be afraid to try out something different and to work it up into acceptable examples. Above all, don't get left behind.

Making approaches for work

With your portfolio arranged and your target audience in mind, compile a list of publishing houses, packagers and magazines which you think may be suitable for your work.

An agent should know exactly where to place your work, and this may be the easier option (see below). However, you may wish to market yourself by making and going to appointments until you crack your first job.

Alternatively, you could make up a simple broadsheet comprising a black and white and two or three colour illustrations, together with your contact details, and have it colour photocopied or printed. Another inexpensive option is to have your own CDs made up and to send them instead. Send a copy to either the Art Director, the Creative Director or the Senior Commissioning Editor (for picture books) of each potential client on your list. Try to find out the name of the person you would like to see your work. Wait at least a week and then follow up your mailing with a phone call to ask if someone would like to see your portfolio.

Also consider investing in your own website which you can easily update yourself.

Know your capabilities

Know your strengths, but be even more aware of your weaknesses. You will gain far more respect if you admit to not being able to draw something particularly well than by going ahead and producing an embarrassing piece of artwork and having it rejected. You will be remembered for your professional honesty and that client may well try to give you a job where you can use your expertise.

Publishers need to know that you can turn out imaginative, creative artwork while closely following a text or brief, and be able to meet their deadline. It may take an illustrator three weeks to prepare roughs for 32 pages, three weeks to finish the artwork, plus a week to make any corrections. In addition, time has to be allowed for the roughs to be returned. On this basis, how many books can an illustrator realistically take on? Scheduling is of paramount importance (see below).

You will need to become familiar with 'publishing speak' – terms such as gutters, full bleed, holding line, overlays, vignettes, tps, etc. If you don't know the meaning of a term, ask – after all, if you have only recently left college you will not be expected to know all the jargon.

In the course of your work you will have to deal with such issues as contracts, copyright, royalties, public lending rights, rejection fees, etc. The Association of Illustrators, which exists to give help to illustrators in all areas, is well worth joining.

Organising your workload

When you have reached the stage when you have jobs coming through on a fairly regular basis, organise a comprehensive schedule for yourself so you do not overburden yourself with work. Include on it when roughs have to be submitted, how much work you can fit in while waiting for their approval, the deadline for the artwork, and so on. A wall chart can be helpful for this but another system may work better for you. It is totally unacceptable to deliver artwork late. If you think that you might run over time with your work, let your client know in advance as it may be possible to reach a new agreement for delivery.

Payment

There are two ways in which an illustrator may be paid for a commission for a book: a flat fee on receipt and acceptance of the artwork, or by an advance against a royalty of future sales. The advance offered could be less than a flat fee but it may result in higher earnings overall. If the book sells well, the illustrator will receive royalty payments twice a year for as long the book is in print.

You need to know from the outset how you are going to be paid. If it is by a flat fee, you may be given an artwork order with a number to be quoted when you invoice. Always read through orders to make sure you understand the terms and conditions. If you haven't been paid within 30 days, send a statement to remind the client, or make a quick phone call to ask when you can expect to receive payment.

With a royalty offer, a contract will be drawn up and this must be checked carefully. One of the clauses will state the breakdown of how and when you will be paid.

Once you have illustrated your first book you should register with the Public Lending Right Office (see page 226) so that you can receive a yearly payment on all UK library borrowings. You will need to cooperate with the author regarding percentages before submitting your own form. The PLR office will give you a reference number, and you then submit details to them of each book you illustrate. It mounts up and is a nice little earner!

Agents

The role of the agent is to represent the illustrator to the best of their ability and to the illustrator's best advantage. A good agent knows the marketplace and will promote illustrators' work where it will count. An agent may ask you to do one or two sample pieces to strengthen your portfolio, giving them a better chance of securing work for you.

Generally speaking, agents will look after you, your work schedules, payments, contracts, royalties, copyright issues, and try to ensure you have a regular flow of work which you not only enjoy but will stretch your talents to taking on bigger and better jobs. Without exposing your weaknesses, check that you have adequate time in which to do a job and that you are paid a fair rate for the work.

Some illustrators manage well without an agent, and having one is not necessarily a pathway to fame and fortune. Choose carefully: you need to both like and trust the agent and vice versa.

Agents' charges range from 25% to 30%. Find out from the outset how much a prospective agent will charge.

Finally

Do not be downhearted if progress is at first slow. Everyone starts by serving an apprenticeship, and it is a great opportunity to learn, absorb and soak up as much of the business as possible. Ask questions, get all the advice you can, and use what you learn to improve your craft and thereby your chances of landing a job. Publishers are always on the lookout for fresh talent and new ideas, and one day your talent will be the one they want.

Maggie Mundy has been representing illustrators for children's books since 1983. Her agency represents 25 European and British illustrators for children's books.

Children's character licensing

Joel Rickett gives an overview of children's character licensing across publishing, broadcasting and merchandising.

Characters that were once dreamt up by desperate parents in a bid to send their children to sleep are now big business. Names such as Peter Rabbit, Winnie the Pooh, Tintin, Babar and Mr Men are loved around the world. Their faces adorn T-shirts, soft toys, board games, pencil cases, milkshakes and even nappies. Barney and Kermit the Frog embark on world-wide stadium tours; in the summer of 2006 the Queen celebrated her 80th birthday by inviting Postman Pat, Mowgli and the BFG (Big Friendly Giant) to Buckingham Palace.

For this we can blame television series and films which carry these characters far and wide. They fuel a seemingly insatiable demand: in the UK alone, the children's licensing business is worth about £2.7 billion a year according to NPD Eurotoys (2004). About 22 per cent of the money spent on children up to the age of 14 is absorbed by character-branded products; for four to five year-olds, that proportion rises to a third.

In this licensed world Disney reigns supreme. Yet many of Disney's characters began with books and inspire children to turn back to the printed page. The healthy two-way flow between books and broadcast has been bolstered by the *Harry Potter* phenomenon and Peter Jackson's *Lord of the Rings* films. The enduring appeal of stories such as *Thomas the Tank Engine* has led to a stream of revivals of old favourites – Noddy, Bagpuss, Basil Brush, Muffin the Mule. No character is safe from a nostalgic resurrection.

The companies that control rights to these characters are serious stock market players. The pioneer is Hit Entertainment, which created all-singing Bob the Builder, and took Angelina Ballerina from the cosy confines of Katherine Holabird's stories to television sets, dolls and duvet covers. Hit is followed by Chorion (owner of Noddy and Mr Men) and Entertainment Rights (Postman Pat, Basil Brush).

The first thing licensing companies seek, after television distribution deals, is publishing partners. Books are still seen as crucial for establishing the character, building its authority, and winning the goodwill of parents. Kathleen Caper, marketing executive at the Copyrights Group, says: 'People hang on to their books and soft toys. Publishing is an essential part of childhood – DVDs become defunct and are not a family heirloom.'

Despite the dominance of television, characters can still exist outside it. Caper points out that only 10 episodes of Peter Rabbit are screened each year, while Paddington Bear has no television series. 'But they still do well – they have longevity. I don't think Teletubbies will be a classic brand. Our aim is for our characters to still be here in 100 years.'

Publishing with character

Children's book and magazine publishers have reacted to and even led this boom in character licensing. They work closely with authors, illustrators, animators and television producers to create a wide range of books and spin-off products around a central character. These span titles for the activity, leisure, educational and gift markets, across ages, and for different distribution channels (e.g. bookshops, supermarkets, school clubs, catalogues). Marketing and publicity strategies are tied closely to broadcast schedules.

Competition is fierce for the lead licences between a handful of UK publishing houses – Egmont, Scholastic, HarperCollins, Macmillan, Random House, Simon & Schuster and

Penguin, which runs Frederick Warne and the BBC's children's books operation. In 2005 the supermarket specialist Parragon poached the Disney books licence from Penguin – marking a significant mass market shift for the biggest brand generator.

But Parragon was too late to win one of the largest licensed franchises in recent years: Narnia. Back in 2000, HarperCollins paid tens of millions of pounds to the C.S. Lewis estate for the licence, gambling that the long-awaited Hollywood film would get the green light. So when Disney and Walden Media's production of *The Lion, the Witch and the Wardrobe* was finally scheduled for Christmas 2005 the publisher was determined to repeat its *Lord of the Rings* success. In the UK it ran pre-release advertisements with the strapline 'read it before you see it'. Then came 17 tie-in titles, from activity books and boxed sets to an official 'making of' guide, designed to appeal to new readers as well as fans of the classic books. For the main £400,000 campaign it created lampposts and life-sized lions for shops, as well as department store Christmas grottos.

Of course, if the film had been a flop then HarperCollins may have been left with piles of unsold stock. But despite a mixed critical reaction people flocked in their droves – it took $224 million in the US in its first three weeks, knocking *King Kong* from the number one spot. The debate around C.S. Lewis' Christian values – and Disney's $150 million marketing budget – also helped the publishing programme; in the UK HarperCollins sold more than 500,000 extra Narnia books and it posted a 24 per cent increase in its fourth-quarter operating profits to $77 million.

Despite such juggernaughts there are still opportunities for smaller publishers in the licensing market. For example the late Max Velthuijs' *Frog* series from tiny Andersen Press is being brought to life as *Frog & Friends* by Telescreen. Tony Ross' *Little Princess*, also from Andersen, has been commissioned by Channel Five and is due to run at end of 2006.

Such screen transitions must be handled with care to avoid damaging perceptions of the original books. Deborah Forte, president of Scholastic's broadcast arm Scholastic Media, says the adaptors should first identify what is 'sacred' about the character or series. She cites Clifford, the preschool character that Scholastic took from bestselling picture books into a major US television show. 'We adapted the property but identified the fundamental values and what was sacred to the author. We did not throw away the look or the character, or change the core relationship between Clifford and [owner] Emily Elizabeth'. Clifford has been the number one preschool show in the US for five years running and sales of Clifford books in the US grew from £4 million a year to £45 million a year after the animation was first broadcast. Forte says a good adaptation can generate a new audience for books: 'If the essence of the storytelling is there, readers will be gained'.

Mobile markets

All the talk among children's character specialists is of new technologies, predominantly video-on-demand and mobile phone formats. While the CD-Rom goldrush led up a blind alley, and the internet has so far proved more a marketing tool than a profit source, there's a strong sense that these new areas will transform the way characters and series are sold and watched. In music, sales of mobile ringtones have already overtaken CD singles; in 2005 the irritating Crazy Frog became the first mobile character to have a number one hit.

Several start-up firms operating in mobile formats are approaching publishers with a view to licensing content; David McKee's Mr Benn books are already being developed for mobile phones and related merchandise. The challenge for publishers is to make the new technology draw people back to real books. To this end Walker Books has created a series of animated DVDs based on some of its best-loved picture books, including Lucy Cousins' *Hooray for Fish*, Sam McBratney's *Guess How Much I Love You* and Martin Waddell's *Owl Babies*. The animations have been created by King Rollo Films, the company behind the Maisie animations.

Selling the spin-offs

Multimedia brands are nothing new. Captain Pugwash started as a comic strip in the 1950s, then became a book, then a television series. It was revived in the late 1990s with a retro feel. The world's oldest literary licensing programme is of course from Beatrix Potter. Within two years of *The Tale of Peter Rabbit* being published in 1902, Mopsy, Cotton-tail and Peter had their own dolls. Now sales of Beatrix Potter products from ceramics to baby food are worth £333 million a year. And soon we'll be treated to a biopic, *Miss Potter*, starring Renée Zellweger.

Kathleen Caper, whose Copyrights Group controls the Beatrix Potter spin-offs, believes its success underlines the need to keep brands consistent. 'In 1910 Peter Rabbit was about beauty and mischievous behaviour. We have been very careful to make sure those values have remained stable. We may brighten up the colours for a nursery age product, but we are still using the same artwork'. She contrasts this approach to *Winnie the Pooh*, where the values have become muddled under Disney's direction. 'He's still a successful character, but I'm not sure what he stands for now'.

So why do some book characters translate smoothly into spin-off products, yet others flop? Caper says there is no way to predict success: 'Sometimes the books do amazingly well, but licensing and merchandising don't'. The prime example is *Harry Potter*, where related products have failed to take off.

To minimise the risk, some licensers and publishers use focus groups to see how children react to new characters. They can then modify the character and advertising according to these 'play patterns' to ensure maximum pressure is put on parents. Some believe this approach has become overly aggressive but Dr Janine Spencer, director of the Centre for Research into Infant Behaviour (CRIB) says: 'Young children are attracted to novelty because that's how they learn. When you test children you find that they are drawn to any new object you introduce into a group of familiar objects. I think the industry should stop feeling guilty about selling to kids, because kids want things'.

One of the most successful UK spin-offs of recent years has been clothing and stationery based on the much-adored books from the current Children's Laureate Jacqueline Wilson and her long-time collaborator Nick Sharratt. Wilson told *Licensing* magazine: 'This not about cash. It's about doing delightful things that children will like. The products are extensions of the books'. Accordingly she took close interest in how they were developed: 'The products must be pretty and modern but also wholesome. I know that girls are conscious about the way they look and how they are seen but I am anxious not to encourage them to squeeze into little sexy tops and things like that. I don't think children need any encouragement to grow up faster than they need to'.

Tweens and tots

Wilson's comments highlight a relentless shift in the market over the last decade: the falling age of the 'consumer'. Whether due to media saturation or social and economic change, children are responsive to certain kinds of characters at ever-younger ages. For example the original Paddington Bear books were written for children aged eight and above, but Paddington has now become mainly a preschool character. 'Everything has shifted down,' Caper says. 'Kids are getting older younger.'

This has fuelled the 'tween' phenomenon, where girls aged 8–12 are fed a diet of music and fashion. But Wilson's series was successful because it provided an alternative to 'tween' marketing. Caper also notes a 'bounceback', where teenagers or adults again become absorbed by younger brands. Paddington T-shirts have recently become a hit with young teenage girls, and Bagpuss has just launched as a fashion brand to adults.

The preschool area has seen a character boom over the last five years, driven by frenetic competition between specialist broadcast slots such as CBeebies and Channel Five's Milkround. The names will be familiar to any parent: Boo-ba, Ballymory, Teletubbies, Pingu, Rubadubber, Fireman Sam. The market has been saturated, leaving little space for new brands.

This is mirrored in the picture book market, the source for much broadcast material. While star characters such as *The Gruffalo* (Julia Donaldson and Axel Scheffler) can shift more copies than ever, children's publishers have cut back heavily on their output. They are finding it tough to win shelf space in retailers who are slimming down their ranges to classic authors like Eric Carle (*The Hungry Caterpillar*) and Shirley Hughes. Picture books also suffer from a lack of media oxygen.

So with publishers and broadcasters both reluctant to take punts on untested properties, how can new creators break through? Caper says the answer is originality and persistence: 'Don't do a "me too" – it's about trying to create something that's original'. One route for young artists is stationery deals – for example winning a card license with a small greeting card house. There are myriad examples of characters that have gone from cards to books to television, such as *Scary Monsters*. Another idea is to self publish: you can then try to build your own audience, perhaps starting at local schools or bookshops.

Even if you make it into print and then sign a television deal, don't get overly excited: only an estimated 2 per cent of optioned books ever reach development stage. As ever, books should be a labour of love and an end in themselves.

Joel Rickett is Deputy Editor of *The Bookseller*, and writes regular columns for the *Guardian* and *Screen International*. At the audiovisual content show Mipcom in 2005, he hosted a seminar on licensing links between children's books and broadcasting.

Illustrators' agents

Before submitting work, artists are advised to make preliminary enquiries and to ascertain terms of work. Commission varies but averages 25–30%. The Association of Illustrators (see page 344) provides a valuable service for illustrators, agents and clients.

*Member of the Society of Artists Agents
†Member of the Association of Illustrators

Advocate

39 Church Road, London SW19 5DQ
tel 020-8879 1166 *fax* 020-8879 3303
email mail@advocate-art.com
website www.advocate-art.com
Director Edward Burns

Has 5 agents representing 110 artists and illustrators. Supplies work to book and magazine publishers, design and advertising agencies, greeting card and fine art publishers, and gift and ceramic manufacturers. Also has an original art gallery, stock library and international licensing agency for the character 'Newton's Law'. Founded as a co-operative in 1996.

Allied Artists/Artistic License

The Gallery@Richmond, 63 Sheen Road, Richmond upon Thames TW9 1YJ
tel 020-8334 1010 *fax* 020-8334 9900
email info@allied-artists.net,
mary@umbrellapublishing.ca
website www.allied-artists.net,
www.umbrellapublishing.ca
Contacts Gary Mills, Mary Burtenshaw

Represents over 40 artists, all of whom illustrate children's books. Specialises in highly finished realistic figure illustrations and stylised juvenile illustrations for children's books. Extensive library of stock illustrations. Commission: 33%. Founded 1983.

Arena*

Quantum Artists Ltd, 108 Leonard Street, London EC2A 4RH
tel 020-7613 4040 *fax* 020-7613 1441
email info@arenaworks.com
website www.arenaworks.com
Contact Tamlyn Francis

Represents 35 artists, half of whom produce children's material. Produces illustrations for picture books and children's fiction for all ages; also for book covers and design groups. Average commission 20%. Founded 1970.

The Art Agency (Wildlife Art Ltd)

The Lodge, Cargate Lane, Saxlingham Thorpe, Norwich NR15 1TU
tel (01508) 471500 *fax* (01508) 470391

email info@the-art-agency.co.uk
website www.the-art-agency.co.uk

Represents more than 40 artists producing top-quality, highly accurate and imaginative illustrations across a wide variety of subjects and for all age groups, both digitally and traditionally. Clients are in the UK and international, mainly in children's books and magazines/partworks, for fiction and non-fiction. Sae must be included with work submitted for consideration. Do not email portfolios. Commission: 30%. Founded 1992.

The Artworks†

40 Frith Street, London W1D 5LN
tel 020-7734 3333 *fax* 020-7734 3484
email info@theartworksinc.com
website www.theartworksinc.com
Contact Lucy Scherer, Stephanie Alexander

Represents 40 artists for illustrated gift books and children's books. Commission: 25% advances, 15% royalties.

Associated Freelance Artists Ltd

124 Elm Park Mansions, Park Walk, London SW10 0AR
tel 020-7352 6890 *fax* 020-7352 8125
email pekes.afa@virgin.net
Directors Eva Morris, Doug FitzMaurice

Freelance illustrators mainly in children's educational fields, and some greeting cards.

Beehive Illustration

42ᴀ Cricklade Street, Cirencester, Glos. GL7 1JH
tel (01285) 885149 *fax* (01285) 641291
email info@beehiveillustration.co.uk
website www.beehiveillustration.co.uk
Contact Paul Beebee

Represents over 70 artists specialising in ELT (English Language Teaching) books, education and general publishing illustration. Commission: 25%. Founded 1989.

Celia Catchpole Ltd

56 Gilpin Avenue, London SW14 8QY
tel 020-8255 4835 *fax* 020-8255 4835
Proprietor Celia Catchpole

Represents 9 artists specialising in artwork for picture books and storybooks for ages 0–12. Submit samples as A4 photocopies. Commission: 15%. Founded 1996. See also entry in *Children's literary agents UK and Ireland.*

The Copyrights Group Ltd
23 West Bar, Banbury, Oxon OX16 9SA
tel (01295) 672050 *fax* (01295) 672060
email enquiries@copyrights.co.uk
Chairman & Ceo Nicholas Durbridge, *Creative Director* Linda Pooley

Leading independent licensing organisation with an international team of staff working together to represent writers, artists and the owners of quality characters, fine art and brand names for licensing to manufacturers of consumer products and for consumer promotions. Properties include *Peter Rabbit, Paddington Bear, Spot, Flower Fairies, Maisy, Jacqueline Wilson, Horrible Histories, Benjamin the Elephant, Ivory Cats, The Snowman* and *The Wombles.*

Graham-Cameron Illustration
The Studio, 23 Holt Road, Sheringham, Norfolk NR26 8NB
tel (01263) 821333 *fax* (01263) 821334
email enquiry@graham-cameron-illustration.com
and Duncan Graham-Cameron, Graham-Cameron Illustration, 59 Redvers Road, Brighton BN2 4BF
tel (01273) 385890
website www.graham-cameron-illustration.com
Partners Mike Graham-Cameron, Helen Graham-Cameron, Duncan Graham-Cameron

Represents 37 artists. Undertakes all forms of illustration for publishing and communications. Specialises in educational and children's information books. Send A4 copies of sample illustrations with sae. No MSS. Founded 1985.

David Higham Associates Ltd – see
Children's literary agents UK and Ireland

John Hodgson Agency
38 Westminster Palace Gardens, Artillery Row, London SW1P 1RR
tel 020-7580 3773 *fax* 020-7222 4468

Represents 6 artists producing children's material. Specialises in children's picture books for 0–8 year-olds. Phone before sending samples. Enclose an sae with samples. Commission: 25%. Founded 1965.

The Illustration Cupboard
401 Langham House, 302 Regent Street, London W1B 3HH
tel/fax 020-7610 5481
email illustrationcupboard@yahoo.com
website www.illustrationcupboard.com
Chief Executive John Huddy

Represents over 50 artists, most of whom produce children's material, largely for ages 12–16. Specialises in the exhibition and sale of original contemporary

book illustration from around the world. Exhibitions are arranged throughout the year in the UK and abroad, and are also featured on the website. Founded 1996.

The Inkshed*
99 Chase Side, Enfield EN2 6NL
tel 020-8367 4545 *fax* 020-8367 6730
email makecontact@inkshed.co.uk
website www.inkshed.co.uk
Partners Andrea Plummer, Gordon Allen, *Contact* Abby Glassfield

Represents 31 artists who work across the board – advertising, design, publishing, editorial. Commission: 25–30%. Founded 1985.

Kathy Jakeman Illustration
Richmond Business Centre, 23–24 George Street, Richmond, Surrey TW9 1HY
tel 020-8973 2000
email kathy@kji.co.uk
website www.kji.co.uk

Represents 15 artists producing illustrations for children's publishing. Send samples by post only, *not* by email. Commission: 25%. Founded 1990.

LAW Ltd (Lucas Alexander Whitley)
14 Vernon Street, London W14 0RJ
tel 020-7471 7900 *fax* 020-7471 7910
website www.lawagency.co.uk
Contacts Philippa Milnes-Smith, Helen Norris

Illustrations for children's publishing for ages 0–16. Submit copies of samples (not originals) together with an sae for their return plus a covering letter and CV. Commission: 15% (20% overseas). Founded 1996.

David Lewis Illustration Agency
Worlds End Studios, 134 Lots Road, London SW10 0RJ
tel 020-7435 7762 *mobile* (07931) 824674
fax 020-7435 1945
email davidlewis34@hotmail.com
website www.davidlewisillustration.com
Director David Lewis, *Associate Director* Ramon Johns

All kinds of material for all areas of children's publishing, including educational, merchandising and toys. Represents approx. 25 artists, half of whom produce children's material. Send A4 colour or b&w copies of samples with return postage. Do not send CDs or emails. Commission: 30%. Founded 1974.

Frances McKay Illustration
15 Lammas Green, Sydenham Hill, London SE26 6LT
tel 020-8693 7006 *mobile* (07703) 344334
email frances@francesmckay.com
website www.francesmckay.com
Proprietor Frances McKay

Represents 20+ artists producing children's material, largely for book publishers and packagers. Also considers MSS for young children. Submit illustrations for age 4+ with an original slant, either as jpg files on CD, as low-res scans by email or send copies by post with sae. Commission: 25%. Founded 1999.

John Martin & Artists

12 Haven Court, Hatfield Peverel, Chelmsford, Essex CM3 2SD
tel (01245) 380337
email bernardjma@aol.com
website www.jm-a.co.uk
Contact Bernard Bowen-Davies

Represents 12 illustrators, mainly producing artwork for children's fiction/non-fiction and educational books. Include return postage with submissions. Founded 1956.

Maggie Mundy Illustrators' Agency

14 Ravenscourt Park Mansions, Dalling Road, London W6 0HG
tel 020-8748-2391
email maggiemundy@compuserve.com

Represents 5 artists in varying styles of illustration for children's books. The Agency's books are closed.

NB Illustration[†]

40 Bowling Green Lane, London EC1R 0NE
tel 020-7278 9131 *fax* 020-7278 9121
email info@nbillustration.co.uk
website www.nbillustration.co.uk
Directors Joe Najman, Charlotte Berens, Paul Najman

Represents 35+ artists, of whom 10% produce children's material for picture books and educational publishing. Submit samples either as 72 dpi jpeg files by email or by post with an sae. Commission: 30%. Founded 2000.

The Organisation*

The Basement, 69 Caledonian Road, London N1 9BT
tel 020-7833 8268 *fax* 020-7833 8269
email lorraine@organisart.co.uk
website www.organisart.co.uk
Contact Lorraine Owen

Represents 60 artists, 75% of whom produce children's material for all age ranges. Both traditional and digital illustration can be supplied to cover all markets, including the children's and educational book markets. Also produces illustrations for other print markets, advertising, packaging and editorial. Before submitting samples research the website. New artists must not have a similar style to one already represented. Send samples either by email or on a CD by post, or send printed images with sae. Average commission: 30%. Founded 1987.

Oxford Designers & Illustrators Ltd

Aristotle House, Aristotle Lane, Oxford OX2 6TR
tel (01865) 512331 *fax* (01865) 512408

email richardcorfield@odi-illustration.co.uk
website www.o-d-i.com
Directors Peter Lawrence (managing), Richard Corfield, Andrew King

Studio of 20 artists, three-quarters of whom produce preschool to A level educational book illustration. Also produces work for other publishers, business and industry. Submit samples by email. Not an agency. Commission: 20%. Founded 1968.

PFD – see *Children's literary agents UK and Ireland*, page 179

Sylvie Poggio Artists' Agency[†]

36 Haslemere Road, London N8 9RB
tel 020-8341 2722 020-8374 1725
website www.sylviepoggio.com

Represents a wide spectrum of professional artists who work in the fields of contemporary, conceptual, cartoony, realistic and digital illustrations.

Linda Rogers Associates

PO Box 330, 163 Half Moon Lane, London SE24 9WB
tel 020-7501 9106
email lr@lindarogers.net
website www.lindarogers.net
Partners Linda Rogers, Peter Sims, Jess Sims

Represents approx. 65 illustrators producing children's material. Specialises in books and magazines, all types, all ages. Looking for contemporary, multi-racial, figurative work. Submit artwork samples by post with sae for their return, *not* by email. Will not view artists' websites. Commission: 25%. Founded 1973.

Elizabeth Roy Literary Agency

White Cottage, Greatford, Nr Stamford, Lincs. PE9 4PR
tel/fax (01778) 560672

Handles illustrations for children's books. Only interested in exceptional material. Illustrators should research the children's book market before sending samples, which must include figure work. Send by post with return postage; no CD, disk or email submissions. Founded 1990. See also entry in *Children's literary agents UK and Ireland*.

SGA Illustration Agency

(formerly Simon Girling & Associates)
18 High Street, Hadleigh, Suffolk IP7 5AP
tel (01473) 824083 *fax* (01473) 827846
email info@sgadesignart.com
website www.sgadesignart.com

Represents over 50 illustrators, all of whom produce children's material. Works mainly within publishing: early learning board books through all ages to teenage, picture books, and educational and trade material. Also manages projects from conception to final film. Especially interested in figurative artists. Submit samples as jpgs or printed copies by post with an sae. Commission: 30%. Founded 1985.

Specs Art
93 London Road, Cheltenham, Glos. GL52 6HL
tel (01242) 515951
email roland@specsart.com
website www.specsart.com
Partners Roland Berry, Stephanie Prosser

Represents 30 artists, all of whom produce children's material for all ages. High-quality illustration and animation work for advertisers, publishers and all other forms of visual communication. Specialises in licensed character illustration. Submit about 6 jpegs by email. Commission: 25%. Founded 1982.

Temple Rogers Artists' Agency
120 Crofton Road, Orpington, Kent BR6 8HZ
tel (01689) 826249 *fax* (01689) 896312

Contact Patrick Kelleher

Illustrations for children's educational books and magazine illustrations. Commission: by arrangement.

Vicki Thomas Associates
195 Tollgate Road, London E6 5JY
tel 020-7511 5767 *fax* 020-7473 5177
email vickithomasassociates@yahoo.co.uk
website www.vickithomasassociates.com
Consultant Vicki Thomas

Represents approx. 50 artists, three-quarters of whom produce children's material for all ages. Specialises in designing gift products and considers images for publishing, toys, stationery, clothing, decorative accessories, etc. Submit samples as photocopies with a covering letter. Commission: 25–30%. Founded 1985.

Winning the greeting card game

The UK population spends £1.2 billion a year on greeting cards. Jacqueline Brown helps to guide artists to success in this fiercely competitive industry.

The UK greeting card industry leads the world on two counts – design and innovation and per capita send. On average people in the UK send 50 cards a year, 85% of which are bought by women.

But just how do you, as an artist, go about satisfying this voracious appetite of the card-sending public? There are two main options: either to become a greeting card publisher yourself or to supply existing greeting card publishers with your artwork and be paid a fee for doing so.

The idea of setting up your own greeting card publishing company may sound exciting, but this decision should not be taken lightly. Going down this route will involve taking on all the set up and running costs of a publishing company as well as the production, selling and administrative responsibilities. This often leaves little time for you to do what you do best – creating the artwork.

There are estimated to be around 800 greeting card publishers in the UK, ranging in size from one-person operations to multinational corporations, roughly 200 of which are regarded as 'serious' publishers (see Card and stationery publishers). Not all of them accept freelance artwork, but a great many do. Remember, whatever the size of the company, all publishers rely on good designs.

Some greeting card language

Own brand/bespoke publishers. These design specific to a retailer's needs.

Spring Seasons. The industry term to describe greeting cards for Valentine's Day, Mother's Day, Easter and Father's Day. Publishers generally launch these ranges all together in June/July.

Greeting card types. Traditional; cute or whimsical; contemporary/quirky art; juvenile; handmade or hand-finished; fine art; photographic, humorous.

Finishes and treatments. Artists will not be expected to know the production techniques and finishes, but a working knowledge is often an advantage. Some of the most commonly used finishes and treatments include: embossing (raised portion of a design), die-cutting (where the card is cut into a shape or includes an aperture), foiling (metallic film) and flitter (a glitter-like substance).

Finding the right publishers

While some publishers concentrate on producing a certain type of greeting card (e.g. humorous, fine art or juvenile), the majority publish a variety of greeting card ranges. Unfortunately, this makes it more difficult for you as an artist to target the most appropriate potential publishers for your work. There are various ways in which you can research the market, quickly improve your publisher knowledge and, therefore, reduce the amount of wasted correspondence:

- **Go shopping.** Browse the displays in card shops, newsagents and other high street shops, department stores and gift shops. This will not only give you an insight into what is already available but also which publishers may be interested in your work. Most publishers include their contact details on the backs of the cards.
- **Trade fairs.** There are a number of trade exhibitions held during the year at which publishers exhibit their greeting card ranges to retailers and overseas distributors. By visiting these exhibitions, you will gain a broad overview of the design trends in the industry,

as well as the current ranges of individual publishers. Some publishers are willing to meet artists and look through their portfolios on the stand but others are not. If you believe your work could be relevant for them, ask for a contact name and follow it up afterwards. Have a supply of business cards handy, perhaps illustrated with some of your work, to leave with publishers.

Types of publishers

There are two broad categories of publisher – wholesale and direct-to-retail – each employing a different method of distribution to reach the retailer.

Wholesale publishers distribute their products to the retailer via greeting card wholesalers or cash-and-carry outlets. They work on volume sales and have a rapid turnover of designs, many being used with a variety of different captions. For example, the same floral design may be used for cards for mothers, grandmothers, aunts and sisters. It is therefore usual for the artist to leave a blank space on the design to accommodate the caption. Until recently, wholesale publishers were generally only interested in traditional, cute and juvenile designs, but they now publish across the board, including contemporary and humorous ranges.

Further information

The Greeting Card Association
United House, North Road, London N7 9DP
tel 020-7619 0396
email gca@max-publishing.co.uk
website www.greetingcardassociation.org.uk

The UK trade association for greeting card publishers. Its website contains leaflets on freelance designing and writing for greeting cards complete with lists of publishers which accept freelance work. The Ladder Club meets once a year for a one-day seminar for would-be/fledgling publishers, many of whom are artists or photographers looking to publish their own work. The seminar covers all aspects of publishing and costs approx. £25.

Trade fairs
Spring & Autumn Fairs Birmingham, NEC
Contact TPS *tel* 020-8277 5830
Takes place First Sunday in Sept and Feb

Top Drawer, Earls Court
website www.topdrawer.co.uk,
www.pulse-london.co.uk
Contact Clarion Events *tel* 020-7370 8374
Takes place 10–12 Sept 2006 (at Olympia),
14–16 Jan 2007, 21–24 May 2007 (tbc)

Home and Gift, Harrogate
website homeandgift.co.uk
Contact Clarion Events *tel* 020-7370 8200
Takes place mid July

Trade magazines
Greetings Today
(formerly Greetings Magazine)
Lema Publishing, Unit 1, Queen Mary's Avenue, Watford, Herts. WD18 7JR
tel (01923) 250909 *fax* (01923) 250995
Publisher-in-Chief Malcolm Naish, *Editor* Vicky Denton
Monthly £45 p.a. (other rates on application)

Articles, features and news related to the greetings card industry. Includes Artists Directory for aspiring artists wishing to attract the eye of publishers. Runs seminars for small publishers and artists.

Progressive Greetings Worldwide
Max Publishing, United House, North Road, London N7 9DP
tel 020-7700 6740 *fax* 020-7607 6411
12 p.a. (£40 p.a.)

The official magazine of the Greeting Card Association. Provides an insight to the industry, including an up-to-date list of publishers, a new product section and a free showcase for artists, illustrators and verses. Special supplements include *Focus on Art Cards*, *Focus on Humorous Cards*, *Focus on Words & Sentiments*, *Focus on Kids* and *Focus on Giftwrap*.

Hosts The Henries, the greeting card industry awards. The September edition includes details of the finalists in the different categories and the November issue features the winners.

Direct-to-retail (DTR) publishers supply retailers via sales agents or reps. Most greeting cards sold through specialist card shops and gift shops are supplied by DTR publishers, which range from multinational corporations down to small, trendy niche publishing companies. These publishers market series of ranges based on distinctive design themes or characters. Categories of DTR cards include contemporary art/fun, fine art, humour, children's, photographic, traditional and handmade.

Approaching a publisher

Unfortunately, there is no standard way of approaching and submitting work to a card publisher. The first step is to establish that the publisher you wish to approach accepts work from freelance artists; then find out their requirements for submission and to whom it should be addressed.

It is always better to send several examples of your work to show the breadth of your artistic skills. Some publishers prefer to see finished designs while others are happy with well-presented sketches. Never send originals: instead send photocopies, laser copies or photographs, and include at least one design in colour. Never be tempted to sell similar designs to two publishers – a bad reputation will follow you around.

Some publishers will be looking to purchase individual designs for specific sending occasions while others will be more intent on looking for designs which could be developed to make up a range. Bear in mind that publishers work a long way in advance, e.g. Christmas ranges are launched to the retailers in January. Development of a range may take up to six months prior to launching.

Also remember that cards in retail outlets are rarely displayed in their entirety. Therefore, when designing a card make sure that some of the 'action' appears in the top half.

When interest is shown

Some publishers respond to submissions from artists immediately while others prefer to deal with them on a monthly basis. A publisher's response may be in the form of a request for more submissions of a specific design style or of a specific character. This speculative development work is usually carried out free of charge. Always meet your deadline (news travels fast in the industry).

A publisher interested in buying your artwork will probably then issue you with a contract. This may cover aspects such as the terms of payment; rights of usage of the design (e.g. is it just for greeting cards or will it include giftwrap and/or stationery?); territory of usage (most publishers want worldwide rights); and ownership of copyright or license period.

There is no set industry standard rate of pay for greeting card artists. Publishers lpay artists either on a per design or per range basis in one of the following ways:

● **Flat fee.** A one-off payment is made to the artist for ownership of a design for an unlimited period. The industry standard is around £200–£250 for a single design, and payment on a sliding scale for more than one design.

● **Licensing fee.** The publisher is granted the right to use a piece of artwork for a specified number of years, after which the full rights revert to the artist. Payment to the artist is approximately £150 upwards per design.

● **Licensing fee** plus royalty. As above plus a royalty payment on each card sold. Artists would generally receive a minimum of £100 for the licensing fee plus 3% of the trade price of each card sold.

- **Advance royalty deal.** A goodwill advance on royalties is paid to the artist. In the case of a range, the artist would receive a goodwill advance of say £500–£1000 plus 5% additional royalty payment once the threshold is reached.
- **Royalty only.** The artist receives regular royalty payments, generally paid quarterly, based on the number of cards sold. Artists should expect to receive a sales report and royalty statement.

The fees stated above should only be regarded as a rough guideline. Fees and advances are generally paid on completion of artwork. Publishers which have worldwide rights pay royalties for sales overseas to artists, although these will be on a pro rata basis to the export trade price.

Jacqueline Brown is editor of *Progressive Greetings Worldwide* and general secretary of the Greeting Card Association.

Card and stationery publishers

Before submitting work, artists are advised to write giving details of the work they have to offer, and asking for requirements.

*Member of the Greeting Card Association

Card Connection Ltd*
Park House, South Street, Farnham, Surrey
GU9 7QQ
tel (01252) 892300 *fax* (01252) 892363
email ho@card-connection.co.uk
website www.card-connection.co.uk
Managing Director Simon Hulme, *Senior Product Manager* Natalie Turner

Everyday and seasonal designs. Styles include cute, fun, traditional, contemporary, humour and photographic. Submit colour copies. Humorous copy and jokes plus sentimental verse. Founded 1992.

Carlton Cards Ltd*
Mill Street East, Dewsbury, West Yorkshire
WF12 9AW
tel (01924) 465200
website www.carltoncards.co.uk
Group Marketing Director Keith Auty, *Product Development Director* Josephine Loughran

All types of artwork, any size; submit as colour roughs, colour copies or transparencies. Especially interested in humorous artwork and ideas.

Carte Blanche Greetings Ltd*
Unit 3, Chichester Business Park, Tangmere, Chichester, West Sussex PO20 2FT
website www.metoyou.co.uk
Contact Stephen Haines

Greetings cards, gifts and stationery in the *Me to You* brand, featuring the toy bear with the blue nose. Founded 1987.

Caspari Ltd*
9 Shire Hill, Saffron Walden, Essex CB11 3AP
tel (01799) 513010 *fax* (01799) 513101
Managing Director Keith Entwisle

Traditional fine art/classic images; 5 x 4in transparencies. No verses. Founded 1990.

Simon Elvin Ltd*
Wooburn Industrial Park, Wooburn Green, Bucks
HP10 0PE
tel (01628) 526711 *fax* (01628) 53148
email rachel.bradley@simonelvin.com
website www.simonelvin.com
Art Director Isabel Scott Evans, *Studio Co-ordinator* Rachel Bradley

Female/male traditional and contemporary designs, female/male cute, wedding/anniversary, birth congratulations, fine art, photographic animals, flowers and male imagery, traditional sympathy, juvenile ages, special occasions and gift wrap.

Looking for submissions that show flair, imagination and an understanding of greeting card design. Artists should familiarise themselves with the ranges, style and content. Submit a small collection of either colour copies or prints (no original artwork) and include an sae for return of work. Alternatively email jpegs to the Studio Co-ordinator.

4C–Charity Christmas Card Council
Cards World Ltd, 49 Cross Street, London N1 2BB
tel (0845) 230 0046 *fax* (0845) 230 0048
email 4c@charitycards.org
website www.charitycards.org

Traditional and contemporary Christmas cards for the corporate market. Submit artwork on CD-Rom or 5 x 4in transparencies. No verses. Charitable not-for-profit organisation. Founded 1966.

Gallery Five Ltd*
The Old Bakery, 1 Bellingham Road, London
SE6 2PN
tel 020-8741 3891 *fax* 020-8741 4444
website www.galleryfive.co.uk

Send samples of work FAO 'Gallery Five Art Studio'. Colour photocopies, Mac-formatted zip/CD acceptable, plus sae. No verses.

Gemma International Ltd*
Linmar House, 6 East Portway, Andover, Hants
SP10 3LU
tel (01264) 388400 *fax* (01264) 366243
website www.gemma-international.co.uk
Directors L. Rudd-Clarke, A. Parkin, T. Rudd-Clarke, W. O'Loughlin, K. Bishop

Cute, contemporary, leading-edge designs for children, teens and young adults. Founded 1984.

Gibson Greetings International Ltd
Gibson House, Hortonwood 30, Telford, Shrops.
TF1 7YF
tel (01952) 608333 *fax* (01952) 605259
email linda-marshall@gibson-greetings.co.uk
Product Director Linda Marshall

All everyday and seasonal illustrations: cute, humorous, juvenile, traditional and contemporary designs, as well as surface pattern. Greeting card traditional and humorous verse. Founded 1991.

Hallmark Cards Plc*
Hallmark House, Bingley Road, Heaton, Bradford
BD9 6SD
tel (01274) 252000
website www.hallmarkuk.com
Freelance submissions Emma Charlesworth

Artwork: All subjects will be considered. Submit
10–12 colour samples (not originals, as work cannot
be returned) which demonstrate the diversity of your
work. Ensure your name is on all work. Words: As
there is an in-house editorial team, only humour
writing submissions will be considered.

Hanson White – Gibson Hanson Graphics
2nd Floor, AMP House, Dingwall Road, Croydon
CR0 2LX
tel 020-8260 1200 fax 020-8260 1213
email hannah.turpin@gibsonhanson.co.uk,
sally.hipkins@gibsonhanson.co.uk
Submissions Editors Hannah Bonomini, Sally Hipkins

Humorous artwork and cartoons for greeting cards,
including Christmas, Valentine's Day, Mother's Day
and Father's Day. Humorous copy lines and
punchline jokes, funny poems and rhymes.
Guidelines available. Founded 1958.

Jarrold Publishing
(incorporating Pitkin and Unichrome brands)
Whitefriars, Norwich NR3 1JR
tel (01603) 763300 fax (01603) 662748
email publishing@jarrold.co.uk
website www.jarrold-publishing.co.uk
Directors Margot Russell-King (managing), Ben
Carter (finance), Steve Plackett (supply chain gift &
stationery)

UK tourism and heritage guide books and souvenirs,
calendars, diaries and gift stationery. Unsolicited
MSS, synopses and ideas welcome but approach in
writing before submitting to Marketing Department.
Founded 1770.

The Monster Factory*
Unit 207, Welsbach House, 3–9 Broomhill Road,
London SW18 4JQ
tel 020-8875 9988 fax 020-8870 4488
email info@themonsterfactory.com
website www.themonsterfactory.com
Directors Martin Grix, Kate Eagar

Publishers of innovative stationery with a funky,
design-led feel. Specialises in handmade ranges,
unusual printing techniques and quirky illustration.
Will consider original new concepts and fresh
artwork styles with bags of character and humour. Do
not send original artwork. No verses. Founded 2000.

The Paper House Group plc*
Waterwells Drive, Gloucester, Glos. GL2 2PH
tel (01452) 888999 fax (01452) 888912

email art@paperhouse.co.uk
website www.paperhouse.co.uk

Specialises in cartoon humour illustration,
contemporary art styles and traditional verse design
for special occasions and family birthday.

Paperlink Ltd*
356 Kennington Road, London SE11 4LD
tel 020-7582 8244 fax 020-7587 5212
email info@paperlinkcards.com
website www.paperlinkcards.com
Directors Louise Tighe, Tim Porte, Tim Purcell

Publishers of ranges of humorous and contemporary
art greetings cards. Produce products under licence
for charities. Founded 1986.

Pepperpot
Royston Road, Duxford, Cambridge CB2 4QY
tel (01223) 836825 fax (01223) 833321
Publishing Controller Linda Worsfold

Gift stationery, photo albums. No submissions
without sae. Division of Copywrite Designs Ltd.

Pineapple Park*
58 Wilbury Way, Hitchin, Herts. SG4 0TP
tel (01462) 442021 fax (01462) 440418
email info@pineapplepark.co.uk
website www.pineapplepark.co.uk
Directors Peter M. Cockerline, Sarah M. Parker

Illustrations and photographs for publication as
greetings cards. Contemporary, cute, humour: submit
artwork or laser copies with sae. Photographic florals
always needed. Humour copy/jokes accepted without
artwork. Also concepts for ranges. Founded 1993.

Nigel Quiney Publications Ltd
Cloudesley House, Shire Hill, Saffron Walden, Essex
CB11 3FB
tel (01799) 520200 fax (01799) 520100
website www.nigelquiney.com
Contact Alison Butterworth, Creative Director

Everyday and seasonal greetings cards and giftwrap
including fine art, photographic, humour, fun art,
contemporary and cute. Submit colour copies,
photographs or transparencies: no original artwork.

Rainbow Cards Ltd*
Kingswood Business Park, Holyhead Road,
Albrighton, Wolverhampton, West Midlands
WV7 3AU
tel (01902) 376000 fax (01902) 376001
email sales@rainbowcards.co.uk
website www.rainbowcards.co.uk

Artwork for humorous and traditional greetings
cards. Founded 1976.

Really Good*
The Old Mast House, The Square, Abingdon, Oxon
OX14 5AR

tel (01235) 537888 *fax* (01235) 537779
email potatoes@reallygood.uk.com
website www.reallygood.uk.com
Director David Hicks

Always looking for fun and funny artwork in a quirky or modern way to publish on cards, stationery or gifts. Send samples on paper rather than on disk, or email website link or small files to view. Allow plenty of time for review. Founded 1987.

Santoro Graphics Ltd

Rotunda Point, 11 Hartfield Crescent, London
SW19 3RL
tel 020-8781 1100 *fax* 020-8781 1101
email enquiries@santorographics.com
website www.santorographics.com
Directors Lucio Santoro, Meera Santoro (art)

Publishers of innovative and award-winning designs for greetings cards, giftwrap and gift stationery. Bold, contemporary images with an international appeal. Subjects covered: contemporary, pop-up, cute, quirky, fashion, fine art, retro. Submit samples as colour photocopies, transparencies, CD-Roms or via email as jpeg or PDF files. Founded 1985.

Wishing Well Studios Ltd*

Kellet Close, Martland Park, Wigan, Lancs. WN5 0LP
tel (01942) 218888 *fax* (01942) 218899
email nickyh@wishingwell.co.uk,
susie.linley@wishingwell.co.uk
website www.wishingwell.co.uk
Artist contact Nicky Harrison, *Writer contact* Susie Linley

Rhyming and prose verse 4–24 lines long; also jokes. All artwork styles considered but do not send originals.

Publishing practice
Publishing agreements

Before signing a publisher's agreement, it should be thoroughly checked. Caroline Walsh introduces the key points of this very important contract.

So, you've done the difficult bit and persuaded a publisher to make an offer to publish your book. But how do you know if you're getting a fair deal? And what should you be looking out for on the contract? I would always advise an author or illustrator to engage an agent. An agent will ensure that the contract gives you the best possible chance of maximising your income from a book. Alternatively, the Society of Authors (see page 333) and the Writers' Guild of Great Britain (see page 361) will both check publishing agreements for their members. In addition, there are lawyers who specialise in publishing contracts and for those who prefer to go it alone, there are some useful books on the subject listed at the end of this article.

What follows is a whistle-stop tour around the key points of a publishing contract, especially for those writing for children. To begin, the offer from the publisher should come in writing clearly setting out exactly what rights the publisher wants to license and what they are willing to pay for those rights. A contract is a business agreement for the supply of goods or performance of work at a specified price. Normally, that payment comes as an advance against royalties. Occasionally, a flat fee payment is appropriate, but a royalty allows the author to share in the income from a book throughout its life and is therefore generally preferable. Perhaps the most important point of all is that you make sure you fully understand which rights are being licensed under the contract and aren't seduced merely into worrying about the advance and royalty (tempting though they may be!)

Publishers' agreements often have useful headings for each clause and I've used some of those headings here for ease of reference.

Licence
The very first thing to be clear about is what is being licensed to the publisher. For a new book one expects to grant to the publisher, for the legal term of copyright, the exclusive right to publish and sell the work in certain forms. The standard grant is of 'volume form', which means all book forms (hardback, paperback, other formats). However, the offer or contract may also state other forms, for example serial (newspaper and magazine rights) or audio rights. Some publishers' contracts include all-encompassing wording such as 'all media forms currently in existence and hereinafter invented'. This in effect hands control to the publisher of a wide range of rights, including electronic, dramatic (film, television, radio), merchandising and so on. In such a case, it's likely that the author's share of income from such rights will be less than it would be were the author to reserve those rights and have them handled separately.

Territory
Territory states *where* the publisher has the right to sell or sub-license the book. For picture books of all kinds, fiction and non-fiction, UK publishers generally require world rights

as the UK market alone is not large enough to sustain the costs of four-colour printing. US publishers are lucky enough to have a sufficiently large home market to mean they are not reliant on foreign sales and therefore will not always require world rights.

For fiction (i.e. novels) a judgement needs to be made about which territories should be granted to the publisher. English language rights are made up of two large mutually exclusive territories: the UK and Traditional British Commonwealth (including or excluding Canada) on the one hand and the USA, its dependencies and the Philippines on the other. The rest of the world is considered an open market. One could grant Traditional British Commonwealth rights in the English Language to a publisher, thereby reserving American and translation rights to be sold separately. Or one could grant World English Language rights, so the publisher can sell on US rights while translation rights are held in reserve to be sold separately. Or again, one could grant world rights to the originating publisher.

When thinking of granting a wide range of territories to a publisher, it is worth checking out how proactive and successful their foreign rights department is. It may be possible to speak to the foreign rights manager and find out for yourself if they have a good track record. An agent will have an informed view on a publisher's expertise in this area and furthermore, they will probably either be experienced themselves in selling foreign and US rights, or will work with associate agencies in all the different language territories. Publishers will take 15%–30% share on US and foreign sales and, if you have an agent too, their commission will also be deducted before you receive your percentage. Agents will generally charge 15%–20% on US and foreign sales.

Advances

We've all read the newspaper headlines about huge advances, but the fact is most children's book advances currently fall within the range of £1000–£25,000. For books that will be published in the trade (i.e. by a mainstream publishing house and where the book will appear in bookshops) most offers are framed as an advance against royalties. Advances may be paid in one go, on signature, but don't be surprised if the publisher proposes paying half on signature and half on publication, or in thirds (signature, delivery and publication), or even in quarters (signature, delivery, hardback publication, paperback publication), though the latter is more common when the advance offered is substantial.

Royalties

As a very basic rule of thumb, hardbacks attract a 10% base royalty and paperbacks 7.5%. Bear in mind that on picture books these figures will be shared between author and illustrator. Sometimes, children's black and white illustrated fiction titles also bear a small royalty for the illustrator, which will come out of the total royalty. Most novelty books, including board books, work on a smaller royalty, for example 5% or even less because of the high production costs and relatively low retail price.

Ideally, the royalty will escalate to a higher level when a certain number of sales have been achieved and this can prove to be very important if a book becomes a long-running success.

For a trade book the royalties should ideally be based on the recommended retail price for home sales. Export sales and sales to book clubs or book fairs are usually calculated on the publisher's price received (or net receipts). The contract should set out each type of sale and list the appropriate royalty rate. Nowadays particular attention needs to be paid to 'high discount' clauses in contracts. However good the main home sales royalty is, a disadvantageous high discount clause can mean that disappointingly few of the sales attract the full royalty and consequently revenues will be much reduced. This is especially important now because retailers are pushing publishers hard on discounts. An agent will be used to negotiating carefully on precisely this kind of area to secure the best possible terms.

Co-edition royalties

As previously mentioned, picture books in the UK are very dependent upon publishers selling American and foreign language co-editions. Therefore, it is important to note on the contract what the author's share of any such co-edition deals will be. These generally fall under two categories in the contract:

• If the UK publisher prints for the foreign publisher, the books are usually sold for a fixed price per copy as 'royalty inclusive' and the author's and artist's share will be expressed as a percentage of the publisher's price received. These deals help to get the book published by bringing the unit cost down and they begin the process of earning out the advance.

• US and foreign language sales also fall under the heading of subsidiary rights. In this case, the UK publisher may or may not print the books, but the US or foreign publisher will have agreed to pay an advance and royalty for the right to sell the book in their territory (a 'royalty exclusive' deal). The author's and artist's share in this instance shouldn't be less than 50% and it could be much more. If a book is particularly sought after by foreign or US publishers, such a royalty exclusive deal could mean that the original UK advance is earned out immediately.

Subsidiary rights

Other subsidiary rights include reprint rights (large print, book club, paperback reprint, etc), serial rights (the right to publish in newspapers and magazines), anthology and quotation rights, educational rights, audio rights and so on. There will usually be a percentage listed against each right and that is the author's share of any deal. Generally the author receives at least 50% on these deals and more in the case of serial, US and translation rights. The rights listed in the sub-rights clause should be checked against the opening grant of rights clause to see that they conform.

Delivery and publication

There should be clauses in the contract that state the agreed delivery date of the book and give some indication of what is expected, for example 'a work for children to be written and illustrated by the said author to a length of not more than 25,000 words plus approximately 50 black and white line illustrations'. There should also be an undertaking by the publisher to publish the work within a stated time period, for example 'within 12 months from delivery of the complete typescript and artwork'. There might also be an indication of what the published price will be.

Copyright and moral rights

As you are licensing your work, you should retain copyright and there should be a clause that obliges the publisher to include a copyright line in every edition of the work published or sub-licensed by them. The author's moral rights are also often asserted within the contract.

Production

Though the publishers will generally insist on having the final decision regarding details of production, publication and advertising, they should agree to consult meaningfully with the author over the blurb, catalogue copy, jacket and cover design. There should also be an undertaking to supply the author with proofs for checking and enough time for the author to check those proofs.

Accounts

Publishers usually account to authors twice a year for royalties earned. Even if the advance has not earned out, the publishers should still send a royalty statement. Royalty statements are notoriously enigmatic and vary from publisher to publisher. Mistakes on royalty statements are more common than one might like to think and an agent will be used to checking royalty statements carefully and taking up any anomalies with the publisher.

In addition to the twice-yearly accounting, once the initial advance has been earned out, an agent will be able to ensure that any substantial income from sub-rights deals (e.g. in excess of £100) will be paid immediately.

Electronic rights

The electronic book market is in its infancy and norms have not yet been established. If a publisher insists on including these rights in the contract, one should aim to negotiate a royalty of 50% of the publisher's price received or, at the very least, leave the royalty rate to be mutually agreed at a later date.

Reversion

It's important to ensure that the author can get back the rights to their book if the publisher either fails to stick to the terms of the contract or lets the book go out of print and leaves it out of print for six to nine months after receiving a written request to reprint it. It is well worth reclaiming rights to out of print books as it may be possible to re-license them later on.

Assignment

A small but important clause that may need to be added states that the publishers shall not assign the rights granted to them without the author's express written consent. This gives the author at least a degree of control over the book's destiny if the publishing company runs into trouble or is sold.

Educational publishers' contracts

Many children's authors begin as writers for educational publishers and quite a number continue to work in this field alongside producing books for the trade market. Educational publishers usually commission tightly briefed work. Advances are generally modest and the royalties are based on the publishers' price received. However, substantial sums can eventually be earned. Educational publishers usually expect to be granted a very wide range of rights and while it makes sense to grant audio or electronic rights where the publisher has the capacity to produce or license such formats for their market, it may be possible and desirable to reserve, for example, dramatic and merchandising rights. However, discretion is needed here. If, for example, the publisher is commissioning writers to create stories about a given set of characters created by the publisher, then the publisher will rightly expect to control such rights.

That really is a scratching of the surface of publishing agreements. Do take advice if you don't feel confident that the contract presented to you is fair. It seems a very obvious thing to say but always read a publishing agreement carefully before signing it and if anything in it isn't clear, ask for an explanation. Remember, too, that it's a negotiation and that despite publishers' talk of 'standard terms' and 'standard agreements', it is always possible to make amendments to contracts.

Caroline Walsh is a literary agent and a director of David Higham Associates Ltd (www.davidhigham.co.uk). She specialises in the children's book market.

Useful reading
The following books provide useful advice on publishing agreements – but don't forget to engage that agent!

Clark, Charles (ed.), *Publishing Agreements: A Book of Precedents*, Tolley, 6th edn, 2002
Flint, Michael F., *A User's Guide to Copyright*, Tottel Publishing, 2005
Legat, Michael, *An Author's Guide to Publishing*, Robert Hale, 3rd edn revised, 1998
Legat, Michael, *Understanding Publishers' Contracts*, Robert Hale, 2nd edn revised, 2002

FAQs about ISBNs

The ISBN Agency receives a large number of enquiries about the ISBN system. The most frequently asked questions are answered here.

What is an ISBN?

An ISBN (International Standard Book Number) is a product identifier used by publishers, booksellers and libraries for ordering, listing and stock control purposes. It enables them to identify a specific edition of a specific title in a specific format from a particular publisher. The digits are always divided into four parts, separated by spaces or hyphens. The four parts can be of varying length and are as follows:

Contact details

UK ISBN Agency
3rd Floor, Midas House, 62 Goldsworth Road, Woking GU21 6LQ
tel (0870) 777 8712 *fax* (0870) 777 8714
email isbn@nielsenbookdata.co.uk
website www.isbn.nielsenbookdata.co.uk

- Group Identifier – Identifies a national, geographic or language grouping of publishers. It tells you which of these groupings the publisher belongs to (not the language of the book).
- Publisher Identifier – Identifies a specific publisher or imprint.
- Title Number – Identifies a specific edition of a specific title in a specific format.
- Check Digit – This is always and only the final digit which mathematically validates the rest of the number.

Prior to 2007 ISBNs were always 10 digits long, but all publications from 1 January 2007 onwards will be assigned a 13-digit ISBN. The change is necessary to cope with the dramatically increasing rate of publications.

Do all books need to have an ISBN?

There is no legal requirement for an ISBN and it conveys no form of legal or copyright protection. It is a product identifier.

What can be gained from using an ISBN?

If you wish to sell your publication through major bookselling chains, or internet booksellers, they will require you to have an ISBN to assist their internal processing and ordering systems. The ISBN also provides access to Bibliographic Databases such as BookData's BookFind–Online, which are organised using ISBNs as references. These databases are used by the book trade: publishers, booksellers and libraries for internal purposes, to provide information for customers and to source and order titles. The ISBN therefore provides access to additional marketing opportunities which assist the sales of books and other published media.

Where can we get an ISBN?

ISBN prefixes are assigned to publishers in the country in which the publisher is based by the national agency for that country. The UK and Republic of Ireland Agency is run by Neilsen BookData. The Agency introduces new publishers to the system, assigns prefixes to new and existing publishers and deals with any queries or problems in using the system. The UK ISBN Agency was the first ISBN agency in the world and has been instrumental in the set up and maintenance of the ISBN. Publishers based elsewhere will not be able to get numbers from the UK Agency but may contact them for details of the relevant agency in their market.

Who is eligible for ISBNs?

Any organisation or individual who is publishing a qualifying product for general sale or distribution to the market is eligible (see 'Which products do not qualify for ISBNs?').

What is a publisher?

It is sometimes difficult to decide who the publisher is and who their agent may be, but the publisher is generally the person or body which takes the financial risk in making a product available. For example, if a product went on sale and sold no copies at all, the publisher is usually the person or body which loses money. If you get paid anyway, you are likely to be a designer, printer, author or consultant of some kind.

How long does it take to get an ISBN?

In the UK the 'Standard' service time is 10 working days. There is also a 'Fast Track' service, which is a three-working day processing period.

How much does it cost to get an ISBN?

In the UK there is a registration fee which is payable by all new publishers. The fees during 2006 are £94 including VAT for the Standard service and £148.05 including VAT for the Fast Track service. A publisher prefix unique to you will be provided and allows for 10 ISBNs. Larger allocations are available where appropriate.

ISBNs are only available in blocks. The smallest block is 10 numbers. It is not possible to obtain a single ISBN.

Which products do not qualify for ISBNs?

Calendars and diaries (unless they contain additional text or images such that they are not purely for time-management purposes); greetings cards, videos for entertainment; documentaries on video/CD-Rom; computer games; computer application programs; items which are available to a restricted group of people, e.g. a history of a golf club which is only for sale to members, or an educational course book only available to those registered as students on the course.

Can I turn my ISBN into a barcode?

Up until 2007, ISBNs will remain only 10 digits long, whereas the appropriate barcode is 13 digits long and is derived from the ISBN by adding a prefix and recalculating the check digit. From 1 January 2007, the appropriate barcode number will be the same as the 13-digit ISBN. Further information about barcoding for books is available on the Book Industry Communication website (www.bic.org.uk).

What is an ISSN?

An International Standard Serial Number is the numbering system for journals, magazines, periodicals, newspapers and newsletters. It is administered by the British Library (*tel* (01937) 546959).

Public Lending Right

Under the PLR system, payment is made from public funds to authors (writers, translators, illustrators and some editors/compilers) whose books are lent out from public libraries. Payment is made once a year, and the amount authors receive is proportionate to the number of times that their books were borrowed during the previous year (July to June).

The legislation

Public Lending Right (PLR) was created, and its principles established, by the Public Lending Right Act 1979 (HMSO, 30p). The Act required the rules for the administration of PLR to be laid down by a scheme. That was done in the Public Lending Right Scheme 1982 (HMSO, £2.95), which includes details of transfer (assignment), transmission after death, renunciation, trusteeship, bankruptcy, etc. Amending orders made in 1983, 1984, 1988, 1989 and 1990 were consolidated in December 1990 (SI 2360, £3.90). Some further amendments affecting author eligibility came into effect in December 1991 (SI 2618, £1), July 1997 (SI 1576, £1.10), December 1999 (SI 420, £1), July 2000 (SI 933, £1.50), June 2004 (SI 1258 £3) and July 2005 (SI 1519, £3).

Further information

Public Lending Right
PLR Office, Richard House, Sorbonne Close, Stockton-on-Tees TS17 6DA
tel (01642) 604699 *fax* (01642) 615641
website www.plr.uk.com,
www.plrinternational.com
Contact The Registrar

Application forms, information, publications and a copy of its *Annual Report* are all obtainable from the PLR Office. See website for further information on eligibility for PLR, loans statistics and forthcoming developments.

PLR Advisory Committee
Advises the Secretary of State for Culture, Media and Sport and the Registrar on the operation of the PLR scheme.

How the system works

From the applications he receives, the Registrar of PLR compiles a register of authors and books which is held on computer. A representative sample of book issues is recorded, consisting of all loans from selected public libraries. This is then multiplied in proportion to total library lending to produce, for each book, an estimate of its total annual loans throughout the country. Each year the computer compares the register with the estimated loans to discover how many loans are credited to each registered book for the calculation of PLR payments. The computer does this using code numbers – in most cases the ISBN printed in the book.

Parliament allocates a sum each year (£7,419,000 for 2005–6) for PLR. This Fund pays the administrative costs of PLR and reimburses local authorities for recording loans in the sample libraries. The remaining money is then divided by the total registered loan figure in order to work out how much can be paid for each estimated loan of a registered book.

Limits on payments

Bottom limit. If all the registered interests in an author's books score so few loans that they would earn less than £5 in a year, no payment is due. This will be reduced to £1 for the February 2007 payments.

Top limit. If the books of one registered author score so high that the author's PLR earnings for the year would exceed £6000, then only £6000 is paid. No author can earn more than £6000 in PLR in any one year. This will increase to £6600 for the February 2007 payments.

Money that is not paid out because of these limits belongs to the Fund and increases the amounts paid that year to other authors.

The sample

The basic sample represents only public libraries (no academic, school, private or commercial libraries are included) and only loans made over the counter (not consultations of books on library premises). It follows that only those books which are loaned from public libraries can earn PLR and make an application worthwhile.

The sample consists of the entire loans records for a year from libraries in more than 30 public library authorities spread through England, Scotland, Wales and Northern Ireland. Sample loans represent around 20% of the national total. Several computerised sampling points in an authority contribute loans data ('multi-site' sampling). This change has been introduced gradually, and began in July 1991. The aim has been to increase the sample without any significant increase in costs. In order to counteract sampling error, libraries in the sample change every two to three years. Loans are totalled every 12 months for the period 1 July to 30 June.

An author's entitlement to PLR depends, under the 1979 Act, on the loans accrued by his or her books in the sample. This figure is averaged up to produce first regional and then finally national estimated loans.

ISBNs

PLR depends on the use of code numbers to identify books lent and to correlate loans with entries on the register so that payment can be made. The system uses the International Standard Book Number (ISBN), which is required for all new registrations. Different

Summary of the 23rd year's results

Registration: authors. When registration closed for the 23rd year (30 June 2005) the number of shares in books registered was 402,835 for 35,822 authors and assignees.

Eligible loans. Of the 341 million estimated loans from UK libraries, 148 million belong to books on the PLR register. The loans credited to registered books – 43% of all library borrowings – qualify for payment. The remaining 57% of loans relate to books that are ineligible for various reasons, to books written by dead or foreign authors, and to books that have simply not been applied for.

Money and payments. PLR's administrative costs are deducted from the fund allocated to the Registrar annually by Parliament. Operating the Scheme this year cost £822,000, representing some 11% of the PLR fund. The Rate per Loan for 2005–6 increased to 5.57 pence and was calculated to distribute all the £6,540,000 available. The total of PLR distribution and costs is therefore the full £7.419 million which the Government provided in 2005–6.

The numbers of authors in various payment categories are as follows:

*349	payments at	£5000–6000
390	payments between	£2500–4999.99
782	payments between	£1000–2499.99
959	payments between	£500–999.99
3725	payments between	£100–499.99
12,379	payments between	£5–99.99
18,584	TOTAL	

* includes 281 authors where the maximum threshold applied.

editions (e.g. 1st, 2nd, hardcover, paperback, large print) of the same book have different ISBNs.

Authorship

In the PLR system the author of a book is the writer, illustrator, translator, compiler, editor or reviser. Authors must be named on the book's title page, or be able to prove authorship by some other means (e.g. receipt of royalties). The ownership of copyright has no bearing on PLR eligibility.

Co-authorship/illustrators. In the PLR system the authors of a book are those writers, translators, editors, compilers and illustrators as defined above. Authors must apply for registration before their books can earn PLR. This can now be done

Most borrowed authors and books

The most borrowed author overall was children's writer Jacqueline Wilson. There were 3 children's writers (*) among the 6 authors who clocked up over 1 million loans in 2004–05

1. Jacqueline Wilson*
2. Josephine Cox
3. Daniel Steel
4. James Patterson
5. Mick Inkpen*
6. Janet & Allan Ahlberg*

The most borrowed children's fiction title overall was by J.K. Rowling. She took first place with *Harry Potter and the Order of the Phoenix*.

online through the PLR website. There is no restriction on the number of authors who can register shares in any one book as long as they satisfy the eligibility criteria.

Writers and/or illustrators. At least one must be eligible and they must jointly agree what share of PLR each will take. This agreement is necessary even if one or two are ineligible or do not wish to register for PLR. Share sizes should be based on contribution. The eligible authors will receive the share(s) specified in the application. PLR can be any whole percentage. Detailed advice is available from the PLR office.

Translators. Translators may apply, without reference to other authors, for a 30% fixed share (to be divided equally between joint translators).

Editors and compilers. An editor or compiler may apply, either with others or without reference to them, to register a 20% share. Unless in receipt of royalties an editor must have written at least 10% of the book's content or more than 10 pages of text in addition to normal editorial work. The share of joint editors/compilers is 20% in total to be divided equally. An application from an editor or compiler to register a greater percentage share must be accompanied by supporting documentary evidence of actual contribution.

Most borrowed children's authors

1.	Jacqueline Wilson	11.	Dick King-Smith
2.	Mick Inkpen	12.	R.L. Stine
3.	Janet & Allan Ahlberg	13.	Terry Deary
4.	Roald Dahl	14.	Martin Waddell
5.	Lucy Daniels	15.	Ian Whybrow
6.	Enid Blyton	16.	Francesca Simon
7.	Nick Butterworth	17.	Colin & Jacqui Hawkins
8.	Eric Hill	18.	Debi Gliori
9.	Lucy Cousins	19.	Shirley Hughes
10.	Rose Impey	20.	David McKee

This list is of the most borrowed authors in UK public libraries. It is based on PLR sample loans in the period July 2004–June 2005. It includes all writers, both registered and unregistered, but not illustrators where the book has a separate writer. Writing names are used; pseudonyms have not been combined.

Dead or missing co-authors. Where it is impossible to agree shares with a co-author because that person is dead or untraceable, then the surviving co-author or co-authors may submit an application without the dead or missing co-author but must name the co-author and provide supporting evidence as to why that co-author has not agreed shares. The living co-author(s) will then be able to register a share in the book which will be 20% for the illustrator (or illustrators) and the residual percentage for the writer (or writers). If this percentage is to be divided between more than one writer or illustrator, then this will be in equal shares unless some other apportionment is requested and agreed by the Registrar.

The PLR Office keeps a file of missing authors (mostly illustrators) to help locate co-authors. Help is also available from publishers, the writers' organisations, and the Association of Illustrators.

Life and death. Authors can only be registered for PLR during their lifetime. However, for authors so registered, books can later be registered if first published within one year before their death or 10 years afterwards. New versions of titles registered by the author can be registered posthumously.

Residential qualifications. With effect from 1 July 2000, PLR is open to authors living in the European Economic Area (i.e. EU member states plus Norway, Liechtenstein and Iceland). A resident in these countries (for PLR purposes) has his or her only or principal home there.

Eligible books

In the PLR system each separate edition of a book is registered and treated as a separate book. A book is eligible for PLR registration provided that:
- it has an eligible author (or co-author);
- it is printed and bound (paperbacks counting as bound);
- copies of it have been put on sale (i.e. it is not a free handout and it has already been published);
- it is not a newspaper, magazine, journal or periodical;
- the authorship is personal (i.e. not a company or association) and the book is not crown copyright;
- it is not wholly or mainly a musical score;
- it has an ISBN.

Notification and payment

Every registered author receives from the Registrar an annual statement of estimated loans for each book and the PLR due.

Sampling arrangements

To help minimise the unfairnesses that arise inevitably from a sampling system, the Scheme specifies the eight regions within which authorities and sampling points have to be designated and includes libraries of varying size. Part of the sample drops out by rotation each year to allow fresh libraries to be included. The following library authorities have been designated for the year beginning 1 July 2006 (all are multi-site authorities):
- London – Harrow, Redbridge/Havering/Wandsworth, Tower Hamlets, Corporation of London;
- Metropolitan Boroughs – Bolton, North Tyneside, Coventry, Newcastle upon Tyne, St Helens;

- Counties: Northern – Nottinghamshire/Nottingham, Derbyshire/Derby, Lincolnshire, Northumberland, Darlington;
- Counties: South West – Hampshire, Worcestershire, Gloucestershire, Stoke on Trent;
- Counties: South East – Oxfordshire, Kent, West Sussex, Windsor and Maidenhead, Essex/Southend/Thurrock;

Most borrowed children's fiction titles

	Author	Title	Publisher	Year
1.	J.K. Rowling	Harry Potter and the Order of the Phoenix	Bloomsbury	2003
2.	Jacqueline Wilson (illus. Nick Sharratt)	Lizzie Zipmouth	Young Corgi	2000
3.	Jacqueline Wilson (illus. Nick Sharratt)	Best Friends	Doubleday	2004
4.	Jacqueline Wilson (illus. Nick Sharratt)	The Story of Tracy Beaker	Yearling	1992
5.	Jacqueline Wilson (illus. N. Sharratt)	Midnight	Doubleday	2003
6.	Jacqueline Wilson (illus. N. Sharratt)	Mum-minder	Yearling	1994
7.	Jennifer Donnelly	A Gathering Light	Bloomsbury	2004
8.	Jacqueline Wilson (illus. Nick Sharratt)	The Dare Game	Corgi Yearling	2001
9.	Jacqueline Wilson (illus. Nick Sharratt)	Vicky Angel	Corgi Yearling	2001
10.	Jacqueline Wilson (illus. Nick Sharratt)	Glubbslyme	Yearling	1995
11.	Jacqueline Wilson (illus. Nick Sharratt)	Bad Girls	Yearling	1997
12.	Jacqueline Wilson (illus. Nick Sharratt)	The Suitcase Kid	Yearling	1993
13.	Jacqueline Wilson (illus. Nick Sharratt)	The Worry Website	Doubleday	2002
14.	Jacqueline Wilson (illus. Nick Sharratt)	The Illustrated Mum	Corgi Yearling	2000
15.	J.K. Rowling	Harry Potter and the Goblet of Fire	Bloomsbury	2001
16.	Francesca Simon (illus. Tony Ross)	Horrid Henry's Underpants	Dolphin	2003
17.	Jacqueline Wilson (illus. Nick Sharratt)	Sleepovers	Young Corgi	2002
18.	Jacqueline Wilson (illus. Nick Sharratt and Sue Heap)	Double Act	Transworld Corgi	1996
19.	Jacqueline Wilson (illus. Nick Sharratt)	Bed and Breakfast Star	Yearling	1995
20.	Jacqueline Wilson (illus. Nick Sharratt and Sue Heap)	Buried Alive!	Corgi Yearling	1999

- Scotland – Orkney, Argyll & Bute, Edinburgh, East Lothian;
- Northern Ireland – all five Education and Library Boards;
- Wales – Conwy, Swansea, Neath Port Talbot.

Participating local authorities are reimbursed on an actual cost basis for additional expenditure incurred in providing loans data to the PLR Office. The extra PLR work mostly consists of modifications to computer programs to accumulate loans data in the local authority computer and to transmit the data to the PLR Office at Stockton-on-Tees.

Most borrowed classic children's titles

	Author	Title	Publisher	Year
1.	Roald Dahl (illus. Quentin Blake)	The BFG	Puffin	2001
2.	Roald Dahl (illus. Quentin Blake)	The Witches	Puffin	2001
3.	Roald Dahl (illus. Quentin Blake)	Matilda	Puffin	2001
4.	Roald Dahl (illus. Quentin Blake)	Charlie and the Chocolate Factory	Puffin	2001
5.	Roald Dahl (illus. Quentin Blake)	Charlie and the Great Glass Elevator	Puffin	2001
6.	Roald Dahl (illus. Quentin Blake)	James and the Giant Peach	Puffin	2001
7.	Roald Dahl (illus. Quentin Blake)	Danny the Champion of the World	Puffin	2001
8.	J.R.R. Tolkien (illus. David Wyatt)	The Hobbit	Collins	1998
9.	Korky Paul and Valerie Thomas	Winnie's Magic Wand	OUP	2002
10.	C.S. Lewis (illus. Pauline Baynes)	The Lion, the Witch and the Wardrobe	Collins	1998
11.	Roald Dahl (illus. Quentin Blake)	The Enormous Crocodile	Puffin	2001
12.	Astrid Lindgren (illus. Tony Ross)	Pippi Longstocking	OUP	2001
13.	Walt Disney Company	Walt Disney's Classic Dumbo	Ladybird	2003
14.	Frances Hodgson Burnett (illus. Robin Lawrie)	The Secret Garden	Puffin	1994
15.	Walt Disney Company	Peter Pan	Ladybird	1994
16.	A.A. Milne (illus. E.H. Shepard)	Winnie-the-Pooh	Mammoth	1991
17.	Ian Beck	Chicken Licken	OUP	2003
18.	Roald Dahl (illus. Quentin Blake)	The Complete Adventures of Charlie and Mr Willy Wonka	Puffin	2001
19.	Anna Sewell	Black Beauty	Puffin	1954
20.	E. Nesbit (illus. H.R. Millar)	Five Children and It	Puffin	1996

Reciprocal arrangements

Reciprocal PLR arrangements now exist with the German, Dutch and Austrian PLR schemes. Authors can apply for German, Dutch and Austrian PLR through the Authors' Licensing and Collecting Society. (Further information on PLR schemes internationally and recent developments within the EC towards wider recognition of PLR is available from the PLR Office or on the international PLR website.)

Most borrowed children's non-fiction titles

	Author	Title	Publisher	Year
1.	Eric Hill	Spot Can Count	Puffin	2000
2.	Terry Deary, Neil Tonge (illus. Martin Brown)	The Terrible Tudors	Scholastic	2003
3.	Mick Inkpen	Kipper's A to Z	Hodder Children's	2000
4.	Terry Deary (illus. Martin Brown)	The Woeful Second World War	Hippo	1999
5.	Terry Deary (illus. Philip Reeve)	Dark Knights and Dingy Castles	Scholastic	1997
6.	Terry Deary & Peter Hepplewhite (illus. Martin Brown)	The Awesome Egyptians	Scholastic	1993
7.	Terry Deary (illus. Martin Brown)	The Vile Victorians	Scholastic	1994
8.	Terry Deary (illus. Martin Brown)	The Rotten Romans	Hippo	1994
9.	Terry Deary (illus. Martin Brown)	The Groovy Greeks	Hippo	1996
10.	A.H. Benjamin & Jane Chapman	Baa Moo: What Will We Do?	Little Tiger	2003
11.	Terry Deary (illus. M. Brown)	The Ruthless Romans	Hippo	2003
12.	Terry Deary (illus. M. Brown)	The Smashing Saxons	Hippo	2000
13.	Simon Adams (photos Andy Crawford)	World War II	Dorling Kindersley	2000
14.	Terry Deary (illus. M. Brown)	Even More Terrible Tudors	Hippo	1998
15.	Mick Inkpen	Kipper's A to Z	Hodder Children's	2002
16.	Terry Deary (illus. M. Brown)	England	Scholastic	2004
17.	Terry Deary (illus. M. Brown)	The Frightful First World War	Hippo	1998
18.	Terry Deary (illus. Kate Sheppard)	The Blitzed Brits	Hippo	1994
19.	Lucy Cousins	Count with Maisy	Walker	1999
20.	Terry Deary (illus. M. Brown)	The Vicious Vikings	Hippo	1994

Copyright
Copyright questions

Copyright is a vital part of any writer's assets, and should never be assigned or sold without due consideration and the advice of a competent authority, such as the Society of Authors, the Writers' Guild of Great Britain, or the National Union of Journalists. Michael Legat answers some of the most commonly asked questions about copyright.

Is there a period of time after which the copyright expires?

Copyright in the European Union lasts for the lifetime of the author and for a further 70 years from the end of the year of death, or, if the work is first published posthumously, for 70 years from the end of the year of publication. In most other countries of the world copyright exists similarly for the lifetime and for either 50 years or 70 years after death or posthumous publication.

If I want to include an extract from a book, poem or article, do I have to seek copyright? How much may be used without permission? What happens if I apply for copyright permission but do not get a reply?

It is essential to seek permission to quote from another author's work, unless that author has been dead for 70 years or more, or 70 years or more has passed from the date of publication of a work published posthumously. Only if you are quoting for purposes of criticism or review are you allowed to do so without obtaining permission, and even then the Copyright, Designs and Patents Act of 1988 restricts you to 400 words of prose in a single extract from a copyright work, or a series of extracts of up to 300 words each, totalling no more than 800 words, or up to 40 lines of poetry, which must not be more than 25% of the poem. However, a quotation of no more than, say, half a dozen words may usually be used without permission since it will probably not extend beyond a brief and familiar reference, as, for example, Rider Haggard's well-known phrase, 'she who must be obeyed'. If in doubt, always check. If you do not get a reply when you ask for permission to quote, insert a notice in your work saying that you have tried without success to contact the copyright owner, and would be pleased to hear from him or her so that the matter could be cleared up – and keep a copy of all the relevant correspondence, in order to back up your claim of having tried to get in touch.

If a newspaper pays for an article and I then want to sell the story to a magazine, am I free under the copyright law to do so?

Yes, provided that you have not granted copyright or exclusive use to the newspaper. When selling your work to newspapers or magazines make it clear, in writing, that you are selling only First or Second Serial Rights, not your copyright.

If I agree to have an article published for no payment do I retain any rights over how it appears?

Whether or not you are paid for the work has no bearing on the legal situation. However, the Moral Rights which apply to books, plays, television and radio scripts, do not cover you against a failure to acknowledge you as the author of an article, nor against the mutilation of your text, when it is published in a newspaper or magazine.

I want to publish a photograph that was taken in 1950. I am not sure how to contact the photographer or even if he is still alive. Am I allowed to go ahead and publish it?

The Copyright, Designs and Patents Act of 1988 works retrospectively, so a photograph taken in 1950 is bound to be in copyright until at least 2020, and the copyright will be owned by the photographer, even though, when it was taken, the copyright would have belonged to the person who commissioned it, according to the laws then in place. You should therefore make every effort to contact the photographer, keeping copies of any relevant correspondence, and in case of failure take the same course of action as described above in relation to a textual extract the copyright owner of which you have been unable to trace.

I recently read an article on the same subject as one I have written. It contained many identical facts. Did this writer breach my copyright? What if I send ideas for an article to a magazine editor and those ideas are used despite the fact that I was not commissioned? May I sue the magazine?

Facts are normally in the public domain and may be used by anyone. However, if your article contains a fact which you have discovered and no one else has published, there could be an infringement of copyright if the author who uses it fails to attribute it to you. There is no copyright in ideas, so you cannot sue a writer or a journal for using ideas that you have put forward; in any case you would find it very difficult to prove that the idea belonged to you and to no one else. There is also no copyright in titles.

Does being paid a kill fee affect my copyright in a given piece?

No, provided that you have not sold the magazine or newspaper your copyright.

Do I need to copyright a piece of writing physically – whether an essay or a novel – or is it copyrighted automatically? Does it have to carry the © symbol?

Anything that you write is your copyright, assuming that it is not copied from the work of someone else, as soon as you have written it on paper or recorded it on the disk of a computer or on tape, or broadcast it, or posted it on the internet. It is not essential for the work to carry the © symbol, although its inclusion may act as a warning and help to stop another writer from plagiarising it.

Am I legally required to inform an interviewee that our conversation is being recorded?

The interviewee owns the copyright of any words that he or she speaks as soon as they are recorded on your tape. Unless you have received permission to use those words in direct quotation, you could be liable to an action for infringement of copyright. You should therefore certainly inform the interviewee that the conversation is being recorded and seek permission to quote what is said directly.

More and more newspapers and magazines have versions both in print and on the internet. How can I ensure that my work is not published on the internet without my permission?

Make sure that any clause granting electronic rights to anyone in any agreement that you sign in respect of your work specifies not only the proportion of any fees received which you will get, but that your agreement must be sought before the rights are sold. Copyright extends to electronic rights, and therefore to publication on the internet, in just the same way as to other uses of the material.

I commissioned a designer to design a business card for me, and I paid her well. Does the design belong to me or to her?

Copyright would belong to the designer, and not to the person who commissioned it (as is also true in the case of a photograph, copyright in which belongs to the photographer). However, copyright in the business card might be transferred to you if a court considered you to have gained beneficially from the card.

Michael Legat became a full-time writer after a long and successful publishing career. He is the author of a number of highly regarded books on publishing and writing.

See also...
- *UK copyright law*, page 236
- *Authors' Licensing and Collecting Society*, page 250
- *Design and Artists Copyright Society*, page 253
- *The Copyright Licensing Agency Ltd*, page 248

UK copyright law

Amanda Michaels describes the main types of work which may qualify for copyright protection, or related protection as a design, together with some of the main problems which may be faced by readers of this *Yearbook* in terms of protecting their own works or avoiding infringement of existing works in the UK. This is a technical area of the law, and one which is constantly developing; in an article of this length, it is not possible to deal fully with all the complexities of the law. It must also be emphasised that copyright is national in scope, and whilst works of UK authors will be protected in many other countries of the world, and works of foreign authors will generally be protected in the UK, foreign laws may deal differently with questions of subsistence, ownership and infringement.

Copyright is a creation of statute, now shaped and influenced significantly by EU harmonisation measures. On 1 August 1989, the Copyright, Designs & Patents Act 1988 ('the Act') replaced the Copyright Act 1956, which in turn replaced the Copyright Act 1911. All three Acts are still relevant to copyright today. Whilst the Act to a large degree restated the existing law, it was also innovative, in particular in the creation of a new 'design right' offering protection (generally speaking in lieu of copyright) for many industrial or commercial designs, and in the wider protection of moral rights.

> ## Useful websites
>
> **www.patent.gov.uk/index.htm**
> Website of the Patent Office.
>
> **www.intellectual-property.gov.uk**
> **www.wipo.int**
> Website of the World Intellectual Property Organisation.
>
> **www.baillii.org**
> Contains judgements from UK courts and with links to equivalent foreign websites. Legislation on the site may be in an unamended form.

The law has changed further since 1989, largely as a result of EU directives. An important change occurred on 1 January 1996, when the duration of copyright protection in respect of most works (see below) was extended from 'life of the author' plus 50 years to life plus 70 years. Further changes came into force on 1 January 1998, when a new 'database right' was created. New Community design rights were brought into effect in 2003 and numerous other amendments were made, in particular to the rules on fair dealing with copyright works, by the Copyright and Related Rights Regulations 2003 (see below).

Continuing relevance of old law

In this article, I discuss the law as it currently stands, but where a work was created prior to 1 August 1989 it will always be necessary to consider the law in force at the time of creation (or possibly first publication) in order to assess the existence or scope of any rights. Particular difficulties arise with foreign works, which may qualify for protection in the UK as a matter of international obligation. Each Act has contained transitional provisions and these, as well as the substantive provisions of any relevant earlier Act, will need to be considered where, for instance, you wish to use an earlier work and it is necessary to decide whether permission is needed and if so, who may grant it. Publishing or licence agreements designed for use under older Acts and prior to the development of modern technologies may be unsuitable for current use.

Copyright protection of works

The overall policy justifying copyright protection is 'to prevent the unauthorised copying of material forms of expression (literary, dramatic, artistic and musical, for example) resulting from intellectual exertions of the human mind…. The important point is that copyright can be used to prevent copying of a substantial part of the relevant form of expression, but it does not prevent use of the information, thoughts or emotions expressed in the copyright work. It does not prevent another person from coincidentally creating a similar work by his own independent efforts' (see Mummery LJ in *Sawkins* v. *Hyperion Records* [2005] IWLR 3281).

Hence, copyright protects the particular form in which an author's idea has been expressed, not the idea itself. Generally speaking, plots or artistic ideas are not protected by copyright, but what is protected is the particular manner in which the idea is presented. For instance, in *Designers Guild Limited* v. *Russell Williams (Textiles) Limited* [2001] FSR 113 a fairly simple fabric design was found to be original and to have been copied: this was an infringement of the copyright in the design. By contrast, in *Baigent & Leigh* v. *The Random House Group*, the 'Da Vinci Code' case, Dan Brown was alleged to have copied a number of historical facts or theories from the earlier book *The Holy Blood and the Holy Grail* but not the language in which they were expressed (the few phrases actually copied did not amount to a 'substantial part' of the *HBHG*). The claim was that there was infringement by copying a 'Central Theme' composed of a series of 15 connected points. However, the judge found that this was not the 'theme' of *HBHG*, and held that in any event the individual points were of too high a level of abstraction to be capable of copyright protection.

Of course, if someone has written an outline, script or screenplay for a television show, film, etc and that idea is confidential, then dual protection may arise in the confidential idea embodied in the documents and in the literary (and sometimes artistic) works in which the idea has taken material form. If the idea is used, but not the form, this might give rise to an action for breach of confidence, but not for infringement of copyright. Copyright prevents the copying of the *material form* in which the idea has been presented, or of a substantial part of it, measured in terms of quality, not quantity.

Section 1 of the Act sets out a number of different categories of works which can be the subject of copyright protection. These are:

- original literary, dramatic, musical or artistic works,
- sound recordings, films, broadcasts or cable programmes, and
- typographical arrangements of published editions.

These works are further defined in ss.3–8 (see box for examples).

However, no work of any description enjoys copyright protection until it has been recorded in a tangible form, as s.3(2) provides that no copyright shall subsist in a literary, musical or artistic work until it has been recorded in writing or otherwise.

On the other hand, all that is required to achieve copyright protection is to record the original work in an appropriate medium. Once that has been done, copyright will subsist in the work (assuming that the qualifying features set out below are present) without any formality of registration or otherwise. There is, for instance, no need to publish a work to protect it. Please note, however, that the law of the United States does differ on this.

Nonetheless, there can be a real benefit in keeping a proper record of the creation of a work. Drafts or preliminary sketches should be kept and dated, as should source or research material, so as to be able to show the development of a work. It may also be beneficial (especially where works are to be submitted to potential publishers or purchasers) to take a complete copy of the documents and send them to oneself or lodge them with a responsible third party, sealed and dated, so as to be able to provide cogent evidence of the form or content of the work at that date. Such evidence may help the author, whether as claimant or defendant, to prove the independence of the creation of his work, and its originality, in a copyright infringement (or indeed breach of confidence) action.

Originality

Literary, dramatic, artistic and musical works must all be 'original' to gain copyright protection, but this does not impose any concept of objective novelty. Just as the law protects the form, rather than the idea, originality relates to the 'expression of the thought', rather than to the thought itself. The policy of copyright protection and its limited scope (set out above) explain why the threshold requirement of an original work does not impose 'any objective standard of novelty, usefulness, inventiveness, aesthetic merit, quality or value'; so, a work may be 'complete rubbish', yet have copyright protection (see again Mummery LJ in *Sawkins*). A work need only be original in the sense of being the product of skill and labour on the part of the author. This can be seen for instance in the definition of certain artistic works, and in the fact that copyright protects works such as compilations (like football pools coupons or directories) and tables (including mathematical tables).

There may be considerable difficulty, at times, in deciding whether a work is of sufficient originality, or has original features, where there is a series of similar designs or amendments of existing works. *Sawkins* was just such a case: the question was whether or not the editorial work by Doctor Sawkins on existing works by the baroque composer, Lalande, had created new musical works. The result turned partly on the definition of 'music', but the nature of Dr Sawkins' input was confirmed to have amounted to creation of an original musical work with its own copyright. See also *L.A. Gear Inc.* [1993] FSR 121, *Biotrading* [1998] FSR 109. Equally, an adaptation of an existing work may have its own copyright protection (see *Cala Homes* [1995] FSR 818). What is clear, though, is that merely making a 'slavish copy' of a work will not create an original work: see *Interlego AG* [1989] AC 217. If the work gives particular expression to a commonplace idea or an old tale, copyright may subsist in it (e.g. *Christoffer* v. *Poseidon Film Distributors Limited* (6/10/99) in which it was held that a script for an animated film of a story from Homer's *Odyssey* was an original literary work). But, as the *Da Vinci* case confirmed, whilst copyright may subsist in the work, use only of the pre-existing facts or ideas contained in it may not infringe that copyright. Copyright protection will be limited to the original features of the work, or those features created or chosen by the author's input of skill and labour.

Definitions under the Act

Literary work is defined as: 'any work, other than a dramatic or musical work, which is written, spoken or sung, and accordingly includes: (a) a table or compilation other than a database, (b) a computer program, (c) preparatory design material for a computer program and (d) a database.'

A musical work means: 'a work consisting of music, exclusive of any words or action intended to be sung, spoken or performed with the music.'

An artistic work means: '(a) a graphic work, photograph, sculpture or collage, irrespective of artistic quality, (b) a work of architecture being a building or model for a building, or (c) a work of artistic craftsmanship.'

These categories of work are not mutually exclusive, e.g. a film may be protected both as a film and as a dramatic work. See *Norowzian* v. *Arks* [2000] FSR 363.

Sound recordings or films which are copies of pre-existing sound recordings or films, broadcasts which infringe rights in another broadcast or cable programmes which consist of immediate retransmissions of broadcasts are not protected by copyright.

'Works' such as the titles of books or periodicals, or advertising slogans, which may have required a good deal of original thought, generally are not accorded copyright protection, because they are too short to be deemed literary works. It also seems that computer 'languages', and the ideas or logic underlying them, are not protected as copyright works; such protection extends only to the computer programs: see *Navitaire* v. *Easyjet* [2004] EWHC 1725.

Qualification

The Act is limited in its effects to the UK (and to colonies to which it may be extended by Order). It is aimed primarily at protecting the works of British citizens, or works which were first published here. However, in line with the requirements of various international conventions, copyright protection in the UK is also accorded to the works of nationals of many foreign states, as well as to works first published in those states, on a reciprocal basis.

As for works of nationals of other member states of the European Union, there is a principle of equal treatment, so that protection must be offered to such works here: see *Phil Collins* [1993] 3 CMLR 773.

The importance of these rules mainly arises when one is trying to find out whether a foreign work is protected by copyright here, for instance, if one wishes to make a film based upon a foreign novel.

Ownership

The general rule is that the copyright in a work will first be owned by its author, the creator of the work. In most cases this is self-explanatory, but the definition of 'author' in relation to films and sound recordings has changed over the years; currently, the author of a sound recording is its producer, and the authors of a film are the producer and principal director.

One important exception to the general rule is that the copyright in a work made by an employee in the course of his or her employment will belong to their employer, subject to any agreement to the contrary. However, this rule does not apply to freelance designers, journalists, etc, and not even to self-employed company directors. This obviously may lead to problems if the question of copyright ownership is not dealt with when an agreement is made to create, purchase or use a work. In the absence of an appropriate agreement, the legal title may simply not be owned by the apparent owner, who will need it if he wishes to sue for infringement, and it is often difficult to formalise the position long after creation of the work. More importantly, perhaps, there have been numerous cases in which the extent of the rights obtained in a 'commissioned' work has been disputed, simply because of the lack of any clear agreement at the outset between the author and the 'commissioner'. It is very important for writers and artists of all kinds to agree about ownership/terms of use at the outset and record them in writing. It is equally important to understand the difference between an assignment and a licence (see below).

Where a work is produced by several people who collaborate so that each one's contribution is not distinct from that of the other(s), then they will be joint authors of the work. Where two people collaborate to write a song, one producing the lyrics and the other the music, there will be two separate copyright works, the copyright of which will be owned by each of the authors separately. But where two people write a play, each rewriting what the other produces, there will be a joint work.

The importance of knowing whether the copyright is joint or not arises:
- in working out the duration of the copyright, and
- from the fact that joint works can only be exploited with the agreement of all the joint authors, so that all of them have to join in any licence, although each of them can sue for infringement without joining the other(s) as a claimant in the proceedings.

Duration of copyright

As a result of amendments brought into effect on 1 January 1996, copyright in literary, dramatic, musical or artistic works expires at the end of the period of 70 years from the end of the calendar year in which the author dies (s.12(1)). Where there are joint authors, then the 70 years runs from the death of the last of them to die. If the author is unknown, there will be 70 years protection from the date the work was first made or (where applicable) first made available to the public. Previously, the protection was for 'life plus 50'.

The extended 70-year term also applies to films, and runs from the end of the calendar year in which the death occurs of the last to die of the principal director, the author of the screenplay or the dialogue, or the composer of any music created for the film (s.13B). This obviously may be a nightmare to establish, and there are certain presumptions in s.66A which may help someone wishing to use material from an old film.

However, sound recordings are still protected by copyright only for 50 years from the year of making or release (s.13A); similarly, broadcasts, cable programmes and computer-generated works still get only 50 years protection.

The new longer term applies without difficulty to works created after 1 January 1996 and to works in copyright on 31 December 1995. The owner of that extended copyright will be the person who owned it on 31 December 1995, unless that person had only a limited term of ownership, in which case the extra 20 years will be added on to the reversionary term.

Where copyright had expired here, but the author died between 50 and 70 years ago, the position is more complicated. EC Directive 93/98 provided that if a work was protected by copyright anywhere in the European Union on 1 July 1995, copyright would revive for it in any other state until the end of the same 70-year period. This may make it necessary to look at the position in the states offering a longer term of protection, namely Germany, France and Spain.

Ownership of the revived term of copyright will belong to the person who was the owner of the copyright when the initial term expired, save that if that person died (or a company, etc, ceased to exist) before 1 January 1996, then the revived term will vest in the author's personal representatives, and in the case of a film, in the principal director's personal representatives.

Any licence affecting a copyright work which subsisted on 31 December 1995 and was then for the full term of the copyright continues to have effect during any extended term of copyright, subject to any agreement to the contrary (paragraph 21 of the Regulations).

The increased term offered to works of other EU nationals as a result of the Term Directive is not offered automatically to the nationals of other states, but will only apply where an equally long term is offered in their state of origin.

Where acts are carried out in relation to such revived copyright works, pursuant to things done whilst they were in the public domain, protection from infringement is available. A licence as of right may also be available, on giving notice to the copyright owner and paying a royalty.

Dealing with copyright works

Ownership of the copyright in a work confers upon the owner the exclusive right to deal with the work in a number of ways, and essentially stops all unauthorised exploitation of the work. Ownership of the copyright is capable of being separated from ownership of the material form in which the work is embodied, depending upon the terms of any agreement or the circumstances. Even buying an original piece of artwork will not in general carry with it the legal title to the copyright, as an effective assignment must be in writing signed by the assignor (although beneficial ownership might pass: see below).

Copyright works can be exploited by their owners in two ways:

● **Assignment**. In an assignment, rights in the work are sold, with the owner retaining no interest in it (except, possibly, for payment by way of royalties). An assignment must be in writing, signed by or on behalf of the assignor, but no other formality is required. One can make an assignment of future copyright (under s.91). Where the author of a projected work agrees in writing that he will assign the rights in a future work to another, the copyright vests in the assignee immediately upon the creation of the work, without further formalities.

These rules do not affect the common law as to beneficial interests in copyright. One possibility may be that a court will, in the right circumstances, find or infer an agreement to assign the copyright in a work, e.g. where a sole trader who had title to the copyright used in his business later incorporated the business and allowed the company to exploit the software as if it were its own, an agreement to assign was inferred (see *Lakeview Computers plc* 26/11/99). Alternatively, if the court finds that a work was commissioned to be made, and that there was a common intention that the purchaser should own the copyright, the court may order the author to assign the copyright to him. Where a freelance designer produced a logo for an advertising agency, a term was implied in the contract between the designer and the agency that the client for which the logo was designed was to be the owner of the worldwide copyrights in the logo: see *R. Griggs Group* v. *Ross Evans* [2005] FSR 31. 'Commission' in this context means only to order a particular piece of work to be done: see *Apple Corps Ltd* v. *Cooper* [1993] FSR 286 (a 1956 Act case).

● **Licensing**. A licence is granted to another to exploit the right whilst the licensor retains overall ownership. Licences do not need to take any form in particular, and may indeed be granted orally. However, an exclusive licence (i.e. one which excludes even the copyright owner himself from exploiting the work) must be in writing, if the licensee is to enjoy rights in respect of infringements concurrent with those of the copyright owner.

Agreements dealing with copyright should make it clear whether an assignment or a licence is being granted. There may be significant advantages for the author in granting a licence rather than an assignment, for where the assignee's rights pass to a third party, for instance on his insolvency, the author cannot normally enforce the original agreement to make a purchaser pay royalties, etc (*Barker* v. *Stickney* [1919] 1 KB 121). If the agreement is unclear, the Court is likely to find that the grantee took the minimum rights necessary for his intended use of the work, quite probably an exclusive licence rather than an assignment (*Ray* v. *Classic FM plc* [1998] FSR 622), unless the work was 'commissioned' from the author (see box). The question of moral rights (see below) will also have to be considered by the parties.

Assignments and licences often split up the various rights contained within the copyright. So, for instance, a licence might be granted to one person to publish a novel in book form, another person might be granted the film, television and video rights, and yet another the right to translate the novel into other languages. Obviously, the author should seek to grant the narrowest possible rights on each occasion, so retaining other rights for future exploitation; this means scrutinising draft publishing agreements carefully and negotiating as best one can.

Assignments and licences may also confer rights according to territory, dividing the USA from the EU or different EU countries one from the other. Any such agreement should take into account divergences between different national copyright laws. Furthermore, when seeking to divide rights between different territories of the EU there is a danger of infringing the competition rules of the EU. Professional advice should be taken, as breach of these rules may attract a fine and can render the agreement void in whole or in part.

Licences can, of course, be of varying lengths. There is no need for a licence to be granted for the whole term of copyright. Well-drafted licences will provide for termination on breach, including the failure of the licensee to exploit the work, and on the insolvency of the licensee and will specify whether the rights may be assigned or sub-licensed.

Copyright may be assigned by will. A bequest of an original document, etc embodying an unpublished copyright work will carry the copyright.

Infringement

The main type of infringement is what is commonly thought of as plagiarism, that is, copying the work. In fact, copyright confers on the owner the exclusive right to do a number of specified acts, so that anyone doing those acts without his permission will normally infringe. It is important to note that it is not necessary to copy a work exactly or use all of it; it is sufficient if a substantial part is used. That question is to be judged on a qualitative not a quantitative basis, bearing in mind that it is the skill and labour of the author which is to be protected (see *Ravenscroft* v. *Herbert* [1980] RPC 193 and *Designers Guild*). It is important to note that primary infringement, such as copying, can be done innocently of any intention to infringe.

The form of infringement common to all forms of copyright works is that of copying. This means reproducing the work in any material form. Infringement may occur where an existing work provides the inspiration for a later one, if copying results, for example by including edited extracts from a history book in a novel (*Ravenscroft*), using a photograph as the inspiration for a painting (*Baumann* v. *Fussell* [1978] RPC 485), or words from a verse of one song in another (*Ludlow Music* v. *Williams* [2001] FSR 271). Infringement will not necessarily be prevented merely by the application of significant new skill and labour by the infringer, nor by a change of medium.

In the case of a two-dimensional artistic work, reproduction can mean making a copy in three dimensions, and vice versa. However, s.51 of the Act provides that in the case of a 'design document or model' (for definition, see 'Design right' below) for something which is not *itself* an artistic work, it is no infringement to make an article to that design. This means that whilst it would be an infringement of copyright to make an article from a design drawing for, say, a sculpture, it will not be an infringement of copyright to make a handbag from a copy of the design drawing for it, or from a handbag which one has purchased. Instead, such designs are generally protected by design right or as registered designs (for both see below). A recent decision suggests that there is in fact a gap in the regime through which some designs may fall. Design right does not protect 'surface decoration', but nor (because of s.51) does copyright protect elements of surface decoration if they are dictated by the shape of the article on which the decoration appears. Hence, the design of stripes on a T-shirt was not protected either by copyright or by design right. See *Lambretta* v. *Teddy Smith* [2005] RPC 6.

Copying a film, broadcast or cable programme can include making a copy of the whole or a substantial part of any image from it (see s.17(4)). This means that copying one frame of the film will be an infringement. It is not an infringement of copyright in a film to reshoot the film (*Norowzian*) (though there would doubtless be an infringement of the copyright in underlying works such as the literary copyright in the screenplay).

Copying is generally proved by showing substantial similarities between the original and the alleged copy, plus an opportunity to copy. Surprisingly often, minor errors in the original are reproduced by an infringer.

Copying need not be direct, so that, for instance, where the copyright is in a fabric design, copying the material without ever having seen the original drawing will still be an infringement, as will 'reverse engineering' of industrial designs, for example to make unlicensed spare parts (*British Leyland* [1986] AC 577; *Mars* v. *Teknowledge* [2000] FSR 138).

Issuing copies of a work to the public when they have not previously been put into circulation in the UK is also a primary infringement of all types of work.

Other acts which may amount to an infringement depend upon the nature of the work. It will be an infringement of the copyright in a literary, dramatic or musical work to perform it in public, whether by live performance or by playing recordings. Similarly, it is an infringement of the copyright in a sound recording, film, broadcast or cable programme to play or show it in public. Many copyright works will also be infringed by the rental or lending of copies of the work.

One rather different form of infringement is to make an adaptation of a literary, dramatic or musical work. An adaptation includes, in the case of a literary work, a translation, in the case of a non-dramatic work, making a dramatic work of it, and vice versa. A transcription or arrangement of a musical work is an adaptation of it.

There are also a number of 'secondary' infringements – see box.

'Secondary' infringements

Secondary infringements consist not of making infringing copies, but of dealing with existing infringing copies in some way. It is an infringement to import an infringing copy into the UK, and to possess in the course of business, or to sell, hire, offer for sale or hire, or distribute in the course of trade an infringing copy. However, none of these acts will be an infringement unless the alleged infringer knew or had reason to believe that the articles were infringing copies. What is sufficient knowledge will depend upon the facts of each case (see *LA Gear Inc.* [1992] FSR 121, *ZYX Records* v. *King* [1997] 2 All ER 132 and *Pensher Security* [2000] RPC 249). Merely putting someone on notice of a dispute as to ownership of copyright may not suffice to give him or her reason to believe in infringement for this purpose. But someone who is informed that he is infringing 'yet carries out no sensible enquiries, and does nothing in the face of continued assertions of the copyright' may become someone with 'reason to believe' the claim: *Nouveau Fabrics* v. *Voyage Decoration* [2004] EWHC 895; *Hutchison* [1995] FSR 365.

Other secondary infringements consist of permitting a place to be used for a public performance in which copyright is infringed and supplying apparatus to be used for infringing public performance, again, in each case, with safeguards for innocent acts.

Exceptions to infringement

The Act provides a large number of exceptions to the rules on infringement which were extended and amended with effect from 31 October 2003 by the Copyright and Related Rights Regulations 2003. They are far too numerous to be dealt with here in full, but they include:

● fair dealing with literary, dramatic, musical or artistic works for the purpose of non-commercial research or private study (s.29);

● fair dealing for the purpose of criticism or review or reporting current events, as to which see e.g. *Pro Sieben Media* [1999] FSR 610; *Hyde Park* v. *Yelland* [2001] Ch. 143; *NLA* v. *Marks & Spencer Plc* [2002] RPC 4) (s.30);

● incidental inclusion of a work in an artistic work, sound recording, film, broadcast or cable programme (s.31);

● educational exceptions (ss.32–36A);

● exceptions for libraries (ss.37–44A) and public administration (ss.45–50);

● making transient copies as part of a technological process (s.28A) and backing-up, or converting a computer program or accessing a licensed database (s.50A–D);

● dealing with a work where the author cannot be identified and the work seems likely to be out of copyright (s.57);

● public recitation, if accompanied by a sufficient acknowledgement (s.59).

The effect of the Human Rights Act on copyright in relation to the right to free speech seems likely to be limited, as sufficient protection is to be found in the fair dealing provisions: *Ashdown* v. *Telegraph Group Limited* [2002] Ch. 149.

There is no defence of parody.

Remedies for infringements

The copyright owner will usually want to prevent the repetition or continuation of the infringement and will want compensation.

In almost all cases an injunction will be sought to stop the infringement. The Courts have useful powers to grant an injunction at an early stage, indeed even before any infringement takes place, if a real threat of damage can be shown. Such an interim injunction can be applied for on three days' notice (or without notice in appropriate cases), but will not be granted unless the claimant has a reasonably good case and can show that he would suffer 'unquantifiable' damage if the defendant's activities continued pending trial. Delay in bringing an interim application may be fatal to its success. An injunction may not be granted where the claimant clearly only wants financial compensation (*Ludlow Music*).

Financial compensation may be sought in one of two forms. Firstly, damages. These will usually be calculated upon evidence of the loss caused to the claimant, sometimes based upon loss of business, at others upon the basis of what would have been a proper licence fee for the defendant's acts. Additional damages may be awarded in rare cases for flagrant infringements and can be substantial. See for example *Notts. Healthcare* v. *News Group Newspapers* [2002] RPC 49.

Damages will not be awarded for infringement where the infringer did not know, and had no reason to believe, that copyright subsisted in the work. This exception is of limited use to a defendant, though, in the usual situation where the work was of such a nature that he should have known that copyright would subsist in it.

The alternative to damages is an account of profits, that is, the net profits made by the infringer by virtue of his illicit exploitation of the copyright. Where an account of profits is sought, no award of flagrant damages can be made. See *Redrow Homes Limited* [1999] 1 AC 197.

A copyright owner may also apply for delivery up of infringing copies.

Finally, there are various criminal offences relating to the making, importation, possession, sale, hire, distribution, etc of infringing copies.

Design right

Many industrial designs are excluded from copyright protection by s.51. Alternatively, the term of copyright protection is limited to 25 years from first industrial exploitation, by s.52. However, they may instead be protected by the 'design right' created by ss.213–64 or by Community design right. Like copyright, design right does not depend upon registration, but upon the creation of a suitable design by a 'qualifying person'.

Design right is granted to original designs consisting of the shape or configuration (internal or external) of the whole or part of an article, not being merely 'surface decoration'. Even very simple designs may be protected. However, a design is not original if it was commonplace in the design field in question at the time of its creation. In *Farmers Build* [1999] RPC 461, 'commonplace' was defined as meaning a design of a type which would excite no 'peculiar attention' amongst those in the trade, or one which amounts to a run-of-the-mill combination of well-known features. Designs are not protected if they consist of a method or principle of construction, or are dictated by the shape, etc of an article to which the new article is to be connected or of which it is to form part, the so-called 'must-fit' and 'must-match' exclusions. In *Ocular Sciences* [1997] RPC 289, these exclusions had a devastating effect upon numerous design rights claimed for contact lens designs. See also *Dyson* v. *Qualtex* [2006] EWCA Civ. 166 in which these exclusions were discussed in relation to spare parts for Dyson vacuum cleaners.

Design right subsists in designs made by or for qualifying persons (see, broadly, 'Qualification', above) or first marketed in the UK or EU or any other country to which the provision may be extended by Order.

Design right lasts only 15 years from the end of the year in which it was first recorded or an article made to the design, or (if shorter) 10 years from the end of the year in which articles made according to the design were first sold or hired out. During the last five years of the term of protection, a licence to use the design can be obtained 'as of right' but against payment of a proper licence fee. Hence, design right may give only five years 'absolute' protection, as opposed to the 'life plus 70' of copyright.

The designer will be the owner of the right, unless it was commissioned, in which case the commissioner will be the first owner. An employee's designs made in the course of employment will belong to the employer. The right given to the owner of a design right is the exclusive right to reproduce the design for commercial purposes. The rules as to assignments, licensing and infringement, both primary and secondary, are substantially similar to those described above in relation to copyright, as are the remedies available.

There have recently been significant changes to the law on registered designs, which coexist with the right given by the unregistered design right discussed above. The Registered Design Act 1949 has been amended (and expanded) in line with EU legislation, and now permits the registration of designs consisting of the appearance of the whole or any part of a product resulting from features of the product itself, such as shape, materials, etc or from the ornamentation of the product. It covers industrial or handicraft items, their packaging or get-up, etc. Designs must be novel and not solely dictated by function. The range of designs which may be registered is wider than under the old law, and designs need not necessarily have 'eye appeal'. Such designs provide a monopoly right renewable for up to 25 years. For further explanation see the useful guidance on the Patent Office website.

EU Regulation 6/2002 created two Community design regimes, one for registered and one for unregistered designs. In some cases, especially where there are problems with relying upon UK unregistered design right, the Community regime may be very helpful. It is not possible in the space available here to describe these new regimes in detail but the Regulation is available online (www.europa.ue.int/eur-lex). In brief, such designs are *very* broadly defined in Article 3 and can include the outward appearance of a product or part of it, shape, texture, materials and/or its ornamentation. 'Products' include any industrial or handicraft item, packaging, graphic symbols and typographic typefaces but not computer programs. However, the designs must be 'new' and have 'individual character'. The registered right may be enjoyed for up to 25 years in five-year tranches, but an unregistered Community design right lasts only three years. The unregistered right protects the design from copying, but the registered right gives 'absolute' exclusivity, in that it may be infringed without copying.

Moral rights

The Act also provides for the protection of certain 'moral rights'.

The right of 'paternity' is for the author of a copyright literary, dramatic, musical or artistic work, or the director of a copyright film, to be identified as the author/director, largely whenever the work is commercially exploited (s.77). See *Sawkins*.

However, the right does not arise unless it has been 'asserted' by appropriate words in writing, or in the case of an artistic work by ensuring that the artist's name appears on the frame, etc (see end). There are exceptions to the right, in particular where first ownership of the copyright vested in the author's or director's employer.

The right of 'integrity' protects work from 'derogatory treatment', meaning an addition to, deletion from, alteration or adaptation of a work which amounts to distortion or mutilation of the work or is otherwise prejudicial to the honour or reputation of the author/ director. Again, infringement of the right takes place when the maltreated work is published commercially or performed or exhibited in public. There are various exceptions set out in s.81 of the Act, in particular where the publication is in a newspaper, etc, and the work was made for inclusion in it or made available with the author's consent.

Where the copyright in the work vested first in the author's or director's employer, he or she has no right to 'integrity' unless identified at the time of the relevant act or on published copies of the work.

These rights subsist for as long as the copyright in the work subsists.

A third moral right conferred by the Act is not to have a literary, dramatic, musical or artistic work falsely attributed to one as author, or to have a film falsely attributed to one as director, again where the work in question is published, etc. This right subsists until 20 years after a person's death.

None of these rights can be assigned during the person's lifetime, but all of them either pass on the person's death as directed by his or her will or fall into his residuary estate.

A fourth but rather different moral right is conferred by s.85. It gives a person who has commissioned the taking of photographs for private purposes a right to prevent copies of the work being issued to the public, etc.

The remedies for breach of these moral rights again include damages and an injunction, although s.103(2) specifically foresees the granting of an injunction qualified by a right to the defendant to do the acts complained of, if subject to a suitable disclaimer.

Moral rights are exercisable in relation to works in which the copyright has revived subject to any waiver or assertion of the right made before 1 January 1996 (see details as to who may exercise rights in paragraph 22 of the Regulations).

NOTICE

AMANDA LOUISE MICHAELS hereby asserts and gives notice of her right under s.77 of the Copyright, Designs & Patents Act 1988 to be identified as the author of the foregoing article.

AMANDA MICHAELS

Amanda L. Michaels is a barrister in private practice in London, and specialises in copyright, designs, trade marks, and similar intellectual property and 'media' work. She is author of *A Practical Guide to Trade Mark Law* (Sweet & Maxwell, 3rd edn 2002).

Further reading

Bainbridge, David, *Intellectual Property*, Longman, 6th edn, 2005

Flint, *A User's Guide to Copyright*, Tottel Publishing, 2005

Garnett, Rayner James and Davies, *Copinger and Skone James on Copyright*, Sweet & Maxwell, 15th edn, 2004

Copyright Acts

Copyright, Designs and Patents Act 1998 (but it is vital to use an up-to-date amended version)

The Duration of Copyright and Rights in Performances Regulations 1995 (SI 1995 No 3297)

The Copyright and Related Rights Regulations 2003 (SI 2003 No 2498)

The Intellectual Property (Enforcement, etc) Regulations 2006 (SI 2006 No 1028)

The Performances (Moral Rights, etc) Regulations 2006 (SI 2006 No 18)

see also Numerous Orders in Council

Council Regulation 6/2002

The Copyright Licensing Agency Ltd

The Copyright Licensing Agency (CLA) collects and distributes money on behalf of artists, writers and publishers for the copying, scanning and emailing of their work. CLA operates on a non-profit basis, and issues licences to schools, further and higher education, business and government bodies so that such organisations can access the copyright material in books, journals, law reports, magazines and periodicals.

Why was CLA established?

CLA was established in 1982 by its members, the Authors' Licensing and Collecting Society (ALCS) and the Publishers Licensing Society (PLS) to promote and enforce the intellectual property rights of British rightsholders both at home and abroad. CLA also has an agency agreement with the Design and Artists Copyright Society (DACS), which represents artists and illustrators.

ALCS has two corporate members – the Society of Authors and the Writers' Guild of Great Britain. It also has a large number of individual authors as members and affiliations with the National Union of Journalists and the Chartered Institute of Journalists. PLS members are the Publishers Association, the Periodical Publishers Association and the Association of Learned and Professional Society Publishers.

How CLA helps artists and writers

CLA allows licensed users access to millions of titles worldwide. In return CLA ensures artists and writers, along with publishers, are fairly recompensed by the licence fees, which CLA collects and forwards to its members for onward distribution to artists, writers and publishers.

The collective management of licensing schemes means that CLA can provide users with the simplest and most cost-effective means of obtaining authorisation for photocopying, while copy limits ensure fair recompense is maintained for rightsholders.

CLA is has developed licences which enable digitisation of existing print material. The licence enables users to scan and electronically send extracts from copyright works.

Further information
The Copyright Licensing Agency Ltd Saffron House, 6–10 Kirby Street, London EC1N 8TS *tel* 020-7400 3100 *fax* 020-7400 3101 *email* cla@cla.co.uk CBC House, 24 Canning Street, Edinburgh EH3 8E9 *tel* 0131-272 2711 *fax* 0131-272 2811 *email* clascotland@cla.co.uk *website* www.cla.co.uk

Licence to copy

CLA's licensees fall into three main categories:
- education (schools, further and higher education);
- government (central, local, public bodies); and
- business (business, industry, professionals).

CLA develops licences to meet the specific needs of each sector and groupings within each sector. Depending on the requirement, there are both blanket and transactional licences available. Every licence allows the photocopying of most books, journals, magazines and periodicals published in the UK.

An international dimension

Many countries have established equivalents to CLA and the number of such agencies is set to grow. Nearly all these agencies, including CLA, are members of the International Federation of Reproduction Rights Organisations (IFRRO).

Through reciprocal arrangements with these organisations, any CLA licence also allows copying from an expanding list of publications in other countries. Currently these countries are: Australia, Austria, Belgium, Brazil, Canada (including Quebec), Denmark, Finland, France, Germany, Greece, Iceland, Ireland, Italy, Japan, Kenya, Malta, The Netherlands, New Zealand, Norway, South Africa, Spain, Sweden, Switzerland, the USA and Zimbabwe.

CLA receives monies from these organisations for the copying of UK material abroad and forwards it to rightsholders.

Distribution

The fees collected from licensees are forwarded to artists, authors and publishers via ALCS, DACS and PLS respectively, and are based on statistical surveys and records of copying activity. For the year 2004/5 £41 million was distributed to rightsholders.

Respecting copyright

CLA also believes it is important to raise awareness of the copyright in published material and the need to protect the creativity of artists, authors and publishers. To this end, CLA organises a range of activities such as copyright workshops in schools, seminars for businesses and institutions and an extensive exhibition programme. A comprehensive website is regularly updated and a bi-annual newsletter, *Clarion*, is posted to all licensees and to those individuals and groups concerned with copyright. A downloadable version is also available on the CLA website (www.cla.co.uk/clarion).

Protecting the value of creativity

CLA believes in working together with all sectors to take into account their differing needs, meaning legal action is rare. However, organisations – especially in the business sector – need to be made aware that copyright is a legally enforceable right enshrined in statute law, not a voluntary option. CLA's compliance division aims to continue the education programme. However, as a last resort it has the power to take legal proceedings on behalf of rightsholders.

Authors' Licensing and Collecting Society

The Authors' Licensing and Collecting Society is the rights management society for UK writers.

The Authors' Licensing and Collecting Society (ALCS) is the UK collective rights management society for writers. Established in 1977, the Society represents the interests of all UK writers and aims to ensure that they are fairly compensated for any works that are copied, broadcast or recorded.

A non-profit company, ALCS was set up in the wake of the campaign to establish a Public Lending Right to help writers protect and exploit their collective rights. Today, it is the largest writers' organisation in the UK with a membership of over 53,000 and an annual distribution of over £14 million in royalties to writers.

The Society is committed to ensuring that the rights of writers, both intellectual property and moral, are fully respected and fairly rewarded. It represents all types of writers and includes educational, research and academic authors drawn from the professions; scriptwriters, adaptors, playwrights, poets, editors and freelance journalists, across the print and broadcast media.

Internationally recognised as a leading authority on copyright matters and authors' interests, ALCS is committed to fostering an awareness of intellectual property issues among the writing community. It maintains a close watching brief on all matters affecting copyright both in the UK and internationally and makes regular representations to the UK government and the European Union.

ALCS works closely with the Writers' Guild of Great Britain, the Society of Authors and by reciprocal agreement with over 50 collecting societies overseas. Owned and controlled by writers, it is governed by a non-executive board of 12 directors, all of whom are working writers. Four of these directors are nominated by the Writers' Guild of Great Britain and four by the Society of Authors. The other four independent members are elected directly by ALCS Ordinary Members.

Membership

Authors' Licensing and Collecting Society Ltd
14–18 Holborn, London EC1N 2LE
tel 020-7395 0600 *fax* 020-7395 0660
email alcs@alcs.co.uk
website www.alcs.co.uk
Chief Executive Owen Atkinson

ALCS membership is open to all writers and successors to their estates at a current annual subscription fee of £10 for Ordinary members. Members of the Society of Authors and the Writers' Guild of Great Britain have free Ordinary membership of ALCS. In addition, members of the National Union of Journalists, Chartered Institute of Journalists, British Association of Journalists and the British Comedy Writers' Association have free Associate membership of ALCS. You may also register direct with ALCS for free Associate membership.

ALCS operations are primarily funded through a commission levied on distributions and membership fees. The commission on funds generated for Ordinary members is currently 10.5%. Writers do not have to become Ordinary members of ALCS to receive funds due to them for the reproduction of their works; however, for Associate members such funds are subject to a levy of 14%. Most writers will find that this, together with a number of other membership benefits, provides excellent value to membership.

The Society collects fees that are difficult, time-consuming or legally impossible for writers and their representatives to claim on an individual basis, money that is nonetheless due to them. To date, it has distributed over £129 million in secondary royalties to writers.

Over the years, ALCS has developed highly specialised knowledge and sophisticated systems that can track writers and their works against any secondary use for which they are due payment. A network of international contacts and reciprocal agreements with foreign collecting societies also ensures that British writers are compensated for any similar use overseas.

The primary sources of fees due to writers are secondary royalties from the following:

Photocopying

The single largest source of income, this is administered by the Copyright Licensing Agency (CLA – see page 248). Created in 1982 by ALCS and the Publishers Licensing Society (PLS), the CLA grants licences to users for the copying of books and serials. This includes schools, colleges, universities, central and local government departments as well as the British Library, businesses and other institutions. Licence fees are based on the number of people who benefit and the number of copies made. The revenue from this is then split between the rightsholders: authors, publishers and artists. Money due to authors is transferred to ALCS for distribution. ALCS also receives photocopying payments from foreign sources.

Digitisation

In 1999, the CLA launched its licensing scheme for the digitisation of printed texts. It offers licences to organisations for storing and using digital versions of authors' printed works, which have been scanned into a computer. Again, the fees are split between authors and publishers.

Foreign Public Lending Right

The Public Lending Right (PLR) system pays authors whose books are borrowed from public libraries. Through reciprocal agreements with VG Wort (the German collecting society), Stichting Leenrecht (the Dutch collecting society) and Literar Mechana (the Austrian collecting society) ALCS members receive payment whenever their books are borrowed from German, Dutch and Austrian libraries. (Please note that ALCS does not administer the UK Public Lending Right, this is managed directly by the UK PLR Office; see page 226.)

ALCS also receives other payments from Germany. These cover the loan of academic, scientific and technical titles from academic libraries; extracts of authors' works in textbooks and the press, together with other one-off fees.

Simultaneous cable retransmission

This involves the simultaneous showing of one country's television signals in another country, via a cable network. Cable companies pay a central collecting organisation a percentage of their subscription fees, which must be collectively administered. This sum is then divided by the rightsholders. ALCS receives the writers' share for British programmes containing literary and dramatic material and distributes this to them.

The BBC

ALCS licenses BBC Worldwide Ltd for the inclusion of material within the ALCS repertoire. The licence covers the direct reception and cable retransmission of BBC Prime, a satellite entertainment channel, in Europe and Africa and other countries.

Educational recording

ALCS, together with the main broadcasters and rightsholders, set up the Educational Recording Agency (ERA) in 1989 to offer licences to educational establishments. ERA collects fees from the licensees and pays ALCS the amount due to writers for their literary works.

Other sources of income include a blank tape levy and small, miscellaneous literary rights.

Tracing authors

ALCS is dedicated to protecting and promoting authors' rights and enabling writers to maximise their income. It is committed to ensuring that royalties due to writers are efficiently collected and speedily distributed to them. One of its greatest challenges is finding some of the writers for whom it holds funds and ensuring that they claim their money.

Any published author or broadcast writer could have some funds held by ALCS for them. It may be a nominal sum or it could run in to several thousand pounds. Either call or visit the ALCS website – see box for contact details.

Design and Artists Copyright Society

The Design and Artists Copyright Society promotes and protects the copyright and related rights of artists and visual creators in the UK and worldwide.

About DACS

The Design and Artists Copyright Society (DACS) was established in 1984 and is the UK's copyright licensing and collecting society for visual creators. It acts as an agent for its members, offering a range of services for copyright consumers. It also negotiates a share of revenue from collective licensing schemes, on behalf of all visual creators, and distributes this through its Payback service.

Contact details

Design and Artists Copyright Society (DACS)
33 Great Sutton Street, London EC1V 0DX
tel 020-7336 8811 *fax* 020-7336 8822
email info@dacs.org.uk
website www.dacs.org.uk

DACS membership represents over 36,000 international fine artists, as well as 16,000 commercial photographers, illustrators, craftspeople, cartoonists, architects, animators and designers. It is a not-for-profit organisation that distributes 75% of licensing revenue back to visual creators. A 25% commission is retained to cover administration costs.

About membership

Membership of DACS is open to all visual creators, their heirs and beneficiaries, working in any medium. Members retain ownership and control of their copyright while DACS manages it by negotiating terms and collecting fees on their behalf. Its experienced licensing team works closely with both artists and consumers to ensure the best balance of interests is achieved when licensing works.

About licensing

DACS is quickly growing to be one of the most well-respected art licensing agencies in its field, promoting and protecting the copyright and related rights of artists and visual creators in the UK and worldwide.

Licensing individual rights

DACS provides a range of licensing services for copyright consumers seeking to license the individual rights of an artist for a one-off use: for example, when a publisher wants to reproduce an artistic work in a book.

Licensing clients come from a diverse range of sectors including advertising, publishing, broadcasting, multimedia, product design and merchandising. Members' works have been licensed for everything from greeting cards to film sets, from websites to silk scarves.

Licensing rights collectively

Licences for secondary uses of artistic works are collectively administered under blanket licensing schemes: for example, when a business needs to photocopy pages of books or magazines. DACS negotiates a share of the revenue from these schemes on behalf of visual creators. Money from these schemes is paid back annually through DACS' Payback service.

Artist's Resale Right

The Artist's Resale Right (or *droit de suite*) entitles artists and visual creators to a percentage share of the price every time their work is resold by a gallery, dealer or auction house. The right is applicable to all professional resales and can be transferred to heirs for up to 70 years after the artist's death. DACS collects and distributes resale royalties on behalf of UK artists through the Artist's Resale Right Service Hub.

Copyright advisory service

DACS has a number of free copyright fact sheets available for download at their website (www.dacs.org.uk). Members are also entitled to use DACS' copyright advisory service where advisers can answer copyright enquiries via telephone or email.

Other benefits

DACS belongs to an international network of collecting societies in 27 countries. Visual creators' rights are administered on the same basis in all these countries and they will receive royalties when their work has been reproduced overseas.

Because DACS is an authoritative voice for visual creators' rights in the UK, new members who join will be strengthening the presence of visual creators and their rights in the copyright community as a whole.

Copyright

- Copyright is a right granted to creators under law.
- Copyright in all artistic works is established from the moment of creation – the only qualification is that the work must be original.
- There is no registration system in the UK; copyright comes into operation automatically and lasts the lifetime of the visual creator plus a period of 70 years after their death.
- After death, copyright is usually transferred to the visual creator's heirs or beneficiaries. When the 70-year period has expired, the work then enters the public domain and no longer benefits from copyright protection.
- The copyright owner has the exclusive right to authorise the reproduction (or copy) of a work in any medium by any other party.
- Any reproduction can only take place with the copyright owner's consent. Permission is usually granted in return for a fee, which enables the visual creator to derive some income from other people using his or her work.
- If a visual creator is commissioned to produce a work, he or she will usually retain the copyright unless an agreement is signed which specifically assigns the copyright. When visual creators are employees and create work during the course of their employment, the employer retains the copyright in those works.

See also...
- *Copyright questions*, page 233
- *UK copyright law*, page 236

Magazines and newspapers
Writing for teenage magazines

Teenage magazines can be a lifeline to adolescent girls but writing for this market is very specialised. Michelle Garnett explains what writers for teenage magazines need to know.

Life for teen girls is tough. Raging hormones, changing body bits, annoying boys and constant peer pressure, all gang up to present one huge challenge for them. And that's where teen magazines come to the rescue, providing escapism and reassurance for their confused readers.

But before even thinking about submitting your work to any teen mag, it's vital to get a firm grasp on what they're all about. Most mags tend to fall into two categories – 'Lifestyle' and 'Entertainment':

The 'Lifestyle' titles (think *Bliss* and *Cosmogirl*) provide info on anything relevant to teen girls' lives, from reports on way-out new style trends and self-help features to dish out advice on coping with bullies to tips on bagging a buff boyfriend and gritty real life stories.

The 'Entertainment' titles (think *It's Hot*) focus on celeb, music, TV and film gossip with lashings of star interviews, celeb quizzes, posters and song words.

However, as an exception to the rule, the teen weekly, *Sneak*, has a rather unique mix of the two categories. As a weekly title it covers the latest celeb gossip but also throws in a chunk of style and boy advice, gripping real life dramas and those all-important problem pages. However, most other mags lean towards either Lifestyle or Entertainment content with just a sprinkling of features related to the other category.

These days, with teens spending piles of their pocket money on mobile phone top-up cards and quick-fix junk food there's heaps of competition amongst the teen mags to be the one title that flies off the shop shelves like a rocket.

There's no excuse – covers *have* to be attention grabbing. Cover lines must offer exclusivity (e.g. a gripping heart-to-heart with the latest Big Brother star), fresh ideas (new revelations about the murky depths of teen boys' minds) and aspirational promises (easy steps to looking fab *whatever* your body shape). Cover images must be non-threatening (girls looking friendly, not bitchy), eye-popping (topless, and most importantly, hairless boy totty is usually a firm favourite) and colourful (you can't beat a flash of fluoro to help you stand out). Most mags (with the exception of *Sneak*) also rely on 'free gifts' to help boost their 'come buy me!' appeal.

Teen mag readership

But who are these teen girls that we're trying to persuade to part with their precious pocket money? If you're intending to aim your features at this discerning group of individuals you'd better get to know all you can about them.

On the whole, teen readers are demanding, streetwise, fickle consumers who want to be treated with respect but view adulthood with apprehension, often clinging to the comforts of childhood to help them feel secure and safe when the pressure gets too much.

Here's the scientific bit... Did you know that typical teen readers tend to fall into four *very* revealing categories? First off, there's the 'Obsessive Fan'. This girl has to be the first to know any gossip. She'll usually be infatuated with one boy in particular – often this will be a celeb whose cute face will be plastered all over her bedroom wall, school locker, books, etc. She'll spend every last penny on anything (including mags) that contains a fleeting mention of him. Sometimes her affections will be focused on a 'real' boy – it's been known for Obsessive Fan types to keep a secret stash of her 'crush souvenirs', containing such gems as a dirty fork that he once used in the school canteen!

Next there's the 'Fashionista'. This girl is crazy about fashion. She'll spend hours flicking through the style pages desperate for inspiration for her weekly shopping trips to New Look and Top Shop. The more creative Fashionista will copy the step-by-step customising guides to give her outfits that individualistic edge. She'll be an expert with her make up brush and unsurprisingly, will be very image conscious. She might pretend that she doesn't need to read features on 'detox diets to make your skin glow' but she'll devour them in secret and then pass on her newly acquired tips to her gang.

Then there's the 'Reality Lover'. This girl is addicted to Jeremy Karl and TV soaps. She'll greedily devour tragic real life stories. It doesn't matter whether the tale relates to a famous celeb or an ordinary 15 year-old from Leeds – so long as it's majorly grim, with a positive ending, she'll be hooked. It's no surprise that she's a fan of reality TV shows and dramas and loves gossiping about the latest shocking antics on *Wife Swap* or *Footballers' Wives*. In fact, it's reading about other people's lives that provides her with some comfort and re-assurance about her own life.

Lastly, there's the 'Info Gatherer'. This girl is a true magazine junkie! She uses her mag fix to get high on knowledge that'll help her make sense of the world around her and will elevate her status in her gang. She's not fussy about what she reads, is less street-sussed than other girls in her class and becomes easily bored. She'll often have three different mags on the go at a time but will just as happily plough through her mum's mags too.

But in case you're thinking, 'Hey, I was a teen once – I *know* what they're like' just remember one thing... 21st century teen readers are very different from those even just 10 years ago. These days' teens have much less to rebel about. The majority are actually best mates with their mothers and instead of shocking them with new pillar-box red highlights they'll be out shopping with their trendy mums and swapping clothes! They're also worldly wise and surprisingly ambitious about their future prospects.

Oh and don't think you can ever pull the wool over teen readers' eyes – they're sharp and quick to judge and if you get even the smallest fact wrong, they'll pick you up on it!

Considering writing for teen mags

So, now you've considered the kind of reader you'll be speaking to via your feature, it's time to get cracking, yes? No! It may sound mind-numbingly obvious but the first step when considering submitting material to a teen mag is to actually read a copy of that magazine! It's amazing how many times I've received suggestions for short fiction pieces when we don't actually feature those kind of stories in the magazine.

Familiarise yourself with the content, the look and the feel of the magazine. Many mags get revamped quite frequently to keep ahead of the competition, so it's wise to regularly browse through the latest issues to stay up to date.

A quick glance at the mag should tell you which kind of teen it's aimed at and therefore how you should tailor your copy or artwork to the targeted reader. As a writer it's vital to soak up the tone of the copy. Is it streetwise and fast-paced or cheesy and fun? Are there any phrases or words that pop up on a regular basis, giving an insight into the kind of language the average reader uses? Most *Sneak* features tend to adopt a punchy, straight-talking tone with, where appropriate, a strong, humorous undercurrent that at times can be just a little bit cruel to unsuspecting celebs! A magazine aimed at younger readers, such as *It's Hot*, veers towards a more excitable, upbeat tone, with the tendency to paint the pop world as bright, crazy and inoffensive.

Consider the tone of the actual subject matter too. Is it serious and gritty? Is it frivolous and tongue-in-cheek? Are there clear sections within the magazine which consist of a running theme? In *Sneak* magazine there's a chunky 'Boy News' section, which highlights the readers' love of discovering inside info about boys in a bid to help them understand them better. *Bliss* magazine features a strong 'real life stories' section which caters for their readers love for a dramatic, juicy read.

Another angle to reflect on is the topicality of the copy and pictures. When contributing ideas to a monthly mag think of a quirky spin you can give your idea to help give what could be a tried and tested subject a fresh makeover. If you're intending to submit ideas to a weekly mag then you need to prove that you've got your finger on the pulse. Think about how you can make your work up to date and relevant. Ask yourself, 'What's affecting teens' lives right *now*?' Are they crumbling under the pressure of exams? Is there a huge blockbuster film on the horizon that's set to capture their imaginations?

When the high school bitch-arama *Mean Girls* was released at the cinemas it was no-ticeable how several titles were quick to spot the potential popularity of the movie. *Sneak* ran style spreads aping the main characters' preppy look plus features on how to get one better on the 'Mean Girls' at your own school. Similarly, by the time the final *Lord of the Rings* instalment hit the big screen, Hollywood star Orlando Bloom had firmly established himself as a teen heartthrob and his appearance in the movie as long-haired lovely Legolas encouraged a stream of Orli-inspired features to whet readers' appetites. Paparazzi and studio shots of the actor were in high demand and real life titbits and Orlando quizzes were a staple diet for several months.

And of course, think seasonal. A few months prior to the summer holidays, monthly teen titles will be dreaming up cover-worthy concepts for the ultimate boredom buster feature. Conjure up a trend-based, original idea and you could find yourself commissioned to produce a hefty eight-page special.

Getting noticed

Finally... how to get yourself noticed amongst a sea of competition from other freelancers. Sometimes it's all about timing. It may be worthwhile to find out if the mag you're hoping to submit work to has a set date each week or month when feature ideas are discussed so that you can ensure your suggestions land in the Features Editor's email box just when he or she is tuned into an ideas brainstorm. Don't go the bother of sending in a fully completed article. If your idea is strong, a catchy headline and brief synopsis will grab their attention and the sheer mention of a juicy real life case study will be enough to get them salivating! And if you have a specialist subject area (style, real life stories, celebrity interviews) it could be worth suggesting a meeting with the relevant team member – if you impress them with your expertise you could bag yourself a regular commission.

But most importantly of all – don't give up. If you don't hear back immediately it doesn't necessarily mean your idea's been discarded. Many teen mag offices are hectic environments in which pressured deadlines often take on a life of their own. Your contact is probably furiously chasing a lead on a reality TV star's love life trauma, while trying to persuade a gang of shy 14 year-old lads to confess their first date hells and batting around that ever niggling question: 'how am I going to make our lovely readers feel entertained, shocked, reassured and hooked by my magazine this issue?' And hopefully that's when *your* life-saving email will come to light!

Good luck!

Michelle Garnett was editor of *Sneak* magazine from April 2002 to May 2005. Previously, she worked for 10 years in various roles in the entertainment industry including deputy editor of *Top of the Pops Magazine*, producer of *cd:uk news*, editor of *worldpop.com* (in the crazy days of the internet boom!), writer of pop band biographies and (her most bizarre job to date...) official news reporter for Reuters on the Backstreet Boys four-day round-the-world promotional trip (2000). She now freelances for various publications.

Cartoons and deadlines

A good cartoon needs only a glance to take in its message. But what makes a good cartoonist? Ros Asquith introduces the world of drawing cartoons for a living.

If anyone had told me, when I was 10 years old, that I'd earn a living by drawing pictures, I'd have thought they were mad. I'd also have believed that I'd never be good enough. After spending nearly 20 years as a cartoonist and illustrator I still worry that both those things might be true – and I live in fear of being found out. I once worked for a newspaper editor who received a letter that said 'My four year-old can draw better than Ros Asquith'. He replied, paraphrasing Groucho Marx: 'Astonishing – send me your four year-old's work post haste.' I was lucky to have such an editor. I could just as easily have been sacked.

I've been both dismissed and defended countless times and if you really want to be a cartoonist you need to learn to take criticism as gracefully as praise. A cartoon is an immediate statement. It must make itself understood in one glance and is therefore more vulnerable to criticism than any article. The phrase 'saw your cartoon' has a very different meaning from 'saw your article'. It means the reader has seen, understood, liked or disliked, all at once. And there will always be readers who dislike or are offended by your work – and a great many of them who think they could do it better.

Not surprising then, that a distinguished colleague once gave the following pearls of wisdom to an eager young woman hoping to get started in the business, 'I always have just two words of advice for young cartoonists: take poison.' And who can blame him? We cartoonists are paid to play and we have to make it look difficult just in case other people get the idea they might be able to do it too.

How do you get started?

First, you must love to draw. Secondly, you must be brimming with ideas. Thirdly, a sense of humour is an asset. But love of drawing, the sheer sensual joy of holding a pencil and the pleasure of guiding it across the page, the endless magic of creating something out of nothing, is the major qualification. Perhaps it's not surprising that I've ended up doing what I do, since my earliest memories are linked to the pictures I drew as a child. I illustrated my own life from an early age, whether the adventures I drew were real or imaginary.

You may say that love of drawing is not enough, surely you must also be *good* at drawing? That's debatable. Almost all small children love to draw but sadly the way we teach art in primary schools soon weeds out those who 'can draw' from those who 'can't'. This is a nail in the coffin of talent for everyone who can't make things look realistic at an early age. If they were encouraged, by peers as well as teachers, to pursue expressiveness and ideas rather than striving for realism, perhaps children would not abandon drawing by the age of 11. We lose a vast amount of creative talent in this way, but it usually means that anyone considering cartooning or illustration as a career is already settled into the little box labelled 'can draw.' You need more than this. If you are someone who can't imagine a day without drawing, then go for it.

There are as many routes to cartooning as there are cartoonists. One thing we have in common, though, is heads full of heroes. I grew up devouring cartoons in every form: Leo Baxendale's fantastic Bash Street Kids in the *Beano*, Ronald Searle's ferocious St Trinian's schoolgirls, Thelwell's recalcitrant ponies, all the *New Yorker* cartoonists but especially James Thurber, Charles Addams (whose fiendish gallows humour inspired the long-running *Addams Family* series on television), and the endlessly inventive, wordlessly eloquent Saul Steinberg. I revelled in the artistry of *Batman* comics and could have probably won *Mastermind* with Superman as my subject when I was about 12. I was a huge fan of Reg Smythe's Andy Capp and my favourite cartoonist ever was the gentle giant of the *Express*, Giles, who could not only draw better than anyone on the planet, but whose drawings also conveyed a huge affection for humanity in all its whimsical and tremulous attempts to make sense of itself. These heroic figures captured for me the essence of the human condition, the little person against the tyrant, whether the tyranny be that of a dictatorship, a cruel boss, or merely a wilful domestic appliance.

Now I'm lucky enough to draw in the same paper as my later heroes: Steve Bell, Posy Simmonds, David Austin, Nicola Jennings and Andrjez Krause.

How on earth did that happen?

Despite drawing all the time, I'd hoped to become a graphic designer. Cartooning was not a career that occurred to me and it still surprises me how few women do it. (In fact I have several letters to 'Rob' or

'Rod' Asquith, which proves that even when you sign your name to a cartoon, people think you're a bloke.) My first cartoons came about by mistake, when I was working for Inter-Action Trust. The director, Ed Berman, wanted some jokes to replace the advertisements on the upper deck of the Fun Art Bus, a magnificent old Route master that had a cinema downstairs, a theatre upstairs, a driver who played keyboard on the bonnet and tickets that were poems. The bus ran a normal route and you could ride it for free. This was art in the community. I did some jokes about dogs. They were pasted up inside the bus and to my amazement the passengers laughed.

I made the drawings into a book (photocopied and spiral bound at Instant Print) and sold some at a dog show(!) and some through *The Times'* late great cartoonist Mel Calman, who was very encouraging when I nervously approached him. He agreed to sell some in his Bloomsbury shop.

On the left are examples of roughs I did for the letters page in the *Saturday Review* section of the *Guardian*. And above is the final artwork of the one they chose. See? Couldn't be simpler.

But still it never occurred to me to take my drawings further into the market-place – I spent the next few years as a mural painter, photographer and theatre critic and only started drawing again in desperation. I was asked to write an article for *Time Out* magazine about why there were no West End plays written by women, but I couldn't think of anything to write that I hadn't written already, so I drew a full-page feminist cartoon instead, which had a much greater impact than anything I'd ever written.

This led to my drawing for a number of publications alongside reviewing theatre. But it was having babies that finally made me turn back to drawing – after all, I didn't want to go out reviewing theatre every night any more. My children made me laugh so much I couldn't resist drawing jokes about them. Optima published these drawings in a collection originally titled *BABY! (the highs, the lows, the runny nose)* and Alan Rusbridger, (now the *Guardian's* editor, but then launching the *Weekend* magazine) liked them and asked me to do a strip.

My favourite creation, Doris, was born. Doris was a cleaner who never spoke but gently satirised the chattering classes (or *Guardian* readership) for whom she worked. I have since been told that cartoons should be recognisable in silhouette (think of Mickey Mouse or Bart Simpson) and, unconsciously, that was true of Doris, whose spotted headscarf and simple profile – I always drew her facing sideways – appeared weekly in the *Guardian* for 10 years. No doubt the readership was divided over Doris – she wasn't perhaps at the cutting edge of political satire and I expect some people found her bland, but I still get a lot of people asking after her – and that is a wonderful reason for becoming a cartoonist. Like an author, you can create a character people feel they know. Myself, I find it difficult not to believe the Simpsons live in a parallel universe and that I might bump into them some day. I've continued to enjoy drawing for sections of the *Guardian* regularly ever since.

My drawings for children's books (usually ones I've written myself) have, like Doris, instantly recognisable trademarks: Trixie Tempest's bunches, or the Teenage Worrier Letty Chubb's hair and nose, or Rover the Cat's pointy ears and whiskers.

Practical tips

If you are doing a strip, it's useful to have something that you'll be able to draw easily time and again, with clothes or hair that readers instantly latch onto: Andy Capp's cap, Claire in the Community's pony tail, Wendy Weber's huge round glasses, Bristow's bowler hat, Tin Tin's quiff. Draw something you will find easy to reproduce again and again. There's no sense giving yourself a hard time.

Your own route to success will be unique but initially you must have lots of ideas about absolutely everything. You need a sense of humour and a love of the absurd, obviously, but who knows if your gags are funny? Humour is as diverse as humanity – as everyone who's argued over a sitcom knows – and since no one can please everyone, you must have the courage to pursue your own vision, however eccentric, and hope there'll be enough takers for it in the real world. Try to find your own style, which should become as instantly recognisable as your signature.

Practise with different styles and ideas. Experiment with all kinds of pencils and pens and all kinds of colours and textures and papers. Doodle on the computer, but don't expect miracles. Be playful. See what suits you. Then, be serious and pursue it!

Most cartoonists draw in pencil and then ink over it – it must be the simplest profession in terms of tools. But still, when cartoonists gather, they will talk of nibs and inks, in search of the elusive pen, the freer flowing, quicker drying inks. (When you're drawing to dead-lines, you need a hair dryer handy.)

Research the market to see what's out there in terms of newspapers and magazines. What do you want to draw? What do you find funny? What do you know a lot about? Are you political? Domestic? Wry? Romantic? Surreal? Can you encompass an idea without any words? Or do you need punchlines? Do you want to do strips? Or single gags?

I'd like a hot meal for everyone who's asked me if I write the words to my cartoons – of course I do. But if you feel you can draw but can't write, then there are a number of successful partnerships who work that way.

Presenting your portfolio

Take a subject. It could be gardening, DIY, giving birth, cats, Shakespeare. Preferably all of these. Then discipline yourself to come up with at least six gags on each subject as this is what you'll have to do if you work on a newspaper. Then you'll give your rough ideas to the editor who will either sneer and send you off to do some more roughs (or possibly another job entirely, like floor sweeping) or will smile enigmatically and choose one. If your editor actually laughs, you will feel foolishly happy – and that is about as near as you are likely to get to your audience. If you want to hear an audience laughing, you would be better off becoming a stand-up comedian.

Once you've created your portfolio of roughs and finished sketches, take it to news-papers and magazines which you think might be interested in your work. Set up appoint-ments in advance as newspapers and magazines are extremely busy places. I think it's better to meet people face to face than to fax or email them, as you can then gauge what they really think of your work and might even pick up some helpful tips.

Listen to what editors say. They will not always be right about your work, because illustration and cartooning are matters of taste, but they are much more often right than not – and they certainly know more about their particular readership than you do, so don't try to tell them how to do their jobs. Good art editors will certainly give helpful advice about presentation and ideas, but what they are looking for is professionalism, vision, and originality.

Don't be put off by rejection. (Everyone knows that Harry Potter was rejected by several editors – you will be too!) Keep trying. Keep improving. Aim your work at suitable places. There are racks and racks of magazines to choose from. Remember that a picture is worth a thousand words and editors like a laugh as much as you do.

A final word of advice: if the names Gary Larsen, Posy Simmonds, Jules Feiffer, James

Thurber, Steve Bell and Matt Groening, mean nothing to you, you may be barking up the wrong tree.

Or you may be that genius I've yet to meet who needs no outside inspiration.

Ros Asquith is a cartoonist and an author. Her cartoons appear regularly in the *Guardian* where her comic strip Doris featured for many years. She wrote and illustrated the bestselling *Teenage Worrier* series (Corgi), which has been translated into 12 languages. Her most recent children's books are about the Trixie Tempest, Tweenage Tearaway character (HarperCollins) and a teenage novel, *Love, Fifteen* (Random House 2005).

Magazines and newspapers for children

Listings of magazines about children's literature and education start on page 278.

Action Hero
BBC Worldwide Ltd, BBC Woodlands, 80 Wood Lane, London W12 0TT
tel 020-8433 2000 *fax* 020-8433 2941
website www.bbcworldwide.com
Editor Paddy Kempshall
Every 4 weeks £1.85

Magazine for boys aged 4–7 featuring popular TV characters and toys joining forces to fight evil. Content includes stories, makes, games, posters, news and reviews of the best toys available and a competition.

Action Man
Panini UK, Panini House, Coach and Horses Passage, Tunbridge Wells, Kent TN2 5UJ
tel (01892) 500100 *fax* (01892) 545666
email paninicomics@panini.co.uk
website www.paninicomics.co.uk
Every 3 weeks £1.75

Every issue has an interactive pull-out combat zone to use with the reader's own Action Man – there's a different mission to complete in every issue. Also quizzes and competitions.

Adventure Box
Bayard, 1st Floor, 2 King Street, Peterborough PE1 1LT
tel (01733) 565 858 *fax* (01733) 427 500
email contact@bayard-magazines.co.uk
website www.bayard-magazines.co.uk
Editor-in-chief Simona Sideri, *Art Director* Pat Carter
10 p.a. £37.50 p.a.

Aimed at 7–9 year-old children starting to read on their own. Each issue contains an illustrated chapter story plus games, an animal feature, nature activity and a cartoon. Length: 2500–3000 words (stories). Specially commissions most material. Founded 1996.

After Hours
RNIB, PO Box 173, Peterborough PE2 6WS
tel (01733) 375000 *fax* (01733) 375001
email editorial@rnib.org.uk
website www.rnib.org.uk

Braille magazine for blind and partially sighted children aged 11–14.

Alias
Titan Publishing Group Ltd, Titan House, 144 Southwark Street, London SE1 0UP
tel 020-7620 0200 *fax* 020-7803 1803
email dead-drop@titanemail.com
website www.titanmagazines.com
Editor Paul Terry
6 p.a. £3.50

Includes interviews, features, pin-ups and merchandise round-ups.

Amy
BBC Worldwide Ltd, Woodlands, 80 Wood Lane, London W12 0TT
tel 020-8433 2000
3-weekly £1.99

The little sister title to *Girl Talk*. Lifestyle magazine for 5–8 year-old girls featuring CBBC characters such as Tracey Beaker and programmes such as *Blue Peter* and the *Really Wild Show*. Also includes film, arts and crafts, stories, puzzles and quizzes. Founded 2006.

Animal Action
RSPCA, Wilberforce Way, Southwater, Horsham, West Sussex RH13 9RS
tel (0870) 7540145
website www.rspca.org.uk
Editor Sarah Evans
Bi-monthly £8 p.a.

RSPCA membership magazine for children under 13 years old with animal news, features, competitions and puzzles.

Animals and You
D.C. Thomson & Co Ltd, Albert Square, Dundee DD1 9QJ
tel (01382) 223131 *fax* (01382) 225511
185 Fleet Street, London EC4A 2HS
tel 020-7400 1030 *fax* 020-7400 1089
Monthly (Fri) £1.90

Features, stories and pin-ups for girls who love animals. Founded 1998.

Aquila
New Leaf Publishing Ltd, PO Box 2518, Eastbourne, East Sussex BN21 2BB
tel (01323) 431313 *fax* (01323) 731136
email info@aquila.co.uk
website www.aquila.co.uk
Editor Jackie Berry
Monthly £35 p.a.

Dedicated to encouraging children aged 8–13 to reason and create, and to develop a caring nature.

Short stories and serials of up to 4 parts. Occasional features commissioned from writers with specialist knowledge. Approach in writing with ideas and sample of writing style, with sae. Length: 700–800 words (features), 1000–1100 words (stories or per episode of a serial). Payment: £75 (features); £90 (stories), £80 (per episode). Founded 1993.

Art Attack

Panini UK, Panini House, Coach and Horses Passage, Tunbridge Wells, Kent TN2 5UJ
tel (01892) 500100 *fax* (01892) 545666
email paninicomics@panini.co.uk
website www.paninicomics.co.uk
Editor Julie Scott
Every 3 weeks £1.99

Magazine to complement the TV show *Art Attack*. Step-by-step instructions on creative things to make and do.

Astonishing Spider-Man

Panini UK, Panini House, Coach and Horses Passage, Tunbridge Wells, Kent TN2 5UJ
tel (01892) 500100 *fax* (01892) 545666
email paninicomics@panini.co.uk
website www.paninicomics.co.uk
Editor Brady Webb
Every 4 weeks £2.50

The Avengers United

Panini UK, Panini House, Coach and Horses Passage, Tunbridge Wells, Kent TN2 5UJ
tel (01892) 500100 *fax* (01892) 545666
email paninicomics@panini.co.uk
website www.paninicomics.co.uk
Editor Scott Gray
Every 4 weeks £2.50

Balamory Magazine

BBC Worldwide Ltd, BBC Woodlands, 80 Wood Lane, London W12 0TT
website www.bbcworldwide.com
Every 4 weeks £1.75

Based on the TV programme *Balamory*, each issue follows an exciting story through Balamory, with colouring, drawing, puzzles and games. *BBC Balamory Magazine* is featured in *Toybox Teach Me* magazine, along with lots of other CBeebies characters.

Barbie

Egmont Magazines, 184 Drummond Street, London NW1 3HP
tel 020-7380 6430 *fax* 020-7380 6444
website www.egmontmagazines.co.uk
Editor Claire Noonan
Every 3 Weeks £1.65

Magazine for 3–7 year old girls with the aim of providing the reader with factual and fantasy material which they can use with their own dolls in the form of fashion and role play. Includes up-to-date fashion and beauty tips, photo dramas and the latest gossip about Barbie, her friends and family.

Batman: Legends

Panini UK, Panini House, Coach and Horses Passage, Tunbridge Wells, Kent TN2 5UJ
tel (01892) 500100 *fax* (01892) 545666
email paninicomics@panini.co.uk
website www.paninicomics.co.uk
Editor Brady Webb
Every 4 weeks £2.40

The Batman Comic

Titan Publishing Group Ltd, Titan House, 144 Southwark Street, London SE1 0UP
tel 020-7620 0200 *fax* 020-7803 1803
email batmanemail@titanemail.com
website www.titanmagazines.com
Editor Richard Matthews
Every 4 weeks £1.75

The Beano

D.C. Thomson & Co. Ltd, Albert Square, Dundee DD1 9QJ
tel (01382) 223131 *fax* (01382) 322214
185 Fleet Street, London EC4A 2HS
tel 020-7400 1030 *fax* 020-7400 1089
Editor Euan Kerr
Weekly 80p

Comic strips for children aged 6–12. Series, 11–22 pictures. Artwork only. Payment: on acceptance.

Big Cook Little Cook

BBC Worldwide Ltd, Woodlands, 80 Wood Lane, London W12 0TT
tel 020-8433 2356
website www.bbcmagazines.com/bigcooklittlecook
4-weekly £1.65

Magazine to give 3–6 year-old children the opportunity to have fun and get excited about food. Based on *Big Cook Little Cook*, shown on CBeebies. Founded 2005.

Blast Off!

RNIB, PO Box 173, Peterborough PE2 6WS
tel (01733) 375000 *fax* (01733) 375001
email editorial@rnib.org.uk
website www.rnib.org.uk
Editor Racheal Jarvis
Monthly 22p (£1.43 overseas)

Braille general interest magazine for blind and partially sighted children aged 7–11. Also available on disk.

Bliss

EMAP Consumer Media, Endeavour House, 189 Shaftesbury Avenue, London WC2H 8JG

tel 020-7437 9011 *fax* 020-7208 3591
website www.blissmag.co.uk
Editor Lisa Smosarski
Monthly £2.10

Glamorous young women's glossy magazine. Bright, intimate, American A5 format, with real life reports, celebrities, beauty, fashion, shopping, advice, quizzes. Payment: by arrangement. Founded 1995.

Bob the Builder
BBC Worldwide Ltd, BBC Woodlands, 80 Wood Lane, London W12 0TT
tel 020-8433 2000 *fax* 020-8433 2941
website www.bobthebuilder.org
Editor Coralie Noakes
Every 4 weeks £1.65

Stories, puzzles, competitions and activities built around Bob and his team for children aged 4–6 and their parents.

Braille at Bedtime
RNIB, PO Box 173, Peterborough PE2 6WS
tel (01733) 375000 *fax* (01733) 375001
email editorial@rnib.org.uk
website www.rnib.org.uk
Editor Racheal Jarvis
Every 2 months 69p (£3.34 overseas)

Braille short fiction magazine for blind and partially sighted children aged 7–11.

Brat
Globalclub Publications, Knockbracken Health Park, Saintfield Road, Belfast BT8 8BH
tel 028-9057 9057
email info@bratmag.com
website www.bratmag.com
Editor Paul McNamee
Monthly £1.90/€2.95

Magazine aimed at 15–16 year-old boys and girls with a mix of celebrity gossip, music, sport, sex, school health and careers advice. There are separate sections for boys and girls and a unisex problem page. Founded 2005.

Bratz
Titan Publishing Group Ltd, Titan House, 144 Southwark Street, London SE1 0UP
tel 020-7620 0200 *fax* 020-7803 1803
email bratzmail@titanemail.com
website www.bratzpack.com
Editor Darryl Curtis
Every 4 weeks £2.50

Buffy & Angel
Titan Publishing Group Ltd, Titan House, 144 Southwark Street, London SE1 0UP
tel 020-7620 0200 *fax* 020-7803 1803
email buffymail@titanemail.com
website www.titanmagazines.com

Editor Natalie Clubb
Monthly £3.75

Interviews, news and other features, including pin-ups, from *Buffy the Vampire Slayer* series.

Cartoon Network
Panini UK, Panini House, Coach and Horses Passage, Tunbridge Wells, Kent TN2 5UJ
tel (01892) 500100 *fax* (01892) 545666
email paninicomics@panini.co.uk
website www.paninicomics.co.uk
Editor Simon Frith
Every 3 weeks £1.99

CBeebies Weekly Magazine
BBC Worldwide Ltd, Woodlands, 80 Wood Lane, London W12 0TT
tel 020-8433 2356
email cbeebiesweekly@bbc.co.uk
website www.cbeebiesmagazine.com
Editor Andrea Wickstead
Weekly £1.75

Magazine to 'enhance a child's experience of the CBeebies programming week'. Aims to encourage family interaction and promote the philosophy of learning through play. Includes a 'child-friendly' TV guide. Founded 2006.

Children's Express UK
Exmouth House, 3–11 Pine Street, London EC1R 0JH
tel 020-7833 2577 *fax* 020-7278 7722
email enquiries@childrens-express.org
website www.childrens-express.org
Director Fiona Wyton

An award-winning news agency charity (does not publish a magazine or newspaper) that offers young people aged 8–18 the opportunity to write on issues of importance to them, for newspapers, radio and TV. It operates after school and at weekends. Founded 1995.

Clifford the Big Red Dog
Egmont Magazines, 184 Drummond Street, London NW1 3HP
tel 020-7380 6430
website www.egmontmagazines.co.uk
Monthly £1.60

Magazine for 3–6 year-olds reflecting the concept of the TV series, with each themed issue teaching an important life lesson such as sharing, respect or being a good friend. The stories and activities reinforce reading, writing and maths in a fun way.

Commando
D.C. Thomson & Co. Ltd, Albert Square, Dundee DD1 9QJ
tel (01382) 223131 *fax* (01382) 322214
8 per month £1.10

Fictional war stories told in pictures. Scripts: about 135 pictures. Synopsis required as an opener. New writers encouraged; send for details. Payment: on acceptance.

CosmoGIRL!

National Magazine House, 72 Broadwick Street, London W1F 9EP
tel 020-7439 5081 *fax* 020-7439 5400
email cosmogirl.mail@natmags.co.uk
website www.cosmogirl.co.uk
Editor Celia Duncan
Monthly £2.10

Little sister to *Cosmopolitan*. Features 'to inspire teenage girls to be the best they can be'. Specially commissions most material. Welcomes ideas for articles and features. Length: 600 words. All illustrations commissioned. Founded 2001.

Cricket Magazine

Carus Publishing Company, Cricket Magazine Group, P0 Box 300, Peru, IL 61354, USA
tel 815-224-5830 *fax* 815-224-6615
email mmiklavcic@caruspub.com
website www.cricketmag.com
Editor Marianne Carus, *Art Director* Ron McCutchan
12 p.a. $35.97

USA award-winning fun magazine for 9–14 year-olds with literary content including original stories, poems and articles by the world's best authors for children (*not* about cricket the sport!). Also includes puzzles, games, activities, plays, music and art. Welcomes ideas for articles and features. Founded 1973.
Submission details Do not query first. Send sase or IRCs with submissions. Allow 12 weeks for a reply. Length: 200–2000 words (stories), 200–1500 words (articles); poems up to 50 lines. Payment: up to 25 cents per word (stories and articles), up to $3 per line (poems). Illustrations: welcomes b&w and colour artwork but do not send originals. Payment by arrangement.

Daisy

Egmont Magazines, 184 Drummond Street, London NW1 3HP
tel 020-7380 6430
website www.egmontmagazines.co.uk
4-weekly £1.85

Aimed at 4–7 year-old girls who like anything pretty or cute! A mix of favourite characters and animals, posters, and puzzles and activities. Founded 2005.

The Dandy

D.C. Thomson & Co. Ltd, Albert Square, Dundee DD1 9QJ
tel (01382) 223131 *fax* (01382) 322214
185 Fleet Street, London EC4A 2HS
tel 020-7400 1030 *fax* 020-7400 1089
Weekly £1.20

Comic strips for children. Picture stories with 7–10 pictures per page, 1–4pp per story. Promising artists are encouraged. Payment: on acceptance.

Discovery Box

The Children's Magazine Company Ltd, Tower House, Soverign Park, Lathkill Street, Market Harborough, Leics. LE94 7ZT
tel (01858) 435319 *fax* (01858) 434958
email childrens.magazines@bayard-presse.com
website www.bayard-magazines.co.uk
Editor Sophie Delbert
10 p.a. £34.75

Photographs and short texts to introduce children aged 8–12 to animals and their habitats. Includes historical events retold as picture stories and a range of topics and experiments to develop children's scientific knowledge; also photographs showing the variety of lifestyles around the world. Plus games, fun facts, short story, recipe, quizz, cartoon. Specially commissions most material. Founded 1996.

Disney & Me

Egmont Magazines UK, 184–192 Drummond Street, London NW1 3HP
tel 020-7380 6430
website www.egmontmagazines.co.uk
Fortnightly £1.65

Entertaining and fun reading source for 4–8 year-olds with authentic illustrations based on original Disney animation. Includes stories, games, puzzles, posters, colouring pages and reader's letters.

Disney Fairies

Egmont Magazines, 184 Drummond Street, London NW1 3HP
tel 020-7380 6430
website www.egmontmagazines.co.uk
Monthly £1.99

Aimed at 5–7 year-old girls. Published under the Disney franchise spawned from the novels *Fairy Dust* and *The Quest for the Egg* by Gail Carson Levine. Founded 2006.

Disney Girl

BBC Worldwide, Woodlands, Wood Lane, London W12 0TT
tel 020-8433 1845 *fax* 020-8433 2941
website www.bbcworldwide.com
Editor Claire Funge
Monthly £1.70

Magazine of Walt Disney cartoons and characters for 5–8 year-old girls. Contains short stories, dressing up, fashion, craft activities, competitions, readers' letters, puzzles. Length: 500 words (fiction). Payment: £75. All material is specially commissioned. Founded 2002.

Disney's Princess

Egmont Magazines UK, 184–192 Drummond Street, London NW1 3HP

tel 020-7380 6430
website www.egmontmagazines.co.uk
Every 2 weeks £1.65

Magazine for 5–8 year-old girls to enter the magical world of Disney heroines through stories, crafts and activities. Founded 1998.

DK FindOut!

Titan Magazines, Titan House, 144 Southwark Street, London SE1 0UP
tel 020-7620 0200 *fax* 020-7803 1803
email karina.barker@titanemail.com
Editor Karina Barker
Monthly

Information magazine covering geography and the natural world, art, history and science.

Doctor Who Adventures

BBC Worldwide Ltd, Woodlands, 80 Wood Lane, London W12 0TT
tel 020-8433 3825
email dwa@bbc.co.uk
Fortnightly £1.99

Magazine for 6–12 year-old fans of the *Doctor Who* series. Readers are immersed into the world of the Doctor, taking them on an adventure into time and space, with monsters and creatures, excitement, action, adventure and humour. Founded 2006.

Doctor Who Magazine

Panini UK, Panini House, Coach and Horses Passage, Tunbridge Wells, Kent TN2 5UJ
tel (01892) 500100 *fax* (01892) 545666
email paninicomics@panini.co.uk
website www.paninicomics.co.uk
Editor Clayton Hickman
Every 4 weeks £3.99

Essential X-Men

Panini UK, Panini House, Coach and Horses Passage, Tunbridge Wells, Kent TN2 5UJ
tel (01892) 500100 *fax* (01892) 545666
email paninicomics@panini.co.uk
website www.paninicomics.co.uk
Editor Scott Gray
Every 4 weeks £2.50

Fifi and the Flower Tots

BBC Worldwide Ltd, Woodlands, 80 Wood Lane, London W12 0TT
tel 020-8433 2356
website www.bbcmagazines.com/fifiandtheflowertots
4-weekly £1.70

Magazine aimed at 3–5 year-old children and based on the *Fifi and the Flowertots* TV programme. It mirrors the values of fun, friendship and creativity with activities and stories. Parent's notes are included to encourage joint participation and added enjoyment to the magazine. Founded 2006.

Fimbles

BBC Worldwide Ltd, BBC Woodlands, 80 Wood Lane, London W12 0TT
tel 020-8433 2000 *fax* 020-8749 0538
website www.bbcworldwide.com
Editor Coralie Noakes
Monthly £1.65

Magazine aimed at 2–4 year-olds. The *Fimbles* are always trying to find out new things and the magic of discovery accompanies everything they do.

First News

First News House, 95 The Street, Horsley, Surrey KT24 6DD
email newsdesk@firstnews.co.uk
website www.firstnews.co.uk
Editor Nicky Cox, *Editorial Director* Piers Morgan
Weekly Fri £1

And inspiring, educational and entertaining national newspaper and website for 8–14 year-olds with news, sport, showbiz, interviews and one in depth feature. Among its aims, it aspires to raise the profile of children's views and opinions in society. Launched May 2006.

Fun to Learn Bag-o-Fun

Redan Publishing Ltd, Canon Court East, Abbey Lawn, Shrewsbury SY2 5DE
tel (01743) 364 433 *fax* (01743) 271 528
email info@redan.com
website www.redan.com
Bi-monthly £3.65

Magazine for preschool children and their parents to encourage early educational activities. Compiled of popular characters including Mr Men, Brum, Spot, Blues Clues and Oswald to help bring to life stories and activities whilst developing basic educational skills.

Fun to Learn Barney

Redan Publishing Ltd, Canon Court East, Abbey Lawn, Shrewsbury SY2 5DE
tel (01743) 364 433 *fax* (01743) 271 528
email info@redan.com
website www.redan.com
4-weekly £1.95

An interactive magazine for girls and boys aged 3–7 with stories, activities and puzzles based on the loveable purple dinosaur, Barney. It supports the National Curriculum's Early Learning Goals and also covers Barney's 5 pillars of sharing, caring, imagining, dancing and learning.

Fun to Learn Best of Barney

Redan Publishing Ltd, Canon Court East, Abbey Lawn, Shrewsbury SY2 5DE
tel (01743) 364 433 *fax* (01743) 271 528
email info@redan.com
website www.redan.com

Bi-monthly £1.99

An interactive magazine for girls and boys aged 3–7 with stories, activities and puzzles based on the loveable purple dinosaur, Barney. It supports the National Curriculum's Early Learning Goals and also covers Barney's 5 pillars of sharing, caring, imagining, dancing and learning.

Fun to Learn Discovery
Redan Publishing Ltd, Canon Court East, Abbey Lawn, Shrewsbury SY2 5DE
tel (01743) 364 433 *fax* (01743) 271 528
email info@redan.com
website www.redan.com
Quarterly £1.99

A magazine covering the National Curriculum's Early Learning Goals. It has a different theme every issue, providing preschool children with stories and activities on themes such as Lions & Tigers, Dinosaurs, Cars & Lorries, Space, Witches & Wizards and Father Christmas.

Fun to Learn Favourites
Redan Publishing Ltd, Canon Court East, Abbey Lawn, Shrewsbury SY2 5DE
tel (01743) 364 433 *fax* (01743) 271 528
email info@redan.com
website www.redan.com
3-weekly £1.99

A magazine for preschool children compiled of stories and activities using popular children's TV characters including Dora the Explorer, Barney, Mr Men, Jakers!, Franny's Feet, Brum, Bear in the Big Blue House and Jay Jay the Jet Plane. It includes a 24-page pull-out workbook based on one of these characters for parent and child inter-activity, with activities including counting, matching, puzzles and colouring.

Fun to Learn Friends
Redan Publishing Ltd, Canon Court East, Abbey Lawn, Shrewsbury SY2 5DE
tel (01743) 364 433 *fax* (01743) 271 528
email info@redan.com
website www.redan.com
3-weekly £1.99

Magazine for preschool children and their parents to encourage early educational activities. Compiled of stories and activities using popular children's TV characters including Barney, Spot, Clifford's Puppy Days, Oswald, Miffy, Engie Benjy, Peppa Pig, Fireman Sam and The Wiggles. Includes a 24-page pull-out workbook based on one of these popular characters for parent and child inter-activity, with activities including counting, matching, puzzles and colouring. The content supports the National Curriculum's Early Learning Goals.

Fun to Learn Letterland
Redan Publishing Ltd, Canon Court East, Abbey Lawn, Shrewsbury SY2 5DE

tel (01743) 364 433 *fax* (01743) 271 528
email info@redan.com
website www.redan.com
4-weekly £1.95

A magazine designed to complement the Letterland early reading skills scheme. It contains stories and activities to entertain and educate children using its story-based phonics system and characters designed to make learning fun.

The Funday Times
1 Pennington Street, London E98 1ST
tel 020-7782 7415 *fax* 020-7782 7416
email funday.news@sunday-times.co.uk
Editor Dave Coombs, *Art Director* Ed White
Free with *The Sunday Times* (£1.40)

Supplement for 8–12 year-old boys and girls. Content is a lively mix of news, features, sport, music and readers' views plus cartoons, puzzles and quizzes. Specially commissions most material but considers unsolicited material and welcomes ideas for articles and features. Length: 300 words (articles), 600 words (features), 100 words (news). Payment: 40p per word. Illustrations: colour transparencies, prints, artwork, cartoons. Founded 1989.

Futurama (UK)
Titan Publishing Group Ltd, Titan House, 144 Southwark Street, London SE1 0UP
tel 020-7620 0200 *fax* 020-7803 1803
email planetexpressmail@titanemail.com
website www.titanmagazines.com
Editor Martin Eden
Bi-monthly £2.10

Girl Talk
BBC Worldwide, Woodlands, Wood Lane, London W12 0TT
tel 020-8433 1845 *fax* 020-8433 2941
email girltalk.magazine@bbc.co.uk
website www.bbcworldwide.com
Editor Samantha McEvoy
Fortnightly £1.30

Magazine for children aged 7–12 years old. Contains pop, TV and film celebrity features, personality features, quizzes, fashion, competitions, stories. Length: 500 words (fiction). Payment: £75. All material is specially commissioned. Founded 1997.

Go Girl Magazine
Egmont Magazines, 184 Drummond Street, London NW1 3HP
tel 020-7380 6430
website www.egmontmagazines.co.uk
Editor Sarah Delmege
Fortnightly £1.85

Magazine for 7–11-year-old girls including fashion, beauty, celebrity news and gossip. Payment: by arrangement. Founded 2003.

Goodie Bag Mag

D.C. Thomson & Co Ltd, Albert Square,
Dundee DD1 9QJ
tel (01382) 223131 *fax* (01382) 225511
185 Fleet Street, London EC4A 2HS
tel 020-7400 1030 *fax* 020-7400 1089
Monthly (Fri) £2.99

Features, fashion, puzzles pin-ups, stories,
competitions. Founded 2003.

Guiding magazine

17–19 Buckingham Palace Road, London SW1W 0PT
tel 020-7834 6242 *fax* 020-7828 5791
website www.girlguiding.org.uk
Editor Wendy Kewley
Monthly £2

Official magazine of Girlguiding UK. Articles of
interest to women of all ages, with special emphasis
on youth work and the Guide Movement. Articles on
simple crafts, games and the outdoors especially
welcome. Length: up to 600 words. Illustrations: line,
half-tone, colour. Payment: £70 per 1000 words.

Hot Wheels

Egmont Magazines, 184 Drummond Street, London
NW1 3HP
tel 020-7380 6430
website www.egmontmagazines.co.uk
Editor Matt Crossick
Monthly £1.85

Magazine for 6–9 year-old boys who love anything on
wheels, with cars, bikes, skateboards and Formula
One action. Based on the Hot Wheels toy brand for
boys. Founded 2004.

It's HOT!

BBC Worldwide Ltd, BBC Woodlands, 80 Wood
Lane, London W12 0TT
tel 020-8433 2000 *fax* 020-8749 0538
website www.bbcworldwide.com
Editor Rosalie Snaith
Monthly £2.10

Entertainment magazine for 9–13 year-old girls
covering TV, pop, films and gossip. Includes 3 comic
strips (*EastEnders*, *S Club 7* and the *Top Of The Pops
Star Bar*) and a day-by-day diary of cool stuff to do.
Founded 2002.

Junior Puzzles

Puzzler Media Ltd, Stonecroft, 69 Station Road,
Redhill, Surrey RH1 1EY
tel (01737) 378700 *fax* (01737) 781800
email reception@puzzlermedia.com
website www.puzzler.co.uk
Editor Jackie Guthrie
7 p.a. £2.20

Entertainment for 7–12 year-old children with a
variety of puzzles, e.g. spot the difference,

wordsearch, kriss kross, dot to dot, crosswords,
mazes.

Kids Alive! (The Young Soldier)

The Salvation Army, 101 Newington Causeway,
London SE1 6BN
tel 020-7367 4910 *fax* 020-7367 4710
email kidsalive@salvationarmy.org.uk
website www.salvationarmy.org.uk/kidsalive
Editor Justin Reeves
Weekly 50p (£25 p.a. including free membership of
the Kids Alive! Club)

Children's magazine: pictures, scripts and artwork for
cartoon strips, puzzles, etc; Christian-based with
emphasis on education re addictive substances.
Payment: by arrangement. Illustrations: half-tone,
line and 4-colour line, cartoons. Founded 1881.

Learn with Bob the Builder

BBC Worldwide Ltd, Woodlands, 80 Wood Lane,
London W12 0TT
tel 020 8433 2356
website www.bbcmagazines.com/learnwithbob
4-weekly £1.99

Educational magazine for 3–5 year-olds to help
develop their reading, writing and number skills,
while supporting the National Curriculum Early
Learning Goals. The educational activities also
prepare children for KS1. Uses young children's
interest in Bob the Builder and his team to make
learning basic skills fun and exciting.

Learn with Toybox

BBC Worldwide Ltd, BBC Woodlands, 80 Wood
Lane, London W12 0TT
tel 020-8433 2000 *fax* 020-8749 0538
website www.bbcworldwide.com
Every 4 weeks £1.99

Educational magazine for 3–5 year-olds offering
children developmentally appropriate challenges,
built on the Early Learning Goals. Makes the best use
of children's interest in their favourite TV characters
to make learning basic skills fun and exciting. Focuses
on literacy, numeracy, knowledge and understanding
of the world.

Learn with Tweenies

BBC Worldwide Ltd, Woodlands, 80 Wood Lane,
London W12 0TT
tel 020-8433 2356
website www.bbcmagazines.com/learnwithtweenies
4-weekly £1.99

Educational magazine using characters from the
Tweenies to help 3–5 year-olds develop their reading,
writing and number skills, while supporting the
National Curriculum Early Learning Goals. The
educational activities also prepare children for KS1.

Learning is Fun!

BBC Worldwide Ltd, BBC Woodlands, 80 Wood
Lane, London W12 0TT

tel 020-8433 2000 *fax* 020-8749 0538
website www.bbcworldwide.com
Editor Stephanie Cooper
Every 4 weeks £2.10

Educational magazine which aims to support children as they progress through KS1 of the National Curriculum, Literacy and Numeracy strategies. Each school subject is depicted in an exciting, fun and stimulating way with colourful illustrations, photographs of children and pictures. It includes a regular feature, written by the Education Editor, which tackles parent/school/child issues.

The Magic Key

BBC Worldwide Ltd, BBC Woodlands, 80 Wood Lane, London W12 0TT
tel 020-8433 2000 *fax* 020-8749 0538
website www.bbcworldwide.com
Every 4 weeks £2.10

Educational magazine devised to help develop the literacy skills of 5–7 year-olds, with stories and activities designed to support their reading and writing skills. Encourages children to develop an interest in words, an understanding of language and a love of reading. Both the National Curriculum and Literacy Strategy at KS1 have been used as a guide to the educational content with the notes on each page enabling parents to support and extend their child's learning. Features the popular children's characters from the Oxford Reading Scheme.

Marvel RAMPAGE

Panini UK, Panini House, Coach and Horses Passage, Tunbridge Wells, Kent TN2 5UJ
tel (01892) 500100 *fax* (01892) 545666
email rampage@panini.co.uk
website www.paninicomics.co.uk
Editor Tom O'Malley
Every 4 weeks £1.99

The Max

RNIB, PO Box 173, Peterborough PE2 6W7
tel (01733) 375336 *fax* (01733) 375001
email editorial@rnib.org.uk
website www.rnib.org.uk
Editor Racheal Jarvis
Fortnightly 40p (monthly £2.60 overseas)

Braille magazine for blind and partially sighted men aged 16–19. Also available in disk and email formats. Includes features on the music scene, sport, interviews with personalities and a problem page. Will consider unsolicited material but most material has previously appeared in mainstream print magazines.

Mighty World of Marvel

Panini UK, Panini House, Coach and Horses Passage, Tunbridge Wells, Kent TN2 5UJ
tel (01892) 500100 *fax* (01892) 545666

email paninicomics@panini.co.uk
website www.paninicomics.co.uk
Editor Scott Gray
Every 4 weeks £2.40

Missy

RNIB, PO Box 173, Peterborough PE2 6WS
tel (01733) 375000 *fax* (01733) 375001
email editorial@rnib.org.uk
website www.rnib.org.uk
Editor Chris James
Monthly 40p (£2.78 export)

Braille general interest magazine for blind and partially sighted girls aged 12–15. Also available on disk.

Mizz

Panini UK, Panini House, Coach & Horses Passage, The Pantiles, Tunbridge Wells, Kent TN2 5UJ
tel (01892) 500100 *fax* (01892) 545666
email mizz@ipcmedia.com
website www.ipcmedia.com
Editor Leslie Sinoway
Fortnightly £1.60

Articles on any subject of interest to girls aged 10–14. Approach in writing. Payment: by arrangement. Illustrated. Founded 1985.

myBOOKSmag

4 Froxfield Close, Winchester SO22 6JW
tel (01962) 620320
email guy@newbooksmag.com
website www.newbooksmag.com
Editor Helen Boyle, *Send material to* Guy Pringle, Publisher
Quarterly £1.50

Activities and extracts from the best new books for 5–7 year-olds. Specially commissions all material. Email for a free introductory copy. Founded 2001.

The Newspaper

Young Media Holdings Ltd, PO Box 8215, Sawbridgeworth, Herts. CM21 9WW
tel/fax (0870) 240 5845
email editor@thenewspaper.org.uk
website www.thenewspaper.org.uk
Editors Buffy Whiting, Tracey Comber
6 p.a. Free; subscription only

Newspaper aimed at 8–14-year-old schoolchildren for use as part of the National Curriculum. Contains similar columns as in any national daily newspaper. Length: 800–1000 words for features and short stories (non-fiction). No payment for contributions. Illustrations: colour. Founded 1999.

Noddy

Egmont Magazines, 184–192 Drummond Street, London NW1 3HP
tel 020-7380 6430 *fax* 020-7380 6444

website www.egmontmagazines.co.uk
Editor Claire Noonan
Monthly £1.85

Preschool magazine. Noddy and his friends introduce children to the basic skills they need before they start school via a variety of stories, activities, colouring, rhymes and games. Founded 1992; relaunched 2006.

Play & Learn Thomas & Friends

Egmont Magazines UK, 184 Drummond Street, London NW1 3HP
tel 020-7380 6430
website www.egmontmagazines.co.uk
Fortnightly £1.65

Magazine for 3–6 year-old children with activities and stories involving Thomas characters. A companion to KS1 programmes of study.

Pokemon World

Highbury Entertainment Ltd, Paragon House, St Peter's Road, Bournemouth BH1 2JS
tel (01202) 299900
email nickr@paragon.co.uk
website www.paragon.co.uk/mags/pokemon.html
Managing Editor Nick Roberts
Monthly £3.99

Magazine devoted to Pokémon. It covers every aspect of the phenomenon, from games and movies through to merchandise and trading cards.

Pony Magazine

Headley House, Headley Road, Grayshott, Surrey GU26 6TU
tel (01428) 601020 *fax* (01428) 601030
Editor Janet Rising
Monthly £2.30

Lively articles and short stories with a horsy theme aimed at readers aged 8–16 . Technical accuracy and young, fresh writing essential. Length: up to 800 words. Payment: by arrangement. Illustrations: drawings (commissioned), photos, cartoons. Founded 1949.

Pop Girl

BBC Worldwide, Woodlands, Wood Lane, London W12 0TT
tel 020-8433 1845 *fax* 020-8433 2941
email girltalk.magazine@bbc.co.uk
website www.bbcworldwide.com
Editor Samantha McEvoy, *Art Director* Carol Gook,
Send material to Bea Appleby
Monthly £1.50

Magazine for girls aged 7–12 years old. Contains pop, TV and film celebrity interviews, pop star style, fan fiction, puzzles, competitions, readers' letters. Length: 500 words (fiction). Payment: £75. All material is specially commissioned. Founded 2003.

Postman Pat

Panini UK, Panini House, Coach and Horses Passage, Tunbridge Wells, Kent TN2 5UJ

tel (01892) 500100 *fax* (01892) 545666
email paninicomics@panini.co.uk
website www.paninicomics.co.uk
Editor Kirsty Grant
Every 4 weeks £1.85

Power Rangers

Egmont Magazines, 184 Drummond Street, London NW1 3HP
tel 020-7380 6430
website www.egmontmagazines.co.uk
Editor Jeanette Ryall
Monthly £1.85

Energetic magazine for *Power Rangers* fans, aimed at 4–7 year-old boys. Features puzzles, stories, games, posters and colouring of the characters.

Pure

RNIB, PO Box 173, Peterborough PE2 6WS
tel (01733) 375336 *fax* (01733) 375001
email editorial@rnib.org.uk
website www.rnib.org.uk
Editor Chris James
Monthly 40p (£2.60 export)

Braille magazine for blind and partially sighted girls aged 16–19. Also available in disk and email formats. Includes real life stories, celebrity interviews and beauty features. Will consider unsolicited material but most material has previously appeared in mainstream print magazines.

Puzzler Quiz Kids

Puzzler Media Ltd, Stonecroft, 69 Station Road, Redhill, Surrey RH1 1EY
tel (01737) 378700 *fax* (01737) 781800
email reception@puzzlermedia.com
website www.puzzler.co.uk
Editor Jackie Guthrie
7 p.a. £1.75

Puzzles and quizzes for 7–11 year-old children to help build reading, writing and mathematical skills.

The Roly Mo Show!

BBC Worldwide Ltd, Woodlands, 80 Wood Lane, London W12 0TT
tel 020-8433 2356
website www.bbcmagazines.com/rolymo
4-weekly £1.99

Magazine using the Roly Mo character to help 3–6 year-old children become confident communicators through word games, rhymes and sounds. Includes activities for parents and children to do together. Founded 2006.

Royal National Institute of the Blind

PO Box 173, Peterborough, Cambs. PE2 6WS
tel (0845) 7023153 *fax* (01733) 375001
textphone (0845) 7585691
helpline (0845) 7669999

email cservices@rnib.org.uk
website www.rnib.org.uk

Published by the Royal National Institute of the Blind, the following titles are available via email, on floppy disk and in braille, unless otherwise stated.
3FM (email and braille), *Access IT, After Hours* (11–14-year-olds; braille), *Aphra, Big Print newspaper* (large print only), *Blast Off!* (children's magazine; disk and braille), *Braille at Bedtime* (7–11-year-olds; braille), *Broadcast Times* (email and disk), *Channels of Blessing* (disk and braille), *Chess Magazine* (braille), *Christmas Radio Guide* (email and braille), *Christmas Television Guide* (email and braille), *Compute IT, Contention, Conundrum* (disk and braille), *Cricket Fixtures, Daily Bread* (disk and braille), *Daisy TV Listings* (Daisy format), *E-Access Bulletin* (email only), *Football Fixtures* (email and braille), *Good Vibrations, Insight* (clear print, audio CD, disk, braille, email), *The Max* (boys aged 16–19), *Missy* (girls aged 12–15), *Money Matters, Music Magazine* (disk and braille), *NB* (print, email, disk, cassette tape, braille), *New Literature on Sight Problems* (print and email), *New Product Guide* (braille, email, tape, disk), *Journal of Physiotherapy, Physiotherapy* (disk, cassette tape, braille), *Physiotherapy Frontline* (cassette tape), *Piano Tuners' Quarterly* (email, disk, cassette tape, braille), *Progress, Proms Guide, Pure* (girls aged 16–19), *Radio Guide* (email and braille), *Ready, Steady, Read* (for new readers of braille in braille only), *Rhetoric, Scientific Enquiry* (disk and braille), *Shaping Up, Shop Window, Shop Window Christmas Guide, Short Stories, Soundings* (cassette tape and web), *SP* (disk and braille), *Television Guide* (email and braille), *Theological Times* (disk, cassette tape, braille), *Upbeat, Vibe* (boys aged 12–15), *You & Your Child, Vision* (clear print, email, disk, cassette tape, braille, Daisy format).

Scooby-Doo
Panini UK, Panini House, Coach and Horses Passage, Tunbridge Wells, Kent TN2 5UJ
tel (01892) 500100 *fax* (01892) 545666
email paninicomics@panini.co.uk
website www.paninicomics.co.uk
Editor Kate Rhead
Every 3 weeks £1.99

Scooby-Doo World of Mystery!
De Agostini UK Ltd, Griffin House,
161 Hammersmith Road, London W6 8SD
tel 020-8600 2015, (0870) 8702567 (customer services) *fax* 020-8741 8927
email enquiries@deagostini.co.uk
website www.deagostini.co.uk
Weekly £1.99

Scooby and the gang go on spooky adventures around the world, every week in a different country. Includes country facts, comics, mysterious site information, scrapbooks and puzzles and games.

Shout
D.C. Thomson & Co. Ltd, Albert Square, Dundee DD1 9QJ

tel (01382) 223131 *fax* (01382) 200880
email shout@dcthomson.co.uk
185 Fleet Street, London EC4A 2HS
tel 020-7400 1030 *fax* 020-7400 1089
Editor-in-Chief Jackie Brown
Fortnightly £2

Colour gravure magazine for 11–14 year-old girls. Pop, film and 'soap' features and pin-ups; general features of teen interest; emotional features, fashion and beauty advice. Illustrations: colour transparencies. Payment: on acceptance. Founded 1993.

Simpsons Comics
Titan Publishing Group Ltd, Titan House,
144 Southwark Street, London SE1 0UP
tel 020-7620 0200 *fax* 020-7803 1803
website simpsonsmail@titanemail.com
website www.titanmagazines.com
Editor Paul Terry
13 p.a. £2.60

Reprints the US *Simpsons Comics* material with localised letters page and some other features.

Simpsons Comics Presents
Titan Publishing Group Ltd, Titan House,
144 Southwark Street, London SE1 0UP
tel 020-7620 0200 *fax* 020-7803 1803
email simpsonsmail@titanemail.com
website www.titanmagazines.com
Editor Paul Terry
Monthly £2.99

Sneak
Emap Performance, Mappin House, 4 Winsley Street, London W1W 8HF
tel 020-7182 8000 *fax* 020-7182 8529
email sneakmail@emap.com
website www.sneakmagazine.com
Editor Lara Palamondian
Weekly £1.40

Teenage magazine with celebrity scandal and photos, TV soap storylines, real-life stories and items on TV, music and film.

Sparkle World
Redan Publishing Ltd, Canon Court East, Abbey Lawn, Shrewsbury SY2 5DE
tel (01743) 364 433 *fax* (01743) 271 528
email info@redan.com
website www.redan.com
3-weekly £2.25

Magazine aimed at 4–9 year-old girls with stories and activities based on a dazzling selection of the most popular licensed characters, including Care Bears, Polly Pocket, Strawberry Shortcake, Little Miss Fairies, My Little Pony and Angelina Ballerina. A fun and educational magazine for young girls who love everything that glitters.

Spectacular Spider-Man

Panini UK, Panini House, Coach and Horses Passage,
Tunbridge Wells, Kent TN2 5UJ
tel (01892) 500100 *fax* (01892) 545666
email paninicomics@panini.co.uk
website www.paninicomics.co.uk
Editor Ed Hammonds
Every 3 weeks £1.99

SpongeBob SquarePants

Titan Magazines, Titan House, 144 Southwark Street,
London SE1 0UP
tel 020-7620 0200 *fax* 020-7803 1803
email spongebob@titanemail.com
Monthly

Star Trek Monthly

Titan Magazines, Titan House, 144 Southwark Street,
London SE1 0UP
tel 020-7620 0200 *fax* 020-7803 1803
Editor Nick Jones
13 p.a. £3.50

Up-to-date news about every aspect of *Star Trek*,
including all TV series and films, cast interviews,
behind-the-scenes features and product reviews.
Payment: by arrangement. Founded 1995.

Star Wars Comic

Titan Publishing Group Ltd, Titan House,
144 Southwark Street, London SE1 0UP
tel 020-7620 0200 *fax* 020-7803 1803
email swcomicmail@titanemail.com
website www.titanmagazines.com
Editor Richard Matthews
Bi-monthly £2.50

Features reprints of the *Dark Horse Star Wars* comics.

Star Wars Magazine

Titan Publishing Group Ltd, Titan House,
144 Southwark Street, London SE1 0UP
tel 020-7620 0200 *fax* 020-7803 1803
email starwarsmail@titanemail.com
website www.titanmagazines.com
Editor Brian J. Robb
Bi-monthly £4.99

Interviews, features, pin-ups and merchandise round-
ups.

Storybox

The Children's Magazine Company Ltd, Tower
House, Soverign Park, Lathkill Street, Market
Harborough, Leics. LE94 7ZT
tel (01858) 435319 *fax* (01858) 434958
email childrens.magazines@bayard-presse.com
website www.bayard-magazines.co.uk
Editor-in-chief Simona Sideri
10 p.a. £34.75 p.a.

Aimed at 3–6 year-old children. A range of stories
with rhyme and evocative pictures to stimulate

children's imagination and introduce them to the
delights of reading. Each issue presents a new, full-
colour, 24-page story created by teams of
internationally acclaimed writers and illustrators for
laptime reading. A non-fiction section linked to a
theme in the story follows, together with pages of
games and craft ideas. Includes games, an animal
feature, science and a cartoon. Founded 1996.
    Submission details Length: 500–1000 words
(stories). Requirements: rhyme, repetition, interesting
language. Specially commissions most material.
Payment: by arrangement.

Sugar

Hachette Filipacchi, 64 North Row, London
W1K 7LL
tel 020-7150 7000 *fax* 020-7150 7001
Editor Annabel Brog
Monthly £2.20

Magazine for young women aged 13–19. Fashion,
beauty, entertainment, features. Send synopsis first.
Will consider unsolicited material. Interested in real-
life stories (1200 words), quizzes. Payment:
negotiable. Founded 1994.

Super Six

Redan Publishing Ltd, Canon Court East, Abbey
Lawn, Shrewsbury SY2 5DE
tel (01743) 364 433 *fax* (01743) 271 528
email info@redan.com
website www.redan.com
Monthly £1.99

Magazine for 4–9 year-old boys compiled of stories
and activities using a number of popular boys' TV
characters including from *Thunderbirds*, SpongeBob,
Pokemon and from *LEGO City*. Includes a 16-page
pull-out workbook based one character designed for
parent and child interaction through counting,
puzzles and colouring.

tBkmag

4 Froxfield Close, Winchester SO22 6JW
tel (01962) 620320
email guy@newbooksmag.com
website www.newbooksmag.com
Editor Helen Boyle, *Send material to* Guy Pringle,
Publisher
Quarterly £1.50

Extracts and activities from the best new books for
8–12 year-olds. Specially commissions all material.
Email for a free introductory copy. Founded 2001.

Teletubbies

BBC Worldwide Ltd, BBC Woodlands, 80 Wood
Lane, London W12 0TT
tel 020-8433 2000 *fax* 020-8749 0538
website www.bbc.co.uk/teletubbies
Editor Helen Mitchell
13 p.a. £1.99

Magazine for very young children (18 months+) who love the *Teletubbies*. The activities included are designed to build children's confidence, creativity and imagination and are clear, colourful and entertaining. Founded 1997.

Thomas & Friends

Egmont Magazines UK, 184 Drummond Street, London NW1 3HP
tel 020-7380 6430
website www.egmontmagazines.co.uk
Fortnightly £1.70

Magazine for 3–6 year-old children designed to encourage early reading skills and all-round child development using stories and activities involving Thomas and all his friends. Each issue contains posters, colouring pages, competitions and readers' letters and drawings as regular features.

Thomas & Friends: Thomas Express Special

Egmont Magazines UK, 184 Drummond Street, London NW1 3HP
tel 020-7380 6430
website www.egmontmagazines.co.uk
Every 3 weeks £1.99

Magazine for children aged 3–6 years. Features basic counting, matching and spotting activities approved by an education expert.

Thunderbirds

Redan Publishing Ltd, Canon Court East, Abbey Lawn, Shrewsbury SY2 5DE
tel (01743) 364 433 *fax* (01743) 271 528
email info@redan.com
website www.redan.com
Monthly £2.25

Magazine with photo stories featuring characters from *Thunderbirds* to encourage boys aged 5+ to have fun reading on their own. Includes an 8pp pull-out 'Mission Pages' section designed to stretch the brain and make learning fun.

Tom and Jerry

Panini UK, Panini House, Coach and Horses Passage, Tunbridge Wells, Kent TN2 5UJ
tel (01892) 500100 *fax* (01892) 545666
email paninicomics@panini.co.uk
website www.paninicomics.co.uk
Editor Jason Quinn
Every 4 weeks £1.99

Toonerang

Panini UK, Panini House, Coach and Horses Passage, Tunbridge Wells, Kent TN2 5UJ
tel (01892) 500100 *fax* (01892) 545666
email paninicomics@panini.co.uk
website www.paninicomics.co.uk
Every 4 weeks £1.75

Top of the Pops

BBC Worldwide Ltd, BBC Woodlands, 80 Wood Lane, London W12 0TT
tel 020-8433 2000 *fax* 020-8749 0538
website www.bbcworldwide.com
Editor Peter Hart
Monthly £2.10

'The celebrity gossip bible for teenagers.' Primarily aimed at teenage girls (ages 10–13), the magazine strives to provide all the celebrity knowledge teenagers could want. It aims to make the reader feel part of an exclusive club, to transport them behind the scenes so they get a real sense of what really goes on in the world of the stars. Founded 1995.

Toxic Magazine

Egmont Magazines UK, 4th Floor, 184–192 Drummond Street, London NW1 3HP
tel 020-7380 6430
website www.toxicmag.co.uk
Editor Matt Yeo
Fortnightly £1.95

Topical lifestyle magazine for 7–12 year-old boys. Includes competitions, pull-out posters, reviews and jokes. Covers boys' entertainments, sports, video games, films, TV, music, fashion and toys. Slapstick humour. Showcases latest products, events and trends. Payment: by arrangement. Founded 2002.

Toybox

BBC Worldwide Ltd, BBC Woodlands, 80 Wood Lane, London W12 0TT
tel 020-8433 2000 *fax* 020-8749 0538
website www.bbcworldwide.com
Associate Publisher Pauline Cooke
Monthly 99p

Fun and interactive magazine for 3–5 year-olds with stories, activities, games and colouring-in. Features a variety of star characters from the BBC.

Tractor Tom

Panini UK, Panini House, Coach and Horses Passage, Tunbridge Wells, Kent TN2 5UJ
tel (01892) 500100 *fax* (01892) 545666
email paninicomics@panini.co.uk
website www.paninicomics.co.uk
Editor Kirsty Grant
Every 4 weeks £1.85

TV Hits! Magazine

Essential Publishing, The Tower, Phoenix Square, Colchester, Essex CO4 9HU
tel (01206) 851117
email hello@tvhitsmagazine.co.uk
website www.tvhits.co.uk
Monthly £2.10

Magazine for teenagers with news on music, TV and film, features on celebrities, interviews with stars, plus gossip. Founded 1989.

Tweenies
BBC Worldwide Ltd, BBC Woodlands, 80 Wood Lane, London W12 0TT
tel 020-8433 2164 *fax* 020-8433 2941
website www.bbcworldwide.com
Editor Andrea Wickstead
Fortnightly £1.65

Magazine based around the *Tweenies* for children aged 2–5, with stories and activities including songs to sing, things to make and colouring-in.

2000 AD
The Studio, Brewer Street, Oxford OX1 1QN
email publicrelations@2000adonline.com
website www.2000adonline.com
Weekly, Wed £1.75

Cult sci-fi comic. A multi-award-winning cocktail of explosive sci-fi and fantasy, infused with a mean streak of irony and wry black humour. 2000AD has been a proving ground for the finest young writers and artists of the generation, and many of the biggest names in comics today honed their skills within its pages. It has won the Best British Comic award at the UK Comic Art Awards, National Comics Awards and Eagle Awards many times. Founded 1977.

Ultimate Fantastic Four
Panini UK, Panini House, Coach and Horses Passage, Tunbridge Wells, Kent TN2 5UJ
tel (01892) 500100 *fax* (01892) 545666
email paninicomics@panini.co.uk
website www.paninicomics.co.uk
Every 4 weeks £1.95

Ultimate Spider-Man & X-Men
Panini UK, Panini House, Coach and Horses Passage, Tunbridge Wells, Kent TN2 5UJ
tel (01892) 500100 *fax* (01892) 545666
email paninicomics@panini.co.uk
website www.paninicomics.co.uk
Editor Brady Webb
Every 4 weeks £1.95

Vibe
RNIB, PO Box 173, Peterborough PE2 6WS
tel (01733) 375000 *fax* (01733) 375001
email editorial@rnib.org.uk
website www.rnib.org.uk
Editor Racheal Jarvis
Monthly 38p (£2.65 export)

Braille general interest magazine for blind and partially sighted boys aged 12–15. Also available on disk.

The Voice
Blue Star House, 8th Floor, 234–244 Stockwell Road, London SW9 9UG
tel 020-7737 7377 *fax* 020-7274 8894
email newsdesk@the-voice.co.uk
website www.voice-online.co.uk
Editor-in-Chief Deidre Forbes, *Head of News* Andrew Clunis, *Deputy Editor* Vic Motune, *Arts & Entertainment Editor* Russell Myrie, *Sports Editor* Rodney Hinds
Weekly 85p

Weekly newspaper for black Britons. Includes news, features, arts, sport and a comprehensive jobs and business section. Illustrations: colour and b&w photos. Open to ideas for news and features on sports, business, community events and the arts. Founded 1982.

Young Voices
website www.young-voices.co.uk
Editor Emelia Kenlock
Monthly, 2nd Tues of each month £1.95
News, features, reviews, showbiz highlights and current affairs for 11–19 year-olds. Founded 2003.

Wallace & Gromit Comic
Titan Magazines, Titan House, 144 Southwark Street, London SE1 0UP
tel 020-7620 0200 *fax* 020-7803 1803
email wallacegromit@titanemail.com
Monthly

Comic based on the Aardman Wallace & Gromit characters.

Winnie the Pooh
Egmont Magazines UK, 184–192 Drummond Street, London NW1 3HP
tel 020-7380 6430
website www.egmontmagazines.co.uk
Monthly £1.85

Interactive early learning magazine (2–5 year-olds) involving parent and child in a visually entertaining read.

W.I.T.C.H.
BBC Worldwide Ltd, Woodlands, 80 Wood Lane, London W12 0TT
tel 020-8433 2000
email witch@bbc.co.uk
Editor Samantha McEvoys
Monthly £1.85

Comic magazine featuring 5 young teenage girls who have special magical powers and want to save the world. They are also interested in all the things teenage girls are interested in – including fashion, boys and gossip. The magazine reflects the W.I.T.C.H. brand values of friendship, magic, action and drama, and features a mix of comic characters and real-life girls with whom the readers can identify.

Wolverine and Deadpool
Panini UK, Panini House, Coach and Horses Passage, Tunbridge Wells, Kent TN2 5UJ
tel (01892) 500100 *fax* (01892) 545666

email paninicomics@panini.co.uk
website www.paninicomics.co.uk
4-weekly £2.40

Young Scot

Rosebery House, 9 Haymarket Terrace, Edinburgh
EH12 5EZ
tel 0131-313 2488
email info@youngscot.org
website www.youngscot.org
Editor Fiona McIntyre
Quarterly Free with *Scottish Daily Record* and at
selected venues

The latest news, features, discounts, and competitions
for Youngs Scots aged 12–26. Young Scot offers
incentives, information and opportunities to people
in this age group to help them make informed
choices, play a part in their community, and make
the most of their free time and learning.

Young Writer

Glebe House, Webley, Herefordshire HR4 8SD
tel (01544) 318901 *fax* (01544) 318901
email editor@youngwriter.org
website www.youngwriter.org
Editor Kate Jones
3 p.a. £3.75 (£10 for 3 issues)

Specialist magazine for young writers under 18 years
old: ideas for them and writing by them. Includes
interviews by children with famous writers, fiction
and non-fiction pieces, poetry; also explores words
and grammar, issues related to writing (e.g. dyslexia),
plus competitions with prizes. Length: 750 or 1500
words (features), up to 400 words (news), 750 words

(short stories – unless specified otherwise in a
competition), poetry of any length. Illustrations:
colour – drawings by children, snapshots to
accompany features. Payment: most children's
material is published without payment; £25–£100
(features); £15 (cover cartoon). Free inspection copy.
Founded 1995.

Your Dog Magazine

BPG (Stamford) Ltd, Roebuck House, 33 Broad
Street, Stamford, Lincs. PE9 1RB
tel (01780) 766199 *fax* (01780) 766416
email s.wright@bournepublishinggroup.co.uk
Editor Sarah Wright
Monthly £3.10

Articles and information of interest to dog lovers;
features on all aspects of pet dogs. Length: approx.
1500 words. Illustrations: colour transparencies,
prints and line drawings. Payment: £80 per 1000
words. Founded 1994.

Your Horse

Emap Active, Bretton Court, Bretton, Peterborough
PE3 8DZ
tel (01733) 264666 *fax* (01733) 465200
email natasha.simmonds@emap.com
Editor Natasha Simmonds
Every 4 weeks £3.30

Practical horse care and riding advice for the leisure
rider and horse owner. Send feature ideas with
examples of previous published writing. Specially
commissions most material. Welcomes ideas for
articles and features. Length: 1500 words. Payment:
£120 per 1000 words. Founded 1983.

Magazines about children's literature and education

Listings of magazines and newspapers for children start on page 264.

Armadillo

Mary Hoffman, c/o Patricia White Rogers, Coleridge & White, 20 Powis Mews, London W11 1JN
email armadillo@maryhoffman.co.uk
website www.armadillomagazine.com
Editor Mary Hoffman
4 p.a.

Magazine about children's books, including reviews, interviews, features and profiles. After 5 years of publication as a paper magazine posted to subscribers, Armadillo is now available only online. New issues will be posted at the end of March, June, September and December. Some material will be accessible as a free sample but full access to the magazine is by subscription (see website for rates). New reviewers and writers are always welcome but the magazine does not pay a fee; reviewers keep the books. Publishers please note: books are not to be sent to the editor; she instructs reviewers to obtain specific titles direct from publishers. Founded 1999.

Books for Keeps

1 Effingham Road, London SE12 8NZ
tel 020-8852 4953 fax 020-8318 7580
email booksforkeeps@btinternet.com
website www.booksforkeeps.co.uk
Editor Rosemary Stones, Send material to Richard Hill
Bi-monthly £23.50 p.a.

Features, reviews and news on children's books. Readership is both professionals and parents. Founded 1980.

The Bookseller

VNU Entertainment Media Ltd, 5th Floor, Endeavour House, 189 Shaftesbury Avenue, London WC2H 8TJ
tel 020-7420 6006 fax 020-7420 6103
email letters.to.editor@bookseller.co.uk
website www.thebookseller.com
Editor-in-Chief Neill Denny, Features Editor Liz Bury
Weekly £179 p.a.

Journal of the UK publishing and bookselling trades. The Children's Bookseller supplement is published regularly and there is news on the children's book business in the main magazine. Produces the Children's Buyer's Guide, which previews children's books to be published in the following 6 months. The website holds news on children's books, comment on the children's sector, author interviews and children's bestseller charts. Founded 1858.

Carousel – The Guide to Children's Books

The Saturn Centre, 54–76 Bissell Street, Birmingham B5 7HX
tel 0121-622 7458 fax 0121-666 7526
email carousel.guide@virgin.net
website www.carouselguide.co.uk
Editor Jenny Blanch
3 p.a. £10.50 p.a. (£15 p.a. Europe; £18 p.a. rest of world)

Reviews of fiction, non-fiction and poetry books for children, plus in-depth articles; profiles of authors and illustrators. Length: 1200 words (articles); 150 words (reviews). Illustrations: colour and b&w. Payment: by arrangement. Founded 1995.

Child Education

Scholastic Ltd, Villiers House, Clarendon Avenue, Leamington Spa, Warks. CV32 5PR
tel (01926) 887799 fax (01926) 883331
website www.scholastic.co.uk
Editor-in-Chief Helen Freeman
Monthly £3.99

For teachers concerned with the education of children aged 4–7. Articles by specialists on practical teaching ideas and methods. Length: 600–1200 words. Payment: by arrangement. Profusely illustrated with photos and artwork; also A1 full colour picture poster. Founded 1924.

Child Education Topics

Scholastic Ltd, Villiers House, Clarendon Avenue, Leamington Spa, Warks. CV32 5PR
tel (01926) 887799 fax (01926) 337322
Editor Michael Ward
Bi-monthly £3.99

Practical articles suggesting project activities for teachers of children aged 4–7; material mostly commissioned. Length: 500–1000 words. Illustrations: colour photos and line illustrations, colour posters. Payment: by arrangement. Founded 1978.

Cricket Magazine – see page 267

Early Childhood Today

Scholastic Canada Ltd, 175 Hillmount Road, Markham, Ontario L6C 1Z7
website www.scholastic.ca

Addresses and anticipates the needs of early childhood educators (pre-K–K). Each thematic issue focuses on a specific aspect of early childhood development, such as literacy or creativity, and provides a 'mini-workshop' on that topic: updates on current research, interviews with leading experts, and easy-to-implement activities broken down by age group.

Early Years Activity Bank

Scholastic Ltd, Villiers House, Clarendon Avenue, Leamington Spa, Warks. CV32 5PR
tel (01926) 887799 *fax* (01926) 883331
email earlyyears@scholastic.co.uk
website www.scholastic.co.uk
Editor Sarah Sodhi
6 p.a. £75 p.a.

Support material for early years professionals. A bank of play-based activities and resources including term-by-term activities with seasonal links, practical ideas covering the Stepping Stones and Early Learning Goals, colour posters and flashcards. Illustrations: transparencies and colour artwork. Length: 500 words (articles). Founded 2000.

Mary Glasgow Magazines

Scholastic UK Ltd, 24 Eversholt Street, London NW1 1DB
tel 020-7756 7756 *fax* 020-7756 7797
email email@maryglasgowmags.co.uk
website www.link2english.com, www.maryglasgowmagazines.com

Publisher of 16 magazines for learners of English, French, German, and Spanish. Also publishes a series of resource books for teachers of English as a foreign language. Wholly-owned subsidiary of Scholastic Inc.

Inis – The Children's Books Ireland Magazine

Children's Books Ireland, 17 Lower Camden Street, Dublin 2, Republic of Ireland
tel (1) 872 7475
email inis@childrensbooksireland.com
website www.childrensbooksireland.com
Editor Ms Paddy O'Doherty
Quarterly €4

Reviews and articles on Irish and international children's books. Readership of parents, teachers, librarians and children's books specialists. Founded 1989.

Instructor

Scholastic Canada Ltd, 175 Hillmount Road, Markham, Ontario L6C 1Z7
website www.scholastic.ca

Professional magazine for elementary (Grades 1–8) classroom teachers that keeps educators abreast of the latest and best ideas about how children learn, and translates that thinking into effective classroom

practice. Includes tips, activities, and strategies to better meet the needs of teachers.

Junior

Future Living, 1 Balcombe Street, London NW1
tel 020-7042 4000 *fax* 020-7761 8901
email editorial@juniormagazine.co.uk
website www.juniormagazine.co.uk
Editor Catherine O'Dolan
Monthly £3.50

Glossy up-market parenting magazine aimed at mothers of children aged 0–8 and reflects the shift in today's society towards older mothers and fathers who have established their careers and homes. Intelligent and insightful features and the best in fashion. Specially commissions most material. Welcomes ideas for articles and features. Payment: £150 per 1000 words (articles/features/short fiction), £300 per feature (colour and b&w photos/artwork). Founded 1998.

Junior Education

Scholastic Ltd, Villiers House, Clarendon Avenue, Leamington Spa, Warks. CV32 5PR
tel (01926) 887799 *fax* (01926) 883331
email juniored@scholastic.co.uk
website www.scholastic.co.uk
Editor Alex Albrighton
Monthly £3.99

For teachers of 7–11 year-olds. Articles by specialists on practical teaching ideas, coverage of primary education news; posters; photocopiable material for the classroom. Length: 800–1000 words. Payment: by arrangement. Illustrated with photos and drawings; includes 2 A2 colour posters. Founded 1977.

Junior Education Topics

Scholastic Ltd, Villiers House, Clarendon Avenue, Leamington Spa, Warks. CV32 5PR
tel (01926) 887799 *fax* (01926) 883331
email jet@scholastic.co.uk
website www.scholastic.co.uk
Editor Alex Albrighton
Monthly £3.99

Aimed at teachers of 7–11 year-olds, each issue is based on a theme, closely linked to the National Curriculum. Includes A1 and A3 full-colour posters, 12 pages of photocopiable material and 16 pages of articles. All material commissioned. Length: 800 words. Illustrations: photos and drawings. Payment: £100 per double-page spread; varies for illustrations. Founded 1982.

The Lion and the Unicorn

Project MUSE, 2715 North Charles Street, Baltimore, MD 21218-4319
tel 410-516-6989 *fax* 410-516-6968
email muse@muse.jhu.edu
website http://muse.jhu.edu/journals/lion_and_the_unicorn/
3 p.a.

A theme- and genre-centred journal of international scope committed to a serious, ongoing discussion of literature for children. The journal's coverage includes the state of the publishing industry, regional authors, comparative studies of significant books and genres, new developments in theory, the art of illustration, the mass media, and popular culture. It has become noted for its interviews with authors, editors, and other important contributors to the field, such as Mildred Wirt Benson, Robert Cormier, Chris Crutcher, Lensey Namioka, Philip Pullman, and Aranka Siegal. Special issues have included 'Violence and Children's Literature' and 'Folklore In/And Children's Literature.' Includes a book review section and each year publishes a general issue and 2 theme issues. Project MUSE is part of the Johns Hopkins University Press.

Literacy

UK Literary Association, Upton House, 4 Baldock Street, Royston, Herts. SG8 5AY
tel (01763) 241188 *fax* (01763) 243785
email admin@ukla.org
email h.dombey@brighton.ac.uk
website www.ukla.org, www.blackwellpublishing.com
Editor Henrietta Dombey, School of Education, University of Brighton, Falmer, Brighton BN1 9PH

3 p.a. (subscription only)

The official journal of the United Kingdom Literacy Association (see page 359) and is for those interested in the study and development of literacy. Readership comprises practitioners, teachers, educators, researchers, undergraduate and graduate students. It offers educators a forum for debate through scrutinising research evidence, reflecting on analysed accounts of innovative practice and examining recent policy developments. Length: 2000–6000 words (articles). Illustrations: b&w prints and artwork. Formerly known as *Reading – Literacy and Language*. Published by Blackwell Publishing. Founded 1966.

Literacy Time

Scholastic Ltd, Villiers House, Clarendon Avenue, Leamington Spa, Warks. CV32 5PR
tel (01926) 887799 *fax* (01926) 883331
website www.scholastic.co.uk/magazines/littime.htm
Editor Helen Watts *tel* (01789) 292112
email helenwatts@redclose.demon.co.uk

A selection of posters for whole class work and multiple group reading leaflets, created to meet specific teachers' objectives for the National Literacy Framework, term by term. There are 3 levels: *Literacy Time Years 1/2*, *Literacy Time Years 3/4* and *Literacy Time Years 5/6*. Texts include fiction, non-fiction, playscripts and poetry. Contact the Editor before submitting material.

NATE News (National Association for the Teaching of English)

NATE, 50 Broadfield Road, Sheffield S8 0XJ
tel 0114-255 5419 *fax* 0114-255 5296

email info@nate.org.uk
website www.nate.org.uk
Editor Ian McNeilly
5 p.a.

The official newsletter of the National Association for the Teaching of English (NATE), available as part of its membership. The newsletter is a topical mix of news of NATE activities and views on current issues. NATE also publishes a twice-yearly magazine, *English Drama Media* and an academic journal, *English in Education*, three times a year.

Nursery Education

Scholastic Ltd, Villiers House, Clarendon Avenue, Leamington Spa, Warks. CV32 5PR
tel (01926) 887799 *fax* (01926) 883331
email earlyyears@scholastic.co.uk
website www.scholastic.co.uk
Editor Sarah Sodhi
Monthly £3.99

News, features, professional development and practical theme-based activities for professionals working with 0–5 year-olds. Activity ideas based on the Early Learning Goals. Material mostly commissioned. Length: 500–1000 words. Illustrations: colour and b&w; colour posters. Payment: by arrangement. Founded 1997.

Nursery World

Admiral House, 66–68 East Smithfield, London E1W 1BX
tel 020-7782 3120
website www.nurseryworld.co.uk
Editor Liz Roberts
Weekly £1.30

For all grades of primary school, nursery and child care staff, nannies, foster parents and all concerned with the care of expectant mothers, babies and young children. Authoritative and informative articles, 800 or 1300 words, and photos, on all aspects of child welfare and early education, from 0–8 years, in the UK. Practical ideas, policy news and career advice. No short stories. Payment: by arrangement. Illustrations: line, half-tone, colour.

Parent & Child

Scholastic Canada Ltd, 175 Hillmount Road, Markham, Ontario L6C 1Z7
website www.scholastic.ca

Covers the essential topics that parents need to know about their child's growth and development (pre-K–K), with expert advice on everything from school transitions to understanding children's feelings to promoting learning at home. Features include Ask the Doctor, Weekend Activities, and a Sibling Sharing Page.

Practical Parenting

IPC Media Ltd, King's Reach Tower, Stamford Street, London SE1 9LS

tel 020-7261 5058 *fax* 020-7261 6542
Editor Mara Lee
Monthly £2.45

Articles on parenting, baby and childcare, health, psychology, education, children's activities, personal birth/parenting experiences. Send synopsis with sae. Illustrations: colour photos, line; commissioned only. Payment: by agreement. Founded 1987.

Publishers Weekly

Publishers Weekly, 360 Park Avenue South, New York, NY 10010
tel 646-746-6758 *fax* 646-746-6631
website www.PublishersWeekly.com
Editor-in-Chief Sara Nelson, *Deputy Editor* Karen Holt, *Contact* Isabell Taylor for general editorial enquiries *tel* 646-746-6758, *email* i.taylor@reedbusiness.com *Children's Books Department: Senior Editor* Diane Roback
tel 646-746-6768 *fax* 646-746-6738

The international news magazine of the $23 billion book industry. Covers all segments involved in the creation, production, marketing and sale of the written word in book, audio, video and electronic formats. In addition to reaching publishers worldwide, it influences all media dealing with the acquisition, sale, distribution and rights of intellectual and cultural properties.

Children's Books Books for review, from preschool to young adult, should be sent to Diane Roback, Children's Books Editor – all reviews are prepublication. Also send her story suggestions on children's publishing, new trends, author or illustrator interviews, etc for the weekly *Children's Books*. Diane also edits the listings for new children's books twice a year for the Spring and Fall Children's Announcements issues. Please fax (do not email) any story pitches or queries concerning review submissions of children's books, review enquiries and editorial guidelines for submission of children's books for review. Founded 1873.

Publishing News

7 John Street, London WC1N 2ES
tel (0870) 870 2345 *fax* (0870) 870 0385
website www.publishingnews.co.uk
Editor Liz Thomson, *Children's Editor* Graham Marks
Weekly by subscription only

Articles and news items on the book publishing and bookselling industry. Approx. 6 articles about children's publishing each year in the special features section. Articles by agreement only. Founded 1979.

Report

ATL, 7 Northumberland Street, London WC2N 5RD
tel 020-7930 6441 *fax* 020-7930 1359
email report@atl.org.uk
website www.atl.org.uk
Editors Guy Goodwin, Victoria Poskitt

10 p.a. £2.50 (£15 p.a. UK; £27 p.a. overseas)

The magazine from the Association of Teachers and Lecturers (ATL). Features, articles, comment, news about nursery, primary, secondary and further education. Payment: minimum £120 per 1000 words.

Right Start

McMillan-Scott plc, 9 Savoy Street, London WC2E 7HR
tel 020-7878 2338 *fax* 020-7379 6261
Editor Lynette Lowthian
Bi-monthly £2.25

Features on all aspects of preschool and infant education, child health and behaviour. No unsolicited MSS. Length: 800–1500 words. Illustrations: colour photos, line. Payment: varies. Founded 1989.

Scholastic Canada Ltd

Scholastic Canada Ltd, 175 Hillmount Road, Markham, Ontario L6C 1Z7
website www.scholastic.ca

Classroom magazines to provide curriculum support. They include current events and engaging stories through to hands-on maths and science investigations.
PreK-K/Primary: *Let's Find Out, Clifford.* Elementary/Junior: *DynaMath* (Grade 3–6), *SuperScience* (Grade 3–6), *Storyworks* (Grade 3–6). Intermediate/Secondary: *Scholastic Math* (Grade 7–9), *Science World* (Grade 7–10), *New York Times Upfront* (Grade 7–12), *Scope* (Grade 7–9). Struggling Reader: *Action* (Grade 7–12), *Literary Cavalcade* (Grade 9–12), *Choices* (Grade 7–12), *Scholastic Art* (Grade 7–12).

The School Librarian

The School Library Association, Unit 2, Lotmead Business Village, Lotmead Farm, Wanborough, Swindon SN4 0UY
tel (0870) 777 0979 *fax* (0870) 777 0987
email info@sla.org.uk
website www.sla.org.uk
Editor Nancy Chambers, Lockwood, Station Road, South Woodchester, Stroud, Glos. GL5 5EQ
Quarterly Free to members (£55 p.a.)

Official journal of the School Library Association. Articles on school library management, use and skills, and on authors and illustrators, literacy, publishing. Reviews of books, CD-Roms, websites and other library resources from preschool to adult. Length: 1800–3000 words (articles). Payment: by arrangement. Founded 1937.

TES Cymru

Sophia House, 28 Cathedral Road, Cardiff CF11 9LJ
tel 029-2066 0201 *fax* 029-2066 0207
email cymru@tes.co.uk
website www.tes.co.uk/cymru
Editor Karen Thornton

Weekly £1.30

Education newspaper. Articles on education, teachers, teaching and learning, and education policy in Wales. Length: up to 800 words (articles). Illustrations: line, half-tone. Payment: by arrangement. Founded 2004.

The Times Educational Supplement

Admiral House, 66–68 East Smithfield, London
E1W 1BX
tel 020-7782 3000 *fax* 020-7782 3202 (news),
020-7782 3199 (features)
email friday@tes.co.uk (feature outlines),
teacher@tes.co.uk (curriculum-related outlines)
website www.tes.co.uk
Editor Judith Judd
Weekly £1.20

Education newspaper. Articles on education written with special knowledge or experience; news items; books, arts and equipment reviews. Check with the news or picture editor before submitting material. Outlines of feature ideas should be faxed or emailed. Illustrations: suitable photos and drawings of educational interest, cartoons. Payment: standard rates, or by arrangement.

TES Teacher Weekly Free with TES: Practical ideas and resources for teachers to inspire more successful lessons.

Times Educational Supplement Scotland

Scott House, 10 South St Andrew Street, Edinburgh
EH2 2AZ
tel 0131-557 1133 *fax* 0131-558 1155
Editor Neil Munro
Weekly £1.30

Education newspaper. Articles on education, preferably 800–1000 words, written with special knowledge or experience. News items about Scottish educational affairs. Illustrations: line, half-tone. Payment: by arrangement. Founded 1965.

Under 5

Pre-school Learning Alliance, The Fitzpatrick Building, 158 York Way, London N7 9AD
tel 020-7697 2500 *fax* 020-7697 8607
email editor.u5@pre-school.org.uk
Contact Anna Roberts
10 p.a. £30 p.a.

Articles on the role of adults – especially parents/preschool workers – in young children's learning and development, including children from all cultures and those with special needs. Length: 750 words. Payment: £60 per article. Founded 1962.

Young People Now

Haymarket Publishing Ltd, 174 Hammersmith Road, London W6 7JP
tel 020-8267 4793 *fax* 020-8267 4728
email ypn.editorial@haynet.com
website www.ypnmagazine.com
Editor Steve Barrett
Weekly £1.80

Informative articles, highlighting issues of concern to all those who work with young people, including youth workers, youth justice workers, the voluntary youth sector, probation and social services, Connexions, teachers and volunteers. Founded 1989.

Young Writer – see page 277

Television, film and radio

Commissioning for children's television

Writing for children's television programmes is a very competitive world. Anna Home offers guidelines for writers considering working in this area.

What are the classic children's television titles? *Blue Peter*, of course, *Magpie*, *Bagpuss*, *Grange Hill*, *My Family Are Aliens*, *Bob the Builder*, *Teletubbies*, etc. Children's television embraces a multitude of different kinds of programming, all of which requires writers. *Blue Peter* is not the kind of programme which gets commissioned cold – it evolved over the years through various production teams – but what is fundamental to its success is its makers' knowledge of its audience and how that audience has changed over the years. *Teletubbies* is exactly the same; its creator Anne Wood spent months researching the target audience and testing ideas before committing to them. So….

Rule One
Know your audience and the age range that you are aiming for.

Rule Two
Know the schedules, be aware of the available slots and the kind of programmes which go into them, study the output and the varying requirements of the different channels. CBBC has a different tone from CITV or Fox Kids or Nick; Five only caters for preschool children. Examine the market, watch the output, go to the 'Meet the Commissioner' meetings (advertised in the trade press, e.g. *Broadcast Magazine*), network and study the broadcaster's websites.

Rule Three
Learn how to write proposals and how to pitch them (remember that commissioners receive hundreds and hundreds of proposals in a year). Presentation, clarity and passion are all important. This is a very competitive world and if you get an opportunity to pitch in person know how to do it as it may be your only chance to impress. Rehearse well, have your props prepared (if appropriate) and don't waffle. You have to convince the commissioner that your project has a real USP (unique selling point) and that you can deliver it.

Rule Four
Have some idea of what your project is going to cost and be prepared to defend that costing. Few broadcasters fully fund commissions any more and you need to be aware of how to find matching deficit funding. Sometimes a writer may team up with an independent producer who will cover this part of it (see page 303 for listings). As a writer you will probably already have an agent, but that agent may not be an expert in terms of accessing television or film work. Check this out as many writers have two agents – one for their publishing activities and another for television and film.

Children's television drama

Children's television drama is probably the most exciting but also the most difficult area in which to succeed. It is expensive and commissioners are wary of taking risks on writers or producers without track records. Most children's television drama is now produced in long running series, e.g. *Grange Hill, Byker Grove, My Family Are Aliens*, etc. Writing for these series is more like writing for adult soaps, with teams of writers working with script editors. If you want to break in to one of these teams, it's worth writing a sample script and sending it to the relevant script editor or producer.

One-off dramas or shorter series like *Feather Boy, Shoebox Zoo* or *Illustrated Mum* are rarer these days and there is a huge amount of competition for the available slots. Big costume pieces like *Little Lord Fauntleroy* or *Children of the New Forest* are even rarer, again because of the cost and because large-scale fantasies like *Harry Potter* and special effects heavy drama have mainly moved to the cinema.

Smaller scale adaptations are still commissioned. If you find a book which you think would work for television, you'll have to buy an option before you take it to the producer or commissioner. As a result of the huge success of *Harry Potter, Lemony Snickett*, etc, the cost of optioning children's books has risen steeply and the potential 'biggies' are snapped up before publication. However, there are a number of excellent children's books published every year which could make good television and you might pick up the next 'big thing', so keep an eye on what is happening in the children's publishing world, read the trade magazines and try to get to know children's publishers. When you are looking at books consider whether they have potential beyond one book or a limited series. Commissioners are always looking for something which has the possibility to go to more than one series and to become a franchise or brand. Once you have secured your option write a brief treatment of how you see the television version working and submit it together with the book either to an independent producer, or to a commissioner – remembering the rules outlined above.

Animation

Animation is the most prolific and potentially the most financially rewarding children's genre, but it is rather specialised. There are certain things that work in cell or model animation and there are things that don't, so it is well worth studying successful animated series. Remember that this really is a visual medium and often words are minimal – think *Pingu*! In fact, the *Yoko Toto Yakamoto* series (which has no words) has won two BAFTA Children's Writer Awards. The alternative is to start with a book or a series of characters and then approach an animation production house. You don't have to provide the visuals, but you do need to remember that animation needs to be a minimum of 26 episodes in the first series with the potential to go to 104 episodes or more. Animation also needs to have international appeal as most animated series are international co-productions. Lastly, if you can, its worthwhile trying to learn a little bit about how animation works technically – it will help you identify the right kind of books or ideas.

Comedy and comedy-drama

Comedy and comedy-drama has become an increasingly popular part of children's television output. It's mainly studio based, relatively cheap to make and it works well in the schedule. The same comments about potential longevity apply in terms of the series and you should always have this in mind. Having said all this however, the main thing is to write something that you really want to write and you think will work for the audience on television, something that you care about and are passionate about and are really able to visualise and able to sell to those cynical commissioners.

Good luck.

Anna Home is Chief Executive of the Children's Film and Television Foundation. Previously she worked in children's programmes at both the BBC and ITV. Latterly she was Head of CBBC for 11 years, responsible for commissioning all the children's output. Her career began on *Playschool*, she started *Grange Hill* and her last commission was *Teletubbies*.

Writing comedy for children's television

Adam Bromley looks at types of comedy, the parameters of writing comedy for children's television and describes the commissioning process.

Writing comedy for children's television presents numerous challenges: it is both liberating and restrictive. Today, this target audience is more discerning than ever and they have a wide choice of television channels and entertainment options. If a comedy show doesn't deliver in a few minutes viewers will look elsewhere and perhaps channel surf or switch on a games console. Budgets for making programmes are ratcheted downwards than upwards. Also, editorial restrictions for children's television are extensive and need to be considered at every stage in the writing process.

But don't be disheartened by these challenges because children are more imaginative than adults and as an audience they will be more receptive to more outlandish ideas than conservative adult audiences.

The first question

Before you start on the time-consuming, frustrating and drawn-out process of 'making it' as a comedy writer, there's one question you should ask yourself: 'Can I write funny material?' It's surprising how many aspiring comedy writers never take a moment to be objective about their own work. You have to be tough on yourself because the chances of getting a show commissioned are low. The majority of scripts never get past the initial filtering process by producers and script readers. At every stage the numbers are whittled down. So the odds of any given script actually becoming a television programme are stacked against a writer from day one. Hard work and dedication will take you a long way, but if you can't deliver the comedy then think again. Try out what you've written on children and observe their reaction. You can rely on children to display their honest opinions. Don't rely on adults to give you mere confidence-boosting words of encouragement about your work. You don't need to wow your audience with the first thing you write. But you do need to raise a laugh somewhere along the way. If, after looking at yourself objectively, you do reckon that you may have that potential, the next step is to find out more about your chosen medium.

Budgets and briefs

Children's television has two special features that a writer should be aware of at every stage of writing: low budgets and a restrictive editorial brief. Budgets for programmes are around a fifth of comparable adult television shows so it's worth considering programme budgets when devising an idea. Commissioners are more likely to be attracted to proposals that can be realised on these lower sums than shows with a cast of hundreds and requiring numerous special effects. But don't make the mistake of thinking that a lower budget means lower quality. For example, Monty Python's *Life of Brian* was shot on a very low budget. The use of coconuts clapped together in place of horses for the knights was an ingenious way of overcoming the lack of funds for the horses. Whilst it's not a writer's job to get mired in the detail of how a scene could be shot, you should try to get a sense of what to avoid. Complex ideas which require large casts, major set builds and extensive use of special effects or large amounts of expensive post production are the obvious pitfalls.

The other unique aspect to children's television is its editorial concerns, which are wide ranging and can be tricky to master. In terms of content, swearing, sexual references, blasphemy or realistic violence are absolutely taboo. Your point of reference should be the content of a U or PG-rated film at the cinema. Watch a good variety of children's television and films to get an innate sense of what the boundaries are. As with the budgets, it's more productive to see these editorial rules as something that will force you to be a better writer than just a burden. Often new comedy writers rely on dark, violent scenarios because mastering a scene that relies on word play and a clever premise is beyond them. This tighter control of content means that the writer cannot fall back on shock tactics or explicit language to achieve a reaction which is, in the long run, a better way to progress.

There is an additional concern known as 'imitative behaviour'. Children are more suggestible and have a lower sense of risk and personal safety. In anything you write avoid any action that, if copied by children, might harm them, for example swallowing lots of tablets, forcing things into their mouths, throwing household objects at people. This may pose problems if you've got slapstick gags, which are a reliable mainstay of children's comedy. Be wary of any highly realistic scenarios as opposed to cartoonish ones. If the above sounds limiting, the flipside is that children will readily make greater leaps of imagination than adults. Don't forget that you're writing for an audience that remains fresh and open-minded in a way few adults are. Working within these ground rules is a small price to pay for an appreciative audience.

Comedy writing itself naturally divides into three main areas: sketches, scripted comedy and gag writing.

Scripted comedy

Scripted comedy covers a number of forms, including comedy narrative that has an unfolding story which links week by week and sitcom in which each episode is largely self contained. The three keys to writing good scripted comedy are number one: character; number two: character; and number three: character.

Everything starts and ends with your principal characters. Witty one-liners and elaborate plot structures are worthless unless they flow from strong central characters. For creating comedy characters, it's useful to think of them as embodying certain key personality traits and to make that inform everything they do. As we're dealing with comedy, don't make your characters too pleasant. There's nothing very amusing, for example, about a family sitcom where everyone gets on wonderfully well, is understanding, supportive and helpful. That may be a good environment to raise children, but it makes for tedious television. Characters don't work in isolation so put together a mix of characters that will spark against one another. Comedy, like drama, needs tension. So if you have a dysfunctional family that lives in a house so huge they never need to interact with one another, there's no friction for comedy to happen. But if you put them in a pokey flat where they're always getting in one another's way, then you've got fertile comic territory.

If you want to devise characters that will appeal to a children's audience, a mix of adults and children will be the most likely to work, preferably of different generations. Children won't be interested in mid-life crises, office politics or single women in their twenties looking for love. Generational conflict with families is an ideal starting point. But as with everything, there are no rules.

So long as your audience can find some point of connection, there's no reason why your lead couldn't be an alien or from another century. It all depends on how that character is presented so consider how your characters will connect with the wider audience. A child's frame of reference is different to that of an adult and children want comedy that reflects that. Remembering that you're writing not just for yourself but for hundreds of thousands of strangers will help guide you towards broader, more accessible characters. Make sure that the comedy flows from the characters themselves and doesn't just happen around them. Your comic leads need to initiate much of the action. In comedy things should go wrong most of the time so the leads should be the authors of their own misfortunes rather than having random events simply happen.

Sketch writing

Sketch writing presents other challenges, not least that many ideas have been done before. Common mistakes new writers make with a sketch is to start with a confused or muddled premise. Alternatively, they have a good premise and do nothing with it. The premise of a sketch is the one-line summary of a funny idea. If you can't summarise the sketch into one line and if that summary doesn't make you laugh, then there's probably something at fault with the original idea. Once you've got a promising sketch idea, it should develop as the piece unfolds. Even though the sketch may be only two minutes of airtime, you'll have to give some kind of twist or progression to sustain the audience's interest over that period. Even 10 seconds of dead air in a television programme can feel like an eternity. Write your sketches longer and then trim them back. Another good rule is to not let a sketch run for longer than two minutes.

Gag writing

Gag writing is a discipline all of its own. When writing standalone jokes, practise does make perfect and it's critical that you test your material on audiences. It can be intimidating but there's no better way to find out if what you've written makes audiences laugh. Your main avenue for gag writing is the scripted links in entertainment shows.

The commissioning process

Once you have material ready to submit, understanding the commissioning process can save a lot of wasted effort. The first hurdle for a writer is to get anyone, whether it's a producer or an agent, to take an interest in their work. Getting a programme commissioned is a long, frustrating process and it's integral to that process to have someone promoting your cause – typically a producer.

From a new writer's perspective, agents can help from an the early stage to get your script past the initial filtering stage. Producers and development executives are generally more receptive to scripts sent to them by agents, as they act as a form of quality control. Don't despair, if you send an unsolicited script or proposal to a producer or editor, it will be read... eventually.

One mistake writers often make is to send out copies of their script to every producer working in children's television with a general covering letter. This is never a good idea. It sends out a signal that the writer in question couldn't be bothered to do some research on who might be interested in their script. Finding out who makes which shows is relatively easy as all the major channels have information lines if you miss the end credits of shows. A bit of research goes a long way. You should follow up that script with a phone call or email. Although your script may represent months of hard toil to you, remember that producers work on other shows and that reading scripts is a low priority for them.

If you are able to get a producer to take an interest in your work, often the next natural step is not to immediately pitch your own programme ideas but to work on existing shows, perhaps writing episodes of a long-running sitcom, devising sketch ideas or writing additional material for entertainment shows. This is a good bridging stage as you'll get a better feel of the production and commissioning process. It's also a great opportunity to improve your writing craft without the exposure of a solo project. Nearly all comedy writers started out writing on other people's shows. The longer you spend writing in a professional environment, the better you'll get. Meeting deadlines and turning work around in a short time frame are not disciplines new writers acquire by writing on their own but they are an important part of being a successful television writer. Being funny on demand is a tough task and it's part of the craft.

In the long run most writers are more interested in getting their own solo ideas commissioned. Be prepared for a lot of frustration and disappointment if you follow this route. There are relatively few programme slots available in any given year. Commissioners tend to favour tried and tested writers over new names. There's no conspiracy to exclude new talent, however. When money is in short supply, opting for a safe pair of hands is a form of insurance policy. All of which means that, as a new writer, you'll have to be that much more impressive than an established one to get noticed. In spite of all this, if you deliver funny, original and accessible scripts, sooner or later you'll be noticed and they will make it on screen.

Adam Bromley is a producer for BBC Entertainment. Recent credits include *CBBC Stupid, The Now Show, The Problem with Adam Bloom* and *Think the Unthinkable* for BBC Radio 4 and *Tiny and Mr Duk's Huge Show.*

Children's literature on radio and audio

The spoken word and the written word in literature require different handling. Neville Teller looks at the radio and audiobook media and explores what a writer for the microphone needs to know and how to break into this market.

'Read me a story' – one of childhood's perennial calls. Parents found little relief from this cry (palming it off on grandma or auntie was perhaps the best bet) until radio appeared on the scene. But from its very beginning radio included in its schedules stories read aloud for children, and the loudspeaker, for part of the time at least, was able to provide a fair substitute for mummy or daddy by presenting professional actors reading literature specially prepared for performance at the microphone.

Very early on, actors learned that performing at the microphone was a new skill that had to be acquired – the techniques were quite different from those required on the stage. Writers, too, had to acquire a whole range of new skills in preparing material for radio. Two things quickly became apparent. First, literature simply read aloud from the printed page often failed to 'come across' to a listening audience, because material produced to be scanned by the eye is often basically unsuited to the requirements of the microphone. Secondly, the time taken to read a complete book on the air would be far too long to be acceptable, and in consequence most books would need to be abridged.

Today there are two main outlets in this country for aspiring radio/audio writers for children: BBC radio and audiobook publishers.

How has this market reached its present position?

Radio

Children's radio in the UK has certainly had its ups and downs. It came into existence in December 1922, just a few weeks after the BBC itself was born, and for some 40 years the daily Children's Hour became an established and much-cherished feature of life in this country. It is no exaggeration to say that during its heyday its presenters, and those who made its programmes, created an indelible impression on the childhood of millions of people.

However, in the 1960s the imminent death of radio was a generally accepted prognostication. So, starting in 1961, children's radio was slowly but surely strangled on the dubious, if not specious, grounds that children no longer had the time or inclination to listen to radio. Television, it was argued, was their medium of choice. So first the much-loved title 'Children's Hour' was dropped, then the time allotted to programmes 'For the Young' (as it was then called) was cut back. Finally, in March 1964, the programme was put out of its agony.

The demise of children's radio naturally evoked a massive groundswell of protest. In response – although the BBC of the day had clearly lost faith in it – they did grant some sort of reprieve. Stories had always featured strongly in its schedules, and *Story Time* – a programme of abridged radio readings – started life in the old Children's Hour slot with a strong bias towards children's literature. After a few years, however, its character changed.

More general literature began to be selected, and then the programme was moved to earlier in the afternoon. That decision, despite a brief experiment with a programme called *Fourth Dimension* and the continued existence of *Listen with Mother* till 1982, effectively left the Radio 4 schedules for nearly 20 years bereft of any specifically children's programmes.

The comeback started slowly, and then suddenly gathered momentum. Early in the new millennium the BBC – moved, doubtless, by mounting evidence of the undiminished popularity of radio – decided to reintroduce a regular programme for children. All they could offer at the time was a 30-minute programme each Sunday evening on Radio 4 called *Go4It*, a magazine-type show that would include a 10-minute reading. Children's literature had – to mix metaphors and create a glorious vision – re-established a toehold on the airwaves and I found myself abridging books ranging from *The Lion, the Witch and the Wardrobe* by C.S. Lewis to *The Fall of Fergal* by Philip Ardagh and *The Wolves of Willoughby Chase* by Joan Aitken for the programme.

Much more was to follow, for in the autumn of 2002 the BBC launched its new digital radio channel, BBC7, which included in its schedules, as a basic ingredient, daily programmes for children using live performers and incorporating readings from children's literature, both current and classic. These abridgements are specially prepared and read for the two daily shows: *The Big Toe Radio Show* for older children and – it goes without saying – *The Little Toe Radio Show* for the youngsters. Since its launch I have prepared a considerable number of books for young listeners, ranging from classical children's literature like *Robinson Crusoe, Huckleberry Finn, Black Beauty* and *The Prince and the Pauper* to up-to-the-moment favourites such as Anthony Horowitz's series about his boy secret agent, *Alex Rider* and the *Artemis Fowl* novels by Eoin Colfer, to say nothing of perennial modern favourites such as the *Wishing Chair* and the *Magic Faraway Tree* series by Enid Blyton and *Stig of the Dump* by Clive King.

Audiobooks

Audiobooks are literary works of all types, some abridged, some unabridged, read by actors and made available in audiocassette or CD form. They are a rapidly growing market: from what was virtually a standing start in the late 1980s, annual sales are now in excess of £70 million. No less than five million audiobooks were purchased in the UK last year and children's literature forms a significant proportion of that total.

Over the past decade and a half an enormous backlist of children's literature has been built up in audiobook format. Nowadays, moreover, it is common for major publishers to launch a fair number of their new books in printed and audiobook form simultaneously. Children's publishers are also increasingly developing the 'twin pack' concept – packaging book and audiobook together – so that children can read and listen at the same time. This development is bound to mushroom, because Customs and Excise decided in 2003 that such products could be zero-rated for VAT.

It was in May 2000 that a consortium thought of putting one modern development (audiobooks) together with another (digital radio), and came up with a revolutionary new radio concept. Oneword is a digital radio channel concerned above all with literature. The core of its programming is the transmission of audiobook readings, both abridged and unabridged, streamed into various segments throughout the day. Its schedules (which, like BBC7's, appear in *Radio Times* as well as in several newspapers) include classical and new books for children.

How children listen

The ways in which children can – and increasingly do – listen to the readings intended especially for them are multiplying. *The Big* and *Little Toe Radio Shows* (unlike *Go4It* which can additionally be accessed by normal AM or FM radio), are transmitted only on digital radio. However, all three programmes are also available online, via the BBC's website, to be heard in what is known as 'simul-streaming' (that is, more or less at the same time as the direct radio transmission). In addition, the readings can be heard for a full week after transmission, by way of the 'Listen Again' facility. More than this, both the older and younger children's digital radio shows have their own dedicated websites, and via these children are able to hear a changing selection of their favourite readings broadcast in the past. As electronic access to the internet becomes increasingly available in portable form, via new generation mobile phones, this flexibility of access to read-aloud literature will certainly increase.

The downloading of audiobooks to MP3, iPod and similar systems is also just around the corner in this country (it is already commonplace in the USA). Stories are likely to prove a popular second-best to music for many children.

The message of all this for writers is simply that the market seems poised for expansion, and if you are keen to break into it, it seems worthwhile to persevere.

Writing for the microphone

Putting unabridged audiobook readings to one side, what does the aspiring radio/audio children's writer need to know, and how can he or she break into the rather specialised world of abridging children's literature for the microphone?

As in all professional fields, the tyro is faced with the classic Catch-22 situation: radio producers and audio publishers are reluctant to offer commissions to people without a track record, while it is of course impossible to gain a track record without having won a commission or two. The only advice is to keep plugging away, hoping for that elusive lucky break – and the only consolation on offer is that even the most experienced of today's professionals was once a complete novice.

But what of the techniques that need to be applied in converting material produced for the printed page into a series of scripts that can be performed by an actor with ease at the microphone, and bring real listening pleasure to the child at the other end?

Getting to grips with abridging books for the microphone requires, in the first instance, the application of some simple arithmetic. Take a book of around 70,000 words. Children's radio these days usually devotes about 10 minutes' airtime to its reading slot, and producers allow up to 14 episodes for each book. In 10 minutes, an actor can read about 1450 words. It is clear, therefore, that normally the abridger will be required to reduce the wordage from 70,000 to no more than 20,300 words. In other words, one can be required to remove up to 70% of the original.

The audio field has different requirements. Most books abridged for audio are still published in the form of two double-sided cassettes, though the changeover to CDs is well under way. Each of the four cassette sides runs for about 45 minutes and uses 7000 words. Thus the normal audiobook contains some 28,000 words. CDs can accommodate well over 60 minutes of airtime, so the 180-minute abridgement is often also presented in the form of three CDs.

An abridgement – is that the same as a précis? I think not. A précis writer's objective is to reproduce the sense of an original in fewer words. The skill of the abridger lies in doing that while, in addition and quite as important, retaining the character of the original writing. That demands the capacity to respond sympathetically to the feel of an author's style and to be able to preserve it, even when large chunks of the original are being cut away. Abridging for radio goes beyond even this, for the writer must fulfil his or her commission through the medium of that highly technical artefact, the radio script.

Some abridgements intended for the printed page are able to boast 'only the words of the original are used'. Radio or audio abridgements that followed that principle could be disastrous. The requirements of eye and of ear do not always coincide; a message easily absorbed from the printed page can become surprisingly garbled if transmitted unamended at the microphone.

In crafting a radio/audio script the needs of the listener must be a prime consideration. The needs of the actor who will read it at the microphone are another. The writer must keep in the forefront of the mind the fact that the script has to be performed. The words must 'flow trippingly on the tongue'.

With audio the listener is in control, and can switch on or off whenever convenient. However, a radio script needs shape. On the air, 10 minutes on an emotional plateau can be pretty boring. *Crescendi* and *diminuendi* are called for. A good plan is to provide a modest peak of interest about halfway through the script, and work up to a climax at the end, leaving the listener anxious for more of the story.

Principles, principles – what about practice? A modest illustration.

'How are you going?' Harriet said, stifling a yawn.

'The Oxford bus,' returned Pam.

Nothing wrong with that – on the printed page. If faced with it, though, the experienced radio or audio writer would feel it necessary to present it somewhat along the following lines:

Harriet stifled a yawn.

'How are you going?'

'The Oxford bus,' said Pam

Why? Let's take the points in order.

Harriet said.

If the speaker's name instantly follows a piece of reported speech, and especially a question, a moment of confusion can arise in the listener's mind. In this instance, it could be unclear for a second whether 'Harriet' is included in, or excluded from, the question. It might be: *'How are you going, Harriet...?'*

The meaning is soon resolved, of course, but impediments to understanding are best eliminated.

'Stifling a yawn' is an indication of the way in which the words were said. If the actor is to provide that indication, he or she needs to know ahead of the speech how it is to be delivered. Moreover, taking the original version, if the actor stifles a yawn while saying Harriet's speech, and then reads 'said Harriet, stifling a yawn,' the passage becomes tautologous.

For this reason it is best to cut back to a bare minimum all indications in the text of how speeches are delivered. It is better to leave it to the actor and the producer to interpret most of them.

There are no apostrophes on the air. By and large, 'said' is the best radio indicator of speech. An alternative is to precede speech by some description of the speaker, and to insert the words spoken with no further indication of who is speaking. Thus:

Harriet stifled a yawn.
'How are you going?'
It is clearly Harriet speaking.
'The Oxford bus,' returned Pamela.

Two points here. Almost all the literary variants of 'said' ring false through the loudspeaker or headphones – cried, riposted, remarked, answered, etc. For reading purposes, most are best replaced with 'said' (or better, wherever possible, omitted altogether) and the speech in question left to the actor to interpret. In this instance, *'returned'* is particularly difficult for the listener – again, for no more than a moment – but is 'returned' part of the speech? *'The Oxford bus returned...?'* It is surely best to eliminate obstacles to understanding.

This peek into the radio/audio abridger's toolbox might leave one thinking that the business is all gimmick and no heart – noses pressed up so hard against tree trunks that there is no time for the wood. It is certainly necessary that in this field, as in any other, basic techniques have to be acquired and then absorbed to the point where they become second nature. Only then can they be applied to ensure that the radio and audio media are used to interpret a writer's intentions as fully and as honestly as possible.

It is, though, equally essential that the abridger of children's books reproduces, as far as possible, the plot, atmosphere and character of the original. The aim must be to leave the listener with as complete a feeling of the original book as possible, given the technical limitations of time and wordage. It is, in short, an essential aspect of the radio/audio writer's craft to keep faith with the author.

Neville Teller has been contributing to BBC radio for over 40 years. He has well over 250 abridgements for radio readings to his credit, some 50 radio dramatisations and over 150 audiobook abridgements. His most recent children's adaptations include *Artemis Fowl* by Eoin Colfer, *Stig of the Dump* by Clive King, *The BFG* by Roald Dahl, *The Wolves of Willoughby Chase* by Joan Aiken and *Stormbreaker* by Anthony Horowitz. Neville Teller is Chairman of the Society of Authors' Broadcasting Committee. He is also on the Committee of the Spoken Word Publishing Association and chairs the SWPA's Contributors' Committee. He is Guest Playwright for Shoestring Radio Theatre, San Francisco.

See also...

- *Children's audio publishers*, page 65
- *Writing to a brief*, page 295

Writing to a brief

Writing to a brief is an exacting process in which the writer has to produce work to satisfy others as opposed to exploring their own project ideas. The writer may work with others as part of a team when script writing or collaborate with an artistic director when adapting a play. Diane Redmond looks at three aspects of writing to a brief for children.

Writing to a brief is enormous fun! I never know what's going to land on my desk – it could be anything: a children's animation series, a set of books, a live action drama script or a stage play. For this kind of writing you must have the ability to absorb a lot of material quickly and you also have to be capable of putting your own ideas on the back burner. You can't twist the brief in order to accommodate what you want to write as opposed to what the commissioner is *paying* you to write.

Animation

Script writing for animation is energising writing – it makes you think in pictures and images which you have to transcribe into words. An animation series is usually commissioned in blocks of 26 or 52 10-minute episodes. Once you've been invited to work on the series, background material is usually sent to you by the commissioning body. This outlining material is often referred to as the 'bible' and it contains everything the writer needs to know in order to write the manuscript: the number of characters, locations, props, sets and costumes. The 'bible' might contain a fully executed script, which is really useful as you can read for yourself a script that's been approved by the commissioner and thereafter use it as a guideline.

The writing team

The writing team meet with the commissioner (the person or company funding the show) to go through the 'bible' in some detail. The commissioner will be looking for scripts that contain humour, warmth, clarity and a real understanding of the age group the writers are pitching at. As a writer, you should never allow yourself to lose track of the main character and the central theme: if it's about garden gnomes then keep it in the garden; if it's about a builder then the building job will be essential to *every* story; if it's about a postman then he has to do his post round. I know it's obvious but you'd be astonished how often writers stray from the central plot in their obsession to create their *own* story! Most scripts, even if they're only 10 minutes long, have a main plot and a sub-plot which have to reconciled. Make sure your sub-plot doesn't swamp your main plot and make doubly sure your main plot echoes the criteria of the series.

Storylines

Sometimes a few storylines are developed when the writing team is together – just enough to get the team kick-started. The writers may be invited to choose a storyline that excites them and develop it into a three- or four-page treatment, i.e. a scene-by-scene breakdown of the 10-minute episode. Alternatively, writers may be asked to think up and develop more storylines at home. When writing like this on a commission your contract should ensure that you're paid for each stage of the writing process.

The very first outline is often the hardest one of all. The writer may have seen the artwork, may even have seen a pilot script and heard a snatch of the opening music but she's coming to the first story *cold*. The characters aren't alive yet – it's the writer at this vital initial stage who breathes life into them. After a couple of scripts, and certainly after a series of 13 episodes, the characters will be alive and kicking! They will have taken up a space in your imagination and will inspire you with ideas for 10 more series! You know what makes them tick because you've created them in the very act of writing. You'll find that within the writing team writers will favour particular characters and bring out the best in that character. It's a heart-lifting experience to work with a team of writers who are open and generous and willing to share their thoughts. By pooling your joint strengths and resources you generate ideas so don't hold back at the writers' meeting. If you've come up with one good idea, think of it as a springboard because you'll need at least another dozen hot on the heels of the first!

The script editor

The script editor is *vital*. He or she coordinates the scripts and makes sure the series has one voice. Four writers will have different styles, which is exactly why they've been chosen to do the job. However, the series itself has the voice – be it that of a ballerina, a robot, or a kind-hearted mule. The script editor has an overall view of the show and will make small changes to scripts so that idiosyncrasies are ironed out. She also has the sensitive task of liaising with the commissioner and the producer on the writers' behalf. Sometimes you *don't* want to see the notes the producer has made: they may be too abrupt or confusing. The script editor will expand and clarify these notes then pass them on to the writers who can then make the necessary alterations to their scripts based on the producer's wishes. The script editor should be valued because she does *a lot* for the writers in the team.

Stages of writing

After the initial idea, followed by a detailed outline (I usually précis mine scene by scene) you may be asked to reconstruct your outline based on changes the animators or the producer have requested. For instance, if you have written an elephant into your script and if that frame (containing your elephant puppet) will cost £8000 you can guarantee someone will want it to go! It's best to sort out all practical problems at this stage and a good producer will go through a script outline with a fine comb, looking for potential problem areas. The animators will tell you what they, in practical terms, can and cannot do so be prepared for notes from them and remember they're the ones who will be shooting the episode when you've been paid off. I usually find animators incredibly helpful, sometimes inspirational as they'll push their puppeteering to the limit and give me brilliant ideas in the process.

Writers expect to get detailed notes on their first draft scripts and shorter notes on their second draft scripts but if problems have been sorted out at the outline stage it's usually a wrap after two drafts. When you get the go-ahead to write the script the real *fun* begins! I have sat at my desk and laughed till I cried at some of the characters I've written for. Behind the lively dialogue there are other things happening simultaneously: movement within the set, expressions, little mutters and mumbles and music too. Sometimes your instructions to camera can be three times as long as a simple piece of dialogue like, 'Oh, all right then.' Occasionally you may wonder, 'How am I going to get all of that information to camera in such a small space?' It's an exacting rigour, which ultimately strengthens your overall writing skills. When your script is approved you get such a sweet feeling of relief. But then you'll start to miss your characters and so begin work on another script idea – and the business starts all over again.

Stage plays

As well as writing my own stage plays I've also adapted stage plays from the classics such as *Hard Times* by Charles Dickens and Homer's *Odyssey*. The Dickens play was commissioned by the Cambridge Youth Theatre for the Edinburgh Festival with a cast of 30, and *The Odyssey* was staged in 1990 and 1994 at the Polka Theatre for Children in London with a cast of six!

When briefed by an artistic director writers should listen hard to his or her requirements and it is imperative that they take on board the limitations of the budget. Theatres usually have to work on a shoestring budget. If too much is spent on props and costumes it may be at the cost of the funding for an actor, so be prepared to adapt and compromise.

Adapting from the classics

Adapting from a text such as a classic is an exacting exercise. The two books I adapted couldn't have been more different but the process was exactly the same. I read both books until I knew them backwards: with that knowledge under my belt I felt at liberty to explore the plotlines within the stories and look for modern day angles on how to dramatise them.

The brief for *The Odyssey* was to write a 90-minute play with a 10-minute interval for children aged between eight and 12 years old. There's a lot of sex in *The Odyssey*. For instance, Odysseus loiters too long with Circe and nearly dies in his desire to reach the Sirens! In order not to shock my young audience I found a way around this sensitive area by bringing in the crew who made humorous references to Odysseus' behaviour. In one of my scenes Eurylochus says, 'It's time we set sail.' Castor nods towards Odysseus locked in the arms of Circe the Witch and says, 'I don't think the captain's ready for that yet, mate!' The language of Homer is hauntingly beautiful but certainly not pitched at children. The hardest part of writing the play was adapting the language and the plot so that the audience could understand what was going on without destroying the nobility of the original piece. Working closely with the artistic director, it took three drafts to get the tone of the play right but by that time I was so familiar with the gods and heroes of Ancient Greece that they felt like my extended family! It's a knowledge I've never lost and have since written three books based on classical Greek heroes. That's another great thing about writing: you can transpose a story from one art form to another!

Book series

A book series may be commissioned as a result of a writer pitching an idea to a publisher, or a publisher may have spotted a gap in the market which a writer has been invited to fill. The books vary in length depending on the age range – they could be anything from 2000 words to 40,000 words.

I've written three series of books based on football which I knew nothing about but finished up the world's expert on the offside trap! I went on to write several more series based on show jumping, a stage school, a veterinary practice, a drama queen, and an eight-book series based on bridesmaids! A lot of research goes into my books. With my show-jumping series I virtually lived at the livery yard, trailing the head groom and asking questions like, 'Where do show jumpers go when they're not show jumping? How do you treat a lame horse? What's the best fitness diet? Do show jumpers need special shoes and saddles?' I've always been very lucky in finding professionals who allowed me into their lives and let me watch them at work, though I have had a few nasty shocks in the process. Once I found myself masked and gloved in a vast operating theatre at a vet's surgery watching a Newmarket racehorse under the scalpel; but I fled the premises (and my note taking) when a couple brought in a large snake that needed treatment! You *really* do have to know your subject when you're writing this kind of specialist book. The readers certainly know their stuff and are very critical of any inaccuracies. I know this first hand because of all the letters I get from children who've read my series and appreciated the accuracy of them.

Diane Redmond has written numerous scripts including *Bob the Builder*, *Angelina Ballerina*, *Magic Key*, *Tweenies* and *The Hoobs*. She has also written for radio, the stage and live action television dramas. She has published over a hundred books, most recently *Joshua Cross and the Queen's Conjuror* (Wizard Books)

See also...
• *Children's literature on radio and audio*, page 290
• *What does an editor do?*, page 129

BBC children's television

During the day, BBC1 runs two children's channels – Cbeebies for a preschool audience and CBBC for older children. Both have designated early morning and afternoon time slots but programmes run continuously on individual channels on digital, cable and satellite networks. These channels have a combined budget of £20 million. To find out about the commissioning process visit www.bbc.co.uk/commissioning

BBC Active

80 Strand, London WC2R 0RL
tel 020-7010 2701 *fax* 020-7010 6965
website www.bbcactive.com,
www.bbcschoolshop.com
Director of BBC Active Susan Ross

The BBC runs a wide range of programmes and websites for schools to encourage children to learn (it also has a separate service for adults.) The programmes aim to inspire learning more broadly and informally on topics such science, history and children's entertainment. The BBC uses interactive TV and internet for these learning services. This department commissions and produces a broad range of online and interactive factual output and is actively looking for new writers.

CBBC

Television Centre, Wood Lane, London W12 7RJ
tel 020-8743 8000
email cbbconline@bbc.co.uk
Submissions CBBC Treatments & Scripts,
Development Executive, CBBC Creates, Room E1200,
East Tower, BBC Television Centre, Wood Lane,
London W12 7RJ
website www.bbc.co.uk/cbbc

Digital channel aimed at 6–12 year-olds (it does not cater for teenagers). Produced by the BBC under the CBBC brand. Broadcasts 7am–7pm on BBC1, BBC2 (known as CBBC1 and CBBC2) and cable/satellite channels. Offers a complete TV and online experience by offering a broad range of content made specifically for the 6–12 age group which is relevant to their daily lives and helps them make sense of the world.

There are opportunities for new writers in this highly competitive area. Unsolicited programme proposals from individual writers and independent production companies are passed to the relevant genre head. The CBBC department is searching for new writing and screen presenting talent, across all CBBC output. CBBC prefer treatments of programme ideas to be sent via email. Presenter enquiries need to send a showreel of approximately 3 minutes on VHS.

Controller, CBBC Richard Deverill
Creative Director Anne Gilchrist
Head of Drama John East
Head of On-Air Paul Smith
Head of Education Sue Nott
Head of CBBC News & Factual Programmes Roy Milani
Head of Preschool Clare Elstow
Creative Director Michael Carrington
Creative Executive Amanda Gabbitas
Cbeebies is CBBC's sister channel for younger viewers. Launched 2002.

Cbeebies

Television Centre, Wood Lane, London W12 7RJ
tel 020-8743 8000
email cbeebiesonline@bbc.co.uk
website www.bbc.co.uk/cbeebies
Creative Director Michael Carrington

Channel produced by the BBC and aimed at children under 6 years old. A range of preschool learning programmes designed to encourage learning through play. Programmes include *The Tweenies* and *Teletubbies*. It transmits on BBC1, BBC2 and the Cbeebies cable/satellite channel (6am–7pm) and features a Cbeebies Bedtime Hour (6pm–7pm). The approach is to entertain and engage children so they learn through play, and to stimulate and encourage participation. CBBC is its sister channel for older viewers. Launched 2002.

Independent children's television

A broad range of independently commissioned and scheduled programmes is available on terrestrial and digital, cable and satellite television networks. ITV, Channel 4 and Channel 5, have allocated children's morning, afternoon and weekend time slots, whereas the digital channels run back-to-back programmes between 12 and 24 hours a day. For channel information, contact Ofcom (www.ofcom.org.uk).

Boomerang

Turner House, 16 Great Marlborough Street, London W1F 7HS
tel 020-7693 1000
email toon.pressoffice@turner.com
website www.boomerangtv.co.uk

Cartoon entertainment broadcast 24 hours a day, including *Scooby-Doo*, *Tom and Jerry*, *The Flintstones* and *Looney Tunes*. Operated by Turner Broadcasting.

Cartoon Network

Turner Entertainments Network Ltd, 16 Great Marlborough Street, London W1F 7HS
tel 020-7693 1000
email toon.pressoffice@turner.com
website www.cartoonnetwork.co.uk

Cartoon entertainment broadcast 24 hours a day, including *Foster's Home for Imaginary Friends*, *Dexter's Laboratory*, *The Powerpuff Girls*, *Codename: Kids Next Door*, *Ed Edd n Eddy* and *HiHi Puffy AmiYumi*. Operated by Turner Broadcasting. Established 1992.

Channel 4 Television Corporation

124 Horseferry Road, London SW1P 2TX
tel 020-7396 4444, 020-7306 8333 (viewer enquiries), 020-7396 4444 (E4 and FilmFour information) *fax* 020-7306 8347
website www.channel4.com/entertainment/t4
Director of Television Kevin Lygo

Commissions and purchases programmes for broadcast during the whole week throughout the UK (except Wales). Also broadcasts subscription film channel FilmFour and digital entertainment channel E4.

Children's early morning viewing is approx. 6–7am and *The Hoobs* and *Spider-man* are programmes shown regularly. Programmes catering for teenagers, such as *Friends*, *Hollyoaks*, *Popworld*, *Shipwrecked*, *The OC* and *Big Brother*, are shown during weekday early evenings and on the weekend show *T4*.

CITV

200 Gray's Inn Road, London WC1X 8HF
tel 020-7843 8000 *fax* 020-7843 8158
website www.itv.com/citv

Encompasses ITV's dedicated children's programming, aimed at 2–12 year-olds, and CITV's new digital free-to-air commercial children's channel for 2–9 year-olds. Featuring CITV's existing slate of children's programming, the channel looks to expand commissioning opportunities and acquisitions. Programmes include drama, factual, preschool, entertainment, comedy and animation series which aim to both entertain and inform its audiences.

Discovery Kids

Discovery Networks Europe, 160 Great Portland Street, London W1W 5QA
tel 020-7462 3600
email mail_us@discovery-europe.com
website www.kids-discovery.co.uk
Contact Valerie Taylor

Satellite and cable network showing mainly science, documentary and nature programmes, such as *Mystery Hunters*, *History Busters* and *Sci-Busters*. Part of the Discovery Channel and owned by Discovery Communications.

Disney Channel UK

3 Queen Caroline Street, London W6 9PE
tel 020-8222 2489 *hotline* (08709) 200020
email studio@disneychannel.co.uk
website www.disney.co.uk/disneychannel, www.disney.co.uk/DisneyChannel/toondisney, www.disney.co.uk/DisneyChannel/playhouse

A cable and satellite network run by the Walt Disney Company. Disney Channel comprises 4 channels: Disney Channel, Disney Channel+1, Toon Disney and Playhouse Disney. Features family-orientated programmes aimed at pre-teens and younger adolescents. Surprisingly, it does not feature many classic Disney cartoons but newer programmes such as *Lizzie McGuire*, *Boy Meets World* and the *Proud Family*. Established 1973; UK version launched 1990s.

Five Broadcasting Ltd

22 Long Acre, London WC2E 9LY
tel 020-7550 5555, (08457) 050505
(comments) *fax* 020-7550 5554
website www.five.tv
website www.five.tv/programmes/milkshake
website www.five.tv/programmes/shake
Director of Programmes Dan Chambers

The fifth and last national 'free-to-air' terrestrial 24-hour TV channel. Commissions a wide range of programmes to suit all tastes.

Milkshake! is Five's weekday children's programme slot, 6.30–9.25am. Programmes include *Noddy, Hi-5, Funky Valley* and *Peppa Pig.* Established 1997.

GMTV

London Television Centre, Upper Ground, London SE1 9TT
tel 020-7827 7000 *fax* 020-7827 7001
email talk2us@gm.tv.
website www.gm.tv
Director of Programmes Peter McHugh

GMTV is ITV's national breakfast TV service, 6–9.25am, 7 days a week. GMTV2 is GMTV's digital, satellite and cable channel shown on ITV2 daily, 6–9.25am. GMTV's children's programming is called *Toonattik* and is broadcast on Saturday 6–9.25am and Sunday 7.30–9.25am. GMTV2 broadcasts children's programmes on weekdays.

ITV Network Ltd/ITV Association

200 Gray's Inn Road, London WC1X 8HF
tel 020-7843 8000 *fax* 020-7843 8158
email info@itv.com
website www.itv.co.uk
Managing Director (Granada) Mick Desmond,
Managing Director (Carlton) Clive Jones, *Director of Programmes* Nigel Pickard

Comprises 16 independent regional TV licensees, broadcasting across 15 regions of the UK. Commissions and schedules its own programmes and from independent production companies, shown across the ITV network. The ITV terrestrial channel is ITV1. See also CiTV (listed) and the following websites:

- **Anglia**
  website www.angliatv.co.uk
- **Border**
  website www.border-tv.co.uk
- **Carlton London, Central and West Country**
  website www.carlton.com
- **Channel Television**
  website www.channeltv.co.uk
- **Grampian**
  website www.grampiantv.co.uk
- **Granada**
  website www.granadatv.co.uk
- **HTV Wales**
  website www.htvwales.co.uk
- **HTV West**
  website www.htvwest.co.uk
- **London Weekend**
  website www.lwt.co.uk
- **Meridian**
  website www.meridian.co.uk
- **Scottish**
  website www.scottishtv.co.uk
- **Tyne Tees**
  website www.tyneteestv.co.uk
- **Ulster**
  website www.u.tv
- **Yorkshire**
  website www.yorkshire-television.co.uk

Jetix Europe

(formerly Fox Kids Europe)
Jetix Europe Ltd, 3 Queen Caroline Street, London W6 9PE
tel 020-8222 3600
email info@jetixeurope.net
website www.jetixeurope.net

Owns and broadcasts programmes for children aged 2–14 in Europe and the Middle East. Programmes are specifically aimed at the needs of different markets, viewing habits, parental sensitivities and cultural trends. Also offers localised websites. Launched 1996.

MTV Network UK & Ireland

17–29 Hawley Crescent, London NW1 8TT
tel 020-7284 7777
email pressinfo@mtvne.com
website www.mtv.co.uk

The world's largest 24-hour music TV network. It has 9 cable/satellite/digital channels in the UK: MTV, MTV Dance, MTV Base, MTV Hits, MTV2, VH1, VH2, VH1 Classic and TMF which show popular rock and music videos. All channels except VH1 Classic are aimed at adolescents and young adults. The company also produces other shows, including animated cartoons such as *Beavis and Butthead* and *Daria,* as well as reality shows and sitcoms such as *The Osbournes.* Owned by Viacom.

Nick Jr

Nickelodeon House, 15–18 Rathbone Place, London W1T 1HU
tel 020-7462 1000
email letterbox@NickJr.co.uk
website www.nickjr.co.uk

Programmes for preschool children to promote social and thinking skills through playful entertainment. Nick Jr. policy is 'play to learn'. Programmes include *Maisy, Kipper, Maggie and the Ferocious Beast* and *Angelina Ballerina.*

Nickelodeon UK

Nickelodeon House, 15–18 Rathbone Place, London W1H 1HU
tel 020-7462 1000
website www.nick.co.uk

American cable/satellite network known for its innovative children's programming. There are 4 channels in the UK: Nickelodeon, Nicktoons TV, Nick Jr and Nick Replay (programmes include *Sabrina the Teenage Witch* and *My life as a Teenage Robot*). Established in the US in 1979; launched in UK 1993. Owned by Viacom.

Nicktoons TV

Nickelodeon House, 15–18 Rathbone Place, London W1T 1HU

tel 020-7462 1000
website www.nick.co.uk/toons

Channel solely devoted to Nick's own produced children's cartoons (e.g. *Rugrats*).

Radio Telefís Éireann (RTÉ)
Donnybrook, Dublin 4, Republic of Ireland
tel (01) 208 3111 *fax* (01) 208 3080
email info@rte.ie
website www.rte.ie

The Irish national broadcasting service operating radio and TV.

Television Ongoing production of an urban drama serial, *Fair City*. Currently of interest: drama series for mainstream audiences, serials (preferably contemporary) and situation comedies (preferably set in Ireland or of strong Irish interest), with preferred length of commercial half hour or one hour. Proposals for serials and series suitable for a young adult RTÉ 2 audience, either cutting edge or humorous, which could exploit a low-cost DV production model are of particular interest. Full scripts will not be considered – treatments and series/ serial outlines only, except in cases where projects are already part funded. Before submitting material to the Drama or Entertainment departments, authors are advised to write to the department in question to establish initial interest, timing of commissioning rounds, etc.

Radio The RTÉ Radio 1 arts, features and drama department regularly produces documentaries, short stories and radio plays. Email ideas or proposals for future radio documentaries (documentaries@rte.ie). RTÉ Radio 1 holds annual competitions for short stories and radio plays; see the RTÉ Radio 1 website (www.rte.ie/radio1) for details. For further information on submissions email radio1@rte.ie

S4C
Parc Ty Glas, Llanishen, Cardiff CF14 5DU
tel 029-20747444 *fax* 029-20754444

email s4c@s4c.co.uk
website www.s4c.co.uk
Chief Executive Iona Jones, *Director of Commissioning* Rhian Gibson

The Welsh Fourth Channel. S4C's analogue service broadcasts 32 hours per week in Welsh: 22 hours are commissioned from independent producers and 10 hours are produced by the BBC. Most of Channel 4's output is rescheduled to complete this service. S4C's digital service broadcasts 12 hours per day in Welsh.

It runs the same children's programmes as Channel 4 but includes Welsh language programmes for both older and younger viewers such as *Bardd Plant Cymru*, *Mas Draw* and *Triong!*.

Smash Hits Channel
Mappin House, 4 Winsley Street, London W1W 8HF
tel 020-7182 8000
email letters@smashhits.net
website www.smashhits.net

24-hour, non-stop music channel where the viewer decides what is played.

Trouble
Flextech Television, 160 Great Portland Street, London W1W 5QA
tel (0870) 043 4027, 020-7299 5000
email enquiries@trouble.co.uk
website www.trouble.co.uk

Channel for teenagers. Shows US programmes such as *2 Guys & a Girl* and UK programmes such as *Date my Mate* and *Playing Tricks*. Also has interactive programmes such as *Talk to the Hand*. The website claims to have some of the busiest teen chatrooms. Owned by Flextech Television, the content division of Telewest Braodband.

Children's television and film producers

The recommended approach for submitting material is through a literary agency. However, if you choose to submit material direct, first check with the company that they may be interested in your work and whether they would like to receive it.

Aardman Animations

Gas Ferry Road, Bristol BS1 6UN
tel 0117-984 8485 *fax* 0117-984 8486
email mail@aardman.com
website www.aardman.com
Head of Script Development Mike Cooper

Produces animated TV series, TV specials, short films, feature films, interstitials and commercials. Half of its programmes/films are aimed at children (40% family, 10% adult). Specialists in model animation. Considers screenplays for cinema and TV. No unsolicited submissions. Only considers proposals via an agent. Founded 1972.

ACP Television

Crosshands, Coreley, Ludlow, Shrops. SY8 3AR
tel (01584) 890893 *fax* (01584) 890810
email mair@acptv.com
website www.acptv.com
Contact Sandra Keating

Documentaries for children aged 12–16. Founded 1993.

Big Heart Media

Unit 22–23, 63 Clerkenwell Road,
London EC1M 5NP
tel 020-7490 2499 *fax* 020-7490 2556
website www.bigheartmedia.com
Contact Colin Izod

Creates TV drama and documentaries for young people. Founded in 1998.

Calon TV

3 Mount Stuart Square, Cardiff CF10 5EE
tel 029-2048 8400
email enquiries@calon.tv
website www.calon.tv
Managing Director Robin Lyons, *Head of Creative Development* Andrew Offiler

Animation and children's programmes for TV.

Children's Film and Television Foundation Ltd

Ealing Studios, Ealing Green, London W5 5EP
tel 020-8567 6655 *fax* 020-8758 6856
website www.ealingstudios.co.uk
Chief Executive Anna Home

Involved in the development and co-production of films for children and the family, both for the theatric market and for TV. Will consider screenplays for cinema. Founded 1951.

Collingwood O'Hare Entertainment

10–14 Crown Street, London W3 8SB
tel 020-8993 3666 *fax* 020-8993 9595
email info@crownstreet.co.uk
website www.collingwoodohare.com
Contact Helen Stroud, Head of Development

Children's animation series for TV for ages 0–12, e.g. *Yoko! Jakamoko! Toto!*, *Gordon the Garden Gnome* and *Animal Stories*. Will only consider material submitted via an agent. Founded 1988.

The Comedy Unit

Glasgow TV & Film Studios, The Media Park,
Craigmont Street, Glasgow G20 9BT
tel 0141-305 6666 *fax* 0141-305 6600
email general@comedyunit.co.uk
website www.comedyunit.co.uk
Contact Gavin Smith

Comedy and entertainment programmes for radio, TV and film. Approx. 20% of output is aimed at children aged 5–12. Will consider scripts for plays, comedy drama scripts for TV or film, and treatments for live-action and animation. Aims to significantly develop children's output. Submit material by post or email. Allow approx. one month for response. Founded 1996.

Cosgrove Hall Films Ltd

8 Albany Road, Chorlton-Cum-Hardy, Manchester M21 0AW
tel 0161-882 2500 *fax* 0161-882 2555
email animation@chf.co.uk
website www.chf.co.uk
Managing Director Anthony Utley

Screenplays for cinema and TV for animation (drawn, model or CGI) or a 'live action'/animation mix. Series material especially welcome, preschool to adult. Founded 1976.

The Walt Disney Company Ltd

3 Queen Caroline Street, London W6 9PE
tel 020-8222 1000 *fax* 020-8222 2795

Screenplays not accepted by London office. Must be submitted by an agent to The Walt Disney Studios in Burbank, California.

Endemol UK

Shepherd's Building Central, Charechrost Way,
London W14 0EE
tel (0870) 333 1700 *fax* (0870) 333 1800
email info@endemoluk.com
website www.endemoluk.com

Entertainment, documentary, children's, arts, factual
entertainment, reality, comedy, live events.

The Farnham Film Company

34 Burnt Hill Road, Lower Bourne, Farnham
GU10 3LZ
tel (01252) 710313 *fax* (01252) 725855
email info@farnfilm.com
website www.farnfilm.com

Television drama, documentaries and film.
Particularly interested in children's programmes:
drama, comedy, factual, game shows (only
exceptionally, and only for children). Send one-page
letter or email describing idea in first instance. Check
website for submission guidelines.

Flick Films Ltd

101 Wardour Street, London W1F 0UG
tel 020-7734 4892, 020-7734 3825 *fax* 020-7287 2307
website www.flicksfilms.com
Contact Terry Ward

Animation for TV commercials. Children's animated
TV series include *Mr Men* series, *Bananaman*, *Little
Miss* and *The Pondles*. Founded 1972.

Ginger Television

1st Floor, 3 Waterhouse Square, 138–142 Holborn,
London EC1N 2NY
tel 020-7882 1020 *fax* 020-7882 1040
email stephen.joel@ginger.com
website www.ginger.com
Executive Producers Stephen Joel, Ed Stobart

Entertainment, factual entertainment and drama.
Producers of *High School Project–USA* teen series.
Part of SMG TV Productions.

HIT Entertainment plc

5th Floor, Maple House, 149 Tottenham Court Road,
London W1T 7NF
tel 020-7554 2500 *fax* 020-7388 9321
website www.hitentertainment.com

One of the world's leading children's entertainment
companies. Its activities span TV and video
production (with studios in the US and the UK),
publishing, consumer products, licensing (properties
include *Bob the Builder*, *Thomas the Tank Engine*,
Barney, *Angelina Ballerina*, *Pingu* and *Guinness World
Records*) and live events. Founded 1989.

Libra Television Ltd

4th Floor, 22 Lever Street, The Northern Quarter,
Manchester M1 1EA

tel 0161-236 5599 *fax* 0161-236 6877
email hq@libratelevision.com
website www.libratelevision.com
Contact Louise Lynch

Children's and education TV programmes.

Lion Television

Lion House, 26 Paddenswick Road, London W6 0UB
tel 020-8846 2000 *fax* 020-8846 2001
website www.liontv.co.uk

Light entertainment, documentaries, drama,
children's, the arts, news/current affairs, religion.

Loonland UK Ltd

Royalty House, 72–74 Dean Street, London
W1D 3SG
tel 020-7434 2377 *fax* 020-7434 1578
email info@loonland.com
website www.loonland.com

See also Telemagination.

Lupus Films Ltd

Studio 212, Blackbull Yard, 24–28 Hatton Wall,
London EC1N 8JH
tel 020-7419 0997 *fax* 020-7404 9474
email info@lupusfilms.net
website www.lupusfilms.net
Head of Development Ruth Fielding

High-quality children's programming across a variety
of genre, from preschool animation to live-action
family drama for up to 12 year-olds. Produces 1–2
programmes/films a year. Will consider screenplays
for cinema and TV and for other TV programmes
submitted *only* from reputable agents or publishers.
'Strong and original ideas will always push through.
Watch children's TV and be aware of different
channels' preferences and scheduling trends.' The
company was set up by Camilla Deakin and Ruth
Fielding, formerly the commissioning team for Arts
and Animation at Channel 4 Television. Lupus prides
itself on being the 'head not the hands' of the
animation production process, acting not as a studio
but as a production company, seeking out the best
ideas and putting together talented teams by
accessing their many useful contacts in the industry.
Founded 2002.

Millimages

6 Broadstone Place, London W1U 7EN
tel 020-7486 9555 *fax* 020-7486 9666
email info@millimages-uk.com
website www.millimages.com
Managing Director John Reynolds

One of the main children's animation production
companies in Europe.

Penguin Television

80 Strand, London WC2R 0RL
tel 020-7010 3000 *fax* 020-7010 6643

email info@penguintv.com
website www.penguintv.com
Marketing Executive Laura Jones

Children's, documentaries/factual, lifestyle and educational programmes. Produces approx. 3 programmes a year (about half the total output) for children aged 0–12. Will consider screenplays for TV and other TV programmes and non-broadcast TV scripts. Send material to Production Dept. Founded 2000.

Pesky Ltd
Studio 46, 2–3 Coleridge Gardens,
London NW6 3QH
tel 020-7372 6600 *fax* 020-7372 2662
website www.pesky.com
Contact Claire Underwood

'Work for hire' interactive design and animation studio. Also designs licensable characters and animation shows. Productions include *The Amazing Adrenalini Brothers* for CBBC. Interested in hearing from animators and scriptwriters by post. Founded 1997.

Praxis Films Ltd
Unit 3N, Leroy House, 436 Essex Road, London
N1 3QP
tel 020-7682 1865
email info@praxisfilms.co.uk
website www.praxisfilms.co.uk
Contact Tony Cook, Head of Development & Training

Documentaries, current affairs, educational, schools programming for TV. New Media, communications consultancy, media training. Founded 1985.

Ragdoll Ltd
Timothy's Bridge Road, Statford-upon-Avon
CV37 9NQ
tel (01789) 404100
email stratford@ragdoll.co.uk
website www.ragdoll.co.uk

Company set up by Anne Wood and best-known for *Teletubbies, Rosie and Jim, Badjelly the Witch, Boohbah, Brum* and *Pob*. Initiated *Open A Door*, a unique international exchange of 5-minute films without words that focus on the perceptions and needs of young children worldwide.

Rubber Duck Entertainment
48 Margaret Street, 3rd Floor, London W1W 8SE
tel 020-7907 3773 *fax* 020-7907 3777
website www.rde.co.uk

A new division of the Contender Entertainment Group, its first animated series for children, *Tractor Tom*, has been broadcast.

Screentiger Ltd
First Floor, 53 Greek Street, London W1D 3DR
tel 020-7434 2487 *fax* 020-7287 7204

email claudine.massin@virgin.net
Animation for TV.

SMG TV Productions
200 Renfield Street, Glasgow G2 3PR
tel 0141-300 3000
email website@smgproductions.tv
website www.smgproductions.tv

Drama, factual/factual entertainment, entertainment and children's programming. The network TV production arm of SMG plc. Incorporates Ginger Television.

Sunset & Vine
30 Sackville Street, London W1S 3DY
tel 020-7478 7300 *fax* 020-7478 7407
email reception@sunsetvine.co.uk
website www.sunsetvine.co.uk

Sports programmes. Music Box subsidiary produces entertainment and children's programming, including *Buzz* series, *Kerrang Awards, Popped In Crashed Out* and *Forever*. Sunset & Vine North subsidiary produces documentaries.

Talent Television
Lion House, 72–75 Red Lion Square,
London WC1R 4NA
tel 020-7421 7800 *fax* 020-7421 7811
website www.talenttv.com
Head of Production Adam Hayes

Current affairs, entertainment, children's.

Telemagination
Royalty House, 3rd Floor, 72–74 Dean Street,
London W1D 3SG
tel 020-7434 1551 *fax* 020-7434 3344
email mail@tmation.co.uk
website www.telemagination.co.uk,
www.loonland.com
Head of Production Beth Parker, *Director of Animation* Alan Simpson

Producer of animated TV series for children such as *The Telebugs* and *The Animals of Farthing Wood*. One of the UK's leading full-service animation studios, the company has particular experience in large-scale international co-productions. Owned by TV-Loonland, a leading international producer and distributor of TV series and animation in the programming market for children, youth and families. Established 1984; bought by Loonland in 2000.

Television Junction
46 Gas Street, Birmingham B1 2JT
tel 0121-248 4466 *fax* 0121-248 4477
email info@televisionjunction.co.uk
website www.televisionjunction.co.uk

Education programmes for TV.

Tiger Aspect Productions

7 Soho Street, London W1D 3DQ
tel 020-7434 6700 *fax* 020-7434 1798
email general@tigeraspect.co.uk
website www.tigeraspect.co.uk
Managing Director Andrew Zein, *Head of Comedy*
Clive Tulloh, *Head of Factual Group* Paul Sommers,
Executive Producer, Entertainment Anastasia Mouzas,
Head of Production, Animation & Children's
Catherine Elliot

Programme genres include comedy, drama,
entertainment, factual, animation, wildlife (Tigress)
and feature films (Pictures). Children's programmes
include *Star* and *Charlie and Lola*. All material should
be submitted through an agent. Founded 1993.

TV4C Ltd

4 Great Chapel Street, London W1F 8FD
tel 020-7734 4302 *fax* 020-7437 3301
email info@chatsworth-tv.co.uk
website www.chatsworth-tv.co.uk
Managing Director Malcolm Heyworth, *Head of
Development* Nick Heyworth

Creates and produces animated programmes for
children aged 1–10. Founded 2000.

Twofour Productions Ltd

Twofour Studios, Estover, Plymouth PL6 7RG
tel (01752) 727400 *fax* (01752) 727450
email enq@twofour.co.uk
website www.twofour.co.uk
Contact Melanie Leach, Development Dept

Factual, factual entertainment, leisure and lifestyle,
and children's TV programmes. Founded 1987.

WarkClements Children's and Youth

IWC Media, Children's, Family & Youth,
3–6 Kenrick Place, London W1U 6HD
tel 020-7317 2230 *fax* 020-7317 2245
website www.iwcmedia.co.uk
Director of Children's, Family & Youth Richard
Langridge

Award-winning children's division of ICW Media.
Programmes include *Captain Abercromby* and
Jeopardy, both commissioned by the BBC and *Help!
I'm a Teenage Outlaw* for CITV. Currently planning
further ventures in children's programming in all
areas, including comedy, factual and drama and
family films. Founded 2001.

Children's radio

The BBC is the main outlet for radio writers with its strong relationship with children's literature. In addition to storytelling, the BBC commissions and produces dramatisations of children's classics and historically based fiction, as well as a wide range of significant works by contemporary children's authors.

BBC RADIO

BBC School Radio
Room 340, Henry Wood House, 3 & 6 Langham Place, London W1 1AA
email schoolradio@bbc.co.uk
website www.bbc.co.uk/schoolradio

Audio resources to support teaching across a wide range of primary curriculum areas. The programmes offer a varied and flexible, convenient resource with learning outcomes which carefully target curriculum objectives. Programmes are available in 3 ways: as prerecorded CDs (due to rights restrictions these are only available to schools in the UK); as 'audio on demand' using the internet site; and transmission.

A range of programmes includes existing copyright material while others require original scriptwriting. Contact the Editor for further details.

CBBC Radio
BBC 7, Room 1003, BBC Broadcasting House, London W1 1AA
tel (0870) 010 0700 *textphone* (07958) 100 700
email bigtoe@bbc.co.uk
website www.bbc.co.uk/music/childrens

Programmes available on the children's radio player include: *Big Toe* – features, music, interviews, Top 40; *Little Toe* (*Big Toe's* little brother or sister) – stories. *Go4It* – Radio 4's weekly show hosted by Barney Harwood, with stories competitions and special features; *Making Tracks* – music show presented by CBBC's Angellica Bell and Adrian Dickson; and *Smile* – pop and urban sounds from the show.

INDEPENDENT RADIO PRODUCERS

The Comedy Unit
Glasgow TV & Film Studios, The Media Park, Craigmont Street, Glasgow G20 9BT
tel 0141-305 666 *fax* 0141-305 6600
email general@comedyunit.co.uk

Contact April Chamberlain, Joint Managing Director

Comedy and entertainment programmes for radio, TV and film. Approx. 20% of output is aimed at children aged 5–12. Submit material by post or email. Allow approx. one month for response. Founded 1996.

Crosshands Ltd/ACP Television
Crosshands, Coreley, Ludlow, Shrops. SY8 3AR
tel (01584) 890893 *fax* (01584) 890893
email mail@acptv.com
Contact Richard Uridge

Radio and TV documentaries.

CSA Word
6ᴀ Archway Mews, London SW15 2PE
tel 020-8871 0220 *fax* 020-8877 0712
email info@csaword.co.uk
website www.csaword.co.uk
Audio Manager Victoria Williams

Produces readings, plays and features/documentaries. Allow approx. 2 months for response to submissions. Founded 1992.

Loftus Productions Ltd
2ᴀ Aldine Street, London W12 8AN
tel 020-8740 4666
email ask@loftusproductions.co.uk
website www.loftusproductions.co.uk
Contact Nigel Acheson

Produces features, documentaries and readings (no drama) for BBC Radio. Programmes are mostly for adults with approx. 5% of output for children aged 5–12, usually documentaries. Also produces audio guides for museums and galleries, some specifically for children. Founded 1996.

Lou Stein Associates Ltd
email info@loustein.co.uk
Contact Lou Stein

Plays for BBC Radio. Founded 2000.

Theatre

Presenting children's theatre

Playwright Kaye Umansky recalls her experiences of staging plays in primary schools.

I love writing plays. I've done it all my life. Once, I loved acting in them – until I got bad stage fright in my thirties and stopped. But I have always loved writing them. At Hooe County Primary, I wrote a version of *Cinderella* with songs – it filled a whole exercise book and I made my friends perform it in the girls' toilets. I think I might have been a bit bossy. I know I got cross when they lost interest and wandered off. But it didn't stop me writing another one.

When I was 11, I wrote a nativity play for my mum, a music teacher, and we performed it in church. It was called *No Room!* and filled four exercise books. I know, because the other day I found them in the loft. I awarded myself the best part (Angel Narrator) just because I could. I must have been an appalling show off because I sang three solos. Janice, my best friend, took dancing lessons and already had a tutu so I let her be The Star. Joan Murphy was Mary because she was nice and we sang duets together in music festivals, which played a large part in my life back then. Jean Lott and her two cousins were Kings. Joey Marks was a shepherd because I hated him. The vicar liked it, so I wrote four more.

At 17 I went to London to train as a teacher. Needless to say, drama was my chosen subject. It was the Sixties and we wore leotards and did a lot of arty posing in front of moving oil slides, emoting and waving our arms around. We also did a lot of improvisation and went on trips to the theatre.

Teaching was a lot more hit and miss in the Seventies – or perhaps it was just me? But I remember education being more 'child led' and generally flowery. We believed in a thing called 'Reading Readiness' which meant that we didn't panic if the children couldn't read *War and Peace* by the time they hit three.

I taught for 14 years in a variety of tough London primary schools. It's a wonder I live to tell the tale – I didn't know what I was doing. Things were so different back then: no National Curriculum, no proper lesson plans, no proper discipline (well, not in my class). We just mostly taught what we fancied.

I really loved putting on the play, though. It's the one thing about being in school I still miss. I compensate by writing them but it's not the same as actually *doing* it. The smell of the greasepaint, the roar of the crowds, the jamming of the tape recorder. You can't beat it.

In my first school, nobody could play the piano except me, which meant I got lumbered with hymn practice while everyone else had a free period. Nobody wanted to take responsibility for drama either. I remember the staff meeting when the subject of the Christmas play was broached. Mrs Morgan, the deputy-head, asked for volunteers and suddenly everyone developed a deep interest in the contents of their Tupperware lunch boxes.

Of course, I said I'd do it. I couldn't wait. I wanted to do everything – write it, direct it, run the auditions, play the piano, record the music, sort out the dances, *everything*. Hey, I was the expert. Drama was my thing, remember? I still did amateur dramatics in my spare time. I was *keen*.

Mrs Morgan gave me a pile of ancient plays that she'd unearthed from a pyramid somewhere, insisting that they had gone down very well in previous years. I looked at them and my heart sank. They were all horribly worthy, with loads of turgid dialogue about Children From Other Lands or The Pilgrim Fathers. No humour, no decent songs and limited opportunities for a disco scene. I'm from Plymouth. I'm fed up with the Pilgrim Fathers. No way, I thought.

I asked my class for suggestions. Weaned on unsuitable films from babyhood, they thought it should be 'something funny and scary with lots of horror in it'. Hmmm … tricky. I didn't think we could cope with the revolving head in *The Exorcist*, funny though the vomiting scene might be. And where would we fit in the disco?

Time was short and an original play would have taken too long so I took the easy way out and decided to adapt a fairy story. After some consideration, I thought I'd have a crack at Hans Andersen's *The Snow Queen*, which I've always loved because of the chill factor. I went through the story, breaking it down into scenes, noting where songs and dances could go and deciding which characters should be given a humorous slant because there had to be something funny, right?

An announcement was made in assembly, calling all would-be thespians to the hall at lunch hour. It rained that day and the hall was a better bet than the playground. Virtually every kid turned up. Alone, I faced an overexcited mob of what felt like thousands. They had to be peeled off the wall bars and nailed down before they were ready to listen. The rest of the staff was closeted in the cosy staff room, drinking coffee and doing the crossword.

Order restored, I told the kids the story and promised there would be a disco scene in there somewhere. I talked about commitment and lost lunch hours and how you really had to think hard about taking on a big role, but it didn't seem to put anyone off.

Auditions next. More chaos. I set them drama exercises and made them act out little scenes. I watched carefully and wrote things down in my trusty exercise book. Then I made

Writing and producing a play for children

1. Choose a story both you and the children love. Make sure it has plenty of dramatic elements – i.e. action, adventure, fear, comedy.
2. Consider the size of your cast. If this is to be a mighty all-school production and you need to flesh out the tale by adding minor roles (trees, flowers, snowflakes, etc) make sure everyone has something interesting to say or do – a funny line, a dance, a song, some comic stage business. Standing around with your branches stuck out is boring.
3. If possible, use the children's own words. If you are not confident with this method and decide to write a proper script, avoid hugely long speeches that take ages to learn.
4. Avoid unnecessary complications. You do not need to construct a hot air balloon for the Wizard of Oz to fly away in: it can happen off-stage.
5. As in pantomime, try to include local references. 'In' jokes about teachers, or the school, are always popular.
6. Spend some time discussing characterisation, pace and timing with the children before you begin. Reading dialogue is very different to reading a story. Each character has an individual voice and a personality which must be maintained throughout.
7. Add topical references to popular culture (for example, Big Brother, Pop Idol).
8. Including a good-natured teacher in a comedy role (especially a cross-dressing male) is always a hit.
9. Children selected for acting roles may not be confident solo singers. It is a good idea to have a choir to lend support. This also enables more children to be actively involved in the production.
10. Additionally, non actors can sing in the choir, play in the orchestra, provide sound effects, stage manage, paint scenery, design the programme, help decorate the venue, be ushers and so on.
11. Stick in a disco dance.

decisions, balancing natural talent against the tendency to muck around or be unreliable. (Or just plain unbearable.) The list went up – and then the real work started.

Other plays by Kaye Umansky

The Fwog Pwince (BBC Educational)
Cruel Times – A Victorian Play (Hodder Wayland Plays)
Humble Tom's Big Trip – A Tudor Play (Hodder Wayland Plays)

I was tempted to write the script but decided not to. A lot of the kids hadn't reached their Reading Readiness stage yet. Learning lines could be problematic so I took the obvious route. I just told them what needed to happen in each scene and allowed them to come up with the words themselves. This is called 'Working Towards A Polished Improvisation'. In effect, it meant that whenever they said or did anything really good, I would leap up and cry 'Hooray! Wonderful! Keep that in!'. Sometimes I would say: 'Er, no, actually, Leroy, we won't say that word. Mrs Morgan won't like it if you swear at Gerda and neither will your grandma. And you can take that smirk off, you're not funny or clever'.

Of course, with the best will in the world, I couldn't do everything. When I was on the point of nervous collapse, a few colleagues kindly put down their coffee cups and came to my rescue. They helped out with the dances and the scenery and the tape recorder and – O thank you, thank you! – the dreaded costumes. I'm not handy with a needle – ask my husband.

Gradually, it all came together.

I made a lot of mistakes, I'm sure, and I know I did a lot of shouting because, sadly, that's my teaching style. But, my goodness, it was fun. Disadvantaged kids who couldn't read, add up or even catch a ball, suddenly turned into Glenda Jackson and Jeremy Irons. Sometimes it was electrifying! I couldn't believe how talented some of them were.

Anyway, the performance? I have to say it was good. No, better than good. It was *great!* The kids were amazing, there were no major disasters, no one swore, the Headmaster was happy, the parents loved it and Mrs Morgan presented me with a bunch of wilting carnations. I felt like Jonathan Miller. No stopping me now!

We did a play every year. Following the success of *The Snow Queen*, we did *The Lion, the Witch and the Wardrobe* (more snow), *The Wizard of Oz* (with balloons), *Dick Whittington* (with bells) and *Aladdin* (with cymbals).

When I gave up teaching I didn't stop writing plays. I took a course at the Central School of Speech and Drama and wrote a film script based on Mervyn Peake's *Gormenghast*, which was a labour of love and took a while, I can tell you. That's up in the loft too, somewhere.

It's over 50 years since I wrote my funny little toilet version of *Cinderella*. These days, I spend most of my time writing children's fiction but I can always find time to write a play. In fact, the characters in my novels frequently get involved in theatrical ventures. The *Pongwiffy* series springs to mind. It's a rare *Pongwiffy* book that doesn't feature some sort of performance. *I'm A Tree* (A & C Black) and *The Time the Play Went Wrong* (Pearson Education) are both about the experience of putting on a school play. Both are written from a child's point of view and feature harassed, overworked teachers, like I was.

So what plays have I written? Well, over the years, I've done quite a few and I like to think they're child friendly. For A & C Black I've done a musical adaptation of *The Snow Queen* in which I tried hard to retain the flavour of the performance the kids came up with so long ago. I've adapted *Cinderella*, *The Emperor's New Clothes*, *Noah's Ark* and *Sleeping*

Beauty for their *Curtain Up* series. I've also written a series of music books for them based largely on traditional stories, with ideas for performance: *Three Tapping Teddies, Three Singing Pigs, Three Rapping Rats* and *Three Rocking Crocs.* Most recently I've written an infant nativity, which brings me full circle to when I wrote *No Room!* back in the long ago.

These days, sadly, I don't get actively involved. I just go along to see them being performed. Every time I get a thrill – and sometimes, as visiting playwright, a bunch of carnations!

Kaye Umansky's nativity musical is included in *Three Little Nativities* (A & C Black 2006) and a new play, *Let's Go to London,* is due to be published in 2007 (White Wolves, A & C Black). Her *Three Rapping Rats* won the 1999 TES Schoolbook Award for Primary Music.

Theatre for children

London and provincial theatres are listed below; listings of touring companies start on page 315.

LONDON

Polka Theatre for Children
240 The Broadway, London SW19 1SB
tel 020-8545 8320 *fax* 020-8545 8365
email info@polkatheatre.com
website www.polkatheatre.com
Artistic Director Annie Wood

Exclusively for children between 18 months and 16 years of age, the Main Theatre seats 300 and the Adventure Theatre seats 80. It is programmed for 18 months–2 years in advance. Theatre of new writing, with targeted commissions. Founded 1967.

Soho Theatre and Writers' Centre
21 Dean Street, London W1D 3NE
tel 020-7478 0117 *fax* 020-7287 5061
email erin@sohotheatre.com
website www.sohotheatre.com
Acting Artistic Director Jonathan Lloyd, *Writers' Centre Director* Nina Steiger

Aims to discover and develop new playwrights, produce a year-round programme of new plays and attract new audiences. Producing venue (144-seat theatre) of new plays and comedy. The Writers' Centre offers an extensive unsolicited script-reading service and provides a range of development schemes including the Writers' Attachment Programme, Launch Pad Workshops, the Verity Bargate Award, the Westminster Prize, a thriving Young Writers' Programme, commissions and seed bursaries and more. Three writers' rooms are available free of charge (Mon–Fri, 10am–6pm). There is also a large self-contained studio space with 85-seat capacity plus theatre bar, restaurant, offices, rehearsal, writing and meeting rooms. Founded 1972.
Primarily for adults but has staged *The Gruffalo* and *Private Peaceful*.

Unicorn Theatre for Children
147 Tooley Street, London SE1 2HZ
tel 020-7645 0500 *fax* 020-7645 0550
email stage.door@unicorntheatre.com
website www.unicorntheatre.com
Executive Director Christopher Moxon, *Artistic Director* Tony Graham, *Associate Director* Rebecca Gatward, *Associate Director & Literary Manager* Carl Miller, *Associate Artist (Literary)* Charles Way

At the end of 2005 Unicorn moved into its new theatre near Tower Bridge, where it produces a year-round programme of theatre for children aged 4–12, their families and schools. In-house productions of full-length plays with professional casts are staged across 2 auditoriums, alongside visiting companies and education work. Unicorn rarely commissions plays from writers who are new to it, but it is keen to hear from writers who are interested to work with the Unicorn in the future. Its aim is for its work to be artistically led, truthful, and insistent on the primacy of imagination. It asks: does the play matter to children; does it have a sense of poetry; does it contain a child's perspective; is it drama; can it transcend and transform?
Do not send unsolicited MSS as Unicorn does not have the resources to read and respond to them in appropriate detail. Send a short statement describing why you would like to write for Unicorn and a CV or a summary of your relevant experience.

Young Vic Theatre Company
66 The Cut, London SE1 8LZ
email info@youngvic.org
website www.youngvic.org
General Manager Mark Feakins

Metropolitan producing theatre producing great plays of the world repertoire. Founded 1969.

PROVINCIAL

The Byre Theatre of St Andrews
Abbey Street, St Andrews KY16 9LA
tel (01334) 476288 *fax* (01334) 475370
email enquiries@byretheatre.com
website www.byretheatre.com
Artistic Director Stephen Wrentmore

Offers an exciting year-round programme of contemporary and classic drama, dance, concerts, comedy and innovative education and community events. Operates a blend of in-house and touring productions. Maintains a policy of producing new and established work. Education programme caters for all ages with Youth workshops and Haydays (for 50+). Offers support for new writing through the Byre Writers, a well-established and successful playwrights group.

Chichester Festival Theatre
Chichester Festival Theatre, Oaklands Park, Chichester, West Sussex PO19 6AP
tel (01243) 784437 *fax* (01243) 787288
email admin@cft.org.uk
website www.cft.org.uk
Artistic Director Jonathan Church

Summer Festival Season April–Sept in Festival and Minerva Theatres together with a year-round education programme, autumn festival of music and youth theatre Christmas show.

Contact Theatre Company

Oxford Road, Manchester M15 6JA
tel 0161-274 3434 fax 0161-274 0640
email info@contact-theatre.org.uk
Artistic Director John E. McGrath

Interested in working with and for young people aged 13–30. Send sae for writers' guidelines.

The Egg

Sawclose, Bath BA1 1ET
tel (01225) 823499 (education officer), (01225) 823433 (administrator), (01225) 448844 (box office)
website www.theatreroyal.org.uk/egg

Part of the Theatre Royal, Bath, the Egg is a purpose-built newly opened theatre for young people and their families. It hosts shows by children and for children. There are also ongoing participatory workshops which explore the breadth and depth of theatre practice.

Everyman Theatre

Regent Street, Cheltenham, Glos. GL50 1HQ
tel (01242) 512515 fax (01242) 224305
email admin@everymantheatre.org.uk
website www.everymantheatre.org.uk
Chief Executive Geoffrey Rowe, Artistic Director Sue Colverd

Regional presenting and producing theatre promoting a wide range of plays. Small-scale experimental, youth and educational work encouraged in The Other Space studio theatre. Contact the Artistic Director before submitting material.

Haymarket Theatre Company

The Haymarket Theatre, Wote Street, Basingstoke, Hants RG21 7NW
tel (0870) 770 1029 fax (01256) 357130
email info@haymarket.org.uk
website www.haymarket.org.uk

Produces up to 8 main house shows a year for Basingstoke, national and regional touring and the West End. New writing is central to the programming policy.

The Haymarket Youth Theatre is a vibrant group of young performers aged 12–18. It is led by a professional director and meets weekly on Thursday evenings, 6–8.30pm during term time. As well as rehearsing for productions, students are trained in drama skills and theatre practice, involving workshops, visiting specialist tutors and residential courses. Entry is by audition only which is in workshop style (no solo performances required!) and lasts about 2 hours. For further information contact Barbara Lilley on (01256) 323073 or barbara@haymarket.org.uk

Leeds Children's Theatre

c/o The Carriageworks, Millennium Square, Leeds LS2 8YQ
email info@leeds-childrens-theatre.co.uk
website www.leeds-childrens-theatre.co.uk

One of the many amateur dramatic societies based at The Carriageworks Theatre. A member of the Leeds Civic Arts Guild, Leeds Children's Theatre stages 2 shows each year. It is dedicated to the principle of quality, affordable children's entertainment in order to encourage the introduction of the theatrical experience to young children. It covers most aspects of theatrical production. Membership is open to all young people. Saturday morning drama workshops offer an excellent introduction but there is currently a waiting list for places. Adult membership is also available. Founded 1935.

Leighton Buzzard Children's Theatre

12 Linslade Road, Heath and Reach, Leighton Buzzard, Beds. LU7 0AU
tel (01525) 237469
email sally@lbct.freeserve.co.uk
website www.lbct.org

A community-based group which exists to introduce young people to the joy of theatre, to develop theatre craft and to enhance enjoyment of performance through community involvement. It offers a unique opportunity to young people aged 5–18 to act, sing, dance, improvise, communicate, have fun and learn.

Library Theatre Company

St Peter's Square, Manchester M2 5PD
tel 0161-234 1913 fax 0161-228 6481
email ltc@libraries.manchester.gov.uk
website www.librarytheatre.com
Contact Artistic Director

Produces mostly contemporary drama with a major play for children and families at Christmas. A recent family production was Neil Bartlett's version of Oliver Twist. Will consider scripts from new writers. Allow 4 months for response.

Norwich Puppet Theatre

St James, Whitefriars, Norwich NR3 1TN
tel (01603) 629921 (box office), 615564 (admin.) fax (01603) 617578
email info@puppettheatre.co.uk
website www.puppettheatre.co.uk
Artistic Director Luis Boy

Norwich Puppet Theatre is the base for a professional company which creates and presents its own productions at the theatre, as well as touring to schools and venues throughout the UK and to international venues and festivals abroad. Founded 1979.

Nottingham Playhouse

Nottingham Theatre Trust Ltd, Wellington Circus, Nottingham NG1 5AF

tel 0115-947 4361 *fax* 0115-947 5759
website www.nottinghamplayhouse.co.uk/playhouse
Chief Executive Stephanie Sirr, *Artistic Director* Giles Croft

Works closely with communities of Nottingham and Nottinghamshire. Takes 6 months to read unsolicited MSS.

Roundabout is the Theatre in Education company of Nottingham Playhouse. Produces plays and workshops for children and young people, and training and support for teachers. Since 1975 Roundabout has created over 250 plays, and performed to over half a million children.

Queen's Theatre, Hornchurch
(Havering Theatre Trust Ltd)
Billet Lane, Hornchurch, Essex RM11 1QT
tel (01708) 462362 *fax* (01708) 462363
email info@queens-theatre.co.uk
website www.queens-theatre.co.uk
Artistic Director Bob Carlton

500-seat producing theatre serving outer East London with permanent company of actors/musicians presenting 8 mainhouse and 4 TIE productions each year. Treatments welcome; unsolicited scripts may be returned unread. Also offers writer's groups at various levels.

The Queen's Youth Theatre Programme provides the opportunity for young people aged 7–18 to become involved in drama. There is no selection process on the basis of experience or ability.

The Sherman Theatre
Senghennydd Road, Cardiff CF24 4YE
tel 029-2064 6901 *fax* 029-2064 6902
email admin@shermantheatre.demon.co.uk
website www.shermantheatre.co.uk
Artistic Director Phil Clark, *General Manager* Margaret Jones, *Programme Coordinator* Kate Perridge

Regional repertory theatre producing a third of its plays for children. Produces work for the very young (under 5s) and Christmas productions for 6–12 year-olds and teenagers. Also participatory work with youth theatres for 15–25 age range. Recent children's productions include *Merlin and the Cave of Dreams* by Charles Way with a cast of 8 and *Pinocchio*, adapted by Mike Kenny with a cast of 3. No unsolicited submissions. Founded 1987.

TOURING COMPANIES

The Hiss & Boo Company Ltd
1 Nyes Hill, Wineham Lane, Bolney, West Sussex RH17 5SD
tel (01444) 881707 *fax* (01444) 882057
email ian@hissboo.co.uk

Not much scope for new plays, but will consider comedy thrillers/chillers and plays/musicals for

children. Produces pantomimes. No unsolicited scripts – telephone first. Plays/synopses will be returned only if accompanied by an sae.

Imaginate
45A George Street, Edinburgh EH2 2HT
tel 0131-225 8050 *fax* 0131-225 6440
email info@imaginate.org.uk
Director Tony Reekie, *General Manager* Tessa Rennie

Imaginate is an arts agency committed to promoting and developing performing arts for children in Scotland. See page 351 for further information.

The Little Angel Theatre
14 Dagmar Passage, London N1 2DN
tel 020-7226 1787 *fax* 020-7359 7565
email info@littleangeltheatre.com
website wwwlittleangeltheatre.com
Artistic Director Peter Glanville

The theatre is committed to working with children and families, both through schools and the local community. It is developing innovative projects to improve access to their work, offer opportunities for participation, and stimulate learning and creativity for all using puppetry. Every term it runs activities for children, families and schools, including the Saturday Morning Puppet Club, family workshops and schools projects such as the highly successful Pupper Power.

The Little Angel shows last about an hour and they tour many of their shows to schools, theatres, arts centres and festivals. Its Education Programme works with schools, youth groups and Education Authorities; it is a strategic plank in the theatre's ongoing work with children and young people. In 2003 the Little Angel gave 579 performances to a total audience of over 63,000 children and adults.

M6 Theatre Company (Studio Theatre)
Hamer C.P. School, Albert Royds Street, Rochdale, Lancs. OL16 2SU
tel (01706) 355898 *fax* (01706) 712601
email info@m6theatre.co.uk
website www.m6theatre.co.uk
Contact Dorothy Wood

Theatre-in-education company providing high-quality theatre for children, young people and community audiences.

Oily Cart
Smallwood School Annexe, Smallwood Road, London SW17 0TW
tel 020-8672 6329 *fax* 020-8672 0792
email oilies@oilycart.org.uk
website www.oilycart.org.uk
Artistic Director Tim Webb

Touring company staging 2 children's productions a year. Multi-sensory, highly interactive work is produced, often in specially constructed installations for 2 specific audiences: children aged 6 months–

6 years and young people with profound and multiple learning disabilities. Considers scripts from new writers but at present all work is generated from within the company. Founded 1981.

Proteus Theatre Company

Queen Mary's College, Cliddesden Road, Basingstoke, Hants RG21 3HF
tel (01256) 354541 *fax* (01256) 356186
email info@proteustheatre.com
website www.proteustheatre.com
Artistic Director Mary Swan, *Associate Director* Deborah Wilding, *General Manager* Nicola Oakley

Small-scale touring company particularly committed to new writing and new work, education and community collaborations. Produces 3 touring shows per year plus several community projects. Founded 1979.

Quicksilver Theatre

4 Enfield Road, London N1 5AZ
tel 020-7241 2942 *fax* 020-7254 3119
email talktous@quicksilvertheatre.org
website www.quicksilvertheatre.org
Joint Artistic Director/Ceo Guy Holland, *Joint Artistic Director* Carey English

A professional touring theatre company which brings live theatre to theatres and schools all over the country. Delivers good stories, original music, kaleidoscopic design and poignant, often humorous, new writing to entertain and make children and adults think. Two to three new plays a year for 3–5 year-olds, 4–7 year-olds and children 8+ and their families. Mission: to make life-changing theatre to inspire and entertain. Founded 1977.

Red Ladder Theatre Company

3 St Peters Buildings, York Street, Leeds LS9 8AU
tel 0113-245 5311 *fax* 0113-245 5351
email rod@redladder.co.uk
website www.redladder.co.uk
Artistic Director Rod Dixon

Theatre performances for young people (13–25) in youth clubs and small-scale theatre venues. Commissions at least 2 new plays each year. Runs the Asian Theatre School, an annual theatre training programme for young Asians in Yorkshire.

Snap People's Theatre Trust

29 Raynham Road, Bishop's Stortford, Herts. CM23 5PE
tel (01279) 461607 *fax* (01279) 506694
email info@snaptheatre.co.uk
Contact Gill Bloomfield

Produces 2 new plays for children and young adults each year. Recent children's productions include *Stepping on the Cracks* by Mike Kenny with a cast of 2, and *Starlight – The Dreamcatchers* by Diane Hancock with a cast of 3. Welcomes scripts from new writers. Allow a few months for response. Founded 1978.

Theatre Centre

Shoreditch Town Hall, 380 Old Street, London EC1V 9LT
tel 020-7729 3066 *fax* 020-7739 9741
email admin@theatre-centre.co.uk
website www.theatre-centre.co.uk
Director Rosamunde Hutt

New writing company producing 3 plays a year and touring nationally and internationally. All productions are for children and/or young people, staged in schools, arts centres and other venues. Recently produced *Trashed* by Noël Greig, *One Dark Night* by Mike Kenny, *Walking on Water* by Sarah Woods and *Journey to the River Sea* by Carl Miller adapted from the novel by Eva Ibbotson. Keen to hear from writers from ethnic minority groups. Response time to submissions can be lengthy. Founded 1953.

Theatre Workshop

34 Hamilton Place, Edinburgh EH3 5AX
tel 0131-225 7942 *fax* 0131-220 0112
Contact Robert Rae

Cutting edge, professional, inclusive theatre company. Plays include new writing/community/ children's/disabled. Scripts from new writers considered.

Resources for children's writers

Learning to write for children

Many people have what they consider to be brilliant ideas for children's books but have no experience of writing. But lack of experience need not get in the way of bringing an idea to fruition as there is guidance available in the form of courses. Alison Sage demystifies what happens on a writing course for children and outlines the benefits to be gained.

Can you teach people to write for children?

There are quite a few who think you can't. There is an implicit idea that writing is a talent you are born with and that one day, sitting at the word processor in your kitchen (why is it always the kitchen?) your innate ability will suddenly surface like a lottery ticket, and you will write a bestseller that will pay your mortgage and take you on exotic holidays for life.

After many years working in publishing and talking to would-be writers, I have come to the conclusion that this is only a tiny fraction of the truth. Writing is like any other talent and it improves with being used. Dancers dance, musicians play and writers have to write and write and write to get better.

There is no doubt that some people have more aptitude for writing than others. But besides natural talent, a writer must have something to say.

Next, a writer needs to have the persistence and self belief to continue to write through all kinds of distractions and discouragement. And finally, if a writer wants to be published successfully, he or she needs a certain amount of luck.

The role of writing classes

First and most importantly, writing classes can give the writer a chance to explore different kinds of writing in a non-judgemental atmosphere. It is the job of the teacher to help students to experiment until they find what suits them.

Students can also meet other people in the same situation. Writing can be a very lonely pursuit. A writer's friends are usually embarrassed to give their honest opinion about a story because it is a recipe for falling out. Every writer knows the despair of writing something which at first sounds wonderful and then on re-reading sounds rubbish. Where can writers find an independent judgement? Whoever they ask must be someone they can trust to be impartial, someone who can suggest where their good ideas become woolly and perhaps even how they might go about improving things. However, these must always be *suggestions*. It is the writer who must decide how, where, and in what way to alter the manuscript.

In an ideal world, the publisher's editor would help new writers endlessly until they achieved a bestselling novel. The reality is that publishers' editors are too busy to nurture every single would-be talent. Therefore, it is up to the writer either to go it alone – which many do – or to find someone else to act as a sounding board. This is where writing classes can help.

Who benefits most from writing classes?

It is impossible to guess at the beginning of a course how far students will develop their talent or even who will actually get published. Obviously, different teachers suit different people, but I have found an astonishing range amongst my students. That is what makes it so exciting and rewarding – and so unpredictable. The only student who is unlikely to be happy is the one who says: 'Teach me to write a bestseller.' This is frankly impossible and anyone who believes that writing is an exact science is bound to be disappointed.

Interestingly enough, the one thing that can indicate how far a student will get – apart from their persistence, of course – is how flexible they are. Often, people who are highly educated are actually at a disadvantage. They believe they have been taught how to write correctly – and that there is a 'right' and a 'wrong' way to do it. Nothing could be further from the truth, particularly when writing for children. Therefore, I have seen an Oxford graduate watch enviously as another student, still at school, sends the whole class into fits of laughter with a perfect story. I have had students who were models, refugees, counsellors, puppeteers, housewives, diplomats, postmen, soldiers, office managers, nurses, with children, without children or simply out of work. One of my best students left school aged 15. He is now editing a magazine and I still wonder if he will ever write his children's novel… Another is now a published author/illustrator, through his own talent and a great deal of effort. Yet another is looking after her children – and one day perhaps the quiet brilliance of her writing will find a publisher.

A typical course outline

Every course is different because every student is asked what they hope to achieve and this obviously affects what we do. However, certain things are always included in some form.

It may sound self evident, but central to a writing course is getting students to write. Students develop through putting new ideas into practice. Therefore, every class includes about 15 minutes' writing time and students read out and talk about what they have written. Most students are nervous at first, because they feel they are unprepared. But this rarely lasts because writing on the spot seems to bring the group closer together. It also relaxes everyone, as no one can be expected to write a bestseller in 15 minutes and at this point, students invariably have brilliant ideas and express them unbelievably well. If anyone gets stuck, they simply explain that the topic hasn't worked for them. Different students shine at different topics and this helps to steer them towards what they ultimately want to write.

Finding a story

The first place to look for a story is in your own experience. All students are asked to write something about their first memories of their baby brothers or sisters because when students genuinely remember their own childhood, their language becomes simpler, their writing more powerful and direct. They write in a way they never would if they were consciously trying to 'write for children'. This is a very important step in trying to discover what is your own voice. Writers need to know not only what they want to say, but also how they are going to put it over.

The class then usually discusses what kinds of story are appropriate for different ages. Perhaps one of the most common mistakes made by new children's writers is that they write about very young topics in a very sophisticated fashion. If you are aiming to write a picture book for a three year-old, you need to understand a little of what a three year-old can cope with. It is no use writing a story that is 10,000 words long.

However, a nine year-old is not going to be interested in stories designed for a three year-old – even if technically they are suitable. In fact, a good rule of thumb is that children are interested in most of the things that adults are – except they are not used to dealing with concepts. A child may love a book about a character who is alone, or brave, or funny. They will not be so interested in loneliness, heroism or humour in the *abstract*. Children are also not very comfortable with irony until they are about nine or 10 years old, tending to take the printed word at its face value. However, when they *do* discover it, they love it.

The beginning

The next thing to stress is the importance of the beginning. Many students think that page one is where a writer finds his feet and that the story proper starts about page six. This is not true. The first paragraph of a book is crucial. Children invest a lot of energy in reading a book and they want to be convinced pretty quickly that this effort is going to be worthwhile. A dull first page means that the book will be put down, never to be opened again. Even more to the point, perhaps, a busy editor reading an unsolicited manuscript will also lose interest if the beginning of the story is dull or confusing and they will make this the excuse they need to return it immediately. The beginning must draw the reader in. If a story is the solving of a problem, then the beginning must make that problem sound exciting and tantalising.

At this point, it is usually a good idea for the class to discuss strategies for keeping going with a story. Finishing a story gives a student a great boost and in itself, is a huge learning curve. Different strategies are helpful for different people. Some students need a writing routine – a special chair or table or cup of coffee. For others this is either no use or impossible to maintain. Some find writing notes at the end of each writing session is helpful, so that they can more easily get into the flow of ideas where they broke off. And most people find a notebook helpful, where they can record interesting ideas and experiences to be used as the raw material for future stories. If you are able to go into a school and help with reading, this can be a great eye opener as you will see first hand which stories children struggle over and which really work.

A vital ingredient

Another vital topic usually covered at this stage of the course is tension. Tension is what makes you want to continue reading and without tension, a story is as dull as a meal without salt. Just as a joke falls flat if the timing is wrong, so a fascinating story can become boringly muddled if the author does not build to a climax. It is about choosing selective details and using the reader's own imagination to create suspense. A description of the monster's claw grasping from behind the door is far more terrifying than a complete rundown of the whole creature.

If you think of your own favourite childhood story, it is often not the end that sticks in your mind. It is the bit just before the climax. That is when the tension and suspense should be strongest. At the end of the story, you can ask a question or add a twist, to give the impression that your characters will continue even after the book has been shut.

Talk about getting published

Finally, most students are interested in the mechanics of getting published, and this is a minefield for would-be authors. It is difficult to get your work singled out from a pile of unsolicited manuscripts and while (eventually) good writers are usually discovered, it can be a long and tortuous process.

There are things you can do to improve your chances and while they are mostly common sense, this is probably an area where a good writing class can help. Look in your local bookshop for the publishers which produce the kind of books you admire. There is an outside chance that if you like them, they might like you. Far too many good manuscripts are sent to the wrong places and if a publisher produces medical books, he or she is not likely to be interested in a children's manuscript, even if it is *Harry Potter*.

Sharing an interest

Perhaps the most important thing is to enjoy writing and to meet other people who are also interested. That way, students can keep each other going through the rejections and at the very least, improve at something they want to do. There are a great many courses which cater for all different kinds of interests, attitudes and expectations. The best place to look is probably at the local adult education institute. If there is no course specifically listed for writing for children, it is worth ringing up and asking if they would like to start one. You could also put up a notice in your local library for anyone else who might be interested and as soon as you are a group, the authority will take notice of you. You could even start your own independent writing group!

There are also several residential courses (such as the Arvon Foundation courses), and they are a very enjoyable and relaxing way to take your ambitions further. Look on the internet, as these courses constantly change and new ones are added every year. Several universities and colleges also run long and short courses in children's writing and you can achieve a diploma in Writing for Children, although this would take you at least a year.

So can writing be taught?

The debate will certainly continue, as people point out that teachers on courses rarely become as famous as some of their students. However, there *are* things which are helpful to discover when you are starting out as a children's writer. And perhaps the encouragement of the group will make sure that you continue writing until instead of your returned manuscript, it is the publisher's contract that drops through your letterbox!

Alison Sage is an experienced commissioning editor of children's books and has worked for a variety of publishers including Oxford University Press, HarperCollins and Random House. Alison is also a writer and anthologist and her *Treasury of Children's Literature* won the NIBBY – the Children's Book of the Year Award in 1995. She has run many courses on creative writing for children for Kensington & Chelsea and Hammersmith adult education institutes.

See also...

- *Children's writing courses and conferences*, page 325
- *Online resources about children's books*, page 327

Indexing children's books

Valerie A. Elliston is an indexer registered with the Society of Indexers.

What is an index?

An index is 'a systematic arrangement of entries designed to enable users to locate information in a document' (British Standard BS ISO 999: 1996). Unlike the general contents page, it is a key to far more specific detail. There are two basic categories of reader: those who have not read the book and those who have. A good index will help the former to decide whether the book suits his or her needs. It will help the latter to revisit any part of it without having to riffle through all the pages. These statements apply equally to publications for children as well as for adults; the benefits can be enjoyed by both, especially if the skill of using an index is learned in the early years.

Further information

Society of Indexers
Blades Enterprise Centre, John Street, Sheffield S2 4SU
tel 0114-292 2350 *fax* 0114-292 2351
email admin@indexers.org.uk
website www.indexers.org.uk
Administrator Wendy Burrow
Registrar Elizabeth Wallis *tel* 020-8940 4771
Membership £80 p.a. UK/Europe, £100 overseas; £160 corporate
Visit the website or contact the Administrator for further information. Publishers and authors seeking to commission an indexer should consult *Indexers Available* on the website or contact the Registrar.

Useful websites
www.nc.uk.net/nc/contents
www.standards.dfes.gov.uk/primary/publications

Why index children's books?

The vital importance of indexing information books for children has been highlighted over many years, at least since the mid-1930s. This was confirmed in a survey sponsored by the British Library Research and Innovation Centre (Williams and Bakewell 1997). All 16 publishers participating in this investigation rated this importance very highly. Yet, fewer than one-third said that they always included an index in publications for children, with reasons for exclusion given chiefly as restrictions on budget, time and space. Sometimes the contents page is considered sufficient, even though this lacks essential details.

Advantages of indexes

Firstly, the National Curriculum (2000) requires that children should be taught sound information retrieval practice, using organisational features and systems to locate texts. Secondly, the Primary National Strategy includes in its non-fiction objectives: understanding the purpose of contents pages and indexes; finding information by page numbers and initial letters of words. Later, the aim includes finding parts of text that give particular information. Children should also use dictionaries to find words by using initial letters, and the teacher is advised to demonstrate scanning the index for information, asking the children to familiarise themselves with the contents pages, indexes and glossaries of the information books. Thirdly, using an index is one of the earliest tools of independent research as well as helping to promote analytical skills. Despite increasing use of the internet, books will be with us for a long time yet, and children are being encouraged more and more to read them, not only for enjoyment but in preparation for future studies. Finally, skill in using indexes can help when searching for information on the internet.

Disadvantages of a book that lacks an index

The Williams and Bakewell survey found a number of negative effects, chiefly that children lose patience and interest if they have to spend time looking through a whole book for specific information. Younger ones often find scanning difficult, and can therefore fail to develop independent searching methods, remaining reliant on the teacher or librarian. The survey also found that primary school children viewed the index as a highly important feature and assumed that every non-fiction book would have one. An 11 year-old asked how they were supposed to find anything in a book without an index. Workshops conducted by an indexer in a secondary school confirmed children's intelligent interest in the use of indexes. They were quick to grasp the importance of choosing relevant terms and of keeping the number of page references to a minimum. In fact, by the end of each session, the participants were able to criticise a selection of books from the school library, rejecting those without an index and rating the rest according to the quality of the index while taking into account the overall layout and appropriateness of the entries. Another indexer worked with groups of 10–11 year-olds who examined a selection of books and decided which were the key topics on each page before checking in the index. They gave points for inclusion and accuracy, becoming ever more discriminating as they progressed.

Quality of the indexes

Indexes for children's books should be just as high quality as for adults' books, perhaps even more so as children need to be taught with the best examples against which future use can be measured. A clear, accurate and well-presented index can encourage their use, just as a disappointing one can reduce their interest. It follows, therefore, that the index should be carefully planned, not tacked on as an afterthought or made by a computer without any consideration for the particular needs of the young user.

● **Terminology** should be appropriate for the age group, using words that children would be expected to know. Most will be taken from the text, but sometimes thought has to be given to the choice between additional entries or cross-referencing which can be a problem for younger users. For example, the text might mention 'currency' but it would be helpful to also include 'money' in the index or to cross-reference it with 'see also money', according to the age group.

● **Subheadings** should be avoided if possible as they can confuse younger children. However, they might be necessary to avoid using too many locators (i.e. page or paragraph numbers).

● **Indexing names** needs careful consideration as there are many options. Should rulers be indexed individually or be listed as subheadings under the main entries 'kings' and 'queens'? Should titles or surnames be inverted as in indexes to adult books? The most suitable form of the name should be chosen for the particular index (e.g. 'Geldof, Bob' as opposed to 'Geldof, Sir Robert'). Correct spelling is essential, of course.

● **Consistency** is also important: should singular or plural terms be used for countable nouns? The British Standard already quoted recommends the use of the plural form for 'countables' and singular for 'non-countables'. For example, the countables 'chairs', 'cars' not 'chair' and 'car'. The plural is unlikely to arise for non-countable nouns, e.g. 'furniture', 'traffic', 'coffee'. The British Standard recommends lower case initial letters except for proper nouns.

● **Omission** of key topics is a major fault as, if children cannot find the item in the index, they will often assume it is not dealt with in the text and will give up. The index needs to be attractive and reliable, to appeal to the eye yet remain an invaluable tool.

Presentation of indexes

Presentation is particularly important to children.

- **Length** is determined by length of text and space available but, ideally, tu... adequately reflect the book.

- If the **font size** is small in proportion to the text, this can make the index seem rel... unimportant and sometimes more difficult to read, another reason for giving up.

- **Alphabetical order** can be used in two ways: word by word or letter by letter, but the chosen style must be used consistently. Many children's books print the entire alphabet on the first or each index page to help them locate the initial letters. Space between each section beginning with the same letter can be helpful, especially if the section is headed with the appropriate large upper case letter.

- **Illustrations** should be indexed but the difference between references to text and references to illustrations needs to be distinguished, perhaps by use of bold or italic type for the latter. If illustrations are also used purely for decoration, confusion should be avoided; the index pages should be as clear as possible. Another source of confusion could be a combined index and glossary; keeping them separate emphasises the different functions of each.

- **Locators (page or paragraph numbers)** can be shown with each page listed individually (4, 5, 6, 7, 8, 10, 11, 12, i.e. a separate reference to the topic on each page) or in ranges indicated by hyphens or en-rules (4–8, 10–12, i.e. a continuous reference over more than one page). This practice can be explained to children early on in their study of indexes so that they become familiar with it as soon as possible.

- **Passing mention** of a topic should be ignored as it is frustrating for children who find it is mentioned only in connection with something entirely different. Again, here is another reason for children giving up using an index. A further source of frustration is a long string of page numbers; children in the index workshop mentioned above were quick to notice them, announcing that they would certainly give up checking each one. Here then, is a sound reason for making more main entries or using subheadings.

- **Cross-references.** Using 'see' and 'see also' is often a problem, especially to younger children for whom additional entries might be more straightforward. The Williams and Bakewell survey found that the majority of respondents were in favour of keeping these traditional terms so that children could become accustomed to them in preparation for using adult books. Others suggested using double or additional entries or introducing different phrases such as 'try the word . . .' or 'also look up . . .' but the latter solution means the children will still have to learn the traditional phrases later on.

In view of all the foregoing, it might not be surprising that one of the 21 recommendations in the Williams and Bakewell report on indexes to children's information books is that such indexes should be compiled by a professional indexer who should have some knowledge of the subject matter. These recommendations appear in the Society of Indexers 'Occasional Paper No. 5' which is derived largely from that investigation.

Valerie A. Elliston is an indexer registered with the Society of Indexers, and a former adult education lecturer in English Language and Literature.

Further reading

Bakewell, K.G.B. and Williams, Paula L. with contributions from Elizabeth Wallis MBE and Valerie A. Elliston, *Indexing Children's Books*, 'Occasional Paper on Indexing No. 5', Society of Indexers, 2000

British Standards Institution, *Information and Documentation: Guidelines for the content, organization and presentation of indexes*, BS ISO 999: 1996, 1997

Department for Educational Standards, *Key Stages 1 & 2 of the National Curriculum*, DfES, 2000

Williams P.L. and Bakewell K.G.B., *Indexes to Children's Information Books: A study of the provision and quality of book indexes for children at National Curriculum Key Stage 2. Final Report on Project RIC/G/330 (British Library Research and Innovation Report 129)*, 1997

Children's writing courses and conferences

Anyone wishing to participate in a writing course should first satisfy themselves as to its content and quality. For day and evening courses consult your local Adult Education Centre.

The Arvon Foundation
Lumb Bank, Heptonstall, Hebden Bridge, West Yorkshire HX7 6DF
tel (01422) 843714 *fax* (01422) 843714
email l-bank@arvonfoundation.org
website www.arvonfoundation.org
Contact Ilona Jones
Moniack Mhor, Teavarran, Kiltarlity, Beauly, Inverness-shire IV4 7HT
tel (01463) 741675 *fax* (01463) 741733
email m-mhor@arvonfoundation.org
Contact Chris Aldridge
The Arvon Foundation, Totleigh Barton, Sheepwash, Beaworthy, Devon EX21 5NS
tel (01409) 231338 *fax* (01409) 231144
email t-barton@arvonfoundation.org
Contact Julia Wheadon
The Hurst – The John Osborne Arvon Centre Clunton, Craven Arms, Shropshire SY7 0JA
tel (01588) 640658 *fax* (01588) 640509
email hurst@arvonfoundation.org

Children's Literature International Summer School
University of Surrey Roehampton, Froebel College, London SW15 5PJ
tel 020-8392 3008 *fax* 020-8392 3819
email ncrcl@roehampton.ac.uk
website www.ncrcl.ac.uk/cliss
Takes place July

Leading academics and authors from the world of children's literature gather for this biennial 5-day event organised by the National Centre for Research in Children's Literature (NCRCL). The purpose of the summer school is to provide a forum in which participants and researchers in the field can exchange ideas and broaden their knowledge of the subject. There is also an optional Creative Writing module. There are places for 100 participants and en-suite accommodation is available on campus.

Essex Literature Development
Essex Libraries, Goldlay Gardens, Chelmsford, Essex CM2 6WN
tel (01245) 244963
email malcolm.burgess@essexcc.gov.uk
website www.essexlivelit.org.uk
Contact Kaveri Woodward

Development and promotion of Essex writers at all levels, plus advice on funding, grants, marketing and opportunities. Includes Essex Book Festival, Essex Writers' Day, Young People's Creative Writing Day, skills development workshops, etc.

The Federation of Children's Book Groups Conference
Details Martin and Sinead Kromer, 2 Bridge Wood View, Horsforth, Leeds LS18 5PE
email info@fcbg.org.uk
website www.fcbg.org.uk
Takes place 3 days in April

Held annually, guest speakers include well-known children's authors as well as experts and publishers in the field of children's books. Publishers also exhibit their newest books and resources.

IBBY Congress
Nonnenweg 12, Postfach, CH-4003-Basel, Switzerland
tel (4161) 272 2917 *fax* (+4161) 272 2757
email ibby@ibby.org
British Section PO Box 20875, GB–London SE22 9WQ
tel 020-8299 1641
email ann@lazim.demon.co.uk
website www.ibby.org

A biennial international congress for IBBY (International Board on Books for Young People) members and other people involved in children's books and reading development. Every other year a different National Section of IBBY hosts the congress and several hundred people from all over the world attend the professional programme.

Forthcoming congresses: 6–10 September 2008 to be held in Copenhagen, Denmark on the theme 'The Story in the History'; 2010 to be held in Santiago de Compostela, Spain. See also page 351.

NCRCL British IBBY Conference
Roehampton University, Froebel College, London SW15 5PJ
tel 020-8392 3008 *fax* 020-8392 3819
email ncrcl@roehampton.ac.uk
website www.ncrcl.ac.uk

Conference held annually in November on a specific theme.

Oxford University Day and Weekend Schools
Department for Continuing Education, Oxford University, Rewley House, 1 Wellington Square, Oxford OX1 2JA

tel (01865) 270368
email ppdayweek@conted.ox.ac.uk
website www.conted.ox.ac.uk
Contact Day School Administrator

Effective Writing: a series of 3-day accredited courses for creative writing. Topics vary from year to year. Courses always held on Fridays.

Pitstop Refuelling Writers' Weekend Workshops – see Winchester Writers' Conference, Bookfair and Weeklong Workshops

Ty Newydd

Ty Newydd, National Writers' Centre for Wales, Llanystumdwy, Criccieth, Gwynedd LL52 0LW
tel (01766) 522811 *fax* (01766) 523095
email post@tynewydd.org
website www.tynewydd.org

Week and weekend courses on all aspects of creative writing. Full programme available.

Winchester Writers' Conference, Bookfair and Weeklong Workshops

University of Winchester, Winchester, Hants SO22 4NR
tel (01962) 827238
email barbara.large@winchester.ac.uk
website www.writersconference.co.uk
Conference Director Barbara Large MBE, FRSA, FUW
Takes place University College, Winchester,
29 June–1 July 2007; Workshops 2–7 July 2007

This Festival of Writing, now in its 27th year, attracts 65 internationally renowned authors, poets, playwrights, agents and commissioning editors who give mini-courses, workshops, talks, seminars and one-to-one appointments to help writers harness their creativity and develop their writing, editing and marketing skills. Fifteen writing competitions, including Writing for Children, are adjudicated and 64 prizes are awarded at the Writers' Awards Reception. All first place winners are published annually in *The Best of* series.

The Bookfair offers delegates a wide choice of exhibits including authors' and internet services, publishers, booksellers, printers and trade associations.

Pitstop Refuelling Writers' Weekend Workshops are planned for 16–18 March and 26–28 October

2007, including Writing Marketable Children's Fiction and Non-fiction; Editing and Marketing your Novel; and How to Self-Publish Your Book day courses on 11 May and 21 September 2007.

Writers Advice Centre for Children's Books – see page 361

YLG Conference

Bromley Central Library, High Street, Bromley BR1 1EX
tel 020-8461 7193 *fax* 020-8313 9975
email ian.dodds@bromley.gov.uk
website www.cilip.org.uk/groups/ylg
Secretary Ian Dodds
Takes place September

This annual conference run by the Youth Libraries Group (YLG) of CILIP is a forum for discussion and debate on current issues for everyone working with and for children in libraries. It also provides an opportunity for experts, authors, illustrators, publishers and all those involved in the children's book trade to meet informally.

POSTGRADUATE COURSES

Bath Spa University

School of English and Creative Studies, Bath Spa University, Newton Park, Newton St Loe, Bath BA2 9BN
tel (01225) 875875 *fax* (01225) 875503
email enquiries@bathspa.ac.uk
website www.bathspa.ac.uk

MA in Writing for Young People, taught by a team of published children's writers. Prize for most promising work awarded by literary agent Rosemary Canter at PFD. Informal enquires to Julia Green, course leader (j.a.green@bathspa.ac.uk). Also MA in Creative Writing and PhD in Creative Writing.

University of Winchester

West Hill, Winchester SO22 4NR
tel (01962) 827235 *fax* (01962) 827406
website www.winchester.ac.uk
Contact Course Enquiries & Admissions

MA in Writing for Children and MA in Creative and Critical Writing.

Online resources about children's books

This is a representation of some of the many websites relating to children's books and reading. Individual author websites can be accessed via the ACHUKA or Booktrusted websites. See *Societies, associations and organisations* on page page 342 for other resources.

About Children's Books
www.childrensbooks.about.com

Part of About.com, this site holds international information on children's books plus a newsletter.

ACHUKA Children's Books UK
www.achuka.co.uk

The most up-to-date and comprehensive online guide to children's books and what's new in children's publishing. With author interviews, children's book news across the globe plus links to many other sites.

Armadillo
email armadillo@siliconhenge.com
website www.armadillomagazine.com
Editor Mary Hoffman, *Website Editor* Rhiannon Lassiter
£5 for 4 issues

Magazine about children's books, including reviews, interviews, features and profiles. After 5 years of publication as a paper magazine posted to subscribers, *Armadillo* is now available only online. New issues will be posted at the end of March, June, September and December. Some material will be accessible as a free sample but full access to the magazine is by subscription. New reviewers and writers are always welcome but the magazine does not pay a fee; reviewers keep the books. Publishers please note: books are *not* to be sent to the editor; she instructs reviewers to obtain specific titles direct from publishers. Founded in 1999 by author Mary Hoffman as a review publication for children's books.

Amazon
www.amazon.co.uk, www.amazon.com

UK and US online bookstore with more than 3 million books available on their websites at discounted prices, plus a personal notification service of new releases, reader reviews, bestsellers and book information.

BBC Education
www.bbc.co.uk/schools

Information about UK schools' curriculum. Essential for those wishing to write for educational publishers but also for keeping abreast of curricular topics.

BBC Teens
www.bbc.co.uk/teens

The Best Kids Book Site
www.thebestkidsbooksite.com

US site 'where children's books, crafts and collectibles intersect with your interests.' Useful links to Children's Book Awards, children's series fiction and author websites. Also gives access to the Book Wizard, an information tool to help track down children's books.

Quentin Blake
www.quentinblake.com

The official Quentin Blake website. Find out about the illustrator who brought many favourite children's characters to life, from Mister Magnolia and Mrs Armitage to the BFG and Matilda. There's also news and information on new books and exhibitions, downloads for children and suggestions for teachers on using books in the classroom. A great site for children, parents, teachers and aspiring children's books' illustrators.

Book Reviews by Kids
www.bookreviewsbykids.com

Website dedicated to children's book reviews written only by children. A great website for children to get their say on the books that they read.

BookHive
www.bookhive.org

US guide to children's books for children, parents, teachers or anyone interested in reading about children's books. Includes book reviews.

Bookheads
www.bookheads.org.uk

The website of the Booktrust Teenage Prize aims to encourage teenagers to express their views on their favourite books. It features celebrity interviews and details of past, present and future Booktrust Teenage Prize shortlists and winners. A good way of finding out what teenagers really like to read!

Books4Publishing
www.books4publishing.com

Shropshire-based e-agent which showcases authors' synopsis and first chapter and then auto-targets publishers and agents for a £49.95 fee.

Booktrusted
www.booktrusted.co.uk

Dedicated children's division of Booktrust and an essential site for professionals working with young readers. Information on events, prizes, books, authors, etc.

Bunyips
www.nla.gov.au/exhibitions/bunyips

National Library of Australia's fun site about Bunyips!

Canadian Children's Book Centre
www.bookcentre.ca

The site of the Canadian Children's Book Centre includes profiles of authors, illustrators, information on recent books, a calendar of upcoming Canadian events, information on publications and tips from Canadian children's authors.

Children's BBC
www.bbc.co.uk/cbbc

'Kid culture' website. Has a section on books, including a behind-the-scenes visit to, and information on, the Blue Peter Book Awards.

The Children's Book Council
www.cbcbooks.org

The Children's Book Council in the USA is an organisation dedicated to encouraging literacy and the enjoyment of children's books. The website includes reviews of children's books published in the USA, forthcoming publications, author profiles and features 'sneak peeks at publishers' newest and hottest titles.' A good site for checking out the US marketplace.

Children's Books Online: the Rosetta Project
www.childrensbooksonline.org

Antique children's books which can read read online or downloaded.

Children's Books UK Info
www.cbuk.info

Children's books news and views.

Children's Literature
www.childrenslit.com

The aim of this US site is to help teachers, librarians, childcare providers and parents make appropriate literary choices for children. Each month there are featured interviews with children's authors and illustrators and several sets of themed reviews. (These are licensed to Barnes & Noble and Borders for use on their websites.)

The Children's Literature Web Guide
www.acs.ucalgary.ca/~dkbrown/

Internet resources related to books for children and young adults created by the University of Calgary, Canada.

Classic Children's Stories
www.childhoodreading.com

Many classic stories that have carried on through generations, including illustrations.

Contemporary Writers
www.contemporarywriters.com

Searchable database containing up-to-date profiles of some of the UK and Commonwealth's most important living writers – biographies, bibliographies, critical reviews, prizes and photographs.

Cool Reads
www.cool-reads.co.uk

Find out what children think are cool reads! A website set up by teenagers with reviews, genres, ideas and much more.

Roald Dahl Club
www.roalddahlclub.com

Everything you ever wanted to know about Dahl's books with a section for teachers, children's activities plus the online Roald Dahl Club magazine *The Gobblefunk Gazette*.

enCompass
www.enCompassCulture.com

The British Council's online worldwide reading group is divided into 3 sections: books for children (ages 3–12), books for ages 12–18 and books for adults. It aims to provide up-to-date information about the contemporary UK and Commonwealth literature that is being talked about. There is the opportunity to read or write book reviews, follow related web links, read about books and to chat with the online reader-in-residence. Books can be selected from the best of contemporary UK and Commonwealth literature.

The Guardian
www.educationguardian.co.uk

The Guardian's education pages online.

Guy's Read
www.guysread.org

US web-based literacy programme to help boys find material they like to read.

Kids' Bookline
www.cllc.org.uk/PAL2002/Kids_Bookline/ HTML_ENG/FramesKB.html

Part of the Welsh Books Council's Children's Books Department. Activities for children, in both Welsh and English.

Kids' Open Book
www.kidsopenbook.co.uk

Independent site of online reviews of children's books and multimedia, set up by an experienced UK bookseller. Selective titles and personal choices.

Kids' Reads and Teen reads
www.kidsreads.com, www.teenreads.com

Two excellent US websites with information, reviews, author links and features on children's and teenage books. Part of The Book Report Network.

KidSpace@The Internet Public Library
www.ipl.org/div/kidspace/browse/rzn0000

Reading Zone of the Internet Public Library (IPL), a public service organisation and learning/teaching environment at the University of Michigan School of Information, USA.

The Looking Glass
www.the-looking-glass.net

An online children's literature journal.

Mrs Mad's Book-a-Rama
www.mrsmad.com

Children's book reviews from an independent reviewer – great fun and informative.

Graham Marks
www.marksworks.co.uk

Children's feature writer for *Publishing News* now has his own website with author features and general children's books trade news.

National Curriculum Online
www.nc.uk.net

This site links every National Curriculum programme of study requirement to resources on the Curriculum Online.

National Grid for Learning: Scotland
www.ngflscotland.gov.uk

National Literacy Trust
www.literacytrust.org.uk

Details of all the NLT's initiatives plus lots of news and information about children's books.

National Reading Campaign
www.readon.org.uk

Information and networking for reading practitioners about promoting reading for all ages and abilities throughout the community. Government funded and part of the National Literacy Trust.

On-Lion for Kids!
http://kids.nypl.org

New York Public Library children's book site which includes 100 Picture Books Everyone Should Know and 100 Favourite Children's Books.

Picturing Books
http://picturingbooks.imaginarylands.org

A website about picture books.

Reading is Fundamental, UK
www.rif.org.uk

An initiative of the National Literacy Trust that helps children and young people (aged 0–19) to realise their potential by motivating them to read.

Ricochet-Litterature Jeunesse
www.ricochet-jeunes.org

This library offers the reader a series of identification sheets about books, authors, illustrators and film adaptations of children's and young people's literature.

Scottish Writers Website
www.slainte.org.uk

Linked to the Scottish Writers project that provides a forum for young readers and Scottish professionals to exchange literary ideas. Includes online writers-in-residence.

Stories from the Web
www.storiesfromtheweb.org

A development between Leeds, Bristol and Birmingham Library Services and the UK office for Library and Information Networking to provide information on library clubs, stories, and a chance to email authors.

Storybook Web
www.itscotland.org.uk/storybook

Access to Scottish Children's authors and book-related activities for children.

Storyzone
www.storyzone.uk

An e-publishing site that makes contemporary children's stories available to the internet generation. Brand new stories as well as old favourites from well-known authors are available. Useful for those nowhere near a bookshop or library. It costs £5 to download up to 5 stories; £10 for 12; £20 for 25 stories and £40 for 50.

TeenSpace@The Internet Public Library
www.ipl.org/div/teen/teenread

Information on books for teenagers on the IPL website (see Kidspace).

UK Children's Books
www.ukchildrensbooks.co.uk

Directory of authors, illustrators and publishers involved in children's books and reading promotion.

The Word Pool
www.wordpool.co.uk

Independent website which profiles authors of children's books and gives information and advice for aspiring writers. Access to the free monthly newsletter.

World of Reading
www.worldreading.org

Website created by Ann Arbor District Library in USA devoted to book reviews written by and for children around the world.

Write4Kids
www.Write4Kids.com

US site with articles and information about the art of writing children's books. Also *Children's Book Insider* newsletter.

YouthBOOX
www.boox.org.uk

A joint venture between The Reading Agency and National Youth Agency to promote reading for pleasure for teenagers through building on their own interests.

Books about children's books

There are many books written about children's books. Some offer practical advice on selecting books. Others provide invaluable research material for those pursuing degrees and diplomas in children's literature. Here is a small selection.

Best Book Guide For Children and Young Adults
Published by Booktrust
Paperback pub. annually

Booktrust's independent annual 'pick of the best' in children's paperback fiction published in the previous calendar year. It is designed to help parents, teachers, librarians, booksellers and anyone interested in children's reading to select books for children, from babies to teenagers. Printed in full colour, each book featured has a short review, colour coding to indicate reading age and interest level, and bibliographic information.

The Book about Books
by Chris Powling
Published by A & C Black Publishers Ltd
ISBN 0 7136 5479 1
Paperback 2001

Using interviews with authors and illustrators, this book asks: what makes a classic? How do you get a book published? How do writers come up with their ideas? A light-hearted and informative book for children, perfect as a resource for Children's Book Week.

The Cambridge Guide to Children's Books in English
Edited by Victor Watson
Published by Cambridge University Press
ISBN 0 5215 5064 5
Hardback 2001

Reference work providing a critical and appreciative overview of children's books written in English across the world. It includes the history of children's books from pre-Norman times to the present, taking on board current developments in publishing practices and in children's own reading. Entries on TV, comics, annuals and the growing range of media texts are included.

The Oxford Companion to Children's Literature
Edited by Humphrey Carpenter and Mari Prichard
Published by Oxford University Press
ISBN 0 1986 0228 6
Paperback 1999

An indispensable reference book for anyone interested in children's books. Over 900 biographical entries deal with authors, illustrators, printers, publishers, educationalists and others who have influenced the development of children's literature. Genres covered include myths and legends, fairy tales, adventure stories, school stories, fantasy, science fiction, crime and romance. This book is of particular interest to librarians, teachers, students, parents and collectors.

The Reading Bug – and how you can help your child to catch it
by Paul Jennings
Published by Penguin Books
ISBN 0 14 131840 6
Paperback 2004

Paul Jennings is a well-known children's author. This book explains, in his unique humorous style, how readers can open up the world through a love of books. He cuts through the jargon and the controversies to reveal the simple truths, which should enable adults to infect children with the reading bug.

The Rough Guide to Books for Teenagers
Edited by Nicholas Tucker and Julia Eccleshare
Published by Rough Guides
ISBN 1 84353 138 0
Paperback 2003, repr. 2005

A resource for teenagers who love reading, this *Guide* is also ideal for adults looking to recommend and buy books for teenagers. More than 200 books are reviewed – mainly fiction – ranging from classics such as *Wuthering Heights* to more controversial and bestselling titles such as Melvin Burgess's *Junk* and Judy Blume's *Forever*. Graphic novels and some narrative non-fiction are also included.

The Rough Guide to Children's Books 0–5
Edited by Nicholas Tucker
Published by Rough Guides
ISBN 1 85828 787 1
Paperback 2002

Comprises reviews of books for this youngest of age groups, including picture books for babies through alphabets and nursery rhymes to classic stories. Each book has a brief synopsis and an evaluation of its special qualities and educational advantages.

The Rough Guide to Children's Books 5–11
Edited by Nicholas Tucker
Published by Rough Guides

ISBN 1 85828 788 X
Paperback 2002

With over 200 entries, this book contains reviews of recommended titles from poetry, non-fiction and classic tales, to fiction dealing with contemporary issues. Each book is roughly subdivided by the different ages within each age band, and by subject matter and genre.

Sticks and Stones: The Troublesome Success of Children's Literature from Slovenly Peter to Harry Potter

by Jack Zipes
Published by Routledge
ISBN 0415938805
Paperback 2002

Jack Zipes – translator of the Grimm tales, teacher, storyteller, and scholar – questions whether children ever really had a literature of their own. He sees children's literature in many ways as being the 'grown-ups' version' – a story about childhood that adults tell kids. He discusses children's literature from the 19th century moralism of Slovenly Peter (whose fingers get cut off) to the wildly successful *Harry Potter* books. Children's literature is a booming market but its success, this author says, is disguising its limitations. *Sticks and Stones* is a forthright and engaging book by someone who clearly cares deeply about what and how children read.

The Ultimate Book Guide

by Anne Fine
Edited by Daniel Hahn
Published by A & C Black Publishers Ltd
ISBN 0 7136 6718 4
Paperback 2004

Over 600 entries covering the best books for children aged 8–12, from classics to contemporary titles published up to the end of 2003. Funny, friendly and frank recommendations written for children by their favourite and best-known authors including Anthony Horowitz, Jacqueline Wilson, Celia Rees, Darren Shan, David Almond and Dick King-Smith. Plus features on the most popular genres.

Societies, prizes and festivals

The Society of Authors

The Society of Authors is an independent trade union, representing writers' interests in all aspects of the writing profession, particularly publishing, but also broadcasting, television and film, theatre and translation.

Founded over 100 years ago, the Society now has more than 8000 members. It has a professional staff, responsible to a Management Committee of 12 authors, and a Council (an advisory body meeting twice a year) consisting of 60 eminent writers.

Specialist groups

There are specialist groups within the Society to serve particular needs: the Academic Writers Group, the Broadcasting Group, the Children's Writers and Illustrators Group (see below), the Educational Writers Group, the Medical Writers Group and the Translators Association. There are also groups representing Scotland and the North of England.

The Children's Writers and Illustrators Group

The Children's Writers and Illustrators Group (CWIG) was formed in 1963. Besides furthering the interests of writers and artists and defending them whenever they are threatened, the Group seeks to bring members together professionally and socially, and in general to raise the status of children's books.

The Group has its own Executive Committee with representation on the Management Committee of the Society of Authors. Meetings and socials are held on a regular basis. Speakers have so far included publishers, librarians, booksellers and reviewers, and many distinguished writers and illustrators for children.

The annual subscription to the Society of Authors includes membership of all its groups. Membership of the CWIG is open to writers and illustrators who have had at least one

Membership

The Society of Authors
84 Drayton Gardens, London SW10 9SB
tel 020-7373 6642
email info@societyofauthors.org
website www.societyofauthors.org
General Secretary Mark Le Fanu

Membership is open to authors who have had a full-length work published, broadcast or performed commercially in the UK and to those who have had a full-length work accepted for publication, but not yet published; and those who have had occasional items broadcast or performed, or translations, articles, illustrations or short stories published. The owner or administrator of a deceased author's copyrights can become a member on behalf of the author's estate. Writers who have been offered a contract seeking a contribution towards publication costs may apply for one year's associate membership and have the contract vetted.

The 2007 annual subscription (which is tax deductible) is £85 (£80 by direct debit after the first year). There is a special rate for partners living at the same address. Authors under 35 not yet earning a significant income from writing, may pay a lower subscription of £60. Authors over 65 may pay at the reduced rate after their first year of membership.

Contact the Society for a membership booklet and copy of *The Author*, or visit the website for an application form.

book published by a reputable British publisher, five short stories or more than 20 minutes of material broadcast on national radio or television. Election is at the discretion of the Committee.

For further details contact the Secretary, Jo Hodder at jhodder @societyofauthors.org

What the Society does for members

Through its permanent staff (including a solicitor), the Society is able to give its members a comprehensive personal and professional service covering the business aspects of authorship, including:

'It does no harm to repeat, as often as you can, "Without me the literary industry would not exist: the publishers, the agents, the sub-agents, the accountants, the libel lawyers, the departments of literature, the professors, the theses, the books of criticism, the reviewers, the book pages - all this vast and proliferating edifice is because of this small, patronised, put-down and underpaid person."' – *Doris Lessing*

• providing information about agents, publishers, and others concerned with the book trade, journalism, broadcasting and the performing arts;

• advising on negotiations, including the individual vetting of contracts, clause by clause, and assessing their terms both financial and otherwise;

• helping with members' queries, major or minor, over any aspect of the business of writing;

• taking up complaints on behalf of members on any issue concerned with the business of authorship;

• pursuing legal actions for breach of contract, copyright infringement, and the non-payment of royalties and fees, when the risk and cost preclude individual action by a member and issues of general concern to the profession are at stake;

• holding conferences, seminars, meetings and social occasions;

• producing a comprehensive range of publications, free of charge to members, including the Society's quarterly journal, *The Author*. *Quick Guides* cover many aspects of the profession such as: copyright, publishing contracts, libel, income tax, VAT, authors' agents, permissions, indexing, and the protection of titles. The Society also publishes occasional papers on subjects such as film agreements, packaged books, revised editions, multimedia, and vanity publishing.

Further membership benefits

Members have access to:

• books and other products at special rates;

• free membership of the Authors' Licensing and Collecting Society (ALCS);

• a group Medical Insurance Scheme with BUPA;

• the Retirement Benefit Scheme;

• the Contingency Fund (which provides financial relief for authors or their dependents in sudden financial difficulties);

• the Pension Fund (which offers discretionary pensions to a number of members);

• membership of the Royal Over-Seas League at a discount.

The Society frequently secures improved conditions and better returns for members. It is common for members to report that, through the help and facilities offered, they have saved more, and sometimes substantially more, than their annual subscriptions (which are an allowable expense against income tax).

What the Society does for authors

The Society lobbies Members of Parliament, Ministers and Government Departments on all issues of concern to writers. Recent issues have included the operation and funding of Public Lending Right, the threat of VAT on books, copyright legislation and European Union initiatives. Concessions have also been obtained under various Finance Acts.

The Society litigates in matters of importance to authors. For example, the Society backed Andrew Boyle when he won his appeal against the Inland Revenue's attempt to tax the Whitbread Award.

The Society campaigns for better terms for writers. With the Writers' Guild, it has negotiated 'minimum terms agreements' with many leading publishers. The translators' section of the Society has also drawn up a minimum terms agreement for translators which has been adopted by Faber and Faber, and has been used on an individual basis by a number of other publishers.

The Society is recognised by the BBC for the purpose of negotiating rates for writers' contributions to radio drama, as well as for the broadcasting of published material. It was instrumental in setting up the ALCS (see page 250), which collects and distributes fees from reprography and other methods whereby copyright material is exploited without direct payment to the originators.

The Society keeps in close touch with the Arts Councils, the Association of Authors' Agents, the British Council, the Institute of Translation and Interpreting, the Department for Culture, Media and Sport, the National Union of Journalists, the Publishers Association and the Writers' Guild of Great Britain.

The Society is a member of the European Writers Congress, the British Copyright Council, the National Book Committee and the Creators' Rights Alliance.

Awards

The Society of Authors administers:
- Travelling Scholarships which give honorary awards;
- four prizes for novels: the Betty Trask Awards, the Encore Award, the McKitterick Prize and the Sagittarius Prize;
- two prizes for a full-length published work: the Somerset Maugham Awards and *The Sunday Times* Young Writer of the Year Award;
- two poetry awards: the Eric Gregory Awards and the Cholmondeley Awards;
- the Tom-Gallon and Olive Cook Awards for short story writers;
- the Authors' Foundation and Kathleen Blundell Trust, which give grants to published authors working on their next book;
- two radio drama prizes: the Richard Imison Award for a writer new to radio drama and the Peter Tinniswood Award;
- awards for translations from French, German, Italian, Dutch, Portuguese, Spanish and Swedish into English;
- the Francis Head Bequest for assisting authors who, through physical mishap, are temporarily unable to maintain themselves or their families;
- medical book awards.

Booktrust

Booktrust is the largest literature organisation in the United Kingdom. It is supported by Arts Council England and has a broad range of activities aimed at promoting books and reading.

Booktrust is an independent national charity that encourages readers of all ages and cultures to discover and enjoy reading. The reader is at the heart of everything it does. Booktrust administers a number of literary prizes, including the Orange Prize for Fiction and the John Llewellyn Rhys Prize for adults, and the Booktrust Teenage and Nestlé prizes for children, as well as promoting books and reading for all ages through numerous campaigns such as Get London Reading (see *Children's book and illustration prizes and awards*, page 363).

Further information

Booktrust, Book House, 45 East Hill, London SW18 2QZ
tel 020-8516 2977 *fax* 020-8516 2978
email query@booktrust.org.uk
website www.booktrusted.com,
www.booktrust.org.uk, www.bookheads.org.uk,
www.bookstart.org.uk,
www.childrenslaureate.org.uk

Booktrust and children

The Children's Literature Team at Booktrust offers advice and information on all aspects of children's reading and books.

● The 'booktrusted' website gives invaluable information on children's books and resources, including annotated booklists; information about organisations concerned with children's books; publishers; children's book news; and events listings for readings, festivals and other children's book events throughout the UK.

● Booktrust also coordinates the national Bookstart (books-for-babies) programme which gives free advice and books to parents/carers attending their baby's health checks (see *Books for babies*, page 90).

● Booktrust publishes the annual *Best Book Guide for Children and Young Adults*, which details the best in children's paperback fiction published in the previous calendar year.

● Booktrust runs the Booktrust Early Years Awards (formerly the Sainsbury's Baby Book Award) which aims to celebrate, publicise and reward the exciting range of books being published today for babies, toddlers and preschool children. With Bookstart, Booktrust hopes to promote and make these books accessible to as wide an audience as possible.

● Booktrust runs the Writing Together programme, which aims to ensure that, during their life at school, every child encounters opportunities to work with professional writers who inspire them creatively.

● Booktrust administers the Children's Laureate (Jacqueline Wilson 2005/6).

● Booktrust administers National Children's Book Week.

Seven Stories, the Centre for Children's Books

At the newly opened Seven Stories the rich heritage of British children's books is collected, explored and celebrated.

sevenstories
the centre for children's books

Once upon a time an idea was born on the banks of the Tyne to create a national home for children's literature – a place where the original work of authors and illustrators could be collected, treasured and celebrated. After 10 years of pioneering work by founding directors Elizabeth Hammill and Mary Briggs, that dream became a reality. In August 2005 Seven Stories, the Centre for Children's Books, opened in an award-winning converted seven storey Victorian granary in the Ouseburn Valley, a stone's throw from Newcastle's vibrant quayside.

The collection

At the heart of Seven Stories is a unique and growing collection of manuscripts, artwork and other pre-publication materials. These treasures record the creative process involved in making a children's book and provide illuminating insights into the working lives of modern authors and illustrators. The collection focuses on work created in postwar Britain and already contains thousands of items by authors such as Joan Aiken, Peter Dickinson, Jan Mark, Philip Pullman, Robert Westall and Ursula Moray Williams; illustrators like Edward Ardizzone, Faith Jaques, Harold Jones, Pat Hutchins, Helen Cooper, Ted Dewan and Jane Ray; and editors and other practitioners such as Kaye Webb. Many more bodies of work are pledged and on their way.

Exhibitions

A celebration of creativity underpins the Seven Stories project: its collection documents the creative act, and its exhibitions and programmes interpret this original material in unconventional but meaningful ways. The aim is to cultivate an appreciation of books and their making, and inspire creativity in its audience.

The Centre for Children's Books was branded Seven Stories in 2004, and for several years previous to this it mounted exhibitions in borrowed venues. Two of its exhibitions have toured regionally and nationally – 'Over the Hills and Faraway' was a retrospective of Kim Lewis, and 'Happy Birthday *Miffy*', which will be travelling until 2007.

Now, in its new home, Seven Stories provides the only exhibition space in the UK wholly dedicated to showcasing the incomparable legacy of British writing and illustrating for children. Its current exhibition is 'What's in the Book?', which celebrates the work of the highly successful children's illustrator/author team of Janet and Allan Ahlberg.

Throughout its seven storeys – from the Engine Room to the bookshop and café to the Artist's Attic, visitors of all ages are invited to engage in a unique, interactive exploration of creativity, literature and art. In this literary playground, they become writers, artists, explorers, designers, storytellers, readers or collectors, in the company of storytellers, authors, illustrators and other facilitators. Visiting school parties are currently met by either a Storycatcher, Burglar Betty or the Jolly Postman.

Seven Stories aims to place children, young people and their books at the heart of the UK's national literary culture. An independent educational charity, it is committed to access for all and has initiated several innovative outreach projects. The Centre has developed close links with the Newcastle and region community, and is currently working with the new Department of Children's Literature at Newcastle University to develop the Seven Stories collection and maximise its potential for research and display.

In Seven Stories, Britain has now found a long needed home dedicated to the celebration of children's literature.

Further information

Seven Stories, the Centre for Children's Books
30 Lime Street, Ouseburn Valley,
Newcastle upon Tyne NE1 2PQ
tel (0845) 271 0777 *fax* 0191-276 4302
email info@sevenstories.org.uk
website www.sevenstories.org.uk
Registered Charity No 1056812

Public opening hours
Mon–Wed 10am–5pm, Thurs 10am–6pm,
Fri 10am–5pm, Sat 10am–5pm, Sun 11am–5pm

Admission charges
Adult (17 and over) £5; child/concession £4;
family £15

The Children's Book Circle

Rachel Wade and Miranda Baker of the Children's Book Circle introduce the organisation.

Are you passionate about children's books? The Children's Book Circle (CBC) provides an exciting forum in which you can develop your interest, build your contacts and enrich your engagement with the children's book world. The CBC's membership consists of publishers, librarians, authors, illustrators, agents, teachers, booksellers and anyone with an active interest in the field. If you're an aspiring author or illustrator, you'll already know how important it is to become as knowledgeable as possible about the current marketplace for children's books. The CBC is the ideal place to broaden your knowledge. It's not the place to try for a publishing contract, but it will give you the opportunity to take part in discussions with people from the industry in an informal and enjoyable context.

> ## Further information
>
> Contact Elv Moody, Children's Book Circle, Scholastic Ltd, Euston House, 24 Evershot Street, London NW1 1DB
> website www.childrensbookcircle.org.uk
> Membership £15 p.a. for those within the M25 and £12 for those outside the M25

The CBC meets regularly at a variety of venues in London. At our speaker meetings, invited guest speakers debate key issues relating to children's books. The wide membership base ensures that these meetings are exciting occasions. Recent events have included a discussion between the bestselling author Paul Stewart and illustrator Chris Riddell about their working relationship and a debate about the relevance of fairy tales, with contributions from Viv French, Elizabeth Laird and Nicholas Tucker.

Members also have the opportunity to attend the annual Eleanor Farjeon Award reception and the Patrick Hardy Lecture. The Eleanor Farjeon Award is awarded for an outstanding contribution to the world of children's books, either by an individual or an organisation. Recent winners include Philip Pullman and editor Miriam Hodgson. The Patrick Hardy Lecture is delivered each year by a distinguished speaker on a relevant topic of their choice. Past speakers have included Anne Fine, David Almond and Jacqueline Wilson.

Other highlights of the CBC calendar include a summer and Christmas party. The summer party offers members a chance to show off their children's book knowledge in a challenging quiz. The Christmas party is a chance for members to get together for an end-of-year celebration based upon a theme – last year's party was a celebration of children's illustration.

The Children's Book Circle is a non-profit making organisation and is run entirely by volunteers.

Federation of Children's Book Groups

The aim of the Federation of Children's Book Groups is to bring children and books together and have fun. David Blanch introduces the organisation.

The Federation of Children's Book Groups (now a registered charity) was formed in 1968 by Anne Wood to coordinate the work of the many different children's book groups that were coming together across the country. Over the next eight years the organisation expanded and a system of regionalisation was introduced to link groups together in each part of the country.

In 1976 National Tell-A-Story-Week was introduced and became an immediate success. This has now grown into National Share-A-Story-Month and takes place in May. It enables groups to focus on the power of story and to hold events which celebrate this. Each year the National Launch is held in a different part of the country and in 2006 a one-day event was held in Reading on the theme of Reading Aloud, and the event was led by the Children's Laureate, Jacqueline Wilson.

The following year, 1977, saw the publication of the first Federation anthology and since then there have been seven more titles. Plans are under way to consider a new anthology for 2008.

In 1981 the Federation inaugurated one of its most successful ventures – the Children's Book Award, a prize given for the best book of the year judged entirely by children. The first winner was *Mr Magnolia* by Quentin Blake and the present holder is American author, Rick Riordan, for his book *Percy and the Olympians – The Lightning Tree*. The Award for 2006 was presented at the Hay Festival in June. This was the first time that the Award had been presented at a major literary festival. Children from all over the country came together to celebrate all that is best in children's books. For the past four years the award has been supported by Red House Children's Books and their financial commitment has enabled the Award to go from strength to strength, providing opportunities for children all over the country, who are not members of the Federation, to become involved in the final round of judging.

Each year the Federation invites a Group to organise the Annual Conference. This ensures that the Conference moves around the country and that its organisation involves many different members. Venues have included Edinburgh, Bradford, Plymouth, Stratford-upon-Avon, Brighton and Cirencester. The 2005 conference was held in Birmingham and was organised by four of the region's groups working together. Over 300 delegates attended during the weekend and listened to speakers as diverse as Morris Gleitzman, Cathy Cassidy, Michelle Paver, Christina Balit and Jacqueline Wilson.

The Children's Book Groups

Further information

Federation of Children's Book Groups
2 Bridge Wood View, Horsforth, Leeds LS18 5PE
tel 0113-258 8910
email info@fcbg.org.uk
website www.fcbg.org.uk
Registered Charity No 268289

So where are the groups and who are its members? Federation Groups exist in many parts of England, Scotland and Wales; from Plymouth to Dundee; from Grantham to St David's and from York to Lewes. Membership of a group is made up of parents, carers, teachers, librarians and, in some cases, children's authors and illustrators. The passion of Federation members for bringing books and children together is the reason that the organisation has continued and developed over the past 36 years. A new venture in 2006 was to have a presence at the Hay Festival throughout the 10 days, where once again the Federation's aim – to bring children and books together and have fun – was at the forefront of the day's activities. The success of this venture has still be to evaluated, but many Federation members willingly gave up their time to help.

Each of the member groups is self supporting in terms of money and organisation, but has the advantage of a parent body to support and encourage its activities. These are as varied and diverse as the groups themselves, serving their own community's needs. They might include author visits, children's events and celebrations. But above all the Federation is an organisation that is passionate about children's books, bringing together ordinary book-loving families, empowering parents, grandparents, carers and their children to become enthusiastic and excited about all kinds of good books. Local groups encourage everyone to talk about books and reading, and thus enthusiasm for good children's literature is passed on at all levels.

David Blanch joined the Federation in 1969 and helped set up the Birmingham Children's Book Group. He remains a committee member of that Group and currently serves as Publicity Officer on the National Executive. He was the National Chair in 1977/8.

Societies, associations and organisations

The societies and associations listed here include appreciation societies devoted to specific authors (see also online resources on page 327), professional bodies and national institutions. Some also offer prizes and awards (see page 363).

Academi (Welsh Academy)

Main Office 3rd Floor, Mount Stuart House, Mount Stuart Square, Cardiff CF10 5FQ
tel 029-2047 2266 *fax* 029-2049 2930
email post@academi.org
and Academi Glyn Jones Centre, Wales Millennium Centre, Cardiff Bay, Cardiff CF10 5AL
tel 029-2047 2266 *fax* 029-2047 0691
email post@academi.org
North West Wales Office Ty Newydd, Llanystumdwy, Cricieth, Gwynedd LL52 0LW
tel (01766) 522817 *fax* (01766) 523095
email academi.gog@dial.pipex.com
South West Wales Office Dylan Thomas Centre, Somerset Place, Swansea SA1 1RR
tel (01792) 463980 *fax* (01792) 463993
website www.academi.org
Chief Executive Peter Finch
Membership Associate: £15 p.a. (waged), £7.50 (unwaged)

Academi is the trading name of Yr Academi Gymreig, the Welsh National Literature Promotion Agency and Society of Writers. With funds mostly provided from public sources, it has been constitutionally independent since 1978. It runs courses, competitions (including the Cardiff International Poetry and Book of the Year Competition), conferences, tours by authors, festivals and represents the interests of Welsh writers and Welsh writing both inside Wales and beyond. Its publications include *Taliesin* (3 p.a.), a literary journal in the Welsh language; *A470* (bi-monthly), a literature information magazine; *The Oxford Companion to the Literature of Wales, The Welsh Academy English–Welsh Dictionary*, and a variety of translated works.

Academi administers a range of schemes including Writers on Tour, Writers Residencies and Writing Squads for young people. Academi also runs services for writers in Wales such as bursaries, critical advice and mentoring. Founded 1959.

AccessArt

38 Mill Lane, Impington, Cambridge CB4 9XN
tel (01223) 520213
email info@accessart.org.uk
website www.accessart.org.uk

A fun, creative and dynamic learning tool for pupils across all the key stages, and for home-users of all ages. AccessArt gives users access to arts educational activities that would otherwise reach only a small audience. The website allows access to:
• a series of visually exciting and innovative 'online workshops' which condense and articulate artist-led teaching which has taken place in schools, museums and galleries; and
• teachers notes and learners' printouts. Each online workshop is accompanied by explanatory notes for the educators and printable resource material which can be used directly by the learner.

Louisa May Alcott Memorial Association

Orchard House, 399 Lexington Road, PO Box 343, Concord, MA 01742–0343, USA
tel 978-369-4118 *fax* 978-369-1367
email info@louisamayalcott.org
website www.louisamayalcott.org

A private, not-for-profit corporation. The Association provides the financial and human resources required to conduct public tours, special programmes, exhibits and the curatorial work which continue the tradition of the Alcotts, a unique 19th century family. Founded 1911.

American Society of Composers, Authors and Publishers

One Lincoln Plaza, New York, NY 10023, USA
tel 212-621-6000 *fax* 212-724-9064
website www.ascap.com
President & Chairman Marilyn Bergman

Amgueddfa Cymru – National Museum Wales

Cathays Park, Cardiff CF10 3NP
tel 029-2039 7951 *fax* 029-2057 3321
website www.museumwales.ac.uk

Arts Council England

14 Great Peter Street, London SW1P 3NQ
tel (0845) 300 6200 *textphone* 020-7973 6564
fax 020-7973 6590
email enquiries@artscouncil.org.uk
website www.artscouncil.org.uk
Chief Executive Peter Hewitt, *Chair* Sir Christopher Frayling

The national development agency for the arts in England, distributing public money from

Government and the National Lottery. Arts Council England's main funding programme is Grants for the Arts, which is open to individuals, arts organisations, national touring companies and other people who use the arts in their work.

Arts Council England has one national and 9 regional offices. It has a single contact telephone and email address for general enquiries (see above). Founded 1946.

East
Eden House, 48–49 Bateman Street, Cambridge CB2 1LR
tel (0845) 300 6200 *textphone* (01223) 306893
fax (0870) 242 1271

East Midlands
St Nicholas Court, 25–27 Castle Gate, Nottingham NG1 7AR
tel (0845) 300 6200 *fax* 0115-950 2467

London
2 Pear Tree Court, London EC1R 0DS
tel (0845) 300 6200 *textphone* 020-7973 6564
fax 020-7608 4100

North East
Central Square, Forth Street, Newcastle upon Tyne NE1 3PJ
tel (0845) 300 6200 *textphone* 0191-255 8585
fax 0191-230 1020

North West
Manchester House, 22 Bridge Street, Manchester M3 3AB
tel (0845) 300 6200 *textphone* 0161-834 9131
fax 0161-834 6969

South East
Sovereign House, Church Street, Brighton BN1 1RA
tel (0845) 300 6200 *textphone* (01273) 710659
fax (0870) 2421257

South West
Senate Court, Southernhay Gardens, Exeter EX1 1UG
tel (0845) 300 6200 *textphone* (01392) 433503
fax (01392) 229229

West Midlands
82 Granville Street, Birmingham B1 2LH
tel (0845) 300 6200 *textphone* 0121-643 2815
fax 0121-643 7239

Yorkshire
21 Bond Street, Dewsbury, West Yorkshire WF13 1AX
tel (0845) 300 6200 *textphone* (01924) 438585
fax (01924) 466522

Arts Council/An Chomhairle Ealaíon
Literature Officer, 70 Merrion Square, Dublin 2, Republic of Ireland
tel (01) 6180200 *fax* (01) 6761302

website www.artscouncil.ie
Arts Programme Director John O'Kane

The national development agency for the arts in Ireland. Founded 1951.

Arts Council of Northern Ireland
MacNeice House, 77 Malone Road, Belfast BT9 5JW
tel 028-9038 5200 *fax* 028-90661715
website www.artscouncil-ni.org
Chief Executive Roisín McDonough, *Literature Officer* Damian Smyth, *Visual Arts Officers* Iain Davidson, Suzanne Lyle

Promotes and encourages the arts throughout Northern Ireland. Artists in drama, dance, music and jazz, literature, the visual arts, traditional arts and community arts, can apply for support for specific schemes and projects. The value of the grant will be set according to the aims of the application. Applicants must have contributed regularly to the artistic activities of the community, and been resident for at least one year in Northern Ireland.

The Arts Council of Wales
9 Museum Place, Cardiff CF10 3NX
tel 029-2037 6500 *minicom* 029-2039 0027
fax 029-2022 1447
email info@artswales.org.uk
website www.artswales.org.uk
Chairman Prof. Dai Smith, *Arts Director* David Alston, *Head of Communications* Sian Phipps, *Wales Arts International* Chris Richetts, *Director of South Wales* David Newland, *Director of North Wales* Simon Lovell Jones, *Director of Mid & West Wales* Sian Tomos

National organisation with specific responsibility for the funding and development of the arts in Wales. ACW receives funding from the National Assembly for Wales and also distributes the National Lottery funds in Wales to the arts. From these resources, ACW makes grants to support arts activities and facilities. Some of the funds are allocated in the form of annual revenue grants to full-time arts organisations. It also operates schemes which provide financial and other forms of support for individual activities or projects. ACW undertakes this work in both the English and Welsh languages.

North Wales Regional Office
36 Princes Drive, Colwyn Bay LL29 8LA
tel (01492) 533440 *minicom* (01492) 532288
fax (01492) 533677

Mid and West Wales Regional Office
6 Gardd Llydaw, Jackson Lane, Carmarthen SA31 1QD
tel (01267) 234248 *minicom* (01267) 223469
fax (01267) 233084

South Wales Office
9 Museum Place, Cardiff CF10 3NX
tel 029-2037 6525 *minicom* 029-2039 0027
fax 029-2022 1447

Association for Library Service to Children

American Library Association, 50 East Huron, Chicago, IL 60611–2795, USA
tel 800-545-2433 ext. 2153 *fax* 312-944-7671
email library@ala.org
website www.ala.org

The Association for Library Service to Children develops and supports the profession of children's librarianship by enabling and encouraging its practitioners to provide the best library service to our nation's children.

Association for Scottish Literary Studies (ASLS)

c/o Dept of Scottish History, 9 University Gardens, University of Glasgow G12 8QH
tel 0141-330 5309
email office@asls.org.uk
website www.asls.org.uk
Hon. President Alan MacGillivray, *Hon. Secretary* Lorna Borrowman Smith, *Publishing Manager* Duncan Jones
Membership £38 p.a. individuals, £10 UK students, £67 corporate

Promotes the study, teaching and writing of Scottish literature and furthers the study of the languages of Scotland. Publishes annually an edited text of Scottish literature, an anthology of new Scottish writing, a series of academic journals and a Newsletter (2 p.a.). Also publishes *Scotnotes* (comprehensive study guides to major Scottish writers), literary texts and commentary CDs designed to assist the classroom teacher, and a series of occasional papers. Organises 3 conferences a year. Founded 1970.

Association of American Publishers Inc.

71 Fifth Avenue, New York, NY 10003, USA
tel 212-255-0200 *fax* 212-255-7007
website www.publishers.org
President & Ceo Patricia S. Schroeder

Founded 1970.

The Association of Authors' Agents

20 John Street, London WC1N 2DR
tel 020-7405 6774 *fax* 020-7831 2154
email aaa@johnsonandalcock.co.uk
website www.agentsassoc.co.uk
President Clare Alexander, *Vice President* Derek Johns, *Treasurers* Caroline Montgomery and Andrew Nurnberg, *Secretary* Anna Power

Maintains a code of professional practice to which all members commit themselves; holds regular meetings to discuss matters of common professional interest; provides a vehicle for representing the view of authors' agents in discussion of matters of common interest with other professional bodies. Founded 1974.

Association of Authors' Representatives Inc.

676A, Suite 312 9th Avenue, New York, NY 10036, USA
tel 212-840-5777
website www.aar-online.org
Founded 1991.

Association of Booksellers for Children

ABC National Office, 62 Wenham Street, Jamaica Plain, MA 02130, USA
tel 617-390-7759 *fax* 617-344-0540
website www.abfc.com

A national membership association that offers a support network for professional independent children's booksellers who share the goal of encouraging quality and service within the children's book industry.

Association of Canadian Publishers

161 Eglinton Avenue East, Suite 702, Toronto, Ontario M4P 1J5, Canada
tel 416-487-6116 *fax* 416-487-8815
email admin@canbook.org,
margaret_eaton@canbook.org
website www.publishers.ca
Executive Director Margaret Eaton

Founded 1976; formerly Independent Publishers Association, 1971.

The Association of Illustrators

2nd floor, Back Building, 150 Curtain Road, London EC2A 3AT
tel 020-7613 4328 *fax* 020-7613 4417
website www.theaoi.com
Contact Membership Coordinator

Exists to support illustrators, promote illustration and encourage professional standards in the industry. Publishes *Varoom* magazine (3 p.a.); presents an annual programme of events; annual competition, exhibition and tour of Images – the Best of British Illustration (call for entries: late spring). Founded 1973.

Audiobook Publishing Association (APA)

(formerly the Spoken Word Publishing Association)
Administrator Charlotte McCandlish, 18 Green Lanes, Hatfield, Herts. AL10 9JT
tel (07971) 280788
website www.theapa.net
Membership £50–£600 p.a. plus VAT

The UK trade association for the audiobook industry, APA brings together all those involved – publishers, performers, producers, distributors, retailers, manufacturers. It aims to increase the profile of the audiobook in the media, the retail trade and among the general public, and to provide a forum for discussion. Founded 1994.

Australia Council
PO Box 788, Strawberry Hills, NSW 2012, Australia
located at 372 Elizabeth Street, Surry Hills, NSW
2010, Australia
tel (02) 9215 9000 *fax* (02) 9215 9111
email mail@ozco.gov.au
website www.ozco.gov.au
Chairperson David Gonski

Provides a broad range of support for the arts in
Australia, embracing music, theatre, literature, visual
arts, crafts, Aboriginal arts, community and new
media arts. It has 8 major Boards: Literature, Visual
Arts/Craft, Music, Theatre, Dance, New Media,
Community Cultural Development, Major
Performing Arts, as well as the Aboriginal and Torres
Strait Islander Arts Board.

The Literature Board's chief objective is to support
the writing of all forms of creative literature – novels,
short stories, poetry, plays and literary non-fiction. It
also assists with the publication of literary magazines,
has a book publishing subsidies programme, and
initiates and supports projects of many kinds
designed to promote Australian literature both within
Australia and abroad.

Australian Copyright Council
PO Box 1986, Strawberry Hills, NSW 2012, Australia
tel (02) 9318 1788 *fax* (02) 9698 3536
email info@copyright.org.au
website www.copyright.org.au

An independent non-profit organisation which aims
to assist creators and other copyright owners to
exercise their rights effectively; raise awareness in the
community generally about the importance of
copyright; research and identify areas of copyright
law which are inadequate or unfair; seek changes to
law and practice to enhance the effectiveness and
fairness of copyright; foster cooperation amongst
bodies representing creators and owners of copyright.

The Council comprises 23 organisations or
associations of owners and creators of copyright
material, including the Australian Society of Authors,
the Australian Writers Guild and the Australian Book
Publishers Association. Founded 1968.

Australian Publishers Association (APA)
60–89 Jones Street, Ultimo, NSW 2007, Australia
tel (02) 9281 9788 *fax* (02) 9281 1073
email apa@publishers.asn.au
website www.publishers.asn.au
Ceo Maree McCaskill

Australian Writers' Guild (AWG)
8/50 Reservoir Street, Surry Hills, NSW 2010
tel (02) 9281 1554 *fax* (02) 9281 4321
email admin@awg.com.au
website www.awg.com.au

The professional association for all performance
writers, i.e. writers for film, TV, radio, theatre, video

and new media. The AWG is recognised throughout
the industry in Australia as being the voice of
performance writers. Established 1962.

Authors' Licensing and Collecting Society Ltd – see page 345

Barnardo's Photographic Archive
Tanners Lane, Barkingside, Ilford, Essex IG6 1QG
tel 020-8498 7345 *fax* 020-8498 7090
email Stephen.pover@barnados.org.uk
website www.barnardos.org.uk

Extensive collection of b&w and colour images dating
from 1874 to the present day covering social history
with the emphasis on children and child care. Also
300 films dating from 1905. Founded 1872.

Hilaire Belloc Society
Contact Dr Grahame Clough, 1 Hillview Cottage,
Elsted, Nr Midhurst, West Sussex GU29 0JX
tel (01730) 825575
email hilairebelloc1@aol.com

Commemorates the French-born English writer of
light verse, history, travel books, biography and
fiction.

Enid Blyton Society
93 Milford Hill, Salisbury, Wilts. SP1 2QL
tel (01722) 331937
email info@enidblytonsociety.co.uk
website www.enidblytonsociety.co.uk
Contact Anita Bensoussane

To provide a focal point for collectors and enthusiasts
of Enid Blyton through its magazine *The Enid Blyton
Society Journal* (3 p.a.) and the annual Society Day
which attracts in excess of a hundred members each
year. Founded 1995.

Book Publishers Association of New Zealand Inc.
PO Box 36477, Northcote, Auckland 1309, New
Zealand
tel (09) 480-2711 *fax* (09) 480-1130
email bpanz@copyright.co.nz
website www.bpanz.org.nz
President Michael Moynahan

The Booksellers Association of the United Kingdom & Ireland Ltd
272 Vauxhall Bridge Road, London SW1V 1BA
tel 020-7802 0802 *fax* 020-7802 0803
email mail@booksellers.org.uk
website www.booksellers.org.uk
Chief Executive T.E. Godfray
Founded 1895.

Booktrust – see page 336

The British Council
10 Spring Gardens, London SW1A 2BN
tel 020-7930 8466 *fax* 020-7839 6347

website www.britishcouncil.org
Chair The Rt Hon. Lord Kinnock, *Director-General*
Sir David Green, *Director of Literature* Susanna
Nicklin, *Director of Arts* Leigh Gibson

The British Council connects people worldwide with
learning opportunities and creative ideas from the
UK, and builds lasting relationships between the UK
and other countries. It works in 110 countries, where
it has over 180 libraries and information centres, each
catering to the needs of the local community with
print and electronic resources. In 2005–6, 300,000
library members borrowed over 7.5 million books
and videos. British Council libraries not only provide
information and materials to users, but also promote
the latest UK publications.

Working in close collaboration with book trade
associations, British Council offices organise book
and electronic publishing exhibitions ranging from
small, specialist displays to participation in major
international book fairs. Other projects include
Global Publishing Information, a collection of online
publishing market reports on international markets
compiled in collaboration with the Publishers
Association. It also provides various resources on its
website for those interested in finding out more
about UK publishing.

Details of the British Council's many publications
are available online (www.britishcouncil.org/
publications/index.htm). The British Council is the
agent for the Department for International
Development (DFID) for book aid projects in
developing countries, and is an authority on teaching
English as a second or foreign language. It also gives
advice and information on curriculum, methodology,
materials and testing.

The British Council promotes British literature
overseas through writers' tours, academic visits,
seminars and exhibitions. It publishes *New Writing*,
an annual anthology of unpublished short stories,
poems, extracts from works in progress and essays;
and a series of literary bibliographies, including *Eyes
Wide Open: New Fiction from the UK 1999–2001*,
*Hunting Down the Universe: A Bibliography of Popular
Science and Literature*, and *Teaching Management
Principles Using Literature*. Through its Literature
Department, the British Council provides an
overview of UK literature and a range of online
resources on its literature website,
www.britishcouncil.org/arts/literature. This includes a
literary portal (www.literature.britishcouncil.org),
directories of postgraduate and short courses in
literature and creative writing, a directory of literary
conferences, information about UK and
Commonwealth authors on
www.contemporarywriters.com and
www.literarytranslation.com, including translation
workshops. A worldwide online book club and
reading group for adults, teenagers and children
(www.encompassculture.com) was launched in 2003,
and also www.youngtranslators.com for young
European translators.

The Visual Arts Department, part of the British
Council's Arts Group, develops and enlarges overseas
knowledge and appreciation of British achievement
in the fields of painting, sculpture, printmaking,
design, photography, the crafts and architecture,
working closely with the British Council's overseas
offices and with professional colleagues in the UK
and abroad.

Further information about the work of the British
Council is available from Press and Public Relations
at the above address, or from British Council offices
overseas.

British Museum

Great Russell Street, London WC1B 3DG
tel 020-7323 8000
email information@thebritishmuseum.ac.uk
website www.thebritishmuseum.ac.uk

Children's Compass

website www.thebritishmuseum.ac.uk/compass

Children's Compass enables children to explore the
British Museum's collections online. It incorporates a
special childrens' search, activities and quizzes for use
in the classroom, noticeboards for children's work,
'Ask the Expert' and articles written specially for 7–11
year-olds. Compass is also available on terminals in
the Reading Room in the Museum's Great Court.
Access to Compass is free. Alongside these terminals
are quiz sheets for children and family groups.
Children are encouraged to find objects on Compass
and then go and look at them in the galleries in order
to complete the quiz. Compass is also available on
specially designed touchscreens in the Reading Room
which have much more than the web version,
including higher quality images, animations, 3D
reconstructions and gallery plans. Launched in
February 2002.

Randolph Caldecott Society

Secretary Kenn Oultram, Clatterwick House,
Clatterwick Lane, Little Leigh, Northwich, Cheshire
CW8 4RJ
tel (01606) 891303 (office), 781731 (evening)
website www.randolphcaldecott.org.uk
Membership £10 p.a. individual, £15 p.a. families/
corporate

Aims to encourage an interest in the life and works of
Randolph Caldecott (1846–86), the Victorian artist,
illustrator and sculptor. Caldecott produced 16
picture books, each based on the words of a nursery
rhyme or well-known nonsense verse. Meetings held
in Chester and London. Liaises with the American
Caldecott Society. Founded 1983.

Canadian Authors Association

320 South Shores Road, PO Box 419, Campbellford,
Ontario K0L 1L0
tel 705-653-0323, 866-216-6222 (toll free)
fax 705-653-0593

email admin@canauthors.org
website www.canauthors.org
President Joan Eyolfson Cadham, *Administrator* Alec McEachern

The Canadian Children's Book Centre (CCBC)

Suite 101, 40 Orchard View Blvd, Toronto, ON M4R 1B9, Canada
tel 416975-0010 *fax* 416-975-8970
email info@bookcentre.ca
website www.bookcentre.ca

A national, not-for-profit organisation dedicated to encouraging, promoting and supporting the reading, writing and illustrating of Canadian books for young readers. CCBC programmes and publications offer a wide range of resources to anyone who is interested in quality reading for children and teens. Founded 1976.

Canadian Magazine Publishers Association

425 Adelaide Street West, Suite 700, Toronto, Ontario M5V 3C1, Canada
tel 416-504-0274 *fax* 416-504-0437
email cmpainfo@cmpa.ca
website www.cmpa.ca

Founded 1973.

Canadian Publishers' Council

250 Merton Street, Suite 203, Toronto, Ontario M4S 1B1, Canada
tel 416-322-7011 *fax* 416-322-6999
email pubadmin@pubcouncil.ca
website www.pubcouncil.ca
Executive Director Jacqueline Hushion

CANSCAIP (Canadian Society of Children's Authors, Illustrators & Performers)

40 Orchard View Boulevard, Suite 104, Toronto, Ontario M4R 1B9, Canada
tel 416-515-1559
email office@canscaip.org
website www.cansaip.org
Office Manager Lena Coakley
Membership $75 p.a. Full member (published authors and illustrators), $45 Insitutional Friend, $35 Friend

A non-profit support network for children's artists. Promotes children's literature and performances through Canada and internationally. Founded 1977.

Careers Writers' Association

Membership Secretary Ann Goodman, 16 Caewal Road, Llandaff, Cardiff CF5 2BT
tel 029-2056 3444 *fax* 029-2065 8190
email ann@ann50.freeserve.co.uk
website www.careerswriters.co.uk

Membership £20 p.a.
Society for established writers on the inter-related topics of education, training and careers. Holds occasional meetings on subjects of interest to members, and circulates details of members to information providers. Founded 1979.

The Lewis Carroll Society

Secretary Alan White, 69 Cromwell Road, Hertford, Herts. SG13 7DP
email alanwhite@tesco.net
website www.lewiscarrollsociety.org.uk
Membership £15 p.a. UK, £18 Europe, £20 elsewhere; special rates for institutions

Aims to promote interest in the life and works of Lewis Carroll (Revd Charles Lutwidge Dodgson) (1832–98) and to encourage research. Activities include regular meetings, exhibitions, and a publishing programme that includes the first annotated, unexpurgated edition of his diaries in 9 volumes, the Society's journal *The Carrollian* (2 p.a.), a newsletter, *Bandersnatch* (quarterly) and the *Lewis Carroll Review* (occasional). Founded 1969.

Lewis Carroll Society (Daresbury)

Secretary Kenn Oultram, Clatterwick House, Clatterwick Lane, Little Leigh, Northwich, Cheshire CW8 4RJ
tel (01606) 891303 (office), 781731 (evening)
Membership £5 p.a.

Aims to encourage an interest in the life and works of Lewis Carroll (1832–98), author of *Alice's Adventures*. Meetings take place at Carroll's birth village (Daresbury, Cheshire). Founded 1970.

Lewis Carroll Society of North America (LCSNA)

PO Box 204, Napa, CA 94559, USA
website www.lewiscarroll.org
Membership $25 p.a.

An organisation of Carroll admirers of all ages and interests and a centre for Carroll studies. It is dedicated to furthering Carroll studies, increasing accessibility of research material, and maintaining public awareness of Carroll's contributions to society. The Society has a worldwide membership and meets twice a year. The Society maintains an active publication programme and members receive copies of the Society's magazine *Knight Letter*. An interest in Lewis Carroll, a simple love for Alice (or the Snark for that matter) qualifies for membership. Founded in 1974.

The Center for Children's Books (CCB)

Graduate School of Library and Information Science, University of Illinois at Urbana–Champaign, 501 East Daniel Street, Champaign, IL 61820, USA
tel 217-244-9331
email ccb@uiuc.edu

website http://ccb.lis.uiuc.edu

CCB houses a non-circulating collection of more than 16,000 recent and historically significant trade books for children, plus review copies of nearly all trade books published in the USA in the current year. There are over 1000 professional and reference books on the history and criticism of literature for youth, literature-based library and classroom programming, and storytelling. Although the collection is non-circulating, it is available for examination by scholars, teachers, librarians, students, and other educators.

Centre for Literacy in Primary Education (CLPE)

Webber Street, London SE1 8QW
tel 020-7401 3382/3 *fax* 020-7928 4624
email info@clpe.co.uk
website www.clpe.co.uk

A centre for children's language, literacy, literature and educational assessment which provides in-service training for teachers and contains a reference library of children's books plus teachers' resources. CLPE also publishes booklists and teaching resources relating to literacy in the primary classroom.

The Children's Book Circle – see The Children's Book Circle

The Children's Book Council (CBC)

12 West 37th Street, 2nd Floor, New York, NY 10018–7480, USA
tel 212-966-1990 *fax* 212-966-2073
website www.cbcbooks.org

The non-profit trade association of publishers and packagers of trade books and related materials for children and young adults. The goals of the CBC are to make the reading and enjoyment of children's books an essential part of America's educational and social goals; to enhance public perception of the importance of reading by disseminating information about books and related materials for young people and information about children's book publishing; and to create materials to support literacy and reading encouragement programs and to encourage the annual observance of National Children's Book Week.

Children's Book Council of Australia

PO Box 765, Rozelle, NSW 2039, Australia
tel (02) 9818 3858 *fax* (02) 9810 0737

Aims to foster children's enjoyment of books through managing the Children's Book of the Year Awards; providing information on and encouragement to authors and illustrators; organising exhibitions and activities during Children's Book Week; supporting children's library services; and promoting high standards in book reviewing.

The Children's Book Guild of Washington DC

website www.childrensbookguild.org
President Catherine Ruf

An association of writers, artists, librarians, teachers, editors, publishers and distributors dedicated to the field of children's literature. Its aims are to uphold and stimulate high standards of writing and illustrating for children; to increase knowledge and use of better books for children in the community; and to cooperate with other groups having similar purposes. Founded 1945.

Children's Books History Society

Secretary Ms Sarah Mahurter, 66 Idmiston Square, Worcester Park, Surrey KT4 7SY
tel 020-8830-6084 *fax* 020-8830-6084
email sjamahuter@hotmail.com
Membership £10 p.a.; apply for overseas rates

Aims 'to promote an appreciation of children's books, and to study their history, bibliography and literary content'. Holds approx. 6 meetings and produces 3 substantial *Newsletters* and an occasional paper per year. The Harvey Darton Award is given biennially for a book that extends knowledge of British children's literature of the past. Founded 1969.

Children's Books Ireland

17 North Great Georges Street, Dublin 1, Republic of Ireland
tel (01) 872 7475 *fax* (01) 872 7476
email info@childrensbooksireland.com
website www.childrensbooksireland.com
Director Mags Walsh, *Administrator* Jenny Murray
Membership €30/£20 p.a. individual, €50/£35 p.a. institutions, €45/£30/$55 p.a. overseas individual, €60/£40/$70 p.a. overseas institutions, €20/£15 p.a. student

Provides leadership and support in the promotion and celebration of books and reading for young people. As a resource and advocacy organisation for adults, CBI is committed to raising awareness of the importance and value of books for children and to bringing young people and books together. Formed in 1996.

Children's Literature Association (ChLA)

PO Box 138, Battle Creek, MI 49016–0138, USA
tel 269-965-8180 *fax* 269-965-3568
website http://chla.wikispaces.com
Membership Open to both individuals and institutions

ChLA's aims are to encourage serious scholarship and research in children's literature; to enhance the professional stature of the graduate and undergraduate teaching of children's literature; and to encourage high standards of criticism in children's literature. Individual members are entitled to the *ChLA Quarterly* and the annual volume of *Children's Literature*.

Children's Literature Centre

Martynas Mazvydas National Library of Lithuania, Gedimino pr. 51, LT–01504, Vilnius, Lithuania

tel (370) 5 2398561 *fax* (370) 5 2496129
email vaikai@lnb.lt
website www.lnb.lt

Martynas Mazvydas National Library of Lithuania Children's Department came into existence in 1963 and in 1994 was reorganised into the Children's Literature Centre (CLC).

It accumulates, processes, and stores children's literature, both original and in translation, as well as works on history, theory and literary criticism, informative and reference publications from various countries related to children's literature. The aim of CLC is to acquire, as fully as possible, earlier Lithuanian and translated children's books and books published by Lithuanian exiles. The CLC collection numbers approximately 102,000 volumes.

The Centre organises children's reading research, analyses book popularity, design, illustrations, quality of translations. CLC arranges international children's book exhibitions, seminars and conferences on children's book and reading. Presentation of new books, meetings with authors, publishers and designers are regularly carried out. CLC is the coordination and monitoring centre of children's libraries in Lithuania.

Children's Writers and Illustrators Group – see The Society of Authors, page 333

CLÉ – Irish Book Publishers' Association

25 Denzille Lane, Dublin 2, Republic of Ireland
tel (01) 639 4868
email info@publishingireland.com
website www.publishingireland.com
President Tony Farmar

Comhairle nan Leabhraichean/The Gaelic Books Council

22 Mansfield Street, Glasgow G11 5QP
tel 0141-337 6211 *fax* 0141-353 0515
email brath@gaelicbooks.net
website www.gaelicbooks.net
Chair Prof. Roibeard Ó Maolalaigh

Stimulates Scottish Gaelic publishing by awarding publication grants for new books, commissioning authors and providing editorial services and general assistance to writers and readers. Has its own bookshop of all Gaelic and Gaelic-related books in print and runs a book club. All the stock is listed on the website and a paper catalogue is also available. Founded 1968.

Curiosity & Imagination 4Children

Bellerive House, 3 Muirfield Crescent, London E14 9SZ
tel 020-7522 6919 *fax* 020-7512 2010
email info@curiosityandimagination.org.uk
website www.curiosityandimagination.org.uk
Manager Alison Coles, *Communications Officer* Nick Austin

Promotes an approach to children's learning which:
• harnesses the power of playful, hands-on experience as a tool for learning;
• empowers parents and carers to support their children's learning;
• encourages community ownership of the provision, giving children a central role in decision-making;
• draws in expertise from local partners across a range of sectors.

This approach fosters children's natural curiosity, stimulating them to discover more about themselves, other people and the world around them. It also inspires children's imaginations, helping them to see what is possible in the future. See website for further information.

Cyngor Llyfrau Cymru – see Welsh Books Council/Cyngor Llyfrau Cymru

Roald Dahl Foundation

81A High Street, Great Missenden, Bucks. HP16 0AL
tel (01494) 892192
website www.roalddahl.com, www.roalddahlfoundation.org

A UK-based registered charity offering a programme of grant-giving to charities, hospitals and individuals in the UK. It supports many varied projects, in the same way Roald Dahl did when he was alive, offering practical assistance to children and families in 3 areas: neurology, haematology and literacy.

The websites are illustrated with the artworks of Quentin Blake, Roald Dahl's principal illustrator and include full information about the author, his life and his works. The Roald Dahl website includes a free online club for children and the online magazine *Dahl-y Telegraph*.

The Roald Dahl Museum and Story Centre

81–83 High Street, Great Missenden, Bucks. HP16 0AI
tel (01494) 892192
website www.roalddahlmusem.com
An exciting hands-on gallery for children.

Walter de la Mare Society

PO Box 25351, London NW5 1ZT
tel 020-7485 2533
website www.bluetree.co.uk/wdlmsociety
Membership £15 p.a.

To promote the study and deepen the appreciation of the works of Walter de la Mare (1873–1956) through a magazine, talks, discussions and other activities. Founded 1997.

Discover

1 Bridge Terrace, London E15 4BG
tel 020-8536 5555
email team@discover.org.uk
website www.discover.org.uk

Discover is designed for children aged 0–8 years and their families, carers and teachers. Discover is about story-building – making stories together. Story-building helps children to use their imaginations and express themselves, both to each other and to grown-ups, through play. Speaking, listening, writing and acting become easy activities. Story-building is fun and breaks down barriers.

Discover has been running its outreach programmes to schools, libraries and community centres since 2000. The Story Garden opened in 2002 and the Story Trail opened in June 2003 in a renovated Edwardian building in the centre of Stratford. Story Trail is full of unique hands-on exhibits. Children's input at every stage of Discover's work is fundamental.

The Arthur Conan Doyle Society

Organisers Christopher and Barbara Roden, PO Box 1360, Ashcroft, B.C., Canada V0K 1A0
tel 250-453-2045 *fax* 250-453-2075
email ashtree@ash-tree.bc.ca
website www.ash-tree.bc.ca/acdsocy.html

Promotes the study of the life and works of Sir Arthur Conan Doyle (1859–1930). Publishes *ACD* journal (bi-annual) and occasional reprints of Conan Doyle material. Occasional conventions. Founded 1989.

Department for Education and Skills

Sanctuary Buildings, Great Smith Street, London SW1P 3BT
tel (0870) 000 2288 *fax* (01928) 794248
email info@dfes.gsi.gov.uk
website www.dfes.gov.uk

Aims to help build a competitive economy and inclusive society by creating opportunities for everyone to develop their learning potential and achieve excellence in standards of education and levels of skills. The department's main objectives are to give children an excellent start in education and enable young people and adults to develop and equip themselves with the skills, knowledge and personal qualities needed for life and work.

The Department also sponsors 11 non-departmental public bodies across a variety of professional disciplines and educational services.

Educational Publishers Council

The Publishers Association, 29ʙ Montague Street, London WC1B 5BW
tel 020-7691 9191 *fax* 020-7691 9199
email mail@publishers.org.uk

Provides a forum for publishers of printed and electronic learning resources for the school and college markets. It runs a series of events and meetings for its members and provides an information service. It also promotes the industry through the media and plays an active role in educational exhibitions.

Educational Writers Group – see The Society of Authors, page 333

English Association

University of Leicester, University Road, Leicester LE1 7RH
tel 0116-252 3982 *fax* 0116-252 2301
email engassoc@le.ac.uk
website www.le.ac.uk/engassoc/
Chair Peter J. Kitson, *Chief Executive* Helen Lucas

Aims to further knowledge, understanding and enjoyment of English literature and the English language, by working towards a fuller recognition of English as an essential element in education and in the community at large; by encouraging the study of English literature and language by means of conferences, lectures and publications; and by fostering the discussion of methods of teaching English of all kinds.

Federation of Children's Book Groups – see page 340

Federation of European Publishers

Rue Montoyer 31 Bte 8, B–1000 Brussels, Belgium
tel (2) 770 11 10 *fax* (2) 771 20 71
email info@fep-fee.be
website www.fep-fee.be
President Dr Arne Bach, *Director* Anne Bergman-Tahon

Represents the interests of European publishers on EU affairs; informs members on the development of EU policies which could affect the publishing industry. Founded 1967.

The Federation of Indian Publishers

18/1–C Institutional Area, Aruna Asaf Ali Marg (near JNU), New Delhi 110067, India
tel 26852263, 26964847 *fax* 26864054
email fip1@satyam.net.in
website www.fipindia.com

Federation of Spanish Publishers' Association

(Federación de Gremios de Editores de España)
Cea Bermúdez, 44–2° Dcha. 28003 Madrid, Spain
tel (91) 534 51 95 *fax* (91) 535 26 25
email fgee@fge.es
website www.federacioneditores.org
President D. Emiliano Martinez

French Publishers' Association

(Syndicat National de l'Edition)
115 Blvd St Germain, 75006 Paris, France
tel (1) 44 41 40 50 *fax* (1) 44 41 40 77
website www.sne.fr

The Gaelic Books Council – see Comhairle nan Leabhraichean/The Gaelic Books Council

The Greeting Card Association
United House, North Road, London N7 9DP
tel 020-7619 0396
website www.greetingcardassociation.org.uk
Administrator Sharon Little

The trade association for greeting card publishers. See website for information on freelance designing and writing for greeting cards. Official magazine: *Progressive Greetings Worldwide* (see page 213).

Guernsey Arts Council
La Fontaine, Courtil de la Fontaine, Kings Road, St Peter Port, Guernsey GY1 1QB, CI
email tdguernsey@cwgsy.net eales@guernsey.net
Chairman Mrs Terry Domrille, *Secretary* Ann Wilkes-Green *tel* (01481) 254144

Hayward Gallery
Belvedere Road, London SE1 8XZ
tel 020-7960 5226 *fax* 020-7401 2664
website www.hayward.org.uk

Imaginate
45A George Street, Edinburgh EH2 2HT
tel 0131-225 8050 *fax* 0131-225 6440
email info@imaginate.org.uk
website www.imaginate.org.uk
Director Tony Reekie, *General Manager* Tessa Rennie

Imaginate is an arts agency committed to promoting and developing performing arts for children in Scotland. Its vision is that all children, by the age of 12, will have had a positive experience of performing arts. Its mission is to act as an advocate for the provision of high-quality performing arts for children across Scotland. Imaginate produces an annual programme of events and initiatives.

Imaginate creates and produces the Bank of Scotland Children's International Theatre Festival for children and young people (see page 375). This annual event attracts an audience of children, their teachers, parents, carers and friends from across Scotland. An outreach programme takes live theatre into schools and communities in Edinburgh and the Lothians during the Festival. It also takes international theatre invited by Imaginate to perform at the Festival to venues across Scotland reaching children in communities from Shetland to Dumfriesshire to the Borders.

Imaginate produces WYSIWYG – What You See Is What You Get, Scotland's annual showcase of children's theatre for funders, artists, producers, programmers, arts and education workers.

In addition, Imaginate brings together practitioners from home and abroad to collaborate, develop skills and share experiences for the future benefit of young audiences. It identifies and develops opportunities and activities to support the growth and development of the performing arts sector for children and young people in Scotland. It has a range of resources accessible to the children's theatre sector.

Imperial War Museum
Lambeth Road, London SW7 5BD
tel 020-7416 5320
website www.iwm.org.uk

Independent Publishers Guild
PO Box 93, Royston, Herts. SG8 5GH
tel (01763) 247014 *fax* (01763) 246293
website www.ipg.uk.com
Membership £150 + VAT p.a. Open to new and established publishers and book packagers; supplier membership is available to specialists in fields allied to publishing (but not printers and binders)

Provides an information and contact network for independent publishers. The IPG also voices the concerns of member companies with the book trade. Founded 1962.

International Board on Books for Young People (IBBY)
Nonnenweg 12, Postfach, CH–4003–Basel, Switzerland
tel (4161) 272 2917 *fax* (+4161) 272 2757
email ibby@ibby.org
British Section PO Box 20875, GB–London SE22 9WQ
tel 020-8299 1641
email ann@lazim.demon.co.uk
website www.ibby.org

IBBY is a non-profit organisation which represents an international network of people from all over the world who are committed to bringing books and children together. Its aims are:
• to promote international understanding through children's books;
• to give children everywhere the opportunity to have access to books with high literary and artistic standards;
• to encourage the publication and distribution of quality children's books, especially in developing countries;
• to provide support and training for those involved with children and children's literature;
• to stimulate research and scholarly works in the field of children's literature.

IBBY is composed of more than 68 National Sections all over the world and represents countries with well-developed book publishing and literacy programmes, and other countries with only a few dedicated professionals who are doing pioneer work in children's book publishing and promotion. Founded in Zurich, Switzerland in 1953.

International Publishers Association
3 avenue de Miremont, CH–1206 Geneva, Switzerland
tel (022) 346-30-18 *fax* (022) 347-57-17
email secretariat@ipa-uie.org
President Ana Maria Cabanellas, *Secretary-General* Mr Jens Bammel

Founded 1896.

The Irish Book Publishers' Association – see CLÉ – Irish Book Publishers' Association

Irish Educational Publishers Association

c/o Gill and Macmillan Ltd, Hume Avenue, Park West, Dublin 12, Republic of Ireland
tel 353 1 500 9509 *fax* 353 1 500 9598
email hmahony@gillmacmillan.ie
Contact Hubert Mahony

Represents 13 publishers of educational materials in Ireland.

Irish Writers' Centre

19 Parnell Square, Dublin 1, Republic of Ireland
tel (01) 8721302 *fax* (01) 8726282
email info@writerscentre.ie
website www.writerscentre.ie
Director Cathal McCabe

National organisation for the promotion of writers and writing in Ireland. It runs an extensive programme of events at its headquarters; it operates the Writer in Community Scheme which funds events throughout Ireland; it runs an education programme which offers courses and workshops in writing; it operates an International Writers' Exchange Programme. See website for further details. Founded 1991.

The Kipling Society

Hon. Secretary Jane Keskar, 6 Clifton Road, London W9 1SS
tel 020-7286 0194
email jane@keskar.fsworld.co.uk
website www.kipling.org.uk
Membership £22 p.a. (£20 p.a. for standing orders)

Aims to honour and extend the influence of Rudyard Kipling (1865–1936), to assist in the study of his writings, to hold discussion meetings, to publish a quarterly journal, and to maintain a Kipling Library in London and a Kipling Room in The Grange, Rottingdean, near Brighton.

C.S. Lewis Society (Oxford)

Pusey House, St Giles, Oxford OX1 3LZ
email oulewis@herald.ox.ac.uk

Meets 8.15pm, Tuesday term-time at Pusey House, to promote knowledge of C.S. Lewis (1898–1963) and the writers who influenced him, including J.R.R. Tolkien, Charles Williams, Dorothy L. Sayers, G.K. Chesterton and George MacDonald. Open to non-University members.

The C.S. Lewis Society (New York)

Secretary Clare Sarrocco, 84–23, 77th Avenue, Glendle, NY 11385–7706, USA
email subscribe@nycslsociety.com
website www.nycslsociety.com

The oldest society for the appreciation and discussion of C.S. Lewis (1898–1963). Founded 1969.

Little Theatre Guild of Great Britain

National Secretary, Barbara Watson, 181 Brampton Road, Carlisle CA3 9AX
tel (01228) 522649
website www.littletheatreguild.org

Aims to promote closer cooperation amongst the little theatres constituting its membership; to act as coordinating and representative body on behalf of the little theatres; to maintain and advance the highest standards in the art of theatre; and to assist in encouraging the establishment of other little theatres. Its yearbook is available to non-members for £5.

The Livesey Museum for Children

682 Old Kent Road, London SE15 1JF
tel 020-7639 5604 *fax* 020-7277 5384
email info@liveseymuseum.org.uk
website www.liveseymuseum.org.uk

An all-new interactive exhibition is shown every year for children under 12 years old, their families, carers and teachers. Children can learn things by experimenting and investigating, by using their imaginations – and by having fun! Exhibitions are designed to support the National Curriculum at Foundation Stage, KS1 and KS2.

L.M. Montgomery Heritage Society

L.M. Montgomery Institute , University of Prince Edward Island, 550 University Avenue, Charlottetown, Prince Edward Island, Canada C1A 4P3
tel 902-628-4346 *fax* 902-628-4345
email lmminst@upei.ca
website www.lmontgomery.ca

The Society is dedicated to protecting L.M. Montgomery's (1874–1942) Prince Edward Island literary and historic legacy for the benefit, education and enjoyment of the public. The Society is a non-profit organisation made up of representatives from Island heritage sites and groups with a mutual interest in preserving and promoting Montgomery's Island home. As part of its mandate, the Society holds events honouring the life and times of Montgomery, including an annual birthday celebration held each November and the L.M. Montgomery Festival held each August. L.M. Montgomery is the author of Anne of Green Gables and Emily of New Moon. Founded 1994.

Museum of London

London Wall, London EC2Y 5HN
tel (0870) 444 3851 *fax* (0870) 444 3853
email info@museumoflondon.org.uk
website www.museumoflondon.org.uk

The Mythopoeic Society

Edith Crowe, Corresponding Secretary, The Mythopoeic Society, PO Box 320486, San Francisco, CA 94132-0486, USA

email edith.crowe@sjsu.edu
website www.mythsoc.org
Membership with Mythprint $20 p.a. (USA), $36 p.a. (rest of world)

A non-profit international literary and educational organization for the study, discussion, and enjoyment of fantastic and mythic literature, especially the works of Tolkien, C.S. Lewis, and Charles Williams. The word 'mythopoeic' (myth-oh-PAY-ik or myth-oh-PEE-ic), meaning 'mythmaking' or 'productive of myth', aptly describes much of the fictional work of the 3 authors who were also prominent members of an informal Oxford literary circle (1930s-1950s) known as the Inklings. Membership is open to all scholars, writers, and readers of these literatures. The Society sponsors 3 periodicals: *Mythprint* (a monthly bulletin of book reviews, articles and events), *Mythlore* (scholarly articles on mythic and fantastic literature), and *Mythic Circle* (a literary annual of original poetry and short stories). Each summer the Society holds an annual conference. Founded 1967.

National Art Library

Victoria and Albert Museum, South Kensington, London SW7 2RL
website www.vam.ac.uk/nal

A major reference library and the Victoria and Albert Museum's curatorial department for the art, craft and design of the book. All are welcome to use the facilities.

National Association for the Teaching of English (NATE)

50 Broadfield Road, Sheffield S8 0XJ
tel 0114-255 5419 *fax* 0114-255 5296
email info@nate.org.uk
website www.nate.org.uk

The professional association for all those working in English education in the UK. NATE provides information about current developments, publications and resource materials. It also funds research, in-service training and holds an annual and regional conferences. Annual membership gives members 5 copies of NATE's journal, newsletter and pupil age-related magazines and well as discounts on publications, courses and conferences. See website for details of how to join.

National Association of Writers' Groups

Headquarters The Arts Centre, Biddick Lane, Washington, Tyne and Wear NE38 2AB
tel (01262) 609228
email nawg@tesco.net
Secretary Mike Wilson, 40 Burstall Hill, Bridlington, East Yorkshire YO16 7GA
website www.nawg.co.uk
Membership £30 p.a. plus £5 registration per group; £12 Associate individuals

Aims 'to advance the education of the general public throughout the UK, including the Channel Islands, by promoting the study and art of writing in all its aspects.' Publishes *Link* bi-monthly magazine. Annual Festival of Writing held in Durham in September. Annual Creative Writing Competition. Founded 1995.

National Association of Writers in Education (NAWE)

PO Box 1, Sheffield Hutton, York YO6 7YU
tel (01653) 618429
website www.nawe.co.uk

Represents and supports writers, teachers and all those involved in the development of creative writing in education. Useful resource of writers who work in schools and communities is held on the website.

National Centre for Language and Literacy (NCLL)

University of Reading, Bulmershe Court, Reading RG6 1HY
tel 0118-378 8820
email ncll@reading.ac.uk
website www.ncll.org.uk

An independent organisation concerned with all aspects of language and literacy learning. The Centre supports teachers, parents and governors through its unique collection of resources, its publications, an extensive programme of courses and conferences, ongoing research and a membership scheme designed to meet the needs of individual schools.

National Centre for Research in Children's Literature (NCRCL)

Roehampton University, Froebel College, Roehampton Lane, London SW15 5PJ
tel 020-8392 3008 *fax* 020-8392 3819
email ncrcl@roehampton.ac.uk
website www.ncrcl.ac.uk

Facilitates and supports research exchange in the field of children's literature. The NCRCL is based in Roehampton University, which houses several collections held in the Children's Literature Centre and in the Froebel Archive for Childhood Studies. The website provides information on resources, activities and children's literature-related individuals and links to websites.

National Galleries of Scotland

National Gallery of Scotland, The Mound, Edinburgh EH2 2EL
tel 0131-624 6200, 0131-624 6332 (press office) *fax* 0131-343 3250 (press office)
email pressinfo@nationalgalleries.org
Scottish National Portrait Gallery, 1 Queen Street, Edinburgh EH2 1JD
Scottish National Gallery of Modern Art, Belford Road, Edinburgh EH4 3DR

The Dean Gallery, Belford Road, Edinburgh
EH4 3DS
website www.nationalgalleries.org

National Gallery
Trafalgar Square, London WC2N 5DN
tel 020-7747 2885 fax 020-7747 2423
website www.nationalgallery.org.uk

National Library for the Blind (NLB)
Far Cromwell Road, Bredbury, Stockport SK6 2SG
tel 0161-355 2000 minicom 0161-355 2043
fax 0161-355 2098
email enquiries@nlbuk.org
website www.nlb-online.org

A registered charity giving visually impaired adults and children access to books and information. The NLB houses Europe's largest collection of Braille and Moon books. It also publishes magazines for children and teenagers (see Magazines and newspapers for children) and spearheads the Right to Read campaign. Also houses a range of giant print books (24 point) which are available for loan.

National Literacy Association
1st Floor, Leonard House, 321 Bradford Street,
Digbeth, Birmingham B5 6ET
tel/fax 0121-622 5143
email mail@nla.org.uk
website www.nla.org.uk

Campaigns to raise awareness of the needs of underachievers and aims to ensure that school leavers will have adequate literacy for their needs in daily life. Produces publications and other resources including The Guide to Literacy Resources, which is distributed free to schools, parent groups, libraries and others.

National Literacy Trust
Swire House, 59 Buckingham Gate, London
SW1E 6AJ
tel 020-7828 2435 fax 020-7931 9986
email contact@literacytrust.org.uk
website www.literacytrust.org.uk, www.rif.org.uk,
www.readon.org.uk
Director Neil McClelland, PA Jacky Taylor

Independent registered charity dedicated to building a literate nation in which everyone enjoys the skills, self-esteem and pleasures that literacy can bring. The only organisation concerned with raising literacy standards for all age groups throughout the UK. Maintains an extensive website with literacy news, summaries of key issues, research and examples of practice nationwide; organises an annual conference, courses and training events, and runs a range of initiatives to turn promising ideas into effective action. Initiatives include the National Reading Campaign, funded by the government; Reading is Fundamental, UK, which provides free books to children; Reading The Game, involving the

professional football community; the Talk To Your Baby campaign; and the Literacy and Social Inclusion Project, a partnership with the Basic Skills Agency. Founded 1993.

National Museum Wales – see page 342

National Museums Liverpool
127 Dale Street, Liverpool L2 2JH
tel 0151-207 0001 fax 0151-478 4790
Venues: World Museum Liverpool, Walker Art Gallery, The Conservation Centre, Merseyside Maritime Museum, HM Customs & Excise National Museum, Museum of Liverpool Life, Lady Lever Art Gallery, Sundley House (re-opens 2007).

National Museums of Scotland
Chambers Street, Edinburgh EH1 1JF
tel 0131-225 7534 fax 0131-220 4819
website www.nms.ac.uk

National Portrait Gallery
St Martin's Place, London WC2H 0HE
tel 020-7306 0055 fax 020-7306 0056
website www.npg.org.uk

National Society for Education in Art and Design
The Gatehouse, Corsham Court, Corsham, Wilts.
SN13 0BZ
tel (01249) 714825 fax (01249) 716138
website www.nsead.org
General Secretary Dr John Steers NDD, ATC, PhD

The leading national authority concerned with art, craft and design across all phases of education in the UK. Offers the benefits of membership of a professional association, a learned society and a trade union. Has representatives on National and Regional Committees concerned with Art and Design Education. Publishes Journal of Art and Design Education (3 p.a.; Blackwells) and Start magazine for primary schools. Founded 1888.

Natural History Museum
Cromwell Road, London SW7 5BD
tel 020-7942 5000
website www.nhm.ac.uk

The Edith Nesbit Society
21 Churchfields, West Malling, Kent ME19 6RJ
email mccarthy804@aol.com
website www.the-railway-children.co.uk
Membership £7 p.a., £14 organisations/overseas

Aims to promote an interest in the life and works of Edith Nesbit (1858–1924) by means of talks, a regular newsletter and and other publications, and visits to relevant places. Founded 1996.

New Producers Alliance
The NPA Film Centre, Unit 1.07, The Tea Building,
56 Shoreditch High Street, London E1 6JJ

tel 020-7613 0440 *fax* 020-7729 1852
email queries@npa.org.uk
website www.npa.org.uk
Membership £75 p.a.

A national membership organisation and registered charity dedicated to providing essential training and networking opportunities for film-makers. Led by industry professionals, the NPA assists independent film-makers in developing their skills, contacts and creativity in line with working industry practices. Founded 1993.

New Writing North

2 School Lane, Whickham, Newcastle upon Tyne NE16 4SL
tel 0191-488 8580 *fax* 0191-488 8576
email mail@newwritingnorth.com
website www.newwritingnorth.com
Director Claire Malcolm

The literature development agency for the North East. Offers advice and support to writers of poetry, prose and plays. See website. Founded 1996.

Newcastle University Library

Robinson Library, Newcastle upon Tyne NE2 4HQ
tel 0191-222 7662
email lib-readersservices@ncl.ac.uk
website www.ncl.ac.uk/library

Historical children's books and other material relevant to the history of childhood and education. Over 100 collections of material ranging from rare books and archives to woodblocks and illustrations, from the mid 15th–21st century.

The Special Collections

tel 0191-222 5146
email lib-specenq@ncl.ac.uk
website www.ncl.ac.uk/library/specialcollections
Contains many historical children's books as well as a wealth of other material relevant to the history of childhood and education, especially 18th and 19th-century chapbooks (cheap, popular pamphlets sold by itinerant traders, and often used by children). Most of these are to be found in the internationally important Robert White Collection. Other collections include the Wallis Collection which contains material designed for the instruction of children; the Crawhall Collection which includes items such as the children's ABC books illustrated with woodcuts by Joseph Crawhall; the Bradshaw-Bewick Collection which contains several books designed for children and illustrated with woodcuts by Thomas Bewick. It also holds collections built up by schools from North-East England since the 16th century.

Special Collections at the Robinson Library is working in conjunction with Seven Stories to collect and preserve neglected collections of historical children's books.

The Booktrust Collection

Since the 1970s, most UK publishers have sent copies of every children's book they publish to Booktrust (see page 336), so that these books may be inspected and researched by the public. The Booktrust Collection is now housed in Newcastle University Library. The Collection currently contains approx. 60,000 items, including examples of toy and board books, picture books, young fiction and non-fiction. This number grows substantially each year. The Collection provides an overview of British children's book publishing of the recent period and therefore of illustration, pedagogy, printing, images of childhood, design, typography, and so on, i.e. all the many areas included in the making of books for children. This is as complete a collection of recent and contemporary British children's books as exists anywhere.

The Seven Stories Archive

Since 1997, Seven Stories (see page 337)has been forming a collection of manuscripts and artwork by British writers and illustrators for children, from 1945 to the present day. The archive includes manuscripts by: Joan Aiken, Peter Dickinson, Eva Ibbotson, Jan Mark, Philip Pullman, Michael Rosen, Sylvia Waugh and Ursula Moray Williams; and original artwork by: Edward Ardizzone, Quentin Blake, Michael Foreman, Shirley Hughes, Harold Jones and Diana Stanley. Major archival deposits to Seven Stories include the Kaye Webb archive, the Ladybird archive and the Robert Westall archive. Some of this archive is housed in the library.

Office for Standards in Education (OFSTED)

Alexandra House, 33 Kingsway, London WC2B 6SE
tel (08456) 404045 *fax* 020-7421 6707

A non-ministerial Government department established under the Education (Schools Act) 1992. Since April 2001 OFSTED has been responsible for inspecting all educational provision for 16–19 year-olds to establish and monitor an independent inspection system for maintained schools in England. Its inspection role also includes the inspection of local educational authorities, teacher training institutions and youth work. In September 2001, OFSTED took over the regulation of childcare providers, from 150 local authorities.

The Office of Communications (Ofcom)

Riverside House, 2A Southwark Bridge Road, London SE1 9HA
tel 020-7981 3040 *fax* 020-7981 3334
email contact@ofcom.org.uk
website www.ofcom.org.uk

Established to regulate the communications sector in the UK. It aims to further the interest of consumers in relevant markets, secure the optimum use of the radio spectrum, ensure the availability throughout the UK of TV and radio services and to protect the public from any offensive or potentially harmful effects of broadcast media, as well as safeguarding people from being unfairly treated in TV and radio programmes. Established 2003.

The Poetry Book Society – see page 159

The Poetry Library – see page 161

The Poetry Society – see page 160

Poetry Society Education – see page 164

The Beatrix Potter Society

Membership Secretary c/o The Lodge, Salisbury Avenue, Harpenden, Herts. AL5 2PS
tel (01582) 769755
email beatrixpottersociety@tiscali.co.uk
website www.beatrixpottersociety.org.uk
Membership £20 p.a. UK (£25 overseas), £25/£30 commercial/institutional

Promotes the study and appreciation of the life and works of Beatrix Potter (1866–1943) as author, artist, diarist, farmer and conservationist. Regular lecture meetings, conferences and events in the UK and USA. Quarterly newsletter. Small publishing programme. Founded 1980.

The Publishers Association

29B Montague Street, London WC1B 5BW
tel 020-7691 9191 *fax* 020-7691 9199
email mail@publishers.org.uk
website www.publishers.org.uk
Chief Executive Ronnie Williams OBE, *Director of International and Trade Divisions (BDCI)* Simon Bell, *Director of Educational, Academic & Professional Publishing* Graham Taylor
Founded 1896.

Qualifications and Curriculum Authority (QCA)

83 Piccadilly, London W1J 8QA
tel 020-7509 5555 *fax* 020-7509 6666
email info@qca.org.uk
website www.qca.org.uk
Chairman Sir Anthony Greener, *Chief Executive* Dr Ken Boston

An independent government agency funded by the DfES. It is responsible for ensuring that the curriculum and qualifications available to young people and adults are of a high quality and are coherent and flexible. Its remit ranges from the under-fives to higher level vocational qualifications.

The Arthur Ransome Society Ltd (TARS)

Abbott Hall Museum, Kendal, Cumbria LA9 5AL
tel (01539) 722464
website www.humbolt1.com/ar
President Norman Willis

To celebrate the life, promote the works, and diffuse the ideas of Arthur Ransome (1884–1967), author of the world-famous *Swallows and Amazons* series of books for children. The Society seeks in particular to encourage children and others to engage, with due regard to safety, in adventurous pursuits; educate the public generally about Ransome and his work; sponsor research in relevant areas; be a communications link for those interested in any aspect of Arthur Ransome's life and works. Founded 1990.

REACH: National Advice Centre for Children with Reading Difficulties

2 Station Road, Gerrards Cross, Bucks SL9 8EL
tel (01753) 888688 *fax* (01753) 888699

Offers advice and assistance on children's reading disability and a comprehensive resource collection of books and materials in a user-friendly environment for both children and adults. Phone first for an appointment during opening hours (Mon–Fri 10am–5pm).

Readathon

The Parsonage, St Mary's, Chalford, Stroud GL6 8QB
tel (0870) 240 1124
email reading@readathon.org
website www.readathon.org

Readathon was set up to encourage children to read more books. Children undertake to read books, or do other literacy-based activities, in return for pledges of money, for charity, from family and friends. Thousands of schools have contributed to this success, and have made the Readathon campaign Britain's largest sponsored literary event. On joining, a free pack containing everything needed to run a successful Readathon is supplied.

Since it began Readathon has raised well over £17 million, which has been shared equally between two charities, the Roald Dahl Foundation and Sargent Cancer Care for Children. Fundraising costs are kept to a minimum because Readathon receives support from booksellers, children's publishers, and many organisations concerned with books and reading. Founded 1984.

Reading is Fundamental, UK

National Literacy Trust, Swire House,
59 Buckingham Gate, London SW1E 6AJ
tel 020-7828 2435 *fax* 020-7931 9986
email rif@literacytrust.org.uk
website www.rif.org.uk

An initiative of the National Literacy Trust that helps children and young people (aged 0–19) to realise their potential by motivating them to read. Working with volunteers, it delivers targeted literacy projects that promote: the fun of reading; the importance of book choice; and the benefits to families of sharing books at home.

Children in each project choose up to 3 free books a year to keep at special events involving families and local volunteers; receive a book bag, bookmark, bookplates and stickers; and enjoy fun activities that highlight the pleasures of reading and often involve authors, poets, storytellers and illustrators.

Established in 1996 following the success of RIF Inc. (the largest children's and family literacy programme in the USA), RIF, UK has distributed 700,000 books to over 234,000 children and young people, and currently supports around 300 projects reaching 24,000 children. RIF, UK projects are set up in schools, libraries, football clubs, early years centres, bookshops, after-school and study support centres, women's refuges, prisons and parents' groups.

The Malcolm Saville Society
Chairman Richard Griffiths, 78A Windmill Road, Mortimer, Berks. RG7 3RL
email mystery@witchend.com
website www.witchend.com
Membership £10 p.a. (£12.50 Europe, £16 elsewhere)

Aims to remember and promote interest in the work of Malcolm Saville (1901–82), children's author. Regular social activities, book search, library, contact directory and magazine (4 p.a.). Founded 1994.

Scattered Authors Society
Secretary Yvonne Coppard, 35 Thornton Way, Girton, Cambridge CB3 0NL
email yvonnecoppard@aol.com

Aims to provide a forum for informal discussion, contact and support for professional writers in children's fiction. Founded 1998.

School Library Association
Unit 2, Lotmead Business Village, Lotmead Farm, Wanborough, Swindon SN4 0UY
tel (01793) 791787 *fax* (01793) 791786

Promotes the development of school libraries and information literacy as central to the curriculum. It publishes booklists and guidelines for library and resource centres, a quarterly journal and provides training and an information service.

Science Museum
Exhibition Road, London SW7 2DD
tel (0870) 870 4868
email sciencemuseum@nmsi.ac.uk
website www.sciencemuseum.org.uk

Scottish Arts Council
12 Manor Place, Edinburgh EH3 7DD
tel 0131-226 6051, (0845) 603 6000 (help desk; local rate) *fax* 0131-225 9833
email help.desk@scottisharts.org.uk
website www.scottisharts.org.uk
Chief Executive Graham Berry, *Head of Literature* Dr Gavin Wallace, *Head of Visual Arts* Amanda Catto

The lead body for the funding, development and advocacy of the arts in Scotland. Offers a unique national perspective on the provision and management of the arts which seeks to balance the needs of all arts sectors and all parts of Scotland. The expertise and experience of Scottish Arts Council in developing sound policy and good practice includes the ability to interrelate arts and socio-economic policy objectives. Also offers a focus on research, information provision and international writing.

The Council invests £60 million from Scottish Executive and National Lottery funding to support and develop artistic excellence and creativity throughout Scotland. Supports a range of artists, arts organisations and projects across Scotland. The Council funds awards, bursaries, fellowships and training opportunities for individuals, as well as for a range of arts projects.

Scottish Book Trust (SBT)
Sandeman House, 55 High Street, Edinburgh EH1 1SR
tel 0131-524 0160 *fax* 0131-524 0161
email info@scottishbooktrust.com
website www.scottishbooktrust.com

With a particular responsibility towards Scottish writing, SBT exists to promote literature and reading, and aims to reach (and create) a wider reading public than has existed before. It also organises exhibitions, readings and storytellings, national author tours, administers the Live Literature Scotland Scheme, operates an extensive children's reference library and provides a book information service for writers and readers. SBT has a range of publications and advises other relevant art organisations. Its latest initiative, BRAW (Books, Reading and Writing), the Network for the Scottish Children's Book, aims to promote books, reading and writing, by authors and illustrators living in Scotland and for young people across Scotland. Founded 1960.

Scottish Publishers Association
Scottish Book Centre, 137 Dundee Street, Edinburgh EH11 1BG
tel 0131-228 6866 *fax* 0131-228 3220
email enquiries@scottishbooks.org
website www.scottishbooks.org
Chairman Janis Adams, *Director* Lorraine Fannin, *Vice-Chair* Neil Wilson, *Finance & Office Administrator* Carol Lothian, *Member Services Manager* Liz Small, *Information & Personal Development Administrator* Katherine A. Naish

Founded 1973.

The Scottish Storytelling Forum
The Scottish Storytelling Centre, 43–45 High Street, Edinburgh EH1 1SR
tel 0131-557 5724 *fax* 0131-557 5224
website www.scottishstorytellingcentre.co.uk

Scotland's national charity for oral storytelling, established to encourage and support the telling and sharing of stories across all ages and all sectors of society, in particular those who, for reasons of poverty or disability, were excluded from artistic experiences. The Scottish Storytelling Centre is the Forum's resource and training centre. The Storytelling Network has over 100 professional storytellers across Scotland. Founded 1992.

Seven Stories – the Centre for the Children's Book – see page 337

Society for Editors and Proofreaders (SfEP)

(formerly Society of Freelance Editors and Proofreaders)
Office Riverbank House, 1 Putney Bridge Approach, London SW6 3JD
tel 020-7736 3278
email admin@sfep.org.uk
website www.sfep.org.uk

Works to promote high editorial standards and achieve recognition of its members' professional status, through local and national meetings, an annual conference, an email discussion group, a regular newsletter and a programme of reasonably priced workshops/training sessions. These sessions help newcomers to acquire basic skills, enable experienced editors to update their skills or broaden their competence, and also cover aspects of professional practice or business for the self-employed. An annual Directory of members' services is available. The Society supports moves towards recognised standards of training and accreditation for editors and proofreaders and has developed its own Accreditation in Proofreading qualification. It has close links with the Publishing Training Centre and the Society of Indexers, is represented on the BSI Technical Committee dealing with copy preparation and proof correction (BS 5261), and works to foster good relations with all relevant bodies and organisations in the UK and worldwide. Founded 1988.

Society for Storytelling (SfS)

PO Box 2344, Reading, Berks. RG6 7FG
tel 0118-935 1381
email sfs@fairbruk.demon.co.uk
website www.sfs.org.uk

Provides information on oral storytelling, events, storytellers and traditional stories. SfS volunteers have specialist knowledge of storytelling in education, health, therapy and business settings. To increase public awareness of the art it promotes National Storytelling Week, which takes place in the first week of February. The SfS provides a network for anyone interested in the art of oral storytelling whether they are full-time storytellers, use storytelling in their work, tell for the love or it or just want to listen. It holds an annual conference each Spring and produces

a quarterly newsletter, a *Directory of Storytellers* and a variety of books and fact sheets. Founded 1993.

Society of Artists Agents

21c Montpellier Row, London SE3 0RL
tel (07870) 628 709
email jennieward@btopenworld.com
website www.thesaa.com
Contact Jennifer Ward

Formed to promote professionalism in the illustration industry and to forge closer links between clients and artists through an agreed set of guidelines. The Society believes in an ethical approach through proper terms and conditions, thereby protecting the interests of the artists and clients. Founded 1992.

The Society of Authors – see page 333

Society of Children's Book Writers and Illustrators (SCBWI)

36 Mackenzie Road, Beckenham, Kent BR3 4RU
tel 020-8249 9716
email ra@britishscbwi.org
website www.britishscbwi.org
Regional Adviser, SCBWI–British Isles Natascha Biebow
Membership £44 p.a. plus a one-off fee of £8.50

An international network for the exchange of knowledge between professional writers, illustrators, editors, publishers, agents, librarians, educators, booksellers and others involved with literature for young people. Sponsors 3 annual conferences on writing and illustrating children's books and multimedia – in New York (February), Los Angeles (August) and Bologna (spring) – as well as dozens of regional conferences and events throughout the world. Publishes a bi-monthly newsletter, *The Bulletin*, and information publications, and awards grants for works in progress. The SCBWI also presents the annual Golden Kite Award for the best fiction and non-fiction books, which is open both to published and unpublished writers and illustrators.

The SCBWI British Isles region meets regularly for speaker or workshop events. Also sponsors local critique groups and publishes *Words and Pictures* quarterly newsletter, which includes up-to-date events and marketing information, interviews and articles on the craft of children's writing and illustrating in the British Isles. The yearly Writers' Day and Illustrators' Day includes workshops and the opportunity to meet publishing professionals. Founded 1971.

Society of Editors

Director Bob Satchwell, University Centre, Granta Place, Mill Lane, Cambridge CB2 1RU
tel (01223) 304080 *fax* (01223) 304090
email info@societyofeditors.org
website www.societyofeditors.org

Membership £230 p.a.

Formed from the merger of the Guild of Editors and the Association of British Editors, the Society has more than 450 members in national, regional and local newspapers, magazines, broadcasting, new media, journalism education and media law, campaigning for media freedom. Founded 1999.

Society of Young Publishers

Contact The Secretary, c/o The Bookseller, Endeavour House, 189 Shaftesbury Avenue, London WC2H 8TJ
email info@thesyp.org.uk
website www.thesyp.org.uk
Membership Open to anyone employed in publishing or hoping to be soon; Associate membership available to those over the age of 35

Organises monthly speaker meetings at which senior figures talk on topics of key importance to the industry today, and social and other events. Runs a job database which matches candidates with potential employers. Meetings are held in Central London, usually on the last Wednesday of the month at 6.30pm. Also a branch in Oxford. Founded 1949.

Speaking of Books

105 John Humphries House, 4 Stockwell Street, London SE10 9JN
tel 020-8858 6616

Arranges school visits by writers, illustrators and storytellers and book-related in-service training activities and bookstalls.

The Robert Louis Stevenson Club

Secretary Dr Alan Marchbank, 12 Dean Park, Longniddry, East Lothian EH32 0QR
tel (01875) 852976 *fax* (01875) 853328
email alan@amarchbank.freeserve.co.uk
website www.rlsclub.org.uk
Membership £20 p.a., £150 10 years

Aims to foster interest in Robert Louis Stevenson's life (1850–94) and works through various events and its newsletter. Founded 1920.

The Swedish Institute for Children's Books (Svenska barnboksinstitutet)

Odengatan 61, SE–113 22 Stockholm, Sweden
tel (0)8-54 54 20 50 *fax* (0)8-54 54 20 54
email info@sbi.kb.se
website www.sbi.kb.se

A special library open to the public and an information centre for children's and young people's literature. The aim is to promote this kind of literature in Sweden as well as Swedish children's and young people's literature abroad. Founded 1967.

Tate

Tate Britain, Millbank, London SW1P 4RG
tel 020-7887 8008, 020-7887 8000 (admin)

email information@tate.org.uk
Tate Modern, Bankside, London SE1 9TG
tel 020-7887 8008
Tate Liverpool, Albert Dock, Liverpool L3 4BB
tel 0151-702 7400
Tate St Ives, Porthmeor Beach, St Ives, Cornwall TR26 1TG
tel (01736) 796226
website www.tate.org.uk

Teenage Magazine Arbitration Panel (TMAP)

28 Kingsway, London WC2B 6JR
tel 020-7405 0819, 020-7405 0819 *fax* 020-7404 4167
website www.ppa.co.uk/tmap

The magazine industry's self-regulatory body which ensures that the sexual content of teenage magazines is presented in a responsible and appropriate manner.

Theatre Museum

National Museum of the Performing Arts, 1E Tavistock Street, London WC2E 7PR
tel 020-7943 4700 *fax* 020-7943 4777
website http://theatremuseum.org

In addition to its exhibitions and extensive education programme, the Museum has an unrivalled collection of programmes, playbills, prints, photos, videos, texts and press cuttings relating to performers and productions from the 17th century onwards. Available by appointment (book 3 weeks in advance), free of charge through the Study Room. Open Wed–Fri 10.30am–4.30pm. Reprographic services available. The Theatre Museum's reading room will be relocated to West Kensington during 2005. Please see website for details.

The Tolkien Society

Secretary Sally Kennett, 210 Prestbury Road, Cheltenham GL52 3ER
email membership@tolkiensociety.org
website www.tolkiensociety.org
Membership Secretary Claire Chambers, 8 Queens Lane, Eynsham, Witney OX29 4HL
Membership 20 p.a.

Union of Welsh Publishers & Booksellers

c/o Honno Press/Editorial Office, Pen Roc, Rhodfa'r Mor, Aberystwyth SY23 2AZ
tel (01970) 623150
Contact Elin Ap Hywel

United Kingdom Literacy Association (UKLA)

Upton House, Baldock Street, Royston, Herts. SG8 5AY
tel (01763) 241188 *fax* (01763) 243785
email admin@ukla.org
website www.ukla.org

UKLA is a registered charity, which has as its sole object the advancement of education in literacy. It is committed to promoting good practice nationally and internationally in literacy and language teaching and research. Its activities include:

• a conference programme of international, national and local conferences reflecting language and literacy interests.

• an active publications committee. Members are kept up to date via UKLA journals and website. Members receive a copy of both the newsletter, *UKLA News* (3 p.a.), and the recently renamed journal *Literacy* (see *Magazines about children's literature*). For an additional subscription, members can receive the *Journal of Research in Reading*. Both of the UKLA journals are refereed and include research reports, both qualitative and quantitative research, and critiques of current policy and practice as well as discussions and debates about current issues. UKLA also produces a range of books, written mainly with teachers and students in mind.

• regular responses to national consultations, including those organised through the DfES or QCA. Consequently, the UKLA often seeks information and responses from its members, as well as establishing a UKLA response to particular issues.

• promoting and disseminating research. UKLA provides support and small grants for literacy research.

• networking – UKLA helps its members to network both in the UK and through its worldwide contacts. UKLA's affiliation to the International Reading Association enables it to keep members in touch with events and ideas in other parts of the world. UKLA is also involved in specific international projects such as Project Connect, for which it provides some support for literacy education in Uganda.

Founded in 1963 as the United Kingdom Reading Association; renamed the United Kingdom Literacy Association in 2003.

V&A Museum of Childhood

Cambridge Heath Road, London E2 9PA
tel 020-8980 2415 (24-hour Information Line)
fax 020-8983 5225
website www.museumofchildhood.org.uk

Holds one of the largest and oldest collections of toys and childhood artefacts in the world. As well as its permanent displays, the museum has temporary exhibitions, and every weekend, has art activities for children aged 5+ and soft play for under 5 year-olds, with additional activities during school holidays.

Victoria and Albert Museum

South Kensington, London SW7 2RL
tel 020-7942 2000
email www.vanda@vam.ac.uk
website www.vam.ac.uk

Voice of the Listener & Viewer Ltd (VLV)

101 King's Drive, Gravesend, Kent DA12 5BQ
tel (01474) 352835 *fax* (01474) 351112

email info@vlv.org.uk
website www.vlv.org.uk
Chairman Jocelyn Hay, *Administrative Secretary* Sue Washbrook

Represents the citizen and consumer interests in broadcasting: it is an independent, non-profit-making society working to ensure independence, quality and diversity in broadcasting. VLV is funded by its members and is free from sectarian, commercial and political affiliations. It holds public lectures, seminars and conferences, and has frequent contact with MPs and other relevant parties. It provides an independent forum where all with an interest in broadcasting can speak on equal terms. It produces a quarterly news bulletin and holds its own archive and those of the former Broadcasting Research Unit (1980–90) and BACTV (British Action for Children's Television). It maintains a panel of speakers, the VLV Forum for Children's Broadcasting, the VLV Forum for Educational Broadcasting, and acts as a secretariat for the European Alliance of Listeners' and Viewers' Associations (EURALVA). VLV does not handle complaints. Founded 1984.

Volunteer Reading Help (VRH)

VRH Central Office, Charity House,
14–15 Perseverance Works, 38 Kingsland Road,
London E2 8DD
tel 020-7729 4087 *fax* 020-7729 7643
email info@vrh.org.uk
website www.vrh.org.uk

A national charity that helps book-shy children become word-wise children. It recruits and trains volunteers to work with children aged 6–11 who find reading a challenge. The reading helpers support the same children every week, giving each an hour of quality, one-to-one time.

Welsh Animation Group (WAG)

Contact Georgia Anderegg, WAG Treasurer,
13 Bangor Street, Cardiff CF24 3LQ
tel 029-2048 1420
website http://wag.sequence.co.uk
Chair Robin Lyons
Membership Waged £25, unemployed £15, student £5, studio/corporate £200

Aims to bring together everybody working in animation in Wales, 'to build on the creative and economic successes of animation in Wales... to promote Welsh animation both nationally and throughout the world... to lobby for economic growth and the creation of jobs in the industry, and nurture the creative talent that has already brought Welsh animation international acclaim.' Holds regular meetings where animators can show their work, network, and voice their opinions. Helps to organise the Animation Day at the International Film Festival of Wales. Founded 1999.

Welsh Books Council/Cyngor Llyfrau Cymru

Castell Brychan, Aberystwyth, Ceredigion SY23 2JB
tel (01970) 624151 *fax* (01970) 625385
email castellbrychan@cllc.org.uk
website www.cllc.org.uk, www.gwales.com
Director Gwerfyl Pierce Jones

A national body funded directly by the Welsh Asssembly Government which provides a focus for the publishing industry in Wales. Awards grants for publishing in Welsh and English. Provides services to the trade in the fields of editing, design, marketing and distribution. The Council is a key enabling institution in the world of books and provides services and information in this field to all who are associated with it. Founded 1961.

The Henry Williamson Society

General Secretary Sue Cumming, 7 Monmouth Road, Dorchester, Dorset DT1 2DE
tel (01305) 264092
email zseagull@aol.com
Membership Secretary Margaret Murphy, 16 Doran Drive, Redhill, Surrey RH1 6AX
tel (01737) 763228
email mm@misterman.freeserve.co.uk
website www.henrywilliamson.org
Chairman John Gregory
Membership £12 p.a.

Aims to encourage a wider readership and greater understanding of the literary heritage left by Henry Williamson (1895–1977). Two meetings annually; also weekend activities. Publishes an annual journal. Founded 1980.

Working Group Against Racism in Children's Resources

Unit 34, Eurolink Business Centre, 49 Effra Road, London SW2 1BZ
tel/fax 020-7501 9992
website www.wgarcr.org.uk

A registered charity dedicated to training anyone working with children in the identification and elimination of racist images, language and sterotypes in children's books, resources and play materials.

Writernet

(formerly New Playwrights Trust)
Cabin V, Clarendon Buildings, 25 Horsell Road, London N5 1XL
tel 020-7609 7474 *fax* 020-7609 7557
email info@writernet.org.uk
website www.writernet.org.uk
Director Jonathan Meth, *Chair* Bonnie Greer, *Administrator* Anne-Marie Draycott

Provides writers for all forms of live and recorded performance – working at any stage in their career, and in diverse contexts – with a range of services that enable them to pursue their careers better. These include: a network connecting dramatic writers to the industry and to each other; online resources to support dramatic writers and those who work with them; providing a wide range of producers with the opportunity to make more informed choices to meet their needs; as well as a script-reading service, publications and guides. It aims to help writers from all parts of the country and a wide diversity of backgrounds to fulfil their potential both inside and outside the new-writing mainstream. Founded 1985.

Writers Advice Centre for Children's Books

16 Smith's Yard, Summerley Street, London SW18 4NR
tel (07979) 9905353
email info@writersadvice.co.uk
website www.writersadvice.co.uk
Editorial Director Louise Jordan

Dedicated to helping new and published children's writers by offering both editorial advice and tips on how to get published. The Centre also runs an online children's writing correspondence course plus a self-publishing service under its own imprint. Founded 1994.

The Writers' Guild of Great Britain

15 Britannia Street, London WC1X 9JN
tel 020-7833 0777 *fax* 020-7833 4777
email admin@writersguild.org.uk
website www.writersguild.org.uk
General Secretary Bernie Corbett
Membership Open to all persons entitled to claim a single piece of written work of any length for which payment has been received under written contract, in terms not less favourable than those existing in current minimum-terms agreements negotiated by the Guild. Candidate membership (£90) is open to all those who are taking their first steps into writing but who have not yet received a contract. The minimum subscription is currently £150, or 1% of an author's income earned from professional writing sources in the previous calendar year, with a cap of £1500. All Full members are automatically members of the Authors Licensing and Collecting Society (ALCS). The Guild is a corporate member of the ALCS and is represented on its board.

A trade union for all professional writers working in TV, radio, film, theatre, books and multimedia, it is affiliated to the Trades Union Congress (TUC) and has more than 2000 members. The Guild represents writers in matters such as terms of pay and credits for their work. The Minimum Terms Agreements and advice services aim to safeguard writers against exploitation. Also offered are professional, cultural and social activities to help provide writers with a sense of community, making writing a less isolated occupation. Further information and advice for writers working in theatre, film, radio or TV can be found in *Writers' and Artists' Yearbook*, also published by A & C Black.

Members receive the *Writers' Bulletin*, which carries articles, letters and reports written by members, plus an email newsletter every Friday. Other benefits include free entry to the British Library reading rooms, and reduced entry to the National Film Theatre and regional film theatres. Founded in 1958.

Youth Libraries Group (YLG)

Bromley Central Library, High Street, Bromley BR1 1EX
tel 020-8461 7193 *fax* 020-8313 9975
email ian.dodds@bromley.gov.uk

Secretary Ian Dodds

The YLG is open to all members of the Chartered Institute for Library and Information Professionals (CILIP) who are interested in children's work. At a national level its aims are:
• to influence the provision of library services for children and the provision of quality literature;
• to inspire and support all librarians working with children and young people; and
• to liaise with other national professional. organisations in pursuit of such aims.

At a local level, the YLG organises regular training courses, supports professional development and provides opportunities to meet colleagues. It holds an annual conference and judges the CILIP Carnegie and Kate Greenaway Awards (see page 366). It also produces the journal *Youth Library Review*.

Children's book and illustration prizes and awards

This list provides details of prizes, competitions and awards for children's writers and artists. See page 375 for a *Calendar of awards.*

The Hans Christian Andersen Awards
Details International Board on Books for Young People, Nonnenweg 12, Postfach, CH–4003 Basel, Switzerland
tel (61) 272 29 17 *fax* (61) 272 27 57
email ibby@ibby.org
website www.ibby.org

The Medals are awarded every 2 years to a living author and an illustrator who by the outstanding value of their work are judged to have made a lasting contribution to literature for children and young people. 2006 award winners: Margaret Mahy (author) and Wolf Erlbruch (illustrator).

Angus Book Award
Details Moyra Hood, Educational Resources Librarian, Educational Resources Service, Angus Council, Leisure Services, Bruce House, Wellgate, Arbroath DD11 3TL
tel (01241) 435008
email hoodm@angus.gov.uk
website www.angus.gov.uk/bookaward

An annual award originally set up as an Angus Council initiative to encourage pupils to read and enjoy quality teenage fiction. It is based on pupils not only voting for the winner but actively participating in all aspects of the award from selection of the shortlist to the award ceremony. The award involves 3rd-year pupils from all 8 secondary schools in Angus in reading 5 shortlisted titles. The shortlist is selected by teachers, librarians and pupils from books appropriate for the 14–15 year-old age group, written by authors living in the UK and published in paperback between July and June of the preceding year. Titles are chosen that reflect the range of themes which interest teenagers whilst challenging and interesting both committed and less enthusiastic readers. As part of the shortlisting process authors agree to visit schools and attend the Award ceremony, which takes place in May. The winner receives a miniature replica of the Aberlemno Serpent stone and £500. 2006 winner: *TWOC* by Graham Joyce (Faber and Faber). Launched 1996.

Arts Council England
Details The Literature Dept, Arts Council England, 14 Great Peter Street, London SW1P 3NQ
tel (0845) 300 6200 *textphone* 020-7973 6564
fax 020-7973 6590
email enquiries@artscouncil.org.uk
website www.artscouncil.org.uk

Arts Council England presents national prizes rewarding creative talent in the arts. These are awarded through the Council's flexible funds and are not necessarily open to application: the Children's Award, the David Cohen Prize for Literature, the Independent Foreign Fiction Prize, John Whiting Award, Meyer Whitworth Award and the Raymond Williams Community Publishing Prize. See the separate entries for details.

Arts Council England, London
Details David Cross, Literature Administrator, Arts Council England, London, 2 Pear Tree Court, London EC1R 0DS
tel 020-7608 6184 *fax* 020-7608 4100
website www.artscouncil.org.uk

Arts Council, England, London, is the regional office for the Capital, covering 33 boroughs and the City of London. Grants are available through the 'Grants for the arts' scheme throughout the year to support a variety of literature projects, concentrating particularly on:
• original works of poetry and literary fiction and professional development for individual writers, including writers of children's books;
• touring and live literature;
• small independent literary publishers; and
• literary translation into English.
    Contact Literature Unit for more information or see website for an application form.

Askews Torchlight Children's Book Award
Details 218–222 North Road, Preston, Lancs. PR1 1SY
tel (01772) 555947 *fax* (01772) 254860
email roberts@askews.co.uk
website www.askews.co.uk

To highlight quality fiction for 9–12 year-olds, written by authors who have not already been shortlisted for major awards. 2006 winner: *Percy Jackson and the Lightning Thief* by Rick Riordan (Puffin).

Association for Library Service to Children Awards
American Library Association, 50 East Huron, Chicago, IL 60611–2795, USA

tel 800-545-2433 ext. 2163 *fax* 312-944-7671
email alsc@ala.org

The following awards are administered by ALSC:
The Caldecott Medal was named in honor of the 19th century English illustrator Randolph Caldecott. It is awarded annually to the artist of the most distinguished American picture book for children.

The Newbery Medal was named after the 18th century British bookseller John Newbery. It is awarded annually to the author of the most distinguished contribution to American literature for children.

The Theodor Seuss Geisel Award is given annually to the author(s) and illustrator(s) of the most distinguished contribution to the body of American children's literature known as beginning reader books published in the United States during the preceding year. The award is to recognise the author(s) and illustrator(s) of a beginning reader book who demonstrate great creativity and imagination in his/her/their literary and artistic achievements to engage children in reading. The Award is named for the world-renowned children's author, Theodor Geisel. 'A person's a person no matter how small,' Theodor Geisel, a.k.a. Dr. Seuss, would say. 'Children want the same things we want: to laugh, to be challenged, to be entertained and delighted.' Established 2004.

The Robert F. Sibert Informational Book Award is given annually to the author of the most distinguished informational book published in English during the preceding year.

The Wilder Medal, a bronze medal, honors an author or illustrator whose books, published in the USA, have made, over a period of years, a substantial and lasting contribution to literature for children.

The Aventis Prizes for Science Books

Details The Royal Society, 6–9 Carlton House Terrace, London SW1Y 5AG
tel 020-7451 2513 *fax* 020-7451 2693
email scott.keir@royalsoc.ac.uk
website www.sciencebookprizes.com

These annual prizes reward books that make science more accessible to readers of all ages and backgrounds. Prizes of up to a total of £30,000 are awarded in 2 categories: General (£10,000) for a book with a general readership; and Junior (£10,000) for a book written for people aged under 14. Up to 5 shortlisted authors in each category receive £1000.

Eligible books should be written in English and their first publication in the UK must have been between 1 January and 31 December each year. Seven copies of each entry should be supplied with a fully completed entry form. Publishers may submit any number of books for each prize. Entries may cover any aspect of science and technology but educational textbooks published for professional or specialist audiences are not eligible. 2006 prize winners: General – *Electric Universe – How Electricity Switched on the Modern World* by David Bodians (Little,

Brown); Junior – *The Global Garden* by Kate Petty, Jennie Maizels and Corina Fletcher (Eden Project). The prizes are managed by the Royal Society in cooperation with the sponsor, Aventis. Founded 1988.

Bardd Plant Cymru (Children's Poet Laureate)

Welsh Books Council, Castell Brychan, Aberystwyth, Ceredigion SY23 2JB
tel (01970) 624151 *fax* (01970) 625385
website www.cllc.org.uk

Basic Skills Book Awards

Welsh Books Council, Castell Brychan, Aberystwyth, Ceredigion SY23 2JB
tel (01970) 624151 *fax* (01970) 625385
website www.cllc.org.uk

As part of the Welsh Assembly Government's National Basic Skills Strategy, awards are made in categories including Primary Age-group, Secondary Age-group and Adult.

The Bisto Book of the Year Awards – see The CBI Bisto Book of the Year Awards

Blue Peter Children's Book Awards

Details Fraser Ross Associates, 6 Wellington Avenue, Edinburgh EH6 7EQ
tel 0131-553 2759 *fax* 0131-657 4412
website www.bbc.co.uk/bluepeter

Awarded annually and judged by a panel of adults and children. There are 3 categories: the Book I Couldn't Put Down, the Best Illustrated Book to Read Aloud and the Best Book with Facts. Books must be published in paperback between 1 May and 31 April the preceding year. Winners are announced in December on a Blue Peter special broadcast by CBBC. 2005 winners: Best Illustrated Book to Read Aloud: *The Snail and the Whale* by Julia Donaldson and Axel Scheffler (Macmillan); the Best Book with Facts: *Explorers Wanted! At the North Pole* by Simon Chapman (Egmont); the Book I Couldn't Put Down and overall winner of Book of the Year: *Private Peaceful* by Michael Morpurgo (Collins).

BolognaRagazzi Award

Piazza Costituzione 6, 40128 Bologna, Italy
tel (051) 282242/282361 *fax* (051) 6374011
email bookfair@bolognafiere.it
website www.bookfair.bolognafiere.it
Takes place April 24–27 2007

Winners of the BolognaRagazzi Award are displayed at the Bologna Children's Book Fair. Prizes are given to encourage excellence in children's publishing in the categories of fiction, non-fiction and 'new horizons' (books from emerging countries). The books are judged on the basis of their creativity, educational value and artistic design.

Booktrust Early Years Awards

Details Booktrust, Book House, 45 East Hill, London SW18 2QZ
tel 020-8516 2972/2960 *fax* 020-8516 2978
email tarryn@booktrust.org.uk,
helen@booktrust.org.uk
website www.booktrusted.org.uk
Contacts Tarryn McKay, Helen Hayes

The winners of each of 3 categories, Baby Book Award, Pre-School Award and Best New Illustrator, each receive £2000. The winning publishers will also receive a commemorative award. Closing date: June 2007. 2005 winners: Baby Book Award – *Poppy Cat's Farm* by Lara Jones (Campbell Books); Pre-School Award – *The Very Dizzy Dinosaur* by Jack Tickle (Little Tiger Press); Best New Illustrator – *The Fantastic Mr Wani* by Kanako Usui (Little Tiger Press). Established 1999 as the Sainsbury's Baby Book Award.

The Booktrust Teenage Prize

Details Booktrust, Book House, 45 East Hill, London SW18 2QZ
tel 020-8516 2986 *fax* 020-8516 2978
email hannah@booktrust.org.uk
website www.bookheads.org.uk
Contact Hannah Rutland

The first annual national book prize to recognise and celebrate the best in young adult fiction. The author of the best book for teenagers receives £2500 and is chosen from a shortlist of 6. Eligible books must be fiction, aimed at teenagers between the ages of 13 and 16 and written in English by a citizen of the UK, or an author resident in the UK. The work must be published between 1 July and 30 June by a UK publisher.

2005 winner: *Century* by Sarah Singleton (Simon & Schuster). 2005 shortlist: *Sugar Rush* by Julie Burchill (Young Picador), *Siberia* by Ann Halam (Orion), *Come Clean* by Terri Paddock (HarperCollins), *The Whisper* by Bali Rai (Corgi), *How I Live Now* by Meg Rosoff (Penguin), *Century* by Sarah Singleton (Simon & Schuster), *The Unrivalled Spangles* by Karen Wallace (Simon & Schuster). Established 2003.

The Branford Boase Award

Details The Administrator, 8 Bolderwood Close, Bishopstoke, Eastleigh SO50 5PG
tel (01962) 826658 *fax* (01962) 856615
email anne.marley@tiscali.co.uk
website www.branfordboaseaward.org.uk

An annual award of £1000 is made to a first-time writer of a full-length children's novel (age 7+) published in the preceding year; the editor is also recognised. Its aim is to encourage new writers for children and to recognise the role of perceptive editors in developing new talent. The Award was set up in memory of the outstanding children's writer Henrietta Branford and the gifted editor and

publisher Wendy Boase who both died in 1999. Closing date for nominations: end of March of each year. 2006 winner: Ruth Alltimes for *Fly by Night* (Macmillan). Founded 2000.

British Book Awards

Details Merric Davidson, PO Box 60, Cranbrook, Kent TN17 2ZR
tel (01580) 212041 *fax* (01580) 212041
email nibbies@mdla.co.uk
website www.britishbookawards.com

Referred to as the 'Nibbies' and presented annually, major categories include: Author of the Year, Publisher of the Year, Bookseller of the Year, WHSmith Children's Book of the Year (2006 winner: *Ark Angel* by Anthony Horowitz, Walker Books). Founded 1989.

Carnegie Medal – see The CILIP Carnegie and Kate Greenaway Awards

The CBI Bisto Book of the Year Awards

Details The Administrator, Children's Books Ireland, 17 Great Georges Street, Dublin 1, Republic of Ireland
tel (01) 8727475 *fax* (01) 8727476
email info@childrensbooksireland.com
website www.childrensbooksireland.com

Annual awards open to authors and/or illustrators who were born in Ireland, or who were living in Ireland at the time of a book's publication. Closing date: December 2006 for work published between 1 January and 31 December 2006. Founded 1990.

The CBI Bisto Book of the Year Award

An award of €6000 is presented to the overall winner (text and/or illustration). 2006 award winner: *The New Policeman* by Kate Thompson (Bodley Head).

The CBI Bisto Merit Awards

A prize fund of €3000 is divided between 3 authors and/or illustrators. 2006 award winners: Oliver Jeffers for *Lost and Found* (HarperCollins), Kevin Keily for *A Horse Called El Dorado* (O'Brien Press), and Eileen O'Hely and Nicky Phelan for *Penny the Pencil* (Mercier).

The CBI Bisto Eilís Dillon Award

An award of €3000 is presented to an author for a first children's book. 2006 award winner: Deirdre Madden for *Snake's Elbows* (Orchard).

The Children's Laureate

Details Booktrust, Book House, 45 East Hill, London SW18 2QZ
tel 023-8516 2985 *fax* 020-8516 2978
email childrenslaureate@booktrust.org.uk
website www.childrenslaureate.org,
www.booktrust.org

A biennial award of £10,000 to honour a writer or illustrator of children's books for a lifetime's achievement. It highlights the importance of children's book creators in developing readers and illustrators of the future. Children's Laureates: Jacqueline Wilson (2005–7), Michael Morpurgo (2003–5), Anne Fine (2001–3), Quentin Blake (1999–2001). Founded 1998.

The CILIP Carnegie and Kate Greenaway Awards
email marketing@cilip.org.uk
website www.ckg.org.uk

Recommendations for the following 2 awards are invited from members of CILIP (the Chartered Institute of Library and Information Professionals), who are asked to submit a preliminary list of not more than 2 titles for each award, accompanied by a 50-word appraisal justifying the recommendation of each book. The awards are selected by the Youth Libraries Group of CILIP.

Carnegie Medal
Awarded annually for an outstanding book for children (fiction or non-fiction) written in English and first published in the UK during the preceding year or co-published elsewhere within a 3-month time lapse. 2005 winner: *Millions* by Frank Cottrell Boyce (Macmillan). 2006 shortlist: *Clay* by David Almond (Hodder), *Framed* by Frank Cottrell Boyce (Macmillan), *The White Darkness* by Geraldine McCaughrean, *Turbulence* by Jan Mark (Hodder), *Tamar* by Mal Peet (Walker).

Kate Greenaway Medal
Awarded annually for an outstanding illustrated book for children first published in the UK during the preceding year or co-published elsewhere within a 3-month time lapse. Books intended for older as well as younger children are included, and reproduction will be taken into account. The Colin Mears Award (£5000) is awarded annually to the winner of the Kate Greenaway Medal. 2005 Medal winner: *Ella's Big Chance* by Shirley Hughes. 2006 shortlist: *Arthur Spiderwick's Field Guide to the Fantastical World Around You* by Tony Diterlizzi (Simon & Schuster), *Wolves* by Emily Gravett (Macmillan), *Traction Man is Here* by Mini Grey (Red Fox), *Lost and Found* by Oliver Jeffers, *Mirrormask* by Dave McKean (Bloomsbury), *Jinnie Ghost* by Jane Ray (Frances Lincoln), *Little Red: A Fizzingly Good Yarn* by David Roberts (Chrysalis), *Russell the Sheep* by Rob Scotton (HarperCollins).

The CLPE Poetry Award
Details CLPE, Webber Street, London SE1 8QW
tel 020-7401 3382/3 fax 020-7928 4624
email ann@clpe.co.uk
website www.clpe.co.uk

A new award that aims to honour excellence in children's poetry. Organised by the Centre for Literacy in Primary Education, it is presented annually in June/July for a book of poetry published in the preceding year. The book can be a single-poet collection or an anthology. Submissions deadline: end of February. 2005 winner: *Sensational! Poems Inspired by the Five Senses* by Roger McGough (ed.) (Macmillan). 2006 shortlist: *The Carnival of Animals* by Gerard Benson, Judith Chernaik and Cicely Herbert (eds) and Satoshi Kitamura (Walker), *The Crocodile is Coming!* by June Crebbin and Mini Grey (Walker), *She's All That! Poems About Girls* by Belinda Hollyer (ed.) and Susan Hellard (Kingfisher), *Cock Crow, Poems About Life in the Countryside* by Michael Morpurgo (ed.) and Quentin Blake (Egmont), and *Why Does My Mum Always Iron a Crease in My Jeans?* by Fiona Waters (ed.) (Puffin).

Costa Book Awards
(formerly the Whitbread Book Awards)
DetailsAnna O'Kane, The Booksellers Association, Minster House, 272 Vauxhall Bridge Road, London SW1V 1BA
tel 020-7802 0801 fax 020-7802 0803
email anna.okane@booksellers.org.uk
website www.costabookawards.co.uk

The awards celebrate and promote the most enjoyable contemporary British writing. Judged in 2 stages and offering a total of £50,000 prize money, there are 5 categories: Novel, First Novel, Biography, Poetry and Children's. They are judged by a panel of 3 judges and the winner in each category receives £5000. Nine final judges then choose the Costa Book of the Year from the 5 category winners. The overall winner receives £25,000. Writers must be resident in Great Britain or Ireland for 3 or more years. Submissions must be received from publishers. Closing date: end of June.

2006 Whitbread Children's Book Award winner: *The New Policeman* by Kate Thompson (Bodley Head).

George Devine Award
Submissions Christine Smith, 9 Lower Mall, London W6 9DJ
tel 020-7267 9793 (evenings)

This annual award of £10,000 is open to any promising playwright for an original new stage play, which need not have been produced. TV and radio plays will not be considered. Applicants should submit 2 copies of the play plus sae for return of scripts and an outline of their their work to date. Closing date: 1 March. Set up in 1966 as a memorial to the life and talent of George Devine, Artistic Director of the Royal court 1956–65.

The Eleanor Farjeon Award
website www.childrensbookcircle.org.uk

An annual award of (minimum) £750 may be given to a librarian, teacher, author, artist, publisher, reviewer, TV producer or any other person working with or for children through books. It was instituted in 1965 by the Children's Book Circle (page 339) for distinguished services to children's books and named after the much-loved children's writer. 2005 award winner: Malorie Blackman.

Foyle Young Poets of the Year Award – see page 367

Kate Greenaway Medal – see The CILIP Carnegie and Kate Greenaway Awards

The Guardian Children's Fiction Prize
tel 020-7239 9694
email books@guardian.co.uk

The Guardian's annual prize of £1500 is for a work of children's fiction for children over 8 (no picture books) published by a British or Commonwealth writer. The winning book is chosen by the Children's Book Editor together with a team of 3–4 authors of children's books. 2005 winner: *The New Policeman* by Kate Thompson (Doubleday).

Killie Writing Competition
Details Killie Writing Competition, Kilmarnock College KA3 7AT
tel (01355) 302160
email enquiries@killie.co.uk
website www.killie.co.uk

Annual competition usually with 4 categories: 5–7 year-olds, 8–11 year-olds, 12–16 year-olds, adults. Free expessive writing (poetry or fiction) with no limit on subject, word count, style or format. See website for guidelines. Work submitted must have been previously unpublished. Various prizes with the overall best entry receiving £1000 and a trophy. Closing date: April. Founded 2000.

Lancashire County Library Children's Book of the Year Award
Details Lancashire Country Library Headquarters, PO Box 61, County Hall, Preston PR1 8RJ
tel (01772) 264040 *fax* (01772) 264043
email library@lcl.lancscc.gov.uk

A prize of £500 and an engraved decanter is awarded to the best work of fiction for 12–14 year-olds, written by a UK author and first published between 1 September and 31 August of the previous year. The winner is announced in June. 2006 winner: *Raven's Gate* by Anthony Horowitz (Walker Books).

The Astrid Lindgren Memorial Award
Swedish National Council for Cultural Affairs, PO Box 7843, SE–103 98 Stockholm, Sweden
tel (08) 519 264 00 *fax* (08) 519 264 99
email literatureaward@alma.se
website www.alma.se

An award to honour the memory of Astrid Lindgren, Sweden's favourite author, and to promote children's

and youth literature around the world. The award is 5 million Swedish crowns, the world's largest for children's and youth literature, and the second-largest literature prize in the world, and will be awarded each year to one or more recipients, regardless of language or nationality.

Authors, illustrators, storytellers and promoters of reading are eligible. The award is for life-long work or artistry rather than for individual pieces. The prize can only be awarded to living people. The body of work must uphold the highest artistic quality and evoke the deeply humanistic spirit that Astrid Lindgren treasured.

The winner is selected by a jury based on nominations for outstanding achievement from selected nominating bodies around the world. The jury has the right to suggest nominees of their own. Neither individuals nor organisations may nominate themselves. 2006 award-winner: Katherine Paterson (US author). The Astrid Lindgren Memorial Award is administered by the Swedish National Council for Cultural Affairs. Founded 2002.

Literary Review Grand Poetry Prize
44 Lexington Street, London W1F 0LW
tel 020-7437 9392 *fax* 020-7734 1844
website www.literaryreview.co.uk

Literary Review runs a competition each month for poems on a given subject which are no more than 24 lines, rhyme, scan and make sense. The Grand Prize of £5000 is awarded to the best of these each year. Closing date: September. Founded 1990.

London Writers Competition
Details Arts Office, Wandsworth Council, Room 224A, Wandsworth Town Hall, High Street, London SW18 2PU
tel 020-8871 8711
email arts@wandsworth.gov.uk
website www.wandsworth.gov.uk/arts

Open to writers who live, work or study in the Greater London area. Awards are made annually in 4 classes (Poetry, Short Story, Fiction for Children and Play) and prizes total £1000 in each class. Entries must be previously unpublished work. Judging is under the chairmanship of Francine Stock.

The Macmillan Prize for Children's Picture Book Illustration
Applications Dianne Pinner, Macmillan Children's Books, 20 New Wharf Road, London N1 9RR
tel 020-7014 6124
email d.pinner@macmillan.co.uk

Three prizes are awarded annually for unpublished children's book illustrations by art students in higher education establishments in the UK. Prizes: £1000 (1st), £500 (2nd) and £250 (3rd).

The Macmillan Writer's Prize for Africa
website www.writeforafrica.com

A biennial competition devoted to previously unpublished works of fiction by African writers from all over the continent which aims to promote and celebrate story writing for children and young people. There are 2 awards for children's literature and teenage fiction, an award for the best new children's writer, and an additional award for illustration.

Entrants may select freely from themes that they consider to be of interest and value to their intended readership but all stories should have a strong African flavour. Entries will be assessed on the depth and originality of the work, the quality of the writing and the story's appeal to its audience. The competition is open to all nationals or naturalised citizens of countries throughout Africa and to those born in those countries. The next competition will be launched in January 2007. Sponsored by Macmillan Education.

2006/7 winners: Junior Award, for 8–12 year-olds – *The Saint in Brown Sandals* by Elizabeth Irene Baitie (Ghana); Senior Award, for 13–17 year-olds – *Voice of a Dream* by Glaydah Namukasa (Uganda); New Children's Writer Award – *The House that Kojo Built* by Ngozi Ifeyinwa Razak-Soyebi (Nigeria). Launched 2005.

Macmillan Children's Illustrator Award for Africa

A competition to recognise the importance of pictures in children's books. 2006/7 winner: Enoch Yaw Mensah (Ghana). Launched 2005.

Marsh Award for Children's Literature in Translation

Administered by National Centre for Research in Children's Literature, Froebel College, Roehampton University, Roehampton Lane, London SW15 5PJ *tel* 020-8392 3008
Contact Dr Gillian Lathey

This biennial award of £1000 is given to the translator of a book for children (aged 4–16) from a foreign language into English and published in the UK by a British publisher. Electronic books, and encyclopedias and other reference books, are not eligible. Next award: January 2007. 2005 award winner: Sarah Adams for *Eye of the Wolf* by Daniel Pennac. Founded 1996.

The Mythopoeic Fantasy Award for Children's Literature

The Award Administrator, The Mythopoeic Society, PO Box 320486, San Francisco, CA 94132-0486, USA *website* www.mythsoc.org

This Award honours books for younger readers (from young adults to picture books for beginning readers), in the tradition of *The Hobbit* or *The Chronicles of Narnia*.

2006 award finalists: *Valiant* by Holly Black (Simon & Schuster), *Wizards at War* by Diane Duane (Harcourt), *By These Ten Bones* by Clare B. Dunkle (Henry Holt), and *The Bartimaeus Trilogy* by Jonathan Stroud (Hyperion).

NASEN & TES Special Educational Needs Book Awards

Details Kerry Paige, NASEN/TES Book Awards, Admiral House, 66–68 East Smithfield, London E1W 1BX
tel 020-7782 3403
email kerry.paige@tsleducation.com
website www.teachingexhibitions.co.uk

The Awards have been created to recognise the authors and publishers of high-quality books that inspire both children with special educational needs and their teachers. The awards will be presented in 3 categories: the Special Educational Needs Children's Book Award; the Special Educational Needs Academic Book Award; and the Books for Teaching and Learning Award. A prize of £500 will be awarded to the winning author of each category and to the publisher a quarter-page advertisement in the *TES* worth £1200 at a ceremony to be held at the British Library.

All books submitted for entry in any category must have been published in the UK between 21 July and 20 July each year. A maximum of 3 books can be submitted per publisher. Closing date: July. 2005 award winners: *Caged in Chaos* by Victoria Biggs (Jessica Kingsley), *Mother – Teachers* by Barbara Ann Cole (David Fulton Publishers) and *Language for Learning Across the Curriculum* by Sue Hayden and Emma Jordan (Language for Learning).

The Nestlé Children's Book Prize

Details Booktrust, Book House, 45 East Hill, London SW18 2QZ
tel 020-8516 2986 *fax* 020-8516 2978
email hannah@booktrust.org.uk
website www.booktrust.org.uk
Contact Hannah Rutland

Three prizes (Gold, Silver and Bronze) are awarded to the 3 shortlisted books in each category (5 and under, 6–8 and 9–11 years). The Gold Award winners each receive £2500, the Silver Award winners receive £1500, and the Bronze Award winners receive £500. Eligible books must be published in the UK in the 12 months ending 30 September of the year of presentation and be a work of fiction or poetry for children written in English by a citizen or resident of the UK. Closing date for entries: June. 2005 winners: 5 and under: *Lost and Found* by Oliver Jeffers (HarperCollins); 6–8 years: *The Whisperer* by Nick Butterworth (HarperCollins); 9–11 years: *I, Coriander* by Sally Gardner (Orion Children's Books). Formerly the Nestlé Smarties Book Prize; established in 1985.

New Zealand Post Book Awards for Children and Young Adults

Details c/o Booksellers New Zealand, PO Box 13248, Johnsonville, Wellington, New Zealand *tel* (04) 478-5511 *fax* (04) 478-5519
email jayne.wasmuth@booksellers.co.nz

website www.nzpostbookawards.co.nz

Annual awards to celebrate excellence in, and provide recognition for, the best books for children and young adults published annually in New Zealand. Awards are presented in 4 categories: non-fiction, picture book, junior fiction and young adult fiction. The winner of each category wins $5000. One category winner is chosen as the *New Zealand Post Book of the Year* and receives an additional $5000. Eligible authors' and illustrators' books must have been published in New Zealand in the calendar year preceding the awards year. Closing date: December. Founded 1990.

North East Book Award

Details Eileen Armstrong, Cramlington High School, Cramlington, Northumberland NE23 6BN
tel (01670) 712311 *fax* (01670) 730598
email earmstrong@cchsonline.co.uk

Awarded to a book first published in paperback between May and the end of June the following year. The shortlist is selected by librarians, teachers and the previous year's student judges, and the final winner by Year 10 students. Winner announced in January. 2006 joint award winners: *Looking for JJ* by Anne Cassidy (Scholastic) and *Roxy's Baby* by Catherine MacPhail (Bloomsbury).

Northern Rock Foundation Writer's Award

Details New Writing North, 2 School Lane, Whickham, Tyne & Wear NE16 4SL
tel 0191-488 8580 *fax* 0191-488 8576
email mail@newwritingnorth.com
website www.newwritingnorth.com
Contact Holly Hooper

An annual award of £60,000 (paid over 3 years as a £20,000 salary) donated by the Northern Rock Foundation and designed to release a writer from commitments such as teaching in order to devote time to a major work. Eligible are writers of poetry, prose, children's books and biography, with at least 2 books published by a nationally recognised publisher. Writers must reside in Northumberland, Tyne & Wear, County Durham, Cumbria or the Tees Valley. Closing date: early January. See website for more details. Founded 2002.

Nottingham Children's Book Awards

Nottingham City Libraries and Information Service, Sneiton Library, Sneiton Boulevard, Nottingham NG2 4FD
tel 0115-915 1173
website www.nottinghamchildrensbookaward.co.uk
Contact Elaine Dykes, Deborah Sheppard

Nottingham children choose their favourite 4 paperbacks of the year. The award is in 4 age groups: Foundation, 5–7 year-olds, 8–9 year-olds and 10–11 year-olds. It attracts upwards of 8000 votes through

libraries, schools and nurseries each year. A shortlist of 20 titles is drawn up by groups of children in November, the shortlisted books are made available in January, promotion takes place through the Spring term and voting takes place in early March. The Award culminates in a grand presentation and celebration day in April. 2006 winners – Foundation: *Duck's Key* by Jez Alborough (HarperCollins); 5–7 year-olds: *Smelly Bill* by Daniel Postgate (Meadowside); 8–9 year-olds: *I Hate School* by Jeanne Willis and Tony Ross (Anderson); 10–11 year-olds: *The Secret Life of Jamie B* by Ceri Worman (Orchard). Launched 1999.

Ottakar's Children's Book Prize

Brewery House, 36 Milford Street, Salisbury, Wilts. SP1 2AP
tel (01722) 428500
email fiona.martin@ottakars.co.uk
Contact Fiona Martin

This prize (£1000) celebrates exciting new or not yet established authors of children's books. It is unique in that booksellers and children select the shortlist and ultimate winner from books not yet published. Submissions deadline: end of March. Winner 2006: *The Diamond of Drury Lane* by Julia Golding (Egmont Press). Founded 2004.

Peterloo Poets Open Poetry Competition

Details Peterloo Poets, The Old Chapel, Sand Lane, Calstock, Cornwall PL18 9QX
tel (01822) 833473 *fax* (01822) 833989
email info@peterloopoets.com
website www.peterloopoets.com

This annual competition offers a first prize of £1500 and 14 other prizes totalling £2600. There is also a 15–19 age group section with 5 prizes each of £100. Founded 1986.

Phoenix Award

Children's Literature Association, PO Box 138, Battle Creek, MI 49016–0138, USA
tel 269-965-8180 *fax* 269-965-3568
website http://chla.wikispaces.com

This Award is presented by the Children's Literature Association (ChLA) for the most outstanding book for children originally published in the English language 20 years earlier which did not receive a major award at the time of publication. It is intended to recognise books of high literary merit. 2006 award winner: *Howl's Moving Castle* by Diana Wynne Jones (Greenwillow 1986). The ChLA publishes an annual electronic journal, *The Phoenix Papers*, about the Award. Founded 1985.

The Red House Children's Book Award

Details Marianne Adey, The Old Malt House, Aldbourne, Marlborough, Wilts. SN8 2DW

tel (01672) 540629 *fax* (01672) 541280
email marianneadey@aol.com
website www.redhousechildrensbookaward.co.uk

This award is given annually to authors of works of fiction for children published in the UK. Children participate in the judging of the award. 'Pick of the Year' booklist is published in conjunction with the award. 2006 winners – Younger Children category: *Pigs Might Fly* by Jonathan Emmett and Steve Cox (Puffin); Younger Readers category: *Spy Dog* by Andrew Cope (Puffin); Older Readers category and overall winner: *Percy Jackson and the Olympians* by Rick Riordan (Miramax). Founded in 1980 by the Federation of Children's Book Groups.

Royal Mail Awards for Scottish Children's Books

Scottish Book Trust, Sandeman House, Trunk's Close, 55 High Street, Edinburgh EH1 1SR
tel 0131-524 0160 *fax* 0131-524 0161
email anna.gibbons@scottishbooktrust.com
website www.braw.org.uk
Contact Anna Gibbons, Manager, BRAW

Awards totalling £5250 are given to new and established authors of published books in recognition of high standards of writing for children in 3 age group categories: younger children (0–7 years), younger readers (8–12 years) and older readers (13–16 years). A shortlist is drawn up by a panel of children's book experts and then a winner in each category is decided by children and young people by voting for their favourites in book groups in schools and libraries across Scotland. An award of £1000 is made for the winner in each category and £250 for runners up. Books published in the preceding calendar year are eligible. Authors should be Scottish or resident in Scotland but books of particular Scottish interest by other authors are eligible for consideration. Posthumous awards cannot be made. Guidelines available on request. Closing date: 31 January. Award presented: December. Administered by BRAW in partnership with the Scottish Arts Council.

RSPCA Young Photographer Awards (YPA)

Details Publications Department, RSPCA, Wilberforce Way, Southwater, Horsham, West Sussex RH13 9RS
tel (0870) 7540455 *fax* (0870) 7530455
email publications@rspca.org.uk
website www.rspca.org.uk/ypa

Annual awards are made for animal photographs taken by young people in 2 age categories: under 12 and 12–18 year-olds. Prizes: overall winner (high-end digital camera), age group winners (camera). Four runners-up in each age group receive a camera. Closing date for entries: 4 September 2006. Sponsored by Warners and Olympus Cameras. Founded 1990.

Saga Children's Book Competition

Details Jane Griffiths, Editorial Assistant, HarperCollins Children's Books, 77–85 Fulham Palace Road, London W6 8JB
tel 020-8307 4080
website www.saga.co.uk/magazine, www.harpercollins.co.uk

A competition run by *Saga Magazine* in association with HarperCollins, is looking for writers aged 50 or over who can write for older children. The winner will have their book published by HarperCollins. Send completed MSS of 20,000–60,000 words and a synopsis of 500 words together with the official entry form to the address published in the September issue (not the above address). Send a sae or see websites for competition rules and detailed terms and conditions of entry. Closing date: 31 January 2007.
2006 winner: *Hybrids* by David Thorpe (HarperCollins).

Sainsbury's Baby Book Award – see Booktrust Early Years Awards

Scottish Arts Council

Scottish Arts Council, 12 Manor Place, Edinburgh EH3 7DD
tel 0131-226 6051
email gavin.wallace@scottisharts.org.uk
website www.scottisharts.org.uk
Contact Gavin Wallace, Head of Literature

A limited number of writers' bursaries – up to £15,000 each – are offered to enable professional writers based in Scotland, including writers for children, to devote more time to writing. Priority is given to writers of fiction and verse and playwrights, but writers of literary non-fiction are also considered. Applications may be discussed with Gavin Wallace. See also Royal Mail Awards for Scottish Children's Books.

Scottish Arts Council Book Awards

These awards are currently undergoing reconfiguration and will be relaunched in 2007.

Sheffield Children's Book Award

Details Book Award Co-ordinator, Schools Library Service, Sheffield
tel 0114-250 6844
email jennifer.wilson@sheffield.gov.uk
website www.sheffield.gov.uk

Presented annually in November to the book chosen as the most enjoyable by the children of Sheffield. There are 3 category winners and one overall winner. 2005 winners – Longer Novel and overall winner: *Looking for JJ* by Anne Cassidy; Picture Book: *Spookyrumpus* by Tony Mitton and Guy Parker-Rees; Shorter Novel: *Avenger* by Pete Johnson and David Wyatt.

WHSmith Children's Book of the Year – see British Book Awards

South Lanarkshire Book Award

Details Literacy Development Co-ordinator, Libraries and Community Learning
tel (01355) 248581 *fax* (01355) 229365
email margaret.cowan@southlanarkshire.gov.uk
website www.slc-learningcentres.org.uk

Awarded to the best teenage book. The initial selection is by librarians and the final winner is chosen by a panel of school students. The shortlist is announced in December and the winner announced in March the following year. 2006 winner: *Paralysed* by Sherry Ashworth (Simon & Schuster).

The Spoken Word Awards

Contact Audiobook Publishing Association,
c/o Charlotte McCandlish, 18 Green Lanes, Hatfield, Herts. AL10 9JT
tel (07971) 280788
email charlotte.mccandlish@ntlworld.com
website www.theapa.net

Annual awards are made for excellence in the spoken word industry. There are over 40 judges from all areas of the industry including audiobook reviewers, radio broadcasters, producers, abridgers, etc. 2005 award winners include – Children's 6 and Under – Contemporary: *The Snail and the Whale* by Julia Donaldson and Axel Scheffler, narrated by Imelda Staunton (Macmillan); and Children's Fiction: *Playtime Rhymes* by Sally Gardner, narrated by Angela Dijksman and Heather Chivers (Orion).

Tir Na N-og Awards

Details Welsh Books Council, Castell Brychan, Aberystwyth, Ceredigion SY23 2JB
tel (01970) 624151 *fax* (01970) 625385
email menna.lloydwilliams@cllc.org.uk
website www.cllc.org.uk

There are 3 annual awards to children's authors and illustrators: best original Welsh-language fiction, including short stories and picture books. 2006 winners – English-language books: *Tirion's Secret Journal* by Jenny Sullivan (Pont Books); Welsh-language books – Primary Sector: *Carreg Ateb* by Emily Huws (Cymdeithas Lyfrau Ceredigion); Welsh-language books – Secondary Sector: *Creadyn* by Gwion Hallam (Gwasg Gomer). Total prize value is £3000. Founded 1976.

Christopher Tower Poetry Prize – see page 164

UKLA Children's Book Awards

Details Debbie Wright
tel (01491) 836631
email dwright@brookes.ac.uk
Submissions Administrative Secretary, United Kingdom Literacy Association, Upton House, Baldock Street, Royston, Herts. SG8 5AY
website www.ukla.org

Biennial awards are presented for excellence in the field of literacy. 'Literacy is interpreted here as being about the expression of meaning and ideas through challenging use of language, imaginative expression, illustration and other graphics.' Three copies of each book should be submitted. The awards are presented at the United Kingdom Literacy Association International Conference in July.

The V&A Illustration Awards

Enquiries The Word & Image Dept, Victoria & Albert Museum, London SW7 2RL
tel/fax 020-7942 2392
email a.villa@vam.ac.uk
website www.vam.ac.uk/illustrationawards
Contact Annemarie Bilclough

These annual awards are given to practising book and magazine illustrators, for work first published in the UK during the 12 months preceding the closing date of the awards. A 1st and 2nd prize winner will be chosen from the following 3 award categories: book illustration, book cover and jacket illustration, and newspaper, magazine and comic illustration. Of the 3 category winners, one will be selected to receive £3500 as the best overall illustration and the other 2 winners will each receive £1500. The 3 second prize winners will each be awarded £750. Closing date late July/early August. Also a Student Illustrator of the Year category: 1st prize winner will receive £1300 and 4 runners up will receive £300. Closing date: March.

Ver Poets Open Competition

Competition Secretary Gill Knibbs, 181 Sandridge Road, St Albans, Herts. AL1 4AH
tel (01727) 762601
email gillknibbs@yahoo.co.uk

A competition open to all for poems of up to 30 lines of any genre or subject matter, which must be unpublished work in English. Prizes: £500 (1st), £300 (2nd), £100 (3rd). Entry fee: £3 per poem or £10 for 4. Send 2 copies of each poem with no name or address; either put address on separate sheet or send sae or email for entry form. Closing date: 30 April. Anthology of winning and selected poems with Adjudicator's Report usually available from mid-June, free to those included.

The High Lights competition for younger poets (15–19 year-olds) is a biennial competition to be run in 2007.

Whitbread Book Awards – see Costa Book Awards

Winchester Writers' Conference Competitions

Faculty of Arts, University of Winchester, Winchester, Hants SO22 4NR
tel (01962) 827238
email barbara.large@winchester.ac.uk

website www.writersconference.co.uk
Contact Barbara Large

Fifteen writing competitions are attached to this major international Festival of Writing which takes place at the end of June. Each entry is adjudicated and 64 sponsored prizes are presented at the Writers' Awards Dinner. Categories are the First Three Pages of the Novel, Short Stories, Shorter Short Stories, Writing for Children, A Page of Prose, Lifewriting, Slim Volume, Small Edition, Poetry, Feature Articles, Retirement, Reaching Out for disabled writers, Local History, and Young Writers' Poetry Competition.

Write A Story for Children Competition

Entry forms The Academy of Children's Writers, PO Box 95, Huntingdon, Cambs. PE28 5RL
tel (01487) 832752
website www.childrens-writers.co.uk

Three prizes (1st £2000, 2nd £300, 3rd £200) are awarded annually for a short story for children,

maximum 1000 words, by an unpublished writer of children's fiction. Send sae for details or see website. Founded 1984.

Young Writers' Programme

Details Young Writers' Programme, Royal Court Young Writers' Programme, Sloane Square, London SW1W 8AS
tel 020-7565 5050 *fax* 020-7565 5001
email ywp@royalcourttheatre.com
website www.royalcourttheatre.com

Anyone aged 13–25 can submit a play on any subject. A selection of plays are professionally presented by the Royal Court Theatre with the writers fully involved in rehearsal and production. Pre-Festival Development Workshops are run by professional theatre practitioners and designed to help everyone attending to write a play. Playwriting projects run all year round.

Calendar of awards

Announcements of awards are subject to change.

January
The Marsh Award for Children's Literature in Translation (biennial)
Costa Book Awards
The Macmillan Writer's Prize for Africa
Macmillan Children's Illustrator Award for Africa
North East Book Award
Ottakar's Children's Book Prize

March
Hans Christian Andersen Awards
Nottingham Children's Book Award
South Lanarkshire Book Award

April
BolognaRagazzi Award
Nottingham Children's Book Awards
WHSmith Children's Book of the Year (British Book Awards)

May
Angus Book Awards
The CBI Bisto Book of the Year Awards
The Macmillan Prize for Children's Picture Book Illustration

June
Aventis Prize for Junior Science Book
The Branford Boase Award
The CLPE Poetry Award
Lancashire County Library Children's Book of the Year Award
Red House Children's Book Award

July
Askews Torchlight Children's Book Award
Carnegie Medal
Kate Greenaway Medal
UKLA Children's Book Awards

September
Booktrust Early Years Award
The Guardian Children's Fiction Prize
Saga Children's Book Competition
The Spoken Word Awards

October
Booktrust Teenage Prize
The Eleanor Farjeon Award
NASEN & TES Special Educational Needs Book Awards
Tir-Na-nog Awards

November
The Nestlé Children's Book Prize
Sheffield Children's Book Award

December
Blue Peter Children's Book Awards
Royal Mail Awards for Scottish Children's Books
The V&A Illustration Awards

Children's literature festivals and trade fairs

Some of the literature festivals in this section are specifically related to children's books and others are general arts festivals which include literature events for children.

Aspects Festival

Town Hall, The Castle, Bangor, Co. Down BT20 4BT
tel (028) 91 278032, 91 271200 (box office)
fax (028) 91 271370
website www.northdown.gov.uk
Contact Gail Prentice, Arts Officer/Festival Co-ordinator
Takes place 20–24 Sept 2006

An annual celebration of contemporary Irish writing with novelists, poets and playwrights. Includes readings, discussions, workshops and an Aspects showcase day for young writers.

Bank of Scotland Children's International Theatre Festival

45A George Street, Edinburgh EH2 2HT
tel 0131-225 8050 *fax* 0131-225 6440
email info@imaginate.org.uk
Director Tony Reekie, *General Manager* Tessa Rennie
Takes place Last week of May and first week of June

This annual event attracts an audience of children, their teachers, parents, carers and friends from across Scotland. If offers more international theatre for children and young people than any other event in the UK. An outreach programme takes live theatre into schools and communities in Edinburgh and the Lothians during the Festival. It also takes international theatre from the Festival to perform at venues across Scotland reaching children in communities from Shetland to Dumfriesshire to the Borders. See also Imaginate on page 351. Founded 1990.

Bath Literature Festival

Bath Festivals Trust, 5 Broad Street, Bath BA1 5LJ
tel (01225) 462231, (01225) 463362 (box office) *fax* (01225) 445551
email info@bathfestivals.org.uk
website www.bathlitfest.org.uk
Director Sarah LeFanu
Takes place 3–11 March 2007

An annual 9-day festival with leading guest writers. Includes readings, debates, discussions and workshops, and events for children and young people. Programme available from box office in December.

Beyond the Border: The Wales International Storytelling Festival

St Donats Arts Centre, St Donats Castle, Nr Llantwit Major, Vale of Glamorgan CF61 1WF
tel (01446) 799095 (marketing), 799100 (box office) *fax* (01446) 799101
email enquiries@stdonats.com, davidambrose@beyondtheborder.com
website www.beyondtheborder.com
Programme Director David Ambrose
Takes place First weekend in July

An international festival celebrating oral tradition and bringing together storytellers, poets and musicians from around the world. This is the largest event of its type in the UK. On the last day there is a competition for young storytellers aged 10–20 to be BTB Young Storyteller of The Year.

Bologna Children's Book Fair

Piazza Costituzione 6, 40128 Bologna, Italy
tel (051) 282242/282361 *fax* (051) 6374011
email bookfair@bolognafiere.it
website www.bookfair.bolognafiere.it
Takes place April 24–27 2007

Held annually, the Bologna Children's Book Fair is the leading children's publishing event. Publishers, authors and illustrators, literary agents, TV and film producers, licensors and licensees, and many other members of the children's publishing community meet in Bologna to buy and sell copyrights, establish new contacts and strengthen their professional relationships, discover new illustrators, develop new business opportunities, learn about the latest trends and developments and explore children's educational materials, including new media products. Approximately 4000 professionals active in children's publishing attend from 70 countries. Entry is restricted to those in the publishing trade.

Selected by a jury, the Bologna Illustrators Exhibition showcases fiction and non-fiction children's book illustrators, both new and established, from all over the world. Many illustrators also visit the Fair to show their latest portfolios to publishers. Winners of the BolognaRagazzi Award are displayed. Prizes are given to encourage excellence in children's publishing in the categories of fiction, non-fiction and 'new horizons' (books from emerging countries), and books are judged on the basis of their creativity, educational value and artistic design. Hans Christian Andersen Award is announced at the Fair.

The Bologna Children's Book Fair, working with The Association of Educational Publishers (US), has created the Global Learning Initiative (GLI), an international business-to-business event created by and for educational publishers serving the K–12 market. The GLI provides a rights and commercial centre specifically for the growing international community of supplemental educational publishers.

Book Now! Literature Festival

Education, Arts & Leisure Department, Orleans House Gallery, Riverside, Twickenham TW1 3DJ
tel 020-8831 6000 *fax* 020-8744 0507
website www.richmond.gov.uk
Takes place Throughout Nov

An annual literature festival covering a broad range of subjects. Leading British and overseas guest writers hold discussions, talks, debates and readings. There are also exhibitions and storytelling sessions for children and adults.

Booktide Children's Arts Festival

Ceredigion County Council, Aberystwyth Library, Corporation Street, Aberystwyth, Ceredigion SW23 2BU
tel (01970) 633702
website www.aber.ac.uk/artscentre
Contact Elinor Ingham
Takes place mid October

A programme of performances, talks and workshops for schools throughout Ceredigion.

Cheltenham Literature Festival

Town Hall, Imperial Square, Cheltenham, Glos. GL50 1QA
tel (01242) 227979 (box office), 237377 (brochure), 263494 (festival office) *fax* (01242) 256457
email clair.greenaway@cheltenham.gov.uk
website www.cheltenhamfestivals.com
Artistic Director Sarah Smyth
Takes place 6–15 Oct 2006

This annual festival is the largest of its kind in Europe. Events include talks and lectures, poetry readings, novelists in conversation, exhibitions, discussions, workshops and a large bookshop. *Book It!* is a festival for children within the main festival with an extensive programme of events. Brochures are available in August.

Chester Literature Festivals

Viscount House, River Lane, Saltney, Chester CH4 8RH
tel (01244) 674020 *fax* (01244) 684060
email info@chesterlitfest.org.uk
website www.chester-literature-festival.org.uk
Festival Administrator Katherine Seddon
Takes place 30 Sept–28 Oct 2006

An annual festival commencing the first weekend in October. Events featuring international, national and local writers and poets are part of the programme, as well as a literary lunch and festival dinner. There is a poetry competition for school children, events for

children and workshops for adults. A Cheshire Prize for Literature is awarded each year; only residents in Cheshire are eligible.

Children's Book Festival

Festival Office, Childrens Books Ireland, 17 North Great Georges Street, Dublin 1, Republic of Ireland
tel (1) 872 7475 *fax* (1) 872 7476
email info@childrensbooksireland.com
website www.childrensbooksireland.com
Contact James Curtain, Festival Coordinator
Takes place 4–28 Oct 2006

Annual nationwide celebration of reading and books in Ireland for young people.

Children's Book Week

Book House, 45 East Hill, London SW18 2QZ
tel 020-8516 2976 *fax* 020-8516 2998
email education@booktrust.org.uk
website www.booktrust.org.uk, www.booktrusted.com
Takes place First full week of October

The annual National Children's Book Week celebrates the wonderful world of children's books. It focuses on the enjoyment of reading, with the aim of encouraging as many children as possible to enjoy books. The Week is based on the belief that designating a special day or week at school, in libraries and at home, for enjoyable book activities can help children to see reading as a source of pleasure – as well as trying to encourage them to write themselves, to discuss and share books and to explore libraries and bookshops. All over the UK, schools, libraries and bookshops hold events and activities.

Edinburgh International Book Festival

5A Charlotte Square, Edinburgh EH2 4DR
tel 0131-718 5666 *fax* 0131-226 5335
email admin@edbookfest.co.uk
website www.edbookfest.co.uk
Director Catherine Lockerbie
Takes place 12–28 Aug 2006, 11–27 Aug 2007

Now established as Europe's largest book event for the public. In addition to a unique independent bookselling operation, over 600 writers contribute to the programme of events. Programme details available in June.

Essex Poetry Festival

tel (01702) 230596
email derek@essex-poetry-festival.co.uk
website www.essex-poetry-festival.co.uk
Contact Derek Adams
Takes place Oct 2006

A poetry festival across Essex. Also includes the Young Essex Poet of the Year Competition.

Folkestone Literary Festival

Church Street Studios, 11 Church Street, Folkestone, Kent CT20 1SE

tel (01303) 211300 fax (01303) 211883
email info@folkestonelitfest.com
website www.folkestonelitfest.co.uk
Takes place September

This annual festival launches with the the announcement of the winner of the Saga Award for Wit, followed by over 40 events. The Children's Day concludes the festival.

Global Learning Initiative – see Bologna Children's Book Fair

The Guardian Hay Festival
Festival Office, The Drill Hall, 25 Lion Street, Hay-on-Wye HR3 5AD
tel (0870) 7872848 (admin)
email ruth@hayfestival.com
website www.hayfestival.com
Takes place May/June

This annual festival aims to celebrate the best in writing and performance from around the world, to commission new work, and to promote and encourage young writers of excellence and potential. Over 200 events in 10 days with leading guest writers. Programme published April.

Guildford Book Festival
c/o Tourist Information Office, 14 Tunsgate, Guildford GU1 3QT
tel (01483) 444334
email deputy@guildfordbookfestival.co.uk
website www.guildfordbookfestival.co.uk
Festival Director Glenis Pycraft
Takes place 16–28 Oct 2006

An annual festival. Diverse, provocative and entertaining, held throughout the historic town. Author events, poetry, workshops for all age groups from 6 months onwards. Its aim is to further an interest and love of literature by involvement and entertainment. Founded 1990.

Hay Festival – see The Guardian Hay Festival

Imagine: Writers and Writing for Children
Purcell Room, South Bank Centre, London SE1 8XX
tel 020-7921 0906 (administration), 020-7921 0971 (programme), (0870) 160 2520 (box office)
fax 020-7928 2049
email Literature&Talks@rfh.org.uk
website www.rfh.org.uk/imagine
Takes place February

An annual festival celebrating writing for children. Three days featuring a selection of poets, storytellers and illustrators.

Jewish Book Week
Jewish Book Council, PO Box 38247, London NW3 5YQ

tel 020-8343 4675 fax 020-8343 4675
email jewishbookcouncil@btopenworld.com
website www.jewishbookweek.com
Administrator Pam Lewis
Takes place 24 Feb–4 March 2007

A festival of Jewish writing, with contributors from around the world and sessions in London and nationwide. Includes events for children and teenagers.

Lincoln Book Festival
City of Lincoln Council, Dept of Development and Environmental Services, City Hall, Beaumont Fee, Lincoln LN1 1DF
tel (01522) 873844 fax (01522) 873553
email Sara.Bullimore@lincoln.gov.uk
website www.lincolnbookfestival.co.uk
Contact Sara Bullimore (Arts & Cultural Sector Officer)
Takes place May

A festival that celebrates books but also includes other art forms that books initiate and inspire – comedy, film, performance, conversation. It aims to celebrate local, national and international writers and artists, historical and contemporary works of art as well as offering the public a chance to see both emerging and well-known writers and artists. Includes a programme of children's events.

Lowdham Book Festival
4th Floor, Arts, County Hall, West Bridgford, Nottingham NG2 7QP
tel 0115-977 4435
email ross.bradshaw@nottscc.gov.uk
website www.lowdhambookfestival.co.uk
Contact Ross Bradshaw, Literature Officer
Takes place June/July

An annual 10-day festival of literature events for adults and children with a daily programme of high-profile national writers. There is a writer-in-residence during the Festival and a book fair on the last Saturday.

Northern Children's Book Festival
22 Highbury, Jesmond, Newcastle upon Tyne NE2 3DY
tel 0191-2813289
website www.ncbf.org.uk
Chairperson Ann Key
Takes place 6–18 Nov 2006

An annual festival to bring authors, illustrators, poets and performers to children in schools, libraries and community centres across the North East of England. About 36 authors visit the North East over the 2-week period for 2–8 days, organised by the 12 local authorities. The climax of the festival is a huge public event in a different part of the North East each year when over 4000 children and their families visit to take part in author seminars, drama workshops, and to enjoy a variety of book-related activities. The Gala Day will be on 18 Nov 2006 at St Hilds C of E School, Hartlepool.

Off the Shelf Literature Festival

Central Library, Surrey Street, Sheffield S1 1XZ
tel 0114-273 4400 *fax* 0114-273 4716
email offtheshelf@sheffield.gov.uk
website www.offtheshelf.org.uk
Contacts Maria de Souza, Su Walker, Lesley Webster
Takes place 14–28 Oct 2006

The festival comprises a wide range of events for adults and children, including author visits, writing workshops, storytelling, competitions and exhibitions. Programme available in September.

Oundle Festival of Literature

2 Herne Road, Oundle, Peterborough, Northants PE8 4BS
tel (01832) 274960
email liz@oundlelitfest.org.uk
website www.oundlelitfest.org.uk
Contact Liz Dillarstone (Publicity)
Takes place March 2007

Featuring a full programme of author events, poetry, philosophy, politics, story-telling, biography, illustrators and novelists for young and old. Includes events for children.

Oxford Literary Festival – see The Sunday Times Oxford Literary Festival

Readathon

The Parsonage, St Mary's Chalford, Stroud GL6 8QB
tel (0870) 240 1124
website www.readathon.org

Run in schools throughout the year, especially for Children's Book Week and World Book Day. Children undertake to read books for pledges of money. All the money raised is donated to children's charities. See page 356.

Redbridge Book and Media Festival

London Borough of Redbridge, Arts and Events Team, 8th Floor, Lynton House, 255–259 High Road, Ilford IG1 1NY
tel 020-8708 3044
email laurence.staig@redbridge.gov.uk
website www.redbridge.gov.uk/leisure/bkmdfest.cfm
Contact Arts and Events Team
Takes place May 2007

Features author talks, performances, panel debates, Urdu poetry events, an exhibition, workshops, children's activities and events and a schools outreach programme.

Royal Court Young Writers' Festival

The Royal Court Young Writers' Programme, Sloane Square, London SW1W 8AS

tel 020-7565 5050
website www.royalcourttheatre.com
Contact The Administrator
Takes place Biennially (2008)

A national festival which anyone aged 13–25 can enter. Promising plays which arise from the workshops are then developed and performed at the Royal Court's Theatre Upstairs.

Scottish International Storytelling Festival

43–45 High Street, Edinburgh EH1 1SR
tel 0131-556 9579 *fax* 0131-557 5224
email reception@scottishstorytellingcentre.com
website www.scottishstorytellingcentre.co.uk
Festival Director Donald Smith
Takes place 25 Oct–5 Nov 2006

A celebration of Scottish storytelling set in its international context complemented by music, ballad and song. The 2006 festival takes an Across the Water theme, celebrating Irish/Scots links, with National Tell A Story Day on 27 October. Takes place in numerous venues across Edinburgh, the Lothians and Scottish Borders.

StAnza: Scotland's Poetry Festival

tel (01333) 360 491 (administration), (01334) 475000 (box office), (01592) 414714 (programmes)
email admin@stanzapoetry.org
website www.stanzapoetry.org
Festival Director Brian Johnstone
Takes place 14–18 March 2007

The festival engages with all forms of poetry: read and spoken verse, poetry in exhibition, performance poetry, cross-media collaboration, schools work, book launches and poetry workshops, with numerous UK and international guests and a full weekend children's programme.

The Sunday Times Oxford Literary Festival

301 Woodstock Road, Oxford OX2 7NY
tel (01865) 514149 *fax* (01865) 514804
email oxford.literary.festival@ntlworld.com
website www.sundaytimes-oxfordliteraryfestival.co.uk
Festival Directors Angela Prysor-Jones, Sally Dunsmore
Takes place 2 weeks prior to Easter

An annual 8-day festival for both adults and children. Presents topical debates, fiction and non-fiction discussion panels, and adult and children's authors who have recently published books. Topics range from contemporary fiction to discussions on politics, history, science, gardening, food, poetry, philosophy, art and crime fiction. There is an additional 2 days of events for schools.

Winchester Writers' Conference, Bookfair and Weeklong Workshops – see page 325

Word – University of Aberdeen Writers Festival

University of Aberdeen, Office of External Affairs, University of Aberdeen, King's College, Aberdeen AB24 3FX
tel (01224) 274444 *fax* (01224) 272086
website www.abdn.ac.uk/word
Artistic Director Alan Spence, *Festival Producer* Elly Rothnie, *Festival Co-ordinator* Fiona Christie
Takes place May

Over 50 of the world's finest writers and artists take part in a packed weekend of readings, music, art exhibitions and film screenings. The Word Kid's Programme hosts some of the UK's best-loved children's writers as well as some of the richest talents in Gaelic literature.

Wordplay Literature Festival for Young People

The Dylan Thomas Centre, Somerset Place, Swansea SA1 1RR
tel (01792) 463980 *fax* (01792) 463993
email dylanthomas.lit@swansea.gov.uk
website www.dylanthomas.org
Contact Derek Cobley (Literature Officer)
Takes place Throughout the year

See website for details.

The Word's Out

Perth and Kinross Council, AK Bell Library, York Place, Perth PH2 8EP
tel (01738) 444949
email cfbeaton@pkc.gov.uk
Contact Caroline Beaton (Community Libraries Manager)
Takes place 23–28 Oct 2006

A festival to celebrate books, reading and libraries. It has a significant Scottish emphasis but has authors attending from across the UK. Includes events for children.

World Book Day

c/o The Booksellers Association, 272 Vauxhall Bridge Road, London SW1V 1BA
tel 020-8987 9370
email cathy.schofield@blueyonder.co.uk
website www.worldbookday.com
Contact Cathy Schofield
Takes place 1 March 2007

An annual celebration of books and reading aimed at promoting their value and creating the readers of the future. Every schoolchild in full-time education receives a £1 book token. Events take place all over the UK in schools, bookshops, libraries and arts centres.

World Book Day was designated by UNESCO as a worldwide celebration of books and reading, and is marked in over 30 countries. It is a partnership of publishers, booksellers and interested parties who work together to promote books and reading for the personal enrichment and enjoyment of all.

A main aim of World Book Day is to encourage children to explore the pleasures of books and reading by providing them with the opportunity to have a book of their own. To support this aim, a Schools' Pack full of ideas and activities, display material and information about how to get involved in World Book Day is mailed to schools from mid-January. There are a range of activities and events organised by thousands of people around the country.

Thanks to the generosity of National Book Tokens Ltd and numerous participating booksellers, schoolchildren are entitled to receive a World Book Day £1 Book Token (or equivalent Euro Book Token in Ireland). The Book Token can be exchanged for one of the specially published World Book Day £1 Books (while stocks last), or is redeemable against any one of the Recommended Reads, or a book or audiobook of their choice at a participating bookshop or book club. Details of the £1 Books and Recommended Reads can be found in the Resources section of the website. See also World Book Day Online Festival and Readathon entries.

Young Readers Birmingham

Children's Office, Central Library, Chamberlain Square, Birmingham B3 3HQ
tel 0121-303 3368 *fax* 0121-464 1004
email patsy.heap@birmingham.gov.uk
website www.birmingham.gov.uk/youngreaders
Contact Patsy Heap
Takes place 19 May–2 June 2007

An annual festival targeted at young people aged 0–19 and adults who care for or work with them. It aims to motivate them to enjoy reading and through this to encourage literacy; to provide imaginative access to books, writers and storytellers; to encourage families to share reading for pleasure; to provide a national focus for the celebration of books and reading for children and young people and help raise the media profile of children's books and writing. Approximately 150 events take place.

Bologna Children's Book Fair 2006

Alex Hamilton reviews the annual book fair dedicated to children's books.

For 43 years Bologna has held a trade fair exclusively for children's books. It is the only city in the world that does, though some children's publishers bravely flaunt their colophon in the vast book fairs held in Frankfurt, London and Tokyo and try not to feel overwhelmed by the adult profusion. A couple of years ago the Bologna Children's Book Fair (generally referred to in the book trade as just 'Bologna') seemed threatened when corporate back-room planners argued that Frankfurt plus London was more than enough. Luckily they recognised the greater good, persuaded perhaps by the general feeling, endorsed by Book Marketing Council figures, that – even ignoring the cascade of *Harry Potter* sales – children's books were on the up.

Participants at Bologna spread out into seven pavilions of a light and airy complex, remote in time from the terracotta glamour of the old town with its 35 kilometres of porticos and clusters of palazzi, but near enough in practice, with free shuttle-bus services and anything up to 630 taxis available. Colossal banks with daunting security operate nearby, but all this was not constructed merely to please the nice folk who work to make children literate. In an average year the Bologna venue may be used by 24,214 traders hustling ceramics, 27,589 creative packagers, 15,799 marketing leather goods and an inexplicably feeble 647 for lingerie. Focusing on the children's books element, this year 4583 exhibitors came from 71 countries (an increase of 15 over the past three decades). The French description of their writers' problem as 'the brute Anglo-Saxon fact' is underlined by the ratio of foreign publishers: 134 British, 120 American, 85 Italian, 80 French, 71 German and 61 Spanish. Behind them, but with increasing influence, came 35 Japanese and 21 Korean publishers.

The Fair does not exist to sell books to the public – indeed it is forbidden until the fourth and last day, when publishers are glad to get rid of them rather than pay the cost of taking them home. But determined people can be seen trundling heavyweight suitcases that open to reveal bundles of editorial schemes, some no more than fragments of works in production. In other words, it is open only to professionals, people who make, however improbably, a living from books (and their related games and toys, like *The Bat Book* with robot bat and its whirring wings). Specifically, these are literary agents (and, this year, one scout representing half a dozen European publishers), film animators, publishers' foreign rights sellers, desk editors, creative directors, art editors, booksellers, distributors, company directors, graphic editors, packagers, authors, translators, award judges, systems engineers, techno-wizards, librarians, teachers, journalists (mainly Italian, making speeches rather than asking questions) and illustrators.

From the First World War on, adult publishing pretty well let illustration go and the art has been sustained by children's books and talented freelances who were often scandalously ill-paid. It has always been the motor of the business, whose buzz every child can understand and, from the tremendous range of variegated displays on the stands, it is clear that it has developed into a highly sophisticated practice. Some illustrators become famous by matching images to their own stories, but the majority wait for a call from a publisher, to complement an in-house idea or to decorate the work of authors they may never even meet. Most publishers are shy of ready-made partnerships.

An opportunity for illustrators...

The ethos of Bologna is sympathetic to illustrators: there is a section in one of the halls for them with a kind of international art gallery showing the best illustrations of the year chosen by a panel of experts. Among the imaginative brilliancies of 92 artists chosen from 2544 applicants, there were no fewer than 27 from Japan, and from 16 other countries, including Ukraine, San Marino and Korea, and half a dozen from Iran. Indeed, the talented multi-award-winning Iranian, Alirezza Goldouzian, was picked for the cover of the 2006 annual. Hungary, the guest of honour, featured only three publishers but a great range of artists, 30 in all, were given a separate show of a lifetime. While admiring these bravura international displays, the big commercial operators were sceptical of their ultimate value. 'Yes, marvellous,' they say, 'but will they travel? Would they sell in America? Doubt it.'

Untouched by these downbeat speculations and to get their identity and style across to the publishers, hardy young illustrators rail in to Bologna from all over Europe. They may never have such an opportunity again and as there are so many of them it seems like a feeding frenzy, as they go in hoping someone will speak their language before falling back on English. If they are organised, and lucky, they may have made appointments. If not, they will doggedly push and bite their lip at disappointments. Some publishers see a use in scanning many at one time: when Gerstenberg of Hildesheim in Germany pinned up a short notice welcoming illustrators to show their work to an editor between 1pm and 3pm each day a line of 15 soon formed in the aisle. They were all women in their twenties from Poland, Czech Republic, Germany, France, Switzerland, Sweden, etc, and patiently stood with large portfolios under their arms. Often the interview is brief and editors will say 'nice, but not for us', but once in a while they want to see more and the trip has been worth it.

... but less a place for authors

In contrast, authors should not even try to interest publishers in their work at Bologna. Egmont Books say they are offered up to 25 manuscripts a day at their stand, decline all offers unseen, and hand applicants a sheet with Egmont's London address advising them to send the MS to their anonymous 'Reader'. This is only slightly more encouraging than the practice of such big publishers as Holt of New York, who say they receive 15,000 unsolicited MSS a year, read none of them, return those that enclose an sae and dump the rest. Not all are quite so cavalier but it is plain that this is an age when only an agent can bridge the gap to a publisher. Of the 100 agents at Bologna, 35 (and the scout) were British, but better not interrupt them in their special enclave where they sit, deeply engaged, in lines of small white tables, facing their opposite numbers like prisoners on visitors' day. The details of contracts are usually finalised at a later date, but all agree that the importance of Bologna is personal contact.

Very occasionally an established author turns up to take the pulse, indulge in the town's famous food culture (40 kinds of pasta are on offer), listen to some opera and tell everybody that it is pure coincidence that their latest title is just out. Or for a celebration, like the veterans David McKee and Tony Ross cheering on Klaus Flugge and 30 years of his Andersen Press. But only very, very established authors have a stand to themselves. Of these I noticed stands dedicated to Dick Bruna (his leg was too painful to come himself but he's working still at the age 79) with 85 million sales in 40 languages of his *Miffy* books, etc; the *Asterix* phenomenon, with a display from Uderzo's former publisher alongside another by his new publisher; the series of umpteen *Mister Men* selling like chopsticks in China; and the late scientologist L. Ron Hubbard, author of 170 books, among them *Dianetics* that has sold 22 million copies, though not many to children.

Perennials and new questions

Year on year, certain elements persist. Dinosaur books are still at large. Fantasy remains solid, 'fun mysteries' are doing well and self-generating series are at a premium. Staples include 'beautiful books that keep little hands busy' – dot-to-dot, sticker books, magic painting, finger puppets, recipes for a wet day (like *Making Models from Burgers*) colossal colouring books and the whole information business moving step by step from *My First Words* to *My First Laptop*. And then there is the extensive medley of books that answer questions you might never have thought of asking, such as *What is the Colour of Air?* Why is Milk White? and *What Makes Packaging Strong Enough to Hold What's Inside?* On the other hand, *The Encyclopedia of the Unexplained* provides no explanations. Challenging questions have been answered by books at Bologna since it began: the *How and Why?* series, bought as an idea on licence by the eponymous founder of Tesslof Verlag of Nurnberg more than 40 years ago, now has 121 titles and world sales of 50 million. A different sort of question, about the personal development of children, is answered in a successful new series from Usborne Publishing, including *How Tall Will I Grow?*, *When Will I Wear a Bra?* and *What's Happening to Me?*, and a book that could be usefully consulted by the snack bars of the Fair is *How to Make a Tasty Sandwich*.

Anxieties at a traumatic level are addressed by publishers with a professional psychological orientation, usually American, like Magination Press, with titles such as *A Terrible Thing Happened* (what?); *A Story for Little Kids About Divorce*; *My Mom and Dad Don't Live Together Anymore*; and *Putting on the Brakes* (a young people's guide to understanding attention deficit disorder). And the great dilemmas of our time figure more and more, dealing with climate change and poverty in developing countries.

Representation from outside the West

On my first visit to Bologna 25 years ago some African publishers had stands but nothing to put on them – Madagascar had decorated theirs with pictures of their national airline. Since then, a variety of organisations have worked to give them a proper start and to encourage their local authors and illustrators. So this year the continent was represented by Egypt, South Africa, Rwanda, Tanzania and francophone Benin and Senegal (still a small contingent and needing to increase). Their problems in finding professional staff and selling their books at a price people can even contemplate are compounded by the fact that in one territory there may be many languages in use and the books must fall back (by the President's ruling) on a *lingua franca* like Kiswahili. Several of the titles from Benin and Rwanda deal in the basic facts of hygiene and survival, deliberately making a crude impact with their covers, like *Le Pipi Rouge* that shows two boys relieving themselves with streams of blood in the river. Five publishers came together to get this one done. The Tanzanian main representative spoke of the warm feelings of children for books and how teachers, when carrying one of the giant flats along the road to school, found themselves being followed by a swarm of eager children. The teachers feel good too, especially those who have written the books. From some 5000 copies, printed in Mauritius, the government would take the bulk for 89 schools and the residue for the trade, selling at around £2 a copy.

This scale of figures would be common in many of the small countries around the world. There were, for example, about 60 titles on show from the Lithuanian Publishers Association from Vilnius. An author would have to be satisfied with sales of 3000 at roughly £3, said one publisher, and produce several books a year to make a living. One trick for authors to increase their revenue is to write books endorsed by the government. In Brazil, for instance, with its population of nearly 150 million, the figures for books 'doing extremely well' in the general retail trade are similar to those in a First World country like Canada (where 'a children's bestseller' means anywhere between 7000 and 10,000); but those picked up by the state, which spends $40 million a year on books, may get orders for several hundred thousand.

The Global Initiative

The Fair has a pavilion dedicated to education and discovery called 'The Global Initiative', with its own 'global classroom'. One of the cultural changes that publishers and translators now have to take into account is that parents across the world want their children to learn English as a lever into higher education. Perhaps they should consider drawing as a useful skill too. In the global classroom I listened to a talk on teaching children to draw: it seems they will find it fun drawing things upside down and must get pencil and eye working at the same speed, never mind if they flap. It was good stuff, but came to an abrupt halt as the speaker acknowledged she had miscalculated the time and run out of slides.

Where to stay

Outside Bologna it is useful to remember that B&B is the saving grace of Bologna accommodation – hotel rates are ruinous, precisely because of the many trade fairs and an annual tourist intake of half a million. There is a large and lively student population and a Communist administration (*Italian* Communist). The Fair is held shortly before Easter and if you want to go, book online, preferably by Christmas. B&Bs charge €50–70 a night, against €200-plus at a hotel. B&B owners are generally pleasant and helpful, though it is sometimes disconcerting to have no key and be told to stay out until 6pm, like the ancient practice of our own seaside landladies.

Alex Hamilton is a journalist, an award-winning travel writer and the author of several novels and volumes of short stories.

Finance for writers and artists

FAQs for writers

Peter Vaines, a chartered accountant and barrister, addresses some frequently asked questions.

What can a working writer claim against tax?

A working writer is carrying on a business and can therefore claim all the expenses which are incurred wholly and exclusively for the purposes of that business. A list showing most of the usual expenses can be found in the article on *Income tax*, starting on page 387 of this *Yearbook*, but there will be other expenses that can be allowed in special circumstances.

Strictly, only expenses which are incurred for the sole purpose of the business can be claimed; there must be no 'duality of purpose' so an item of expenditure cannot be divided into private and business parts. However, HM Revenue & Customs (formerly the Inland Revenue) is usually quite flexible and is prepared to allow all reasonable expenses (including apportioned sums) where the amounts can be commercially justified.

Allowances can also be claimed for the cost of business assets such as a motor car, personal computers, fax, copying machines and all other equipment (including books) which may be used by the writer. An allowance of 25% of the cost can be claimed on the reducing balance each year and for most assets (except cars) an allowance of 50% can be claimed in the first year of purchase. Some expenditure on information technology now benefits from a special 100% allowance. See the article on *Income tax*, starting on page 387, for further details of the deductions available in respect of capital expenditure.

Can I request interest on fees owed to me beyond 30 days of my invoice?

Yes. A writer is like any other person carrying on a business and is entitled to charge interest at a rate of 8% over bank base rate on any debt outstanding for more than 30 days – although the period of credit can be varied by agreement between the parties. It is not compulsory to claim the interest; it is up to you to decide whether to enforce the right.

What can I do about bad debts?

A writer is in exactly the same position as anybody else carrying on a business over the payment of his or her invoices. It is generally not commercially sensible to insist on payment in advance but where the work involved is substantial (which will normally be the case with a book), it is usual to receive one third of the fee on signature, one third of the fee on delivery of the manuscript and the remaining one third on publication. On other assignments, perhaps not as substantial as a book, it could be worthwhile seeking 50% of the fee on signature and the other 50% on delivery. This would provide a degree of protection in case of cancellation of the assignment because of changes of policy or personnel at the publisher.

What financial disputes can I take to the Small Claims Court?

If somebody owes you money you can take them to the Small Claims Section of your local County Court, which deals with financial disputes up to £5000. The procedure is much less formal than normal court proceedings and involves little expense. It is not necessary to have a solicitor. You fill in a number of forms, turn up on the day and explain the background to why you are owed the money. See www.courtservice.gov.uk for full details of the procedure.

If I receive an advance, can I divide it between two tax years?

Yes. There used to be a system known as 'spreading' but in 2001 a new system called 'averaging' was introduced. This enables writers (and others engaged in the creation of literary, dramatic works or designs) to average the profits of two or more consecutive years if the profits for one year are less than 75% of the profits for the highest year. This relief can apply even if the work takes less than 12 months to create and it allows the writer to avoid the higher rates of tax which might arise if the income in respect of a number of years' work were all to be concentrated in a single year.

How do I make sure I am taxed as a self-employed person so that tax and National Insurance contributions are not deducted at source?

To be taxed as a self-employed person under Schedule D you have to make sure that the contract for the writing cannot be regarded as a contract of employment. This is unlikely to be the case with a professional author. The subject is highly complex but one of the most important features is that the publisher must not be in a position to direct or control the author's work. Where any doubt exists, the author might find the publisher deducting tax and National Insurance contributions as a precaution and that would clearly be highly disadvantageous. The author would be well advised to discuss the position with the publisher before the contract is signed to agree that he or she should be treated as self-employed and that no tax or National Insurance contributions will be deducted from any payments. If such agreement cannot be reached, professional advice should immediately be sought so that the detailed technical position can be explained to the publisher.

Is it a good idea to operate through a limited company?

It can be a good idea for a self-employed writer to operate through a company but generally only where the income is quite large. The costs of operating a company can outweigh any benefit if the writer is paying tax only at the basic rate. Where the writer is paying tax at the higher rate of 40%, being able to retain some of the income in a company at a tax rate of only 19% is obviously attractive. However, this will be entirely ineffective if the writer's contract with the publisher would otherwise be an employment. The whole subject of operating through a company is complex and professional advice is essential.

When does it become necessary to register for VAT?

Where the writer's self-employed income (from all sources, not only writing) exceeds £61,000 in the previous 12 months or is expected to do so in the next 30 days, he or she must register for VAT and add VAT to all his/her fees. The publisher will pay the VAT to the writer, who must pay the VAT over to the Customs and Excise each quarter. Any VAT the writer has paid on business expenses and on the purchase of business assets can be deducted. It is possible for some authors to take advantage of the simplified system for VAT payments which applies to small businesses. This involves a flat rate payment of VAT without any need to keep records of VAT on expenses.

Income tax

Despite attempts by successive Governments to simplify our taxation system, the subject has become increasingly complicated. Peter Vaines, a chartered accountant and barrister, gives a broad outline of taxation from the point of view of writers and other creative professionals. The proposals in the March 2006 Budget are broadly reflected in this article.

How income is taxed
Generally

Authors are usually treated for tax purposes as carrying on a profession and are taxed in a similar fashion to other professionals, i.e. as self-employed persons taxed under Schedule D. This article is directed to self-employed persons only, because if a writer is employed he or she will be subject to the much less advantageous rules which apply to employment income.

Attempts are often made by employed persons to shake off the status of 'employee' and to attain 'freelance' status so as to qualify for the advantages of Schedule D, such attempts meeting with varying degrees of success. The problems involved in making this transition are considerable and space does not permit a detailed explanation to be made here – individual advice is necessary if difficulties are to be avoided.

Particular attention has been paid by HM Revenue & Customs to journalists and to those engaged in the entertainment industry with a view to reclassifying them as employees so that PAYE is deducted from their earnings. This blanket treatment has been extended to other areas and, although it is obviously open to challenge by individual taxpayers, it is always difficult to persuade HM Revenue & Customs to change its views.

There is no reason why employed people cannot carry on a freelance business in their spare time. Indeed, aspiring authors, painters, musicians, etc, often derive so little income from their craft that the financial security of an employment, perhaps in a different sphere of activity, is necessary. The existence of the employment is irrelevant to the taxation of the freelance earnings although it is most important not to confuse the income or expenditure of the employment with the income or expenditure of the self-employed activity. HM Revenue & Customs is aware of the advantages which can be derived by an individual having 'freelance' income from an organisation of which he or she is also an employee, and where such circumstances are contrived, it can be extremely difficult to convince an Inspector of Taxes that a genuine freelance activity is being carried on. Where the individual operates through a company or partnership providing services personally to a particular client, and would be regarded as an employee if the services were supplied directly by the individual, additional problems arise from the notorious IR35 legislation and professional advice is essential.

For those starting in business or commencing work on a freelance basis HM Revenue & Customs produces a very useful booklet, *Starting in Business (IR28)*, which is available from any tax office.

Income

For income to be taxable it need not be substantial, nor even the author's only source of income; earnings from casual writing are also taxable but this can be an advantage, because occasional writers do not often make a profit from their writing. The expenses incurred in connection with writing may well exceed any income receivable and the resultant loss may then be used to reclaim tax paid on other income. There may be deducted from the income certain allowable expenses and capital allowances which are set out in more detail below. The possibility of a loss being used as a basis for a tax repayment is fully appreciated by HM Revenue & Customs, which sometimes attempts to treat casual writing as a hobby so that any losses incurred cannot be used to reclaim tax; of course by the same token any income receivable would not be chargeable to tax. This treatment may sound attractive but it should be resisted vigorously because HM Revenue & Customs does not hesitate to change its mind when profits begin to arise. In the case of exceptional or non-recurring writing, such as the autobiography of a sports personality or the memoirs of a politician, it could be better to be treated as pursuing a hobby and not as a professional author. Sales of copyright cannot be charged to income tax unless the recipient is a professional author. However, the proceeds of sale of copyright may be charged to capital gains tax, even by an individual who is not a professional author.

Royalties

Where the recipient is a professional author, a series of cases has laid down a clear principle that sales of copyright are taxable as income and not as capital receipts. Similarly, lump sums on account of, or in advance of royalties are also taxable as income in the year of receipt, subject to a claim for averaging relief (see below).

Arts Council awards

Arts Council category A awards

- Direct or indirect musical, design or choreographic commissions and direct or indirect commission of sculpture and paintings for public sites.
- The Royalty Supplement Guarantee Scheme.
- The contract writers' scheme.
- Jazz bursaries.
- Translators' grants.
- Photographic awards and bursaries.
- Film and video awards and bursaries.
- Performance Art Awards.
- Art Publishing Grants.
- Grants to assist with a specific project or projects (such as the writing of a book) or to meet specific professional expenses such as a contribution towards copying expenses made to a composer or to an artist's studio expenses.

Arts Council category B awards

- Bursaries to trainee directors.
- Bursaries for associate directors.
- Bursaries to people attending full-time courses in arts administration (the practical training course).
- In-service bursaries to theatre designers and bursaries to trainees on the theatre designers' scheme.
- In-service bursaries for administrators.
- Bursaries for actors and actresses.
- Bursaries for technicians and stage managers.
- Bursaries made to students attending the City University Arts Administration courses.
- Awards, known as the Buying Time Awards, made not to assist with a specific project or professional expenses but to maintain the recipient to enable him or her to take time off to develop his personal talents. These at present include the awards and bursaries known as the Theatre Writing Bursaries, awards and bursaries to composers, awards and bursaries to painters, sculptures and print makers, literature awards and bursaries.

Copyright royalties are generally paid without deduction of income tax. However, if royalties are paid to a person who normally lives abroad, tax must be deducted by the payer or his agent at the time the payment is made unless arrangements are made with HM Revenue & Customs for payments to be made gross under the terms of a Double Taxation Agreement with the other country.

Arts Council grants

Persons in receipt of grants from the Arts Council or similar bodies will be concerned whether or not such grants are liable to income tax. HM Revenue & Customs has issued a Statement of Practice after detailed discussions with the Arts Council regarding the tax treatment of the awards. Grants and other receipts of a similar nature have now been divided into two categories (see box) – those which are to be treated by HM Revenue & Customs as chargeable to tax and those which are not. Category A awards are considered to be taxable; awards made under category B are not chargeable to tax.

This Statement of Practice has no legal force and is used merely to ease the administration of the tax system. It is open to anyone in receipt of a grant or award to disregard the agreed statement and challenge HM Revenue & Customs view on the merits of their particular case. However, it must be recognised that HM Revenue & Customs does not issue such statements lightly and any challenge to their view would almost certainly involve a lengthy and expensive action through the Courts.

The tax position of persons in receipt of literary prizes will generally follow a decision by the Special Commissioners in connection with the Whitbread Book Awards (now called the Costa Book Awards). In that case it was decided that the prize was not part of the author's professional income and accordingly not chargeable to tax. The precise details are not available because decisions of the Special Commissioners were not, at that time, reported unless an appeal was made to the High Court; HM Revenue & Customs chose not to appeal against this decision. Details of the many literary awards that are given each year start on Children's book and illustration prizes and awards, and this decision is of considerable significance to the winners of each of these prizes. It would be unwise to assume that all such awards will be free of tax as the precise facts which were present in the case of the Whitbread awards may not be repeated in another case; however it is clear that an author winning a prize has some very powerful arguments in his or her favour, should HM Revenue & Customs seek to charge tax on the award.

Allowable expenses

To qualify as an allowable business expense, expenditure has to be laid out wholly and exclusively for business purposes. Strictly there must be no 'duality of purpose', which means that expenditure cannot be apportioned to reflect the private and business usage, e.g. food, clothing, telephone, travelling expenses, etc. However, HM Revenue & Customs does not usually interpret this principle strictly and is prepared to allow all reasonable expenses (including apportioned sums) where the amounts can be commercially justified.

It should be noted carefully that the expenditure does not have to be 'necessary', it merely has to be incurred 'wholly and exclusively' for business purposes. Naturally, however, expenditure of an outrageous and wholly unnecessary character might well give rise to a presumption that it was not really for business purposes. As with all things, some expenses are unquestionably allowable and some expenses are equally unquestionably not allowable – it is the grey area in between which gives rise to all the difficulties and the outcome invariably depends on negotiation with HM Revenue & Customs.

Great care should be taken when claiming a deduction for items where there may be a 'duality of purpose' and negotiations should be conducted with more than usual care and courtesy – if provoked the Inspector of Taxes may well choose to allow nothing. An appeal is always possible although unlikely to succeed as a string of cases in the Courts has clearly demonstrated. An example is the case of *Caillebotte* v. *Quinn* where the taxpayer (who normally had lunch at home) sought to claim the excess cost of meals incurred because he was working a long way from his home. The taxpayer's arguments failed because he did not eat only in order to work, one of the reasons for his eating was in order to sustain his life; a duality of purpose therefore existed and no tax relief was due.

Other cases have shown that expenditure on clothing can also be disallowed if it is the kind of clothing which is in everyday use, because clothing is worn not only to assist the pursuit of one's profession but also to accord with public decency. This duality of purpose may be sufficient to deny relief – even where the particular type of clothing is of a kind not otherwise worn by the taxpayer. In the case of *Mallalieu* v. *Drummond* a barrister failed to obtain a tax deduction for items of sombre clothing that she purchased specifically for wearing in Court. The House of Lords decided that a duality of purpose existed because clothing represented part of her needs as a human being.

Allowances

Despite the above, Inspectors of Taxes are not usually inflexible and the following list of expenses are among those generally allowed.

(a) Cost of all materials used up in the course of preparation of the work.

(b) Cost of typewriting and secretarial assistance, etc; if this or other help is obtained from one's spouse then it is entirely proper for a deduction to be claimed for the amounts paid for the work. The amounts claimed must actually be paid to the spouse and should be at the market rate although some uplift can be made for unsocial hours, etc. Payments to a wife (or husband) are of course taxable in her (or his) hands and should therefore be most carefully considered. The wife's earnings may also be liable for National Insurance contributions and it is important to take care because otherwise you may find that these contributions may outweigh the tax savings. The impact of the National Minimum Wage should also be considered.

(c) All expenditure on normal business items such as postage, stationery, telephone, email, fax and answering machines, agent's fees, accountancy charges, photography, subscriptions, periodicals, magazines, etc, may be claimed. The cost of daily papers should not be overlooked if these form part of research material. Visits to theatres, cinemas, etc, for research purposes may also be permissible (but not the cost relating to guests). Unfortunately, expenditure on all types of business entertaining is specifically denied tax relief.

(d) If work is conducted at home, a deduction for 'use of home' is usually allowed providing the amount claimed is reasonable. If the claim is based on an appropriate proportion of the total costs of rent, light and heat, cleaning and maintenance, insurance, etc (but not the Council Tax), care should be taken to ensure that no single room is used 'exclusively' for business purposes, because this may result in the Capital Gains Tax exemption on the house as the only or main residence being partially forfeited. However, it would be a strange household where one room was in fact used exclusively for business purposes and for no other purpose whatsoever (e.g. storing personal bank statements and other private papers); the usual formula is to claim a deduction on the basis that most or all of the rooms in the house are used at one time or another for business purposes, thereby avoiding any suggestion that any part was used exclusively for business purposes.

(e) The appropriate business proportion of motor running expenses may also be claimed although what is the appropriate proportion will naturally depend on the particular circumstances of each case; it should be appreciated that the well-known scale of benefits, whereby employees were taxed according to the size and cost of the car (and are now taxed on the basis of their CO_2 emissions), do not apply to self-employed persons.

(f) It has been long established that the cost of travelling from home to work (whether employed or self-employed) is not an allowable expense. However, if home is one's place of work then no expenditure under this heading is likely to be incurred and difficulties are unlikely to arise.

(g) Travelling and hotel expenses incurred for business purposes will normally be allowed but if any part could be construed as disguised holiday or pleasure expenditure, considerable thought would need to be given to the commercial reasons for the journey in order to justify the claim. The principle of 'duality of purpose' will always be a difficult hurdle in this connection – although not insurmountable.

(h) If a separate business bank account is maintained, any overdraft interest thereon will be an allowable expense. This is the only circumstance in which overdraft interest is allowed for tax purposes and care should be taken to avoid overdrafts in all other circumstances.

(i) Where capital allowances (see below) are claimed for a personal computer, fax, modem, television, video, CD or tape player, etc, used for business purposes the costs of maintenance and repair of the equipment may also be claimed.

Clearly many other allowable items may be claimed in addition to those listed. Wherever there is any reasonable business motive for some expenditure it should be claimed as a deduction although it is necessary to preserve all records relating to the expense. It is sensible to avoid an excess of imagination as this would naturally cause the Inspector of Taxes to doubt the genuineness of other expenses claimed.

The question is often raised whether the whole amount of an expense may be deducted or whether the VAT content must be excluded. Where VAT is reclaimed from the Customs and Excise by someone who is registered for VAT, the VAT element of the expense cannot be treated as an allowable deduction. Where the VAT is not reclaimed, the whole expense (inclusive of VAT) is allowable for income tax purposes.

Capital allowances

Allowances

Where expenditure of a capital nature is incurred, it cannot be deducted from income as an expense – a separate and sometimes more valuable capital allowance being available instead. Capital allowances are given for many different types of expenditure, but authors and similar professional people are likely to claim only for 'plant and machinery'; this is a very wide expression which may include motor cars, personal computers, fax and photocopying machines, modems, televisions, CD, video and cassette players used for business purposes. Plant and machinery generally qualify for a 50% allowance in the year of purchase and 25% of the reducing balance in subsequent years. Expenditure on information technology for the purposes of the business now benefits from a special 100% allowance in the year of purchase. Where the useful life of an asset is expected to be short, it is possible to claim special treatment as a 'short life asset' enabling the allowances to be accelerated.

The reason these allowances can be more valuable than allowable expenses is that they may be wholly or partly disclaimed in any year that full benefit cannot be obtained – ordinary business expenses cannot be similarly disclaimed. Where, for example, the income of an author does not exceed his personal allowances, he would not be liable to tax and a claim for capital allowances would be wasted. If the capital allowances were to be disclaimed their benefit would be carried forward for use in subsequent years. Careful planning with claims for capital allowances is therefore essential if maximum benefit is to be obtained.

As an alternative to capital allowances, claims can be made on the 'renewals' basis whereby all renewals are treated as allowable deductions in the year; no allowance is obtained for the initial purchase, but the cost of replacement (excluding any improvement element) is allowed in full. This basis is no longer widely used, as it is considerably less advantageous than claiming capital allowances as described above.

Leasing is a popular method of acquiring fixed assets, and where cash is not available to enable an outright purchase to be made, assets may be leased over a period of time. Whilst leasing may have financial benefits in certain circumstances, in normal cases there is likely to be no tax advantage in leasing an asset where the alternative of outright purchase is available. Indeed, leasing can be a positive disadvantage in the case of motor cars with a new retail price of more than £12,000. If such a car is leased, only a proportion of the leasing charges will be tax deductible.

Books

The question of whether the cost of books is eligible for tax relief has long been a source of difficulty. The annual cost of replacing books used for the purposes of one's professional activities (e.g. the cost of a new *Children's Writers' & Artists' Yearbook* each year) has always been an allowable expense; the difficulty arose because the initial cost of reference books, etc (e.g. when commencing one's profession) was treated as capital expenditure but no allowances were due as the books were not considered to be 'plant'. However, the matter was clarified by the case of *Munby* v. *Furlong* in which the Court of Appeal decided that the initial cost of law books purchased by a barrister was expenditure on 'plant' and eligible for capital allowances. This is clearly a most important decision, particularly relevant to any person who uses expensive books in the course of exercising his or her profession.

Pension contributions

Personal pensions

Where a self-employed person pays annual premiums under an approved personal pension policy, tax relief was available for the year 2005/6 for the following amounts:

Age at 6/4/2005	Maximum %
35 and under	17.5% (max) £18,480
36–45	20% (max) £21,120
46–50	25% (max) £26,400
51–55	30% (max) £31,680
56–60	35% (max) £36,960
61–74	40% (max) £42,240

These figures do not apply to existing retirement annuity policies; these remain subject to the old limits which are unchanged.

These arrangements were extremely advantageous in providing for a pension as premiums were usually paid when the income is high (and the tax relief is also high) and the pension (taxed as earned income when received) usually arises when the income is low and little tax is payable. There was also the opportunity to take part of the pension entitlement as a tax-free lump sum. It is necessary to take into account the possibility that the tax advantages could go into reverse. When the pension is paid it could, if rates rise again, be taxed at a higher rate than the rate of tax relief at the moment. From 6 April 2006 there is a whole new regime for pensions. All the old rules were swept away and there is now a much simpler system. Each individual has a lifetime allowance (set at £1.5 million for 2006/7 but rising annually). When benefits crystallise, which will generally be when a pension begins to be paid, this is measured against the individual's lifetime allowance; any excess will be taxed at 25%, or at 55% if the excess is taken as a lump sum.

Each individual also has an annual allowance for contributions to the pension fund which is set at £215,000 for 2006/7 but will increase in later years. If the annual increase in an individual's rights under all registered schemes of which he is a member exceeds the annual allowance, the excess is chargeable to tax at 40%.

For most writers and artists this means that they can effectively contribute the whole of their earnings to a pension scheme (if they can afford to do so) without any of the previous complications. It is still necessary to be careful where there is other income giving rise to a pension because the whole of the pension entitlement has to be taken into account.

Flexible retirement is possible allowing members of occupational pensions schemes to continue working while also drawing retirement benefits. As part of this reform, however, the normal minimum pension age will be raised from 50 to 55 by 6 April 2010.

Class 4 National Insurance contributions

Allied to pensions is the payment of Class 4 National Insurance contributions, although no pension or other benefit is obtained by the contributions; the Class 4 contributions are designed solely to extract additional amounts from self-employed persons and are payable in addition to the normal Class 2 (self-employed) contributions. The rates are changed each year and for 2006/7 self-employed persons will be obliged to contribute 8% of their profits between the range £5035–£33,540 per annum. This amount is collected in conjunction with the Schedule D income tax liability.

Since 6 April 2003 there has been a further 1% charge on earnings above £33,540 limit to correspond with the increase in employees' contributions.

Averaging relief
Relief for copyright payments

For many years special provisions enabled authors and similar persons engaged on a literary, dramatic, musical or artistic work for a period of more than 12 months, to spread certain amounts received over two or three years depending on the time spent in preparing the work.

On 6 April 2001 a simpler system of averaging was introduced. Under these rules, professional authors and artists engaged in the creation of literary, dramatic works or designs may claim to average the profits of two or more consecutive years if the profits for one year are less than 75% of the profits for the highest year. This new relief can apply even if the work took less than 12 months to create and is available to people who create works in partnership with others.

The purpose of the relief is to enable the creative artist to utilise his allowances fully and to avoid the higher rates of tax which might apply if all the income were to arise in a single year.

Collection of tax
Self-assessment

In 1997, the system of sending in a tax return showing all your income and HM Revenue & Customs raising an assessment to collect the tax was abolished. So was the idea that you pay tax on your profits for the preceding year. Now, when you send in your tax return you have to work out your own tax liability and send a cheque; this is called 'self-assessment'. If you get it wrong, or if you are late with your tax return or the payment of tax, interest and penalties will be charged.

Under this system, HM Revenue & Customs rarely issue assessments; they are no longer necessary because the idea is that you assess yourself. A colour-coded tax return was created, designed to help individuals meet their tax obligations. This is a daunting task but the term 'self-assessment' is not intended to imply that individuals have to do it themselves; they can (and often will) engage professional help. The term is only intended to convey that it is the taxpayer, and not HM Revenue & Customs, who is responsible for getting the tax liability right and for it to be paid on time.

The deadline for sending in the tax return is 31 January following the end of the tax year; so for the tax year 2005/6, the tax return has to be submitted to HM Revenue & Customs by 31 January 2007. If for some reason you are unwilling or unable to calculate the tax payable, you can ask HM Revenue & Customs to do it for you, in which case it is necessary to send in your tax return by 30 September 2006.

Income tax on self-employed earnings remains payable in two instalments on 31 January and 31 July each year. Because the accurate figures may not necessarily be known, these payments in January and July will therefore be only payments on account based on the previous year's liability. The final balancing figure will be paid the following 31 January together with the first instalment of the liability for the following year.

When HM Revenue & Customs receives the self-assessment tax return, it is checked to see if there is anything obviously wrong; if there is, a letter will be sent to you immediately. Otherwise, HM Revenue & Customs has 12 months from the filing date of 31 January in which to make further enquiries; if it doesn't, it will have no further opportunity to do so and your tax liabilities are final – unless there is something seriously wrong such as the omission of income or capital gains. In that event, HM Revenue & Customs will raise an assessment later to collect any extra tax together with appropriate penalties. It is essential for the operation of the new system that all records relevant to your tax returns are retained for at least 12 months in case they are needed by HM Revenue & Customs. For the self-employed, the record-keeping requirement is much more onerous because the records need to be kept for nearly six years. One important change in the rules is that if you claim a tax deduction for an expense, it will be necessary to have a receipt or other document proving that the expenditure has been made. Because the existence of the underlying records is so important to the operation of self-assessment, HM Revenue & Customs will treat them very seriously and there is a penalty of £3000 for any failure to keep adequate records.

Interest

Interest is chargeable on overdue tax at a variable rate, which at the time of writing is 6.5% per annum. It does not rank for any tax relief, which can make HM Revenue & Customs an expensive source of credit.

However, HM Revenue & Customs can also be obliged to pay interest (known as repayment supplement) tax-free where repayments are delayed. The rules relating to repayment supplement are less beneficial and even more complicated than the rules for interest payable but they do exist and can be very welcome if a large repayment has been delayed for a long time. Unfortunately, the rate of repayment supplement is only 2.25%, much lower than the rate of interest on unpaid tax.

Value added tax

The activities of writers, painters, composers, etc are all 'taxable supplies' within the scope of VAT and chargeable at the standard rate. (Zero rating which applies to publishers, booksellers, etc on the supply of books does not extend to the work performed by writers.) Accordingly, authors are obliged to register for VAT if their income for the past 12 months exceeds £61,000 or if their income for the coming month will exceed that figure.

Delay in registering can be a most serious matter because if registration is not effected at the proper time, the Customs and Excise can (and invariably do) claim VAT from all the income received since the date on which registration should have been made. As no VAT would have been included in the amounts received during this period the amount claimed by the Customs and Excise must inevitably come straight from the pocket of the author.

The author may be entitled to seek reimbursement of the VAT from those whom he or she ought to have charged VAT but this is obviously a matter of some difficulty and may indeed damage his commercial relationships. Apart from these disadvantages there is also a penalty for late registration. The rules are extremely harsh and are imposed automatically even in cases of innocent error. It is therefore extremely important to monitor the income very carefully because if in any period of 12 months the income exceeds the £61,000 limit, the Customs and Excise must be notified within 30 days of the end of the period. Failure to do so will give rise to an automatic penalty. It should be emphasised that this is a penalty for failing to submit a form and has nothing to do with any real or potential loss of tax. Furthermore, whether the failure was innocent or deliberate will not matter. Only the existence of a 'reasonable excuse' will be a defence to the penalty. However, a reasonable excuse does not include ignorance, error, a lack of funds or reliance on any third party.

However, it is possible to regard VAT registration as a privilege and not a penalty, because only VAT registered persons can reclaim VAT paid on their expenses such as stationery, telephone, professional fees, etc, and even typewriters and other plant and machinery (excluding cars). However, many find that the administrative inconvenience – the cost of maintaining the necessary records and completing the necessary forms – more than outweighs the benefits to be gained from registration and prefer to stay outside the scope of VAT for as long as possible.

Overseas matters

The general observation may be made that self-employed persons resident and domiciled in the United Kingdom are not well treated with regard to their overseas work, being taxable on their worldwide income. It is important to emphasise that if fees are earned abroad, no tax saving can be achieved merely by keeping the money outside the country. Although exchange control regulations no longer exist to require repatriation of foreign earnings, such income remains taxable in the UK and must be disclosed to HM Revenue & Customs; the same applies to interest or other income arising on any investment of these earnings overseas. Accordingly, whenever foreign earnings are likely to become substantial, prompt and effective action is required to limit the impact of UK and foreign taxation. In the case of non-resident authors it is important that arrangements concerning writing for publication in the UK, e.g. in newspapers, are undertaken with great care. A case concerning the wife of one of the great train robbers who provided detailed information for a series of articles in a Sunday newspaper is most instructive. Although she was acknowledged to be resident in Canada for all the relevant years, the income from the articles was treated as arising in this country and fully chargeable to UK tax.

The United Kingdom has double taxation agreements with many other countries and these agreements are designed to ensure that income arising in a foreign country is taxed either in that country or in the UK. Where a withholding tax is deducted from payments received from another country (or where tax is paid in full in the absence of a double taxation agreement), the amount of foreign tax paid can usually be set off against the related UK tax liability. Many successful authors can be found living in Eire because of the complete exemption from tax which attaches to works of cultural or artistic merit by persons who are resident there. However, such a step should only be contemplated having careful regard to all the other domestic and commercial considerations and specialist advice is essential if the exemption is to be obtained and kept; a careless breach of the conditions could cause the exemption to be withdrawn with catastrophic consequences.

Further information concerning the precise conditions to be satisfied for exemption from tax in Eire can be obtained from the Revenue Commissioners, Blocks 3–10, Dublin Castle, Dublin 2, or from their website (www.revenue.ie).

Companies

When an author becomes successful the prospect of paying tax at the higher rate may drive them to take hasty action such as the formation of companies, etc, which may not always be to their advantage. Indeed some authors seeing the exodus into tax exile of their more successful colleagues even form companies in low tax areas in the naive expectation of saving large amounts of tax. HM Revenue & Customs is fully aware of the opportunities and have extensive powers to charge tax and combat avoidance. Accordingly, such action is just as likely to increase tax liabilities and generate other costs and should never be contemplated without expert advice; some very expensive mistakes are often made in this area which are not always able to be remedied.

To conduct one's business through the medium of a company can be a most effective method of mitigating tax liabilities, and providing it is done at the right time and under the right circumstances very substantial advantages can be derived. However, if done without due care and attention the intended advantages will simply evaporate. At the very least it is essential to ensure that the company's business is genuine and conducted properly with regard to the realities of the situation. If the author continues his or her activities unchanged, simply paying all the receipts from his work into a company's bank account, he cannot expect to persuade HM Revenue & Customs that it is the company and not himself who is entitled to, and should be assessed to tax on, that income.

It must be strongly emphasised that many pitfalls exist which can easily eliminate all the tax benefits expected to arise by the formation of the company. For example, company directors are employees of the company and will be liable to pay much higher National Insurance contributions; the company must also pay the employer's proportion of the contribution and a total liability of over 23% of gross salary may arise. This compares most unfavourably with the position of a self-employed person. Moreover, on the commencement of the company's business the individual's profession will cease and the possibility of revisions being made by HM Revenue & Customs to earlier tax liabilities means that the timing of a change has to be considered very carefully.

The tax return

No mention has been made above of personal reliefs and allowances; this is because these allowances and the rates of tax are subject to constant change and are always set out in detail in the explanatory notes which accompany the Tax Return. The annual Tax Return is an important document and should be completed promptly with extreme care, particularly since the introduction of self-assessment. If filling in the Return is a source of difficulty or anxiety, comfort may be found in the Consumer Association's publication *Money Which? – Tax Saving Guide*, which is published in March of each year and includes much which is likely to be of interest and assistance.

Peter Vaines FCA, ATII, barrister, is a partner in the international law firm of Squire Sanders & Dempsey LLP and writes and speaks widely on tax matters. He is Managing Editor of *Personal Tax Planning Review*, on the Editorial Board of *Taxation*, tax columnist of the *New Law Journal* and author of a number of books on taxation.

Social security contributions

In general, every individual who works in Great Britain either as an employee or as a self-employed person is liable to pay social security contributions. The law governing this subject is complicated and Peter Arrowsmith FCA gives here a summary of the position. This article should be regarded as a general guide only.

All contributions are payable in respect of years ending on 5 April. See box (below) for the classes of contributions.

Employed or self-employed?

The question as to whether a person is employed under a contract *of* service and is thereby an employee liable to Class 1 contributions, or performs services (either solely or in partnership) under a contract for service and is thereby self-employed liable to Class 2 and Class 4 contributions, often has to be decided in practice. One of the best guides can be found in the case of *Market Investigations Ltd* v. *Minister of Social Security* (1969 2 WLR 1) when Cooke J. remarked:

> '... the fundamental test to be applied is this: "Is the person who has engaged himself to perform these services performing them as a person in business on his own account?" If the answer to that question is 'yes', then the contract is a contract for services. If the answer is 'no', then the contract is a contract of service. No exhaustive list has been compiled and perhaps no exhaustive list can be compiled of the considerations which are relevant in determining that question, nor can strict rules be laid down as to the relative weight which the various considerations should carry in particular cases. The most that can be said is that control will no doubt always have to be considered, although it can no longer be regarded as the sole determining factor; and that factors which may be of importance are such matters as:

> * whether the man performing the services provides his own equipment,
> * whether he hires his own helpers,
> * what degree of financial risk he takes,
> * what degree of responsibility for investment and management he has, and
> * whether and how far he has an opportunity of profiting from sound management in the performance of his task.'

The above case has often been considered subsequently – notably in November 1993 by the Court of Appeal in the case of *Hall* v. *Lorimer*. In this case a vision mixer with around 20 clients and undertaking around 120–150 separate engagements per annum was held to be self-employed. This follows the, perhaps surprising, contention of the former Inland Revenue that the taxpayer was an employee.

Classes of contributions

Class 1 These are payable by employees (primary contributions) and their employers (secondary contributions) and are based on earnings.

Class 1A Payable only by employers in respect of all taxable benefits in kind (cars and fuel only prior to 6 April 2000).

Class 1B Payable only by employers in respect of PAYE Settlement Agreements entered into by them.

Class 2 These are weekly flat rate contributions, payable by the self-employed.

Class 3 These are weekly flat rate contributions, payable on a voluntary basis in order to provide, or make up entitlement to, certain social security benefits.

Class 4 These are payable by the self-employed in respect of their trading or professional income and are based on earnings.

Exceptions

There are certain exceptions to the above rules, those most relevant to artists and writers being:

- The employment of a wife by her husband, or vice versa, is disregarded for social security purposes unless it is for the purposes of a trade or profession (e.g. the employment of his wife by an author would not be disregarded and would result in a liability for contributions if her salary reached the minimum levels). The same provisions also apply to civil partners from 5 December 2005.

- The employment of certain relatives in a private dwelling house in which both employee and employer reside is disregarded for social security purposes provided the employment is not for the purposes of a trade or business carried on at those premises by the employer. This would cover the employment of a relative (as defined) as a housekeeper in a private residence.

In general, lecturers, teachers and instructors engaged by an educational establishment to teach on at least four days in three consecutive months are regarded as employees for social security purposes, although this rule does not apply to fees received by persons giving public lectures.

Freelance film workers

There is a list of grades in the film industry in respect of which PAYE need not be deducted and who are regarded as self-employed for tax purposes.

Further information can be obtained from the guidance notes on the application of PAYE to casual and freelance staff in the film industry issued by the former Inland Revenue. In view of the Inland Revenue announcement that the same status will apply for PAYE and National Insurance contributions purposes, no liability for employee's and employer's contributions should arise in the case of any of the grades mentioned above.

However, in the film and television industry this general rule was not always followed in practice. In December 1992, after a long review, the DSS agreed that individuals working behind the camera and who have jobs on the Inland Revenue Schedule D list are self-employed for social security purposes.

There are special rules for, *inter alia*, personnel appearing before the camera, short engagements, payments to limited companies and payments to overseas personalities.

Artistes, performers/non-performers

The status of artistes and performers for tax purposes will depend on the individual circumstances but for social security new regulations which took effect on 17 July 1998 require most actors, musicians or similar performers to be treated as employees for social security purposes, whether or not this status applies under general and/or tax law. It also applies whether or not the individual is supplied through an agency.

Personal service companies

From 6 April 2000, those who have control of their own 'one-man service companies' are subject to special rules. If the work that the owner of the company does for the company's customers would – but for the one-man company – be considered as an employment of that individual (i.e. rather than self-employment), a deemed salary may arise. If it does, then some or all of the income of the company will be treated as salary liable to PAYE and National Insurance contributions. This will be the case whether or not such salary is actually paid by the company. The same situation may arise where the worker owns as little as 5% of a company's share capital.

The calculations required by HM Revenue & Customs are complicated and have to be done very quickly at the end of each tax year (even if the company's year-end is different). It is essential that affected businesses seek detailed professional advice about these rules which may also, in certain circumstances, apply to partnerships.

Class 1 contributions

As mentioned above, these are related to earnings, the amount payable depending upon whether the employer has applied for his employees to be 'contracted-out' of the State earnings-related pension scheme; such application can be made where the employer's own pension scheme provides a requisite level of benefits for his or her employees and their dependants or, in the case of a money purchase scheme (COMPS) certain minimum safeguards are covered. Employers with employees contributing to 'stakeholder pension plans' continue to pay the full not contracted-out rate. Such employees have their contracting out arrangements handled separately by government authorities.

Contributions are payable by employees and employers on earnings that exceed the earnings threshold. Contributions are normally collected via the PAYE tax deduction machinery, and there are penalties for late submission of returns and for errors therein. From 19 April 1993, interest is charged automatically on PAYE and social security contributions paid late.

Employees liable to pay

Contributions are payable by any employee who is aged 16 years and over (even though they may still be at school) and who is paid an amount equal to, or exceeding, the earnings threshold. Nationality is irrelevant for contribution purposes and, subject to special rules covering employees not normally resident in Great Britain, Northern Ireland or the Isle of Man, or resident in EEA countries or those with which there are reciprocal agreements, contributions must be paid whether the employee concerned is a British subject or not provided he is gainfully employed in Great Britain.

Employees exempt from liability to pay

Persons over pensionable age (65 for men; 60 – until 2010 – for women) are exempt from liability to pay primary contributions, even if they have not retired. However, the fact that an employee may be exempt from liability does not relieve an employer from liability to pay secondary contributions in respect of that employee.

Employees' (primary) contributions

From 6 April 2003, the rate of employees' contributions on earnings from the earnings threshold to the upper earnings limit is 11% (9.4% for contracted-out employments). Certain married women who made appropriate elections before 12 May 1977 may be entitled to pay a reduced rate of 4.85%. However, they will have no entitlement to benefits in respect of these contributions.

From April 2003, earnings above the upper earnings limit attract an employee contribution liability of 1% – previously, there was no such liability.

Employers' (secondary) contributions

All employers are liable to pay contributions on the gross earnings of employees. As mentioned above, an employer's liability is not reduced as a result of employees being exempted from contributions, or being liable to pay only the reduced rate (4.85%) of contributions.

For earnings paid on or after 6 April 2003 employers are liable at a rate of 12.8% on earnings paid above the earnings threshold (without any upper earnings limit), 9.3% where the employment is contracted out (salary related) or 11.8% contracted out (money purchase). In addition, special rebates apply in respect of earnings falling between the lower earnings limit and the earnings threshold. This provides, effectively, a negative rate of contribution in that small band of earnings. It should be noted that the contracted-out rates of 9.3% and 11.8% apply only up to the upper earnings limit. Thereafter, the not contracted-out rate of 12.8% is applicable.

The employer is responsible for the payment of both employees' and employer's contributions, but is entitled to deduct the employees' contributions from the earnings on which they are calculated. Effectively, therefore, the employee suffers a deduction in respect of his or her social security contributions in arriving at his weekly or monthly wage or salary. Special rules apply to company directors and persons employed through agencies.

Items included in, or excluded from, earnings

Contributions are calculated on the basis of a person's gross earnings from their employment. This will normally be the figure shown on the deduction working sheet, except where the employee pays superannuation contributions and, from 6 April 1987, charitable gifts under payroll giving – these must be added back for the purposes of calculating Class 1 liability.

Earnings include salary, wages, overtime pay, commissions, bonuses, holiday pay, payments made while the employee is sick or absent from work, payments to cover travel between home and office, and payments under the statutory sick pay, statutory maternity pay, statutory paternity pay and statutory adoption pay schemes.

However, certain payments, some of which may be regarded as taxable income for income tax purposes, are ignored for Class 1 purposes. These include:
- certain gratuities paid other than by the employer;
- redundancy payments and some payments in lieu of notice;
- certain payments in kind;
- reimbursement of specific expenses incurred in the carrying out of the employment;
- benefits given on an individual basis for personal reasons (e.g. wedding and birthday presents);
- compensation for loss of office.

Booklet CWG 2 (2006 edition) gives a list of items to include in or exclude from earnings for Class 1 contribution purposes. Some such items may, however, be liable to Class 1A (employer only) contributions.

Rates of Class 1 contributions and earnings limits from 6 April 2005

Earnings per week	Rates payable on earnings in each band			
	Not contracted-out		Contracted-out	
	Employee	Employer	Employee	Employer
£	%	%	%	%
Below 84.00	–	–	–	–
84.00–96.99	–	–	– (*)	– (*)
97.00–645.00	11	12.8	9.4	9.3 or 11.8
Over £645.00	1	12.8	1	12.8

* Special rebates deductible in respect of this band of earnings.

Miscellaneous rules

There are detailed rules covering a person with two or more employments; where a person receives a bonus or commission in addition to a regular wage or salary; and where a person is in receipt of holiday pay. From 6 April 1991 employers' social security contributions arise under Class 1A in respect of the private use of a company car, and of fuel provided for private use therein. From 6 April 2000, this charge was extended to cover most taxable benefits in kind. The rate is now 12.8%. From 6 April 1999, Class 1B contributions are payable by employers using PAYE Settlement Agreements in respect of small and/or irregular expense payments and benefits, etc. This rate is also currently 12.8%.

Class 2 contributions

Class 2 contributions are payable at the weekly rate of £2.10 as from 6 April 2005. This rate did not change in 2006. Exemptions from Class 2 liability are:

- A man over 65 or a woman over – until 2010 – 60.
- A person who has not attained the age of 16.
- A married woman or, in certain cases, a widow either of whom elected prior to 12 May 1977 not to pay Class 2 contributions.
- Persons with small earnings (see below).
- Persons not ordinarily self-employed (see below).

Small earnings

Application for a certificate of exception from Class 2 contributions may be made by any person who can show that his or her net self-employed earnings per his profit and loss account (as opposed to taxable profits):

- for the year of application are expected to be less than a specified limit (£4465 in the 2006/7 tax year); or
- for the year preceding the application were less than the limit specified for that year (£4345 for 2005/6) and there has been no material change of circumstances.

Certificates of exception must be renewed in accordance with the instructions stated thereon. At HM Revenue & Customs' discretion the certificate may commence up to 13 weeks before the date on which the application is made. Despite a certificate of exception being in force, a person who is self-employed is still entitled to pay Class 2 contributions if they wish, in order to maintain entitlement to social security benefits.

Persons not ordinarily self-employed

Part-time self-employed activities (including as a writer or artist) are disregarded for contribution purposes if the person concerned is not ordinarily employed in such activities and has a full-time job as an employee. There is no definition of 'ordinarily employed' for this purpose but a person who has a regular job and whose earnings from spare-time occupation are not expected to be more than £1300 per annum may fall within this category. Persons qualifying for this relief do not require certificates of exception but may be well advised to apply for one nonetheless.

Method of payment

From April 1993, Class 2 contributions may be paid by monthly direct debit in arrears or, alternatively, by cheque, bank giro, etc following receipt of a quarterly (in arrears) bill.

Overpaid contributions

If, following the payment of Class 2 contributions, it is found that the earnings are below the exception limit (e.g. the relevant accounts are prepared late), the Class 2 contributions that have been overpaid can be reclaimed, provided a claim is made between 6 April and 31 January immediately following the end of the tax year.

Class 3 contributions

Class 3 contributions are payable voluntarily, at the weekly rate of £7.55 per week from 6 April 2006, by persons aged 16 or over with a view to enabling them to qualify for a limited range of benefits if their contribution record is not otherwise sufficient. In general, Class 3 contributions can be paid by employees, the self-employed and the non employed.

Broadly speaking, no more than 52 Class 3 contributions are payable for any one tax year, and contributions cannot be paid in respect of tax years after the one in which the individual concerned reaches the age of 64 (currently 59 for women). Class 3 contributions may be paid in the same manner as Class 2 (see above) or by annual cheque in arrears.

Class 4 contributions

In addition to Class 2 contributions, self-employed persons are liable to pay Class 4 contributions. These are calculated at the rate of 8% on the amount of profits or gains chargeable to income tax which exceed £5035 per annum but which do not exceed £33,540 per annum for 2006/7. Profits above the upper limit of £33,540 attract a Class 4 charge at the rate of 1%. The income tax profit on which Class 4 contributions are calculated is after deducting capital allowances and losses, but before deducting personal tax allowances or retirement annuity or personal pension or stakeholder pension plan premiums.

Class 4 contributions produce no additional benefits, but were introduced to ensure that self-employed persons as a whole pay a fair share of the cost of pensions and other social security benefits, yet without those who make only small profits having to pay excessively high flat rate contributions.

Payment of contributions

In general, Class 4 contributions are now self-assessed and paid to HM Revenue & Customs together with the income tax as a result of the self-assessment income tax return, and accordingly the contributions are due and payable at the same time as the income tax liability on the relevant profits. Under self-assessment, interim payments of Class 4 contributions are payable at the same time as interim payments of tax.

Class 4 exemptions

The following persons are exempt from Class 4 contributions:
- Men over 65 and women over – until 2010 – 60 at the commencement of the year of assessment (i.e. on 6 April).
- An individual not resident in the United Kingdom for income tax purposes in the year of assessment.
- Persons whose earnings are not 'immediately derived' from carrying on a trade, profession or vocation (e.g. sleeping partners).
- A child under 16 on 6 April of the year of assessment.
- Persons not ordinarily self-employed.

Married persons and partnerships

Under independent taxation of husband and wife from 1990/91 onwards, each spouse is responsible for his or her Class 4 liability.

In partnerships, each partner's liability is calculated separately. If a partner also carries on another trade or profession, the profits of all such businesses are aggregated for the purposes of calculating their Class 4 liability.

When an assessment has become final and conclusive for the purposes of income tax, it is also final and conclusive for the purposes of calculating Class 4 liability.

Maximum contributions

There is a form of limit to the total liability for social security contributions payable by a person who is employed in more than one employment, or is also self-employed or a partner.

Where only not contracted-out Class 1 contributions, or not contracted-out Class 1 and Class 2 contributions, are payable, the maximum contribution payable at the main rates (11%, 9.4% or 4.85% as the

Further information

Further information can be obtained from the many booklets published by HM Revenue & Customs, available from local Enquiry Centres and on their website (www.hmrc.gov.uk).

National Insurance Contributions Office, Centre for Non-Residents
Newcastle upon Tyne NE98 1ZZ
tel (08459) 154811 (local call rates apply)
Address for enquiries for individuals resident abroad.

case may be) is limited to 53 primary Class 1 contributions at the maximum weekly not contracted-out standard rate. For 2006/7 this 'maximum' will thus be £3194.84 (amounts paid at only 1% are to be excluded in making this comparison).

However, where contracted-out Class 1 contributions are payable, the maximum primary Class 1 contributions payable for 2006/7 where all employments are contracted out are £2719.11 (again excluding amounts paid at only 1%).

Where Class 4 contributions are payable in addition to Class 1 and/or Class 2 contributions, the Class 4 contributions payable at the full 8% rate are restricted so that they shall not exceed the excess of £2391.70 (i.e. 53 Class 2 contributions plus maximum Class 4 contributions) over the aggregate of the Class 1 and Class 2 contributions paid at the full (i.e. other than 1%) rates.

Transfer of government departmental functions

The administrative functions of the former Contributions Agency transferred to the Inland Revenue from 1 April 1999. Responsibility for National Insurance contribution policy matters was also transferred from DSS Ministers to the Inland Revenue and Treasury Ministers on the same date. The DSS is now known as the Department for Work and Pensions (DWP). From 18 April 2005, the functions of the former Inland Revenue and former HM Customs and Excise were merged to become HM Revenue & Customs.

Peter Arrowsmith FCA is a sole practitioner specialising in National Insurance matters. He is chairman of the Employment Taxes and National Insurance Committee of the Institute of Chartered Accountants in England and Wales, and Consulting Editor to *Tolley's National Insurance Contributions 2006/7*.

Social security benefits

In this article, K.D. Bartlett FCA summarises some of the more usual benefits that are available.

Benefits available fall into two categories: non-contributory and contributory. To receive a non-contributory benefit certain criteria has to be met, be it financial, physical, etc.

To receive a contributory benefit the claimant must have met the prescribed contribution condition over a period of time by way of National Insurance.

Contributory benefits are: Jobseeker's Allowance, Incapacity Benefit, Widowed Parent's Allowance (formerly Widowed Mother's Allowance), Bereavement Payment (formerly Widow's Payment), Bereavement Allowance (replaced by Widow's Pension), Child's Special Allowance (where applicable), Maternity Allowance and Category A and B Retirement Pensions.

Non-contributory benefits are: Attendance Allowance, Carer's Allowance, Disability Living Allowance, Industrial Injuries Disablement Benefit, Severe Disablement Allowance, Guardian's Allowance and Category C and D Retirement Pensions.

It is usual for only one periodical benefit to be payable at any one time. If the contribution conditions are satisfied for more than one benefit it is the larger benefit that is payable. Benefit rates shown below are those payable from the week commencing 6 April 2006. Self-employed persons (Class 2 contributors) are covered for all benefits except second state pensions and benefits paid in respect of an industrial injury. Most authors are self employed.

Family benefits

Child Benefit is payable for all children who are either under 16 or under 19 and receiving full-time education at a recognised educational establishment. The rate is £17.45 for the first or eldest child and £11.70 a week for each subsequent child. It is payable to the person who is responsible for the child but excludes foster parents or people exempt from UK tax. Furthermore, one-parent families receive £17.55 per week for the eldest child.

Those with little money may apply for a maternity loan or grant from the Social Fund. Those claiming Working Families Tax Credit or Disabled Person's Tax Credit can apply for a Sure Start Maternity Grant of £500 for each baby expected, born, adopted or subject to a parental order. Any savings over £500 are taken into account. This grant will only be paid on the provision of a relevant certificate from a doctor, midwife or health visitor.

A Guardian's Allowance is paid at the rate of £12.50 a week to people who have taken orphans into their own family. Usually both of the child's parents must be dead and at least one of them must have satisfied a residence condition.

The allowance can only be paid to the person who is entitled to Child Benefit for the child (or to that person's spouse). It is not necessary to be the legal guardian. The claim should be made within three months of the date of entitlement.

Disability Living Allowance

Disability Living Allowance has replaced Attendance Allowance for disabled people before they reach the age of 65. It has also replaced Mobility Allowance.

Those who are disabled after reaching 65 may be able to claim Attendance Allowance. The Attendance Allowance Board decide whether, and for how long, a person is eligible for this allowance. Attendance Allowance is not taxable. The care component is divided into three rates whereas the mobility component has two rates. The rate of benefit from 6 April 2006 is as follows:

Care component	Per week
Higher rate (day and night, or terminally ill)	£62.25
Middle rate (day or night)	£41.65
Lower rate (if need some help during day, or over 16 and help preparing a meal)	£16.50

Mobility component	Per week
Higher rate (unable or virtually unable to walk)	£43.45
Lower rate (can walk but needs help when outside)	£16.50

Benefits for the ill

Incapacity Benefit replaced Sickness Benefit and Invalidity Benefit. The contribution conditions haven't changed but a new medical test has been brought in which includes a comprehensive questionnaire. The rates from 11 April 2006 are:

Long-term Incapacity Benefit	£78.50
Short-term Incapacity Benefit	£59.20
Increase of long-term Incapacity Benefit for age:	
Higher rate	£16.50
Lower rate	£8.25

Carer's Allowance, formerly Invalid Care Allowance, is a taxable benefit paid to people of working age who cannot take a job because they have to stay at home to look after a severely disabled person. The basic allowance is £46.95 per week. An extra £9.40 is paid for the first dependent child and £11.35 for each subsequent child.

Pensions

The state pension is divided into two parts – the basic pension, presently £84.25 per week for a single person or £134.75 per week for a married couple.

Women paying standard rate contributions into the scheme are eligible for the same amount of pension as men but five years earlier, from age 60. The Pensions Act 1995 incorporated the provision for an equal state pension age of 65 for men and women to be phased in over a 10-year period beginning 6 April 2010. If a woman stays at home to bring up her children or to look after a person receiving Attendance Allowance she can have her basic pension rights protected without paying contributions.

Pension Credit is a new entitlement for people aged 60 or over. It guarantees everyone aged 60 and over an income of at least:

- £114.05 a week if you are single; or
- £174.05 a week if you have a partner.

For the first time, people aged 65 and over will be rewarded for some of their savings and income they have for their retirement. In the past, those who had saved a little money were no better off than those who had not saved at all. Pension Credit will change this by giving new money to those who have saved – up to £17.88 if you are single, or £23.58 if you have a partner.

The person who applies for Pension Credit must be at least 60 but their partner can be under 60. Partner means a spouse or a person with whom one lives as if you were married to them.

Widowed Parent's Allowance

This is a new system of bereavement benefits for men and women introduced in April 2001. Women who were receiving benefits under the previous scheme are unaffected as long as they still qualify under the rules. A Widowed Parent's Allowance is:

- based on the late husband's or wife's contributions;
- for widows or widowers bringing up children;
- a regular payment.

The main conditions for receiving this benefit are:

- You must be aged over 45 and must have a dependent child or children.
- If you were over the state pension age when you were widowed you may receive Retirement Pension based on the husband's or wife's National Insurance contributions.
- If the spouse died as a result of their job, it is possible to receive bereavement benefits even if they did not pay sufficient National Insurance contributions.
- You cannot receive bereavement benefits if you remarry or if you live with a partner as if you are married to them.
- Bereavement benefits are not affected if you work.
- The allowance is £84.25 for those over 55 and varies for those aged between 45 and 54.

There are increases for dependent children. You receive £9.40 for the oldest child who qualifies for child benefit and £11.35 for each child who qualifies.

Bereavement Payment and benefits

From 9 April 2001 bereavement benefits are payable to both widows and widowers but the benefits are only paid to those without children. Benefits are based on the National Insurance contributions of the deceased. No benefit is payable if the couple were divorced at the date of death or if either of the survivors remarries or cohabits.

Widows and widowers bereaved on or after 9 April 2001 are entitled to a tax-free Bereavement Payment of £2000.

The death grant to cover funeral expenses was abolished from 6 April 1987. It has been replaced by a funeral payment from the Social Fund where the claimant is in receipt of Income Support, income-based Jobseeker's Allowance, Disabled Person's Tax Credit, Working Families' Tax Credit or Housing Benefit. The full cost of a reasonable funeral is paid, reduced by any savings of over £600 held by the claimant.

Child Tax Credits and Working Tax Credit

Child Tax Credits were introduced on 6 April 2003. To obtain them a claim form has to be submitted (Tax Credit Form TC600 is available by either telephoning 0845 366 7820 or applying online – see below).

Child Tax Credit has replaced the Children's Tax Credit previously claimed through tax paid. It is paid directly to the person who is mainly responsible for caring for the child or children. To ascertain which tax credits you could be entitled to apply online (www.taxcredits.inlandrevenue.gov.uk).

Child Tax Credits are especially complicated for those on variable income and the self employed. The tax credit for the tax year 2006/7 is initially based on the income earned in the tax year 2004/5. If the income is now lower in 2006/7 than in 2004/5 then potentially you should be receiving more tax credit or even be eligible for it when before you were earning too much. In this situation you should make a protective claim by completing and sending off a Tax Credit Form TC600.

Working Tax Credit

Working Tax Credit is paid to support people in work and is administered by HM Revenue & Customs (formerly the Inland Revenue). It is not necessary to have paid National Insurance contributions to qualify. The following do qualify:

• Those over 16 who are responsible for a child or young person and work at least 16 hours a week.

People without children can claim if:

• they are over 25 and work at least 30 hours a week;

• they are aged 16 or over and work at least 16 hours a week and have a disability that puts them at a disadvantage in obtaining a job;

• a person or their partner are aged 50 or more and work at least 16 hours a week and are returning to work after time spent on obtaining a qualification.

Working Tax Credit is paid as well as any Child Tax Credit you are entitled to. The calculations on how much you receive are complicated but it will depend on how many hours you work and your income or joint income.

If you are employed then you will receive the payment via your employer and if self employed you will be paid direct. If you think you are eligible to receive Working Tax Credit, either telephone 0845 764 6646 or visit Tax Credits Online (see above).

K.D. Bartlett FCA qualified as a Chartered Accountant in 1969 and became a partner in a predecessor firm of Horwath Clark Whitehill LLP in 1972.

Index